Documents on Nazism, 1919-1945

Documents on Nazism, 1919–1945

Introduced and Edited by

JEREMY NOAKES
and
GEOFFREY PRIDHAM

THE VIKING PRESS   NEW YORK

Published in 1975 by The Viking Press, Inc.
625 Madison Avenue, New York, N.Y. 10022

LIBRARY OF CONGRESS CATALOGING IN PUBLICATION DATA

Noakes, Jeremy.
    Documents on Nazism, 1919–1945.

    Bibliography: p.
    Includes index.
    1. National socialism—History—Sources.
2. Nationalsozialistische Deutsche Arbeiter-Partei—
History—Sources.   3. Germany—History—1933–1945—
Sources.   I. Pridham, Geoffrey, 1942–   joint
author.   II. Title.

DD256.5.N59   943.086   74-5514
ISBN 0-670-27584-0

Printed in U.S.A.

Contents

Preface

The editors are well aware that in seeking to assemble in one volume a collection of documents illustrating the rise of Nazism and the Third Reich they have taken on a formidable task. The documentation of the subject is vast, both published and unpublished. Nazi Germany was defeated and occupied. Her conquerors, bent on proving that the Nazi State and its rulers were guilty of crimes against humanity, captured as many government and Party documents as they could lay hands on. These documents were then sifted for evidence to provide a case for the prosecution and to a lesser extent for the defence. In this way much valuable material was found, and used at the Nuremberg trials, and some of it was later published. But inevitably, the nature of the inquiry and the time available set limits to the usefulness of what was produced at Nuremberg, so far as historical research is concerned. Both the prosecution and the defence were trying to prove a case, and the methods of lawyers acting as counsel are not those of the historian. The argument is, of course, particularly relevant to the interpretation of documents as that emerged in the course of the trials, but to some extent it is true also of the selection of the documents themselves. For the issues which concerned the Allies, such as war guilt and war crimes, dictated the selection of the material. With other areas such as social policy and the nature of the political system—for example, relations between Party and State—they had much less concern.

Over the past twenty years or so, the huge quantity of material captured by the Allies has become available to scholars. Gradually historians in Germany and elsewhere have been subjecting more and more aspects of the subject to scholarly inquiry. Collections of documents and monographs with documentary appendixes have already appeared which throw new light on the means by which the Nazis succeeded in winning power, and also on the nature of the regime which they established. In particular, the conventional view of the Third Reich as a monolithic totalitarian state, a view perpetuated by numerous popular accounts of the regime, has been shown to bear little resemblance to reality. This monolithic impression of the Third Reich was, of course, just what the Nazi authorities wished to convey to the outside world. They wished foreigners, and particularly those from democratic states, to compare the apparent discipline and order of the Third Reich with the political, economic and social conflicts which were so evident in their own societies. On the whole, they were successful in conveying this image.

Only the shrewdest observers of the German scene managed to see behind
the façade.[1] It was not until after the war, when the documents became
available and when important members of the regime, such as the Armaments Minister Speer, began to talk about their experiences, that the real
picture began to emerge.

The first challenge to the image of the Third Reich as a monolith on the
basis of first-hand evidence came in 1947 from Hugh Trevor-Roper in his
The Last Days of Hitler. He argued that the Third Reich was a 'confusion of
private empires, private armies and private intelligence services', and he gave
an explanation for this situation. He argued that 'irresponsibility of the ruler
causes irresponsibility of the subject; the conception of the commonwealth
no longer exists outside propaganda; and politics becomes the politics of
feudal anarchy, which the personal power of an undisputed despot may
conceal but cannot alter'. He suggested that in contemporary dictatorships
differences at the apex of the power pyramid take the place of public opinion
in an open society. Yet since Trevor-Roper's book dealt with the death
throes of the regime, it was conceivable that his picture of it was not applicable to earlier phases. Recent research, particularly by German scholars such
as Karl-Dietrich Bracher, Martin Broszat, Hans Buchheim and Hans
Mommsen, has shown that the Third Reich was characterized by a mixture
of both monocratic and pluralist elements. The documents unearthed by this
research, together with the editors' own personal researches and the published material from the Nuremberg trials, form the basis of this book.
In joint works of this kind it is not always easy to disentangle individual
contributions. Broadly speaking, however, Jeremy Noakes was responsible
for the Introductions to the several Parts and for Chapters 2, 5–10, 13–14,
19–24. Geoffrey Pridham was responsible for Chapters 11–12 and 15.
Chapters 1, 3–4, 16–18 were a joint production. Where possible we have
preferred to include material which has not previously been translated into
English or is not easily accessible. We have, for example, included only one
excerpt from *Mein Kampf* and none from *Hitler's Tabletalk* since both these
works have been published in English paperback.

We are aware of the dangers of selecting documents for the purpose of
illustrating general points. Each historical document has a particular context,
within which alone it can be fully understood. The danger is particularly
acute in the case of the Third Reich, in which the situation was so complex
and fluid that the choice of 'typical' documents can easily result in a distorted
view. Nevertheless, we believe that the advantages outweigh the dangers.
Documents have the advantage of conveying the colour and atmosphere of a
period—they enable one to get the 'feel' of a period in a way which is
essential to a real understanding of the issues involved. We hope that this

[1] Notably Hans Gerth, 'The Nazi Party: Its Leadership and Composition' in *American Journal
of Sociology*, 1940; Franz Neumann, *Behemoth: The Structure and Practice of National Socialism*
(London 1942) and Ernst Fraenkel, *The Dual State* (London/New York 1941).

collection of documents will succeed in conveying something of the complexity of political and social reality in Germany during these years, the frequent glaring contrast between idea and reality and the more occasional horrifying coincidence, and also something of the human drama of the individuals who had the misfortune to live through the Third Reich.

The editors owe much to the Institute of Contemporary History and Wiener Library in London for the loan of a considerable amount of material for long periods. We are especially indebted to Dr T. W. Mason for the loan of his manuscript collection of documents on Nazi labour policy between 1936 and 1940 which is to be published in Germany under the title *Arbeiterklasse und Volksgemeinschaft*. We are also grateful to Miss Jill MacIntyre for the loan of material on which she based an article entitled 'Women and the Professions in Germany, 1930–1940' in *German Democracy and the Triumph of Hitler*, edited by Antony Nicholls and Erich Matthias (London 1971). We acknowledge helpful suggestions from Dr Michael Duffy, who read the bulk of the manuscript, from Dr Albrecht Tyrell, who read the proofs of Parts 1 and 2, and from Mr Martin Crouch, who read Chapters 11 and 12. Finally, our thanks are due also to Mrs Marjorie Dale, Mrs Anne Walters, Mrs Jan Nicholas and Mrs Mary Woods, who generously typed the manuscript, and to Mr Herbert Rees, who provided invaluable assistance in the preparation of the manuscript for the printers.

J.N.
G.P.

Acknowledgements

We wish to express our gratitude to the Bundesarchiv in Koblenz, the Staatsarchiv in Bremen, the Niedersächsisches Hauptstaatsarchiv in Hanover, the Niedersächsisches Staatsarchiv in Oldenburg, the Bayerisches Hauptstaatsarchiv in Munich and the Bayerisches Staatsarchiv in Neuburg an der Donau, the Forschungstelle für die Geschichte des Nationalsozialismus in Hamburg and the Imperial War Museum, London, for permission to quote from unpublished documentary material, and to the publishers, authors, editors and agents concerned for permission to quote from the following books:

H.M. Stationery Office: *Documents on British Foreign Policy*, series 2, volumes 2 and 6; *Documents on German Foreign Policy*, series C, volumes 1, 3, 4; series D, volumes 1, 2, 4, 5, 7, 10, 11, 13.

Deutsche Verlags-Anstalt: *Vierteljahrshefte für Zeitgeschichte*, 1958, 1959, 1960, 1963; Ernst Deuerlein, *Der Hitler-Putsch*; Peter Hüttenberger, *Die Gauleiter*; Albert Krebs, *Tendenzen und Gestalten der NSDAP*; H. Mommsen, *Beamtentum im Dritten Reich*; H. Heiber, *Reichsführer, Briefe an und von Himmler*; Ursula von Gersdorff, *Frauen im Kriegsdienst*; Dieter Petzina, *Autarkiepolitik im Dritten Reich*; Rudolf Diels, *Lucifer ante portas . . . es spricht der erste Chef der Gestapo*.

Oxford University Press under the auspices of the Royal Institute of International Affairs: Norman Baynes (ed.), *The Speeches of Adolf Hitler 1922–39*; Royal Institute of International Affairs, *Documents on International Affairs 1930*.

Fischer Taschenbuch Verlag: Walther Hofer, *Der Nationalsozialismus 1933–45*; Ilse Staff, *Justiz im Dritten Reich*; A. Mitscherlich and F. Mielcke, *Medizin ohne Menschlichkeit*.

Harald Boldt Verlag: F. J. Heyen, *Nationalsozialismus im Alltag*.

Karl Rauch Verlag: Ernst Deuerlein, *Der Aufstieg der NSDAP 1919–1933*.

Hoffmann u. Campe Verlag: Otto Meissner, *Staatssekretär unter Ebert-Hindenburg-Hitler*.

Günter Olzog Verlag: Wilhelm Hoegner, *Der Schwierige Aussenseiter*.

Alfred A. Knopf Inc.: William Shirer, *Berlin Diary*.

Macmillan & Co. Ltd: Ivone Kirkpatrick, *The Inner Circle*.

Victor Gollancz Ltd and Henry Regnery Co., Chicago: *Memoirs of Ernst von Weizsäcker* (trans. John Andrews).

Hutchinson Publishing Group Ltd and Houghton Mifflin Co.: Adolf Hitler, *Mein Kampf* translated by Ralph Manheim. Copyright 1943 and 1971 by Houghton Mifflin Company. Reprinted by permission of the publisher.

Praeger Publishers Inc., New York: Karl Demeter, *The German Officer Corps in Society and State 1650–1945* (copyright 1962, Bernard & Graefe Verlag für Wehrwesen; English translation, copyright 1965, George Weidenfeld & Nicolson Ltd).

Atlantis Verlag AG: *The Von Hassell Diaries 1938–1944.*

Laurence Pollinger Ltd: Kurt Ludecke, *I Knew Hitler.*

Hurst & Blackett: Joseph Goebbels, *My Part in Germany's Fight.*

Weidenfeld & Nicolson Ltd and Deutsche Verlags-Anstalt: Helmut Heiber (ed.), *Diary of Joseph Goebbels 1925–26.*

The Bodley Head Ltd: Roger Manvell and Heinrich Fraenkel, *The July Plot.*

Wehr und Wissen Verlagsgesellschaft: Hans-Adolf Jacobsen, *Der Zweite Weltkrieg in Chronik und Dokumenten.*

Opera Mundi: Paul Schmidt, *Hitler's Interpreter.*

National Bureau of Economic Research Inc., New York: G. Bry, *Wages in Germany 1871–1945.*

Doubleday, New York: Louis Lochner, *The Goebbels Diaries 1942–43.*

Süddeutscher Verlag: Aretin, *Krone und Ketten.*

Abelard-Schuman Ltd: M. Maschmann, *Account Rendered.*

Mouton & Co. N.V., The Hague: B.A. Carroll, *Design for Total War, Arms and Economics in the Third Reich.*

In a few cases it has proved impossible to locate sources of copyright control. Otherwise, all sources are listed above; if there are any quotations which have been incorrectly acknowledged, we hope that those concerned will accept our apologies.

Introduction

Fascism was not unique to Germany. Fascism had its roots in a prewar movement of ideas which found expression in many other European countries. Social Darwinism, social imperialism, racism and antisemitism were rife in France, Austria-Hungary, Italy and even in Britain and America. Similarly, Fascism developed in a postwar context of economic crisis, political breakdown, and social disorientation which was common to Europe as a whole and which produced similar movements in a number of other countries. Nevertheless, while bearing in mind the European dimension, it is also true to say that Fascism developed in Germany because the conditions there were peculiarly favourable to it. This was not because of some evil inherent in the German character, but as a result of particular historical circumstances. And it was these historical circumstances which shaped the German variant of Fascism–Nazism.

Nazism triumphed at a time when the problems which had confronted prewar Germany had been intensified by the crises of the war and the postwar years. Prewar Germany had suffered under a double burden: in the first place, it had only recently been unified as a nation state and this (only partial) unification had come about through wars waged by one German state, Prussia, against other German states and against her European neighbours. There were elements within the new Reich which were unenthusiastic if not hostile towards it—Catholics and particularists in the South German states, supporters of the deposed Guelph dynasty in the rural areas of Hanover, and national minorities such as the Poles and the Danes. Moreover, the formation of a new and large German nation state in the centre of Europe had destroyed the international balance of power besides alienating those states, in particular France, which had been defeated in the process. Thus, the new Germany tended to be acutely sensitive to the possibility of disruption from within and also to anticipate danger from outside, which made the need for internal unity appear all the more important. This sensitivity reinforced the growing nationalism which had accompanied unification; it reinforced also the official claim that to support the existing order was a patriotic duty. Secondly, to the burden imposed by the problems of national unification were added the strains induced by the rapid industrialization which accompanied it. The old economic and social order was disrupted, shifting the balance of economic power between agriculture and industry, creating new classes and forcing old ones into decline, and in particular threatening the economic position of the Prussian ruling class.

The regime which was obliged to deal with these problems consisted of a semi-autocratic monarchy and a ruling class dominated by the Prussian Junkers, a gentry which, despite their economic role as agricultural entre-preneurs, retained the values of the old hierarchical agrarian society and of the Prussian army, of which they traditionally formed the officer corps and which, in the final analysis, represented the main pillar of the regime. Since Germany had just been united by Prussia, the new state came to be identified with these values. Faced with the fact that their dream of national unification had been realized by the old political order, and sensing a growing threat to their position from the rapidly mounting numbers of the urban proletariat, the middle class increasingly abandoned what vestiges of liberal values they had retained. German nationalism reverted to the association with reactionary ideas which had characterized its origins at the beginning of the nineteenth century in reaction against the French Revolution and the Enlightenment. The majority of the middle class adopted the authoritarian values of the old order, competing, for example, for the honour of becoming an officer of the reserve, in a process which has been aptly termed the 'feudalization of the bourgeoisie'.

Yet it would be a mistake to see this process simply in terms of the 'Prussianization' of Germany. For the development was a dialectical one in which Prussia itself was compelled to compromise with the forces of a new age, most notably with nationalism to which the old Prussian Conservatives had been bitterly opposed. To this extent Prussia was Germanized as much as Germany was Prussianized. But the system created by this compromise between the Prussian monarchy, the Junker aristocracy and the bulk of the middle class was seriously flawed. The fact that the Government was not responsible to Parliament and was composed of civil servants rather than the political representatives of the people created a gap between the State and society which the political parties were incapable of filling. It tended to produce parties which were characterized by rigid ideologies and represented narrow interests, since they were never obliged to face the responsibilities of office and come to terms with political reality. The role of the parties was restricted to one of criticism and of lobbying, and their influence was increasingly undermined by the emergence of powerful interest groups such as the agrarians and heavy industry which dealt directly with the bureaucracy and which came to dominate politics—a development encouraged by Bismarck as a means of weakening Parliament and the parties. As a result, the system failed to provide a framework within which the conflicts between social groups could be mediated and a consensus reached. Instead, this responsibility devolved on the State. The problem was that the official values of the State, rooted in a traditional patriarchal and agrarian society, corresponded less and less to the economic and social realities of a modern and industrialized Germany. In particular, the industrial working class were regarded as a growing threat and, apart from sporadic attempts to win their allegiance by social reform, their political and economic aspirations were ignored or repressed. In short, the State encouraged and perpetuated social divisions.

Yet the Government was aware of its need of mass support both to ensure a compliant Reichstag (the lower House of Parliament) and more generally to legitimize the regime in an era in which traditional deference was losing its force. In order to achieve this support without at the same time yielding on the fundamental issue of the distribution of power within the State, a number of techniques were evolved which were of crucial importance in shaping the political culture of the new Germany.

In the first place, the issue of national security was exploited by playing upon the popular fears of both external and internal enemies. Under Bismarck the Government's election slogan was often 'The Reich in peril!'; under his successors the cry became 'Encirclement!' But Bismarck and his successors exploited not only fear but also national pride and ambition which were running strong in the decades following unification. Thus the programme of imperialism which first emerged in the 1880s was in part motivated by a desire to shore up the *status quo* both by creating emotional identification between the masses and the state and by attempting to guarantee the prosperity of the masses at the expense of the colonial peoples rather than through a redistribution of wealth within Germany itself. As Admiral Tirpitz put it, 'The general naval interests must be advanced ... because in the new national task and the economic gain bound up with it lies a strong palliative against educated and uneducated Social Democrats.'

But social solidarity within Germany was not only sought through the exploitation of national fear and pride in regard to other peoples; Bismarck endeavoured to achieve it also by exploiting the fear and suspicion of minorities within Germany. Those who were opposed to his system he labelled 'enemies of the Reich': the industrial workers who had come to accept modernization but wanted a greater share both in its material benefits and in the running of their country and who therefore turned to Socialism; many politically interested Catholics, some of whom shared the Conservatives' resentment at modernization and yet also disliked the domination of the new Germany by Protestant, militarist, and autocratic Prussia; and a section of the commercial and professional middle class who continued to uphold the old liberal values of the 1848 revolution. Under William II the 'enemies of the Reich' became 'the enemy within', the Social Democrats became 'fellows without a fatherland'. But the result of conceiving of politics in terms of 'friends' and 'enemies' was to create a style of political behaviour which remained pervasive even after the fall of the regime which had formed it, and which helped to undermine later attempts to achieve a degree of consensus.

Another aspect of the attempt to win the acquiescence of the masses was

the growing tendency towards personal rule and the projection of the image
of government by a strong-willed leader as superior to government by
parliamentary parties which were portrayed as selfish and divisive. This
'Bonapartist' trend developed first under Bismarck. But Bismarck shared the
limelight with an aged emperor held in the highest respect by his subjects.
In the reign of William II both the exigencies of the system and the influence
of the Kaiser's own personality combined to produce the apotheosis of
personal rule. And it was significant that when during the war the eclipse of
the Kaiser created a power vacuum, it was soon filled by another such
'strong man' with whom the nation could identify, in the shape of Field-
Marshal von Hindenburg. Here was another aspect of a pattern of politics
which helped to condition the political culture of postwar Germany.

Opposition to the system came from two directions. On the Left were the
Social Democrats, some Catholics, particularly those associated with the
Catholic trade unions, and the left-wing Liberals. They advocated constitutional reform as a solution to Germany's problems—the introduction of a
parliamentary democracy on Western European lines. On the Right a
movement emerged that was equally discontented with the *status quo*, the
various manifestations of which can be subsumed under the term '*völkisch*
(racialist) movement'. This movement, actually a number of separate
organizations united only by a common outlook, reflected the attitudes of
those sections of the population which felt most threatened by the process of
modernization: peasants, artisans, and small shopkeepers whose economic
basis was menaced by the growth of large-scale enterprises and also by the
difficulty of adjusting to the increasing influence of often unpredictable
market forces in a rural economy which had hitherto been comparatively
isolated. The reactionary Prussian Junker landowners attempted to win a
mass base for the defence of their economic and political position by exploiting this mood, and an important role in spreading *völkisch* propaganda
among the rural population was played by the Farmers' League, an agricultural pressure group established in 1893 and closely associated with the
Junker-dominated German Conservative Party. In addition, there were other
organizations—such as the Reichshammerbund, for which the antisemitic
programme was the most important element—which also derived their main
support from these groups. One group particularly sympathetic to *völkisch*
ideas were teachers who resented changing social values, and intellectuals
and professional men who resented Jewish and other competitors with
progressive ideas. These men clamoured also for German expansion and
their mood found expression in the Pan-German League founded in 1893
as an imperialist pressure group.

The *völkisch* movement expressed a feeling that the authorities were
compromising with forces believed to be undermining traditional German
values and ways of life—with the forces of capitalism, liberalism, internationalism, and even Socialism. They wanted to return to an idealized

pre-industrial society in which everyone knew his own place in a static hierarchy of estates, and traditional authority was respected in every sphere. They believed that the new trends were associated with what they saw as the growing influence of the Jews who, since their relatively recent emancipation, had taken a lead in many modern economic and cultural developments. The Jews came to personify all the aspects of modernization to which the movement objected. The solutions to Germany's problems advocated by the *völkisch* movement included measures against the Jews, such as the withdrawal of German citizenship, and against Socialist 'agitators'; a reform of the electoral law to reduce the influence of Parliament and of the liberalism stemming from it; and above all a programme of imperialism both as a means of resolving Germany's domestic tensions and as an expression of Germany's claim to the status of a world power. As the threat from the Social Democrats seemed to grow – in 1912 they became the largest party in the Reichstag – the views of the movement came to be shared by more and more groups within the German establishment including the Emperor himself. But the Government was unwilling to risk the confrontations at home and abroad inherent in the full *völkisch* programme and was therefore criticized by the movement for its vacillation and half-measures.

The First World War, the defeat, and the revolution which followed represented the bankruptcy of the Wilhelmine system, which had clearly failed to solve the problems with which it was confronted. In 1918, the forces of the Left filled the political vacuum with a western-style parliamentary democracy. But defeat and the peace terms which were imposed had brought national humiliation, while the revolution had sharpened social tensions. Moreover, the introduction of parliamentary democracy ensured that the conflicts were now transferred via the political parties to the Government itself. Given a period of economic prosperity, it might have been possible to achieve a relaxation of tension and a compromise between the various groups. Indeed the years 1924–28 saw a degree of stability. But the economic crises of the postwar years increased class antagonism, and German society, which had found only a temporary unity in the first two years of the war, now finally disintegrated into warring components – interest groups whose political representatives paralysed the democratic system by their refusal to compromise.

The paralysis of Parliament and the collapse of the economy in 1930 created a new political vacuum and into this vacuum moved the old elites – the Army leadership, the Civil Service, the Junkers, and the industrialists – whose political power had been weakened by the revolution but who otherwise had been left more or less intact. After their failure to exploit the crisis years 1918–23 successfully, these groups had been waiting in the wings, hoping for an opportunity to restore their former power. Now, with the crisis in the parliamentary system, they had a second chance to destroy parliamentary democracy and they determined to use it. The means lay ready to hand in the person of the old Field-Marshal Hindenburg, President of the Reich since 1925. Under Article 48 of the Weimar Constitution the President could in a crisis situation rule by decree, by-passing the legislature which retained only the power of veto. This was the weapon with which the Right planned to destroy the democratic system through their influence with the President.

But 1930 saw a vacuum developing not only at government level but also within the political community at large. Under the impact of economic crisis a large section of the community which had never been fully integrated in the new postwar democratic order became totally alienated from the system. They had become disillusioned with their traditional political repre- sentatives. Young people, in particular, were contemptuous of traditional conservative and liberal ideas, which they regarded as the hopelessly anachronistic ideologies of a dying order, and they disliked the rigidities of the old class structure. Many people were looking for a prophet to lead them out of the wilderness and for a new deal.

Into this vacuum moved the Nazi Party, the heir of the prewar *völkisch* movement, though differing from its precursor in structure and style, above all in its determination and ability to mobilize the masses and to appeal to youth. Yet the programme of the Nazi Party was essentially the same as that of the prewar *völkisch* movement—hostility to the Jews and 'Marxists', the creation of a 'national community', and imperialist expansion. Before the war, support for the more extreme elements of the *völkisch* movement had been small; broadly speaking, the traditional groups were contented despite the impact of modernization. The effects of this had been to some extent cushioned by the fact that their traditional values were upheld by the ruling classes—their status was assured. Under Weimar this was no longer true; the crisis jeopardized not only the economic existence of these groups but their social status and self-esteem. In conditions of acute anxiety and social disintegration, the appeal of a movement which stressed the need for national integration and social solidarity was strong and touched deep chords in a society where the liberal ethos had never really taken root and where *Gemeinschaft* or community values had far stronger foundations.

Part I of this book deals with the rise of Nazism to power. There are three main phases in the rise of Nazism before the appointment of Hitler as Chancellor in January 1933. The first phase, from 1919 to 1923, saw the emergence of the Nazi Party, though still largely confined to Bavaria, as the most extreme and most effective group within the *völkisch* movement. This was due partly to the favourable conditions within Bavaria and partly to its leader, Adolf Hitler. During this period Hitler was beginning to acquire the self-confidence which would turn him from a man who regarded himself as merely 'the drummer' of the Right, preparing the way for the dictatorship of a more substantial figure, to a man who gradually became convinced of his destiny to be Germany's 'Führer'. And during this period under his direction the Party was developing the political style which set it off so markedly from the other parties, with the partial exception of the Communists. For, while others merely talked of the need to win mass support, Hitler developed the techniques with which to exploit the discontent within a large section of the Munich population.

This phase ended with the abortive putsch of 1923. The following period, from 1924 to 1928, is one of relative obscurity in which the Party remained a fringe group, making little electoral progress. For this reason, the period has hitherto been often neglected; yet what followed cannot be understood without an awareness of the events of those years. For although it has long been recognized that the rise of Nazism between 1930 and 1933 can be largely attributed to the economic depression, there has been a tendency to state the connexion and assume that it is self-explanatory. What is not explained is how a party which until 1929 was virtually unknown was suddenly able to exploit the economic situation to such effect. During these years a nationwide cadre organization was being created and Hitler was imposing his authority on the Party to such an extent that it became in effect a 'Führer' party, the cohesion of which depended not so much on adherence to a set of principles or a programme as on the unquestioning acceptance of his leadership. It was this cadre organization of fanatical activists that provided the basis from which the economic crisis of 1928–29 could be exploited to such effect. It was also this form of personal authority which was to characterize Hitler's rule after 1933.

The years 1929–33 see the Nazi Party emerging from obscurity to take over power. Its rise to power was by no means inevitable. For although in 1932 the Nazis succeeded in winning the largest percentage of the vote of any party, they did not win an overall majority. Moreover, just before they came to power they encountered a severe setback. In fact, the take-over of power occurred through a compromise with members of the old elites— the Army, the Prussian Junker landowners, the Civil Service, and a section of the industrialists—and the form of this take-over was of considerable significance for the future development of the regime. There are therefore two aspects to be considered. First, how and why did the Party win so much electoral support? Which groups proved most vulnerable and why? What significance did age, religion, class and occupation have in deciding who supported and who opposed the Nazis? In what ways did their propaganda techniques and themes contribute to their success? Secondly, why were the Conservatives prepared to compromise? What did they envisage as the relationship between themselves and the Nazis? Finally, there is the question of the Nazis' tactics during this period. Hitler's insistence on nothing less than the Chancellorship provoked a grave crisis within the Party and might well have led to disaster. Yet his instinct was proved triumphantly right, and, in any case, given the nature of his objectives, had he any alternative?

Part II deals with the take-over, or 'seizure of power' as the Nazis liked to call it, after Hitler's appointment as Chancellor on 30 January 1933. Although Hitler quickly established his supreme authority, the process was by no means as smooth as is sometimes supposed. The Party had no blueprint which it could impose on coming into office. There had been very little forward planning, since the Party had been too involved in the business of winning votes to go in detail into what would happen when it achieved power. In any event, initially Hitler had to operate within the restrictions imposed by the existing power structure. The main difficulty lay in the question of what was to be the role of the Party militants in the new regime. In the first eighteen months or so of the new regime the local Party and SA[1] units were determined to assert their authority. They had fought for power and now they wished to enjoy its fruits and to see implemented those parts of the Party programme which most appealed to them—help for the small businessman, measures against the Jews (who were in many cases economic rivals), jobs, and official status for the SA as the military arm of the new state. Yet, in order to ensure total control for the Party in every sphere, Hitler would have been obliged to carry out a radical restructuring of the whole state and economy and this he was unwilling to do. He had come to power by means of a compromise with the existing elites and, since they shared many of his objectives, a revolution was unnecessary; or rather, it could take place gradually and, as the regime consolidated itself, the existing institutions could be drained of power. His main objective was to mobilize the nation for war—militarily, economically, and psychologically. He needed the expertise of the existing Army, industrial and administrative leadership to achieve it. Finally, he needed to achieve economic recovery in order to fulfil his part of the bargain with the German people, in return for which they would follow him wherever he led and would make his position impregnable against any threat from the Conservatives. Party and SA interference in the economic sphere, such as attacks on department stores and Jewish businesses, would jeopardize economic recovery. Hitler's purge of the SA in 1934 was an assertion of his decision not to carry out a full-scale revolution all at once.

Part III deals with the relations between the Party and the State in the light of this decision. On the one hand, during the next few years, the Party had to be kept in check as a potentially disruptive force. Thus, although the State apparatus was 'coordinated' in the sense that its leading positions were in the hands of those, whether members of the Party or not, who accepted the authority of Hitler, its position as compared with that of the Party apparatus was for some time stronger than has often been supposed, particularly by those who have followed the totalitarian model and equated the Nazi Party with the Russian Communist Party. Yet at the same time Hitler was determined not to allow himself to be circumscribed by the Civil Service and the judiciary and by their bureaucratic and legal norms and

[1] *Sturmabteilungen*, lit. 'storm detachments'.

procedures. His solution to this dilemma was twofold. On the one hand, although the Party was not allowed to dictate to the State, its *apparat* remained intact and so at all levels of the administration it acted as a rival to the State authorities and could exert effective pressure upon them. Secondly, he allowed the SS[1] under Heinrich Himmler to absorb the police functions of the civil administration and to undermine the powers of the judiciary through the use of so-called 'protective custody'. Since the Party Gauleiters and the Chief of the SS were directly subordinate to him as Führer, this meant that Hitler could rely on two executive agencies entirely independent of the Civil Service and the judiciary.

The most characteristic way in which the traditional power structure was eroded was by the increasing personalization of power – the concentration of power in the hands of individuals who could claim to exercise the authority of Hitler as 'Führer' rather than the authority of the State as represented by a particular office. Increasingly as problems arose, individuals were appointed by Hitler in a totally *ad hoc* way to solve them. In order to carry out these tasks, these individuals created their own *apparat* in rivalry with the organization which was traditionally responsible for that particular sphere. They then drained power away from, or absorbed elements of, that organization, leaving it emasculated. This happened, for example, with Hermann Göring's Four-Year Plan Office and the Ministry of Economics, and with the SS which took over the police functions of the Ministry of the Interior. Essentially, this process represented the application by Hitler to the whole State of the form of organization and the style of authority which had characterized the Nazi Party before 1933. For after 1934 Hitler was not only Führer of the Party; he was now also officially Führer of the German people. The basis of the legitimacy of the regime was now charismatic; inevitably, therefore, the position of the State administration based on legal-rational norms was progressively eroded.

As a result of this development, the whole structure became extremely complex and power was remarkably fluid. The structure was complex because two different forms of authority coexisted. On the one hand, remnants of the old legal-bureaucratic authority of the State continued to exist; but on the other hand, this authority was being undermined by the growth of a Führer-authority represented by individuals who had the confidence of the Führer and whose organizations had acquired official status without fitting into the traditional hierarchy. Power was fluid because the Führer had a way of shifting his support from one individual and organization to another, and ministries could no longer count to any extent on the authority derived from their traditional position within the hierarchy of the State.

This system enabled Hitler to avoid the danger of being circumscribed by the Civil Service. It also had the virtue of flexibility – the ability to respond to new situations as they arose. It did, however, pose serious problems for the

[1] *Schutzstaffel*, lit. 'guard squadron'.

carrying out of coherent policies. Since there were so many individuals and organizations competing for power in every sphere, each with different views on what should be done and how, a coherent policy could not be achieved unless Hitler gave consistent backing to one or another of the competitors. This happened only in spheres where Hitler had a direct interest — an instance is his support of Speer as Armaments Minister during 1942–43; and even here the position was complicated by Hitler's constant interference in matters of detail. Otherwise, it was left to the individuals to fight it out with one another — leading to stalemate or to the victory of the most ruthless and unscrupulous.

This total absence of clear lines of jurisdiction produced duplication and therefore waste of effort and confusion. This duplication, however, appears to have been, in part at least, intentional — an indirect way of exercising control. For Hitler's leadership took the form of a loose control. While his unquestioned authority was always in the background, he preferred to exercise control by leaving one organization to check another rather than by close and active supervision. To what extent this was an intentional policy of 'Divide and Rule' or rather a question of indecisiveness is in dispute among scholars. A quasi-feudal system emerged, therefore, of rival baronies — the Party, the SS-Police, the Labour Front, the Four-Year Plan Office and later the Speer Ministry, the Propaganda Ministry, the Army, and the Interior administration, to name only the most powerful. From being the supreme representative of the sovereign authority of the State the Civil Service was degraded to one bureaucracy among several. These baronies or empires all derived their authority from the Führer and all were competing with one another for the Führer's support against their rivals. They were not monoliths; they often contained rival sections within their own structures. The Party, for example, contained the office of the Deputy Führer (successively, Rudolf Hess and Martin Bormann), the Gauleiters, Robert Ley's Political Organization, and the Party treasury under Franz Schwarz, all to some extent in competition with one another. Nor were these empires entirely distinct — they tended to overlap. No one of them dominated the others. The Third Reich was neither an SS-Police state nor a Party state in the sense that either of these two organizations monopolized power.

Active opposition to the regime came from three main sources — from former Socialists and Communists, from the Churches, and from Conservatives in the Army and in parts of the administration. The Socialists and Communists succeeded in creating temporary networks for the distribution of pamphlets and in meeting together from time to time in small groups. In the Protestant Church there was opposition from certain members of the so-called 'Confessional Church'. This Church was in itself a protest, since it had been established in reaction against the attempt by the Government to 'coordinate' the Protestant Church by exploiting a pro-Nazi element within it in order to establish a Reich Church under a pro-Nazi Reich Bishop. The most notable examples of such Protestant Churchmen were Dietrich Bonhoeffer and Pastor Martin Niemöller. The most remarkable example of Catholic opposition was the sermons by the Bishop of Münster, Count von Galen, protesting against the activities of the Gestapo and against the euthanasia programme. There were also examples of resistance by the Catholic population to attempts by the regime to interfere with Church customs. But the Conservatives involved in the movement leading up to the 1944 bomb plot against Hitler are perhaps the most interesting of the opposition groups, since by studying their ideas and attitudes it can be established more clearly what distinguished such Conservatives, many of whom had initially supported Hitler, from the Nazis.

The picture of the political structure outlined in Part III helps to illuminate another aspect of the regime – its relations with the population – which forms the subject of Part IV. The conventional image of the Third Reich is of a regime which had absolute control over its subjects. While we have no wish to deny the reality and effectiveness of terror, of which the following pages provide numerous examples, the real picture was much less clear-cut. In the first place, although the regime was committed to the imposition of its ideology in every sphere of social and cultural life, in practice the confusion of responsibilities made it difficult to establish uniformity, while considerations of tactics often dictated compromise. Moreover, elements of the ideology were contradictory. For instance, the conviction of the need to acquire living space and the consequent determination to mobilize the nation for the likelihood of war necessitated a programme of rearmament which conflicted with the anti-urban and anti-industrial elements in the Party's ideology.

Finally, it is a mistake to assume that the regime was capable of imposing itself on society as if it operated from some position outside. Although the regime had absorbed within itself most of the channels whereby popular opinion had previously found expression – the political parties and pressure groups – these pressures did not cease, but now came to be articulated by the particular organizations within the regime which had taken over the old channels. To give an example, this meant, in effect, that the Nazi Party, which had become the only party, and the Labour Front, which had become the only representative of labour, acquired to some extent the functions of representing the will of the population and the labour force in regard to other organizations of the regime. That is to say, the Party saw its role as that of ensuring a contented population, and itself wished to be popular; the Labour Front saw its role as that of securing a contented labour force. And both the Party and the Labour Front were anxious to strengthen their influence within the machine. They tended, therefore, to fight policies which in their view produced unpopularity and made it difficult for them to carry out their functions, *even though such policies might be in the overall interest of the regime* – such as the fight against inflation. Nevertheless, it would be a mistake not to take ideology seriously as a component of policy, and the history of the policy on antisemitism is an indication that ideological principle could override all other considerations and could be carried into effect in the teeth of all the difficulties it involved. The pursuit of its ideological enemies, notably the Jews and the Left, provided a cement for the regime and compensated its followers for the failure to realize other aspects of the ideology which quickly revealed themselves as utopian or at least as incompatible with the requirements of the major goal—the mobilizing of the nation for war.

The relationship of ideology to practice also arises in the domain of foreign policy, which is dealt with in Part V. Here it is shown that Hitler's programme was formulated on the basis of a combination of ideological principle on the one hand with, on the other, an assessment of Germany's strategic situation and of the various possibilities open to her within that situation. The ideological principle was his conviction that the life of states, as the life of individuals, was a struggle for survival and that owing to the growing size of her population in relation to her resources Germany would soon lack the means to continue that struggle. She must therefore either expand and acquire 'living space' or be conquered. But the direction which that expansion should take and the way in which it should be brought about were determined primarily on the basis of Hitler's reading of Germany's diplomatic and strategic situation. On coming to power, he endeavoured to carry out the programme he had drawn up, but, when thwarted, he was quite prepared to adapt the methods for achieving his goal. The evidence suggests that, while strategic factors were of more importance in the shaping of his foreign policy than has often been supposed, it would be a mistake to see him as a pure opportunist for whom ideology was merely a convenient rationalization.

With the war, which is covered in Part VI, the various trends within the Third Reich were greatly accelerated. Already in the years immediately preceding the war, there had been a significant shift in the balance of power within the regime, which saw a further decline in the power of the old conservative leadership and the old institutions. Thus, in the winter of 1937 control over the economy passed from the Conservative Hjalmar Schacht, who as Minister of Economics had resisted Party interference, to Göring and his Four-Year Plan organization; in February 1938 the leadership of the Army was purged and Hitler assumed actual, as distinct from nominal, control of the armed forces, with the creation of the High Command of the Armed Forces (OKW)[1] and the appointment of a nonentity, General Wilhelm Keitel, as his deputy; the same month saw the replacement of the Conservative Constantin von Neurath by the Nazi Joachim von Ribbentrop, as Foreign Minister, which gave official confirmation to the process whereby

---

[1] *Oberkommando der Wehrmacht.*

the authority of the Foreign Ministry had been continuously whittled away by the Ribbentrop Bureau. It was also during 1938 that the campaign against the Jews began to be intensified.

But it was the exceptional situation created by the outbreak of war which enabled the regime to realize to the full their most important ideological principles—the elimination of the Jews and of the handicapped, and the resettlement of parts of Poland by removing the indigenous Slav population and replacing it with German-speaking settlers from other parts of Europe. It was also during the war that the State administration lost whatever power and independence it still possessed. From 1939 onwards, the remaining authority of the Ministry of the Interior was eroded by the accretion of power in the hands of the Party and the SS. Thus, it is significant for the future intentions of the regime that Hitler transferred the civil authority in the annexed regions not to the State administration but to Party leaders, who were permitted to act independently of the Ministry of the Interior, and to the SS, which took over all security and police functions in these areas. In 1942, the Party assumed increasing authority within the Reich itself owing to the delegation by Hitler of wide powers to the Gauleiters, who, in the capacity of Reich Defence Commissioners, were responsible for coordinating civil defence in their areas. Finally, in 1943, with Himmler's appointment as Reich Minister of the Interior, the SS at last acquired the remnants of power which had been left to the civil administration after the loss of its police powers.

It was during the war too that the characteristically personal nature of Hitler's rule became even more evident. After his consolidation of power in 1934, the number of Cabinet meetings had declined drastically and it met for the last time in 1937. From then onwards Hitler conducted business entirely with individuals and *ad hoc* groups with the exception of his military conferences. The coordination of civilian matters was provided by Lammers as head of the Reich Chancellery and by Göring as Chairman of the Reich Defence Council. During the war, as Hitler concentrated more and more on strategy and military detail, he became increasingly isolated in his military headquarters. Other leaders were obliged to maintain their own head-quarters near by, but even so power gradually accumulated in the hands of Hitler's secretary, Martin Bormann, who remained with him all the time. Towards the end of the war Bormann had contrived to control to a large extent access to the Führer and the drafting of his orders.

Finally, the war also brought into focus the nature of the regime's relationship with the German population. Despite its claim to have created a 'national community' in which the whole nation was united behind the Führer, the regime showed itself extremely unwilling to put this loyalty to the test by fully mobilizing the nation for war. Thus, in 1939, when the authorities seized the opportunity created by the war to insist on restrictions in order to halt inflation, they withdrew them almost at once in the face of

hostility from the workers, which, significantly, was taken up by the Gauleiter of the area most affected. Later on when, according to the reports of its
own security service, the country was far more willing for total mobilization,
Hitler and the Party still resisted attempts to cut down the civilian sector and
to mobilize women. This was partly for fear of antagonizing the population,
partly from unwillingness to admit the seriousness of the situation for fear of
losing prestige, and, in the case of female mobilization, partly for ideological
reasons.

In a sense, then, by accelerating the existing trends, the war produced
Nazism in its pure form. The façade provided by Conservative figures
during the 1930s had been removed, and the traditional centres of power had
finally been sapped and consumed by the cancerous growths of organizations
representing the authority of the Führer. Nazism had owed its success to the
backing of a conservative establishment and lower-middle class which had
seen it as a means of preserving the Wilhelmine social order through what
they saw as a traditional programme of social imperialism. When pursued
to its logical conclusion in war, however, the racial element in the Nazi
version of social imperialism was leading to the overthrow of the established
order, which the old establishment was powerless to prevent. Only the defeat
of Nazism through war enabled them to escape the consequences of their
initial misjudgement.

PART I The Rise of Nazism, 1919–33

1 The Founding of the Party and the Putsch, 1919-23

The Nazi Party was founded in Munich in 1919 against a background of military defeat and revolution. The German army, the pride of every German nationalist, had been forced to surrender. The military collapse had been followed in November 1918 by a revolution which forced the Kaiser to abdicate. The semi-autocratic regime of the Second Empire was now replaced by a constitution accepted by a National Assembly meeting at Weimar, which established a parliamentary democracy similar to those of Germany's enemies in the West. This represented a victory for the opposition forces of the Empire—Social Democrats, Catholics, and left-wing Liberals. They benefited from the fact that the majority of the population associated the Kaiser and his government with the defeat and felt that Germany needed a new start. Many hoped that the new form of government would at least conciliate the Allies and produce more favourable peace terms.

There were, however, a considerable number of Germans who responded to the new situation with a refusal to accept the triumph of the Left and a determination to reverse it at the earliest possible opportunity. They believed that Germany had been defeated not by military means but by disaffection among the workers in the factories at home, disaffection which had culminated in revolution. Germany had been 'stabbed in the back'. Among these right-wing opponents of the new order, the most extreme were the members of the so-called *völkisch* (racialist) movement, which had existed in Germany before and during the war. It was a movement characterized by pan-German nationalism, by uncompromising hostility towards liberalism, parliamentary democracy, and Marxist Socialism, and above all by an extreme and racialist form of antisemitism. These racialists, who now found themselves confronted with the victory of their bitterest enemies both at home and abroad, believed that the disaffection which had led to defeat had been stirred up by Marxist agitators working wittingly or unwittingly in the service of the Jews, who had wanted the defeat of Germany because German racial values represented the greatest barrier to their domination of the world. But the racialists also believed that the defeat represented the culmination of a long period of decay in the German body politic, caused by the infection of liberalism, which had undermined the true German values of national and social solidarity in which the individual saw his fulfilment in the service of the State. The Socialist agitators had, they thought, been

able to exploit the class barriers which had divided the country before and
during the war, and for which the bourgeoisie and its liberal and capitalist
ideology of individualism and profit-seeking bore a great responsibility. In
this context the racialists found it significant that the Jews were among the
most committed supporters of liberalism.

The experience of defeat and revolution, however, had taught some
members of the *völkisch* movement a lesson. The lesson they drew from their
interpretation of events was that they must now concentrate on trying to win
over the 'masses' – the workers and the lower-middle class – to the nationalist
and racialist cause. They must convince them that the Socialists and Liberals
were lackeys of the Jews, and that even the Conservatives had been corrupted
by Jewish ideas, as was clear from their compromise with parliamentarism
and democracy. They must replace the selfish individualism of liberalism
and the class-warfare doctrines of the Socialists with an ideology which
emphasized racial and therefore social solidarity. All classes must join
together in order to make Germany strong. Individuals must subordinate
themselves and their personal interests to the community. Jewish influence
must be eliminated. Unless this was achieved, Germany would never be
able to mobilize sufficient energy and strength to win back the territory she
had lost and go on to create a world empire.

But the racialists believed that this internal mobilization would be
impossible under the new political system established at Weimar in 1919.
In their view, parliamentary democracy merely ensured that divisions within
the community received the fullest possible expression through a party
system which served only to divide the nation. Moreover, under this system
government had to be based on compromises and parliamentary majorities
which inhibited decisive action. In a democracy, they argued, politics was
reduced to a counting of heads with no distinction made between the
strongest and most able and the weakest and most incompetent. The type
of political leader bred by this system was the man who was good at intrigue
and manoeuvring, the man who was prepared to compromise his principles
in order to keep his position. Yet what was required was a heroic leader,
ruthless and singleminded, a man who would lead by the sheer force of his
personality rather than by his ability to operate effectively in smoke-filled
committee rooms. Such a man could not emerge through the parliamentary
system; he would be dragged down by mediocrities jealous of his abilities.
The present political system must therefore be overthrown and replaced by a
dictatorship. What was needed was a leader and an elite who would have the
drive and willpower to achieve the internal mobilization of Germany. Such
an elite would be made up of those prepared to be utterly ruthless in the
racial and ideological purification of Germany which would be necessary to
achieve these goals. Such were the ideas beginning to crystallize in the minds
of some racialists in the year 1919.

During 1919, as the population became increasingly disillusioned with the performance of the moderates of Left and Right, the political mood in Germany shifted further and further to the extremes. The Peace Settlement of Versailles had imposed severe conditions on Germany and had met with a wave of protest. In particular, the 'war-guilt clause' by which Germany was obliged to accept full blame for the war stuck in the throats of the German people. Some of the unpopularity of the treaty was transferred to the Government which had been obliged to sign it. It was also transferred to the new democratic political system itself which had been expected to pacify the Allies but was now associated with national humiliation. In March 1920, an attempt was made to overthrow the National Government by a right-wing *coup* or 'putsch' carried out by a rebellious Free Corps[1] in collaboration with high-ranking army officers and Conservative politicians, and led by a Prussian civil servant named Kapp. The putsch proved unsuccessful, partly as a result of a general strike called by the deposed Socialist government and the trade unions, partly because of the incompetence of its leaders. But, although it failed to establish its authority at national level, the Right was far more successful in the state of Bavaria.

The founding of the Nazi Party

The Nazi Party was merely one of a number of similar *völkisch* groups which sprang up all over Germany during 1919. But it had the particular advantage of being based in Bavaria. There events had been especially turbulent. The swing to the Left had been even more marked than elsewhere; the swing to the Right was correspondingly strong. From the beginning of November 1918, there were four different left-wing regimes within a period of six months, including one established by Russian Communists on 7 April 1919. But on 1 May 1919 all revolutionary activity was crushed by troops sent by the Socialist central government, including the Free Corps. This force put down the revolution with considerable ferocity and restored the previous moderate Socialist government in Bavaria. In the meantime, however, the revolutionary events of these months had alienated the traditionally conservative population, the majority of whom were Catholic peasants. They too resented the removal of Bavaria's constitutional privileges by the Weimar Constitution. In March 1920, a right-wing group exploited the disorder caused by the Kapp putsch to carry out their own *coup* in Bavaria and they replaced the Socialist government by a right-wing regime under a Conservative, Gustav von Kahr. Under the Weimar Constitution the police were responsible to the federal states rather than to the central government. So, for the next few years, Bavaria became a haven for

[1] The Free Corps were paramilitary formations composed of ex-army officers and volunteers, mostly young men from the middle and lower middle classes. Though extremely right-wing, they were recruited by the Socialist central government to suppress left-wing revolutionary activity and to defend the eastern territories against Polish encroachment.

right-wing extremists from all over Germany. In most other states, and particularly in Prussia (which covered three-fifths of Germany), they were harried by the police at the orders of Socialist state governments. But in Bavaria the state authorities regarded their activities with benevolence. The early months of left-wing extremism had produced an excessive pre-occupation with the threat of Bolshevism and an atmosphere in which the Nazi Party, unlike similar groups elsewhere, could flourish.

The German Workers' Party originated in Munich as a small group mainly of workers from the railway repair sheds, known as the Workers' Political Society and led by Karl Harrer and Anton Drexler. Harrer (1890–1926) was a journalist who belonged to the Thule Society, the headquarters of the *völkisch* movement in Bavaria. Drexler (1884–1942) was a railway mechanic who during the war had tried to persuade his fellow workers to support the extreme annexationist programme of the Right. The group's activities were self-contained, consisting mainly of discussions among its own members with occasional invitations extended to guests. Drexler decided that the group should broaden its appeal and late in 1918 he suggested that they should found a political party to propagate their nationalist and antisemitic ideas among a wider audience. On 5 January 1919, the German Workers' Party[1] was founded with Harrer as chairman of the national party and Drexler as chairman of the Munich branch, the only one as yet in existence.

1   *Hitler joins the Party*

In September 1919 the DAP was joined by a soldier – Adolf Hitler. Before the war Hitler had acquired in his native Austria the extreme nationalist and antisemitic views widely prevalent there owing to bitter Czech/German rivalry and the dislike felt by the Catholic lower middle class in Vienna for the large Jewish bourgeoisie there. Shortly before the war, Hitler had moved to Munich and on the outbreak of war he joined a Bavarian regiment. His experience as a soldier taught him the importance of morale and of the part played by propaganda in politics. He believed that the Allies had been more successful in mobilizing the energy and enthusiasm of their own people and that the Germans had lost the war as a result of Socialist propaganda which had undermined their morale in the interests of international Jewry. He believed that Germany must learn from the Allies and that the first task must be to win the masses for nationalism and antisemitism. Only when this had been achieved would she be able to assert herself abroad.

After the war, Hitler came to the attention of his superiors as a dedicated nationalist and an extremely effective speaker, and after undergoing a course of political instruction he was employed by the Army to counter left-wing tendencies in its ranks. In September 1919, he was asked to report on the

[1] *Deutsche Arbeiter Partei* (DAP).

activities of the German Workers' Party and attended one of its meetings. Drexler described what happened:

On 12 September 1919, the German Workers' Party held a monthly meeting in the Veterans' Hall of the Sterneckerbräu, in the so-called 'Leiber Room'. Gottfried Feder[1] spoke on the 'Breaking of Interest Slavery'. The first National Socialist pamphlet, *My Political Awakening: From the Diary of a German Socialist Worker*, had just appeared. I had collected a few proof copies from the publisher, Dr Boepple, and was standing with five copies in my hand at the bar of the pub, listening with growing enthusiasm to the second speaker in the evening's discussion, who was a guest. He was dealing with the first speaker in the discussion, a Professor Baumann, who had urged the secession of Bavaria from Germany, and he was tackling the Professor in a way which it was a joy to watch. He gave a short but trenchant speech in favour of a greater Germany which thrilled me and all who could hear him. When the speaker had finished I rushed towards him, thanked him for what he had said and asked him to take the pamphlet I had away with him to read. It contained, I said, the rules and basic ideas of the new movement; if he was in agreement with them, he could come again in a week's time and work in a smaller circle, because we could do with people like him.

This was Hitler, and his outburst against the speaker's proposal for the secession of Bavaria from Germany made an immediate impression. Drexler, who had already transformed the DAP into an organization which sought to attract wider public support, recognized Hitler's usefulness as a public speaker and persuaded him to join the Party. The Party membership was still very small, and Hitler rose rapidly to become a member of the executive and by the end of the year its propaganda chief. The DAP provided him with an outlet for his political energies, and it was small enough to enable him to make his influence felt immediately. It attracted him because of its emphasis on antisemitism and on the need to win over the masses.

2   *Hitler's first political tract, 16 September 1919*

In the same month that he joined the Party, Hitler produced the first significant statement of his which has survived and which was concerned with the Jewish question. He wrote it at the request of his military superiors in reply to a letter asking for information on the Jewish problem from one of his fellow-participants in the Army political course, Adolf Gemlich. It expressed a number of ideas which were to remain basic to his thought for the rest of his life. Important, for example, was his emphasis on the fact that the Jews were a racial community rather than a religious group. Secondly, there was the emphasis on the need for the 'rebirth of the moral and spiritual energies of the nation ... through the ruthless action of

[1] Gottfried Feder was a civil engineer with cranky economic ideas, who believed that Germany's problems could be solved by what he called the 'breaking of interest slavery', a phrase which implied an attack on high finance which, he claimed, was in the hands of Jews.

personalities with a capacity for national leadership', though there is no evidence that he yet saw himself in such a role.

If the danger represented by the Jews today finds expression in the undeniable dislike of them felt by a large section of our people, the cause of this dislike is on the whole not to be found in the clear recognition of the corrupting activity of the Jews generally among our people, whether conscious or unconscious; it originates mainly through personal relationships, from the impression left behind him by the individual Jew and which is almost invariably unfavourable. Antisemitism thereby acquires only too easily the character of being a manifestation of emotion. But this is wrong. Antisemitism as a political movement must not be, cannot be, determined by emotional criteria, but only through the recognition of facts. The facts are as follows: First, the Jews are definitely a race and not a religious community. The Jew himself never calls himself a Jewish German, a Jewish Pole, a Jewish American, but only a German, a Polish, an American Jew. From the foreign nations in whose midst he lives the Jew has adopted very little more than their language. A German who is compelled to use French in France, Italian in Italy, Chinese in China, does not thereby become a Frenchman, an Italian, or a Chinese; similarly a Jew who happens to live among us and is thereby compelled to use the German language cannot be called a German. Even the Mosaic faith, however important for the maintenance of this race, cannot be considered as absolutely decisive in the question of whether or not someone is a Jew. There is hardly a single race whose members belong exclusively to one particular religion.

Through a thousand years of inbreeding, often practised within a very narrow circle, the Jew has in general preserved his race and character much more rigorously than many of the peoples among whom he lives. And as a result, there is living amongst us a non-German, foreign race, unwilling and unable to sacrifice its racial characteristics, to deny its own feeling, thinking and striving, and which none the less possesses all the political rights that we ourselves have. The feelings of the Jew are concerned with purely material things; his thoughts and desires even more so. The dance round the golden calf becomes a ruthless struggle for all those goods which, according to our innermost feelings, should not be the highest and most desirable things on this earth.

The value of the individual is no longer determined by his character, by the importance of his achievements for all, but solely by the amount of his possessions, by his money.

The value of the nation is no longer to be measured in terms of the sum of its moral and spiritual forces, but solely on the basis of the wealth of its material goods.

From this feeling emerges that concern and striving for money and for the power which can protect it which makes the Jew unscrupulous in his choice of means, ruthless in his use of them to achieve this aim.

In an autocratically governed state he whines for the favour of the 'Majesty' of the prince and abuses it to batten on his subjects like a leech. In a democracy he courts the favour of the masses, crawls before the 'majesty of the people' and yet knows only the majesty of money.

He destroys the character of the prince with byzantine flattery, and national pride, which is the strength of a nation, with mockery and shameless training in vice. His weapon is that public opinion which is never given utterance by the press, but is always led by it and falsified by it. His power is the power of money which in the form of interest effortlessly and interminably multiplies itself in his hands and forces upon nations that most dangerous of yokes, the sad consequences of which are so difficult to perceive because of the initial gleam of gold. Everything which makes men strive for higher things, whether religion, socialism or democracy, is for him only a means to an end, to the satisfaction of a lust for money and domination. His activities produce a racial tuberculosis among nations.

And this has the following result: Antisemitism stemming from purely emotive reasons will always find its expression in the form of programs [sic]. But antisemitism based on reason must lead to the systematic legal combating and removal of the rights of the Jew, which he alone of the foreigners living among us possesses (legislation to make them aliens). Its final aim, however, must be the uncompromising removal of the Jews altogether. Both are possible only under a government of national strength, never under a government of national impotence.

The Republic in Germany owes its birth not to the united national will of our people but to the cunning exploitation of a series of circumstances which combined to produce a deep general discontent. But these circumstances were independent of the form of the State, and are still active today; more active, indeed, today than before. And a large section of our people is aware that no mere change in the form of the State as such can alter or improve our position, but only the rebirth of the moral and spiritual energies of the nation.

This rebirth will be set in motion not by the political leadership of irresponsible majorities under the influence of party dogmas or of an irresponsible press, nor by catchwords and slogans of international coinage, but only through the ruthless action of personalities with a capacity for national leadership and an inner sense of responsibility.

But this fact robs the Republic of the internal support of the spiritual forces of the nation which are so necessary. And so the present leaders of the State are compelled to seek support from those who alone benefited from the changed situation in Germany and do so now, and who for this reason have been the driving forces of the revolution, namely, the Jews. Taking no account of the Jewish peril, which has certainly been recognized by present-day leaders—proof of this is the various statements of present leading figures—they are compelled to accept the support readily offered by the Jews for their own benefit, and therefore to pay the required price. And this price consists not only in giving the Jews every possible encouragement, but above all in hampering the struggle of the duped nation against their brother Jews—in the neutralizing of the antisemitic movement.

3 Programme of the NSDAP,[1] 24 February 1920

Apart from antisemitism, extreme nationalism and a form of anti-capitalism predominated in the Party's propaganda at this stage. All these elements were present in the Party programme which was presented on 24 February 1920 to a public meeting in the Hofbräuhaus, a big Munich beer cellar. The authorship of the programme has often been erroneously ascribed to Gottfried Feder, who played an influential role in the early years of the

[1] *Nationalsozialistische Deutsche Arbeiter Partei*: National Socialist German Workers' Party.

Party. In fact the programme was almost certainly composed by Drexler and Hitler and only Point 11 derives from Feder.

The Programme of the German Workers' Party is designed to be of limited duration. The leaders have no intention, once the aims announced in it have been achieved, of establishing fresh ones, merely in order to increase, artificially, the discontent of the masses and so ensure the continued existence of the Party.

1. We demand the union of all Germans in a Greater Germany on the basis of the right of national self-determination.

2. We demand equality of rights for the German people in its dealings with other nations, and the revocation of the peace treaties of Versailles and Saint-Germain.

3. We demand land and territory (colonies) to feed our people and to settle our surplus population.

4. Only members of the nation may be citizens of the State. Only those of German blood, whatever their creed, may be members of the nation. Accordingly, no Jew may be a member of the nation.

5. Non-citizens may live in Germany only as guests and must be subject to laws for aliens.

6. The right to vote on the State's government and legislation shall be enjoyed by the citizens of the State alone. We demand therefore that all official appointments, of whatever kind, whether in the Reich, in the states or in the smaller localities, shall be held by none but citizens.

We oppose the corrupting parliamentary custom of filling posts merely in accordance with party considerations, and without reference to character or abilities.

7. We demand that the State shall make it its primary duty to provide a livelihood for its citizens. If it should prove impossible to feed the entire population, foreign nationals (non-citizens) must be deported from the Reich.

8. All non-German immigration must be prevented. We demand that all non-Germans who entered Germany after 2 August 1914 shall be required to leave the Reich forthwith.

9. All citizens shall have equal rights and duties.

10. It must be the first duty of every citizen to perform physical or mental work. The activities of the individual must not clash with the general interest, but must proceed within the framework of the community and be for the general good.

We demand therefore:

11. The abolition of incomes unearned by work.

The breaking of the slavery of interest

12. In view of the enormous sacrifices of life and property demanded of a nation by any war, personal enrichment from war must be regarded as a crime against the nation. We demand therefore the ruthless confiscation of all war profits.

13. We demand the nationalization of all businesses which have been formed into corporations (trusts).

14. We demand profit-sharing in large industrial enterprises.

15. We demand the extensive development of insurance for old age.

16. We demand the creation and maintenance of a healthy middle class, the immediate communalizing of big department stores, and their lease at a cheap rate to

small traders, and that the utmost consideration shall be shown to all small traders in the placing of State and municipal orders.

17. We demand a land reform suitable to our national requirements, the passing of a law for the expropriation of land for communal purposes without compensation; the abolition of ground rent, and the prohibition of all speculation in land.

18. We demand the ruthless prosecution of those whose activities are injurious to the common interest. Common criminals, usurers, profiteers, etc., must be punished with death, whatever their creed or race.

19. We demand that Roman Law, which serves a materialistic world order, be replaced by a German common law.

20. The State must consider a thorough reconstruction of our national system of education (with the aim of opening up to every able and hard-working German the possibility of higher education and of thus obtaining advancement). The curricula of all educational establishments must be brought into line with the requirements of practical life. The aim of the school must be to give the pupil, beginning with the first sign of intelligence, a grasp of the notion of the State (through the study of civic affairs). We demand the education of gifted children of poor parents, whatever their class or occupation, at the expense of the State.

21. The State must ensure that the nation's health standards are raised by protecting mothers and infants, by prohibiting child labour, by promoting physical strength through legislation providing for compulsory gymnastics and sports, and by the extensive support of clubs engaged in the physical training of youth.

22. We demand the abolition of the mercenary army and the formation of a people's army.

23. We demand legal warfare on deliberate political mendacity and its dissemination in the press. To facilitate the creation of a German national press we demand:

(a) that all editors of, and contributors to newspapers appearing in the German language must be members of the nation;

(b) that no non-German newspapers may appear without the express permission of the State. They must not be printed in the German language;

(c) that non-Germans shall be prohibited by law from participating financially in or influencing German newspapers, and that the penalty for contravening such a law shall be the suppression of any such newspaper, and the immediate deportation of the non-Germans involved.

The publishing of papers which are not conducive to the national welfare must be forbidden. We demand the legal prosecution of all those tendencies in art and literature which corrupt our national life, and the suppression of cultural events which violate this demand.

24. We demand freedom for all religious denominations in the State, provided they do not threaten its existence nor offend the moral feelings of the German race.

The Party, as such, stands for positive Christianity, but does not commit itself to any particular denomination. It combats the Jewish-materialist spirit within and without us, and is convinced that our nation can achieve permanent health only from within on the basis of the principle: *The common interest before self-interest.*

25. To put the whole of this programme into effect, we demand the creation of a strong central state power for the Reich; the unconditional authority of the political central Parliament over the entire Reich and its organizations; and the

formation of Corporations based on estate and occupation for the purpose of carrying out the general legislation passed by the Reich in the various German states.

The leaders of the Party promise to work ruthlessly—if need be to sacrifice their very lives—to translate this programme into action.

4 *Hitler's description of the DAP*

When Hitler joined the DAP the Party was small and insignificant. No doubt he later exaggerated its weakness in order to emphasize his own impact upon it, but the following description, written in a newspaper article in 1929, is probably fairly accurate, at least for the very early period up to about October 1919:

Our little committee, which with its seven members in reality represented the whole party, was nothing but the managing committee of a small whist [*Skat*] club. The procedure was very simple. Every Wednesday a committee meeting took place. To start with, we met in a pathetic little room in a small pub, 'Rosenbad', in the Herrenstrasse. . . . In 1919, Munich was still in a bad way. Not much light, a good deal of dirt, refuse, shabby people, down-at-heel soldiers, in short the sort of picture which could be expected after four-and-a-half years of war, especially if, as in the case of Germany, the war had been followed by a shocking revolution. So it was a very poor 'committee room' in which we met. . . . The committee's proceedings consisted in reading out letters received, discussing replies to them, and registering the letters that were sent off following this discussion, i.e., reading them out also. Since that time I have developed a deadly hatred of writing letters and of letter writers.

It was always the same people, probably the chairmen of associations similar in size. We were sent comradely greetings, we were told that in their particular place the seed had been sown or had even sprouted. We were asked if we could say the same of ourselves and the necessity of joint action was stressed.

We had also 'association funds'. These consisted of material goods and cash. The cash fluctuated around 5 marks, and when times were good it rose to 12, 13, 15, and once, I remember, even to 17 marks. The material goods consisted of a cigar box in which the money was kept, notepaper, envelopes, a few stamps and the 'statutes' of the association.

5 *A Nazi handbill advertising a Hitler speech*

Hitler's main contribution to the Party in this early period was his ability as a political speaker and his drive and energy. From now onwards, he concentrated on a well-advertised campaign of public meetings. In Munich alone, in the eleven months beginning in February 1920, the Party staged 46 meetings with an average attendance of 1,350. Hitler was the principal speaker, with themes such as 'the Bolshevik menace', the Jews, and the peace treaties. The following is a typical handbill:

NATIONAL SOCIALIST GERMAN WORKERS' PARTY

With untiring activity the agents of the Jewish international stock exchange and moneylenders are trying to make Germany ripe for collapse, so that they may hand over the state and the economy to the

International Finance Trusts

This requires the division and thereby the weakening of our people at home. Hence also the embittered struggle of the

MERCENARIES

of international high finance against a party which, unlike all the other parties, is not composed of

'BOURGEOIS' or 'PROLETARIANS'

but of the creative mental and manual workers of our people. They alone can and will be the supporters of the future Germany.

Fellow Citizens!

A great public MASS MEETING will take place on Friday, November 19, 1920, in the Hofbräuhausfestsaal (Platzl),

'THE WORKER IN THE GERMANY OF THE FUTURE'

Speaker: Herr Adolf Hitler

6 *A speech by Hitler, 26 October 1920*

The following excerpt from a speech by Hitler, based on notes taken by a member of the Bavarian political police, indicates some of the main themes which he emphasized during this period. The speech, entitled 'National Welfare and Nationalist Idea', was given in the Kindlkeller, a Munich beer cellar:

We need some national pride again. But who can the nation be proud of these days? Of Ebert[1] perhaps? (*laughter*) Of the Government? We need a national will just as much. We must not always say: We can't do that. We must be able to do it. In order to smash this disgraceful peace treaty, we must regard every means as justified (*loud applause*). First, there must be a nationalist mood and then will come the economic prosperity of the nation. We must have blind faith in our future, in our recovery.

Now Hitler turned to deal with the Right and the Left. The Nationalists on the Right lack a social sense, the Socialists on the Left a nationalist one. He appeals to the parties on the Right: If you want to be nationalist then come down among your people and put away all your class pride. To the Left he appeals: You who proclaim your solidarity with the whole world, first show your solidarity with your own compatriots, be Germans first and foremost. Do they look like heroes who want to smash the world and yet crawl before foreigners for fear they might not like something they see here? (*applause*) You who are real revolutionaries, come over to us and fight with us for our whole nation (*loud applause*). Your place is not over there with the procurers of international capital, but with us, with your own people!! (*stormy applause*).

[1] Friedrich Ebert, Social Democrat President of the Weimar Republic, 1919–25.

Then Hitler turned to the future of Germany, to the youth of Germany, and, in particular, with warm words for their intellectual leaders, the German students. Your place is with us, with the people. You who are still young and still have the fire of enthusiasm in your veins, come over to us, join our fighting party, which pursues its aims ruthlessly, with every means, even with force! (*loud applause*) We are not a class party, but the party of honest workers (*Schaffenden*). Our strength does not lie in the International but in our own strength, that is to say in our people! (*long and stormy applause*)

7 *Hitler as a public speaker*

Hitler succeeded in establishing a notable *rapport* with the Munich masses whose economic plight was worsening during this period owing to progressive inflation. He showed remarkable intuition in sensing and articulating their hopes and fears so accurately. He succeeded in projecting himself as a representative figure—an ex-soldier now drifting without a regular job, filled with hatred and resentment against those considered responsible for the plight of Germany, which he in turn identified with the personal plight of his audience. But he not only showed his hearers that he understood their mood and their predicament and gave them an emotionally convincing explanation for their problems; he also conveyed to them his own willpower and determination to change things, to restore Germany to her former greatness and to destroy those who were responsible for the present situation. Kurt Ludecke, one of Hitler's early associates, later recorded his impressions on first hearing him speak in 1922:

My critical faculty was swept away. Leaning from the rostrum as if he were trying to impel his inner self into the consciousness of all these thousands, he was holding the masses, and me with them, under an hypnotic spell by the sheer force of his conviction. . . . I do not know how to describe the emotions that swept over me as I heard this man. His words were like a scourge. When he spoke of the disgrace of Germany, I felt ready to spring on any enemy. His appeal to German manhood was like a call to arms; the gospel he preached, a sacred truth. He seemed another Luther. I forgot everything but the man; then glancing around, I saw that his magnetism was holding these thousands as one. Of course I was ripe for this experience. I was a man of thirty-two, weary with disgust and disillusionment, a wanderer seeking a cause, a patriot without a channel for his patriotism, a yearner after the heroic without a hero. The intense will of the man, the passion of his sincerity, seemed to flow from him into me. I experienced an exaltation that could be likened only to religious conversion.

In February 1920 the Party had changed its name to 'National Socialist German Workers' Party', thereby emphasizing its attempt to combine both a nationalist and a socialist appeal. An early membership list of some 200 names showed a fair cross-section of the city's population: tradesmen, craftsmen, shopkeepers, bank and post-office employees, and a few doctors and engineers as well as a number of soldiers and workers. Largely as a result of Hitler's successful oratory, the membership gradually increased. At the end of 1920 it had reached 2,000 and by August 1921 3,300, and branches were beginning to be founded outside Munich. The first was established in Rosenheim, 40 miles from Munich, as early as April 1920. In July 1921 a branch was founded in Hanover and one or two others followed elsewhere. In November 1922, however, the Party was banned in Prussia and in some other states; Bavaria, and Munich in particular, remained the main centre. The success of the Party drew the attention of military circles. At the end of 1920, with the assistance of funds from the Reichswehr, the Party purchased a newspaper. Having appeared since 1887 as the *Münchener Beobachter*,[1] a racialist weekly, the *Völkischer Beobachter* (*VB*), as it had been renamed on 9 August 1919, was now published twice a week as the organ of the NSDAP. It did not become a daily until 8 February 1923. The state of the Party's finances was at the moment precarious. Funds were derived from membership dues, very small, collections at meetings and occasional contributions from wealthy sympathizers. Nearly all the staff were unpaid.

Hitler takes over the Party leadership, August 1921

By the middle of 1921 Hitler had clearly established himself as the key figure in the Party. Not only did the Party owe its rise in membership to his abilities as a speaker, but he also possessed extremely useful connexions with the Army, which he had left on 31 March 1920, but with which he remained in touch through Captain Ernst Röhm, who acted as a political liaison officer for the Army HQ and was a member of the NSDAP. Yet Hitler was still officially only the propaganda chief. In January 1920 Harrer had been obliged to resign as chairman of the Party. He had disagreed with Hitler and Drexler about the intensive propaganda activities of the Party, wishing it to remain a select group on the lines of a Masonic lodge. Harrer had been replaced as chairman by Drexler. Drexler recognized Hitler's ability and, as he told Feder on 13 February 1921, wanted him to assume more responsibility in the organization, 'though without my being pushed into the background in consequence'.[2] Hitler himself, however, rightly regarded his propaganda activities as the most important function in the Party, particularly since he still saw his objective as the winning of 'the masses' for more important nationalist figures. He was not tempted by the routine work of chairman as carried out by Drexler and declined Drexler's offer of the post.

---

[1] The *Munich Observer*.
[2] cf. Albrecht Tyrell, 'Vom "Trommler" zum Führer. Eine Untersuchung zum Wandel von Hitlers Selbstverständnis zwischen 1919 und 1924' (Dissertation, Bonn 1972), p. 53. In this section we have followed Tyrell's arguments.

A few months later, however, the question of the organization of the Party and of Hitler's position within it was brought to a head when the committee began to pursue a course of action to which Hitler strongly objected. This brought home to him for the first time the importance of the formal distribution of power within the organization and forced him not only to take over the chairmanship of the Party but to establish a new structure of authority within it in which the chairman was no longer merely *primus inter pares* within a committee, but a leader, superior to the committee. The crisis persuaded him that only in this way could he ensure that the Party pursued the policies which he believed were the right ones. And then, having established his position as leader, he rationalized this development with a theory of political leadership which condemned the traditional form of committee organization and insisted on the need for a dominant leader.

8 *Hitler's ultimatum, July 1921*

The issue which brought the conflict to a head was the fusion of the NSDAP with other National Socialist parties, which had been discussed at conferences in August 1920 at Salzburg and in March 1921 at Zeitz. Other parties involved were the German Socialist Party,[1] whose organization was more widespread throughout Germany than that of the NSDAP, and National Socialist groups from Austria and Bohemia such as the German National Socialist Party. Drexler and other NSDAP leaders favoured a union of such parties on the ground that a unified *völkisch* movement would be more effective than various groups operating on their own. Hitler, however, was contemptuous of the other racialist groups which he regarded as too bourgeois in their political style and too academic in their antisemitism. He was convinced that a merger would merely dilute the energy and drive of the Nazi Party. It would also of course threaten the position which he had built up for himself as the indispensable motor of the Nazi Party, a role where at last he found personal fulfilment.

During a long absence of Hitler in Berlin in the early summer of 1921, Drexler was persuaded by a Dr Dickel, the leader of a *völkisch* group in Augsburg, to merge the NSDAP with Dickel's own group, the *Abendländischer Bund* (Western League). Informed of this development by one of his Munich colleagues, Hitler returned at once from Berlin and tried to persuade the committee to change their minds. When they refused, he resigned on 11 July and threatened to set up his own party. Three days later he issued an ultimatum stating his conditions for rejoining. These included a stipulation that the headquarters of the Party should remain in Munich. If a merger with the *Abendländischer Bund* or the DSP were carried through, the headquarters would be moved to Augsburg or Berlin, thereby depriving Hitler of much of his influence since his main personal following was in Munich. The terms of his ultimatum were as follows:

[1] *Deutschsozialistische Partei* (DSP).

1. That an extraordinary membership meeting be immediately summoned within eight days from today with the following agenda: The present committee of the Party to resign their offices. At the new election I demand the post of chairman with dictatorial powers for the immediate establishment of an action committee which must ruthlessly purge the Party of foreign elements which have now penetrated it.[1] The action committee to consist of three people.

2. That the unalterable rule be laid down that the headquarters of the movement is and always shall be Munich. Finally, that the Party leadership shall be vested in the Munich local branch until the movement has reached a size sufficient to enable it as a whole to finance its own Party leadership.

3. That any further alteration of the name or programme of the Party shall be absolutely avoided for the next six years. Members working in this direction or to this end shall be excluded from the movement.

4. All further attempts at such a fusion between the National Socialist German Workers' Party and the movement which unjustifiably calls itself the German National Socialist Party must in the future cease. The Party can never agree to a fusion with those who wish to make contact with us; they must join the Party. Reciprocal gestures on our part are out of the question. . . .

I do not make these demands because I am hungry for power, but rather because recent events have convinced me now more than ever that without iron leadership the Party will in a very short time cease to be what it ought to be: a National Socialist German Workers' Party and not an *Abendländischer Bund*.

9 *Extraordinary membership meeting of the NSDAP, 29 July 1921*

A sharp struggle followed, during which Drexler attempted to defeat Hitler's move by expelling some of his colleagues from the Party. Hitler's victory was swift. Drexler changed his mind and threw in his lot with Hitler and the opposition was split. Drexler had long agreed with Hitler on the need for vigorous mass propaganda and he realized that the Party could not dispense with Hitler's superior talent as a public speaker. Hitler had also the backing of the younger and more activist element in the Party who had been attracted by his drive. The dispute had already been settled when a special meeting of the Party was called on 29 July. Hitler dominated the meeting and was elected chairman of the Party. According to the minutes:

The chairman of the meeting was the previous chairman of the association, Herr Anton Drexler.

Secretary: Comrade Herr Hermann Esser.[2]

Participants: 554 members of the Munich local branch who had paid an entrance fee.

Comrade Hitler took over the chair of the meeting and announced the following agenda:

[1] The attribution of the conflict to 'foreign elements' is an example of the paranoia characteristic of the racialists. Whether or not Hitler himself believed it, he clearly thought it was a telling point for his Party comrades.

[2] Hermann Esser, a young ex-Social Democrat (born in 1900), reputed to be a procurer, admired Hitler's skill as a speaker and his radicalism. Since October 1920 he had become the most active speaker in the Party.

1. Report on recent events.
2. Amendments or additions to the statutes.
3. A new election of the committee.

He then read out the draft of the new statutes. Comrade Hitler as chairman of the meeting then proceeded to take the vote on the new statutes. The statutes were with one exception (Comrade Posch) unanimously adopted (*enthusiastic applause*). Comrade Drexler then began to speak and proposed the election of Comrade Hitler as Chairman of the Party. The election is unanimously confirmed with loud applause.

10 *Article 5 of the Statutes*

Drexler was made honorary president. The statutes adopted at this meeting formalized the dictatorial powers of the Party chairman. The committee of Party officers created by the first statutes of 1920 was retained merely for the purposes of registration of the NSDAP as a legal organization, while Hitler's responsibility to the membership meeting was a formality:

The headquarters of the National Socialist German Workers' Association is in Munich. The leadership of the Party as such will be combined with the leadership of the Munich branch so long as the Association does not have sufficient funds flowing in from the individual branches to finance a leadership for the Party itself.

Since the Munich branch is the mother group of the whole movement, generous use will be made of its income as before in order to promote the movement as a whole.

The association is subdivided into local branches which are subordinate to the main headquarters.

These will be combined to form *Gau* organizations and the *Gaue* to form state organizations as required.

In order to facilitate a decisive leadership of the movement, the I. Chairman is made responsible for the leadership of the movement as a whole. The leadership of the individual branches is the responsibility of the chairmen of the local branches.

The I. Chairman of the movement as a whole is its legal representative. In his absence the II. Chairman will deputize for him.

The Party headquarters section

The Party headquarters section consists of: (1) the committee to be legally elected by the membership meeting and composed of the first and second chairmen, the first and second treasurers, and the first and second secretaries; (2) the subordinate committees. Since the real responsibility for the leadership of the association lies in the hands of the first chairman, his position must be regarded as standing above the committee. He is responsible solely to the membership meeting.

Hitler buttressed his leadership by placing his leading supporters in positions of authority. Hermann Esser was put in charge of propaganda, and Max Amann, Hitler's former army sergeant, became business manager.

The development of the Party, 1921–23

11 *A different kind of party*

In a memorandum of 7 January 1922 Hitler emphasized the fundamental differences of character between the traditional parties and the NSDAP. The NSDAP had not the limited appeal of the bourgeois parties of prewar Germany – it was a new kind of party, a party of action, a movement of the people:

The ninth of November[1] meant above all the complete collapse, not of party life in itself but of bourgeois party life, of that mixture of goodwill, harmless naïvety, theoretical knowledge and utter lack of instinct. The racialist movement also, just like the bourgeois national parties, utterly failed in its main task of winning the broad masses for the national cause. Responsibility for the collapse lies with the bourgeoisie. The racialists [*Völkische*] were not capable of drawing the practical conclusions from correct theoretical judgements, especially in the Jewish question. In this way the German racialist movement developed a pattern similar to that of the 1880s and 1890s. As in those days, its leadership gradually fell into the hands of highly honourable but fantastically naïve men of learning, professors, district councillors, schoolmasters and barristers – in short a bourgeois, idealistic and refined class. It lacked the warm breath of the nation's youthful vigour. The impetuous force of headstrong fire-eaters was rejected as demagogy. The new movement was therefore a nationalist movement but no longer a movement of the people. . . . There reappeared in the new movement the distressing characteristics of our bourgeois parties, lacking any uniform discipline or form. . . .

This utter failure in all the matters mentioned led to the founding of the NSDAP. The new movement aimed at providing what the others did not: a racialist movement with a firm social base, a hold over the broad masses, welded together in an iron-hard organization, instilled with blind obedience and inspired by a brutal will, a party of struggle and action. . . . If this new kind of movement is to become great and important, its aims must be propagated with fanatical ardour and the total energy of its few supporters must be placed at the service of its propaganda as there is nothing there yet to organize.

Having acquired power over the Munich party, Hitler determined to consolidate his authority by abolishing the autonomy enjoyed by the local branches under Drexler's leadership. By May 1922 there was a total of 45 branches, though most of them were in Bavaria. At a meeting of branch leaders in January 1922 Hitler insisted on their subordination to the Munich headquarters. But in actual fact he found it impossible to exercise effective control over the Party outside Bavaria because the situation in the racialist movement elsewhere was so confused. Nevertheless, his authority over the Party in Munich was now absolute.

[1] 9 November 1918 – the date of the declaration of the Republic.

12 *The founding of the SA, 3 August 1921*

In the summer of 1921, the armed squads employed to protect Party meetings from disruption by opponents were formally organized in a special unit under the cover name of 'Gymnastic and Sports Section', renamed in October the 'Storm Detachments' (SA). In the SA Hitler provided a form of organization which appealed to the considerable number of ex-soldiers and ex-Free Corps men who had no use for conventional political activity, but were looking for the type of violent action which they could no longer find since the dissolution of the Free Corps by the Government. The SA was paramilitary in both organization and appearance—it had military ranks, its men wore uniform and marched in formation. The founding of the unit was formally announced in the *Völkischer Beobachter*:

The NSDAP has created its own gymnastic and sports section within the framework of its organization. It is intended to bind our young party members together to form an organization of iron, so that it may put its strength at the disposal of the whole movement to act as a battering ram. It is intended to uphold the idea of the importance of the military for a free people. It is intended to provide protection for the propaganda activity of the leaders. But above all it is intended to develop in the hearts of our young supporters a tremendous desire for action, to drive home to them and burn into them the fact that history does not make men, but men history, and that he who allows himself to be put in the chains of slavery without any resistance deserves the yoke of slavery. But it [the SA] will also encourage mutual loyalty and cheerful obedience to the leader.[1]

13 *The stormtrooper's pledge*

A good indication of the nature of the organization is provided by the pledge which every stormtrooper was obliged to make on joining:

As a member of the storm troop of the NSDAP I pledge myself by its storm flag [*Sturmfahne*]: to be always ready to stake life and limb in the struggle for the aims of the movement; to give absolute military obedience to my military superiors and leaders; to bear myself honourably in and out of service; to be always companionable towards other comrades!

14 *The Nazis break up a meeting*

The SA was employed to protect Nazi meetings from disruption, to assist in propaganda activities, and to disrupt the meetings of other parties. On 14 September 1921, for example, a meeting of the federalist Bavarian League was disrupted, as described by a correspondent of the *Münchner Neueste Nachrichten*:

The meeting, which was well attended, came to a premature end owing to an attack systematically planned by the National Socialists. National Socialist youths had early

---

[1] The word 'leader' probably refers here rather to the immediate superior SA officer than to Hitler, since it was still of too general application to be used specifically of Hitler.

on taken the seats near the speakers' platform, and numerous National Socialists were distributed as well throughout the hall. When Hitler, the leader of the National Socialists, appeared in the hall, he was greeted by his followers with demonstrative applause. His arrival gave the cue for the violence that followed. The former editor of the *Völkischer Beobachter*, Esser, climbed on a chair and declared that Bavaria owed the situation it was in to the Jews. Ballerstedt[1] had always avoided the Jewish question. The National Socialists therefore saw themselves 'forced' to stop Ballerstedt from speaking and let Hitler speak instead. Hitler's followers, bent on making it a National Socialist meeting, thereupon occupied the platform. But a large section of the meeting protested and demanded that Ballerstedt should speak. He had pushed his way through to the platform, but could not begin because the National Socialists were all the time shouting, 'Hitler!' The uproar grew even worse when someone tried to prevent the fight which was feared by switching off the electricity. When the lights came on again, Ballerstedt declared that anybody who tried to disturb the meeting would be charged with disturbing the peace. After this the young people on the platform, many of them hardly in their teens, surrounded him, beat him up and pushed him down the platform steps. Ballerstedt received a head injury which bled badly. As the audience were naturally growing more and more excited, three members of the state police appeared in the hall. A [plain-clothes] detective declared the meeting dissolved. A fairly strong group of state police then cleared the hall; this operation went smoothly without further incident after an announcement that the charge for admission would be refunded.

Intimidation of political opponents became a regular activity of the SA, involving especially members of left-wing parties—notably, the vicious brawl with Social Democrats in the Hofbräuhaus in November 1921. Opponents who demanded the right to speak in the so-called 'discussion' at Nazi meetings were often given rough treatment.

It became the practice to ban the attendance of Jews at Nazi functions—'Jews are not admitted' was included as a matter of course in the text of Nazi posters. Political violence, whatever its outcome, was to Hitler's advantage: it gave him and his party publicity, and the Bavarian authorities were surprisingly tolerant of such disorder. After the assassination of the Jewish German Foreign Minister, Walther Rathenau, by right-wing fanatics in June 1922, the NSDAP was prohibited in almost every state in Germany. Yet no action was taken by the Government in Bavaria, where the Party's activities continued unabated. In the autumn of 1922, Julius Streicher, a notorious antisemite from Nuremberg, declared his allegiance to Hitler. Streicher, who controlled the DSP in northern Bavaria, was an important acquisition and became one of the Party's most popular speakers.

15 *The first NSDAP rally, 27–29 January 1923*

The NSDAP arranged for its first Party rally in Munich in January 1923. The Bavarian Government took fright at the possible consequences and

[1] The leader of the Bavarian League.

declared martial law in the city. The rally was banned, but, thanks to the intercession of Röhm and a last-minute assurance by Hitler that he would not attempt a 'putsch', the meetings were allowed to go ahead as planned. Karl Alexander von Müller, a Munich professor of history, was present at the rally.

On the 28th, 6,000 S A men instead of 5,000 lined up on the Marsfeld. The previous evening Hitler had dashed in his car from one meeting to another. In the 'Löwen-bräu' I heard him speak in public for the first time. How often I had attended public meetings in this hall! But neither during the war nor during the revolution had I been met on entering by so hot a breath of hypnotic mass excitement. It was not only the special tension of these weeks, of this day. 'Their own battle songs, their own flags, their own symbols, their own salute,' I noted down, 'military-like stewards, a forest of bright red flags with black swastika on white ground, a strange mixture of the military and the revolutionary, of nation-alist and socialist—in the audience also: mainly of the depressed middle class of every level—will it be welded together again here?' For hours, endless booming military music; for hours, short speeches by subordinate leaders. When was he coming? Had something unexpected happened? Nobody can describe the fever that spread in this atmosphere. Suddenly there was a movement at the back entrance. Words of command. The speaker on the platform stopped in mid-sentence. Everybody jumped up, saluting. And right through the shouting crowds and the streaming flags the one they were waiting for came with his followers, walking quickly to the platform, his right arm raised stiffly. He passed by me quite close and I saw. This was a different person from the one I had met now and then in private houses; his gaunt, pale features contorted as if by inward rage, cold flames darting from his protruding eyes, which seemed to be searching out foes to be conquered. Did the crowd give him this mysterious power? Did it emanate from him to them? 'Fanatical, hysterical romanticism with a brutal core of willpower,' I noted down. 'The declining middle class may be carrying this man, but he is not of them; he assuredly comes from totally different depths of darkness. Is he simply using them as a jumping-off point. . . .?

Hitler's growing self-confidence

The 1923 rally was a triumph for Hitler, who showed signs of increasing self-confidence. There has been a tendency among historians to see him in his early years in the Party in terms of the position which he held later on. But his early years were, in fact, a period of development both of his ideology and programme and also of his self-confidence as a political leader. Initially, it is doubtful whether he saw himself as more than a 'drummer' for the extreme Right, a man who could use his gift of oratory to win for his ideas a support which could then be used by some more substantial figure of the Right such as General Ludendorff, the old German war leader who had become a prominent racialist.

16 *Hitler's bohemian habits*

In the early years, his behaviour had been distinctly bohemian, as one of his associates, Kurt Ludecke, recalled:

Hitler loved beauty and appreciated good taste, but it never occurred to him to consider himself as an object that people might examine with curiosity. I soon gave up my futile attempts to induce him to give more heed to his person and his dress, though it might have been advantageous for the leader of the Party not to look so much like a displaced person. He clung to his shapeless trenchcoat and clumsy shoes. At every vehement gesture during his speeches his hair would fall over his eyes. He continued to eat in a hurry, some messy stuff or other, while he ran from place to place. If you succeeded in making him stand still for long enough to confer on important matters, he would take a piece of greasy sausage and a slice of bread out of his pocket and bolt them while he talked. . . . In the long run it was unfortunate for the Party that Hitler had this typical Austrian *Schlamperei*, this lackadaisical casualness. Aside from his many ingratiating qualities, and of course his political genius, he suffered from total disorderliness. Naturally, this lessened with time; but at the beginning it was obvious in everything.

17 *Hitler moves into society*

Gradually, as Hitler acquired an ever larger personal following, his self-confidence and his ambitions increased. Through Party contacts he gained access to Munich society and attracted the attention of wealthy families, some of which like the Bechsteins, the piano manufacturers, helped him financially. Although he never really abandoned his irregular style of life, his appearance began to change. His pretentiously bourgeois manners were, however, still accompanied by a certain awkwardness of behaviour in private which contrasted sharply with his self-confidence as a public speaker. He frequently visited Ernst Hanfstaengl, a Wagner enthusiast who came from a family of wealthy art publishers. The historian von Müller met Hitler at Hanfstaengl's house:

My foreboding about Hitler grew only slowly and uncertainly. The second time I met him was peaceful enough: it was for coffee at Erna Hanfstaengl's at the request of Abbot Alban Schachleiter[1] who wanted to meet him; my wife and I were domestic decoration. The four of us had already sat down round the polished mahogany table by the window when the bell rang; through the open door we could see him greeting his hostess in the narrow passage with almost obsequious politeness, putting down his riding whip, taking off his velour hat and trenchcoat and finally unbuckling a belt with a revolver and hanging it on a peg. It looked comic and reminded me of Karl May.[2] None of us knew then how minutely all

[1] Abbot Schachleiter (1860–1937) was one of the first Roman Catholic priests to work actively for the Nazi movement. Previously head of a monastery in Prague, he moved to Munich after the war and first met Hitler in 1922.

[2] A popular German writer of adventure stories particularly of the Wild West, which Hitler read passionately as a boy.

these little details in dress and manner were calculated for their effect, just like his striking short trimmed moustache which was narrower than his unattractive broad nose. The man who entered was no longer the stubborn and gauche instructor in a badly fitting uniform who had stood before me in 1919. His look expressed awareness of public success; but a peculiar gaucherie still remained, and one had the uncomfortable feeling that he was conscious of it and resented its being noticed. His face was still thin and pale with an expression almost of suffering. But his protruding pale blue eyes stared at times with a ruthless severity and above his nose between the eyebrows was concentrated a fanatical willpower. On this occasion too he spoke little and for most of the time listened with great attention. . . .

18 *Hitler's inability to relax*

According to Ludecke, Hitler's inability to relax in private stemmed from an intensity which found its main outlet in public declamation:

The fact that he was always the centre of a spellbound audience explained why for many years Hitler was unable to listen to anyone or carry on a normal conversation. In Hitler's circle he alone talked; others listened. There he aired his ideas and practised his speeches, but at the same time his character became set in a mould of intellectual isolation which proved one of his weaknesses.

19 *Hitler attends a party*

One guest at a party in Munich in 1923 later described the experience:

Hitler had sent word to his hostess that he had to attend an important meeting and would not arrive until late: I think it was about eleven o'clock. He came none the less in a respectable blue suit and carrying an extravagantly large bouquet of roses, which he presented to his hostess as he kissed her hand. While he was being introduced, he wore the expression of a public prosecutor at an execution. I remember being struck by his voice when he thanked the lady of the house for tea or cakes, of which, incidentally, he ate an amazing quantity. It was a remarkably emotional voice, and yet it made an impression of harshness rather than of conviviality or intimacy. However, he said hardly anything but sat there in silence for about an hour; he seemed to be tired. Not until the hostess was rash enough to let fall a remark about the Jews, whom she jestingly defended, did he begin to speak and then he spoke without stopping. After a while he thrust back his chair and stood up, still speaking, or rather yelling, in a powerful penetrating voice such as I have never heard from anyone else. A child woke up in the next room and began to cry. After he had for more than half an hour delivered quite a witty but very one-sided oration on the Jews, he suddenly broke off, went up to his hostess, begged to be excused and kissed her hand as he took his leave. The rest of the company, whom he seemed not to like, were only vouchsafed a curt bow from the doorway.

The Hitler putsch, 8–9 November 1923

During 1923, the political situation in Germany became increasingly critical. At the end of 1922, Germany had been in arrears in the reparations owed to the Allies under the Versailles Treaty and subsequent agreements. The amount was small but on 11 January 1923 French and Belgian troops occupied the Ruhr area, the main centre of Germany's heavy industry, with the intention of acquiring coal and using the Ruhr as a pawn. The German Government retaliated by ordering the inhabitants of the Ruhr to offer passive resistance to the French.

The economic disruption caused by the Ruhr occupation gave the final blow to the value of the German mark which had been rapidly deteriorating since the war. The war had left a national debt of 150 billion marks and between 1919 and 1923 Germany had paid for the foreign exchange she needed with which to meet reparations by printing more and more German currency. As a result, at the beginning of 1920 the mark had already fallen to one-tenth of its prewar value and by the beginning of 1923 a prewar gold mark was equivalent to 2,500 new paper marks. The French invasion now accelerated this trend. In January 1923 the dollar was equivalent to 10,000 marks, in April to 25,000, in May to 50,000, in June to 110,000, in July to 350,000 and in August to 4·6 million paper marks.

The effects of the inflation were felt most acutely by the middle class, particularly those living on fixed incomes from investments or on rents which had been frozen by the Government; their savings were wiped out. There was full employment, but workers also suffered to some extent from the failure of wages and salaries to keep up with spiralling prices. The only people who profited from the inflation were industrialists and, for a time, farmers. Industrialists could export goods and use the foreign exchange acquired to invest in new plant, which did not decline in value. The peasantry too found their mortgages and other debts wiped out almost overnight. One of the most important results of the inflation therefore was to alienate a substantial section of the middle class from the Republic, which was held responsible for the inflation.

In the situation created by the Ruhr occupation the Army authorities became increasingly concerned that France or other states on Germany's borders might try to annex parts of German territory. In an attempt to mobilize all available German forces to meet this threat, the Army secretly took under its wing many of the extreme right-wing paramilitary leagues to form a so-called 'Black Reichswehr'. Among these groups was the SA, which, as a result, became increasingly militarized during 1923, a tendency to which it had been prone from the beginning. Hitler himself did not approve of this development. He believed that the Ruhr occupation and the inflation were polarizing political opinion in Germany and that civil war was imminent. In view of this he now felt obliged to work with other nationalist groups. But he did not wish to be forced into a position of cooperating with the Government against the French. He wished the nationalist forces to be used to defeat any *coup* by the Left and to replace the Republican regime with a right-wing dictatorship.

In August 1923, the crisis came to a head. It had now become clear that the policy of passive resistance had failed and, after pressure from the Social Democrats, the rather conservative government of Wilhelm Cuno, a Hamburg shipping magnate, resigned. It was replaced by a government under a right-wing Liberal, Gustav Stresemann, which included the Social Democrats. On 26 September, the Government announced the ending of passive resistance in the Ruhr. These developments met with great hostility from the Right, particularly in Bavaria. Hitler himself believed that they represented the first stage in the establishment of a Communist regime, particularly in view of the fact that the Communists had already allied themselves with the Socialist state governments of Thuringia and Saxony to form proletarian paramilitary units. In the meantime, Hitler had become political head of the Kampfbund, an organization which coordinated the activities of the NSDAP and other paramilitary groups in Bavaria. Under pressure from the Kampfbund, the Bavarian Government now declared a state of emergency and appointed Kahr (who had resigned from the Government in 1921) as State Commissioner with dictatorial powers. There now developed an uneasy relationship between the Bavarian authorities and the Kampfbund. Both groups shared a determination to bring down the national government in Berlin. It was thought that this could be best achieved by a march on Berlin, using the excuse of the need to crush the left-wing governments in Thuringia and Saxony which lay between Bavaria and Berlin. They hoped that they could coordinate an action with right-wing groups in north Germany and in particular the Army.

20 *The refusal to ban the* Völkischer Beobachter, *October 1923*

Clearly the attitude of the Army authorities in Bavaria would be of vital importance to the success of such an enterprise; it was soon to be put to the test. The national government in Berlin had replied to the declaration of a state of emergency in Bavaria by declaring a state of emergency in the Reich as a whole and by handing over emergency powers to the Army Commander, General von Seeckt. Acting under these emergency powers, the Reich authorities now attempted to get the Bavarian authorities to ban the *Völkischer Beobachter*, which had launched a series of bitter and mendacious attacks on the new Chancellor, Stresemann. Kahr refused to comply with the order and in a letter of 4 October to General von Lossow, commander of the Bavarian division of the Army, gave his reasons in an attempt to persuade him to follow suit:

Because of the untruths and attacks in Nos. 200 and 201, I have considered banning the *Völkischer Beobachter* in Bavaria too. But in the interests of the unification of all patriots and German-thinking circles, I have refrained from a ban for the time being and have had the chief editor emphatically warned. He has been told that ruthless measures will be taken at the slightest attempt to continue the present policy of criticizing the tasks and intentions of the General State Commissioner

[Kahr]. Since the *Völkischer Beobachter* has given no fresh cause for complaint, I have not been in a position to issue a ban. . . . Independent action by the Reichswehr against the *Völkischer Beobachter* would inevitably arouse public opinion very strongly in its favour and against the Reichswehr, and would give the impression of a *coup* by the Reich in fact, if not in law. Had I banned the *Völkischer Beobachter* without a valid reason, new splits and difficulties would certainly have appeared in the patriotic movement, embitterment against the Reichswehr would have been created among some of the leagues really concerned with the preservation of the unity of the Reich, and harm would therefore have been done to the idea of the Reich. My aim and task, on the contrary, is to unite all nationalist forces, in order to preserve peace and order with their support and to do as much as I can to smooth the path out of this difficult situation for the building up of the Reich.

The Army authorities in Berlin then intervened and ordered General von Lossow to carry out the ban by force. Lossow, however, refused to comply, was dismissed, and thereupon swore an oath of loyalty to the Bavarian authorities, who reinstated him.

21 *Differences over tactics between Kahr and the Kampfbund*

Although Kahr and the Kampfbund were basically in agreement on their objectives, they differed in what they believed to be the necessary tactics. In October 1923, the national government had carried out a pre-emptive stroke by ordering the Army to crush the left-wing regimes in Saxony and Thuringia. This caused the authorities in Bavaria to hesitate. They were uncertain of the attitude of the Army outside Bavaria and they now no longer had an excuse to march on Berlin since the national government had shown its determination to deal with the extreme Left. Kahr therefore decided to warn the leaders of the Kampfbund against independent and precipitate action and held a meeting with the Bavarian paramilitary groups or leagues on 6 November:

To introduce the discussion, Kahr said the first priority is the creation of a nationalist government. We agree on that. Now we have to divide the work between us. The Stresemann Government is not nationalist and therefore must be fought from the start. Kahr then dealt with the fact that various leagues—the Kampfbund was not mentioned by name—had acted somewhat independently during the last few days and it was rumoured that the leagues would start the attack independently. He warned them against this, for he counted on the cooperation of the leagues, if the abnormal path was chosen. For, in the present situation, it was doubtful whether the normal path could be followed. The abnormal path would have to be prepared. Preparations had already been made. But if this abnormal path was to be followed everybody must stand together. A uniform, well-prepared and well-thought-out plan must be followed. . . .

22 *Eyewitness accounts of the Hitler putsch, 8 November 1923*

But while Kahr could afford to wait, Hitler had worked the enthusiasm and expectations of his followers up to fever pitch and he could not afford a long delay. Furthermore, the crisis would not last for ever; there were signs that the national government was getting a grip on the situation. Once conditions had returned to normal, Hitler would have lost his opportunity, possibly for ever. In view of these factors, therefore, he decided to take the initiative himself by creating a situation in which Kahr and Lossow would be forced to join him. He used the opportunity of a public meeting held in the Bürgerbräukeller, a big Munich beer cellar, on the evening of 8 November. The meeting was held to protest against the growth of Bolshevism in Germany. Kahr was to speak at the meeting and General von Lossow, Colonel von Seisser (the head of the Bavarian Landespolizei or paramilitary police) and the rest of the leading citizens of Bavaria were to be present. Some six hundred armed SA men were posted outside the meeting hall as Hitler burst in and interrupted Kahr's speech to announce that 'the national revolution' had begun. The historian von Müller, who later on was a witness at the trial, gave the following account of what happened:

(a) The hall was packed and one had the impression that the whole event had got beyond the control of the organizers. Obviously, more people had come than was planned for. I got a seat opposite the platform, this side of the main gangway, so that I could see the main events very clearly. . . .

Herr von Kahr had spoken for half an hour. Then there was movement at the entrance as if people were wanting to push their way in. Despite several warnings, the disturbance did not die down. Herr von Kahr had to break off speaking. Eventually, steel helmets came into sight. From this moment on, the view from my seat was rather obscured. People stood on chairs so that I didn't see Hitler until he had come fairly near along the main gangway; just before he turned to the platform, I saw him emerge between two armed soldiers in steel helmets who carried pistols next to their heads, pointing at the ceiling. They turned towards the platform, Hitler climbed on to a chair on my left. The hall was still restless, and then Hitler made a sign to the man on his right, who fired a shot at the ceiling. Thereupon Hitler called out (I cannot recollect the exact order of his words): 'The national revolution has broken out. The hall is surrounded.' Maybe he mentioned the exact number, I am not sure. He asked the gentlemen Kahr, Lossow, Seisser to come out and guaranteed their personal freedom. The gentlemen did not move. The General State Commissioner [Kahr] had stepped back and stood opposite Hitler, looking at him calmly. Then Hitler went towards the platform. What happened I could not see exactly. I heard him talk to the gentlemen and I heard the words: Everything would be over in ten minutes if the gentlemen would go out with him. To my surprise the three gentlemen went out with him immediately. . . .

Göring[1] remained in charge of the meeting while Hitler took Kahr, Lossow and Seisser into a side room to persuade them to throw in their lot with him.

[1] Hermann Göring, the last commander of the famous Richthofen fighter squadron and a war hero, had come to Munich after the war to study economics at the university. There he met Hitler in 1921 and in March 1923 was made commander of the SA.

Hitler's excited behaviour contributed to the melodramatic atmosphere of the evening, but Kahr refused to be browbeaten when Hitler threatened violence. The whole affair was very much improvised. General Ludendorff, who was to play a major part in Hitler's plans for a national government, had not yet arrived. According to the official account prepared by the Bavarian police:

(b) ... Apart from Hitler and Major Hunglinger,[1] three men from Hitler's bodyguard followed the three gentlemen into the adjoining room. Major von Hösslin, who also wanted to follow them, was stopped at the exit by Captain Göring with the words: 'You are not allowed to go any farther.' Captain Rüdel was also unable to follow at first because of the throng which had amassed in the hall.

After the three gentlemen had entered the room, Adolf Hitler called out: 'No one leaves the room alive without my permission.' At the door a member of the bodyguard walked up and down continually, holding a pistol.

Then Hitler turned to Excellency von Kahr with the statement: 'The Reich Government has been formed, the Bavarian Government has been overthrown. Bavaria is the springboard for the Reich Government. There must be a Reich governor in Bavaria. Pöhner[2] is to become Minister-President with dictatorial powers. You will be Reich governors. Reich Government – Hitler; national army – Ludendorff; Lossow – army minister; Seisser – police minister.

'I know this step is a difficult one for you, gentlemen, but the step must be taken, it must be made easier for the gentlemen to take the jump. Everybody must take up the post which he is allotted. If he does not, then he has no right to exist. You must fight with me, achieve victory with me, or die with me. If things go wrong, I have four bullets in my pistol, three for my colleagues if they desert me, the last bullet for myself.' While saying this, he put the pistol which he had been holding all the time to his head. While he was speaking to Excellency von Kahr, he noticed Major Hunglinger in the room and motioned with his hand for him to leave. Kahr declared to Herr Hitler: 'You can arrest me, you can have me shot, you can shoot me yourself. Whether I live or die is unimportant.' Whereupon Hitler turned to Colonel von Seisser who accused him of not keeping his promise [not to attempt a putsch]. Hitler replied: 'Yes, that's true, but I did it in the interests of the fatherland. Forgive me.'

Herr von Lossow tried to say something to the other two gentlemen. But this was prevented by a shout: 'You gentlemen are not allowed to talk to one another.'

Lossow then stepped back to the window, disgusted with the proceedings. While looking out between the curtains, he noticed in front of every window a group of armed men, some of whom looked into the room with their guns at the ready. Hitler, who clearly saw the unpleasant impression made, waved them away with his hand. Excellency von Lossow asked: 'What is Ludendorff's attitude to the affair?' Hitler replied: 'Ludendorff is ready and will soon be fetched.' Hitler then left the room. He got no answer during this time, either from Herr von Kahr or from the other gentlemen. ...

[1] Major Franz Hunglinger, Seisser's adjutant.
[2] Ernst Pöhner, the former Munich police chief who had been sympathetic to the Nazis.

The crowd in the hall was becoming impatient. Hitler could not go back on his plans as he had staked his prestige on success and his supporters expected much of him. He returned to the hall and, in an effort to put pressure on Kahr and his colleagues, announced that they had agreed to his plans. The effect of Hitler's speech was electric. According to von Müller, the crowd was not entirely on Hitler's side and was aware of his clever tactics:

(c) . . . There was great agitation in the hall. It was clear that nobody could leave the hall. From the middle one could not see exactly in what way it was barred. But there was a general feeling that we were sitting in a sort of trap. The disturbance was so great that nobody could address the audience. Several gentlemen attempted to, the chairman tried to calm people down, several gentlemen tried to speak. They did not succeed.

Only when Pöhner was asked to step on to the platform did it seem to become quiet. But before he had begun he was called away by an armed man, I think, who asked him to come with him, and Pöhner left the hall. Only Captain Göring succeeded in getting silence for a few sentences by shouting and with a certain brutal energy. Among the things he said there were two, so far as I can remember, that impressed the audience: the first was that he stressed emphatically that this action was in no way directed against Kahr, on the contrary it was hoped he would join in; and the second, that it was not directed against the troops, the Reichswehr or the police; on the contrary, they were already coming over from the barracks with flying colours. In my opinion, that impressed the audience. All the same, the general mood—I can of course only judge from my surroundings, but I think that this represented the general feeling in the hall—was still against the whole business. One heard: 'Theatrical!' 'South America!' 'Mexico!' That was the prevailing mood. The change came only during Hitler's second speech when he entered about ten minutes later, went to the platform and made a short speech. It was a rhetorical masterpiece. In fact, in a few sentences it totally transformed the mood of the audience. I have rarely experienced anything like it. When he stepped on to the platform the disturbance was so great that he could not be heard, and he fired a shot. I can still see the gesture. He got the Browning out of his back pocket and I think it was on this occasion that the remark about the machine gun was made. When things did not become quiet, he shouted angrily at the audience: 'If you are not quiet, I shall have a machine gun put up on the gallery.' In fact he had come in to say that his prediction of everything being over in ten minutes had not come true. But he said it in such a way that he finally went out with the permission of the audience to say to Kahr that the whole assembly would be behind him if he were to join. It was a complete reversal. One could hear it being said that the whole thing had been arranged, that it was a phoney performance. I did not share this opinion because Kahr's attitude seemed to contradict it. Seeing him at close quarters, one got the impression of confusion, of great dismay. . . .

Hitler went off stage once more. Ludendorff had just arrived, and, pretending to be surprised by the affair, joined him in persuading Kahr, who, after much hesitation, finally agreed. The official police account continues:

(d) . . . After a while Hitler returned, this time without a pistol, talked about his second speech in the hall and the jubilation it had produced, and pressed the gentlemen further. Suddenly words of command could be heard outside: 'Attention!' and shouts of 'Heil! Heil!' Ludendorff then entered the room in a hat and coat and, without asking any questions, with obvious excitement and with a trembling voice, declared: 'Gentlemen, I am just as surprised as you are. But the step has been taken, it is a question of the fatherland and the great national and racial cause, and I can only advise you, go with us and do the same.'

With the appearance of Ludendorff the character of the proceedings in the adjoining room changed completely. The pistols had disappeared. It took the form of friendly persuasion. (Because of this, Ludendorff, who was not a witness of the initial attack in the hall, may have got the impression that no force had been used, whereas Kahr, Lossow, and Seisser had no doubt that Ludendorff was accessory to the enterprise which had been essentially arranged for him.)

Shortly after Ludendorff, Pöhner entered the room. Hitler, Ludendorff and Weber[1] now began a process of urgent persuasion. Excellency von Kahr, in particular, was besieged on all sides. Moved by the feelings previously described, Lossow at last gave Ludendorff the consent he wanted with the dry comment, 'All right'. After some hesitation, Colonel von Seisser also nodded his agreement. Then Hitler, Ludendorff, and Dr Weber, with Pöhner also, worked on Excellency von Kahr with coaxing and pleading. Lossow and Seisser were asked to take part in the coaxing, but neither replied. Ludendorff took Major Hunglinger on one side and asked him to persuade Herr von Kahr. But still no discussion with Ludendorff or discussion between the three gentlemen was allowed; they only wanted to hear 'Yes' from them. Hitler could no longer go back, whatever the position of Kahr, Lossow, and Seisser might prove to be. Hitler kept bringing this out with statements like: 'The deed has been done, there is no going back. It has already passed into history.'

After long urging, Kahr declared: 'I am ready to take over the destiny of Bavaria as the representative of the monarchy.' Hitler insisted that this statement should be made in the hall. Herr von Kahr replied that after the way in which he had been led out of the hall he refused to go back into the hall. He wanted to avoid any public fraternizing. But Hitler insisted with the words: 'You will be carried shoulder high, you will see what jubilation will greet you: the people will kneel before you.' Kahr replied: 'I can do without that.' They then went into the hall.

The leaders of the putsch returned to the hall and put on a show of solidarity, but von Müller noticed the difference in behaviour between them:

(e) . . . An hour after Hitler's first appearance the three gentlemen came back into the hall with Hitler and Ludendorff. They were enthusiastically received. On the platform Kahr began to speak first without being requested to and gave the speech which was printed word for word in the papers. Ludendorff too in my opinion spoke without being requested to, whereas Lossow and Seisser only spoke after repeated requests—I can't remember the words, but only the gestures—on Hitler's

---

[1] Dr Friedrich Weber, leader of the paramilitary league, Bund Oberland, was also taking part in the putsch.

part. If I am to depict the impression made by the gentlemen on the platform, I would say that Kahr was completely unmoved. His face was like a mask all evening. He was not pale or agitated, he was very serious, but spoke very composedly. I got the impression that there was a melancholy look about his eyes. But that is perhaps being subjective. Hitler, on the other hand, during this scene was radiant with joy. One had the feeling that he was delighted to have succeeded in persuading Kahr to collaborate. There was in his demeanour, I would say, a kind of childlike joy, a very frank expression which I shall never forget. Excellency Ludendorff by comparison was extremely grave; when he came in he was pale with suppressed emotion. His appearance as well as his words were those of a man who knew it was a matter of life and death, probably death rather than life. I shall never forget his expression. It was such that when I heard in town on the following day the rumour that he had been killed, I said to myself: That's what he looked like last night. Lossow's expression was very different; there was something detached, relaxed about his whole attitude. I don't want to make a party point but, if I am to describe it, it struck me that he made a slightly ironical fox face. A certain impenetrable smile never left his features. Seisser was pale and upset. He was the only one who gave the impression of personal agitation, of external agitation. His words were merely a variant of Lossow's. The report in the papers of the words of these two gentlemen was not correct: it was somewhat touched up. . . .

Hitler's apparent triumph was short-lived. The situation changed completely overnight. Ernst Röhm had occupied Army headquarters in Munich and there was sympathy for the putsch among junior officers, but the attitude of the Reichswehr as a whole never remained in doubt and when Lossow returned to his headquarters reinforcements were ordered to the Bavarian capital. Kahr followed suit by revoking the agreement he had been forced to make at gunpoint. In spite of these setbacks, arrangements went ahead for a march into the city centre of a few thousand supporters of Hitler in the forlorn hope of winning sufficient support among the population to force Kahr, Lossow and Seisser to join them. Hitler and Ludendorff led the procession. An official report prepared for the subsequent committee of inquiry related what happened:

(f) . . . The action took place in two parts, separate from one another both in time and place: the events at the Ludwigsbrücke and the confrontation at the Residenz.

At the Ludwigsbrücke a weak section of police had arrived just before noon on 9 November with orders to prevent armed sections of National Socialists from crossing the bridge. At around noon several, initially small, sections of National Socialists tried to get into the centre of the town. They obeyed the order of the police officer in command at the bridge to stop and lined up near the bridge. Between 12.15 and 12.30 p.m. a long column in ranks of twelve came from the Bürgerbräu cellar. The police officer himself went to meet the column and asked its leader to give the order to halt. The leader ordered them to proceed slowly, whereupon the police officer declared he would give the order to shoot if they did not stop. He gave the order to his section about ten yards behind him: 'Load with live bullets!' The National Socialists called out: 'Don't shoot your comrades!'

Simultaneously at the sound of a trumpet signal, stormtroops of the National Socialists rushed towards the police officers, while the smaller sections which had previously stopped attacked them from the sides and the rear. The police were forcibly disarmed, after a short struggle during which no gun was used. The disarmed men were then taken to the Bürgerbräu cellar, though on the way the officer succeeded in escaping. Another police officer going towards the bridge a little later to reconnoitre was fired at, but the shot missed.

Meanwhile, the column of National Socialists about 2,000 strong, nearly all armed, moved on through the Zweibrückenstrasse across the Marienplatz towards the Theatinerstrasse. Here it split up, the majority going down the Perusastrasse to the Residenz, the rest going on along the Theatinerstrasse.

The police stationed in the Residenz tried to cordon it off as well as the Theatiner-strasse by the Preysingstrasse. Numerous civilians hurried on ahead of the actual column in Residenzstrasse and pushed the police barricade. The ceaseless shouts of 'Stop! Don't go on!' by the state police were not obeyed. Since there was the danger of a breakthrough here, a police section, originally in the Theatinerstrasse, hurried round the Feldherrenhalle to give support. They were received with fixed bayonets, guns with the safety catches off, and raised pistols. Several police officers were spat upon, and pistols with the safety catches off were stuck in their chests. The police used rubber truncheons and rifle butts and tried to push back the crowd with rifles held horizontally. Their barricade had already been broken several times. Suddenly, a National Socialist fired a pistol at a police officer from close quarters. The shot went past his head and killed Sergeant Hollweg standing behind him. Even before it was possible to give an order, the comrades of the sergeant who had been shot opened fire as the Hitler lot did, and a short gun battle ensued during which the police were also shot at from the Preysingpalais and from the house which contains the Café Rottenhöfer. After no more than thirty seconds the Hitler lot fled, some back to the Maximilienstrasse, some to the Odeonsplatz. General Ludendorff apparently went on towards the Odeonsplatz. There he was seen in the company of a Hitler officer by a police officer barring the Briennerstrasse, who went up to General Ludendorff and said to him: 'Excellency, I must take you into custody.' General Ludendorff replied: 'You have your orders. I'll come with you.' Both gentlemen were then accompanied into the Residenz.

The putsch had failed. Its leaders were arrested and the Nazi Party, whose membership had grown to 55,000, was banned. Hitler had become prisoner of the public enthusiasm which he had encouraged, but he had not succeeded in gaining control over events. The attempt failed because of the lack of support from the Army and the police.

23 *Hitler's closing speech at his trial, 27 March 1924*

On 26 February 1924, Hitler, Ludendorff, Pöhner and the leaders of the Kampfbund were put on trial for high treason in Munich, with the conservative nationalist leaders, Kahr, Lossow and Seisser, as the chief witnesses for the prosecution. The trial received enormous publicity and Hitler's bravado enabled him to turn the ignominious failure of the putsch into a considerable propaganda victory. For, while asserting that Kahr and the others had pursued a similar goal, he did not deny his own part—he claimed it was a patriotic act and he blamed the failure of the enterprise on the pusillanimity of the nationalist leaders. As a result of this stand, Hitler now became a hero to many antisemites in other parts of Germany who before had never heard of him. They saw him as the one man who had had the courage and energy to act. This ensured that when the Party was refounded after his release, numerous new branches could be established outside Bavaria.

... Lossow said here that he had spoken with me in the spring and had not noticed then that I was trying to get something for myself and had thought that I only wanted to be a propagandist and a man who would rouse people.

How petty are the thoughts of small men! You can take my word for it, that I do not consider a ministerial post worth striving for. . . .

From the very first I have aimed at something more than becoming a Minister. I have resolved to be the destroyer of Marxism. This I shall achieve and once I've achieved that, I should find the title of 'Minister' ridiculous. When I first stood in front of Wagner's grave, my heart overflowed with pride that here lay a man who had forbidden any such inscription as 'Here lies State Councillor, Musical Director, His Excellency Richard von Wagner'. I was proud that this man and so many others in German history have been content to leave their names to posterity and not their titles. It was not through modesty that I was willing to be a 'drummer' at that time for that is the highest task [*das Höchste*]: the rest is nothing.

Mr Public Prosecutor! You emphasize in the indictment that we had to wait with clenched teeth until the seed ripened. Well, we did wait and when the man came, we cried: 'The seed is ripe, the hour has come.' Only then, after long hesitation, did I put myself forward. I demanded for myself the leadership in the political struggle; and secondly, I demanded that the leadership of the organization for which we all longed and for which you inwardly long just as much should go to the hero who, in the eyes of the whole of German youth, is called to it. The witness Seisser declared cynically that we had to have Ludendorff so that the Reichswehr would not shoot. Is that a crime? Was it treason that I said to Lossow, 'The way you are beginning it must come to a conflict; as I see it, there need be no conflict'? . . .

... What did we want on the evening of 8 November? All these gentlemen wanted a Directory in the Reich. If one has striven for something in the Reich, one cannot condemn it in Bavaria. The Directory already existed in Bavaria, it consisted of Messrs Kahr, Lossow and Seisser. We no longer knew anything of a legal government, we only feared that there might be scruples over the final decision.

I am no monarchist, but ultimately a Republican. Pöhner is a monarchist, Ludendorff is devoted to the House of Hohenzollern [Prussia-Germany]. Despite our different attitudes we all stood together. The fate of Germany does not lie in the choice between a Republic or a Monarchy, but in the content of the Republic and the Monarchy. What I am contending against is not the form of a state as such, but its ignominious content. We wanted to create in Germany the precondition which alone will make it possible for the iron grip of our enemies to be removed from us. We wanted to create order in the state, throw out the drones, take up the fight against international stock exchange slavery, against our whole economy being cornered by trusts, against the politicizing of the trade unions, and above all, for the highest honourable duty which we, as Germans, know should be once more introduced—the duty of bearing arms, military service. And now I ask you: Is what we wanted high treason? . . .

Now people say: But His Excellency von Kahr, von Lossow and von Seisser did not want the events of the evening of 8 November. The bill of indictment says that we pushed these gentlemen into an embarrassing situation. But it was through these gentlemen that we ourselves had got into an embarrassing situation; *they* had pushed *us* into it. Herr von Kahr should have said honourably: Herr Hitler, we understand something different by a *coup d'état*, we mean something different by a march on Berlin. He had a duty to say to us: In what we are doing here we mean something different from what you think. He did not say that, and the consequences should be borne solely by these three gentlemen. . . .

. . . The army which we have formed grows from day to day; it grows more rapidly from hour to hour. Even now I have the proud hope that one day the hour will come when these untrained [*wild*] bands will grow to battalions, the battalions to regiments and the regiments to divisions, when the old cockade will be raised from the mire, when the old banners will once again wave before us: and the reconciliation will come in that eternal last Court of Judgement, the Court of God, before which we are ready to take our stand. Then from our bones, from our graves, will sound the voice of that tribunal which alone has the right to sit in judgement upon us. For, gentlemen, it is not you who pronounce judgement upon us, it is the eternal Court of History which will make its pronouncement upon the charge which is brought against us. The verdict that you will pass I know. But that Court will not ask of us, 'Did you commit high treason or did you not?' That Court will judge us . . . as Germans who wanted the best for their people and their fatherland, who wished to fight and to die. You may pronounce us guilty a thousand times, but the Goddess who presides over the Eternal Court of History will with a smile tear in pieces the charge of the Public Prosecutor and the verdict of this court. For she acquits us.

The judges, who were right-wing and sympathized with the motives of the conspirators, acquitted Ludendorff and gave Hitler the minimum sentence of five years' imprisonment, with the clear understanding that he would be released early on probation.

2 The Creation of a Nationwide Party Organization, 1924–28

With the failure of the Hitler putsch the threat from the extreme Right had been removed for the time being at any rate; certainly henceforward Bavaria no longer threatened the Republic. The political situation was further improved by the stabilization of the mark which followed in November 1923 with the replacement of the paper mark by a new so-called 'Rentenmark', which was backed by the whole of German agricultural and industrial real estate. At the end of February 1924, the improvement in the situation was officially recognized by the lifting of the state of emergency. Although the Reichstag election of May 1924 resulted in an increase in support for the extreme Right and Left, this was essentially a reflection of the previous discontent and also a result of the unemployment which followed the ending of inflation. During the rest of the year, however, the economic situation improved as a result of a settlement of the reparations issue in the form of the Dawes Plan, by which the Allies laid down methods for ensuring the payment of reparations. The acceptance of the Dawes Plan by the German Government on 30 August ensured the return of international confidence in the German economy, and investors, particularly in America, hurried to take advantage of the high interest rates which they could obtain in Germany. With the help of these loans, the German economy made a marked recovery during the autumn of 1924 and this, together with the more stable political situation, was reflected in the results of the Reichstag election of December 1924 which produced an increase in votes for the pro-republican forces and a decline in support for the extremists, both racialists and Communists.

The next four years, until 1928–29, saw a period of relative economic prosperity and political stability in Germany. The election of the old war hero, Field-Marshal Paul von Hindenburg, as President of the Republic in 1925, which seemed at the time to represent a triumph of the anti-republican Right, had if anything contributed to this stability. Hindenburg was punctilious in his observance of the Constitution and now, with this respected figure at its head, the Republic could seem more tolerable even to some of the more conservative middle class. The period of 1924–28 saw also notable diplomatic achievements by the Foreign Minister Gustav Stresemann—first in 1925, in securing a *détente* in the West with the Treaty of Locarno, without tying Germany's hands in the East, and then in 1926, with Germany's gaining admittance to the League of Nations and thereby international respectability. While these achievements failed to win the approval of the more rabid nationalists, they reduced international tension and contributed to business confidence and to economic prosperity.

These developments created an atmosphere in which extremist politics were not in demand and the Nazi Party found it very difficult to make any impact. They were regarded by the general public with a mixture of indifference and contempt. The significance of this period is that, despite the difficulties, the Party succeeded in building up a skeleton organization of dedicated, indeed fanatical, activists, an organization which for the first time covered the whole of Germany instead of being limited almost wholly to Bavaria. The result was that, when the economic situation began to deteriorate in the years 1928–29 and the population became totally disillusioned not only with their particular political representatives but with the political system as a whole, the Nazi Party had an organization on which it could build. Moreover, it was during these years that the nature of the Nazi movement was finally determined. The patterns of authority within the Party, the significance of its programme, and the character of the Party cadres were all defined in this period.

The survival of the Nazi movement during 1924

During Hitler's imprisonment the banned Nazi Party disintegrated into rival factions. Hitler had nominated Alfred Rosenberg, the editor of the *Völkischer Beobachter*, to act as his deputy during his imprisonment. Rosenberg allied himself with other Bavarian racialists to form a *völkisch* block in Bavaria largely as a means of participating in the spring elections to the Reichstag and the Bavarian Landtag. Rosenberg's authority was challenged, however, by Esser, Streicher and other former Nazis who established a rival organization—the Greater German National Community (*Grossdeutsche Volksgemeinschaft*) which attacked the decision to take part in elections and what they saw as the bourgeois style of the *völkisch* block.[1]

Outside Bavaria the situation was dominated by a racialist party known as the German Racialist Freedom Party,[2] founded in 1922 by three Reichstag deputies who were former members of the main extreme right-wing party, the German Nationalist Party. During the elections, the DVFP worked with the former Nazis in an electoral alliance, the so-called *Völkisch*-Social Block. But the ambitions of the DVFP were bitterly resisted by many former Nazis, particularly young people, who considered the party too bourgeois both in its social composition and in its political style. For a time they worked together with Esser and Streicher until personal differences caused a bitter row. These opponents of the DVFP looked to Hitler as their leader and appealed to him for support. But Hitler, finding that he could not control

---

[1] For the '*völkisch* movement', see above, 'Introduction', pp. 18ff.

[2] *Deutschvölkische Freiheitspartei* (DVFP).

events from prison and unwilling to compromise himself with any commitment, decided to withdraw from active politics until his release. The confusion in the *völkisch* movement strengthened his own position.

During August the DVFP managed to unite with a group of former Nazis
to establish a National Socialist Freedom Movement.[1] It was led by a so-
called 'Reich leadership'—a triumvirate of General Ludendorff, Albrecht
von Graefe (a leader of the DVFP), and Gregor Strasser (the representative
of those members of the former NSDAP who had accepted the amalgamation, and a Bavarian deputy elected on the ticket of the *Völkisch*-Social
Block). Strasser became a Reichstag deputy in December.

1 Hitler's claim to sole leadership, September 1924

Hitler, who was determined to retain absolute control of the Party, had no
intention of allowing this 'Reich leadership' to become a permanent arrangement. His views were made clear in a letter of 21 September 1924 from
Hermann Fobke, a Nazi student of Göttingen University, who was in prison
with Hitler for his part in the putsch, to Adalbert Volck, the leader of the
opponents of the DVFP in north Germany:

... Herr Hitler wishes me to pass on his thanks for your information. After his
release he will summon all the men in leading positions in order to make a clean
break. This will be achieved through the response to a single question: Who
should be the political leader? He does not recognize a Reich leadership and he
will never participate in such a Soldiers' Council-type creation. So there will
never be any question of a Hi./v.G./L. leadership combination. In the consultations
with the subordinate leaders after Hitler's release, there will be only one simple
point at issue—Who recognizes him as the sole leader? ...

2 Hitler's decision to adopt the parliamentary tactic

While in Landsberg Prison, Hitler was working out his plans for the Party
after his release. He was impressed by the fact that in the Reichstag election
of May 1924 the coalition of antisemitic groups formed for the election won
9 per cent of the vote which entitled them to send thirty-two deputies,
although of these only ten were former Nazis. In the spring election to the
Bavarian state diet the racialists were even more successful, becoming as a
result the second largest party in the diet. The putsch had proved unsuccessful because of the failure of the Army to cooperate and, with the end of the
political and economic crisis, an attempt to seize power by force looked less
and less feasible. Clearly a new policy was necessary as Hitler told Ludecke
when he received a visit from him in Landsberg:

... I noticed that he barred in particular any reminder of the putsch and any
question concerning his policy towards the Party schism. ... I gladly eschewed

---

[1] *Nationalsozialistische Freiheitsbewegung* (NSFB).

the subject as too delicate. But the lesson it taught was another matter, which Hitler himself took up.

'From now on,' he said, 'we must follow a new line of action. It is best to attempt no large reorganization until I am freed, which may be a matter of months rather than of years.'

I must have looked at him somewhat incredulously. 'Oh yes,' he continued, 'I am not going to stay here much longer. When I resume active work it will be necessary to pursue a new policy. Instead of working to achieve power by armed conspiracy, we shall have to hold our noses and enter the Reichstag against the Catholic and Marxist deputies. If outvoting them takes longer than outshooting them, at least the results will be guaranteed by their own Constitution! Any lawful process is slow. But already, as you know, we have thirty-two Reichstag deputies under this new programme, and are the second largest party in the Bavarian Landtag diet. Sooner or later we shall have a majority and after that we shall have Germany. I am convinced that this is our best line of action now that conditions in the country have changed so radically. . . .

Although he now accepted the need to participate in elections and to enter Parliament, Hitler did not in any way give up his hostility to Parliament. His former attempt to carry out a putsch made it much easier for him to pursue a constitutional course since he could never be accused of weakness. This was important in view of the fact that it was the extremism of the Nazis which distinguished them from similar groups and contributed so much to their success.

The refounding of the Party, 27 February 1925

Hitler was released in December 1924 and, after promising to work within the Constitution, was permitted to refound the Nazi Party. The authorities assumed that now the crisis was over the Party would be harmless. The Party was refounded at a meeting in the same Bürgerbräu beer cellar in Munich on 27 February 1925. On the previous day, Hitler had published in the *Völkischer Beobachter* the following two documents. He began with a flattering reference to General Ludendorff, whom he had succeeded in winning as the Nazi candidate for the forthcoming Reich presidential election. This was something of a *coup* in view of Ludendorff's prestige within the *völkisch* movement. He then made it clear that he was not concerned with past quarrels nor with the personal characters of his supporters — a veiled reference to Esser and Streicher. Both men had made themselves unpopular with large sections of the *völkisch* movement during the previous year, but they had proved themselves loyal to Hitler and also very successful propagandists. Hitler made it clear that he was interested only in what the individual could offer him in terms of abilities and in whether he was prepared to obey the leader without preconditions. He justified this demand for absolute control with a promise to render an account in a year's time and take the responsibility whatever the outcome. Finally, unlike the other anti-semitic groups, particularly in north Germany, he was not interested in fighting Roman Catholicism. This would only limit the potential support of the Party particularly in Bavaria itself and it would antagonize the Bavarian Government, which was now dominated by the Catholic Bavarian People's Party and which he was trying to conciliate in order to secure freedom for the Party to operate effectively:

3 Hitler's call to the former members of the NSDAP, 26 February 1925

National Socialists! Party Comrades!

... In this hour we do not only want to remember again those who in November 1923 became blood witnesses of our political beliefs and aims; we also want to thank all those who in this past year did not despair of the movement and what it stands for, but laboured in its service regardless of whatever camp they felt drawn to.

Above all, we want to remember the one man who had nothing to gain but rather stood to lose the fame of being the undying leader of the heroic German armies in the greatest war on earth, and who despite all this decided to make the great sacrifice of giving his name and his energy to a movement which had no leader.

In General Ludendorff the National Socialist movement will for ever honour its most faithful and unselfish friend. The movement will be bound to him not by the memory of friendship given in happy times but by loyalty maintained in persecution and misery.

My task as leader of the movement is not to look for the causes of a previous quarrel or to assess who was right, but to mould the movement into a unified weapon regardless of the interests of individuals. Thus I shall not inquire into the past of those comrades who rejoin, but only work to ensure that the past will not repeat itself in the future. From our supporters I demand that if they are willing to join the new movement they should feel themselves once more to be brothers in a great fighting community and stand together loyally shoulder to shoulder as before.

But I expect the leaders, in so far as they come from the old camp, to give me the same obedience as we all give to the common idea.

Those who cannot forget the past are not worthy of serving a better future.

I myself promise to render an account to the comrades in a year's time as to whether the Party has become a movement or whether the movement has suffocated by being a party.

In either case I shall take the responsibility.

Long live the National Socialist German Workers' Party!

Long live our German fatherland!

4 'On the revival of our movement'

... I do not consider it to be the task of a political leader to try and improve, let alone make uniform the human material which he has at hand. The temperaments, characters, and talents of individual people are so various that it is impossible to unify a large number of completely similar people. It is also not the task of a political leader to try and remove these deficiencies by 'training' people to be united. All such attempts are condemned to failure. Human nature is a given quantity which does not lend itself to alteration in particulars, but can only transform itself through a process of development lasting for centuries. But even then the prerequisite for such a change is generally alterations in the basic racial elements. . . .

If a political leader departs from this awareness and if instead he attempts only to seek people who come up to his ideal, he will not only wreck his plans, but also in a very short time leave behind him chaos instead of an organization. The guilt which he then attributes to individual supporters or subordinates is in reality only his own lack of awareness and ability.

For this very reason, if I try today to revive the old NSDAP, I cannot recognize commitments which derive from past events. I am not prepared to accept conditions, whose fulfilment would only represent that lack of psychological awareness and ability which I described above.

I shall, therefore, see it as my particular task to direct the various temperaments, talents and qualities of character in the movement into those channels in which by supplementing one another they benefit everybody.

In the future, the movement's struggle must once more take the form which we intended at its foundation. With all its forces concentrated together it must be turned against that power to which above all we owe the collapse of our fatherland and the destruction of our people. This does not mean an alteration in or a 'postponement' of the old and main aim of our struggle, but simply its re-assertion.

At this point, I must object particularly to the attempt to drag religious quarrels into the movement, or even to go so far as to equate the movement with such things. I have always opposed the collective description 'racialist' [völkisch], because the extremely vague definition of this term has opened the way to damaging activities. For this reason, earlier on, the movement placed more emphasis on its clearly defined programme as well as on the unified trend of its struggle than on a term which was incapable of being clearly defined and which was conducive to a more or less verbose interpretation.

I see in the attempt by various people to turn the racialist movement into a struggle about religion the beginning of the end of that movement.

Religious reformations cannot be carried out by political infants and these people are rarely anything but that.

I am quite clear about the possibility of beginning such a struggle, but I doubt if the gentlemen involved are clear about its probable end result.

In any case, it will be my main task to make sure that in the newly awakened NSDAP members of both confessions can live peacefully side by side and can stand together in the common struggle against that power which is the deadly enemy of every form of Christianity, no matter what confession.

No movement has fought harder against the Centre Party and its supporting groups than our own, not for religious reasons but solely from political considerations. And so from now onwards we must fight the Centre not because it claims to be 'Christian' or 'Catholic' but solely because a party which has allied itself with atheistic Marxism for the suppression of its own people is neither Christian nor Catholic.

We do not declare war on the Centre for religious reasons, but solely for national-political ones.

History will pass judgement on who will be successful, we or the advocates of a cultural struggle.

Finally, I demand of the movement's supporters that from now onwards they direct all their energies outwards and do not weaken themselves in a fratricidal struggle.

The best local branch leadership is not the one which 'unites' the other nationalist organizations or 'wins them over' to the movement, but the one which wins anti-nationalists back to the German people.

The success of our movement must be measured not by the number of Reichstag or Landtag seats we win, but by the extent to which Marxism is destroyed and by the degree of enlightenment about its originator, the Jews.

Let those who wish to join in this struggle do so; let those who do not, stay away.

The assertion of the primacy of the 'Führer'

After the refounding of the Party, Hitler, who was soon banned from public speaking in Bavaria and many other states, concentrated on writing the second volume of *Mein Kampf*. During the summer of 1925, the Munich branch of the Party became involved in bitter factional squabbles in which personalities played a major part. Hitler had left the day-to-day running of the Party in the hands of the Party officials—Bouhler (the secretary), Schwarz (the treasurer), Amann (the head of the publishing house) and Esser (the propaganda chief). In addition, Julius Streicher, the branch leader of Nuremberg, and Artur Dinter, Gauleiter or regional leader of Thuringia, were influential. This group had fought a bitter feud with other Bavarian antisemites and former Nazis during 1924 and this feud now broke out again. But Esser, Streicher and Dinter were also extremely unpopular among many Party members throughout Germany and particularly in the north and west. Some of the Gauleiters here, where the Party was now growing more rapidly than in Bavaria, resented the authority of what they regarded as an unsavoury Munich clique. This conflict dated back to the previous year when Esser's abrasive personality had alienated many Nazis, particularly when he committed the cardinal sin of washing the Party's dirty linen in the pages of the big 'Jewish' newspaper, the *Frankfurter Zeitung*.

But apart from questions of personality, important issues of principle now emerged. Some leading members of the Party outside Bavaria disagreed on aspects of Party policy. In the first place, the Party leaders in Göttingen and Hanover disagreed with participation in elections. This represented a challenge to the new parliamentary tactics now being followed by the Party. Secondly, Gregor Strasser, the Gauleiter of Lower Bavaria, who had met many of the north and west German Party leaders while acting as Hitler's

A NATIONWIDE PARTY ORGANIZATION

deputy in the refounding of the Party there, felt that the Party programme was too vague and should be defined more concretely in a 'Socialist' direction. He was supported by some of the local Party leaders in the industrial areas of north and west Germany who wanted to compete with the Left for the support of the workers.

5 Gregor Strasser: 'How does one become a National Socialist?'

The 'Socialism' of Gregor Strasser was in fact typical of that of most racialists—a determination to try to win the workers for nationalism by giving them a greater sense of belonging to the nation. It sprang from his experience in the trenches during the war, as he told a meeting in 1927:

... How did all those tens of thousands in all parts of Germany become National Socialist? Perhaps I may be allowed to recall how I became one ... because I am a test case here! Before the war we did not bother with politics. I grew up the son of a low-ranking civil servant. I had no ambition other than to get on through hard work. In the war we became Nationalists, that is to say, out of that vague feeling that the fatherland had to be defended, that it was something great and sacred, the protector of the existence of the individual, out of this vague notion which for many of us was not clear, we became nationalists on the battlefield. When I saw all the nations of the earth rushing against the German trenches with blood-thirsty destruction, when the international stock exchange armed one country after another and set them going against the single German nation in the trenches — Americans, Portuguese, Blacks, Yellows, against the little group of Germans fighting for their existence, it became clear to me: if Germany wants to survive, every German must *know what it means to be a German and must defend this idea to the limits of self-sacrifice.* Companies and batteries reduced from 250 to 60 men did not have to be told about the *community of need*; they knew: if we do not stand together the Blacks will be on us. We knew that the first priority of manhood is to defend oneself, and the second, all who speak the same language must stick together, must organize themselves to be strong by being united!

And why did we become Socialists?

This notion was still as far from many who today stand in our ranks as the notion of nationalism in terms of its real significance. We learnt all sorts of things at school. But nobody told us that half the German people were hostile to the nation *because they had been denied the most basic needs of life by the other half.* Not a word were we told about that tragic hour for the German people *when the growing German workers' movement was nothing but the cry of millions of German fellow countrymen for acceptance into the nation on equal terms (loud applause).* So these millions of people were left to the Jew Marx who created Marxism out of the German workers' movement, who intended to do nothing but *destroy the German nation* with the strength of these millions *and to make it a colony of world capital.*

We must always regard *one* principle as fundamental: to be ready to recognize mistakes, to see that when a nation goes under, it is mainly the *fault of the rulers* of that nation. They had the power to prevent everything which in the long run forced people to become hostile to the nation and state.

This person, whom the Jew Marx had perverted into a 'Social Democrat', a

Marxist, was suddenly found standing next one in the platoon, in the battery, by the guns. During the long hours of sentry duty there would be discussion: What are you? A mechanic. Politically? A red, a Marxist. And we who came from the bourgeoisie, we who had been told nothing, were surprised.

Why am I a Marxist? Because you have never bothered with us! Then one started thinking, then came the great realization how brave the man is, and how well he does his duty! It was my experience that the best soldiers were frequently those who had least to defend at home (*applause*). He cooperated, he did his duty unfailingly, and from conversations with him we understood *the mistakes of our great-grandfathers. Because we had become nationalists in the trenches we could not help becoming Socialists in the trenches*, we could not help coming home with the brutal intention of gathering the whole nation round us and teaching them that the greatness of a nation depends on the willingness of the individual to stand up for this nation and say to it: Your fate is indissolubly linked with the fate of your people, with the fate and greatness of your nation. We could not help coming home from this war with this resolve: *Those who have fought together with us and who are hostile towards the nation because it has not bothered with them must be emancipated so that Germany will in future be strong and the master of her enemies!* (*loud applause*).

6 *The founding of the NSDAP working group of the north and west German Gaue, 11 September 1925*

In order to further his attempt to change the programme and as a counter-weight to the Party bureaucracy in Munich, Strasser now took the initiative in establishing a so-called 'working group' (*Arbeitsgemeinschaft*) of the Gauleiters in north and west Germany. In fact, however, as is clear from the following report, written by Fobke, a Göttingen leader, of the first meeting, held at Hagen in Westphalia on 10 September, there were deep disagreements between these Gauleiters over the various points at issue, particularly over the question of elections which was the main issue for the Göttingen leaders. The only aim on which most of them were agreed was cooperation in matters of organization among regions with similar problems and the development of new ideas appropriate to their needs which the bureaucrats in the Munich headquarters were apparently incapable of doing. These would, it was hoped, meet with Hitler's approval and it is significant that Point 4 of the statutes of the working group shows that they had been careful to gain Hitler's general approval for the organization:

... The movement is at the moment undergoing a crisis associated mainly with the name of Hermann Esser. This extremely dubious character, of obscure political as well as moral background, is at the moment absolute boss in the Party leadership. The result is a continual diminution of all the good elements in the movement, which today, for example, in the city of Munich only comprises 700 members. Thousands stand aside without joining any group, others—the smaller part—have joined together in the National Socialist People's League [*Nationalsozialistische Volksbund*] under the leadership of Dörfler and Anton Drechsler [*sic*], which parted from the NSDAP some time ago under the slogan 'With Hitler but without Esser!' when Hitler did *not* do without Esser. In the last few days, an open conflict has developed between Alfred Rosenberg, editor of the *Völkischer Beobachter* and publisher of the *Weltkampf*, and Adolf Hitler, the origin of which must be sought in the prominent position in the Party of Esser, Amann and Streicher. Of my personal acquaintances with me in the prison at Landsberg, the best are standing aside in convinced opposition.

Hitler himself, whom I met on 26 and 27 August, adopts a completely passive attitude towards the business; this, under the circumstances, is equivalent to supporting Esser. At the moment his activity is entirely confined to the completion of the second volume of his book, *Mein Kampf*. Any suggestion of getting rid at last of Esser & Co., including above all Streicher and Dinter, he counters with the insubstantial objection that for him their usefulness is the decisive factor. He overlooks the fact that the total rejection of them throughout the Reich is being outweighed by their theoretical usefulness within a limited area. Outside Bavaria too the movement is in my opinion in a stagnant condition, which, apart from the general political indifference, has its origin in the sorry state of things at the Munich headquarters.

Opposition to the Esser dictatorship is naturally making itself evident. To create a counterbalance to this dictatorship was the purpose of a meeting which Gregor Strasser, Hitler's honest and extremely hard-working, even if not exactly inspired colleague, summoned for 10 September at Hagen in Westphalia. Strasser himself was prevented from attending, with the result that the discussion was perhaps not as far-reaching as it would have been had he been there....

As convener, Herr Strasser originally intended to use the negotiations at the meeting to play off the block formed by those invited against the pernicious Munich line. Of this plan, apart from Haase [Gauleiter] of Göttingen, only Dr Goebbels[1] and a man unknown to us by name who chaired the meeting,[2] were aware. Since Strasser did not attend, the real purpose of the meeting was not touched on; instead, to begin with, the only decision reached was the setting up of a close association between the *Gaue* mentioned above, with the name 'Working Group of the north and west German Gauleiters of the NSDAP'. Cooperation was planned through an exchange of speakers, and organizational help of every kind was arranged by setting up a headquarters and by the publication of the 'National Socialist Letters' [*NS Briefe*]. These are intended for the leadership and are meant to effect a uniform clarification of basic questions, to be achieved by a free exchange of views. At the head of this working group is Strasser.

When it looked as if in Strasser's absence the question of Esser would not be mentioned, I brought it up with the agreement of Herr Haase. This produced a general reaction of horror. Some people strongly opposed such a 'palace revolution', and the representative from Rhineland-North, who was chairing the meeting, suggested postponing discussion of the matter. Haase and I agreed to this postponement intentionally because by pressing the point we had sown a seed which could be cultivated at the monthly meetings which were planned to follow. Consultation with the chairman who was deputizing for Strasser and with Dr Goebbels produced unanimity on this point.

Haase had travelled to Hagen with the firm intention of bringing about at all

[1] A party activist in Elberfeld.
[2] Dr Hellmuth Elbrechter, a pro-Nazi from Elberfeld.

events a clarification of the question of participation in any elections, whether local council, county council, regional diet or Reichstag, in view of the Prussian elections which were coming up. A preliminary sounding produced the situation that at the moment Telschow[1] (Hanover-East) and Lohse[2] (Schleswig-Holstein) were supporting us in opposing, whereas Vahlen[3] (Pomerania) and Haake[4] (Cologne) were against us and in favour of electoral participation. Already some time back we had had Rust's[5] (Hanover-Brunswick) pledge to support non-participation.

Haase therefore made a short statement to the effect that we and those gentlemen who agreed with our position *would under no circumstances participate in any elections, no matter what directives had been given by Munich headquarters. The other* Gaue *would have to adapt themselves to our attitude.* This declaration produced a shocked and embarrassed pause. But the discussion produced a majority agreement on a resolution to Hitler which this time was unanimously approved. This stated that *all* the Gauleiters meeting in Hagen absolutely rejected participation in elections and demanded a clear statement from the Party leadership, which so far had sent three different sets of instructions to three different places. . . .

To conclude, the newly founded working group offers the possibility of securing further recognition for our position in the National Socialist movement. Haase is determined to exploit this possibility to the limit and, next to the question of Parliament, to try also to settle the case of Esser, that is the purging of the movement in accordance with our views. . . .

7 Statutes of the working group

1. The Working Group of the North and West German *Gaue* of the NSDAP comprises the *Gaue*: Rhineland-North, Rhineland-South, Westphalia, Hanover, Hanover-South, Hesse-Nassau, Lüneburg-Stade, Schleswig-Holstein, Greater-Hamburg, Greater-Berlin and Pomerania.
2. The aim and purpose of the Working Group is: the greatest possible uniformity among the affiliated *Gaue* in organization and propaganda; the creation of uniform propaganda methods, the swapping of speakers; the good-neighbourly encouragement of friendly personal relations among the Gauleiters; the exchange of ideas on questions of politics and organization by letter and by regular meetings; when necessary, joint statements on current political issues.
3. The journal of the Working Group is the bi-monthly *NS Briefe*, to be published by Comrade Gregor Strasser and edited by Comrade Dr Goebbels.
4. Both Working Group and *NS Briefe* exist with the express approval of Adolf Hitler.
5. The director of the Working Group is Comrade Gregor Strasser, Landshut.
6. The secretary of the Working Group is Comrade Dr Goebbels, Elberfeld.
7. The office of the Working Group is until further notice at Elberfeld, Holzerstrasse 4. Tel. 6526.
8. The Gauleiters affiliated to the Working Group meet for joint discussions, when necessary, in a city in one or another of the above-mentioned *Gaue*.

[1] Otto Telschow, Gauleiter of Lüneburg-Stade 1925-28, Gauleiter of Hanover-East 1928-45.
[2] Hinrich Lohse, Gauleiter of Schleswig-Holstein 1925-45.
[3] Professor Vahlen, Gauleiter of Pomerania 1925-27.
[4] Heinz Haake, a Party leader in the Rhineland.
[5] Bernhard Rust, Gauleiter of Hanover-North 1925-28, of Hanover-South-Brunswick 1928-45, after 1933 Minister of Education first in Prussia and then in the Reich.

9. In order to enable the individual Gauleiters to acquire an overall view of the position of the movement and to simplify the common task, the individual Gauleiters bind themselves to send in to the Working Group office 15 copies of every important announcement by their *Gau*, whether political statement, organizational circular, pamphlet, or press statement, so that it can be conveniently forwarded to the individual *Gaue*.

10. Every affiliated Gauleiter is not only entitled but obliged to pass on to the Working Group leadership proposals and suggestions which seem to him important, so that they may have fruitful effect.

11. So long as the organizing work of the Working Group does not claim disproportionate resources, the *Gau* Rhineland-North will provisionally meet the costs of the Working Group administration.

12. The affiliated Gauleiters bind themselves in honour to subordinate all self-interest to the framework of common action and in a comradely spirit to serve the idea of National Socialism under its leader Adolf Hitler.

At a meeting of the Working Group which took place in Hanover on 22 November 1925, Gregor Strasser was invited by the members to draft a new Party programme. Two months later, however, on 24 January 1926, a second meeting in Hanover rejected his draft as unsatisfactory and a sub-committee was set up to consider a new programme. Strasser's draft was considered too vague and verbose and he had clearly proved unable to reconcile the differing views of the members of the Working Group on such questions as the structure of a future National Socialist state and foreign policy. A number of members, including Goebbels, favoured an alliance with Russia against the 'Jewish-capitalist' West. They now regarded Russia under Stalin as a 'nationalist' power. The Göttingen group, on the other hand, regarded Russia as a field for German expansion.

8 *Resolution on compensation for the princes*

Another important issue discussed at this meeting was the need to decide whether or not to support a referendum organized by the Left to demand the expropriation of the royal princes. It was recognized that the Group's attitude on this question would be regarded as a test of how seriously the Nazis were to be considered as a genuinely workers' and Socialist party. The meeting passed the following resolution which, despite its equivocation, went some way towards committing the Party to the principle of expropriation. In the event, this did not prove sufficient to persuade many workers to support the Nazi Party but it does indicate that the Working Group, led by Strasser, Goebbels and the other Elberfeld leaders, were serious in their intention of winning working-class support.

The study group holds the view, without in any way wishing to anticipate the decision of Party headquarters, that the so-called question of compensation for the princes is not a question of fundamental importance for the Party as such.

It is guided by the view that the question of so-called compensation for the princes is not only a legal but also a social matter. In a state in which law and justice prevailed, one would obviously regard it only from the legal standpoint. This state of Weimar, however, which has perpetrated upon pensioners, war-loan recipients and state creditors the enormous injustice of confiscating their property and calling it revaluation, has violated the very basis of law and property, and this not in the interests of the community, but, on the contrary, in the service of speculative, immoral stock exchange capital which is in the hands of only a few.

The distressing circumstances in which the German people find themselves, owing to the criminal policy of the government parties of all shades, do not permit, simply with reference to formal law, the granting of hundreds of millions of Reichsmarks to former princes, the majority of whom did not understand or further the racial tasks of Germany.

But this attitude makes it doubly necessary to point out the crude mendacity of the parties of the Left, who want to exploit this question for sordid party purposes.

One must remember the position of these same parties at the time when they were still in the Government. On 28 July 1919 the Socialist Government of the Reich replied to the request of the People's Council of Reuss for the expropriation of the Royal Houses without compensation: 'The Reich Government is not in a position to grant this petition since they cannot propose a law whose content cannot be reconciled with the future constitution of the German Reich.'

And on 3 December 1918 the Ebert–Scheidemann Reich Government wrote to the Workers' and Soldiers' Council in Lippe-Detmold:

'The question of whether the property of the former Prince of Schaumburg-Lippe situated in Lippe-Detmold is the private property of his family is a legal question on which the decision is reserved to the appropriate courts.'

The mendacity of the present petition of these parties is strikingly evident from this: the one-sidedness, no less than the deception.

For such wealth, which is immoral in view of the present distress of the German people, is not only in the hands of former princes, but above all is in the possession of Jewish financiers great and small. Therefore, if the Marxist petition for the expropriation of the Royal Houses without compensation is accepted, we demand also the expropriation without compensation of all Eastern Jews who have entered Germany as immigrants since 1 August 1914, as well as the confiscation of all increases in property after 1 August 1914, paying particular attention to bank and stock exchange profits.

We ask all Party members in public discussions to adopt on this question a position in accordance with this point of view.

Hitler received a report of the Hanover meeting from his representative, Gottfried Feder. Feder regarded himself as the leading ideologist of the Party and therefore resented the criticism levelled at the programme by the Working Group. His report on the support given by the meeting to the referendum, on their determination to rewrite the programme, and above all on their critical attitude towards the Munich headquarters, which may or may not have included the leader himself, forced Hitler to act. He was in the process of trying to win the approval of businessmen, a tactic which would be undermined by Party support for the expropriation of the princes. Furthermore, while Hitler regarded the details of the Party programme as of relatively minor significance, he was not prepared to have the programme itself discussed since this would tend to give it undue importance; if the programme could be altered as a result of discussion and pressure from the membership, the Party would be liable to endless doctrinal disputes such as those that bedevilled the parties of the Left over the correct party line. This would detract from the main aim of winning power. Above all, if the programme was made to appear so important and was subject to alteration by the membership, then it would inevitably restrict the freedom of the leader to act as he thought fit in any given circumstances. Instead of the party line being defined by the leader, the leader would be bound by a party programme whose interpretation would be in the hands of the party membership. In short, the issue at stake in this struggle was whether the party was to be a 'Führer party' in which the leader was the source of all authority, or whether authority was to be ultimately derived from the programme as interpreted by the membership. Finally, Hitler was afraid of the growth of the Working Group into a regional organization which might challenge the authority of Munich headquarters. In order to meet this challenge, therefore, he summoned a conference of Party leaders at Bamberg in Bavaria at which, without actually attacking the Working Group, he made it clear that their policies were unacceptable. Goebbels described the occasion in his diary:

9 *The Bamberg conference, 14 February 1926*

Leaving Saturday morning. In Bamberg we shall have to act the part of the bashful maiden and lure Hitler on to our territory. I am glad to notice that our [i.e. the Socialist] spirit is on the march in all towns. Not a soul has faith in Munich. Elberfeld must become the Mecca of German Socialism. . . .

. . . Sunday morning. Strasser comes to fetch me in the morning. He is hopeful. Plan for action ready. With Rust and Vahlen. Then tour of Bamberg. Charming town. Old, Jesuit. Hitler's car tears past us. A handshake. Well, well, Schlange-Berlin,[1] Streicher, Esser, Feder. Then to work. Hitler speaks for two hours. This pretty nearly finishes me. What kind of Hitler? A reactionary? Amazingly clumsy and uncertain. Russian question: altogether beside the point. Italy and Britain the natural allies. Horrible! It is our job to smash Bolshevism. Bolshevism is a Jewish creation! We must become Russia's heirs! A hundred and eighty millions!!! Compensation for princes! Law is law. Also for the princes. Question of not weakening private property [*sic*]. Horrible! Programme will do! Happy with it. Feder nods. Ley[2] nods. Streicher nods. Esser nods. It hurts me deeply to see you in that company!!! Short discussion. Strasser speaks. Hesitant, trembling, clumsy, good, honest Strasser; Lord, what a poor match we are for those pigs down there! Half an hour's discussion after a four-hour speech! Nonsense, you

[1] Dr Schlange, Gauleiter of Berlin 1925–26.
[2] Dr Robert Ley, Gauleiter of Rhineland-South 1925–31; 1931–33, posts in Munich headquarters; after 1933, head of the German Labour Front and of Party organization.

will win! I cannot say a word! I am stunned! By car to the station. Strasser is quite beside himself! Waving and *Heil*. My heart aches! Farewell from Strasser. We meet again in Berlin the day after tomorrow. I want to cry! Journey home. Sad journey home. With Haake and Dr Ley. I say hardly a word. A horrible night! Probably one of my greatest disappointments. I can no longer wholly believe in Hitler. This is terrible. I have lost my inner support. I am only half myself. Grey dawn appears. Elberfeld. A few hours' sleep. Kaufmann.[1] I want to embrace him. We all say all there is to be said. Schmitz and Toni join us. The result: we are Socialists. We don't want to have been it in vain! Telegram from Lohse, Strasser, Vahlen. Do nothing hasty. Tomorrow discussion in Göttingen. Then Wednesday to Strasser. Proposal: Kaufmann, Strasser and I go to Hitler to impress on him: he must not allow those rogues down there to tie him hand and foot. Well then, train again tomorrow. Into battle. I despair! Sleep! Sleep! Sleep!

Although for a few weeks Goebbels and some other members of the Working Group still hoped that they would win over Hitler, this proved impossible. At the Party Congress in May 1926 the programme was once again declared immutable and in July working groups within the Party were forbidden. In the meantime Goebbels had made his peace with Hitler and in November was appointed Gauleiter in Berlin.

The creation of the Party cadre

The importance of the period 1925-29 in the history of the Nazi Party lies in the creation of a cadre of dedicated activists scattered in towns and villages throughout Germany. The basic framework had been laid before 1925 in the sense that the Party began with a number of supporters who had already been involved in the *völkisch* movement either in the Nazi Party before its ban or in the German *Völkisch* Freedom Party (DVFP). These men now, rather than join the new DVFP, joined the refounded Nazi Party largely because of its reputation for activism and also because of the prestige won by Hitler during his trial. Significantly, those who joined the Nazi Party tended to be younger than those joining its rival. The basic pattern of Nazi organization was regional. Germany was divided into *Gaue* or regions, and regional Party leaders or Gauleiters were appointed. These were usually men who had already succeeded in establishing their leadership in the area and who were in effect confirmed by the Party headquarters in Munich. Until 1928, the boundaries of the *Gaue* had been arranged on a largely *ad hoc* basis depending partly on the existing political and administrative divisions but partly also on the extent of the area over which the respective Gauleiters had succeeded in establishing their authority. In 1928, however, the *Gaue* were reorganized to correspond with the Reichstag electoral districts of which there were thirty-five. Below the *Gaue* came the local branches and 'strongpoints' which varied in size from a few hundred members

[1] Karl Kaufmann, Gauleiter of the Ruhr 1926-28, Gauleiter of Hamburg 1929-45.

down to one or two, who did not form a branch but carried out propaganda in their area as best they could. In time, a district (*Kreis*) organization developed between the *Gau* headquarters and the local branches but this did not become fully effective until after 1929. The main burden of Party work during this period fell on the *Gau* headquarters which kept in touch with Munich on the one hand and the local branches on the other. In the early period the main correspondence with Munich concerned membership forms and subscriptions. As far as propaganda was concerned, the *Gaue* could expect only an occasional speaker from headquarters. Most of the propaganda work was carried out by the Gauleiters and a few leading local activists. It entailed speaking at meetings arranged by the local branches, often in neighbouring towns and villages where there was not yet a branch. Sometimes the meeting would produce enough new members to found a branch—usually a minimum of fifteen. Once a branch had been founded it would canvass support in the neighbouring villages by holding periodic meetings and distributing pamphlets.

10 *The Affinghausen/Diepholz local branch, November 1929*

A typical example of the way the movement spread was the village of Affinghausen in the district of Diepholz in Lower Saxony. The history of the local branch written in 1937 records the founding as follows:[1]

In the year 1928–29 the National Socialist speaker, Jan Blankemeyer [a peasant] from Oldenburg came and talked to us about Adolf Hitler and his movement. Comrade Blankemeyer then came every two months and in winter even more frequently. He was living then in Uenzen, Kreis Grafschaft Hoya [a neighbouring district]. Comrades from the Uenzen branch ran the meetings here. Then Dincklage, the deputy Gauleiter, came. In October 1929, after a Blankemeyer meeting, eleven people joined the Party. Then in November 1929 the SA from Borstel near Nienburg [in a neighbouring district] held a propaganda march, which was followed by a meeting with Comrade Leister from Nienburg, and a branch was founded with farmer Hermann Menke as branch leader. Then we carried out propaganda in the surrounding villages.

Before 1928–29 it was a slow process and it was characterized by much conflict within the various local Party organizations. But the important thing is that a cadre organization was being created, for this provided the organizational framework which was essential if the Party was to be capable of successfully exploiting the economic and social discontent which resulted from the depression of 1929–33. It was the character of these men, who were to form the political leadership of the Third Reich, which helped to shape the future development of National Socialism. In particular, their youth, their radicalism, their sense of commitment, helped to determine the charismatic nature of the Party organization, expressed in the emphasis on

[1] This document is given in a compressed form.

the absolute authority of Hitler as leader, which rooted itself in the Party during these years. It was essentially this fact which had ensured the failure of the Working Group. For the members of the group themselves and notably its most dynamic leader, Joseph Goebbels, shared this commitment to Hitler's leadership. These people wanted a leader and they recognized that Hitler was by far the most effective leader in the *völkisch* movement. He offered them the type of political action which they enjoyed. Politics for them was not a matter of discussion, bargaining and compromise within established bodies and procedures. It was the thrill of physical action in the streets and beer halls or of inspiring an audience with a speech; the sense of comradeship induced by the struggle against an enemy; the glow of self-righteousness springing from a comparison of one's own self-sacrifice for the sake of the nation with the 'philistinism' of the citizen going about his ordinary daily life.

11 *The change of generations, 1926–28*

This style of politics appealed to many young people and to many who during the postwar crisis had become uprooted from normal ties of family and job and for whom their alienation now became a source of pride, rationalized by an ideology which condemned the established order and glorified them as an elite. These men now ousted the older generation of *völkisch* leaders whose political style had been shaped by the prewar years, as the young Dr Albert Krebs, who became for a short time Gauleiter in Hamburg, later recalled:

Characteristic of this period was the steady disappearance of all leaders and subordinate leaders (with the exception of a few parliamentary deputies) whose views and methods of struggle were still rooted in prewar days. Their places were taken by the young men of what was known as the front generation of 25–35 years old.

The importance of this changing of the guard can hardly be overemphasized. The openness of the feeling and judgement of these young men, their unweakened power of faith, their sheer physical energy and pugnacity lent the Party an impetus which the bourgeois parties above all could not match. Only rarely can the attack of youth be parried with the wire entanglement of grey-haired experience or the barbed-wire barricades of bitter scepticism. For the youth of the twenties these were nothing but a new provocation to their defiance and revolutionary enthusiasm. The quickest to feel it were those racialist groups and parties whose leadership represented conservative, or rather reactionary, views taken over from the past. Within only two short years they no longer had any political role whatsoever, even though such of them as the 'German Racialist League of Defence and Defiance'[1] had at one time several hundred thousand followers. Even in Hamburg, where the development of the NSDAP progressed rather slowly. the Racialist Freedom Party was already after one year in total disintegration. 'Without young people,' one of their representatives confessed to me, 'nothing can be organized, not even the distribution of leaflets.'

[1] A large antisemitic organization established by the Pan-German League in 1919.

12 *Thoughts of a young Hitler supporter*

A young member from Bad Harzburg who joined the SA during this period described his 'conversion' as follows:

For me this was the start of a completely new life. There was only one thing in the world for me and that was service in the movement. All my thoughts were centred on the movement. I could talk only politics. I was no longer aware of anything else. At the time I was a promising athlete; I was very keen on sport, and it was going to be my career. But I had to give this up too. My only interest was agitation and propaganda.

13 *Tensions within the Party organization*

The radical nature of the Party membership created problems of discipline for the organization. Indeed the structure of the local Party organizations during these early years bore in some ways a closer resemblance to a street gang than to a conventional political party. The situation of a leader was a fiercely competitive one in which he would be constantly required to prove himself in the eyes of his followers by his drive and radicalism. When things were going well this competition tended to contribute to the dynamic of the Party, but when things went badly, it could cause serious internal conflict as the following account by Ludolf Haase, Gauleiter of Göttingen, indicates:

When in the year 1914 our magnificent army went to war, leadership was conferred by rank. . . . But as the years went by, and the period of the great *Material-schlachten*[1] arrived with their incredible spiritual and physical demands, the only real leader, so far as his troops were concerned, was the man who proved himself in a crisis. The thing that now counted in an officer was not his uniform but the example he set people and his readiness to die for them. Here in blood, pain and mud, was born National Socialism, to which similar laws later applied, though under apparently quite different conditions. But basically in the movement it is only the true man, not the official, who is leader.

This explains why there was very often tension in the Party. The movement wanted to see men at the top who understood how to master conflict and opposition and who would yield to no one. If the leadership appeared to fall short, they were soon discontented and, because their obedience had been voluntarily given, there was risk of serious disturbance. The falling short might not even be real, only suspected; but still, if some individual had personal designs and spread accusations in the attempt to secure a following, serious damage could be done.

The quieter things were, the greater was this continual threat of internal unrest in the still immature party; the revolutionary spirits wanted to find an outlet, and as soon as the external enemy was less active or less under attack they turned their energy inwards. This hidden process, constantly at work within the movement, was the death of many a local branch in the early period and more than one Gauleiter fell victim to it. The leader of an area grew in the struggle and learned his lessons both from his opponents and from his own troop.

[1] i.e. battles involving massive quantities of war material, artillery, etc.

14 *Branch leaders are not 'appointed' but must win their position*

Hitler thoroughly approved of this situation which reflected his own Social Darwinist view of life. Indeed, he himself encouraged the emergence of leaders through a type of natural selection. Gustav Seifert, a Party member who had founded the Hanover branch in 1921 and who asked to be re-appointed leader in 1925, was told by Max Amann from Munich headquarters in a letter dated 27 October 1925:

You know from your earlier activity as a branch leader of the National Socialist German Workers' Party that Herr Hitler takes the view on principle that it is not the job of the Party leadership to 'appoint' Party leaders. Herr Hitler is today more than ever convinced that the most effective fighter in the National Socialist movement is the man who wins respect for himself as leader through his own achievements. You yourself say in your letter that almost all the members follow you. Then why don't you take over the leadership of the branch?

Hitler did not like intervening personally in conflicts of this kind; he preferred to leave the combatants to fight it out until one or another had come out on top. He believed that leaders would prove themselves by the success with which they maintained and extended their position and he particularly admired ruthlessness in the pursuit of power. On the other hand, he qualified this approach by a tendency to show loyalty to those with whom he had been associated from an early stage even if later they had shown themselves to be not entirely competent.

15 *Goebbels is made responsible for restoring order in the Berlin Party organization in 1926*

Sometimes, for the sake of the stability of the organization, it became necessary for Party headquarters to intervene to uphold the authority of a local leader who was being threatened with faction, and very occasionally Hitler would have to intervene personally and appoint someone from outside to restore order. This occurred, for example, in 1926 with the Berlin branch where there had been continuing conflict. Hitler appointed Joseph Goebbels as the new Gauleiter of Berlin. He recognized Goebbels's ability and was anxious to conciliate him after the affair of the Working Group. Goebbels, who had soon become reconciled to the failure of the Working Group and whose admiration for Hitler was unbounded, accepted with alacrity. The following reports written by Reinhold Muchow, a leading member of the Berlin organization, describe the impact of Goebbels's appointment. The first is for October 1926:

The internal party situation has not been good this month. The state of affairs which has developed in our *Gau* reached such a climax this time that a complete disruption of the Berlin organization seemed likely. The tragedy of the *Gau* has been that it has never had a proper leader, particularly necessary in this city of millions. With all respect to the first Gauleiter, Comrade Dr Schlange, who has worn himself out, he never succeeded in establishing a clear line in the *Gau*. He lacked the gift of oratory and his work was paralysed by much unjust hostility. There began slowly to develop in the *Gau* an opposition which strongly criticized the bad state of affairs. Such criticism is always the driving force behind any opposition, but this was unable to make any positive suggestions, and the main thing was that it could propose no other suitable person as Gauleiter. This opposition was partly justified, but it was unruly rather than positive or objective, and when Comrade Dr Schlange transferred the management of the *Gau* to the deputy Gauleiter, Comrade Schmiedicke, it spread further and further. This comrade was even less capable of the determination required to master the confused situation. The result was that the opposition gathered fresh strength and Comrade Heinz Oskar Hauenstein put himself at the head of it and was put forward as the new Gauleiter. The meetings of branch leaders which should have been devoted to positive work became arenas in which two sides of almost equal strength spent the evenings in passionate debate of which at least 75 per cent was concerned with personalities. The fighting efficiency of the Party sank to nil. Only a very few branches in the *Gau*—Neukölln and Spandau—looked at things dispassionately and persevered patiently, partly on their own responsibility. The unity of both these branches was preserved by the complete isolation of their membership from the details of the personal intrigues which went on in the meetings of the branch leaders. These two branches have an especial significance in that both, particularly Neukölln, are situated in the largest centres of Marxism.

When it proved impossible to establish order in the general chaos and when the local opposition groups went so far as to ignore all the decisions of the deputy Gauleiter, negotiations were started with the Reich party leadership in Munich with the request for a new Gauleiter. We received at length the news that Comrade Dr Goebbels would probably become the future Gauleiter of Berlin. A genuine sigh of relief went up from the disorganized *Gau*, proving how much all the comrades had felt the lack of a real leader. An official statement has not yet been made, but all Berlin comrades confidently hope that Comrade Dr Goebbels will definitely come.

In view of this internal party situation, there was no question of the NSDAP appearing in public in Berlin. Let us hope that the coming weeks will bring the new Gauleiter the success which National Socialism in Berlin deserves.

16 *Goebbels and the Communists*

Goebbels solved the problem by diverting the energy and violence of the Party activists away from internal conflict and against the Party's political opponents in Berlin, of whom the Communists were the most active. In view of the strength of the Left in Berlin, it was an uphill struggle, but the important fact was that the members were now engaged against the enemy under a leader whose energy and radicalism they could admire. This is clear from the following report dated 'February 1927':

On the 11th of this month the Party held a public mass meeting in the 'Pharus [Beer] Halls' in Wedding, the real working-class quarter, with the subject: 'The

Collapse of the Bourgeois Class State'. Comrade Dr Goebbels was the speaker. It was quite clear to us what that meant. It had to be visibly shown that National Socialism is determined to reach the workers. We succeeded once before in getting a foothold in Wedding. There were huge crowds at the meeting. More than 1,000 people filled the hall whose political composition was four-fifths SA to one-fifth KPD.[1] But the latter had gathered their main forces in the street. When the meeting was opened by Comrade Daluege, the SA leader, there were, as was expected, provocative shouts of 'On a point of order!'. After the KPD members had been told that *we*, not they, decided points of order, and that they would have the right to ask questions after the talk by Comrade Dr Goebbels, the first scuffling broke out. Peace seemed to be restored until there was renewed heckling. When the chairman announced that the hecklers would be sent out if the interruptions continued, the KPD worked themselves into a frenzy. Meanwhile, the SA had gradually surrounded the centre of the disturbance, and the Communists, sensing the danger, suddenly became aggressive. What followed all happened within three or four minutes. Within seconds both sides had picked up chairs, beer mugs, even tables, and a savage fight began. The Communists were gradually pushed under the gallery which we had taken care to occupy and soon chairs and glasses came hurtling down from there also. The fight was quickly decided: the KPD left with 85 wounded, more or less: that is to say, they could not get down the stairs as fast as they had calmly and 'innocently' climbed them. On our side we counted 3 badly wounded and about 10–12 slightly. When the police appeared the fight was already over. Marxist terrorism had been bloodily suppressed. . . .

As a result of his success in reviving the Berlin *Gau*, Goebbels was later appointed head of the Party's propaganda organization on 27 April 1930.

17 *Heil Hitler!*[2]

The following document written, significantly by Gregor Strasser, on 9 January 1927 for his paper *Der Nationale Sozialist für Sachsen* indicates the progress already made by the cult of the Führer. Despite the tensions which often existed within the local Party organizations, Hitler had now succeeded in establishing for himself an unchallenged position, and the respect of the rank and file for his leadership now provided the main cohesive force within the Party:

How could a National Socialist start this new year in any other way than with a salute to our honoured leader, a salute which expresses not only a personal devotion which is proof against any attempt to dim its flame but also the loyal pledge: To fight the battle for National Socialism with our life and soul this year like last year. For this is the great secret of our movement: an utter devotion to the idea of National Socialism, a glowing faith in the victorious strength of this doctrine of liberation and deliverance, is combined with a deep love of the person of our leader who is the shining hero of the new freedom-fighters. The tremendous

[1] *Kommunistische Partei Deutschlands*, the German Communist Party.
[2] First used occasionally at the end of 1923, this greeting was now sufficiently widespread to be used in this way.

superiority which the NSDAP has as a fighting instrument compared with all the other formations which instinctively pursue the same aim of German liberty and the rebirth of the German people, is due to the fact that we have the outstanding leader, who holds not only supreme power but also the love of his followers —a much stronger binding force.

'Duke and vassal!' In this ancient German relationship of leader and follower, fully comprehensible only to the German mentality and spirit, lies the essence of the structure of the NSDAP, the driving force of this aggressive power, the conviction of victory!

Heil Hitler! This is our first salute in the new year as it was the last one in the old year: Heil Hitler! In this salute lies the pride in the success of the past year which in all the *Gaue* of our beloved fatherland saw the powerful, irresistible progress of the National Socialist idea! In thousands of public meetings, members' evenings, in many hundreds of mass meetings the idea of National Socialism, the name of Adolf Hitler, was hurled among the masses of the German people and a hush fell on the ranks of this enslaved, exploited, starved people. An awareness of this glowing will for the struggle, the struggle to preserve the German people, the struggle for that people's freedom, freedom both within and without—for the one is worthless and impossible without the other—an awareness of those metallic accents of a brutal harshness which call things by their real names and challenges those things to a struggle, a relentless struggle giving no quarter. . . .

Friends, a new year lies before us. Let us join hands in a silent vow to struggle in the new year with redoubled, with threefold vigour, each one at his post, for the victory of National Socialism, that is for the inward and outward freeing of the German people, to struggle without wavering, without flinching, in selfless devotion and true comradeship. And then, friends, raise your right arm and cry out with me proudly, eager for the struggle, and loyal unto death, 'Heil Hitler'.

18 *The Annual General Meeting, 2–3 September 1928*

This account of the Annual General Meeting in 1928 shows how the Party prided itself on its rejection of democratic procedures in favour of the acclamation of a leader:

. . . Above all, Hitler notes the gradual penetration of the whole movement with the basic concepts of our ideas. He stresses primarily the gradual consolidation of the leadership principle [*Führerprinzip*]. The movement can be proud of the fact that it is the only one based on a logical foundation. This was necessary in order to make up for our numerical minority by a maximum degree of inner discipline, stability, fighting power, in short, energy. . . .

. . . The disintegration spreads slowly but surely; there is hardly any serious resistance. But antisemitism grows as an idea. What was hardly there ten years ago is there today: the Jewish question has been brought to people's notice, it will not disappear any more and we shall make sure that it becomes an international world question; we shall not let it rest until the question has been solved. We think we shall live to see that day (*enthusiastic applause*). . . .[1]

[1] This paragraph is a direct quote from Hitler's speech.

The chairman of the meeting, Gregor Strasser, expresses the mood of the meeting very well by remarking that any other party would now say that they had heard the reports of the chairman, whereas we National Socialists have heard the speech of the leader. And there is the same difference between the chairman of the old parties and the leader of the movement as there is between the report of a chairman of a party and the speech we have just heard.

The party business is now quickly dealt with according to the regulations. First, 'the election of the statutory executive committee'. To the amusement of the audience, Strasser proposes NSDAP member Hitler as Chairman. He notes that he has been unanimously elected by a show of hands (*laughter*). In the place of Comrade Schneider, who has been transferred by his employer away from the city, Comrade City Councillor Fiehler is elected Secretary in the same way. Also Reich treasurer Comrade Schwarz, who had 'resigned', is elected as first Treasurer, whereupon Strasser declares the acceptance of the election by the person nominated.

19 *The role of the SA*

The main burden of Party activity fell on the SA, and at this period nearly all members of the Party who were fit and active belonged to it. Hitler took his time about its refounding, which officially took place in the autumn of 1926. He wanted to make sure that it did not become either a military-style formation, as had happened during 1923, or a group of revolutionary conspirators, since in either event there would have been a danger of the Government's using this as an excuse to ban the Party. In his first orders to the new SA, therefore, on 1 November 1926, he made it clear that it was to be purely a propaganda weapon and a strong-arm squad:

A. *Chief SA Leader: SA Order* 1

Letter from Adolf Hitler to Captain von Pfeffer

To conclude our discussions about the programme of your reorganization, I would like to sum up briefly my main instructions.

The training of the SA must be carried out, not on a military basis, but in accordance with the needs of the Party.

In so far as the members undergo physical training, the main emphasis must be, not on military drill, but far more on sports activities. Boxing and Jiu-Jitsu have always seemed to me far more important than any ineffective, because only incomplete, shooting practice. Physical training must implant in the individual the conviction of his superiority and give him that self-assurance which lies only in confidence in one's own strength; furthermore, it should give him those athletic skills which serve as a weapon for the defence of the movement.

The organization of the SA as well as its clothing and equipment must accordingly be carried out, not on the model of the old army, but in a way appropriate to its task.

In order right from the start to prevent the SA acquiring any secretive character, quite apart from the fact that its clothing is recognizable to everybody, the size of its membership must define the path which assists the movement, one which is known to the public. It must not meet in secret but should march in the open air and thereby be channelled into activities which conclusively destroy all legends of a 'secret organization'. To provide a mental diversion from any temptation to satisfy its activism by petty conspiracies, it must from the very beginning be initiated into the great idea of the movement and be trained in the task of representing this idea to such a degree that the horizon is widened right from the start and the individual SA man does not see his mission in the elimination of some crook or other whether big or small, but in helping to build a new National Socialist racialist state. Thereby the struggle against the present state will be raised above the atmosphere of petty acts of revenge and conspiracy to the greatness of an ideological war of extermination against Marxism, its constructions and its string pullers.

What we need is not a hundred or two hundred daring conspirators, but a hundred thousand and hundreds of thousands more fanatical fighters for our *Weltanschauung*. We must not work in secret conventicles but in huge mass marches, and neither by dagger nor poison nor pistol can the path be cleared for the movement, but only by conquering the street. We have to teach Marxism that National Socialism is the future master of the streets, just as it will one day be master of the State.

[signed] ADOLF HITLER

I hereby bring this letter to the notice of the SA leaders as a directive.

B. *The SA and the public: SA Order* III

1. The SA will appear in public only in closed formation. This is at the same time one of the most powerful forms of propaganda. The sight of a large number of men inwardly and outwardly uniform and disciplined, whose total commitment to fighting is clearly visible or can be sensed, makes the deepest impression on every German and speaks a more convincing and inspiring language to his heart than speech, logic, or the written word is ever capable of doing.

Calm composure and natural behaviour underline the impression of strength—the strength of marching columns and the strength of the cause for which they are marching.

The inner strength of the cause makes the German conclude instinctively that it is right: 'for only what is right, honest and good can release real strength'. Where whole crowds purposefully risk life and limb and their livelihood for a cause (not in the upsurge of sudden mass suggestion), the cause must be great and true!

Here lies the task of the SA from the point of view of propaganda and recruiting. The SA leaders must gear the details and forms of their appearances to a common line.

2. This instinctive 'proof of truth' is not underlined but disturbed and dissipated by the addition of logical arguments and propaganda. The following should be avoided: cheers and heckling, posters about day-to-day controversies, abuse, accompanying speeches, leaflets, festivals, public amusements.

3. It is inappropriate for the SA to work in one way one day and differently the next, according to circumstances. The SA must always and on principle refrain from all actual political propaganda and agitation. This should remain the task of the political leadership alone. However, each SA man is also a member of the

Party and as such of course must cooperate as much as he can in the propaganda of the political leadership. But not the SA as such. Not the SA men on duty and in uniform.

The SA man is the holy freedom fighter. The member of the Party is the clever propagandist and skilled agitator. Political propaganda tries to enlighten the opponent, to argue with him, to understand his point of view, to enter into his thoughts, to agree with him to a certain extent. But when the SA arrives on the scene, this stops. It makes no concessions. It goes all out. It only recognizes the motto (metaphorically): Kill or be killed!

4. It is forbidden for an SA to appeal to the public (or its opponents) orally or in writing, either through proclamations, announcements, leaflets, press 'corrections', letters, advertisements, invitations to festivals or meetings, or in any other way.

Public consecrations of the colours and sports competitions must take place within the framework of an event organized by a local branch, which alone issues the invitations or announcements for it. . . .

3 The Emergence of Nazism as a Mass Movement, 1928–33

By the year 1928, the Weimar Republic appeared, on the surface, to have acquired a degree of political stability and economic prosperity which few could have anticipated in the stormy years of 1919–23. Yet, although the years 1928–29 are often seen as the high point of economic prosperity in Germany before the disastrous slump following the Wall Street crash in 1929, this view requires qualification. In the first place, it must be emphasized that this economic prosperity was based on very insecure foundations. During the years 1924–28, German industry, agriculture and local government had borrowed vast sums of money on the American money market at high rates of interest and largely on a short-term basis. In the event of economic difficulties occurring in the United States, many of these loans were liable to recall at short notice. Secondly, by the end of 1927, certain sections of German society were already being subjected to economic difficulties. These were primarily peasants, artisans and small shopkeepers. These groups had tended to borrow heavily during the post-inflation period at very high interest rates. They then found that, in addition to the burden of interest, they had to pay high taxes and social insurance contributions for their employees. Finally, at the beginning of 1928 a world-wide agricultural depression began in which prices for agricultural produce slumped. This was exacerbated by trade treaties arranged with countries such as Poland by which Germany agreed to import agricultural produce in return for German industrial goods. The farmers now discovered that it was increasingly difficult to meet their interest and tax payments out of income. Inevitably, this crisis soon involved those economic groups dependent on agriculture— the artisans and small traders in rural areas. These economic difficulties provided the background to the growth of parties which had been formed to represent specific economic interests and therefore appealed to those groups which felt they had been neglected by other parties. But these new interest parties were not alone in seeing possibilities in this crisis. It was an opportunity which the Nazis did not miss.

The breakthrough, 1928–30

The relative prosperity and political stability of the years 1924–28 had created a climate which was not conducive to the growth of Nazism. This problem had been exacerbated by the tactics followed by the Party in concentrating on trying to win over the industrial workers. By the end of 1927, it had become clear that this policy had failed to achieve results: the workers remained loyal to the parties of the Left—the Social Democrats and the Communists. Moreover, the majority of the middle class were suspicious of the Party's working-class and 'Socialist' image. Although the Party had succeeded in building up a nucleus of diehard supporters, they were still fewer than 75,000 in the whole of Germany. With only seven deputies the Party was a negligible quantity in Parliament. In short, the Nazi Party was a fringe group on the far right of German politics and without influence.

1 *The change in emphasis from the workers to the middle class*

In view of this situation, a new tactic was clearly necessary if the energies of the Party were not to turn inwards in self-destructive internal conflict. In fact, by the beginning of 1928, a change of emphasis was occurring in which the Party, while continuing to try to attract workers, concentrated increasingly on the middle class, which they now recognized as more responsive to their propaganda than the workers. In December 1927 the deputy Gauleiter of Hanover-North, Karl Dincklage, wrote to Franz Stöhr, a Nazi Reichstag deputy, and referred to the line which Hitler had taken at a conference of Party leaders in Weimar on 27 November:

... In full agreement with the remarks of our leader in Weimar we too believe that we shall not yet succeed in winning much ground from the Marxists in the coming election. We shall receive most sympathy from the small businessman as the strongest opponent of department stores and consumer cooperatives. Further, from the white-collar worker, who, being in the DHV,[1] is already an antisemite ...

In the winter of 1927–28 a movement of discontent began among the rural population of north-west Germany and soon spread to other parts of the Reich. It was sparked off by an increase in the salaries of civil servants which came into effect on 16 December 1927. This infuriated the rural population which regarded itself as grossly overtaxed. The Nazis were quick to exploit the possibilities offered by this movement and in December 1927 Hitler made a major speech to a protest meeting of farmers from Schleswig-Holstein.

2 *A middle-class protest demonstration*

The following police report of a mass demonstration on 26 January 1928, in the city of Oldenburg, which lay in the middle of a big livestock farming area in north-west Germany, describes the grievances of these groups. It also shows the way in which the Nazis exploited them by trying to discredit the professional organizations which had organized the meeting, and to convince their members that the whole parliamentary system was at fault

[1] *Deutschnationaler Handlungsgehilfen-Verband*: the German National Commercial Employees' Association, a white-collar workers' union.

and that only a political movement dedicated to the overthrow of that system could bring relief:

... In meetings of the rural population which were held in many places in the state of Oldenburg during the past weeks, the majority of those participating demanded again and again that an open-air protest meeting should be held in the state capital of Oldenburg, in order to give weight to the demands of the rural population, outlined below, which emerged in the meetings and were in the meantime formulated by a committee. It would also open the eyes of the state government to the masses of discontented who stand behind these demands. The Rural League [*Landbund*], the Farmers' Association [*Bauernverein*], the League of Small-holdings, the Artisans' League, the Settlers' Association, and the Shopkeepers' Guild had therefore called their members to a combined mass demonstration which took place in the Horsefair on 26 January. According to fairly accurate estimates, approximately 20,000 country people had assembled in the Horsefair by 12 noon. ...

After the speeches of the representatives of various trade associations, the general secretary of the Oldenburg Farmers' Association, a farmer named Brendebach, announced the following fourteen demands of the rural population and said that during the next few days a delegation was to go to Berlin to convey these demands to the Reich Government and to demand radical measures for improving the situation of the rural population:

1. An embargo on all superfluous foreign imports.
2. Protection of agriculture through tariffs equivalent to those already applied to industry.
3. Simplification of the tax system; replacement of current direct taxes by income tax and property tax after suitable alterations; furthermore, the right for states and parishes to impose surcharges on these taxes.
4. Tax remission for farmers, craftsmen, and shopkeepers who are in distress.
5. Speedy radical reduction of government activity and expenditure.
6. Economical management in all branches of public administration, and reduction in the number of officials.
7. Temporary suspension of the pay regulations for civil servants of 16 December 1927.
8. We do not see in the incorporation of Oldenburg into Prussia[1] a measure making for cheaper administration.
9. Reduction of social insurance contributions to a level which business can stand.
10. Permission for voluntary overtime work after the 8-hour working period. Loyal application of the Reich regulations on contracts. Radical measures against non-guild work.
11. Planned reduction of controlled housing policy and promotion of building programmes.
12. The prerequisite for any settlement activity must be its profitability.
13. Availability of long-term cheap credit for improvement of the debt situation with the aim of wiping out debts.

[1] This had been suggested as part of a reform of the federal structure of the Reich.

14. The privileged treatment of civil servants in Parliament who receive a salary in addition to allowances and a substitute must cease.

The reading out of the demands drew loud and prolonged applause from the majority of the participants. . . .

A certain Münchmeyer,[1] formerly pastor of Borkum, as well as the National Socialists, had used the assembly of large numbers of the rural population for propaganda purposes for their parties. After ineffective appeals to the leadership of the protest meeting to be allowed to speak at the Horsefair, Münchmeyer called a public meeting at the Lindenhof for 10 a.m., which was attended by approximately 800 people. . . .

The NSDAP had scheduled two public meetings at the Lindenhof and the Ziegelhof at 3 p.m. At the meeting at the Lindenhof which was attended by over 1,000 people, Reichstag Deputy Kube[2] of Berlin was the speaker; Reichstag Deputy Gottfried Feder of Munich spoke at the meeting at the Ziegelhof which was attended by about 500 people. . . .

All the speakers at the Kube meeting expressed the view that the rural population could not be satisfied with the form and outcome of the demonstration. At the end the following resolution was read out and adopted unanimously:

'The thousands of Oldenburg farmers and middle-class people assembled today in the Lindenhof, together with the tens of thousands of their fellow-countrymen, who have come here in the most bitter distress to give visible expression of their despair, having listened to the speech of the National Socialist Reichstag Deputy Wilhelm Kube of Berlin, declare their absolute determination not to be deceived, misled, exploited and expropriated.

'We have recognized that the distress of agriculture is inseparably bound up with the *political misery* of the whole German people; that parliamentarism which is corrupt through and through and a weak government are unable to overcome the the German political and economic emergency.

'Let us do away with this Marxist-capitalist extortion system that has made Germany, our homeland, powerless, without honour, defenceless, and that has turned us free German farmers and middle-class people into poor, misused slaves of the world stock exchange.

'But let us also do away with the professional federations who only throw dust in our eyes and neutralize any vigorous action because politically they stand in the camps of those parties who have caused all this misery by accepting the Dawes Plan. The middle class and the farmers of Oldenburg see in the German National Socialist Hitler movement the only salvation from the parliamentary morass, from the pathetic and cowardly fulfilment policy.

'Only when Germany is reborn in power, freedom and honour, led by unselfish German men who are not burdened by the contemptible policy of the last few years, only then will the German farmer stand as a free man on free soil serving the great German community as the backbone of our people.'

It was noted that after the meeting several farmers approached Reichstag Deputy Kube to secure him for talks in the countryside.

---

[1] A leading antisemite who was to join the Nazis in April.
[2] Wilhelm Kube, Gauleiter of Kurmark 1928–36, General Commissioner of White Russia 1941–43.

3 *Declaration by Adolf Hitler, 13 April 1928*

This rural campaign of the Nazis prompted their opponents to accuse them of being a radical, socialistic, working-class party, which of course was the image which the Party had been trying to convey hitherto. In particular, the opponents tried to frighten the peasants with Point 17 of the Nazi programme.[1] As a result, Hitler was forced to give the following official 'clarification' of Point 17. This alteration in the Party programme gives an indication of the significance attached by Hitler to the reorientation of the Party:

In view of the false interpretations on the part of our opponents of Point 17 of the Programme of the NSDAP, it is necessary to make the following statement:
Since the NSDAP accepts the principle of private property, it is self-evident that the phrase 'confiscation without compensation' refers simply to the creation of possible legal means for confiscation, when necessary, of land acquired illegally or not managed in the public interest. It is, therefore, aimed primarily against Jewish companies which speculate in land.

This new middle-class campaign did not have time to take effect before the Reichstag election in May 1928. The results of this election appeared to reflect the improvement in the situation over the previous four years. The extreme Right suffered a serious defeat. The Nazis lost 100,000 votes compared with December 1924 and were reduced to 2·6 per cent of the total vote (although such a comparison is not entirely accurate since it was the German Racialist Freedom Movement rather than the Nazis which had campaigned in December 1924). The ultra-conservative German Nationalists lost 25 seats and were now reduced to 78. The Left, on the other hand, increased their vote to over 40 per cent of the total. The Social Democrats won 21 seats and now had 152; the Communists won 9 seats and now had 54. The result was greeted both at home and abroad as a victory for Weimar democracy. Yet, looked at more closely, the results indicated that under the surface the situation was by no means as satisfactory as appeared at first sight. For it was not only the Right that had lost support; the parties of the Centre—the Democrats or left-wing Liberals, the German People's Party or right-wing Liberals, and the Catholic Centre Party—had all lost seats. Their voters had either stayed away from the polls—the percentage of those voting declined sharply—or they voted for new economic interest parties which had been established during the years 1924–28, notably the Economic Party which catered for artisans and small shopkeepers and which increased its number of seats from 17 to 23.

In the context of the existing political situation this was an ominous result. For the past four years Germany had been ruled by a coalition of the Right

[1] For Point 17 see above p. 39.

and Centre—German Nationalists, German People's Party, Democrats, and Catholic Centre Party. In other words, the vote for the Left and against the Centre and Right, far from being a vote of confidence in the existing government, had been, if anything, a vote against the Government or at least an abstention. This need not have been an unfortunate result, had it not been for the conclusions which the Right and Centre parties drew from it. They interpreted the result to mean that participation in the Government would only have the effect of alienating their own supporters.

This reaction reflected the nature of the German party system. German parties tended to represent specific interests: the German Nationalists—agriculture, and particularly the big arable landowners of the east, the Junkers; the German People's Party—industry, and particularly heavy industry; the Centre Party—the Catholics; the Social Democrats—the trade unions. At the same time, the parties competed with one another within a broad segment of the population—the German Nationalists, the People's Party and the Democrats competed for the support of the upper and middle classes; the Social Democrats and Communists competed for the support of the workers. This situation, in which the parties were committed to specific interests and competed against rivals for support within the same segment of the population, made the formation of coalitions difficult at the best of times. The result of the election of 1928 now made the position even worse. The parties were confirmed in their view that by participating in government they would damage their electoral prospects; they would be forced to compromise the interests of their voters and members in order to maintain a coalition with parties which represented other and often conflicting interests. This would play into the hands of rivals who were not members of the Government, as had been shown by the growth of the economic interest parties which were regarded as dangerous new competitors. In this situation the party bureaucracies, which were primarily concerned about retaining the backing of interests and voters, applied increasing pressure on the parliamentary groups to stay in opposition in order to enable the party to assert without compromise the interests of their supporters. The parliamentary party groups in turn put pressure on their colleagues in the Government coalition to leave the Government rather than compromise.

These considerations were to determine the trend of politics from now onwards. The German Nationalists had previously compromised their hostility to the Republic by participating in government in order to protect the interests of their mainly agrarian supporters in the formulation of tariff legislation. From now onwards, they began to move to the Right, back to the uncompromisingly anti-Republican position which they had adopted in the first years of the Republic. The People's Party did not follow this trend to the Right immediately. Indeed, it now entered a coalition with the Social Democrats. But this was largely because of the leadership of Gustav Stresemann, who was aware that the democratic system depended on a strong Centre and on a willingness to compromise with the moderate Left. Pressure, however, continued to build up within the party against this coalition, particularly in view of the competition from the intransigent Nationalists on the Right. And, when Stresemann died on 3 October 1929, it was to be only a matter of time before the coalition broke down under the strain of the rightward drift of the People's Party.

Finally, even the Catholic Centre Party began to move towards the Right, particularly after it acquired a new and more conservative leader, Ludwig Kaas, at the end of 1928. This drift of the parties of the Centre towards the Right was paralleled by a corresponding leftward trend of the Social Democrats. This was the result of increasing competition from the Communists on the left, as was evident from their election gains in 1928. In short, after the election of 1928 a polarization of politics began to take place which threatened to paralyse the parliamentary system by making the formation of coalition governments impossible. Whether or not it would continue would depend on future economic developments; a deterioration in the economic situation would force the parties to uphold, even more rigidly, the particular interests of their members and voters.

4 *Excerpt from the* Völkischer Beobachter, *31 May 1928: after the election*
Although the new middle-class campaign had not had time to take effect before the May 1928 election, the low average vote of 2 per cent disguises district variations. In some rural districts in the north-west, for example, where the protest movement had been strong, they gained over 10 per cent. The Party summed up the lessons of the election as follows:

... The election results from the rural areas in particular have proved that with a smaller expenditure of energy, money and time, better results can be achieved there than in the big cities. In small towns and villages mass meetings with good speakers are events and are often talked about for weeks, while in the big cities the effects of meetings with even three or four thousand people soon disappear. Local successes in which the National Socialists are running first or second are, surprisingly, almost invariably the result of the activity of the branch leader or of a few energetic members....

During the eighteen months after the 1928 election the Party's membership steadily increased from 100,000 to 150,000 between October 1928 and 1 September 1929. The next turning-point came in the autumn of 1929. At this point, with the Wall Street crash, the economic situation in Germany rapidly deteriorated. American financiers, themselves under pressure, now called in the numerous short-term loans made to Germany since 1924. Numerous bankruptcies followed. Moreover, since the crisis was international, export markets disappeared and businesses were forced to shed labour or close down altogether. This in turn reduced home demand, making the situation even worse. Unemployment figures began to soar. And, just at this point, an issue emerged which was ideally adapted for a right-wing attack on the Republic—the Young Plan.

The plan drawn up by the Allied Reparations Commission under the chairmanship of the American banker General Young envisaged a final settlement of German war reparations in which Germany would pay less than originally intended but would still make substantial annual payments for another generation. This issue was now seen by the extreme Right as an excellent opportunity to exploit the growing discontent and regain the support which they had lost in the 1928 election. They would claim that Germany's children were being sold in slavery to the Allies. The German Nationalists now had a new leader in the press and film magnate Alfred Hugenberg, who had used the Party's electoral failure and subsequent financial difficulties to impose himself and his extreme anti-Republican views on the Party. Hugenberg now organized a referendum for a law rejecting the Young Plan and making any politician who agreed to the plan face trial as a traitor. In order to win maximum support for the referendum, he invited the help of all those willing to cooperate, including the Nazis.

Hitler saw this as an ideal opportunity for his party. It would give him access to the funds of the Right and national publicity in the Hugenberg press. More important, the association of the Nazis with the conservative and upper-class Nationalists would remove the stigma of its being a radical and working-class party and make it more acceptable to the middle class. Finally, because the Nazis were the most active of all the groups participating in the campaign, they gave the impression of being the most dynamic of the anti-Republican groups on the Right and therefore appeared more attractive than their conservative rivals to the growing number of those discontented with the Republican parties owing to the deteriorating economic situation. The fact that the referendum failed to win anything like sufficient support did not detract from these advantages.

5 'News from the Hamelin Town Council'

The Young Plan campaign coincided with the state and local government elections of November–December 1929, in which the Nazis made significant gains. In the election in the state of Thuringia in December, for example, they won 11·3 per cent of the vote and participation in the Government. In their local government propaganda the Nazis used rumour and scandal as one of their main propaganda means of discrediting opponents. Whether the scandal was true or not did not matter; they hoped to benefit from the belief that 'there's no smoke without fire'. Their aim was to discredit the local establishment whether it was Conservative or Social Democrat. The following article from the Nazi newspaper for the Hanover area gives a typical example of the style of Nazis' local government activity:

The cry for 'strict standing orders' which the Social Democrat newspaper, *Niedersächsische Volksstimme*, bellowed out after the first public session of the new council did not go unheard. Now, after the second session, this paper which addles the minds of the masses could note with satisfaction that the first great deed of the council was the passing of the 'Little Law for the Defence of the Republic' for Hamelin by a unanimous vote with the exception of the two National Socialists. Even the seven 'middle class [*bürgerlich*]' representatives were all in favour. This is intended to muzzle our two councillors, Ziesenitz and Schmidt.

With the remarkable lack of instinct characteristic of the two 'government parties' (seven middle class, nine Social Democrats) they appear not to have realized that these new standing orders were the greatest stupidity on the part of the council; with them they have achieved the precise opposite of what they intended, which was to persuade us to cooperate in a positive way. We as the sole opposition:

1. have now acquired the best opportunity for agitation.
2. will exploit every means of pointing out to the inhabitants of Hamelin just how pathetic 'middle class' and Social Democrat government really is.

The inhabitants of Hamelin will expect from us nothing less than enlightenment from time to time about what is going on; we will make sure of giving it them clearly.

There was a minor row at this session as well:

Public interest in this session was even stronger than in the previous one. The public gallery was overcrowded. There were 200 people standing outside the chamber who wanted to get in. In view of this, before the opening of the session our Comrade Schmidt proposed that since there were vacant seats in the chamber, the public gallery should be enlarged. The Oberbürgermeister, Jürgens, however, did not accede to this request and, significantly, Comrade Schmidt found no support either on the Left or on the Right so that for the time being the gallery was not enlarged. Those gentlemen wanted to keep themselves to themselves for what they term their 'constructive work'. But they had not reckoned with the people. Again and again from the gallery and from the street the cry went up: 'Open the doors'. Eventually, a nice row developed and the Oberbürgermeister's threat to clear the gallery only produced more noise. Comrades Schmidt and Ziesenitz were delighted. . . . Now people could see how the city fathers liked keeping themselves to themselves. What a bad conscience they must have that they prefer to hide from their electors behind locked doors rather than to meet in full view of the public!

Finally, they agreed that the public gallery should be enlarged for this session. Comrade Schmidt's further proposal to permit the gallery to be enlarged for all subsequent sessions was rejected by all with the exception of the two Nazis. . . .

Comrade Schmidt declared: The way in which the unemployed are being treated by the council is disgraceful. We consider all the motions are inadequate and with the permission of the chairman I wish to move our motion: 'That the town council decides that the motion of the committee for the unemployed shall be accepted without any cuts, and that all other motions be rejected.' I wish to point out that yesterday during the preliminary debate the motion was blocked by the Social Democrats with the help of the Combined Economic Groups. We also put forward suggestions for raising the necessary funds: a special tax on the consumer cooperative, a poster tax, an advertisement tax, a department store tax etc., so that if the unemployed get nothing for Christmas it is entirely the fault of the aldermen and councillors.

Senator Müller [SPD]: Herr Schmidt accuses us of lack of goodwill and sympathy for the unemployed. We were unemployed when Herr Schmidt was still at school. . . .

Müller then felt obliged to refer disparagingly to the profession of Herr Ziesenitz [NSDAP] who is a clerk at the district court.

Comrade Ziesenitz: Even if I am only a court clerk and don't earn 22,000 marks a year like Herr Müller, I am not prepared to tolerate people making snide remarks about my profession. In any case I do not visit the Baustrasse (the street in which Müller's mistress lives).

Müller makes a very feeble defence. He says he does not earn 22,000 marks. 'Then it's probably 21,000,' shouts Ziesenitz. 'What about giving the unemployed 1000 marks – after all, you're a Social Democrat!' Müller thereupon claims that the unemployed ought to be content.

6 *Hitler versus Otto Strasser on the relationship between leader and ideology*

There were, however, a few within the Party who resented this reorientation of its propaganda towards the middle-class and rural areas. They continued to press for a more definite 'socialist' commitment; they also objected to the subordination of the Party and its ideology to the leader. A leading spokesman for this group was Otto Strasser, the brother of Gregor Strasser. The newspapers of the Kampfverlag, the Strasser publishing house, continued to adopt a comparatively 'left-wing' line and caused complications for Hitler in his appeal to the middle class. The issue was finally fought out at an interview between Hitler and Otto Strasser in 1930. First, Hitler challenged the claim of Strasser's associates that the 'idea', i.e. the ideology, of the Party was distinct from and superior to the leader:

'How do you justify Blank's[1] theories?' he demanded. 'His conception of loyalty, the distinction he makes between the Leader and the Idea, are incitements to Party members to rebel.'

'No,' I said, 'it is not a question of diminishing the Leader's prestige. But for the free and Protestant German the service of the Idea first and foremost is an ingrained necessity. The Idea is divine in origin, while men are only its vehicles, the body in which the Word is made flesh. The Leader is made to serve the Idea, and it is to the Idea alone that we owe absolute allegiance. The Leader is human, and it is human to err.'

'You are talking monumental idiocy. You wish to give Party members the right to decide whether or not the Führer has remained faithful to the so-called Idea. It's the lowest kind of democracy, and we want nothing to do with it! For us the Idea is the Führer, and each Party member has only to obey the Führer.'

'No,' I replied. 'What you say is all very well for the Roman Church, from which, incidentally, Italian Fascism took its inspiration. But I maintain that for Germany the Idea is the decisive thing, and that the individual conscience should be called upon to decide if there is any divergence between the Idea and the Leader.'

[1] Herbert Blank was a friend of Otto Strasser.

'On that point we disagree', barked Hitler. He sat down and began rubbing his knees with a circular motion that grew quicker and quicker. 'What you say would lead to the dissolution of our organization, which is based on discipline. I have no intention of allowing our organization to be disrupted by a crazy scribbler. You have been an officer; you see that your brother accepts my discipline, even if he doesn't always see eye to eye with me. Take a lesson from him; he's a fine man.'

He seized my hands, as he had done two years before. His voice was choked with sobs, and tears ran down his cheeks. . . .

7 *Hitler versus Otto Strasser on the interpretation of Socialism*

Next, the argument turned to the question of the definition of Socialism about which Hitler and Strasser had very different views:

'All that is very simple for you, Herr Hitler, but it only serves to emphasize the profound difference in our revolutionary and Socialist ideas. The reasons you give for destroying the Kampfverlag I take to be only pretexts. The real reason is that you want to strangle the social revolution for the sake of legality and your new collaboration with the bourgeois parties of the Right.'

At this Hitler grew violent.

'I am a Socialist, and a very different kind of Socialist from your rich friend Reventlow. I was once an ordinary working-man. I would not allow my chauffeur to eat worse than I eat myself. But your kind of Socialism is nothing but Marxism. The mass of the working classes want nothing but bread and games. They will never understand the meaning of an ideal, and we cannot hope to win them over to one. What we have to do is to select from a new master-class men who will not allow themselves to be guided, like you, by the morality of pity. Those who rule must know they have the right to rule because they belong to a superior race. They must maintain that right and ruthlessly consolidate it. . . .

'What you preach is liberalism, nothing but liberalism. There is only one possible kind of revolution, and it is not economic or political or social, but racial, and it will always be the same: the struggle of inferior classes and inferior races against the superior races who are in the saddle. On the day the superior race forgets this law, it is lost. All revolutions—and I have studied them carefully—have been racial. . . .'

'Let us assume, Herr Hitler, that you came into power tomorrow. What would you do about Krupp's? Would you leave it alone or not?'

'Of course I should leave it alone', cried Hitler. 'Do you think me so crazy as to want to ruin Germany's great industry?'

'If you wish to preserve the capitalist regime, Herr Hitler, you have no right to talk of Socialism. For our supporters are Socialists, and your programme demands the socialization of private enterprise.'

'That word "socialism" is the trouble', said Hitler. He shrugged his shoulders, appeared to reflect for a moment and then went on:

'I have never said that all enterprises should be socialized. On the contrary, I have maintained that we might socialize enterprises prejudicial to the interests of the nation. Unless they were so guilty, I should consider it a crime to destroy essential elements in our economic life. Take Italian Fascism. Our National Socialist state, like the Fascist state, will safeguard both employers' and workers' interests while reserving the right of arbitration in case of dispute.'

'But under Fascism the problem of labour and capital remains unsolved. It has not even been tackled. It has merely been temporarily stifled. Capitalism has remained intact, just as you yourself propose to leave it intact.'

'Herr Strasser,' said Hitler, exasperated by my answers, 'there is only one economic system, and that is responsibility and authority on the part of directors and executives. I ask Herr Amann to be responsible to me for the work of his subordinates and to exercise his authority over them. Herr Amann asks his office manager to be responsible for his typists and to exercise his authority over them; and so on to the lowest rung of the ladder. That is how it has been for thousands of years, and that is how it will always be.'

'Yes, Herr Hitler, the administrative structure will be the same whether the state is capitalist or socialist. But the spirit of labour depends on the regime under which it lives. If it was possible a few years ago for a handful of men not appreciably different from the average to throw a quarter of a million Ruhr workers on the streets, if this act was legal and in conformity with the morality of our economic system, then it is not the men but the system that is criminal.'

'But that—' Hitler replied, looking at his watch and showing signs of acute impatience, 'that is no reason for granting the workers a share in the profits of the enterprises that employ them, and more particularly for giving them the right to be consulted. A strong State will see that production is carried on in the national interests, and, if these interests are contravened, can proceed to expropriate the enterprise concerned and take over its administration.'

On 27 March 1930, the polarization on the Right and on the Left within the Reichstag finally brought about the breakdown of the coalition government of the right-wing liberal People's Party and the Social Democrats which had ruled Germany since 1928. The issue on which the Government split was the question of who should finance the deficit in the unemployment benefit fund which was daily becoming larger as the numbers of unemployed rose. On this issue the interest groups behind the two parties made their weight felt. The People's Party under the influence of the industrialists wished to reduce the benefits, thereby putting the whole burden on the unemployed. The Social Democrats, on the other hand, under the pressure of the trade unions insisted on an increase in the social insurance contributions, of which the employers would have to pay half. After months of negotiation compromise proved impossible and the Government was forced to resign.

Three days later, the President appointed a new Chancellor, a Catholic Centre Party leader—Heinrich Brüning. Although Brüning's Government included many of the non-SPD members of the old cabinet, the appearance of continuity was deceptive. Brüning had been recommended to the President by General Kurt von Schleicher, who had emerged as the political expert of the Army. Brüning had been a moderate member of the Centre, but his background as a volunteer machine-gun officer in the war had given him a great respect for the Army and he regarded President Hindenburg with considerable awe. Brüning sympathized with the view, which had become increasingly prevalent among the Centre and moderate Right over the previous months, that the parliamentary system had broken down and that a rather more authoritarian regime was required. Parliament should not be abolished but it was necessary to shift the balance of power between legislature and executive in favour of the latter, more along the lines of the prewar system. Initially, he hoped to achieve this with the help of a Right/Centre coalition which would have a majority in the Reichstag and would therefore exclude the Social Democrats from influence. But the key to such a coalition lay with the German Nationalists and they were split into those who supported Hugenberg in his intransigent opposition to the Republic and a more moderate rebel group. Brüning hoped to strengthen the moderates and thereby acquire a majority.

The new Government's policy for solving the economic crisis reflected the emphasis of traditional economic theory on the need to balance the budget. It was a rigidly deflationary programme of increasing taxation and reducing Government expenditure. Brüning made no attempt to reach a compromise with the Social Democrats because, although without the Nationalists he did not possess a majority in the Reichstag, the President had promised him that he would be able to legislate by emergency decree. Thus, when on 16 July 1930 part of the Government's budget was rejected by the Reichstag, the President implemented it by decree. The Reichstag responded by passing a motion demanding that the decree be revoked. Brüning retaliated by dissolving the Reichstag and fixing elections for 14 September. He hoped that this would result in a reduction in the Socialist vote since they would probably be blamed for the economic crisis which had occurred under an SPD Chancellor. He also hoped that the German Nationalist rebels would be strengthened and that it would then be possible to form a Right/Centre coalition with a majority in Parliament. This proved a disastrous miscalculation with far-reaching consequences.

8 *The Prussian Ministry of the Interior on Nazi propaganda activity, May 1930*

As the following memorandum indicates, Nazi propaganda was already geared to a high pitch of efficiency and the campaign had merely to be intensified among a population now acutely anxious about the economic situation and disillusioned with the failure of their professional and political representatives. The rest of the parties, on the other hand, were obliged to turn from their legislative activities and face a hostile electorate which had little sympathy for their political manœuvring:

Hardly a day passes on which there are not several meetings even in narrowly restricted local areas. Carefully organized propaganda headquarters in the individual *Gaue* ensure that the speaker and the subject of his talk are adapted to the local and economic circumstances. The Reichstag and Landtag deputies of the Party and many other Party speakers travel about every day to undertake and build up this agitation. Through systematic training courses, through correspondence courses and recently through a school for NSDAP speakers established on 1 July 1929, such agitators are trained for this task over a period of months, even years. If they prove themselves, they receive official recognition from the Party and are put under contract to give at least thirty speeches over a period of eight months and receive as an incentive a fee of 20 Reichsmarks or more per evening in addition to their expenses. Rhetorical skill combined with subjects carefully chosen to suit the particular audience, which in the countryside and in the small towns is mainly interested in economic matters, ensure, according to our observations, halls which are almost invariably overcrowded with enthusiastic listeners. Meetings with an audience of between 1000 and 5000 people are a daily occurrence in the bigger towns. Frequently a second or several parallel meetings have to be held because the halls provided cannot hold the numbers who attend.... On such occasions the network of local branches is extended as far as possible or at all events contact men are recruited who are intended to prepare the ground through intensive propaganda by word of mouth for the spread of the movement which can be observed everywhere. Frequently such propaganda squads stay in a certain place for several days and try to win the local population for the movement through the most varied sorts of entertainment such as concerts, sports days, tattoos in suitable places and even church parades. In other places an outside propaganda speaker is stationed for a certain time; with a car at his disposal, he travels systematically through the surrounding district. National Socialist theatre groups travelling from place to place serve the same purpose.

At the Reichstag Election on 14 September 1930 the most striking result was the increase in votes for the Nazi Party from 810,000 at the previous election in 1928 to 6½ million. Much of the increase came from new voters who had not voted in the previous election because they were disaffected or too young to qualify. Some of their support, however, came from those who had previously voted for the middle-class Liberal and Conservative parties (People's Party, Democrats, and Nationalists), who lost 67 seats between them. The Catholic parties (Centre and Bavarian People's Party) increased their support slightly, while the Social Democrats lost support mainly to the Communists who gained 23 seats. But there could be no doubt about the main significance of the result – the Nazi Party with its 107 seats had become the second largest party in the Reichstag. The breakthrough for which the Party had been working for so long had at last been achieved.

Propaganda, 1930–32

Nazi propaganda was controlled by a special propaganda department which was represented at all levels of the Party. At the top was the Reich Propaganda Department in the Party headquarters in Munich, headed by Goebbels from 27 April 1930 onwards. Below this level each *Gau* or Party regional headquarters had its propaganda department with its own chief and then, below that, each branch had an official in charge of propaganda. Although this propaganda department was subject to the overall authority of the political leadership at the various levels, it also had its own separate chain of command. Directives were sent out from the Reich propaganda head-quarters to the propaganda departments of the *Gaue* which in turn relayed them to the propaganda officials in the local branches in their region. Similarly, reports of propaganda activity, information on political opponents, and suggestions were passed up the chain in the reverse direction. The Reich propaganda headquarters exercised a tight control over all aspects of propaganda, particularly at election times. A stream of directives went out specifying precise details of what themes were to be emphasized, and what slogans were to be used at what stage in the campaign. Furthermore, a selection of standard leaflets and posters were produced which the *Gaue* were expected to order. The use of important speakers was centrally con-trolled and they were deployed where headquarters felt they would be most effective.

9 *Nazi instructions for the Presidential election of 1932*
The following excerpts from Reich Propaganda Department directives, signed by Goebbels, for the Presidential elections of March–April 1932, in which Hitler was challenging Hindenburg,[1] give an indication of the high degree of efficiency and attention to detail which was characteristic of the Nazi propaganda machine during these years:

(a) Reich Propaganda Department to all *Gaue* and all *Gau* Propaganda Depart-ments.
... A striking slogan:
Those who want everything to stay as it is vote for Hindenburg. Those who want everything changed vote for Hitler.
...

(b) Reich Propaganda Department to all *Gaue* and all *Gau* Propaganda Depart-ments.
... Hitler Poster. The Hitler poster depicts a fascinating Hitler head on a com-pletely black background. Subtitle: white on black—'Hitler'. In accordance with the Führer's wish this poster is to be put up only during the final days [of the campaign]. Since experience shows that during the final days there is a variety of coloured posters, this poster with its completely black background will contrast with all the others and will produce a tremendous effect on the masses. ...

(c) Reich Propaganda Department
Instructions for the National Socialist Press for the election of the Reich President
  1. From Easter Tuesday 29 March until Sunday 10 April inclusive, all National Socialist papers, both daily and weekly, must appear in an enlarged edition with a tripled circulation. Two-thirds of this tripled circulation must be made available,

[1] For details see below, p. 126.

without charge, to the *Gau* leadership responsible for its area of distribution for propaganda purposes. . . .

2. From Easter Tuesday 29 March until Sunday 3 April inclusive, a special topic must be dealt with every day on the first page of all our papers in a big spread. Tuesday 29 March: Hitler as a man. Wednesday 30 March: Hitler as a fighter (gigantic achievements through his willpower, etc.). Friday 1 April: Hitler as a statesman—plenty of photos. . . .

3. On Sunday 3 April, at noon (end of an Easter truce), the great propaganda journey of the Führer through Germany will start, through which about a million people are to be reached directly through our Führer's speeches. . . . The press organization is planned so that four press centres will be set up in Germany, which in turn will pass on immediately any telephone calls to the other papers of their area, whose names have been given them. . . .

10 *A Hitler meeting in Hamburg, 23 April 1932*

The Party surpassed itself in the stage-management of mass rallies, particularly when Hitler himself was speaking. In the following account written at the time Frau Luise Solmitz, a Hamburg school teacher married to a former army officer, gives her impression of such a meeting:

. . . The April sun shone hot like in summer and turned everything into a picture of gay expectation. There was immaculate order and discipline, although the police left the whole square to the stewards and stood on the sidelines. Nobody spoke of 'Hitler', always just 'the Führer', 'the Führer says', 'the Führer wants', and what he said and wanted seemed right and good. The hours passed, the sun shone, expectations rose. In the background, at the edge of the track there were columns of carriers like ammunition carriers. What they carried were crates of beer. Aeroplanes above us. Testing of the loudspeakers, buzzing of the cine-cameras. It was nearly 3 p.m. 'The Führer is coming!' A ripple went through the crowds. Around the speaker's platform one could see hands raised in the Hitler salute. A speaker opened the meeting, abused the 'system', nobody listened to him. A second speaker welcomed Hitler and made way for the man who had drawn 120,000 people of all classes and ages. There stood Hitler in a simple black coat and looked over the crowd, waiting—a forest of swastika pennants swished up, the jubilation of this moment was given vent in a roaring salute. Main theme: Out of parties shall grow a nation, the German nation. He censured the 'system' ('I want to know what there is left to be ruined in this state!'). 'On the way here Socialists confronted me with a poster, "Turn back, Adolf Hitler". Thirteen years ago I was a simple unknown soldier. I went my way. I never turned back. Nor shall I turn back now.' Otherwise he made no personal attacks, nor any promises, vague or definite. His voice was hoarse after all his speaking during the previous days. When the speech was over, there was roaring enthusiasm and applause. Hitler saluted, gave his thanks, the Horst Wessel song sounded out across the course. Hitler was helped into his coat. Then he went.—How many look up to him with touching faith! as their helper, their saviour, their deliverer from unbearable distress—to him who rescues the Prussian prince, the scholar, the clergyman, the farmer, the worker, the unemployed, who rescues them from the parties back into the nation.

But although Hitler spared no effort in his personal campaigning, particularly at the time of the Presidential elections in 1932, the main burden of propaganda lay on the *Gaue* and local Party organizations. It was their energy and resourcefulness which kept the Party firmly in the public eye. The Party could rely on numerous speakers from all classes, graded according to ability and deployed either at local, regional or national level. Beside their expenses they were paid a graded fee for their pains, and, since many were unemployed, they had an incentive to speak as often as possible.

11 *The organization of rural propaganda*

An indication of the care devoted to local propaganda is provided by the instructions for the organization of rural propaganda contained in the July 1931 issue of *Wille und Weg*, the monthly magazine of the Reich Propaganda Department:

The first meeting in a village must be prepared in such a way that it is well attended. A prerequisite is that the speaker should be fairly well informed about specifically rural questions. Then, it is most advisable to go to a neighbouring village some time after, but to advertise the meeting in the first village as well, then many people will certainly come over for it. After this, one holds a big German Evening in a central hall for a number of villages with the cooperation of the SA and the SA band. . . . The German Evening, provided it is skilfully and generously geared to producing a big public impact, has the primary task of making the audience enthusiastic for our cause; secondly, it is intended to raise the money necessary for the further build-up of propaganda. The preparation of the village meetings is best carried out in the following way: most effectively through written personal invitations to every farmer or inhabitant; in the bigger villages through a circular carried from farm to farm by Party comrades. For the meeting itself the question of finance has to be considered. Our movement is so poor that every penny counts. Collections must therefore be held during all discussion evenings and also in the big mass meetings if permitted by the police, either in the interval or at the end, even when an entrance fee has been taken at the beginning of the meeting. In this way, especially when plates and not caps are used, surprising amounts can sometimes be got out of a meeting.

One of the keys to the Nazis' success in acquiring mass support was their awareness of the extent to which German society had disintegrated into its sectional components, a process accelerated by the postwar economic crises of inflation and then depression. By developing separate departments to organize the various economic interests and social groups, they succeeded in posing simultaneously as more effectively representative of individual interests and as a party of integration which would succeed in creating a unified national community of which they claimed the Party was already a microcosm. Thus, there were Party organizations for, among others, doctors, lawyers, teachers, war-disabled and war-pensioners, and civil servants. Perhaps the most successful of these specialist departments were the Agrarian Office and the *Mittelstand* Office (for artisans and retail traders), later known as the Combat League of Middle Class Tradespeople. These organizations acquired networks of specialists, often leading farmers or leading representatives of particular trades, whose function was to canvass their colleagues and to ensure that the Party's propaganda was effective in reaching their particular interests.

12 *Propaganda aimed at artisans and retail traders*

In the propaganda of the *Mittelstand* Office, for example, the emphasis was on the Nazis' determination to preserve small businesses in face of the competition from the large department stores which had become intense during the depression. They were particularly astute at exploiting local issues:

> *Draft pamphlet [undated: c. April 1932]*
> Attention! Gravediggers at work!
> Middle-class citizens! Retailers! Craftsmen! Tradesmen!
> A new blow aimed at your ruin is being prepared and carried out in Hanover!
> The present system enables the gigantic concern
>   WOOLWORTH (America)
> supported by finance capital, to build a new vampire business in the centre of the city in the Georgstrasse to expose you to complete ruin. This is the wish and aim of the black-red[1] system as expressed in the following remarks of Marxist leaders.
> The Marxist Engels declared in May 1890: 'If capital destroys the small artisans and retailers it does a good thing. . . .'
> That is the black-red system of today!
> Put an end to this system and its abettors! Defend yourself, middle-class citizen! Join the mighty organization that alone is in a position to conquer your arch-enemies. Fight with us in the Section for Craftsmen and Retail Traders within the great freedom movement of Adolf Hitler!
> Put an end to the system!
> *Mittelstand, vote for List 8!*

13 *The Nazis take over the North-West German Artisans' Association*

These departments also had the function of encouraging the infiltration of the main professional organizations and of securing a purge of their leadership by pressure from below. Thus, the agrarian office was very successful in taking over the main professional organization of agriculture, the *Land-bund*. An example of the tactics used is provided by the Party's take-over of the North-West German Artisans' Association in 1932:

---

[1] Black for the Catholic Centre Party and red for the Social Democrats, who together formed the coalition government in the state of Prussia.

(a) *Urgent circular to the District Leaders and District Representatives of the* Mittelstand *Office in* Gau *Hanover-South-Brunswick*

The Gauleiter   *Hanover, 11 January 1932*
CONFIDENTIAL!
A discussion between the Gauleiter and the executive committee of the North-West German Artisans' Association resulted in a decision to arrange the entry of NSDAP members into the executive committee and Association leadership. Since the general meeting of the representatives of the Association is to be held in three weeks' time, the following must be clarified immediately:
1. The political attitude and personal qualities of the chairman and secretary of your particular district Artisans' Association.
2. Which Party members, or, if there aren't any available, which artisans of the National Socialist persuasion are eligible for membership of the executive committee and Association leadership.
3. Which members of the NSDAP are organized in the North-West German Artisans' Association and therefore what influence can be thrown into the scales. The situation requires an immediate meeting of the district leaders and district experts with the *Gau* leadership on 14 January 1932 in Hanover.

Three weeks later Gauleiter Rust reported to Party headquarters in Munich that his attempt to penetrate the Artisans' Association from below had succeeded and that its leaders would be replaced by National Socialists or Nazi sympathizers:

(b) *NSDAP*

Gau *Hanover-South-Brunswick*   *1 February 1932*

The Gauleiter

Dear Herr Wagener,[1]
I take note with interest of your acceptance of the invitation to Brunswick. I hope to be able to introduce to you a mainly National Socialist executive committee of the North-West German Artisans' Association. For about ten weeks we have had a major fight to win control of the Association. On 8 and 9 February an extraordinary meeting of delegates will take place in Hanover at which I have demanded the removal of the present president, Freidel of the Economic Party[2], his replacement by a president who, though not a member of the NSDAP, is working completely along our lines, and two vice-presidential posts for members of the NSDAP. Meetings of artisans, usually overcrowded, have taken place in all the county towns [*Kreisstädte*] of the *Gau* which set things in motion. Furthermore, two meetings of all district experts of the *Mittelstand* Office have made this subject an issue in the *Gau*.
I take this opportunity of telling you that the executive committee of the

---

[1] Otto Wagener was head of the NSDAP's Economics Section in the Nazi Reich Headquarters.
[2] The Economic Party was a small pressure group party established in 1924 by artisans and shopkeepers dissatisfied with their representation in the larger middle-class parties.

Chamber of Industry and Commerce—a rare selection of first-rate economic reactionaries—have applied to me to arrange for the Führer to have a personal discussion with them. Here too the reason for this is pressure from below.

Heil!   BERNHARD RUST

The penetration and politicizing of economic associations by the Nazi Party was a most effective way of winning new supporters. It also helped to prepare the way for the 'coordination' of these groups after the Nazi take-over of power in Germany.

14 *The attitude of young people to Nazism*

One group to whom the Nazi appeal proved particularly strong was youth. With its dynamic and colourful style of politics, its proclaimed aim of breaking down class barriers, its leader–follower relationship, and its remarkably young membership and leadership,[1] the Nazi Party offered young people the type of commitment in politics which they were seeking and which they did not find in the other parties with their traditional parliamentary methods. Only the Communists offered anything similar and they, because of their class commitment, remained largely confined to the working class. Young people, particularly from the middle class, saw the Nazi movement as a national crusade to restore Germany to greatness. The basis of the Nazi appeal to this group was emotional, as is shown by the following report from 1931 on the problems of containing the growth of Nazism in the Protestant youth movement:

The cause which at the moment is most closely associated with the name of National Socialism and with which, at a moderate estimate, certainly 70 per cent of our young people, often lacking knowledge of the facts, are in ardent sympathy, must be regarded, as far as our ranks are concerned, more as an ethical than a political matter. Our young people show little political interest. Fifth-formers are not really much concerned with the study of Hitler's thoughts; it is simply something irrational, something infectious that makes the blood pulse through one's veins and conveys an impression that something great is under way, the roaring of a stream which one does not wish to escape: 'If you can't feel it you will never grasp it. . . .'

All this must be taken into account when we see the ardour and fire of this move-ment reflected in our ranks. A pedantic and nagging approach seems to me useless, and so do all attempts, however well-intentioned, by the leader to refute the policy of National Socialism in detail. The majority of the young fight against this with a strange instinct. We must, in keeping with our responsibility, though it is difficult in individual cases, try first to influence the ethos, and in this we must maintain an attitude above parties. We must educate in such a way that this enthusiasm is duly tempered by deeper understanding and by disenchantment, that words like 'national honour and dignity' do not become slogans but arouse individual respon-sibility so that no brash demagogues grow up among us.

[1] For statistics on the age of the Party membership see below, p. 111.

15 *Nazi activity in the schools*

In order to exploit this appeal to youth the Nazis developed the Hitler Youth movement for those under 18, a pupils' league for boys in grammar schools, and a students' league. As a result of the activities of these organizations, schools and universities became increasingly politicized. In the state of Oldenburg, for example, there were complaints that the children of Republicans were being harassed by their fellow pupils.

To the Oldenburg Ministry for Churches and Schools: 21 November 1930

The Committee of the Oldenburg branch of the Reichsbanner Black-Red-Gold[1] submits the following matter to the State Ministry with a request for a prompt comment:

Leaflets have recently been distributed in the playgrounds of the schools of the city of Oldenburg and its vicinity, inviting people to join a National Socialist Pupils' Association. We enclose one of these leaflets.

A number of pupils have already followed the appeal to join this pupils' association. These consider themselves pledged, in the spirit of the leaflet, to bully those who disagree with them. In the playground these pupils join together and sing National Socialist combat songs. Children of Republicans are called names, their satchels are smeared with swastikas, and they are given leaflets with swastikas or 'Heil Hitler' or 'Germany awake' written on them. In the school in Metjendorf the son of a Republican was beaten up during the break by members of the pupils' association so badly that he had to stay at home for over a week. Grown-ups who are known to be members of a Republican party are called names by the pupils when they pass by the school. In one case this even happened out of the window of a classroom.

Since the children of Republicans are unfortunately in a minority in secondary schools they cannot defend themselves against these combined attacks. With an effort they preserve their self-control, but as soon as the child gets home, this too collapses. He then seeks refuge in tears and complaints. The parents find that lessons following breaks in which their child has been molested by his classmates are useless because he is too preoccupied with the events of the break. Sometimes teachers, not knowing the reason for the child's inattention, punish him as well. The same state of mind influences his homework, which therefore cannot be of a standard which a child in a good, cheerful mood would normally achieve. Again this has its effects at school.

It might be answered that parents and children have the right to make a complaint. This is true and yet at the same time not true. It must unfortunately be said that apart from a group of teachers who would treat such a complaint objectively, there are a number from whom this cannot be counted on and to whom one does not turn because they too are National Socialists or are active in other right-wing associations. The relationship of trust necessary between teachers and parents and their children has completely gone.

[1] The *Reichsbanner* Black-Red-Gold was a pro-Republican paramilitary organization set up in 1924 by Social Democrats and Democrats to defend the Republic against the right-wing paramilitary organizations.

Since we have heard that some headmasters have already declared that they are not in a position to deal with these incidents as required, since they have still received no instructions from the Ministry, we request that such instructions should be issued as soon as possible. We can presumably be sure that the State Ministry will adopt an attitude which does justice to all concerned and will decree that pupils' associations of political organizations are forbidden.

Yours faithfully,

The Committee of the Oldenburg Branch of the Reichsbanner Black-Red-Gold.

16 *The nationalist and classless appeal of Nazism*

Yet, although the Nazis concentrated much of their propaganda on specific groups, one of their main themes was a general appeal to nationalism and a claim that they, alone of all the parties, had succeeded in bridging the barriers between class and occupation. An example of such propaganda was the way in which they used the Kaiser's fourth son, Prince August-Wilhelm of Hohenzollern, as a speaker. He was always paired with an 'ordinary citizen', usually a farmer or a worker. At a meeting in Öttingen in central Bavaria such a meeting drew a crowd of between 900 and 1000 people, according to the police report:

(a) *Report on the NSDAP Meeting with Prince August-Wilhelm on 21 June 1931 in the Crown Hall in Öttingen*

The speakers were: Prince August-Wilhelm of Prussia
Farmer Stegmann from Schillingsfürst
Julius Streicher—NSDAP Gauleiter of Franconia

The speech of Prince August-Wilhelm, which was kept short and matter-of-fact, was followed by the national anthem which was sung standing up in the hall, whereas the Streicher speech had been followed by the Hitler song. The meeting did not have the character of a political but rather of a patriotic meeting or rally. The audience had arrived in large numbers from far and wide on motor cycles and by car.

The effect of such propaganda is clear from an entry in the diary of the upper middle class Hamburg lady already referred to:

(b) *1.vi.32*

... I myself also know that not only the desperate but also those who purposely contract debts in our neighbourhood are enthusiastic Hitler people—as are all those who hope for something from a swing to the Left or the Right or anywhere. Nevertheless, every person who thinks and feels as a German, the bourgeois, the farmer, the aristocrat, the prince, and the intelligentsia, stands by Hitler. It is the nationalist movement.

17 *Age of Nazi Party membership as of 1 January 1935, divided according to date of joining*

		Date of Party membership										Percentage of total population
		Before seizure of power						After seizure of power				
Date of birth	Age	Before 14.ix.30		From 14.ix.30 to 30.i.33		Total		After 30.i.33		Total		
		Number	Per cent	Number	Per cent	Number	Per cent	Number	Per cent	Number	Per cent	
1916–1914	18–20	468	0·5 0·4	14,972	17·0 2·1	15,440	17·5 1·8	72,648	82·5 4·4	88,088	100·0 3·5	5·8
1913–1904	21–30	47,167	5·5 36·4	296,438	34·8 41·3	343,605	40·3 40·4	508,869	59·7 31·0	852,474	100·0 34·1	25·3
1903–1894	31–40	40,700	5·9 31·4	193,937	28·0 26·9	234,637	33·9 27·8	459,780	66·1 27·9	694,417	100·0 27·9	22·0
1893–1884	41–50	22,835	4·7 17·6	122,884	25·2 17·1	145,719	29·9 17·1	342,338	70·1 20·8	488,057	100·0 19·6	17·1
1883–1874	51–60	12,546	4·5 9·7	66,454	23·9 9·2	79,000	28·4 9·3	199,491	71·6 12·1	278,491	100·0 11·2	14·5
1873 and earlier	61 and over	5,847	6·3 4·5	24,761	26·8 3·4	30,608	33·1 3·6	61,755	66·9 3·8	92,363	100·0 3·7	15·3
Total		129,563	5·2 100·0	719,446	28·9 100·0	849,009	34·1 100·0	1,644,881	65·9 100·0	2,493,890	100·0 100·0	100·0

NOTE. In the percentage columns, the upper of the two figures shows the percentage of Party membership on 1 January 1935; the lower figure shows the percentage of Party membership within the period of time covered by each pair of vertical columns.

18 *Party members as of 1 January 1935, divided according to jobs and date of membership*

Job	Before seizure of power — Before 14.ix.30 No.	%	%	Before seizure of power — From 14.ix.30 until 30.i.33 No.	%	%	Up to 30.i.33 No.	%	%	After seizure of power — After 30.i.33 No.	%	%	Total No.	%	%	Society June 1933 %
I Persons in employment	121,151	5·1	93·5	660,678	28·4	93·1	790,829	33·5	93·1	1,567,055	66·5	95·3	2,357,884	100·0	94·5	
1 Workers	33,944	4·5	26·3	233,479	30·8	32·5	267,423	35·3	31·5	488,544	64·7	29·7	755,967	100·0	30·3	46·3
2 White-collar employees	31,067	6·4	24·0	147,855	30·6	20·6	178,922	37·0	21·0	305,132	63·0	18·6	484,054	100·0	19·4	12·4
3 Self-employed	24,563	5·2	18·9	124,579	26·2	17·3	149,142	31·4	17·6	326,081	68·6	19·8	475,223	100·0	19·0	9·6
Artisans	11,059	5·3	8·5	55,814	26·8	7·7	66,873	32·1	7·9	141,309	67·9	8·6	208,182	100·0	8·3	
Tradesmen	9,918	5·3	7·6	48,920	26·0	6·8	58,838	31·3	6·9	128,776	68·7	7·8	187,614	100·0	7·5	

divided into

divided into

Table (rotated 90°). Column headers are printed in the top margin and are largely cut off at the page edge; each data cell lists the absolute number (top figure), then two percentage figures (upper = % of Party membership on 1 January 1935; lower = % of Party membership within the period of time).

Category	Col. 1 (no. / upper % / lower %)	Col. 2	Col. 3	Col. 4	Total	Extra
divided into — Civil servants	7,992 / 3·6 / 6·2	36,088 / 16·2 / 5·0	44,080 / 19·8 / 5·2	179,033 / 80·2 / 10·9	223,113 / 100·0 / 9·0	
Teachers	2,023 / 2·4 / 1·5	10,879 / 12·9 / 1·5	12,902 / 15·3 / 1·5	71,190 / 84·7 / 4·3	84,092 / 100·0 / 3·4	
5 Peasants	17,181 / 6·7 / 13·2	89,800 / 35·2 / 12·5	106,981 / 41·9 / 12·6	148,310 / 58·1 / 9·0	255,291 / 100·0 / 10·2	20·7
6 Others	4,381 / 5·5 / 3·4	26,998 / 33·7 / 3·7	31,379 / 39·2 / 3·7	48,765 / 60·8 / 3·0	80,144 / 100·0 / 3·2	6·2
II Persons not in employment — 7 Pensioners	2,453 / 6·5 / 1·9	11,684 / 30·7 / 1·6	14,137 / 37·2 / 1·7	23,736 / 62·8 / 1·4	37,873 / 100·0 / 1·5	
III Family dependents without a full-time job	5,959 / 6·1 / 4·6	38,084 / 38·8 / 5·3	44,043 / 44·9 / 5·2	54,090 / 55·1 / 3·3	98,133 / 100·0 / 4·0	
divided into — 8 Housewives	4,706 / 7·3 / 3·6	29,304 / 45·3 / 4·1	34,010 / 52·6 / 4·0	30,617 / 47·4 / 1·9	64,627 / 100·0 / 2·6	
9 Students and school children	1,253 / 3·7 / 1·0	8,780 / 26·2 / 1·2	10,033 / 29·9 / 1·2	23,473 / 70·1 / 1·4	33,506 / 100·0 / 1·4	
Total	129,563 / 5·2 / 100·0	719,446 / 28·8 / 100·0	849,009 / 34·0 / 100·0	1,644,881 / 66·0 / 100·0	2,493,890 / 100·0 / 100·0	

NOTE. In the percentage columns, the upper of the two figures shows the percentage of Party membership on 1 January 1935; the lower figure shows the percentage of Party membership within the period of time covered by each pair of vertical columns.

Statistics on the social and geographical bases of Nazism

Between 1928 and 1930 the Nazi Party had concentrated largely on trying to win over sections of the middle class, notably the peasantry, the artisans, and the small retailers, and this is how they had achieved their breakthrough. After 1930, while still continuing much of their propaganda for these groups, they now revived their pre-1928 efforts to win over the workers. In January 1931, for example, they established a Factory Cell Organization in an attempt to challenge the Left in their factory strongholds. This organization, however, had little success. The majority of the workers remained loyal to the Social Democrats and Communists and if under the pressure of unemployment they became more extreme, they tended to move leftwards to the Communists rather than to the Right. Apart from the white-collar workers (clerks and shop assistants) and young unorganized workers it was not so much the unemployed workers who supported the Nazis as the middle classes which felt threatened by the crisis—in economic terms, e.g. fear of bankruptcy, in terms of a threat to their status, and through fear of Bolshevism.

The statistics on Party membership show that, in relation to their proportion of the population as a whole, workers were much under-represented, while the middle-class occupations were correspondingly over-represented. Between 1930 and 1933 the workers increased their proportion of the Party, while that of most other groups correspondingly declined. But this shift was marginal and workers continued to be heavily under-represented—32·5 per cent of the Party compared with 46 per cent of the population. The statistics on age show the predominance of youth within the Party membership.

19 *The vote for the Nazi Party in the Reichstag Elections, 1924–33*

This picture of the Nazi Party as a predominantly middle-class movement is confirmed by electoral statistics which also show the significance of the factor of religion. The main strength of Nazism lay in the Protestant and predominantly rural areas of the north German plain stretching from East Prussia to Schleswig-Holstein. Eight out of the ten districts with the largest Nazi vote in July 1932 are in this area; the exceptions are Liegnitz (Silesia) and Chemnitz-Zwickau. Nazism was weakest in the big cities (e.g. Berlin and Hamburg) and in industrial areas generally, particularly in predominantly Catholic ones (e.g. Düsseldorf East and West). It was also weakest in overwhelmingly Catholic rural areas (e.g. Koblenz-Trier). The religious factor is most evident in Bavaria, where the predominantly Protestant north (Franconia) was a Nazi stronghold, while in the Catholic south (Upper and Lower Bavaria) the Nazi vote was among the lowest in Germany, despite the fact that this was where the Party had originated.

There are, however, certain exceptions to this general pattern. Thus, the
Nazi vote was unusually high in much of Silesia (Liegnitz and Breslau)
which was a predominantly Catholic area with industry, and also in the
Palatinate, a mainly Catholic and rural area. Here the border issue may have
played a part. Silesia had been hotly contested with Poland a few years
before and, after a plebiscite ordered under the Versailles treaty, Upper
Silesia had been awarded to Poland. The Nazis, therefore, probably benefited
from the intense nationalism generated by this conflict. In the Palatinate,
France's attempt to establish a separatist regime in the early 1920s had also
generated nationalist feelings which may help to account for the vote.
Another factor was that in mixed Protestant and Catholic areas Nazism
tended to unify the Protestants, who had long resented the dominance of the
Catholic Centre in their area, but whose vote had been split among several
parties and therefore was less able to influence events.

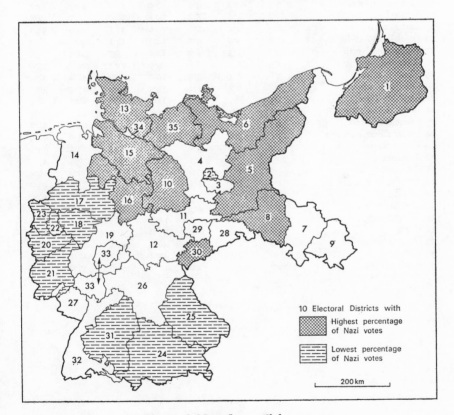

Electoral Map for 31 July 1932

Percentage of votes cast in favour of the NSDAP

Reichstag elections:	4.v.24	7.xii.24	20.v.28	14.ix.30	31.vii.32	6.xi.32	5.iii.33
Number of seats:	32	14	12	107	230	196	288
National vote:	6·5	3·0	2·6	18·3	37·3	33·1	43·9
District							
1 East Prussia	8·6	6·2	0·8	22·5	47·1	39·7	56·5
2 Berlin	3·6	1·6	1·4	12·8	24·6	22·5	31·3
3 Potsdam II	6·5	2·9	1·8	16·7	33·0	29·1	38·2
4 Potsdam I	5·8	2·8	1·6	18·8	38·2	34·1	44·4
5 Frankfurt a.d. Oder	5·0	3·2	1·0	22·7	48·1	42·6	55·2
6 Pomerania	7·3	4·2	1·5	24·3	48·0	43·1	56·3
7 Breslau	4·0	1·4	1·0	24·2	43·5	40·4	50·2
8 Liegnitz	1·5	1·5	1·2	20·9	48·0	42·1	54·0
9 Oppeln	2·6	1·5	1·0	9·5	29·2	26·8	43·2
10 Magdeburg	4·9	3·0	1·7	19·5	43·8	39·0	47·3
11 Merseburg	8·7	4·3	2·7	20·5	42·6	34·5	46·4
12 Thuringia	9·9	5·4	3·7	19·3	43·4	37·1	47·2
13 Schleswig-Holstein	7·4	2·7	4·0	27·0	51·0	45·7	53·2
14 Weser-Ems	7·4	4·8	5·2	20·5	38·4	31·9	41·4
15 East Hanover	8·6	4·4	2·6	20·6	49·5	42·9	54·3
16 South-Hanover-Brunswick	7·6	3·4	4·4	24·3	46·1	40·6	48·7
17 Westphalia-North	3·5	1·3	1·0	12·2	25·7	22·3	34·9
18 Westphalia-South	1·5	1·1	1·6	13·9	27·2	24·8	33·8
19 Hesse-Nassau	5·6	2·5	3·6	20·8	43·6	41·2	49·4
20 Cologne-Aachen	1·5	0·6	1·1	14·5	20·2	17·4	30·1
21 Koblenz-Trier	1·3	—	2·1	14·9	28·8	26·1	38·4
22 Düsseldorf-East	3·9	1·6	1·8	17·0	31·6	27·0	37·4
23 Düsseldorf-West	2·6	0·9	1·2	16·8	27·0	24·2	35·2
24 Upper Bavaria-Swabia	17·0	4·8	6·2	16·3	27·1	24·6	40·9
25 Lower Bavaria	10·2	3·0	3·5	12·0	20·4	18·5	39·2
26 Franconia	20·7	7·5	8·1	20·5	39·9	36·4	45·7
27 Palatinate	5·7	1·9	5·6	22·8	43·7	42·6	46·5
28 Dresden-Bautzen	4·5	1·5	1·8	16·1	39·3	34·0	43·6
29 Leipzig	7·9	1·8	1·9	14·0	36·1	31·0	40·0
30 Chemnitz-Zwickau	7·7	4·2	4·3	23·8	47·0	43·4	50·0
31 Württemberg	4·1	2·1	1·9	9·4	30·3	26·2	42·0
32 Baden	4·8	1·9	2·9	19·2	36·9	34·1	45·4
33 Hesse-Darmstadt	2·9	1·3	1·9	18·5	43·1	40·2	47·4
34 Hamburg	6·0	2·3	2·6	19·2	33·7	27·2	38·9
35 Mecklenburg	20·8	11·9	2·0	20·1	44·8	37·0	48·0

4 The Struggle for Power, 1930–33

Electoral success was a prerequisite for the acquisition of power, but by itself it was not enough in view of the Party's failure to achieve an absolute majority. Now that parliamentary government had broken down and power lay with the President under Article 48 of the Weimar Constitution, it was just as important to win the approval of the conservative elites whose influence increased in proportion to the decline of that of Parliament. The Army, senior members of the bureaucracy, big landowners and particularly the Junkers of east Germany (among whom the President could now count himself after industry's gift to him of his old family estate), industry itself — all these groups, the power of which the revolution of 1918 had failed to destroy, now found a sympathetic hearing from the President and from the camarilla which surrounded him, notably his State Secretary, Otto Meissner, and his son, Oskar. These groups saw the paralysis of the parliamentary system as an opportunity to replace Weimar democracy with a more authoritarian regime, to undo the results of the revolution. On what form such a regime should take there were different views. Some toyed with the idea of restoring the monarchy; others wished to restore the political system of the Second Reich but with a president in place of the emperor. But common to most of these views was the determination to reduce Parliament to a subordinate role and thereby to exclude the Left from effective political influence. In these plans the Nazi movement came to have an important function.

Initially, it had been hoped that it would be possible to secure a majority for a presidential regime with the moderate Right and Centre — this was Brüning's plan. But as the regime based on Article 48 established itself more and more firmly, and as political opinion became increasingly polarized with the resultant erosion of the Centre groups and the moderate Right, so it became clear that it would be impossible to achieve a majority on such a basis. Instead the Brüning Government was sustained in a negative fashion by the unwillingness of the Social Democrats and all groups to the left of the German Nationalists to bring down the Government for fear of the election that would follow. But the idea of permitting the Social Democrats to wield influence had now become anathema to the German Right. The presidential regime, run by the bureaucracy, open to the influence of conservative pressure groups and largely independent of Parliament, had become congenial to them — it fitted in with the German tradition of the

State ruling above the parties, though of course in practice the State invariably represented the conservatives. They wanted to give this regime a permanent basis so that it was no longer dependent on the toleration of the moderate Left.

Yet it was realized that an authoritarian government seeking to secure a permanent basis would need mass support. When it became clear that the Brüning experiment had failed, and that its policies were beginning to threaten conservative interests, as with a plan to break up bankrupt Junker estates and settle them with peasants, the Right began to base their hopes on the Nazi movement as the means of acquiring mass support. Brüning himself had tried to use the Nazis and tame them by securing their participation in government; now the Right decided that Brüning had become an obstacle to this policy. There were many aspects of the Nazi movement of which the Right disapproved. It was too radical, too violent, its economic policies smacked too much of Socialism, and the characters of some of its leaders were dubious, to say the least. But, on the other hand, it was a nationalist movement and a movement hostile to the 'Marxist' Left. It offered the chance of 'conquering the streets' and wresting them from the Left. It contained large numbers of young people with the right ideas about the need to restore German greatness and who, apart from anything else, would provide excellent recruits for the Army. It was essential therefore to harness this movement for a new regime of the Right. If Hitler were brought into the Government in a subordinate capacity, he would be forced to become more 'responsible'. While power would continue to lie in the hands of the conservative establishment, Hitler would use his gifts as a propagandist to sell the policies of the Government to the masses. There was also another factor. If Hitler was not brought into the Government, there was a danger that the Nazis might attempt to come to power by force. This would lead to a civil war between Right and Left which would destroy the social order and ruin Germany's chances of regaining her military strength. There was even the possibility of the radical elements in the Nazi movement getting the upper hand and making common cause with the Communists against the conservative Right, and the Army might well find it impossible to deal with such a combined front. These were some of the considerations in the minds of the Right which lay behind their objective of trying to persuade Hitler to join the Government or at least give it his support.

Hitler, on the other hand, was determined to avoid being harnessed in this way. He was not prepared to come into a Conservative Government in a subordinate capacity—if he was to bear the responsibility he wanted to have the power as well. Initially, he insisted on a government dominated by Nazis. By the end of 1932, however, the crisis in the Party caused largely by the failure to achieve office persuaded him to settle for less. Provided he had the Chancellorship and one or two key ministries, he was prepared to allow the rest of the Government to be dominated by Conservatives. The Conservatives, banking on their majority in the Cabinet, on their influence with the President, and on their greater political experience, assumed that they had managed to harness him to their cause. Hitler was content with the compromise. He was confident that it would not take him long to break out of the frame within which they had tried to fetter him.

The path of legality and the problem of the SA

The success in the 1930 election appeared to have justified the policy of 'legality' which Hitler had followed since 1925. Yet the fact that the Party now had a substantial representation in the Reichstag raised the question of how it was to reconcile its revolutionary aims and its contempt for parliamentary democracy with its participation in the parliamentary process.

1 *Hitler's oath of legality at the Leipzig trial, September 1930*

The issue was raised shortly after the election at the trial of three Army lieutenants accused of working for the Nazi Party, a trial whose importance was signified by the fact that it took place before the Supreme Court at Leipzig. Hitler, called as a witness, made the following statement in which he carefully distinguished between means and ends:

The National Socialist movement will try to achieve its aim with *constitutional means* in this state. The constitution prescribes only the *methods*, not the *aim*. In this constitutional way we shall try to gain decisive majorities in the legislative bodies so that the moment we succeed we can give the *state the form* that corresponds to our ideas.

* * *

The chairman [of the court] summed up the statement to the effect that the setting up of the Third Reich was being worked for in a constitutional way. . . .

This was an important statement. It helped to forestall a possible prohibition of the Party, for it enabled the State authorities and the Army from now onwards to rationalize their unwillingness to take action against the movement, however wild its excesses. It convinced them that co-operation with the Party was possible.

2 *The Stennes Rebellion, April 1931*

Yet there were those in the Party who resented the limitations imposed by the tactics of legality. This resentment was particularly strong in the SA. Before 1930, the majority of the Party membership were in the SA. In this early period the Party and the SA had formed a fringe group of zealots whose very isolation in a hostile environment welded them together in comrade-ship. Their attitude was characterized by a rather crude form of anti-capitalism in the sense of hostility to big business and banks and a suspicion of and hostility towards 'bosses' of all kinds. They shared a total contempt for conventional parliamentary politics and politicians—the Reichstag was regarded as a sink of corruption. It was an aggressively male world and its supreme values were physical courage, comradeship, loyalty and discipline. After September 1930, the question was, How would the SA react to the need to move within the world of conventional politics? How would they react to the growth of a new kind of party—no longer a collection of small groups of like-minded individuals, but a huge organization in which bureau-cracy proliferated, in which they would have to take orders from some Party official whose sole claim to importance was his ability at paper work? The answer was that many of them bitterly resented these changes. They resented the fact that they were expected to do all the dirty work—to risk injury, even their lives, fighting political opponents, to spend long hours in arduous marches and parades while the political wing of the Party had the influence and even the 'perks' such as a majority of the Reichstag seats in the 1930 election; their contempt for Parliament did not prevent them from wishing to acquire seats in it.

Hitler was obliged to move carefully between the twin dangers of, on the one hand, alienating the conservative pressure groups by appearing to condone the military and revolutionary ambitions of the SA, and, on the other hand, of alienating the SA by appearing to renege the revolutionary goals of the movement, through a compromise with the conservative establishment. The former danger had been dealt with for the time being by the Leipzig oath. This was given official recognition when, in January 1931, the Army removed the ban on the employment of Nazis in Army installa-tions and on Nazi enlistment. But the other danger remained. Just before the elections in September 1930, the Berlin SA had mutinied and it had required all Hitler's powers of persuasion and a promise of a higher subsidy to pacify them. Now, after the elections, the danger recurred. On 20 February 1931, as an earnest of the sincerity of his policy of legality, Hitler issued an order forbidding the SA to take part in street fighting. To many in the SA this seemed to be a typical instance of the way in which the ideals of the movement were being compromised in the interests of cooperation with the 'system'. In the spring of 1931, the leader of the SA in east Germany, Walter Stennes, who wished Hitler to return to the revolutionary path, was dismissed. Some of his SA units, however, remained loyal to him and tried to resist his dismissal:

National Socialists of Berlin!

The Munich party leadership of the NSDAP yesterday ordered the dissolu-tion of the Berlin SA and dismissed the supreme SA leader, Captain Stennes, whom Hitler had repeatedly assured of his trust.

The news has provoked indignation, embitterment and a deep feeling of shock in the Berlin SA and beyond that in SA sections throughout the Reich.

What is at stake?

Is it only a conflict of personalities, a leadership struggle?

No, the cause of National Socialism is at stake!

In the person of Captain Stennes the whole SA is being attacked. Munich has forgotten that readiness for sacrifice and simplicity once created the Party and made it strong. Today they build the 'Brown House' in Munich at a cost of millions whereas the individual SA men have not a penny with which to repair their torn boots.

In the face of the emergency decree, in the face of daily sacrifices of blood by the SA, while the fight against the movement and the terror have reached their peak, a Munich clique brings fratricidal warfare into the ranks of the Party.

The SA has helped the Party in its struggle to gain thousands of seats in the Reich, states and communes.

Now the SA have done their duty, they can go. They are now a cumbersome conscience, reminding people of the betrayed Party programme and demanding the fight for the old ideals of National Socialism, in contrast to the opportunistic policy of interests in Munich.

This is not illegal putschism, as the Jewish press wants to represent it, but only in order to prevent the Party's betrayal of the SA and of National Socialism.

The SA leadership has no intention of letting their SA comrades be misused for the financing of the Brown House and as a pawn in political bargains. With a sense of deep responsibility towards every single SA man and towards the whole German people, it acts according to the great fundamental law of National Socialism:

The common welfare comes before individual welfare and according to the deepest law of comradeship, loyalty for loyalty.

'With our flag held high and our ranks tightly closed.'

The SA marches.

Stennes takes over command.

The Stennes revolt failed because Hitler had little difficulty in reasserting his position as leader. (It is significant that in their appeal to the SA in Silesia the rebels insisted that 'our struggle is not directed against Adolf Hitler but against those round him whom he has not yet recognized for what they are'.) Hitler moved quickly to prevent the spread of support for Stennes and made a strong personal appeal to the SA, demanding declarations of loyalty from each of its leaders. The affair brought a decisive victory for the political leadership and resulted in some important reforms in organization, including a tighter control over the membership and activities of local branches, the introduction of training schools for SA leaders, and the further centralizing of administration in the SA which had begun after Röhm's appointment as SA chief of staff at the beginning of 1931.

3 Party/SA conflict over finance

Conflict between the political organization and the SA did not end with the Stennes affair. It remained endemic at all levels of the Party, and was most commonly expressed in rivalry over finance. The SA tended to make frequent collections without the authority of the political organization with the result that when the latter tried to collect money it discovered that the SA had been there already:

Gau *Schleswig-Holstein*   *7 October 1931*

At membership meetings and district conferences recently there were strong complaints about the collecting activities of the SA and SS formations. We emphasize here for the last time that all collections by the SA and SS are forbidden by the Reich leadership and that only the political authorities from the local branch leadership upwards have the right to make them. The political authorities from the local branch leadership upwards must watch carefully to see that this order of the Reich leadership is observed in future. In the event of its being disregarded, the *Gau* leadership must in all cases be informed, so that they can make corresponding monthly deductions [i.e. from the SA grant]. The *Gau* leadership has at the moment about 10,000 Reichsmark arrears of membership dues, a large part of which could have been raised by collections made by the local branches if the SA and SS had not pre-empted this.   H. LOHSE

Relations between Nazis and Nationalists in 1931

During 1931 the Nazis were confronted by the Brüning Government which appeared to be firmly established as a result of its toleration by the moderate Left and Right in the Reichstag. In this situation Hitler had the difficult task of maintaining some contact with the reactionary Nationalists and of cultivating powerful interest groups such as industry—all of whom had growing political influence in the vacuum left by the breakdown of the parliamentary system—without at the same time alienating his activist and radical followers and without allowing himself to be used as a pawn by the reactionaries who were bent on counter-revolution.

4 *The Harzburg Front*

In the summer of 1931 Hitler and Hugenberg, the leader of the Nationalists, made tentative moves towards a revival of the cooperation between their two parties which had begun with the Young Plan campaign of 1929. In July they announced their decision to work together to overthrow the existing 'system'. This cooperation bore fruit in a big demonstration of the extreme Right at Bad Harzburg on 11 October. The demonstration, however, was dominated by the reactionaries, with whom Hitler basically had little sympathy. He went out of his way to show the Nazi Party's determination to preserve its independence by leaving the rostrum after the SA march past and before the nationalist ex-servicemen's association, the Stahlhelm, had arrived. Sir Horace Rumbold, the British ambassador in Berlin, commented on the Harzburg meeting in his report of 14 October:

The Harzburg meeting, which has been a theme of conversation in political circles for many weeks, was expected to mark a turning-point in the political history of Germany. For the first time all the parties of the Right were to join forces, and it was expected that the outcome would be a spectacular reconciliation between the Nazis and Nationalists, followed by the issue of a joint programme on which all the parties of the Right had agreed to unite. This was counted upon to win over the small wavering parties of Right tendency. So far, however, as one can gather from the reports of the meeting, little in the way of unity was achieved beyond the outward show, and it remains to be seen whether any real working agreement can be established between the two main Opposition parties. It is true that a joint resolution was passed to the effect that the parties of the Right were ready to take over the responsibility of governing the Reich and Prussia and the other federal states. Implacable opposition to the present Brüning Government constituted, so far as one can ascertain, the main plank of the political platform on which the groups and parties present agreed to unite. The National Socialist press publishes the speeches of the Nazi leaders as well as the text of the joint resolution in many columns, but devotes only half a column to Herr Hugenberg's speech, while the Stahlhelm are scarcely mentioned as participating. The Nationalist press returns the compliment, and is at pains to emphasize the leading part played by Hugenberg.

There is nothing in Herr Hitler's speech to suggest that he has sacrificed any part of the Socialist section of his programme in order to fall into line with Herr Hugenberg and the big industrialists. He began by stating that he had spent twelve years in an unbroken struggle 'against the November revolt'. He had prophesied catastrophe, both political and economic, and his prophecy had been fulfilled to the letter. The end of the present system must be brought about at all costs if the country was not to lapse into Bolshevism. All previous German Governments, and above all the present Government, were responsible for the disastrous condition of the country. After the usual vehement denunciation of the Treaty of Versailles, 'that instrument for the destruction of the German people', Herr Hitler declared that France, bristling with arms, was compelling the other nations of the world to spend their substance in arming themselves.

Determined to save the country from Bolshevism, the National Socialists were ready to accept responsibility and take over the Government in the Reich and in the federal states. They were prepared to join hands with the National Opposition and with all those who were prepared to fight the international spirit of Marxism. Above all, the distinction between nationalism and Bolshevism must now be made clear....

There appears to have been no settled programme at Harzburg. Hitler issued the address summarized above to a gathering of his own followers before noon. It was prefaced by a cynical speech on the part of Herr Frick, who sought to allay 'the very comprehensible misgivings of his party friends' by assuring them that the Nazi leaders were merely using the Nationalists as a convenient ladder to office. Mussolini, he asserted, had done the same thing before assuming sole control of the Government of Italy.

5 *Hitler addresses Düsseldorf Industry Club, January 1932*

At the same time, although Hitler insisted on retaining his Party's independence from the other sections of the Right, he was also anxious to win the sympathy of powerful interests. This was also necessary in order to acquire the finance necessary for the elaborate Party organization and propaganda. With this in mind, Hitler cultivated relations with industrialists and financiers in the Rhineland in an endeavour to remove the radical image of the Party. The most notable of these attempts was the speech he made to the influential Industry Club in Düsseldorf in January 1932, on an invitation by Fritz Thyssen, a major Ruhr industrialist and keen Nazi supporter:

... People say to me so often: 'You are only the drummer of national Germany.' And supposing that I were only the drummer? It would today be a far more statesmanlike achievement to drum once more into this German people a new faith than gradually to squander the only faith they have.... The more you bring a people back into the sphere of faith, of ideals, the more will it cease to regard material distress as the one and only thing that counts. And the weightiest evidence for the truth of that statement is our own German people. We will never forget that the German people waged wars of religion for 150 years with prodigious devotion, that hundreds of thousands of men once left their plot of land, their property, and their belongings simply for an ideal, simply for a conviction. We will never forget that during those 150 years there was no trace of even an ounce of material interest. Then you will understand how mighty is the force of an idea, of an ideal. Only so can you comprehend how it is that in our movement today hundreds of thousands of young men are prepared to risk their lives to withstand our opponents. I know quite well, gentlemen, that when National Socialists march through the streets and suddenly in the evening there arises a tumult and a commotion, then the bourgeois draws back the window-curtain, looks out, and says: 'Once again my night's rest is disturbed: no more sleep for me. Why must these Nazis always be so provocative and run about the place at night?' Gentlemen, if everyone thought like that, then, true enough, no one's sleep at night would be disturbed, but then also the bourgeois today would not be able to venture into the street. If everyone thought in that way, if these young folk had no ideal to move them and drive them forward, then certainly they would gladly be rid of these nightly fights. But remember that it means sacrifice when today many hundreds of thousands of SA and SS men of the National Socialist movement have every day to mount on their lorries, protect meetings, undertake marches, sacrifice themselves night after night and then come back in the grey dawn to workshop and factory, or as unemployed to take the pittance of the dole: it means sacrifice when from the little they possess they have further to buy their uniforms, their shirts, their badges, yes and even pay their own fares. Believe me, there is already in all this the force of an ideal—a great ideal! And if the whole German nation today had the same faith in its vocation as these hundreds of thousands, if the whole nation possessed this idealism, Germany would stand in the eyes of the world otherwise than she stands now! (*loud applause*). For our situation in the world in its fatal effects is but the result of our own underestimate of German strength. ('*Very true!*') Only when we have once more changed this fatal undervaluation of ourselves can Germany take advantage of the political possibilities which, if we look far enough into the future, can place German life once more upon a natural and secure basis—and that means either new living space [*Lebensraum*] and the development of a great internal market or protection of German economic life against the world without and utilization of all the concentrated strength of Germany. The labour resources of our people, the capacities, we have them already: no one can deny that we are industrious. But we must first refashion the political preconditions: without that, industry and capacity, diligence and economy are in the last resort of no avail; an oppressed nation will not be able to spend on its own welfare even the fruits of its own economy but must sacrifice them on the altar of exactions and of tribute.

And so in contrast to our own official Government I see no hope for the resurrection of Germany if we regard the foreign politics of Germany as the primary factor: our primary need is the restoration of a sound national German body politic armed to strike. In order to realize this end I founded thirteen years ago the National Socialist movement: that movement I have led during the last twelve years and I hope that one day it will accomplish this task and that, as the fairest result of its struggle, it will leave behind it a German body politic completely renewed internally, intolerant of anyone who sins against the nation and its interests, intolerant of anyone who will not acknowledge its vital interests or who opposes them, intolerant of and pitiless towards anyone who shall attempt once more to destroy or undermine this body politic, and yet ready for friendship and peace with anyone who has a wish for peace and friendship (*long and tumultuous applause*).

Hitler's *tour de force* at Düsseldorf resulted soon after in new contributions from big business, though the extent to which industry supported the Nazis has been exaggerated. Before 1933 they won the favour of only a minority of industrialists.

6 *Hindenburg and Hugenberg discuss the Nazis, 1 August 1931*

Cooperation with the Nationalists and attempts to win the sympathy of powerful pressure groups were, however, no substitute for, and as yet made only a limited contribution towards, the main task, which was that of convincing the President. Hindenburg was persuaded to see Hitler in October 1931 but the interview was not a success. Earlier, in a meeting with the Nationalists' leader, Hugenberg, Hindenburg had expressed his scepticism about the Nazis:

The Reich President referred to the cooperation of the German Nationalists with the National Socialists who, he feared, were more socialist than nationalist and whose behaviour in the country he could not approve. He, the Field-Marshal and liberator of East Prussia, had during his East Prussian journey, particularly on the drive across the battlefield of Tannenberg, been repeatedly insulted by scandalous demonstrations of National Socialists and had had to comment very unfavourably on these young people who had been misled. He did not regard them as a reliable national party.

To this Privy Councillor Dr Hugenberg replied that it was for this very reason —to bind the National Socialists to the nationalist side and prevent their slipping towards socialism or communism—that he had decided to work with the Nazis over the past one-and-a-half years and he took credit for this. He believed also that the National Socialists had been politically educated thereby. The demonstrations which the Reich President deplored had probably not been meant so badly. Meetings held by him, Hugenberg, were also often accompanied by National Socialist demonstrations and the shout of 'Germany, awake!' He could not stop these demonstrations either. To a suggestion by the Reich President that Hugenberg should use his press to oppose these demonstrations which were particularly embarrassing in view of the age and standing of the Reich President, he gave us no definite reply.

In the spring of 1932 Hindenburg's seven-year term as President came to an end. Brüning and the parties of the Centre and moderate Left wished to extend Hindenburg's term of office for a year or two in order to keep Hitler from the presidency and provide more time in which to solve the crisis and thereby undermine the Nazi Party. But under the Constitution an extension of the President's term of office required a two-thirds majority in the Reichstag and for this the agreement of the Nazis would be necessary. It was hoped to persuade Hitler by a hint that he could replace Brüning as Chancellor in a year or two and by the difficulty of defeating Hindenburg in an election. The Nazi leadership was divided on the issue. The SA leader, Röhm, and Goebbels wanted to reject the plan and try and defeat Hindenburg in the election, while Gregor Strasser, the head of the Party's organization, argued that Hitler would not be able to defeat Hindenburg and that they should therefore accept the plan. Hitler hesitated for a time and entered into negotiations with General Groener who was both Minister of the Interior and Minister of Defence. But when Hugenberg rejected the idea in the name of the Nationalists, Hitler felt obliged to follow suit in order not to be outflanked by Hugenberg. He counterattacked, however, by offering to support Hindenburg if he would agree to replace Brüning with a right-wing government comprising Nazis and Nationalists and to hold new elections for the Reichstag and Prussian Landtag. When Hindenburg rejected this plan, Hitler had to face the decision of whether or not to enter the election against Hindenburg, knowing that he would almost certainly lose. Although he hesitated for a month, in fact he had little choice. A refusal to fight Hindenburg would have been widely interpreted as cowardice and this was something Hitler could afford even less than defeat.

In the Presidential elections of March–April 1932 Goebbels surpassed all previous Nazi propaganda campaigns.[1] But it was to no avail. In the first ballot on 13 March Hindenburg polled 18,661,736 votes (49·45 per cent) against Hitler's 11,338,571 votes (30·23 per cent). The remaining votes were divided between the Stahlhelm leader, Düsterberg, the candidate of the Nationalists (6·81 per cent), and Thälmann, the Communist leader (13·23 per cent). Since Hindenburg had just failed to win the absolute majority needed, a second ballot was held on 10 April in which Hindenburg gained

[1] For the Nazi propaganda campaign in the Presidential elections see above, pp. 103-4.

52·9 per cent and Hitler 36·6 per cent. Düsterberg did not run and his votes were divided between Hitler and Hindenburg, the majority of them going to Hitler. Thälmann too appears to have lost votes to Hitler, slipping back to 10·1 per cent.

From Brüning to Papen

With their direct assault on the citadel of power thwarted by Hindenburg's re-election, the Nazis were forced to return to their campaign against Brüning. Brüning and his supporters had reason to believe that for the time being their position was secure. But the very fact that Brüning had made himself entirely dependent on the President's support was to prove fatal to his survival in office. For Hindenburg, though relieved at his re-election, had resented the fact that it had been achieved by the very groups which had opposed his first election in 1925—the Social Democrats, Catholic Centre and Democrats—while the Right, to which he had owed his election in 1925 and with whom he had far more in common, had now opposed his re-election. Thus, instead of being grateful to Brüning for having engineered his re-election, he tended to blame him for the manner of it and increasingly lent his ear to the conservative pressure groups who urged the replacement of Brüning by an uncompromisingly right-wing government which would not rely on the toleration of the Centre and moderate Left, but instead would count on the support of the Nazis.

7 *Schleicher opposes action against the SA*

The issue which opened the breach between Hindenburg and Brüning was the Government's decision to ban the SA. Pressure from the state governments for action against the SA had been mounting over the previous months. After the first ballot in the Reich presidential election, Prussian police, acting on instructions from Severing, the Social Democrat Prussian Minister of the Interior, had raided Nazi headquarters throughout the state and found evidence that the SA had planned to carry out a *coup* in the event of Hitler's securing a majority. The evidence was forwarded to the Supreme Court in Leipzig and as a result pressure on the Reich Government increased. The decision whether or not to impose such a ban lay in the hands of General Wilhelm Groener who, as Reich Minister of the Interior, had overall responsibility for internal security in the Reich. Groener, however, relied heavily upon the advice of his chief political adviser, General von Schleicher. Schleicher had played a significant part in the appointment of Brüning, but had become increasingly disillusioned with the Chancellor's dependence on the Left. He had already established contact with the Nazis and in particular with the SA, which he was anxious to harness by integrating it into a new state organization for pre-military training. He also believed it would be possible to win the support of the Nazis for a more right-wing government which would then be able to dispense with the Left. Schleicher, therefore, was furious at Severing's move against the SA, which, as he told Groener on 23 March, he saw as an attempt to force the Reich Government to come out against the Right in the Prussian elections which were fixed for 24 April:

Your Excellency!

First, [I wish you] many nice Easter eggs, but not the sort of cuckoo eggs which Severing–Badt & Co. have hatched out in Leipzig. Seldom has such a perfidious attempt been made to salvage an abortive operation. I am only afraid that my particular friends in the Reich Ministry of the Interior are themselves not entirely innocent. Basically their aim is to win Your Excellency for the struggle against the Right in the Prussian elections so that you will be branded as a faithful ally of the Socialists. To achieve this end they regard any means as permissible, such as mysterious hints about the Border Guard to French correspondents [i.e. that Germany was evading the Versailles restrictions] and naked threats by the SPD party headquarters and by the Prussian Ministry of the Interior that they will not vote for Hindenburg on 10 April if your Excellency does not take up the struggle against the SA. Naturally, attempts have not been lacking to portray the basically amiable Groener as a victim of the devilish Schleicher. But in the long run that no longer has any effect; the lie is too brazen. I am really looking forward to 11 April[1] —then we will really be able to deal with this pack of liars. Severing started a campaign against the Reich Ministry of War at a secret press conference and I have made an appointment to see him straight after Easter. It's a pity that even this man still can't shake off certain practices which he picked up in his period as a Socialist campaigner. A journalist who attended this conference told us that as regards the Prussian elections Severing has completely lost his head. After the events of the past few days, I am quite glad that a counterweight exists in the shape of the Nazis though they too are naughty boys and must be handled with extreme care. If they did not exist one would really have to invent them. The course which Your Excellency is following—no one's friend and no one's enemy—is, I believe, in these circumstances the only correct one. In order to maintain this position above the parties and lay emphasis upon it, I have used your authority to turn down all invitations to speak. Everybody knows where you stand as regards the Old Gentleman [Hindenburg], but were you to take an active part in the public election campaign it would create an unfortunate precedent. . . .

8 Groener advocates a ban on the SA

Groener, however, was afraid that if he did not act against the SA, the State Ministries of the Interior would go ahead with their own separate bans. Moreover, he envisaged a ban on the SA as a means of taming the Nazi Party as he explained in a letter to a friend, Alarich von Gleich, on 2 April 1932:

On Monday or Tuesday, the Ministers of the Interior of the states are coming to a meeting about the SA. I have no doubt that we will master it—one way or the

[1] i.e. the day after the second ballot in the Presidential election, when they would no longer have to take account of the need to retain the votes of the Socialists for Hindenburg.

other. I think we have already drawn its poisonous fangs. One can make good tactical use of the endless declarations of legality made by the SA leaders, which they have handed to me in thick volumes. The SA is thereby undermining its credibility. But there are still difficult weeks of political manoeuvring until the various Landtag elections are over. Then, one will have to start working towards making the Nazis acceptable as participants in a government because the movement, which will certainly grow, can no longer be suppressed by force. Of course the Nazis must not be allowed to form a government of their own anywhere, let alone in the Reich. But in the states an attempt will have to be made here and there to harness them in a coalition and to cure them of their utopias by constructive government work. I can see no better way, for the idea of trying to destroy the Party through an anti-Nazi law on the lines of the old anti-Socialist law I would regard as a very unfortunate undertaking. With the SA of course it is different. They must be eliminated in any event, and ideally the so-called Iron Front[1] as well. . . .

9 General Schleicher's intrigue against the SA ban

The conference with the State Ministers on 5 April finally persuaded Groener to go ahead with a ban. At this point, however, he came up against opposition from Schleicher. Schleicher was anxious to avoid a confrontation with the Nazi Party and therefore suggested the idea of first sending an ultimatum to demand changes in the SA; only if these were rejected would it be necessary to go ahead with the ban. When Hindenburg rejected this idea and accepted an immediate ban, Schleicher intrigued to have the decision reversed. Groener noted down at the time what followed:

In the afternoon of the 10th, State Secretary Zweigert rang me up to inform me that State Secretary Meissner of the Reich President's Office had told him while at breakfast with Reich Minister of Transport Treviranus that the President had changed his mind under the influence of General von Schleicher brought to bear on him by his own son. . . .
12 April. . . . I met Col. von Hindenburg who was in a state of great agitation about the fact that once again his father was expected to sign a decree, although he had only just been appointed Reich President. His father would only have dirt thrown at him again by the Right. They might at least wait a little. He did not bring up any objective reasons, in fact he emphasized that he was not interested in the SA. In view of his excitement, it was impossible to have an objective discussion with him. But I was in no doubt about the fact that his opinion was based purely on naive and sentimental feelings. . . .
At five o'clock in the afternoon, the Reich Chancellor and I went to see the Reich President. State Secretary Meissner was present at the interview. The Chancellor gave a lengthy explanation of why the ban was necessary. I supplemented it by slowly reading out the official explanation which was later released. The Reich President made no substantial objections; in fact his attitude was in no way one of fundamental opposition. . . . At the end, the Reich President stated that

[1] The Iron Front was a propaganda organization formed by the Social Democrats and the Reichsbanner at the end of 1931.

it should not be held against his son if he tried to protect his father. He was prepared to sign the decree if the Chancellor and the Reich Minister of the Interior considered it necessary.

The decree banning the SA and the SS was issued on 13 April. The intrigue, however, continued:

15 April. General von Schleicher reported to me that opposition to the decree was building up in the Reich President's entourage and in the Reich Ministry of Defence. He spoke with reserve, but according to him the following were involved: the former commander of the 3. Division, von Stülpnagel, now with the *Börsenzeitung*, a financial newspaper whose sympathy with the Nazis was well known, General von Horn of the Kyffhäuserbund [an ex-servicemen's organization], and the commander of the 2. Division, von Bock. General von Schleicher did not mention any other names. He maintained that the Reichswehr would not swallow the ban and he was afraid that my position would soon be at risk. He did not accept my objection that the Reichswehr must obey. From various indications I suspect that the Reichstag Nationalist deputy, Schmidt-Hanover, has played a leading role in the intrigue which has now developed against me. I have no doubt that influence was exercised on the Scherl Press by members of the Reich President's entourage.

Later Groener was to reflect:

My hands were tied as regards these manoeuvres because any attempt to get the Reich President to take action against these officers would have met with such resistance that there would have been nothing left but immediate resignation. But this would have also brought about the fall of the Brüning Government even before the Prussian elections, before the Reichstag had convened, and in the middle of the Geneva negotiations on disarmament. . . . I knew very well that the intention was to bring down the Chancellor. In the course of the winter, the Reich President had twice mentioned to me that Dr Brüning did not quite represent his ideal as Reich Chancellor. He did not accept my comment that at the moment he would not find a better one. General von Schleicher had also made no bones about the fact that he was thinking in terms of a change of Chancellor. In view of his connexions with the Reich President's entourage, it can be assumed that he took part in the removal of Dr Brüning as Chancellor. During the absence of the Reich President in Neudeck, his country estate, where Brüning's fall was decided upon, General von Schleicher was in continual contact by telephone with Hindenburg's son.

Schleicher succeeded in bringing about Groener's fall on 13 May. But, as Groener noted, this was only a preliminary move towards the main objective of securing the dismissal of Brüning. Brüning was particularly vulnerable because of his total dependence on the President. He had failed to win popular support because he had consistently subordinated domestic politics to foreign affairs. His main aim had been to secure the end of reparations. He assumed that such a diplomatic victory would secure his position with public opinion at home and in particular against his right-wing critics. But in order to end reparations, he was forced to pursue rigidly orthodox financial policies which alone would satisfy the financial experts of the Allies. Moreover, it was necessary for him to emphasize the economic crisis in Germany in order to make out a convincing case for the necessity of shelving reparations. In short, Brüning's main stress on foreign policy reinforced his commitment to deflationary economic policies at home which only resulted in the growing alienation of many of the population not only from his own government but from the political system itself.

But it was not only his lack of popular support which had made him dependent on the President. After his failure in 1930 to secure a new right-of-centre majority in the Reichstag, he had neglected the Reichstag. The increasingly presidential regime associated with rule by decree accorded with his own sympathy for the prewar system of a government of civil servants ruling 'above the parties' under the direction of the emperor.

By the spring of 1932, however, he had lost the support of the President. In addition to the elements of intrigue already mentioned, a final factor emerged which prompted Hindenburg to act. This was the bitter hostility of the Junker landowners to the Government's plans to take over bankrupt Junker estates and divide them up among landless peasants. The Junkers could now claim Hindenburg's particular sympathy because they had recently presented him with his old family estate which had been bought with funds subscribed by the industrialists. But before Hindenburg could be persuaded to dismiss Brüning an acceptable alternative had to be provided. Schleicher proposed Franz von Papen, a Catholic aristocrat from Westphalia who had been a member of the same regiment as Hindenburg's son. He was a member of the Centre Party but only on account of his Catholicism. His political views had far more in common with those of the Nationalists than with even the right wing of his own party. Papen's aristocratic background and manner appealed to Hindenburg and so he was agreeable to the change.

10 Goebbels on the fall of Brüning

Before engineering the replacement of Brüning by Papen, Schleicher had conducted extensive negotiations with the Nazis in an attempt to secure their toleration of the new government. In return he had promised that Papen would lift the ban on the SA and call an election. Without committing himself on paper, Hitler succeeded in conveying the impression that he would be sympathetic to such a bargain. Goebbels's diary provides an insight into the atmosphere of intrigue which preceded Brüning's fall:

8 May 1932. On Saturday the delegates come and give us some information. The Führer has an important interview with Schleicher in the presence of a few gentlemen of the President's immediate circle.

All goes well. The Führer has spoken decisively. Brüning's fall is expected shortly. The President of the Reich will withdraw his confidence from him.

The plan is to constitute a Presidential Cabinet. The Reichstag will be dissolved. Repressive enactments are to be cancelled. We shall be free to go ahead as we like, and mean to outdo ourselves in propaganda.

11 May 1932. The Reichstag drags on. Groener's position is shaken; the Army no longer supports him. Even those with most to do with him urge his downfall.

This is the beginning; once one of these men falls, the whole Cabinet, and with it the system, will crash. Brüning is trying to salvage what he can. He speaks in the Reichstag, and cleverly beats a retreat on foreign politics. There he becomes aggressive. He believes himself within sight of the goal. He does not mention Groener at all. So he too has given him up!

The whole debate turns on the lifting of the ban on the S A. Groener strongly objects to this. It will be his undoing. I proceed as if the Reichstag were already dissolved. Our preparations are being made on quite a large scale. . . .

The ban on the S A has suddenly become the pivot upon which home affairs would seem to turn. . . .

24 May 1932. The Prussian Diet is convened. Through our confidential agents we are assured that we stand a good chance. Saturday will see the end of Brüning. Secretary of State Meissner leaves for Neudeck. Now we must hope for the best. The list of Ministers is more or less settled: von Papen, Chancellor; von Neurath, Minister of Foreign Affairs, and then a list of unfamiliar names. The main point as far as we are concerned is to ensure that the Reichstag is dissolved. Everything else can be arranged. The Prussian question can only be solved in this way. . . .

29 May 1932. . . . At noon Brüning is to call on Hindenburg. A decision will be reached. Even yesterday he made a speech in which he made light of the rumours of a crisis. But he will soon stop smiling. Nevertheless we still have some slight misgivings. We have been disappointed so often, we can hardly believe things will turn out well this time. I shall only feel secure when victory is actually ours. . . .

30 May 1932. The bomb has exploded. Brüning has presented the resignation of the entire Cabinet to the President, at noon. The system has begun to crumble. The President has accepted the resignation. I at once ring up the Führer. Now he must return to Berlin at once. . . .

Meet the Führer at Nauen. The President wishes to see him in the course of the afternoon. I get into his car and give him a good all-round summary. We are tremendously delighted. . . . Pay our S A at Wilmersdorf a short visit. The Führer is already waiting for me at home. The conference with the President went off well. The S A prohibition is going to be cancelled. Uniforms are to be allowed again. The Reichstag is going to be dissolved. That is of the first importance.

Von Papen is likely to be appointed Chancellor, but that is neither here nor there. The Poll! the Poll! It's the people we want. We are all entirely satisfied.

2 June 1932. All through the morning and afternoon we wait for news from Berlin. It arrives at four. The Opposition demands a written undertaking from the Führer that he will work smoothly with von Papen even after the election. Such a statement cannot be made. . . .

After the meetings we have long consultations with the Führer. He has no intention of writing either letter or memorandum. The main thing is dissolution and re-election.

If the election is not to miscarry, we must contest it unhampered by any such pledges.

On the opposite side also there are men who need to be tackled with circumspection. Intrigues are everywhere afoot. We are playing a risky game. So much the more must the dissolution of the Reichstag be a *sine qua non*.

The Führer estimates his opponents very exactly. He is very logical and an amazingly quick worker.

4 June 1932. Friday. The Führer has nevertheless dictated a memorandum on the question of dissolution of the Reichstag. Résumé: it must come off, otherwise further development is impossible. The Führer meets Schleicher on a neighbouring estate. He wants me to go through the note again. It is then sent after him by express. The motor-cyclist gets there too late. The conference is already over, so that it is impossible to deliver it.

When the Führer gets back, he is beaming with contentment. Everything went off well. The Reichstag is going to be dissolved and the SA prohibition cancelled. (But not until 16th.)

11 *Propaganda for the July 1932 election*

After the fall of the Brüning Government and the lifting of the ban on the SA, the main problem of winning power remained for the Nazis. New Reichstag elections were called for 31 July and Hitler's confidence in success was confirmed by results in the June state elections. For Goebbels, the new Papen Cabinet, with its strong aristocratic image, presented a new quandary — how to campaign as a party of opposition without losing support from conservative bourgeois circles and alienating the President and his entourage. His answer was to ignore the new Government and concentrate on attacking the political system in general:

Reich Propaganda Department   *4 June 1932*
To all Party Offices for their confidential information

During this *Reichstag* election no judgement is to be passed on the actions of the von Papen Cabinet but instead on the acts of those governments and parties responsible for the crime of November 1918 [i.e. the revolution] and who from then until now have as a system to bear the responsibility for the greatest historical collapse of recent centuries. This election will be the moment for dealing with the people responsible for the thirteen years behind us, but not, as the propaganda of our opponents wants to pretend, for the few bridging weeks of the von Papen Cabinet. All our party offices must refrain from any discussion of the von Papen Cabinet during this campaign and any attempt by our opponents to discuss it must be negatived right from the start.

In the light of Brüning's *Memoirs*, his replacement by Papen was not perhaps quite such a turning-point in the history of the Republic as has often been maintained. Brüning had relied heavily on the President's authority and he was basically out of sympathy with the Weimar 'System'. He wished to introduce a stronger executive, ideally through a restoration of the monarchy. Nevertheless, while in office he had maintained the constitutional proprieties and he was tolerated by the democratically minded

parties—the Social Democrats, the Catholic Centre and the Democrats—
as a barrier against what they feared would inevitably be a more authoritarian
alternative. With the appointment of Papen their worst fears were realized;
Papen was bent on replacing the democratic system of Weimar with an
authoritarian dictatorship as soon as possible. On 20 July 1932, he took the
first major step in this direction by using the President's emergency powers
to depose the Prussian Government, which, as a coalition of Social Democrats and Catholic Centre, had long been a target of right-wing hostility. He
appointed himself as Reich Commissioner for Prussia, and Bracht, the
Mayor of Essen and a Nationalist, as his deputy and Prussian Minister of
the Interior. This was followed by a purge of the Prussian administration
in which civil servants who were loyal to the Republic were replaced by
Nationalists. Since Prussia formed three-fifths of the Reich, this was a
devastating blow to the Republic and helped in fact to prepare the way for
the Nazi take-over of power in 1933.

12 *Hindenburg rejects Hitler's demand for the Chancellorship, 13 August 1932*
Papen's Government was vulnerable, however, because of its extremely
narrow basis of support. The Cabinet contained so many aristocrats that it
was dubbed by its opponents 'the Cabinet of the barons'. Papen hoped, as
did his mentor Schleicher, that the Nazis would provide a basis of mass
support for the regime. In this hope they were to be disappointed. Initially,
it is true, the Nazis did exercise some restraint towards the Government.
But after the SA ban had been lifted and the election had been held on
31 July, the Party refused to become lobby fodder for Papen. The election
saw for the Party a big advance on the result of the previous election of
September 1930. The Nazis won 37 per cent of the vote as against 18 per
cent; with 230 seats as against 107 they were now by far the largest party
in the Reichstag. But they still did not possess an overall majority and the
question was, could this increased vote be turned into concrete political power?
Hitler felt in a strong position, particularly in view of the fact that the parties
supporting the Government—the Nationalists and some of the People's
Party—had lost heavily to the Nazis and now held only 44 seats between
them, out of 608. At a meeting with Schleicher on 5 August he demanded the
Chancellorship for himself and other key posts for Nazis. Papen, however,
failed to react and once again Hitler came up against the problem that,
because he could not form a government with a majority in the Reichstag,
power still lay with the President who had the use of Article 48 and the right
to appoint the Chancellor. At an interview on 13 August, Papen rejected
Hitler's demands, and this was confirmed by Hindenburg in the afternoon.

Papen's strength was that, unlike Brüning in the last months of his
Chancellorship, he had the full confidence of the President. On 13 August
Hindenburg listened calmly to Hitler's case for forming a government but
refused to be swayed. Hitler's hope that his large popular following would

convince the President proved of no avail. The meeting was a personal disaster for Hitler and ended with his threatening more uncompromising opposition to the Papen Government. Otto Meissner, head of the Presidential Chancellery, took minutes of the second meeting between Hitler and Hindenburg:[1]

The President of the Reich opened the discussion by declaring to Hitler that he was ready to let the National Socialist Party and their leader Hitler participate in the Reich Government and would welcome their cooperation. He then put the question to Hitler whether he was prepared to participate in the present government of von Papen. Herr Hitler declared that, for reasons which he had explained in detail to the Reich President that morning, his taking any part in cooperation with the existing government was out of the question. Considering the importance of the National Socialist movement he must demand the full and complete leadership of government and state for himself and his party.

The Reich President in reply said firmly that he must answer this demand with a clear, unyielding No. He could not justify before God, before his conscience or before the fatherland the transfer of the whole authority of government to a single party, especially to a party that was biased against people who had different views from their own. There were a number of other reasons against it upon which he did not wish to enlarge in detail, such as fear of increased unrest, the effect on foreign countries, etc.

Herr Hitler repeated that any other solution was unacceptable to him.

To this the Reich President replied: 'So you will go into opposition?'

Hitler: 'I have now no alternative.'

The Reich President: 'In that case the only advice I can give you is to engage in this opposition in a chivalrous way and to remain conscious of your responsibility and duty towards the fatherland. I have had no doubts about your love for the fatherland. I shall intervene sharply against any acts of terrorism or violence such as have been committed by members of the SA sections. We are both old comrades and we want to remain so, since the course of events may bring us together again later on. Therefore, I shall shake hands with you now in a comradely way.'

This discussion was followed by a short conversation in the corridor between the Reich Chancellor and me, and Herr Hitler and his companions, in which Herr Hitler expressed the view that future developments would lead to the solution suggested by him and to the overthrow of the Reich President. The Government would get into a difficult position; the opposition would become very sharp and he could assume no responsibility for the consequences.

The conversation lasted for about twenty minutes.

13 *Goebbels on the outcome of the interview*

Goebbels commented in his diary:

... The Führer is back in under half an hour. So it has ended in failure. He has gained nothing. Papen is to remain Chancellor and the Führer has to content himself with the position of Vice-Chancellor!

[1] See also the account in Rumbold to Simon, 15.viii.32, in *Documents on British Foreign Policy, 1919–39*, 2nd series, vol. 4, doc. no. 14.

A solution leading to no result! It is out of the question to accept such a proposal. There is no alternative but to refuse. The Führer did so immediately. Like the rest of us, he is fully aware of the consequences. It will mean a hard struggle, but we shall triumph in the end. . . .

In the back room the SA leaders assemble at the command of the Chief of Staff. The Führer and he give them a fairly full outline of events. Their task is the most difficult of all. Who knows if their units will be able to hold together? Nothing is harder than to tell a troop with victory already in their grasp that their assignment has come to nothing!

A grim task, but we have to go through with it. There is no other way. The idea of the Führer as Vice-Chancellor of a bourgeois Cabinet is too ludicrous to be treated seriously. Rather go on struggling for another ten years than accept that offer.

The Führer maintains an admirable calm. He stands above all vacillations, hopes, vague ideas, and conjectures; a point of rest in a world of unrest.

The first game is lost.

Well, the fight goes on! In the end the Wilhelmstrasse will give in. There is no Cromwell in the Cabinet, and in the long run, despite everything, strength and tenacity will win the day. . . .

The crisis months, August–December 1932

Hindenburg's refusal to appoint Hitler Chancellor was, as Goebbels recognized, a serious blow to the Party. After waging an incessant and exhausting propaganda campaign for nearly three years, the whole movement had assumed that they had at last reached their goal. The shock of disappointment had very damaging effects on Party morale and particularly on its most active members in the SA. It appeared as if the policy of legality which the Party had pursued since 1925 had led to a cul-de-sac. The question was, what tactics could the Party now pursue? Gregor Strasser, the head of the Party's organization, advocated a coalition with the Catholic Centre Party, some of whose members believed that the Nazi Party should be brought into the government either to make it 'responsible' or to discredit it with the masses. Hitler agreed to negotiations but primarily with the aim of putting pressure on Papen. These contacts bore fruit in the election of Göring to the Reichstag presidency with Centre support. Meanwhile, Papen, who was aware of the decline in Nazi morale, decided to apply pressure on the Party by calling another election in which he reckoned they would lose votes. He hoped that they would then be in more of a mood for cooperation. On 12 September, therefore, he dissolved Parliament. The Nazis could only retaliate rather futilely by holding up the dissolution until a motion of 'no confidence' proposed by the Communists had been passed by 513 votes to 32.

14 *Nazi propaganda against the Papen Government*

Since Papen had captured the conservative ground, Goebbels decided to launch a radical campaign against the reactionary nature of the Papen regime. This was also a line to which he himself was most sympathetic. On the day of the dissolution, therefore, he issued the following instructions:

Reich Propaganda Department   *12 September 1932*
To all Gauleiters and Gau *Propaganda Directors:*

As we have already stated in our express circular, dated 3 September, the struggle against the Papen Cabinet and the reactionary circles behind it must now begin all along the line.... We have no reason to defend ourselves against Herr von Papen and his policy. On the contrary, in accordance with old National Socialist tactics we are now going over to the attack.... The aim is to isolate the Papen regime from the people and prove to the world that it is only a small feudal clique with no other aim than to isolate the National Socialist movement and thereby make its impact ineffectual. The struggle which is now beginning must be carried out ruthlessly and is restricted only by the existing laws and not by any tactical considerations. The NSDAP has no reason whatsoever to spare the Papen regime in any way....

15 *Hess's observations (undated) on propaganda for the Election*

Yet the dangers of a radical campaign were that it would alienate the middle class, which had hitherto provided the Party's main support, without capturing the working class. It might also alienate the influential elites who held part of the key to the appointment of Hitler as Chancellor. Hess, possibly acting for Hitler, pointed out some of these dangers in a memorandum:

It is inexpedient to gear the campaign to the slogan: 'Against the rule of the barons', as has already happened in some cases in the Party's propaganda and press. This slogan is welcome ammunition to the Government, the German Nationalists, and other opponents who can, with some appearance of justification, maintain that the NSDAP, having already 'given up the fight against the Centre', having 'stood by parliamentary methods',[1] is now 'showing class war tendencies'....

The electoral damage produced by this would be greater than any advantage gained. A large number of voters on the Right will undoubtedly be impressed by the partly justified claim that the NSDAP is going over to class-war slogans. We cannot expect to make up for this by extra votes from the Left. For the majority of those who are impressed by this slogan will gravitate towards or stay with the party which expresses it in the most radical way. And that means now, as before, the Marxist parties, for class war is one of the basic points in their programme....

The [Nazi] movement has now won over just about all the voters it can by the methods of propaganda pursued hitherto, that is to say, by means of its general ideological line and propaganda based on general aims. In addition, in this election campaign we are confronted by a government that has succeeded in creating the impression among part of the electorate, and no doubt among some of our former supporters, that it is they who are now putting into practice, or in some cases have

[1] This refers to the Nazis' cooperation with the Centre Party in the Reichstag against the Papen Government.

already carried out, the things which the National Socialists aimed for but were not themselves in a position to carry out. They claim that the National Socialists have no clear and practical goals and that in so far as their aims are known, they represent dangerous experiments; the Nazis can certainly damn the measures taken by the Government but they do not explain how they propose to do better. . . .

Criticism of the Government, therefore, must above all not be phrased in too general terms such as 'Government of the Barons', 'reactionary legacy hunters', but must always be supported with concrete examples. . . .

16 *Goebbels advises against class-warfare propaganda*

Whether or not as a result of this memorandum, Goebbels was obliged to tone down the radical campaign slightly:

Reich Propaganda Department

Strictly Confidential Information No. 8, valid 12–14 October

IMPORTANT!

Through the attempt of the Papen Government to exclude Adolf Hitler from power, we have come into sharp conflict with a certain kind of anti-social and therefore capitalistic concept of economics. This opposition is justified and must be carried out with all our strength.   •

But it must not lead to a complete condemnation of all employers as such and thereby get into the deep waters of Marxist class war. For instance, it is wrong to equate, as Marxism does, employers with exploiters, just as it is wrong to spread details of the unjustifiable salaries of leading industrial figures. . . .

It is also wrong to make industry as a whole responsible for the deficiency of the Papen agrarian programme, as has happened now and then. . . .

In every political situation we must adhere to the old, tried guidelines of National Socialism; not treating all business alike in the Marxist way, but distinguishing strictly between healthy business leadership, which is indispensable to the economy, and exploiters. To talk of the expropriation of all industrial concerns is, of course, a direct contravention of National Socialist principles.

Moreover, the fight against the Papen Cabinet must not develop into a fight against the aristocracy as such. We must always be aware of the fact that the best part of the German aristocracy fights in our own ranks and therefore does not deserve to be demoted from the German front just because of a few black sheep.

Nevertheless, during the last few weeks of the campaign, the radical line culminated in cooperation with the Communists in support of the Berlin transport workers' strike, which had broken out in protest against the wages policy of the Government.

17 *Middle-class disillusionment with Nazism*

The extent to which the radical campaign against Papen had alienated the upper and lower middle classes, who had hitherto supported or at least been sympathetic to the Nazis, is apparent in the following document. In her diary Frau Luise Solmitz gives an insight into the attitude of many of the upper middle class during the autumn of 1932:

13. viii. 32. . . . Goebbels in the National Socialist *Angriff*![1] We know this language only too well from Socialist and Communist papers; we don't want to hear it from Goebbels! This is just what deters many; these are the objections which bourgeois-orientated Hitler supporters have to fight again and again. Perhaps this language is necessary to bring in the masses who tend to the Left, but it alienates the valuable bourgeois element; to embrace them all becomes impossible. Hitler, remain master in your own house!

29. ix. 32. The trade unions are no longer Marxist enough for the Nazis; they demand that the trade unions should call a strike against the underbidding of wage tariffs—and thus against the re-employment of the unemployed. And they want to expel every employer from their ranks who lowers wages in order to enlarge the number of employees. Can an employer remain a Nazi at all?! . . .

3. xi. 32. E.M. said, shaking his head, 'One can't possibly vote for Hitler.' He met a Herr von S., whom he knows from the war: 'I voted for Hitler twice; it's no longer the thing to do.' Our old carrier: 'Hitler? He is far to the Left! I have always voted for Hugenberg.' Old Professor H. persists in voting for his stale old *Volkspartei*,[2] his daughter is fanatically pro-Hitler. . . .

If only one could summon up some enthusiasm for the German Nationalist Party and Hugenberg! With the National Socialist Party we had a love match. The German Nationalist marriage which we are about to enter is a marriage of convenience and without passion [*Schwung*].

31. xii. 32. This year has robbed us of a great hope—this *year*, not death. Adolf Hitler. Our reviver and great leader towards national unity . . . and the man who in the end turns out to be the leader of a party sliding more and more into a dubious future. I still cannot come to terms with this bitter disappointment. . . .

Hampered by the decline in morale and by shortage of money now that the Party had alienated the upper classes with its radical line, the Party's propaganda machine found the going hard. In October, Goebbels noted in his diary that 'the organization has naturally become a bit on edge through these everlasting elections. It is as jaded as a battalion which has been too long in the front trenches, and just as nervy.' And the election held on 6 November was indeed a setback for the Nazis. Their percentage of the vote fell from 37 to 33 and their number of seats from 230 to 196. But even more important than the number of votes lost was the fact that for the first time they had actually lost votes. The myth of invincibility which they had projected so successfully hitherto and which had played a substantial part in their appeal had been broken. Nothing could now disguise the fact that they were in trouble.

Yet although his gamble had paid off, Papen had not really solved his

[1] *Der Angriff*, the daily paper of Goebbels's *Gau*, Berlin.
[2] The *Deutsche Volkspartei* (German People's Party), the right-wing liberal party.

problems. For, while the Nationalists had gained slightly, the Government
still rested on an extremely narrow basis of support. Moreover, contrary to
Papen's hopes, Hitler was still not prepared to join the Government in a
subordinate capacity nor was he prepared to become Chancellor except
with a Cabinet dominated by his party and with full freedom to use the
powers contained in Article 48. This, however, was unacceptable to President
Hindenburg. Frustrated in his attempt to acquire a mass base, Papen
contemplated a *coup d'état* by which the Weimar constitution would be
replaced by an authoritarian presidential dictatorship. This plan, however,
would require the elimination of both the Nazis and the Communists since
they would both be bound to resist such a development by force. President
Hindenburg, wishing to retain Papen for whom he had developed a great
affection, was prepared to acquiesce in this solution. General von Schleicher,
however, now Minister of Defence, did not believe the Army would be
capable of dealing with the SA and the Communists simultaneously,
particularly in view of the fact that the junior officer corps was now permeated with Nazi ideas. Furthermore, unlike Papen who was a traditional
reactionary, Schleicher was aware of the fact that in an advanced industrial
society it is impossible to rule without some degree of mass support, however
that support is acquired. This was particularly essential if Germany's armed
strength was to be fully restored. Schleicher believed that mass support
could be won for a regime sympathetic to rearmament if such a regime
pursued social and economic policies which were more attractive to the
masses than those of the reactionary Papen Government, policies such as a
more vigorous attempt to solve the unemployment problem, if necessary by
state finance. He also believed that he could acquire such mass support by
splitting the mass movements of the Right and the Left. He believed he
could split the Nazi Party by winning over elements within the Party, of
whom Gregor Strasser was the most notable, which were primarily interested
in making a practical contribution to solving the economic and political crisis
and in particular the problem of unemployment, and which were afraid that
the possibility of their making such a contribution might be jeopardized by
Hitler's stubborn insistence on all or nothing so far as political power was
concerned. He also thought that he could split the Left by winning over the
trade unions and the right wing of the Social Democrats for whom the
solution of the unemployment problem would be more important than
doctrinaire principles. He believed that the fact that his government would
be more socially concerned than that of Papen and would avoid the danger
of either Papen or Hitler establishing a dictatorship would be sufficient to
commend it to these groups.

Of the alternatives offered by Papen and Schleicher, Hindenburg preferred the former and, after Papen had formally resigned following the
election, the President asked him to form another government. At this point,
however, Schleicher intervened and declared that the Army could not carry

out the *coup d'état* envisaged by Papen. As a result, the President was forced, regretfully, to accept Papen's resignation and to appoint Schleicher in his place to see if his solution would work. Schleicher at once began to try to put his plan into operation. He appointed a Reich Commissioner for Employment and persuaded Parliament to repeal the deflationary measures which Papen had introduced on 4 September such as cuts in wages and benefits.

18 *The Strasser affair, December 1932*

Yet Schleicher's attempts to win support from a section of the Left and to split the Nazis were both abortive. The trade unions were forced to end the negotiations under pressure from the Social Democrats who were suspicious of Schleicher. In view of his previous role as an intriguer this was understandable, but none the less short-sighted. On 4 December, Schleicher offered Strasser the Vice-Chancellorship which he was anxious to accept. In this he had the sympathy of some of the Nazi deputies and notably their leader, Frick. Göring and Goebbels, however, were strongly opposed and Hitler, though agreeing to continue negotiations with Schleicher, took them out of Strasser's hands. After a stormy interview on 7 December, Strasser wrote Hitler a letter of resignation and on the morning of the 8th called a meeting of the Party's regional inspectors – the senior Gauleiters – in the Reichstag building. It was attended by Dr Ley, the No. 2 in the Party organization, Bernhard Rust of Lower Saxony, Heinrich Haake of Cologne, Jacob Sprenger of Hesse-Nassau, Martin Mutschmann of Saxony, Hinrich Lohse of Schleswig-Holstein, Wilhelm Loeper of Anhalt, and finally, by Strasser's closest associate, Paul Schulz, Reich Inspector I of the Political Organization. To this group Strasser announced his resignation and, according to a postwar account by Lohse, gave the following explanation of his action:

> For some time I have been aware of a development which affects not so much the programme or the final goal but rather the way of achieving this goal, and which I can no longer go along with. At least since August, since the time of his first meeting with Papen, Schleicher and Hindenburg, the Führer has not been following a clear line of policy in his endeavour to achieve power. He is only clear about one thing – he wishes to become Reich Chancellor. He should, however, have become aware of the fact that he is being consistently refused this post by everybody and that in the foreseeable future there is no prospect of his attaining this goal. As a result of this situation, the movement is being put under considerable stress which is undermining its unity and may expose it to splits and disintegration. In view of the appalling distress of our supporters, we cannot let our SA men and our ordinary Party comrades wait for ever or they will become impatient and in the end leave the movement in a mood of disappointment. There is no doubt that our enemies have been waiting for this moment, not just recently but for a long time. The Party must, therefore, come to a decision one way or the other.

There are two paths which can lead to a solution of this serious crisis and if the collapse of the movement is to be avoided one of them must be followed: the legal or the illegal path. I would be prepared to follow either path. But I refuse to wait until the Führer is made Reich Chancellor, for by then the collapse will have occurred. If the legal path was to be followed, the Führer should have accepted Hindenburg's offer in August to make him Vice-Chancellor. From this basis the attempt should have been made to secure new positions. The Vice-Chancellor should have made it clear to the coalition Cabinet in which the National Socialists were participating that without the carrying out of National Socialist ideas there could be no recovery for Germany. The same thing should have happened in a Prussian coalition government and in other state governments.

Had Vice-Chancellor Hitler not succeeded in this task, he would have been weighed and found wanting; his departure from the political stage and the collapse of the government would have been deserved. History does not concern itself with methods but only with success.

The second method is the illegal path. I would have been prepared to follow this path as well. The National Socialist stormtroops of the SA and SS are still intact; they are prepared for the final march and will be at the ready the moment the order comes. This conquest of power by force would also have had a chance of success even if it had been bloody and confronted by serious resistance from the State. For who could withstand this well-organized army which has a firm ideological commitment, which has already passed the half-million mark, and the whole of which is under the leadership of front-line officers and soldiers? But this path has also been rejected and for my part I no longer see any possibility of future activity.

So far as the personal aspect of the problem is concerned, I am aware of an increasingly prevalent game of intrigue within the entourage of the Führer and of personal insults and slights which I am simply no longer able to put up with. I also naturally want to see and speak with the Führer occasionally—both for personal and for official reasons. If I go to the Kaiserhof[1] or to the Brown House in Munich, I always find the same people there. During such visits I usually learn little, at any rate nothing detailed about the current issues of the day, about political meetings or the current state of discussions being carried on with individuals or with groups and parties.

I have no desire to take second place to Göring, Goebbels, Röhm, and others. If they are invited, I expect also to be honoured with an invitation. This the Führer has never done. I regard this as a slight, as a personal humiliation which I have not deserved and which I am no longer prepared to tolerate. Apart from this, I am at the end of my strength and nerves. I have resigned from the Party and am now going to the mountains to recuperate. I ask you all not to draw any conclusions for yourselves from my action but rather to continue to carry out your duties.

Strasser's speech caused consternation among his hearers; they reminded him of the obligations of loyalty to the Führer and of comradeship and begged him to think again. He declared, however, that his step was final and

[1] The Berlin hotel where Hitler stayed.

irrevocable. Gauleiter Rust, the regional inspector of Lower Saxony, then went to the Kaiserhof and reported to Hitler what had happened. Hitler immediately called a meeting in the Kaiserhof at twelve o'clock for those who had been present at the Strasser meeting. Strasser and Schulz did not attend. Lohse continues:

Hitler received the Regional Inspectors in his suite with extreme reserve. He did not ask them to sit down. Those who had been invited stood around him in a semicircle. He too betrayed signs of great emotion, if not shock. His sharp, searching eyes moved from one person to the next, weighing up the emotions aroused and seeming to ask, Are you still loyal to me or are you too already on the side of the faithless traitors and opponents? His facial muscles were rigid, his gaze was penetrating. After a pause for thought and slowly working himself up, he began the interview as follows:

'Since I have received Strasser's resignation this morning without any explanation, we must talk the matter over, gentlemen, so that we know how we stand with one another. You are the pillars of the movement. If one of these pillars breaks, it does not necessarily mean that the whole building will collapse. If one is unfaithful and deserts me in the darkest hour of the Party, I can bear it and overcome it. But if you all want to desert me then my life's work and my struggle for it no longer have any point; the movement will collapse. Without this movement and my life's task associated with it, I shall then have nothing more which could bind me to this earth'—as if in a dream he looked at the bust of his niece on the mantelpiece, the daughter of his half-sister with whom he had had close relations and who had shot herself. 'I shall then take the consequences and shall ask only that my corpse and my coffin be draped with the flag which I created for the movement as a symbol of a new Germany. . . .'

Dr Ley then gave an account of what Strasser had said to the Regional Inspectors and Hitler made the following comments:

'I thought Gregor Strasser was much cleverer than that; I am shocked by the position he adopts and even more by the fact that, after twelve years' acquaintanceship and comradeship in the Party, he did not consider it necessary to let me know about these things and discuss them with me. I find it very difficult to accept this account as an adequate explanation for his momentous decision.

'I will answer you point by point:

'1. The path to the conquest of power depends upon imponderables which Strasser, according to his own account, either completely ignores or does not wish to see, or is simply not aware of. With a man of his calibre one would have thought that was impossible. He spoke to you about the legal path to the conquest of power and declared that it was my duty in August to accept the office of Vice-Chancellor. Herr Strasser knows quite well that Herr von Papen and Herr von Schleicher are not National Socialists and therefore are not willing to follow National Socialist policies. Judging by the measures introduced by and the results of the policy of Reich Chancellor von Papen, as Vice-Chancellor I would have had serious differences with him within the first week. If I did not want to abdicate all influence, betray my movement and make my position in the eyes of the public impossible, I would have had to protest against his policies. I would have had to make demands concerning a whole range of burning issues in economics and the administration, in social, labour and financial policies, demands which would have been turned down flat. Herr von Papen would have declared to me with a smile, "Forgive me, Herr Hitler, but I am Chancellor and head of the Cabinet. If my political course and the measures which result from it do not suit you, I am not forcing you to stay. You can resign your office. But in any case I reject your demands and proposals." Gentlemen, can you imagine the effect of such a conclusion to my Vice-Chancellor-ship on the Party and on public opinion? Herr von Papen and his backers, on the other hand, would have achieved their goal—the proof of the incapacity of Hitler and his subordinates would have apparently been provided. The Party comrades and the electorate would have turned their backs on me in fury, the movement would have collapsed, and in the end over its body not Herr von Papen but, as the last elections show, Bolshevism would have triumphed. I reject this path and intend to wait until I am offered the post of Chancellor. That day will come—it is probably nearer than we think.

'Whether or not the movement disintegrates does not depend on the Party comrades and is not encouraged by them. It lies entirely in our own hands; it depends on our unity and on our unshakeable faith in victory; it depends on our leadership.

'2. The illegal path to the conquest of power is even more dangerous and more fatal. It cannot be said that I do not have the courage to carry out a *coup* by force and, if necessary, by a bloody revolution. I tried it once in Munich in 1923. Herr Strasser knows that; he was there.

'But what was the result and what would the result be now? Our formations are without weapons and, if there are some which have been kept hidden here and there against my wishes and without my knowledge, they would have no effect against the united action of the police and the Reichswehr which are armed with the most modern weapons. You surely do not believe that they would stand by. The police will shoot at the command of Herr von Papen and the Reichswehr at the command of its Supreme Commander, Reich President Hindenburg, for they have taken their oath to him and not to me.

'In the past the police have invariably obeyed the existing political power in the State completely irrespective of the political tendency within the State.

'General [*sic*] von Reichenau[1] said to me recently: "Herr Hitler, you have wonderful troops whose discipline is voluntary. The fact that it is not based on the law and that the leaders do not possess any State authority makes it even more worthy of recognition. The Reichswehr is different. It is under oath and is sub-ordinate to the Field-Marshal as Reich President. If your columns march against the law, the Reichswehr would be compelled to shoot and would carry out the order even though its heart would bleed to do so. If you were Reich President and the Reichswehr was under oath to you, we would obey your orders in just the same way and shoot at the enemies of your State if you gave the order. We are

[1] Colonel von Reichenau was Chief of Staff of the Wehrkreis I (East Prussia). An ambitious man, he was already pro-Nazi, and with the appointment of his Commanding Officer, General von Blomberg, as Minister of Defence in Hitler's Cabinet he came to play an influential role in politics, notably in the so-called Röhm 'putsch' of June 1934.

unpolitical, obey the law, obey orders and keep the oath we have given. I urge you to keep within the law. One day power will inevitably fall into your lap."

'Gentlemen, I am not irresponsible enough to drive German youth and the generation of front-line soldiers who are the best representatives of the nation's manhood into the machine guns of the police and the Reichswehr. Gregor Strasser will not see that happening!

'3. I distribute political tasks to my closest colleagues according to specific principles. The nearer we come to the decision, the more attempts are made by our opponents to create divisions within our own camp and to break us. Whether or not they have already succeeded with Gregor Strasser is a subject I will not go into.

'If I am here in the Reich capital I carry out the most important discussions with ministers, generals, and party and pressure group [Verband] leaders myself. If I am not here, we cannot have a situation in which one moment Strasser is negotiating with the Centre in a certain direction, while tomorrow Goebbels is negotiating with Hindenburg in another direction, and the day after Göring is negotiating with the Reichswehr in a completely opposite direction. During my absence from Berlin, my authorized representative is Reichstag President Göring, who knows my intentions, who knows where I am, who can therefore inform me at once about any important discussions and to whom I can if necessary give an immediate counter-order. . . .

'Furthermore, I do not like the reorganization of the Party leadership and their spheres of operation put forward by Strasser, although I approved it in order to avoid a dispute.[1] It is completely wrong that you as Regional Inspectors have given up your office as Gauleiters and are left hanging completely in the air. You are the oldest and most experienced Gauleiters. You must remain rooted in the soil in which you have grown and developed through the fulfilment of your assignment. I shall cancel the order in order to avoid upheaval and damage to the movement. . . .

'4. . . . I do not issue invitations to any particular Party comrades. Anyone who visits me is welcome. I receive, as soon as I am available, anyone who wishes to and has to speak to me. Naturally I feel closer to some than to others. But is this not normal in human life?

'For some time I have noticed that Gregor Strasser has been avoiding me and when we see each other he is reserved, serious and uncommunicative. Is that my fault? Am I to blame for the fact that Göring and Goebbels visit me uninvited more often than Strasser? Did I not receive you when you wanted to speak to me? Did I not ask you to dine with me if you were with me and I had time for you? Is that sufficient reason for one of my closest and oldest colleagues to turn his back on the movement?'

Hitler became quieter and more personal, more amiable and appealing. At the end of the two-hour-long interview he had found that comradely tone which those present knew and found completely convincing. Now he was their friend, their comrade, their leader, who had shown them the way out of the hopeless situation which Strasser had portrayed, who had won them over both emotionally and intellectually. During his speech, Strasser with his dark prophecies had receded more and more into the nebulous distance, although in view of these prophecies those present had come with considerable reservations. . . . He, Hitler, triumphed and

[1] Strasser had recently appointed some of the more senior Gauleiters to new posts as 'Regional Inspectors' who were intended to supervise the *Gaue* in their regions.

proved to his indispensable comrades, who in the most serious crisis of the movement first wavered and then recovered their nerve, that he was the master and Strasser the journeyman. . . . Those present once more sealed their old bond with him with a handshake. . . .

Strasser's unwillingness to lead a revolt against Hitler together with the total commitment of the Party leadership to Hitler as Führer ensured that the crisis was contained. The loss of confidence throughout the Party continued, however, and on 15 December Goebbels noted in his diary that it was 'very difficult to hold the stormtroopers and the departmental officials on a straight course. It is high time we attained power and at the moment there is no sign of it.'

The appointment of Hitler as Chancellor, 30 January 1933

Just at the lowest point in the fortunes of the Party the tide turned. The previous Chancellor, Franz von Papen, had not overcome his resentment at the way in which he had been elbowed aside by Schleicher. He was determined to bring down Schleicher and return to office himself, even if not as Chancellor. But to achieve this he would have to prove to the President that he could secure the mass support which his previous government had lacked and which Schleicher had promised but failed to get. Since he could get support neither from the Left nor from the Catholic Centre Party, the only possibility was the Nazis. The decline of the Nazis implied both the danger that the crisis would pass without having been used to change the regime and the likelihood of the Nazis' now proving more cooperative and amenable. During December, therefore, Papen opened negotiations with Hitler through various contacts, including Wilhelm Keppler, Hitler's economic adviser and a liaison with industry, Schacht, the former President of the Reichsbank, and Kurt von Schroeder, a Cologne banker and member of the Party.

19 *The meeting between Papen and Hitler, 4 January 1933*

As a result of these contacts, Hitler agreed to meet Papen on 4 January at Schroeder's house in Cologne. After the war Schroeder gave an account to the Nuremberg Tribunal of the background to the meeting and of what transpired at it:

On 4 January 1933 Hitler, von Papen, Hess, Himmler and Keppler arrived at my house in Cologne. Hitler, von Papen and I went into my study where a two-hour discussion took place. Hess, Himmler and Keppler did not take part but were in the adjoining room. Keppler, who had helped to arrange this meeting, came from Berlin; von Papen came by himself from his house in the Saar; and Hitler brought

Himmler and Hess with him as they were on their way to an election meeting in Lippe. The negotiations took place exclusively between Hitler and Papen. I took no part in them. The conference started at about 11.30 a.m. and the first point raised by Hitler was the question why it had been necessary to punish the two Nazis who had killed the Communist in Silesia[1]. . . .

Papen went on to say that he thought it best to form a government in which the conservative and nationalist elements that had supported him were represented together with the Nazis. He suggested that this new government should, if possible, be led by Hitler and himself together. Then Hitler made a long speech in which he said that, if he were to be elected Chancellor, Papen's followers could participate in his (Hitler's) Government as Ministers if they were willing to support his policy which was planning many alterations in the existing state of affairs. He outlined these alterations, including the removal of all Social Democrats, Communists and Jews from leading positions in Germany and the restoration of order in public life. Von Papen and Hitler reached agreement in principle whereby many of the disagreements between them could be removed and cooperation might be possible. It was agreed that further details could be worked out later either in Berlin or some other suitable place. This happened, as I learned later, at a meeting with Ribbentrop. The conference in my house ended at about 1.30 p.m. The three of us then went to lunch together with Hess, Himmler and Keppler during which we talked about general matters. At about 4 p.m. all the guests left my house. . . .

This meeting between Hitler and Papen on 4 January 1933 in my house in Cologne was arranged by me after Papen had asked me for it on about 10 December 1932. Before I took this step I talked to a number of businessmen and informed myself generally on how the business world viewed a collaboration between the two men. The general desire of businessmen was to see a strong man come to power in Germany who would form a government that would stay in power for a long time. When the NSDAP suffered its first setback on 6 November 1932 and had thereby passed its peak, the need for support from German business became particularly urgent. Business had a common interest in the fear of Bolshevism and in the hope that the National Socialists, once in power, would create lasting political and economic foundations in Germany. Another common interest was the wish to put Hitler's economic programme into practice, one of the main points of which was that business should manage its own affairs in solving the problems posed by the political leadership. In order to put this programme into practice, it was expected, as happened later on, that the whole economy would be organized on a new basis, that is to say, in associations which all economic enterprises would have to join, as contrasted with the associations then existing, and which would be managed by economists and businessmen themselves, who would themselves have to ensure a balance in production, so that these new associations could inevitably exert more influence than before. Furthermore, big State orders were expected to achieve an economic improvement.

Papen now arranged for the NSDAP to receive financial assistance from industry. This help came at a crucial moment as Hitler had decided to stake

[1] This referred to the 'Potempa affair' in which on 10 August SA men had brutally murdered a Communist in Potempa, Silesia. Papen commuted the death sentence to life imprisonment.

his prestige on the outcome of the state elections in Lippe-Detmold on 15 January. Although the electorate was no more than 90,000, Hitler needed an election victory to dispel the defeatist mood which still affected the Party and to convince the President and his advisers that the Party was not a spent force. He, therefore, concentrated all his propaganda resources there during the week before polling and his efforts brought an increase in the vote for the NSDAP (39,000 votes compared with 33,000 in November). This result deprived his opponents of an excuse to block his ambition.

20 *Otto Meissner on Schleicher's fall and Hitler's appointment*

Papen now concentrated on trying to win over the President to the idea of a Hitler Government of which he himself would be Vice-Chancellor. In order to achieve this, the President's camarilla and, in particular, his son Oskar had to be persuaded to work on Hindenburg. It has been suggested that the decisive factor in persuading Oskar von Hindenburg was a motion tabled by the Centre Party that the Reichstag should conduct an investigation into the distribution of the emergency funds given to East German agriculture. This was something the Hindenburgs wished to avoid because such an investigation, apart from being unwelcome to their fellow-Junkers, might uncover and publicize the fact that the Hindenburg estate had been registered under Oskar von Hindenburg's name in order to avoid death duties. It is possible that Hitler offered to prevent such an investigation, in the event of his becoming Chancellor. Otto Meissner, the State Secretary in the Reich President's office, gave the Nuremberg Tribunal an account of the developments leading to the appointment of Hitler:

... The weakening of Schleicher's position as Chancellor is best understood by referring to the foregoing review of the situation which led to his elevation to that position, namely, the fact that Papen was dismissed because he wanted to fight the National Socialists and did not find in the Reichswehr the necessary support for such a policy, and the fact that Schleicher came to power because he believed he could form a government which would have the support of the National Socialists. When it became clear that Hitler was not willing to enter Schleicher's Cabinet and that Schleicher on his part was unable to split the National Socialist Party, as he had hoped to do with the help of Gregor Strasser, the policy for which Schleicher had been appointed Chancellor was shipwrecked. Schleicher was aware that Hitler was particularly embittered against him because of his attempt to break up the Party, and would never agree to cooperate with him. So he now changed his mind and decided to fight against the Nazis—which meant that he now wanted to pursue the policy which he had sharply opposed when Papen had suggested it a few weeks before. Schleicher came to Hindenburg therefore with a demand for emergency powers as a prerequisite of action against the Nazis. Furthermore, he believed it to be necessary to dissolve, and even temporarily eliminate, the Reichstag, and this was to be done by Presidential decrees on the basis of Article 48—the transformation of his government into a military dictatorship, and government to be carried on generally on the basis of Article 48.

Schleicher first made these suggestions to Hindenburg in the middle of January 1933, but Hindenburg at once evinced grave doubts as to its constitutionality. In the meantime Papen had returned to Berlin, and by an arrangement with Hindenburg's son had had several interviews with the President. When Schleicher renewed his demand for emergency powers, Hindenburg declared that he was unable to give him such a blank cheque and must reserve to himself decisions on every individual case. Schleicher for his part said that under these circumstances he was unable to stay in office and tendered his resignation on 28 January.

In the middle of January, when Schleicher was first asking for emergency powers, Hindenburg was not aware of the contact between Papen and Hitler—particularly, of the meeting which had taken place in the house of the Cologne banker, Kurt von Schroeder. In the latter part of January, Papen played an increasingly important role in the house of the Reich President, but despite Papen's persuasions, Hindenburg was extremely hesitant, until the end of January, to make Hitler Chancellor. He wanted to have Papen again as Chancellor. Papen finally won him over to Hitler with the argument that the representatives of the other right-wing parties which would belong to the Government would restrict Hitler's freedom of action. In addition Papen expressed his misgivings that, if the present opportunity were again missed, a revolt of the National Socialists and civil war were likely.

Many of Hindenburg's personal friends, such as Oldenburg-Januschau,[1] worked in the same direction as Papen, also General von Blomberg.[2] The President's son and adjutant, Oskar von Hindenburg, was opposed to the Nazis up to the last moment. The turning-point at which his views changed came at the end of January. At Papen's suggestion, a meeting had been arranged between Hitler and Oskar von Hindenburg in the house of Ribbentrop. Oskar von Hindenburg asked me to accompany him; we took a taxi, in order to keep the appointment secret, and drove out to Ribbentrop's home. On our arrival we found a large company assembled; among those present were Göring and Frick.

Oskar von Hindenburg was told that Hitler wanted to talk to him *tête à tête*; as Hindenburg had asked me to accompany him, I was somewhat surprised at his accepting this suggestion and vanishing into another room for a talk which lasted quite a while—about an hour. What Hitler and Oskar von Hindenburg discussed during this talk I do not know.

In the taxi on the way back Oskar von Hindenburg was very silent; the only remark he made was that there was no help for it, the Nazis had to be taken into the Government. My impression was that Hitler had succeeded in getting him under his spell. I may add the amusing fact that early next morning Schleicher telephoned and asked me what had been discussed with Hitler the evening before; this shows that all our precautions to keep the matter secret had been of no avail.

To sum up, the following factors were involved in the winning over of the President: In the first place, the economic policies which Schleicher was

---

[1] A leading and ultra-reactionary Prussian Junker.

[2] The district commander in East Prussia, who had come into contact with Hitler during 1932 through the Protestant Chaplain Müller, who was an ardent Nazi. As a result, Blomberg had become very sympathetic to Nazism.

pursuing in an attempt to win mass support were alienating powerful interests. Industry objected to his labour policies which were regarded as inflationary and too favourable to the workers; the Junkers bitterly opposed his attempt to revive Brüning's plan of breaking up bankrupt Junker estates and settling them with peasants. These interests pressed their views vigorously with the President. Secondly, Hindenburg had never really forgiven Schleicher for forcing Papen's resignation. He wanted his 'Fränzchen' back in the Government. Finally, Schleicher had patently failed in his objective of acquiring a mass base for his government. As a result, he now had no alternative to offer other than another election, action against the Nazis and a dictatorship through Article 48. This had been not far from the policy which he had prevented Papen from carrying out and the President did not see why he should allow Schleicher to do what Papen had been prevented from doing. Hindenburg's refusal to grant a dissolution of the Reichstag forced Schleicher to resign on 28 January.

Yet, despite his growing disenchantment with Schleicher, Hindenburg was still not happy about the idea of Hitler as Chancellor. As late as 26 January, he told the Army generals that they surely did not believe he would make this 'Austrian corporal' Reich Chancellor. Hindenburg was finally persuaded by the structure of the proposed government. In the first place, Papen had persuaded Hitler that the Nazis should have only two ministries in the Cabinet apart from the Chancellorship – the Reich Ministry of the Interior (Frick) and a Minister without Portfolio (Göring) who was also Prussian Minister of the Interior; secondly, Papen became Reich Commissioner in Prussia, i.e. Göring's superior, and had the right of being present at Hitler's audiences with the President; thirdly, the Ministry of Defence was given to a general acceptable to Hindenburg (Blomberg); and finally, Papen persuaded both the Nationalists and the right-wing ex-servicemen's organization, the Stahlhelm, of which Hindenburg was the honorary head, to cooperate in forming the Government. The Nationalist leader, Hugenberg, was won over by the offer of the Ministries of Economics and Agriculture, which had been refused him by Schleicher and which he thought would make him virtually economic dictator; the Stahlhelm leader, Seldte, was made Minister of Labour. In short, Hindenburg believed that, as Papen put it, Hitler would be 'framed' within the Cabinet by Conservatives who would be able to control the policies which Hitler would 'sell' to the country through his Party and propaganda machine. To a doubter, Papen remarked: 'Don't worry, we've hired him.'

Hitler, however, was content with this solution. He himself, as Chancellor, had the supreme position in the Government; Göring, as Prussian Minister of the Interior, controlled the police in three-fifths of the Reich; and General von Blomberg, unbeknown to Hindenburg, was a pro-Nazi. Finally, as one of his conditions for taking office, he had insisted that the new Cabinet and the President should agree to an immediate dissolution. These were, he believed, adequate weapons for the consolidation of power. Time was to prove him right.

The composition of Hitler's first Reich Cabinet was as follows:

Reich Chancellor	Adolf Hitler (NSDAP)
Vice-Chancellor and Reich Commissioner for Prussia	Franz von Papen
*†Reich Foreign Minister	Constantin von Neurath
Reich Minister of the Interior	Dr Wilhelm Frick (NSDAP)
Reich Minister of Defence	General Werner von Blomberg
*†Reich Finance Minister	Count Schwerin von Krosigk
Reich Minister of Economics, Food and Agriculture	Dr Alfred Hugenberg
Reich Minister of Labour	Franz Seldte
*†Reich Minister of Posts and Transport	Paul von Eltz-Rübenach
Reich Minister without Portfolio, Reich Air Commissioner, and acting Prussian Minister of the Interior	Hermann Göring (NSDAP)
*†Reich Commissioner of Employment	Dr Günther Gereke
*†Reich Minister of Justice	Dr Franz Gürtner

*Member of the previous administration.
†Conservative civil servant.

NOTE. Gürtner was not reappointed until 1 February; he therefore did not attend the first meetings of the Cabinet on 30 and 31 January. Goebbels became a Cabinet Minister as Minister of Propaganda on 13 March 1933. Hess was named Deputy Führer on 21 April, and as such was given the power of independent decision on all Party questions; but neither he nor Röhm was nominated to the Cabinet, as Reich Minister, until 1 December. Hugenberg resigned on 27 June 1933 and was replaced by Walter Darré as Minister of Agriculture and Kurt Schmitt as Minister of Economics.

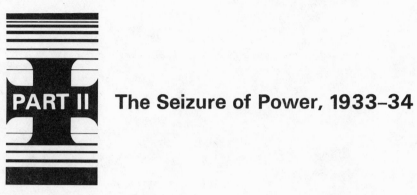

PART II   The Seizure of Power, 1933–34

Though Hitler had now been appointed Chancellor, he had not yet achieved absolute power. Only two other members of his Cabinet were Nazis, his Party had not a majority in the Reichstag, and he could be dismissed at any time by the Reich President. On the other hand, he had a number of important advantages. Göring as Prussian Minister of the Interior controlled the internal administration, including the police, in three-fifths of the Reich; Frick as Reich Minister of the Interior had certain limited powers of supervision over the remainder. With General von Blomberg as Minister of Defence he had little to fear from the Army. But, above all, there was no obvious alternative candidate to represent the forces of the Right. The years 1930–32 had seen several attempts by the Right to establish a government which was at the same time effective, amenable to the right-wing pressure groups—the Army, the Junkers, and Industry—and able to command a degree of mass support. None had managed to fulfil all these requirements, certainly not the last. The fact that Hitler could provide the Right with mass support had led to his appointment; and the other right-wing politicians' awareness of their lack of a popular following gave them a sense of inferiority in regard to the Nazis which helped to paralyse their will.

Hitler had no blueprint or timetable for the take-over of power. Recent research is providing more and more evidence of the spontaneous and unco-ordinated way in which the 'seizure of power' occurred, with measures of far-reaching importance emerging from the pressures of immediate and unforeseen developments. Yet clearly Hitler had certain broad objectives. His main objective during his first weeks in office was to try to build up his mass support in the country in order to legitimize his own position with direct democratic sanction independent of the indirect form provided by the Constitution. This would increase his leverage not only against the right-wing politicians and pressure groups, who could command no such popular support, but against the President himself. Since Hitler's electoral support had consistently been shown to be less than 40 per cent, he now used the propaganda machine provided by his Party, assisted by the resources of the State, to project the idea that the new Government represented a 'national uprising' in which the nation was united behind a Government determined to end the crisis and to lead Germany towards a new and glorious future. In this way, he could create the myth of overwhelming support for the new regime even in the face of hard fact.

Once this myth was established, opposition to the regime wore the appearance of treason, and added weight was given to this impression by the way in which the Government exploited the alleged threat of Bolshevism. To many this appeared a real threat. But the Nazis in effect used the 'Marxists' and the Jews as an 'outgroup' in order to solidify the 'national community'. Here the Nazis were building on a tradition which went back fifty years to Bismarck's division of Germans into 'friends' and 'enemies' of the Reich, the latter including Left-Liberals, Catholics and Socialists, and later the Jews. The Weimar Republic, born out of defeat and revolution, had represented in the eyes of the Right the triumph of Bismarck's *Reichsfeinde* (enemies of the Reich). Thus to many it appeared as if Hitler was now restoring the situation which obtained before November 1918.

The psychological pressure on individuals created by this myth of a 'national uprising', particularly in the context of a desperate national crisis, was considerable: individuals and groups tended to 'coordinate' themselves, sometimes with enthusiasm, sometimes with a sense of resignation. This pressure towards conformity was increased by the knowledge that overt opposition would be mercilessly crushed. Those whom their political background marked out as unlikely to conform were intimidated into silence by the strong-arm methods of the SA and SS.

The degree of violence and intimidation exercised by the Nazi organizations has sometimes been underestimated in those accounts of the Nazi seizure of power which have stressed its pseudo-legality. The maintenance of an appearance of legality was undoubtedly an important element in Hitler's strategy for the consolidation of his power. But the element of legality was only one aspect of the situation; it was not always the one most evident at the time. The 'seizure of power' was in fact anything but peaceful. There was of course no fighting in the streets because the Left offered no resistance. During March, however, there began a 'revolution from below' on the part of the local Nazi organizations who interfered in a totally arbitrary manner with the State administration, with the course of justice and with commercial life; and this interference continued to a lesser extent throughout 1933.

It is as contrasted with the violence against individuals and the arbitrary interference on the part of the local Party organizations that the importance of this aspect of legality is most clearly seen. Hitler had been appointed Chancellor by the President acting under Article 48 of the Weimar Constitution; he headed a government which was legal in the narrow definition of that word. Once in office, he used the power to issue emergency decrees vested in the Reich President under Article 48 to strip the Constitution of its guarantees for civil liberties. In doing so he could claim to be merely taking a stage further the emergency powers used by his three predecessors. He was keeping to the letter of the Constitution even if he flouted its spirit. Moreover, maintaining the appearance of legality, he removed any qualms which might otherwise have been felt by the State officials obliged to carry out his policies. Indeed, for the civil servants and businessmen, faced with the 'revolution from below', the fact that Hitler was keeping to the letter of the law was an incentive to cooperate with the regime in the hope that this would encourage the 'moderate' Hitler to keep his local militants in check.

As far as Hitler's Nationalist partners were concerned, the fact that he moved first against the Left lulled the Right into a sense of security. In the myth of the 'national uprising' they saw a reassertion of the conservative and nationalist values to which they adhered. By the time they had become fully aware of the fact that Nazism was a totalitarian not a conservative movement, it was too late. They were now forced to realize that in co-operating with the Nazis in projecting the image of a 'national uprising' and in identifying it with Hitler's rule, they had fatally undermined their own position. They were now isolated. The only centres of power to which they could look for help were the President and the Army. The President was by now senile and unwilling to face the upheaval which would be caused by dismissing Hitler. In any case, he appears to have been fed carefully selected information by his entourage. The Army was under a Minister of Defence who sympathized with the Nazi movement, its numbers were too small in comparison to those of the SA to guarantee success, and its younger officers were increasingly falling under Nazi influence.

Nevertheless, although Hitler was not prepared to tolerate a rival political organization representing the conservative nationalists, he appreciated that he could not do without the traditional elites such as the Civil Service, Industry and the Army if he was to achieve his major goal of territorial expansion. He was therefore obliged to allow them to remain largely intact for the time being. His problem was that his rank-and-file followers in the SA and the Party, having provided the mass support and the drive which had enabled him to come to power and having then helped him to consolidate his power by terrorizing their opponents, now wished to depose these elites, take over or destroy their organizations and introduce economic policies reflecting their hostility to big business. This would clearly jeopardize Hitler's major goal of rearmament, and he was prepared, if necessary, to use drastic methods to prevent such a development.

Instead of producing a thorough-going social and economic revolution, therefore, the Nazi take-over represented a compromise between, on the one hand, the Nazi leadership who had acquired political power, and on the other, the traditional elites who retained their positions but put themselves at the service of the new regime. They were encouraged to do so by the fact that Hitler's initial objectives—the repression of the Left, rearmament, and the revision of various parts of the Versailles treaties—reflected their own wishes. But by assisting Hitler during these early years they increased his power and prestige and rendered themselves progressively superfluous. As the regime later moved towards its final goals of unbridled conquest and racial extermination, the Conservatives were replaced by technocrats or racialist fanatics who did not share their qualms at such revolutionary policies. The bravest of the Conservatives tried to make amends for their previous collaboration by going into active opposition, but once again it was too late.

5 The 'National Uprising'

1 *The Cabinet meeting of 31 January 1933*

On his appointment as Chancellor, Hitler's first objective was the elimination of the Reichstag as an effective organ either of legislation or of opposition. This could only be achieved by passing an Enabling Act for which, however, a two-thirds majority would be necessary. The first Cabinet meetings, therefore, were concerned with the question of how to secure this majority. One possibility would have been an alliance with the Catholic Centre Party. Negotiations were begun, but neither the Nazis nor the Nationalists wanted them to succeed because they knew that the Centre would demand concessions which would limit their freedom of action. Hitler therefore broke off negotiations at an early stage with the excuse that the Centre's demands were too high. Other possibilities were the suppression of the Communist Party and the confiscation of their seats, or new elections. As a condition for his acceptance of the appointment as Chancellor, Hitler had insisted on the dissolution of the Reichstag. He favoured new elections because he hoped an increased Nazi vote would add an aura of democratic legitimacy to his gradual assumption of absolute power, and would correspondingly undermine the position of the Nationalists who could claim no such sanction. Hugenberg, the Nationalist leader, had been aware of the danger of new elections in view of the fact that the Nazis now had the full power of the State behind them. However, on receiving confirmation of Hitler's promise that the composition of the Cabinet would not be altered after the election irrespective of the outcome, he acquiesced and indeed went further. According to the Cabinet minutes, the initiative for the abolition of the parliamentary system and for the deposition of the Social Democratic Government of Otto Braun in Prussia came from the non-Nazis Papen and Hugenberg, so that the Nazis, far from being restrained by their 'conservative' colleagues, merely had to acquiesce in their requests. The election was scheduled for 5 March. The Government made it clear to the electorate that the coalition would continue after the election but the Nazis and Nationalists fought the campaign as separate groups:

. . . (2) Political Situation

The Reich Chancellor reported on his conversation held on the morning of 31 January with representatives of the Centre Party, Dr Kaas and Dr Perlitius. The representatives had told him that they did not wish to join the Government at this time, although the Centre Party might abstain from opposition to the Cabinet.

The Reich Chancellor had immediately asked them whether they would consent to an extended adjournment of the Reichstag, perhaps for a year. He had received the reply that the Centre Party could not immediately consent to an adjournment for a whole year, but at the most for two months at a time. In any event, it was not inconceivable that in this way an adjournment for a whole year might be obtainable. But such an attitude on the part of the Centre Party would depend on the replies to a series of questions which Mgr Kaas wanted to send the Reich Chancellor today in writing. As Dr Kaas further stated, the Centre Party would consider a coalition only if this would include Prussia. The Centre Party representatives had been unable tó deny during the conversation that a very large part of the German people stood behind the present Government.

He would sum up the result of the conversation with the representatives of the Centre Party to the effect that a year's adjournment could not be obtained with certainty. Perhaps he could talk again about the course of the conversation and the further development of the political situation with Reich Minister Dr Hugenberg, personally.

The Reich Minister of Economics, Food and Agriculture stated he would be very glad to have such a talk.

The Reich Chancellor further stated that if a new election were held he thought that 51 per cent of the Reichstag might be found backing the present Government. He had talked on the morning of 31 January with a number of Gauleiters of the NSDAP, who had confirmed this. In his opinion, further negotiations with the Centre Party were useless; there was no alternative to a new election.

The Vice-Chancellor and Reich Commissioner of Prussia stated that it would be best to decide now that the coming election of the Reichstag would be the last one and that a return to the parliamentary system was to be avoided permanently.

The Reich Chancellor declared that he would make the following binding promises:

(a) The outcome of the new election of the Reichstag is to have no influence on the composition of the present Government;

(b) The forthcoming election of the Reichstag is to be the last election. Any return to the parliamentary system is to be absolutely avoided.

The Reich Minister of Finance pointed out that the votes in the committees of the Reichstag were gradually bringing the Reich Government into some impossible situations. The Government parties must immediately declare that, in view of the political situation, they demanded the adjournment of the committees. If an adjournment could not be obtained, the representatives of the Government parties must dissolve the committees of the Reichstag and in this way prevent them from passing resolutions.

No objections were made to this proposal of the Reich Minister of Finance.

The Reich Chancellor then read a letter received in the meantime from Dr Kaas, containing the questions to the Reich Government promised by him. The Reich Chancellor declared that it was not possible to go into the details at this time. To deal with the individual questions satisfactorily, if it was really desirable, would mean several weeks' work. In his opinion, a detailed substantive reply could not be given.

The Reich Minister of Economics, Food and Agriculture pointed out that it was urgently necessary to depose the so-called sovereign Braun Government[1] in Prussia as soon as possible. Otherwise, the civil servants in Prussia would get into an intolerable situation.

The Chancellor agreed in principle to this point of view. He then turned to the future work of the Reich Government and stated that an extension of the protection against distraint was urgently needed in the interest of the German farmer.[2] In his view, distraint proceedings against farming property must be suspended, with great respect to all claims that had arisen prior to the appointment of the present Cabinet. . . .

State Secretary Meissner pointed out that it was possible to dissolve the Prussian Diet by a decree based on Article 48 of the Reich Constitution. Such a decree will have to be based on the decision of the Supreme Court for Constitutional Questions that unity in the leadership of the State, the Reich, and Prussia, was required.

The Vice-Chancellor and Reich Commissioner of Prussia stated that in his opinion it would be best if the President were to appoint himself State President in Prussia.

State Secretary Meissner expressed certain objections to this proposal and said it would be best to obtain a voluntary dissolution of the Prussian Diet. If such a voluntary dissolution could not be obtained, a dissolution on the basis of Article 48 of the Reich Constitution could then be considered. In any case it would be necessary for the so-called Braun Government to disappear soon.

The Cabinet approved these statements.

2 A middle-class reaction to Hitler's appointment as Chancellor

The attitude of many of the upper middle class to Hitler's appointment is well summed up in the following extracts from the diary of Frau Solmitz. Her approval of the coalition aspect of the new Government, uniting Nationalists and Nazis, is significant. Her ecstatic account of the torchlight processions in Hamburg is an indication of the success of the Nazis in the projection of their take-over, at least among the middle class, as a 'national uprising', this being an essential element in their campaign.

30. i. 33

And what did Dr H. bring us? The news that his double, Hitler, is Chancellor of the Reich! And what a Cabinet!!! One we didn't dare dream of in July. Hitler, Hugenberg, Seldte, Papen!!!

On each one of them depends part of Germany's hopes. National Socialist drive, German National reason, the non-political Stahlhelm, not to forget Papen. It is so incredibly marvellous that I am writing it down quickly before the first discordant note comes, for when has Germany ever experienced a blessed summer after a

---

[1] The German Supreme Court had ruled on 25 October 1932 that the Presidential Decree of 20 July 1932, appointing a Reich Commissioner for Prussia and removing Prussian Minister-President Otto Braun and his Cabinet from office, was constitutional, but that the Decree could not deprive the Prussian Cabinet of the power to represent Prussia in her relations with the Reich, the Prussian Diet and other German States.

[2] As a result of the depression large numbers of farmers were being foreclosed for debt.

wonderful spring? Probably only under Bismarck. What a great thing Hindenburg has achieved! How well he neutralized Hammerstein[1] who was presumptuous enough to bring politics into the Reichswehr!

Huge torchlight procession in the presence of Hindenburg and Hitler by National Socialists and Stahlhelm, who at long last are collaborating again. This is a memorable 30 January!

6. ii. 33

Torchlight procession of National Socialists and Stahlhelm! A wonderfully elevating experience for all of us. Göring says the day of Hitler's and the nationalist Cabinet's appointment was something like 1914, and this too was something like 1914; after Dr H. had only recently remarked that damned little of this spirit had survived on the way from Berlin to Hamburg between 30 January and 3 February.

On Sunday, the Reds waded through relentless rain—Gisela saw them—with wives and children to make the procession longer. The Socialists and Reds will inevitably have to give in now.

But now the weather was beautiful. Dry and calm, a few degrees above freezing. At 9.30 p.m. we took up our position, Gisela with us. I said she should stay till the end for the sake of the children. So far the impressions they had had of politics had been so deplorable that they should now have a really strong impression of nationhood, as we had once, and store it in their memories. And so they did. It was 10 p.m. by the time the first torchlights came, and then 20,000 brown shirts followed one another like waves in the sea, their faces shone with enthusiasm in the light of the torches. 'Three cheers for our Führer, our Chancellor Adolf Hitler. . . .' They sang 'The Republic is shit' and called the colours 'black-red-mustard'[2] and 'The murderous reds have bloody hands and we won't forget the murder at the Sternschanz.' Dreckmann was murdered there and I happened to spot his name on one of the flags, probably the one of the section he had belonged to. The military standards are much too Roman in appearance.

Now came the Stahlhelm, a grey stream; quieter, more spiritual perhaps. On their beautiful flags they carried our old colours black-white-red,[3] with mourning crêpe at the top. Every time flags came past Fr. raised his hat, and, on the other side, four young Nazis saluted the Stahlhelm, both flags and leaders, every time by raising their arms. How wonderful and uplifting it is that the quarrels between brothers that once so depressed us have been settled! It should always be like tonight. But between the SA and the Stahlhelm there was marching a delegation of nationalist students. And they won the hearts of Hamburg. The women at the greengrocery stalls and their customers, all the women there were saying the same thing: 'Those students! Simply charming. They were the best, weren't they?'

And it was a magnificent picture, the snow-white, scarlet, moss-green and black colours, the fantastic berets, boots and gauntlets in the dancing light of the torches, the swords, the flags. They were followed by the Stahlhelm with shining *Schellenbaum*,[4] playing the old Prussian army marches.

---

[1] It had been rumoured (erroneously) that General von Hammerstein had been preparing to use the Army to avert a Nazi take-over.

[2] Black-red-gold were the colours of the Republican flag. 'Mustard' is particularly derogatory since the German word can be used colloquially to mean 'nonsense'.

[3] The colours of the old imperial flag.

[4] A musical instrument.

The SS brought up the rear of the procession.

We were drunk with enthusiasm, blinded by the light of the torches right in our faces, and always enveloped in their vapour as in a cloud of sweet incense. And in front of us men, men, men, brightly coloured, grey, brown, a torrent lasting an hour and 20 minutes. In the wavering light of the torches one seemed to see only a few types recurring again and again, but there were between twenty-two and twenty-five thousand different faces!

Next to us a little boy of three kept raising his tiny hand: 'Heil Hitler, Heil Hitlerman!'

An SA man said to Gisela that morning: 'One doesn't say Heil Hitler any more, one says Heil Germany.' 'Death to the Jews' was also sometimes called out and they sang of the blood of the Jews which would squirt from their knives. (*subsequent addition:* Who took that seriously then?)

Opposite the Eimsbüttel Sports Hall (what a pity we could not see it) stood the leader of the Hamburg National Socialists—and beside him with his hand touching his hat, the leader of the Hamburg Stahlhelm, Lieutenant-Commander Lauenstein, who a few months before had been stabbed by SA men (ten minutes from where he now stood) and now saluted the procession of the SA, just as the SA leader saluted that of the Stahlhelm. What moments! What a marvellous thought!

The National Socialists have much more new blood and young people than the Stahlhelm. Good looking, fresh, gay youths in the procession.

When everything was over, it was actually not yet over, for the last SS men were joined by a crowd of gay people with left-over torches, who made their own procession, happy to join in the occasion.

Finally, the torches were thrown together at the Kaiser Friedrich embankment, after a march from the Lübeck Gate. It was 11.30 p.m. before all was over.

Unity at last, at long last, but for how long? We are after all Germans.

What must Hitler feel when he sees the hundred thousand people whom he summoned, to whom he gave a national soul, people who are ready to die for him. Not only metaphorically speaking but in bitter earnest . . .

And these floods of people in Hamburg are only a small fraction of Hitler's support in the whole Reich. . . .

3 '*Appeal to the German People*', *31 January 1933*

The following 'Appeal to the German People' formed part of this attempt to project the image of a 'national uprising' by creating the impression of national unity and a determined Government and by describing the previous epoch as one of unmitigated disaster. By sticking to vague generalities the Government avoided specific commitments which might have alienated certain sections of the population and limited its freedom of manoeuvre. It also disguised the fact that at this stage the Government had no specific plans.

Over fourteen years have passed since that unhappy day when the German people, blinded by promises made by those at home and abroad, forgot the highest values of our past, of the Reich, of its honour and its freedom, and thereby lost everything. Since those days of treason, the Almighty has withdrawn his blessing from our nation. Discord and hatred have moved in. Filled with the deepest distress, millions of the best German men and women from all walks of life see the unity of the nation disintegrating in a welter of egoistical political opinions, economic interests, and ideological conflicts.

As so often in our history, Germany, since the day the revolution broke out, presents a picture of heartbreaking disunity. We did not receive the equality and fraternity which was promised us; instead we lost our freedom. The breakdown of the unity of mind and will of our nation at home was followed by the collapse of its political position abroad.

We have a burning conviction that the German people in 1914 went into the great battle without any thought of personal guilt and weighed down only by the burden of having to defend the Reich from attack, to defend the freedom and material existence of the German people. In the appalling fate that has dogged us since November 1918 we see only the consequence of our inward collapse. But the rest of the world is no less shaken by great crises. The historical balance of power, which at one time contributed not a little to the understanding of the necessity for solidarity among the nations, with all the economic advantages resulting therefrom, has been destroyed.

The delusion that some are the conquerors and others the conquered destroys the trust between nations and thereby also destroys the world economy. But the misery of our people is terrible! The starving industrial proletariat have become unemployed in their millions, while the whole middle and artisan class have been made paupers. If the German farmer also is involved in this collapse we shall be faced with a catastrophe of vast proportions. For in that case, there will collapse not only a Reich, but also a 2000-year-old inheritance of the highest works of human culture and civilization.

All around us are symptoms portending this breakdown. With an unparalleled effort of will and of brute force the Communist method of madness is trying as a last resort to poison and undermine an inwardly shaken and uprooted nation. They seek to drive it towards an epoch which would correspond even less to the promises of the Communist speakers of today than did the epoch now drawing to a close to the promises of the same emissaries in November 1918.

Starting with the family, and including all notions of honour and loyalty, nation and fatherland, culture and economy, even the eternal foundations of our morals and our faith—nothing is spared by this negative, totally destructive ideology. Fourteen years of Marxism have undermined Germany. One year of Bolshevism would destroy Germany. The richest and most beautiful areas of world civilization would be transformed into chaos and a heap of ruins. Even the misery of the past decade and a half could not be compared with the affliction of a Europe in whose heart the red flag of destruction had been planted. The thousands of injured, the countless dead which this battle has already cost Germany may stand as a presage of the disaster.

In these hours of overwhelming concern for the existence and the future of the German nation, the venerable World War leader [Hindenburg] appealed to us men of the nationalist parties and associations to fight under him again as once we did at the front, but now loyally united for the salvation of the Reich at home. The revered President of the Reich having with such generosity joined hands with us in a common pledge, we nationalist leaders would vow before God, our conscience and our people that we shall doggedly and with determination fulfil the mission entrusted to us as the National Government.

It is an appalling inheritance which we are taking over.

The task before us is the most difficult which has faced German statesmen in living memory. But we all have unbounded confidence, for we believe in our nation and in its eternal values. Farmers, workers, and the middle class must unite to contribute the bricks wherewith to build the new Reich.

The National Government will therefore regard it as its first and supreme task to restore to the German people unity of mind and will. It will preserve and defend the foundations on which the strength of our nation rests. It will take under its firm protection Christianity as the basis of our morality, and the family as the nucleus of our nation and our state. Standing above estates and classes, it will bring back to our people the consciousness of its racial and political unity and the obligations arising therefrom. It wishes to base the education of German youth on respect for our great past and pride in our old traditions. It will therefore declare merciless war on spiritual, political and cultural nihilism. Germany must not and will not sink into Communist anarchy.

In place of our turbulent instincts, it will make national discipline govern our life. In the process it will take into account all the institutions which are the true safeguards of the strength and power of our nation.

The National Government will carry out the great task of reorganizing our national economy with two big Four-Year Plans:

saving the German farmer so that the nation's food supply and thus the life of the nation shall be secured.

saving the German worker by a massive and comprehensive attack on unemployment.

In fourteen years the November parties have ruined the German farmer.

In fourteen years they created an army of millions of unemployed.

The National Government will carry out the following plan with iron resolution and dogged perseverance.

Within four years the German farmer must be saved from pauperism.

Within four years unemployment must be completely overcome.

Parallel with this, there emerge the prerequisites for the recovery of the economy.

The National Government will combine this gigantic project of restoring our economy with the task of putting the administration and the finances of the Reich, the states, and the communes on a sound basis.

Only by doing this can the idea of preserving the Reich as a federation acquire flesh and blood.

The idea of labour service and of settlement policy are among the main pillars of this programme.

Our concern to provide daily bread will be equally a concern for the fulfilment of the responsibilities of society to those who are old and sick.

The best safeguard against any experiment which might endanger the currency lies in economical administration, the promotion of work, and the preservation of agriculture, as well as in the use of individual initiative.

In foreign policy, the National Government will see its highest mission in the preservation of our people's right to an independent life and in the regaining thereby of their freedom. The determination of this Government to put an end to the chaotic conditions in Germany is a step towards the integration into the community of nations of a state having equal status and therefore equal rights with the rest. In so doing, the Government is aware of its great obligation to support, as the Government of a free and equal nation, that maintenance and consolidation of peace which the world needs today more than ever before.

May all others understand our position and so help to ensure that this sincere desire for the welfare of Europe and of the whole world shall find fulfilment.

Despite our love for our Army as the bearer of our arms and the symbol of our great past, we should be happy if the world, by restricting its armaments, made unnecessary any increase in our own weapons.

But if Germany is to experience this political and economic revival and conscientiously to fulfil its duties towards other nations, a decisive act is required: *We must overcome the demoralization of Germany by the Communists.*

We, men of this Government, feel responsible to German history for the reconstitution of a proper national body so that we may finally overcome the insanity of class and class warfare. We do not recognize classes, but only the German people, its millions of farmers, citizens and workers who together will either overcome this time of distress or succumb to it.

With resolution and fidelity to our oath, seeing the powerlessness of the present Reichstag to shoulder the task we advocate, we wish to commit it to the whole German people.

We therefore appeal now to the German people to sign this act of mutual reconciliation.

The Government of the National Uprising wishes to set to work, and it will work.

It has not for fourteen years brought ruin to the German nation; it wants to lead it to the summit.

It is determined to make amends in four years for the liabilities of fourteen years.

But it cannot subject the work of reconstruction to the will of those who were responsible for the breakdown.

The Marxist parties and their followers had fourteen years to prove their abilities.

The result is a heap of ruins.

Now, German people, give us four years and then judge us.

Let us begin, loyal to the command of the Field-Marshal. May Almighty God favour our work, shape our will in the right way, bless our vision and bless us with the trust of our people. We have no desire to fight for ourselves; only for Germany.

4 *A middle-class reaction to the 'Appeal to the German People'*

Again, the reaction of Frau Solmitz is probably typical of many of the educated middle class. On the one hand, there is the feeling that Hitler is not entirely reliable; on the other, the feeling that for all his lack of culture he is the only man who can galvanize the country and make Germany strong again. And there is the awareness that without him the Conservatives are powerless. 'Let him act first and then later we shall teach Hitler good, pure

German'—this illustrates the fatal delusion of the German upper classes that Hitler could be tamed.

7.ii.33
... His [Hitler's] appeal, signed by the whole Government, contains too many words of foreign derivation used in an uneducated way. But I say: let him act first, and then later we shall teach Hitler good, pure German.

19.ii.33
Unfortunately, I must say that the political scales do not come to rest.... I see Hitler exchanging bureaucrats [Bonzen] for bureaucrats, party book for party book. I hear him talk of Socialism....

The black-white-red battle front[1] represents responsibility, represents the solid citizens, morality, protection of individuality, property, free enterprise, without experiments, without the use of force—it is a powerless little group outside Hitler's mighty shadow. What can be done?

5 Georg von Schnitzler on Hitler's speech to industrialists

Although the Nazis could now command the resources of the State for their campaign in the shape of the radio and the police, Hitler insisted, in order to avoid accusations of corruption, that the election campaign should not be financed by the State. Instead, industry was requested to subsidize the campaign, as Georg von Schnitzler informed the Nuremberg Tribunal after the war:

At the end of February 1933,[2] four members of the board of I. G. Farben, including Dr Bosch, the chairman of the board, and myself, were asked by the office of the President of the Reichstag [Göring] to attend a meeting in his house, the purpose of which was not revealed. I do not remember who were the two other colleagues of mine also invited. I believe the invitation reached me during one of my business trips to Berlin. I went to the meeting which was attended by about twenty persons who, I believe, were mostly leading industrialists from the Ruhr.

Among those present I remember:
Dr Schacht, who at that time was not yet head for the second time of the Reichsbank and not yet Minister of Economics;
Krupp von Bohlen, who at the beginning of 1933 presided over the Reich Association of German Industry, which later on was changed into the semi-official organization 'Reich Group Industry';
Dr Albert Vögler, the leading man in the United Steel Works [Vereinigte Stahlwerke];
von Löwenfeld, from an industrial firm in Essen;
Dr Stein, head of the Gewerkschaft Auguste Victoria, a mine which belongs to the I.G.; Dr Stein was an active member of the German People's Party.
I remember that Dr Schacht acted as a kind of host.

[1] The 'Kampffront Schwarz-Weiss-Rot', formed on 10 February for the election out of the German Nationalist Party and the Stahlhelm.
[2] On 20 February.

Whereas I had expected Göring to appear, Hitler entered the room, shook hands with everybody and took a seat at the head of the table. In a long speech he talked mainly about the danger of Communism over which he claimed to have just won a decisive victory.

He then talked about the alliance into which his party and the German National People's Party had entered. This latter party had in the meantime been reorganized by Herr von Papen. At the end he came to the point which was apparently the purpose of the meeting. He stressed how important it was that the two aforementioned parties should gain the majority in the forthcoming Reichstag election. Krupp von Bohlen thanked Hitler for his speech. After Hitler had left the room, Dr Schacht proposed to the meeting the raising of an election fund of, as far as I remember, RM 3,000,000. The fund should be distributed between the two allies according to their relative strength at that time. Dr Stein suggested that the German People's Party should be included and this suggestion was, if I remember rightly, accepted. The amount which the individual firms had to contribute was not discussed. . . .

6 *Excerpts from Hitler's speech*

. . . Private enterprise cannot be maintained in the age of democracy; it is conceivable only if the people have a sound idea of authority and personality. Everything positive, good and valuable, which has been achieved in the world in the field of economics and culture, is solely attributable to the importance of personality. When, however, the defence of the existing order, its political administration, is left to a majority, it will go under irretrievably. All the worldly goods which we possess we owe to the struggle of the chosen. Had we had the present conditions in the Middle Ages, the foundations of our German Reich would never have been laid. The same mentality that was the basis for obtaining these values must be used to preserve these values. . . . It is, however, not enough to say: We do not want Communism in our economy. If we continue on our old political course, then we shall perish. We have fully experienced in the past years that economics and politics cannot be separated. The political conduct of the struggle is the primary, decisive factor. Therefore, politically clear conditions must be reached. As economics alone has not made the German Reich, so politics did not make economics. But each one built steadily higher upon the other. Just as politics and economics working hand in hand brought us to the top, so the working of one against the other, as we experienced it after the revolution, meant our continuous decline. As I lay in hospital in 1918, I went through the revolution in Bavaria. From the very beginning I saw it as a crisis in the development of the German people, as a period of transition. Life always tears humanity apart. It is, therefore, the noblest task of a leader to find ideals that are stronger than the factors which pull people apart. I recognized, even while in hospital, that new ideas must be sought conducive to reconstruction. I found them in Nationalism, in the value of personality, in the denial of reconciliation between nations, in the strength and power of individual personality. . . .

Now we are facing the last election. No matter what the outcome, there will be no retreat, even if the coming election does not bring about a decision. If the election does not decide, the decision must be brought about in one way or another by other means. I have intervened in order to give the people once more the chance of deciding their fate for themselves. This determination is a strong asset for whatever may happen later. If the election brings no result, well, Germany will not be ruined. Today, as never before, everyone is under an obligation to pledge themselves to success. The need to make sacrifices has never been greater than now. As for the economy, I have only one wish—that together with the internal political structure it may look forward to a calm future. The question of the restoration of the armed forces will not be decided at Geneva[1] but in Germany, when we have gained internal strength through internal peace. There will, however, be no internal peace until Marxism is eliminated. Here lies the decision which we must face up to, hard as the struggle may be. I put my life into this struggle day after day as do all those who have joined me in it. There are only two possibilities: either to resist the opponent by constitutional means, and for this purpose, once again, the election is necessary; or the struggle will be conducted with other weapons, which may demand greater sacrifices. I would like to see them avoided. I hope therefore that the German people recognize the greatness of the hour. It will be decisive for the next ten or probably even the next hundred years. It will prove a turning-point in German history, to which I pledge myself with burning energy.

At the same meeting Göring was even more specific:

Göring: He counted on the fact that with political appeasement, the domestic economy would also settle down. No experiments would be made. However, to attain the goal, all forces must be mustered on 5 March. Above all, it is important to penetrate into those circles which are still under the influence of Marxism and slumber uselessly in an aggrieved and bitter state. Most of the internal political obstacles have been removed after the achievement of unity on one platform with the other groups with a similar ideology. This existing unity should be made stronger. No matter how the election turned out, the distribution of forces should remain the same. In the coming struggle everyone must perform in his own field. The German Nationalists will attack where successes can no longer be achieved by the National Socialists. On the other hand, the National Socialists will be given a task which the others cannot carry out. Undoubtedly we must do the most work, for we must penetrate with our SA men into the darkest quarters of the cities and operate there by word of mouth and fight for every single soul.

Göring considered some of the great dangers associated with this election battle. He then led on very cleverly to the necessity of other circles, which were not taking part in this political battle, making at least the financial sacrifices so necessary at this time. These were all the more necessary because not one penny of the taxpayers' money would be requested. Government funds would not be used. The sacrifices asked for would be the easier for industry to bear if it was realized that the election of 5 March would certainly be the last for the next ten years, probably even for the next hundred years.

7 *Göring's order to the Prussian police, 17 February 1933*

In the meantime Göring, through his control of the Prussian administration and police, had taken the initiative against the Nazis' opponents. A purge was

[1] Where a Disarmament Conference was being held.

carried out among the numerous SPD, Centre and Liberal police chiefs, and in the provincial administration in general. Even those who were not immediately affected were clearly intimidated. Moreover, on 17 February Göring issued the following order to the police throughout Prussia:

I assume that it is unnecessary to point out especially that the police must in all circumstances avoid giving even the appearance of a hostile attitude, still less the impression of persecuting the patriotic associations [the Nazi Storm Detachments and the Stahlhelm]. I expect all police authorities to maintain the best relations with these organizations which comprise the most important constructive forces of the State. Patriotic activities and propaganda are to be supported by every means. Police restrictions and impositions must be used only in the most urgent cases.

The activities of subversive organizations are on the contrary to be combated with the most drastic methods. Communist terrorist acts and attacks are to be proceeded against with all severity, and weapons must be used ruthlessly when necessary. Police officers who in the execution of this duty use their firearms will be supported by me without regard to the effect of their shots; on the other hand, officers who fail from a false sense of consideration may expect disciplinary measures.

The protection of the patriotic population, which has been continually hampered in its activities, demands the most drastic application of the legal regulations against banned demonstrations, illegal assemblies, looting, instigation to treason and sedition, mass strikes, risings, press offences, and the other punishable acts of the disturbers of order. Every official must constantly bear in mind that failure to act is more serious than errors committed in acting. I expect and hope that all officers feel themselves at one with me in the aim of saving our fatherland from the ruin which threatens it by strengthening and unifying the patriotic forces.

8 Intimidation of the Social Democrats

On 22 February, Göring issued an order authorizing the employment of SA and SS men and Stahlhelmers as auxiliary police, in order to give them official status and as a means of controlling them. They were issued with armbands and firearms and were officially placed under the authority of the police. But since they were employed as units rather than as individuals, they were in fact able to act to some extent independently, particularly since they could claim to be the true representatives of the new regime.

The new attitude of the police brought about by Göring, together with the activities of the SA, did not fail to have its effects on the Party's opponents:

24.ii.33: Grzesinski (former SPD Police-President in Berlin)
to the SPD Secretaries Franz Klupsch (Dortmund),
Paul Röhle (Frankfurt am Main), Paul Bugdahn (Altona)
and Richard Hansen (Kiel) on the need to cancel meetings.

Dear Comrade,
The incidents of the past few days in the meetings of those comrades who might

be called prominent have prompted the Party committee this morning to examine the question whether, in the interests of our audiences, it would not be better to withdraw these speakers, of which I am one, for the time being. Several of my meetings have been disrupted and a considerable section of the audience had to be taken away badly injured. In agreement with the Party committee, I therefore request the cancellation of meetings with me as speaker. As things are, there is obviously no longer any police protection sufficient to check the aggressive actions of the SA and SS at my meetings.

In Hindenburg Comrade Nölting barely escaped being killed. I had a similar experience in Langenbielau. One of my companions was knocked down. In Breslau last night a terrible disaster was only prevented by the chance delay of SA formations which had been mobilized. None the less, a great number were injured, and in a city which has so far been able to prevent the disruption of meetings by opponents.

I myself deeply regret having to inform you of this and having to reach this decision. It was only made after thorough consultation with members of the Party committee and after similar decisions were made about other comrades. The dog whip[1] seems to have annoyed the Nazis quite a bit.

Nevertheless, with Party greetings and Freedom!

9 *Resignations from the Hanover branch of the SPD*

17 February 1933

I hereby return my membership card and signify my resignation from the Party.

I am and remain a 'religious socialist'. Under the pressure of circumstances the SPD, even against its will, will be pushed aside and into the methods of left-wing radicalism. On the other hand, pressure from the opposite side will grow. The only thing left for me to do in all conscience as a teacher, a Christian, and a German is to try to evade the double pressure and, as ten years ago, try to live for my job, my family and my books, without being a member of a party.

Yours faithfully, GEORGE M.

4 March 1933

The development of the political situation in the last few years has left me rather tired. I would like some peace and hereby signify my resignation from your organization.

I shall of course fulfil my duties as a citizen as before.

Yours truly, KARL M.

9 March 1933

In accordance with Paragraph 9 of the organization statutes, I hereby signify my resignation and that of my wife with immediate effect. . . .

As a civil servant I have to make a choice. On the one hand, I see how the tendency is growing on the part of my employer, the Reich, not to tolerate those employees belonging to anti-Government associations. On the other hand, there is my loyalty to the Party. Unfortunately, I see no other solution but my resignation. The existence of my family is at stake. If the fate of unemployment, which in

[1] On 7 February 1932, in a speech in Leipzig, Grzesinski had said Hitler should be driven out of Germany with a dog whip.

my experience can be *very*, *very* hard, is unavoidable, I need not reproach myself for not having done everything in the interests of my wife and child.

                                                             HANS J.

10 *The Chief of the Gestapo on the Reichstag fire, 27 February 1933*

Then, on 27 February, a week before the election, the Reichstag building was set on fire and a young Dutch Communist named van der Lubbe was caught apparently red-handed in the building. The fire came very conveniently for the Nazis who could use it to claim the Communists were plotting revolution and so justify wholesale arrests. So convenient was it that until recently it was thought probable that the Nazis themselves started the fire and blamed it on the Communist van der Lubbe, whom they had used as a dupe. Recently, however, Fritz Tobias has argued[1] that van der Lubbe himself was solely responsible and the majority of historians now accept this version. One contemporary witness who believed this was the police chief in charge of the investigation, Rudolf Diels, the head of the Prussian political police soon to become known as the Gestapo. Looking back after the war, he wrote:

On that rainy evening in early spring, I was called away from a cosy and highly unofficial rendezvous in the Café Krantzler, Unter den Linden, by my old colleague, Schneider, with the cry, 'The Reichstag is on fire!' When I pushed my way into the burning building with Schneider, we had to climb over the bulging hoses of the Berlin fire brigade, although, as yet, there were few onlookers. A few officers of my department were already engaged in interrogating Marinus van der Lubbe. Naked from the waist upwards, smeared with dirt and sweating, he sat in front of them, breathing heavily. He panted as if he had completed a tremendous task. There was a wild triumphant gleam in the burning eyes of his pale, haggard young face. I sat opposite him in the police headquarters several times that night and listened to his confused stories. I read the Communist pamphlets he carried in his trouser pockets. They were of the kind which in those days were publicly distributed everywhere. And from the primitive hieroglyphics of his diary I tried to follow his trips down to the Balkans.

The voluntary confessions of Marinus van der Lubbe prevented me from thinking that an arsonist who was such an expert in his folly needed any helpers. Why should not a single match be enough to set fire to the cold yet inflammable splendour of the Chamber, the old upholstered furniture, the heavy curtains, and the bone-dry wooden panelling! But this specialist had used a whole knapsack full of inflammable material. He had been so active that he had laid several dozen fires. With a firelighter, the 'Industrious Housewife', he had set the Chamber aflame. Then he had rushed through the big corridors with his burning shirt which he brandished in his right hand like a torch to lay more fires under the old leather sofas. During this hectic activity he was overpowered by Reichstag officials.

He also confessed to several smaller arson attacks in Berlin, the mysterious

---

[1] In *The Reichstag Fire* (London 1965).

cause of which had aroused the attention of the Criminal Investigation Department. Several details suggested that Communist arsonists who had helped him in Neukölln and the Berlin Town Hall might have helped him with the Reichstag. The interrogating officers had pointed their investigations in this direction. But meanwhile things of a quite different nature had happened.

Shortly after my arrival in the burning Reichstag, the National Socialist elite had arrived. Hitler and Goebbels had driven up in their large cars; Göring, Frick and Helldorf[1] arrived; Daluege, the police chief, was not there.

One of Hitler's chief adjutants came to look for me in the maze of corridors, now alive with the fire brigade and the police. He passed me Göring's order to appear in the select circle. On a balcony jutting out into the Chamber, Hitler and his trusty followers were assembled. Hitler stood leaning his arms on the stone parapet of the balcony and stared silently into the red sea of flames. The first hysterics were already over. As I entered, Göring came towards me. His voice was heavy with the emotion of the dramatic moment: 'This is the beginning of the Communist revolt, they will start their attack now! Not a moment must be lost!'

Göring could not continue. Hitler turned to the assembled company. Now I saw that his face was purple with agitation and with the heat gathering in the dome. He shouted uncontrollably, as I had never seen him do before, as if he was going to burst: 'There will be no mercy now. Anyone who stands in our way will be cut down. The German people will not tolerate leniency. Every Communist official will be shot where he is found. The Communist deputies must be hanged this very night. Everybody in league with the Communists must be arrested. There will no longer be any leniency for Social Democrats either.'

I reported on the results of the first interrogations of Marinus van der Lubbe—that in my opinion he was a maniac. But with this opinion I had come to the wrong man; Hitler ridiculed my childish view: 'That is something really cunning, prepared a long time ago. The criminals have thought all this out beautifully; but they've miscalculated, haven't they, Comrades! These gangsters have no idea to what extent the people are on our side. They don't hear the rejoicing of the crowds in their rat holes, from which they now want to emerge', and so it went on.

I pulled Göring aside; but he did not let me start. 'Police on an emergency footing; shoot to kill; and any other emergency regulations which might be appropriate in such a case.' I said again that a police radio message would be sent to all police stations in his name, putting the police in a state of alert and ordering the arrest of those Communist officials whose imprisonment had been intended for some time in the event of a ban on the Party. Göring was not listening: 'No Communist and no Social Democrat traitor must be allowed to escape us' were his last words. When I met Schneider again I tried to collect my thoughts:

'This is a mad-house, Schneider, but apart from that the time has come: all Communist and Social Democrat officials are to be arrested, big raids, a state of alert and all that goes with it!'

Schneider forgot the Social Democrats when he passed on Göring's order as a radio message. When I returned to the 'Alex'[2] after midnight it was buzzing like a beehive. The alerted operational battalions of the police stood lined up in long rows in the entrance drives with steel helmets and rifles. While squad vans arrived

---

[1] Count Wolf von Helldorf, the Berlin SA Chief.
[2] The police headquarters in the Alexanderplatz.

and whole troops of detectives with registers prepared many years before jumped on the ramps, joined by uniformed officers, the first cars were arriving back at the entrance of the building with dazed prisoners who had been woken up from their sleep. In my room I met Count Schimmelpfennig, Goebbels's adjutant. He had come to take me to his boss. Goebbels wanted to hear my account of the affair. I had again become uncertain as to whether the Communist Party was behind the arson and whether it was meant as a signal for the uprising, though there were several pointers to it. Despite his steadfast proletarian confession, the flickering eyes of Marinus van der Lubbe puzzled me. 'I did it and I want my punishment' was his stereotype phrase, repeated in broad German-Dutch. But my reflections were completely irrelevant to the course of events. During my conversation with Goebbels, whom I met on this occasion, Göring had already achieved a *fait accompli*. He had not accepted the matter-of-fact account which his press adviser had drafted and which left all the possibilities for judging the deed open. He had himself composed a wild flourish of trumpets as he had done a week after the Liebknecht House[1] had been given a good going over. At midnight it was broadcast through the Wolf telegraph office and the Telegraph Union.

11 *Presidential Decree for the Protection of People and State, 28 February 1933*

Whoever was responsible, there is no doubt that the Nazis exploited their opportunity to the full. Yet it appears, both from Diels's account and from other evidence, that the measures which followed were not carefully planned and coordinated but were rather spontaneous and largely irrational responses to an imagined threat of a Communist uprising. The arrests of the Communists, for example, were carried out on the basis of lists drawn up by the political police before 1933 and they were not as successful as was subsequently claimed. In fact, the Nazis had hoped to postpone the elimination of the Communists until after the election when they would be in a stronger position to deal with them. But their fear of an uprising prompted them to take precipitate and drastic action which resulted not only in these arrests, but in the most important single legislative act of the Third Reich, the Decree of the Reich President for the Protection of People and State, of 28 February 1933.

The origins of this decree are not entirely clear. It appears that the original impulse came from a German Nationalist, Ludwig Grauert, who was a top official in the Prussian Ministry of the Interior. During the night of the 27th, wishing to legalize the arrests, Grauert suggested an 'emergency decree against arson and terrorist acts'. Hitler accepted the suggestion and put it on the agenda of the Reich Cabinet meeting to be held on the following day. It seems probable that at this stage both Grauert and Hitler had conceived the decree as a purely defensive measure directed specifically against the Communists. Before the Cabinet meeting, however, the Reich Minister of the Interior, Frick, took over the drafting of the measure. Under the Weimar Constitution the powers of the Reich Minister of the Interior were

---

[1] The Communist Party headquarters in Berlin.

restricted. Direct authority over the police and internal administration was in the hands of the state governments. Frick now decided to use the opportunity presented by this decree to strengthen his control over the states. He decided to base the new decree on the Prussian decree of 20 July 1932 which had legalized the *coup* against the Social Democrat/Centre Party Government and he thereby gave it a far wider scope than originally intended. Thus Article 2 enabled Frick, as Reich Minister of the Interior, to take over power in the states and, unlike Papen's Prussian decree of July 1932, the Reich Government and not the Reich President decided when Article 2 should be applied. This Article was to be of crucial importance in the seizure of power in the states during the first half of March. But no less important was Article 1. This represented 'a kind of *coup d'état*'[1] and the suspension of civil rights which it contained provided a quasi-legal foundation for the regime of terror and intimidation which was to follow. In particular, it provided the legal warrant for the expedient of 'protective custody' used by the Gestapo to imprison without trial:

By the authority of Section 48 (2) of the German Constitution the following is decreed as a defensive measure against Communist acts of violence endangering the State:

1. Sections 114, 115, 117, 118, 123, 124 and 153 of the Constitution of the German Reich are suspended until further notice. Thus restrictions on personal liberty, on the right of free expression of opinion, including freedom of the press, on the right of assembly and association, and violations of the privacy of postal, telegraphic and telephonic communications, and warrants for house-searches, orders for confiscations as well as restrictions on property rights are permissible beyond the legal limits otherwise prescribed.

2. If in any German state the measures necessary for the restoration of public security and order are not taken, the Reich Government may temporarily take over the powers of the supreme authority in such a state in order to restore security.

3. States and local authorities have to comply to the limits of their responsibilities with the orders issued by the Government of the Reich under the powers conferred on it by Paragraph 2. . . .

12   *A Hamburg lady on Government actions against the Communists*

Although the Government failed to produce any concrete evidence of a Communist plot, its propaganda had a receptive audience among the middle class. Frau Solmitz recorded in her diary:

1.iii.33
. . . The Reich Government spoke. . . . Göring, like an old greying civil servant,

---

[1] cf. the important article by Hans Mommsen, 'Der Reichstagsbrand und seine politischen Folgen' in the *Vierteljahrshefte für Zeitgeschichte*, vol. 12, no. 4 (October 1964), on which this analysis is based.

reported dryly and very gravely the dreadful murder plans of the Communists—
who have withdrawn into the stronghold of Hamburg. It started with the going
over of the Karl Liebknecht House, where a whole system of underground tunnels
was discovered, as well as galleries above ground. . . . Proof was brought to light by
the hundredweight. Hostages from bourgeois circles, wives and children of police
officers were to be taken and used as shields, all cultural monuments were to be
destroyed as in Russia: palaces, museums, churches. They started with the
Reichstag. Fire broke out in twenty-eight places. All the Communist Party leaders
have been taken into custody. Thälmann has fled to Copenhagen. They wanted to
send armed gangs to murder and start fires in the villages; in the meantime terrorism
was to take over the big cities stripped of their police forces. Poison, boiling water,
every tool from the most refined to the most primitive, were to be used as weapons.
It would sound like a fairy tale of robbers—if it wasn't for Russia having experienced methods and orgies of torture which a German mind, even when sick,
is incapable of devising, and, when healthy, is unable to believe.

If Italy, America and England were wise, they should send us money to fight
Bolshevism—our ruin will be their ruin!

Göring said he had not lost his nerve nor would he lose it. I hope the voters
won't lose their nerve and stay away from the polling booths out of fright. The
streets really are dangerous these days.

In the Reichstag election on 5 March 1933 the Nazis won 288 seats compared with 196 in the November 1932 election and increased their percentage of the vote from 33·1 to 43·9. Thus despite the fact that Hitler was
now Chancellor of Germany and despite the Party's control over the radio
and the Prussian police, they had still failed to win an absolute majority.
The Nationalists had gained only one seat, winning 52, and their percentage
of the very heavy poll of 88 per cent had declined slightly. However, the
Government coalition between Nazis and Nationalists had now a bare overall
majority of 51·7 per cent, though this was not sufficient to pass an Enabling
Act for which a two-thirds majority was necessary.

The opposition parties maintained their position remarkably well,
particularly in view of such difficult circumstances. The Catholic Centre
actually gained three seats, winning 73, and its percentage of the larger poll
declined only slightly. The SPD lost only one seat, still retaining 120, and
their proportion of the poll declined by only 2 per cent. It was significant
that in Prussia, where the impact of the new regime had had most effect as a
result of Göring's ruthless measures, Nazi success was more limited. In the
State Diet election which took place on the same day as the Reichstag election
the Nazis only managed to increase their vote from 36·3 per cent to 43·2
per cent and to win 49 additional seats. Here the Nationalists managed to
win 12 more seats, which suggests that some people hoped to strengthen the
Conservative wing of the coalition in the light of their experience with
Göring and the Nazis. It was in the south German states that the electoral
success of the Nazis was most striking, notably in Bavaria, most of which had
hitherto been resistant to Nazism. Here the anti-Bolshevist campaign

appears to have paid dividends with the very conservative rural voters. This breakthrough in the south German states offered the Nazis an opportunity to demand that these states now adjust their politics to the new regime, an opportunity which they were not slow to exploit.

6 The Seizure of Power in the States and the SA/Party 'Revolution from Below' of March 1933

While covering the election campaign, the *Times* correspondent in Germany had remarked on 'the starkness of the contrast between conditions in Prussia and in states where the Reich Government have not yet taken charge of the State affairs, or where the Nazis have not yet obtained local control'.[1] In fact the majority of the federal states were not yet controlled by the Nazis, and here the authorities which had responsibility for the police and for public order in general endeavoured to maintain an attitude of neutrality towards the various and conflicting forces and to preserve the basic liberties.

The Nazis, however, were determined to remove this contrast between Prussia and the other states and now proceeded to exploit the momentum created by the election campaign to seize power in the states. For this purpose, they used a combination of intimidation from below by mass action on the part of the Party and the SA, and pressure from above by the Reich Ministry of the Interior which was in the hands of a Nazi, Wilhelm Frick. The SA created disorder, usually culminating in the hoisting of the swastika on the town hall, and then the local Party leadership requested the Reich Ministry of the Interior to intervene on the ground that the existing state authorities were incapable of maintaining order and showed insufficient sympathy with the new Reich Government. The Reich Minister of the Interior then appointed a leading local Nazi as a Reich Police Commissioner. This possibility was explicitly provided for in the Presidential Decree of 28 February (Art. 2).[2] Once they were in control of the police, the local Nazis could intimidate the state governments into resignation, leading to the formation of Nazi governments.

1 *The seizure of power in Hamburg*

The first state to experience this technique was Hamburg, where it occurred just before the election. The process was begun by a demand from Frick for a ban on the SPD newspaper, the *Hamburg Echo*. What then happened is recounted by a Nationalist senator, Paul de Chapeaurouge, in a letter of complaint to Papen, written on 9 March:

Having retired from the Senate and a new Senate having been elected, my sense of honour and of duty towards the Reich Government obliges me to refer once again to the events which took place in Hamburg on 3–5 March. I take the

[1] *The Times*, 21 February 1933.
[2] See above, p. 174.

liberty of sending this letter to you because, on account of my convictions, I feel closest to you among all the leading gentlemen of the Reich Government.

My impression of the events of these days is as follows:

On the morning of 3 March, the Social Democrat senators resigned from the Senate because they did not want to consent to the ban on the *Echo* contemplated by the Reich Government. The remaining bourgeois senators pronounced this ban, which was undoubtedly permissible by law, as their first official act.

After the resignation of the Social Democrat senators, I, as the previous deputy police chief, had to take over the police. I knew that I had taken on a very difficult office. But I had no idea that my administration would prove as difficult as it at once became owing to the activities of the Reich Ministry of the Interior. . . .

After the resignation of the Social Democrat senators, the Senate's first duty was to continue to carry out its functions in accordance with a strict observance of the Constitution and the laws until the new election, and to try its best to achieve an early election [of the senate]. This I was determined to do.

The Reich Government had the clear duty of supporting the Senate as the official organ of legal power. In my opinion, the Reich Ministry of the Interior, which is mainly responsible for relations with the states, failed in its task. To a large extent it bears the responsibility for the developments in Hamburg. The city was quite calm; according to absolutely reliable information given to the police, no serious disturbance of public order was to be expected from the Left. The course of events has proved the correctness of this opinion held by the police authorities.

Unrest occurred in Hamburg only because a few authorities, especially the *Gau* leadership of the NSDAP, sent alarmist reports to Berlin and caused the Reich Minister of the Interior to ask the Senate officially to transfer the command of the police to the former police lieutenant, Richter.[1] This suggestion was apparently passed on from Berlin simultaneously to the NSDAP and the press. In Hamburg it was underlined by wild press articles and by pressure on the members of the Senate in personal discussions in a most questionable way, and thus the situation was aggravated.

The course which the Senate should have followed was laid down in the Constitution. According to the Constitution and the law, it was unable to meet the request which had been made. In my opinion, since the election to the Senate was obviously to take place shortly, it was the Reich Minister's duty to urge the *Gau* leadership of the NSDAP, which prided itself on its constant contact with the Ministry, to maintain law and order so that the Constitution and the law would not be broken before the forthcoming election. But, so far as I could observe events, there were no such attempts at persuasion. Despite the alarmist press articles, Hamburg remained completely peaceful; only the police, among whom the NSDAP had begun an active propaganda campaign some time before, began to waver.[2] . . .

. . . The Hamburg events were, in my opinion, determined by the NSDAP's intention, known to me since 3 March, of gaining control of the police before the election of the Senate. This aim could not be achieved owing to the present legal position in Hamburg. Therefore, the NSDAP tried to reach their goal via the Reich. Owing to the fact that the NSDAP did not want to wait over the police

[1] An SA leader.

[2] A section of the police sympathetic to the Nazis hoisted the swastika on the town hall.

question, circumstances have developed in Hamburg which are very regrettable from the point of view of police discipline and public order in the future.

The fact was noted that the final order of the Reich Minister of the Interior to the Senate to give the command of the police to Police Lieutenant Richter apparently reached the *Gau* headquarters of the NSDAP before it reached the Senate. Furthermore, the way in which Gauleiter Kaufman and Harry Hennigsen, [NSDAP] member of the city council, conveyed the order of the Reich Ministry of the Interior to the Senate was in no way appropriate to the importance and gravity of the moment.

It is my firm conviction that, if the Reich Ministry of the Interior had used its full authority to persuade the NSDAP to keep the peace, Hamburg would have been spared the events of 5 March, so constitutionally and politically unsatisfactory. The situation now is that, contrary to the solemn promises of the Reich Government, an interference in Hamburg's sovereignty has taken place which could have been avoided and is undesirable from the point of view of the initial work on the Reich reform. . . .

I must add a few personal remarks: I regard the procedure of the Reich Ministry of the Interior towards Hamburg as at the same time an injustice towards myself. The Reich Ministry knows who I am and where I stand politically and as a soldier. I met State Secretary Pfundtner only a few weeks ago at a dinner of the local Nationalist Club, of which I have been a member since its foundation, given in honour of the presence of His Royal Highness the Duke of Coburg-Gotha. In former times there was a way by which a German officer, a German graduate could take the law into his own hands. Today, unfortunately, I have to confine myself to asking you, Vice-Chancellor, to inform the Reich Government of my letter in the hope that they will then adopt the correct attitude towards me. . . .

During the next few days, all the other states were taken over in a similar fashion. The most important state, Prussia, was already effectively under the control of the new regime. In the first place, the administration had already been purged of Social Democrats and Democrats after Papen's *coup* in July 1932.[1] Secondly, although Papen as Reich Commissioner for Prussia was theoretically superior to Göring as Minister of the Interior, in practice Papen did not interfere because at this stage Göring's activities were directed against the Left. Furthermore, immediately after the appointment of Hitler as Chancellor, on 6 February, all the representative bodies within Prussia were dissolved and new elections were ordered; on 5 March for the Landtag, on 13 March for the provincial and local councils.

Once the 'coordination' was complete, the Nazis proceeded to provide more solid legal foundations for their power in the states. First, they ensured themselves a majority in the other state assemblies through a law of 31 March. Secondly, by a law of 7 April, special Reich Governors (*Reichsstatthalter*) were appointed to the states, and these were nearly all chosen from the senior Gauleiters in the area.[2]

[1] See above, p. 134.
[2] For this law see below, pp. 239–40.

2 *The SA/Party revolution in March 1933*

The pressure from below which emerged at the time of the election, and which was necessary for the coordination of the states, erupted into an orgy of violence against the Party's opponents, particularly those on the Left. It is uncertain to what extent this violence was initiated from above or whether it occurred largely spontaneously. What is clear is that it rapidly got out of control. Essentially, it represented the unleashing of all the frustration which had been pent up in the SA and local Party organizations during the pre-1933 period through the need to follow a policy of strict legality. Now the Party's rank and file, who had fought so hard and for so long and whose hopes had been frustrated so often, saw at last the possibility both of taking revenge on their opponents and of acquiring the prizes of power. As far as they were concerned, it was now their state and they were not in a mood for compromise or half-measures. As a result, during the following weeks trade union offices were smashed and Social Democrat officials were 'arrested' by SA men, cruelly beaten up and dragged off to hastily improvised concentration camps. The SA and local Party officials also seized the opportunity to exploit their position by intimidating Business into giving them employment in one form or another. A kind of protection racket developed. The following account by the first head of the Gestapo, Rudolf Diels, gives a good impression of the confusion and violence which characterized the first months of the allegedly peaceful national uprising:

The uprising of the Berlin SA electrified the remotest parts of the country. Around many big cities in which the authority of the police had been transferred to the local SA leaders, revolutionary activities took place beyond the periphery of these cities throughout the whole area of their regiments [*Standarten*] and groups. The higher the rank of these police-presidents, the farther afield extended the noisy abuses of these parhelions of the revolution. In Lower Silesia, the SA Gruppenführer [Edmund Heines] carried on a regime of violence from Breslau. In the North Rhineland, SS Gruppenführer Weitzel, the newly appointed police president of Düsseldorf, displayed violent radicalism together with the SA leader Lobek; in Essen and the cities of the Ruhr area, the SA of Terboven[1] held sway.

In East Prussia, Gauleiter Koch had allowed neither the SA nor the SS to come to power. Here the political leaders ruled. They were opposed to the 're-actionary' elements. The country was in a sort of state of war in which the aristo-cracy, as the imagined enemy, had to put up with a flood of arrests. From Stettin, the example of the SS Standartenführer, Engel, encouraged the Pomeranian SA to terrorize the country. From the cities of Rostock, Stargard and Greifswald, cases of beatings up were reported in which Communists and Social Democrats had been subjected to mock drownings and hangings. The torments had cost some victims their lives. In Silesia, the Rhineland, Westphalia and the Ruhr area unauthorized arrests, insubordination to the police, forcible entry into public buildings,

[1] Josef Terboven, Gauleiter of Essen 1928-45.

disturbance of the work of the authorities, the smashing up of dwellings and nightly raids had begun before the Reichstag fire at the end of February. . . .

It was no longer possible to tell which public or private spheres had been penetrated by the SA, and scarcely possible to guess the purposes for which it allowed itself to be hired and employed. There was hardly a single business undertaking which had not employed an 'old fighter' of the SA for protection against the dangers of coordination, denunciation and threats. They were present everywhere as self-appointed directors, special commissars and SA delegates. . . .

3 The first concentration camps

. . . No order and no instruction exists for the establishment of the concentration camps; they were not established, one day they were simply there. The SA leaders put up 'their' camps because they did not want to trust the police with their prisoners or because the prisons were overcrowded. No information about many of these *ad hoc* camps ever got as far as Berlin. Years after my departure from Berlin I heard of the existence of some camps of which I had no knowledge in 1933. We first heard of a camp in Kemma in the Ruhr area through the foreign press. It was the American journalist Lochner who informed the state police office that the [SA] group leader Heines had established a concentration camp near Dürrgoy in Silesia. . . .

4 The occupation of the Volksfreund House in Brunswick

In the state of Brunswick, where the Nazis had formed a coalition government with the Nationalists since 1930, relations between the Nazis and their opponents had always been particularly bad. The Nazis now took their revenge, as the following account published by the SPD in exile indicates:

From 3 March 1933 the atmosphere in the town and the countryside became unbearable. One brawl after another. There were growing rumours that the *Volksfreund*[1]—the [SPD] Party, trade union and publishing house building of the workers—was to be raided by National Socialists. All demonstrations were banned. On 9 March at 11 a.m. a fight started between an SS member, obviously sent out for the purpose of provocation, and a member of the *Reichsbanner*. At about 12 noon a small police car appeared in front of the *Volksfreund* building with about ten policemen and the SS man who was alleged to have been beaten up. They searched the *Volksfreund* for the member of the *Reichsbanner* who had taken part in the fight and who, according to them, was in the building. The search of course was fruitless.

At about 3 p.m. the [SPD] parliamentary group of the provincial diet held a meeting. Meanwhile the SA and the SS continued their activities of the previous day; under the eyes of the authorities they hoisted swastika flags on public buildings. The Nazis also tore a large poster off the boathouse of the *Reichsbanner* in the presence of the police and carried it through the town, heading for the *Volksfreund*.

There, lorries with SA and SS had driven up at 4.05 p.m. The porter promptly closed the doors. But the Nazis broke the big display windows and pushed into

[1] The SPD paper.

the building through the holes. They opened fire inside the building with a number of rifles and revolvers. During this, the 28-year-old salesman, Hans Saile, the advertising manager of the Advertising Union, Berlin, was killed by a shot in the stomach. He had received an order from his superiors to leave the threatened district of Brunswick and to travel to Saarbrücken on the same day. . . .

The intruders rushed up the stairs and smashed in the locked doors with their rifle butts. Union secretaries, employees, typists, Co-op salesgirls were all driven together with cudgels, rifles, revolvers and daggers. Then, with the order 'Hands up!', they were locked up for hours, before being released with kicks and slaps.

Although the leadership of the organization had endeavoured for weeks to remove important and valuable material and funds from the building, they did not succeed in securing all the money, books and documents in time. So several thousand Reichsmarks were confiscated by the intruders on their own authority. The whole building was searched for valuables. Then the swastika flag was hoisted. A certain worker, A.P., had hidden behind a cupboard as the Nazis broke in. He had seen from there how the account books had been destroyed in childish vandalism. He had heard the men grumbling that their booty of money and valuables had been far too small. A.P. was discovered, badly beaten up and then thrown out of the building.

The former police lieutenant, Richard Neuenfeldt, now a driver with the *Volksfreund*, who lived in the *Volksfreund* apartment building, Oelschlägern 27 in Brunswick, was busy doing car repairs in the yard at the outset of the occupation. He was recognized and beaten on his head and face with cudgels, steel pipes, revolver butts and metal tools until he collapsed unconscious. Even then he was kicked, dragged across the yard and thrown out. Neuenfeldt is an ex-serviceman, who served at the front and fought right through the war. Those who beat him up —a typical case that was repeated countless times—were 20-year-old boys. As a result of this beating up, Neuenfeldt is a broken man, physically and mentally.

During the course of the action, the private tenants of the *Volksfreund* building were raided in their flats, abused, threatened with weapons and beaten up.

The regular police had meanwhile blocked off the surrounding streets with a strong force. The Nazis looted the building in front of their very eyes. They destroyed the furniture and equipment. Anything that was movable they dragged out into the yard. Documents, pieces of furniture, valuable administrative material, the book supplies of the *Volksfreund* bookshop, many hundredweight of expensive propaganda film, records, account books, and flags were heaped up on a pyre and set alight. The fire burned for three days and nights.

Immediately after the raid on the building, Comrade Dr Heinrich Jasper, the former Minister-President of Brunswick, rang up the Police-President from the diet and informed him of what had happened. He accused the solicitor and deputy, Alpers, leader of the SS in Brunswick, of armed riot, unlawful assembly, housebreaking and disturbance of public order.

Police-President Lieff replied that these actions were completely legal. Deputy Alpers had been provided with a police warrant for this action.

After this phone call, the regular police units were withdrawn from the *Volksfreund*, so Alpers's hordes had a free hand.

After that, Comrade Dr Jasper got in touch with Nazi Minister Klagges and sought redress. Klagges replied that he knew nothing of these events. Jasper should file a written complaint in the usual way. He refused to intervene before the complaint had been dealt with.

There was of course no redress. On the contrary, Alpers became Minister of Justice [in Brunswick] under the Hitler regime.[1]

In the evening of this eventful day the city of Brunswick resembled a military camp. Hundreds of heavily armed Nazi patrols marched through the town, chased passers-by and beat up members of the public. In the course of this a member of the National Air Association was shot dead. The young man had allegedly raised only one hand on being told to put his hands up. . . .

The bourgeois papers in Brunswick reported the occupation the following morning. According to them it had been carried out quite legally, for the building had been a centre of unrest for a long time. Moreover, it was alleged that masses of treasonable material and ammunition had been found. Not one of these statements is true. . . .

5 *Hitler's appeal to the SA and SS, 10 March 1933*

Such violence, however, was not peculiar to Brunswick. It occurred throughout Germany, though not uniformly. Many towns escaped it. In the course of this violence, a number of foreigners, particularly Jews, were molested, producing protests from their diplomatic representatives. There are also indications that the Government was becoming concerned about the excesses of the 'revolution from below' over which they appeared to have little control. Hitler in particular seemed torn between loyalty to his followers, with whose actions against their opponents he entirely sympathized, and the need not to alienate the conservative elites and in particular the President. He therefore issued an appeal for an end to the violence, in which he tried to distinguish between 'legitimate' and 'illegitimate' violence. This was mainly intended as a gesture to demonstrate to conservative opinion at home and to foreign opinion the good intentions of the Government.

Comrades, SA and SS men! A revolution has taken place in Germany. It is the result of hard struggles, the greatest tenacity, but also the tightest discipline. Unscrupulous characters, mainly Communist spies, are trying to compromise the Party by individual actions which have no relation to the great work of the national uprising, but could discredit and detract from the achievements of our movement. In particular, they try to bring the Party or Germany into conflict with foreign countries by molesting foreigners and cars with foreign flags. SA and SS men, you yourselves must immediately stop such creatures and take them to task. Furthermore, you must hand them over to the police, whoever they may be.

From this day onwards the National Government has executive power throughout Germany. The further progress of the national uprising will therefore be guided and planned from the top. Only where these orders are resisted or where individuals or marching columns are ambushed must this resistance be crushed, as before, thoroughly and immediately. The molesting of individuals, the obstruction or disturbance of business life, must cease on principle. You, Comrades, must

[1] Dr Jasper was soon afterwards arrested and sent to Dachau concentration camp where he later died of ill-treatment.

see to it that the national revolution of 1933 cannot be compared in history with the revolution of the knapsack Spartacists in 1918. Apart from this, do not be deterred for a second from our slogan. It is: The extermination of Marxism.

The effect of this appeal, however, was to a large extent neutralized by a speech made by Göring on the same day in Essen in which he declared: 'For years past we have told the people: "You can settle accounts with the traitors." We stand by our word. Accounts are being settled.' Significantly, the *Völkischer Beobachter* published Hitler's appeal less prominently than Göring's speech. Hitler was, therefore, obliged to reaffirm his appeal in a broadcast on the 12th. This appears to have had some effect. The correspondent of *The Times* reported on the 14th that 'for the first time since the General Election there is today a marked diminution in "individual actions".' It is probable, however, that this slackening off was mainly attributable to the fact that by now virtually all the centres of power had been captured.

6 *The concentration camps at Esterwegen and Papenburg*

In practice the situation remained extremely confused. As Rudolf Diels, who was head of the Prussian political police, indicates in the following account, the SA and SS continued to act as independent powers with complete disregard for the police and the administration under Göring, confident that in the last resort the Führer would protect them against proceedings:

At the beginning of October we heard that in Esterwegen and Papenburg prisoners had been shot while escaping. . . . I was refused access to the Esterwegen camp by the SS. I had announced my visit to the camp a week before. But Göring's order, which I had to show, had not impressed the SS. When I appeared at the entrance of the camp, as far as they were concerned I was a civilian without position or rank in their mighty organization. Only when Weitzel, the SS group leader in Düsseldorf, had given the commandant permission by telephone was I allowed to enter the camp.

The Papenburg camp granted me admission. But what can an 'inspection' of such an institution reveal? The prisoners' replies to the questions put by the inspector are determined by the fear of displeasing their tormentors in whose power the prisoners remain. The food is always adequate and the shining cleanliness of floors and barracks and the scrupulous tidiness of the beds do not tell that they are a means of tormenting the inmates. Nobody can see in the ridiculous straightness of the freshly raked expanses of sand that a violation of such orderliness means 'bunker' and corporal punishment. In Papenburg the unusual happened; a few of the prisoners' spokesmen 'let themselves go'. They not only complained of the food, but they made it clear that they had been subjected to ill-treatment.

In Papenburg, the mayor too had told me of the excesses of the SS towards the population. SS men roamed through the district pillaging like the Swedes in the

Thirty Years War. They 'confiscated' arrested people who had incurred their displeasure and started brawls with the youths of the surrounding villages.

My visit had also encouraged the *Regierungspräsident*[1] in Osnabrück to inform me of the misdeeds of the S S in the camp.

Then, just at the right time, came a serious complaint by a Cologne lawyer, Dr Pünder, made to the Reich Minister of the Interior, Frick, on behalf of his brother, State Secretary Pünder, who was in the hands of the S S thugs in Papenburg. Frick had Pünder's complaint passed on to me and Gürtner[2] by *Oberregierungsrat* Erbe. Erbe promised me his support and Hanfstaengl[3] promised to work on Hitler. At the same time, the Chief Prosecutor Halm of Osnabrück had reported that investigations in the camps which he had wanted to undertake because of the ill-treatment of the innkeeper, Hillig, by S S men in Papenburg had been refused with severe threats. By-passing S S and Police Chief Daluege, I went with Joel, the public prosecutor, to Göring's representative, State Secretary Grauert. He gave us fifty Berlin police officers armed with carbines with whom Joel set off for Papenburg. A delegate sent by Joel was told that if the police approached the camp they would be received with machine guns. When Joel attempted to get into the camp, bullets flew round his ears. On his informing Grauert of this state of affairs, he was told to wait for further instructions. Meanwhile, Himmler had protested to Göring against the use of the police against the S S. Göring would have given in, had Joel not informed him that the S S were fraternizing with the prisoners in the camp and were going to arm them. This brought a new element into the revolutionary situation. Mention of the mutinous S S put all other arguments in the shade. Göring asked me to report to Hitler in his presence on what had happened. Hitler ordered the 'take-over' of the camps by the police. When I had informed Grauert, he sent 200 Osnabrück police off to the Dutch border. But they had to make ready to lay siege, as it were, to the camps, especially as a representative of S S Group Leader Weitzel appeared on the scene and tried to intimidate the police officers with threats from Himmler. I now went to ask Hitler straight whether the police could not use force of arms against the S S. Hitler let me see him and after my renewed account of the excesses in the camps, he interrupted me in a military voice of command and ordered me to ask the Reich Defence Minister for army artillery, and to shoot up the camps, the S S and their prisoners without mercy. My colleagues were horrified when I arrived with this order from the Führer. It was clear to me that I could not take it seriously.

I asked my superior, *Ministerialdirektor* Fischer in the Ministry of the Interior, to negotiate with the mutinous S S about their 'demands' which, like freebooters, they had made the conditions of their departure. They had demanded coats, blankets, and back pay. After he had informed the S S, through an S S leader of Weitzel's, of the fulfilment of their demands, Joel took possession of the camps without bloodshed. He then spent some time in Papenburg to begin investigations into the violence of the S S guards.

... At this time Joel also went to Kemma near Wuppertal at Grauert's and my instigation. The S A had tortured the Communists there in a particularly 'original' way. They were forced to drink salty herring solution and then left to pant in vain

---

[1] The senior government official for the area.
[2] The Minister of Justice.
[3] A German-American friend of Hitler's.

for a sip of water throughout the hot summer days. One of my officers who had accompanied Joel reported that the SA there had also played the 'joke' of getting their prisoners to climb trees; they had to hang on in the treetops for hours on end and at certain intervals cry 'cuckoo'. The public prosecutor Winckler in Wuppertal, who proposed to act against the SA, had to flee with his wife and child from their threats. The *Regierungspräsident* Schmidt in Düsseldorf poured out his heart to me about the atrocities. With Joel, I succeeded in getting Göring to have the 'responsible' SA Group Leader relieved of his office, to ensure that Joel had a free hand in the prosecution of the SA guards. After a few months, Joel succeeded, despite the opposition of the Gauleiter Florian, in starting proceedings against the guilty SA men. But the struggle against Hitler, who finally terminated the proceedings, he was bound to lose.... In reality, there were neither commands nor prohibitions. Before or after my reports to Göring and Hitler on acts of violence in the country, SA and SS leaders talked about the bravery of their men on the field of revolution. These acts were approved of and laughed over just as they were disapproved of when I represented them as excesses against the authority of the new state.... Already, the SA were breaking into the police prisons, to get hold of the Communist leaders who had been arrested after the Reichstag fire, and who, they intended, should be the victims of their special revenge. From the police headquarters they took the files which could incriminate their leaders; the frightened officials handed over what they were asked for.

7 Oswald Spengler on the 'National Uprising'

The fact, however, that this violence was directed primarily against the Left and mostly took place behind closed doors enabled the middle class to overlook it or rationalize it by referring to the crisis of the moment. A common expression at the time was, 'Where planing is going on there are bound to be shavings', the German equivalent of 'You can't make an omelette without breaking eggs.' Even so, the official version of the take-over contrasted the 'bloodless national uprising' of 1933 with the 'bloody revolution' of November 1918. Oswald Spengler, though he later came to dislike the Nazis, was typical of the majority of the middle class in his acceptance of this version in a comment made during October 1933:

> ... But now it can already be said: the national revolution of 1933 was something tremendous and will remain so in the eyes of the future because of the elemental supra-personal force with which it occurred and because of the mental discipline with which it was carried out. That was Prussian through and through, like the awakening of 1914 which, in an instant, had transformed men's minds. The German dreamers arose quietly with impressive self-composure and opened up a path to the future.

8 The Potsdam ceremony of 21 March 1933

The image of a glorious and bloodless national revolution received new support from the spectacle which was staged in the garrison church at Potsdam to celebrate the opening of the new Reichstag. Otto Meissner, the

State Secretary of the Reich President, has described the scene and the intention behind it:

On 21 March 1933, after a service of celebration in the Catholic and the Protestant churches in the city, the new Reichstag was opened with a solemn ceremony in front of the tomb of Frederick the Great in the historic Potsdam garrison church. Apart from the members of the Government and the Reichstag, it was attended by the aged Reich President von Hindenburg in the uniform of a Prussian Field-Marshal, by the former Crown Prince in a Prussian General's uniform, and by numerous generals and officers of the old army, as well as of the Reichswehr. Hitler, who for the first time in his political career appeared in tails and a top hat instead of the usual Party uniform, gave an address. He began by paying homage to Hindenburg and then with a great gesture paid tribute to those forces which had preserved the State in the past and to the need to preserve world peace. Hindenburg made a guarded reply which contained words of earnest admonition. This ceremony, celebrated by the right-wing press as 'the hour of birth of the Third Reich', had an emphatically nationalist character. Hitler, Göring and Goebbels, the planners of Potsdam Day, were therewith pursuing the aim of convincing the Reichswehr, the Civil Service, and the nationalist-inclined elements of the bourgeoisie, who were still hesitating, that the course now being taken meant no revolutionary change of system in the sense of the slogans of National Socialist mass propaganda, but a national transformation. By referring in this ceremony to the Christian foundations and the conservative past of Prussia and Germany, and by recalling the memory of the great Prussian king, Hitler wished to express symbolically his intention of regenerating the German people on a broad national basis, in which the Army and the traditional forces which preserved the State would keep their influence. . . .

7 The 'Coordination' of the Reichstag and of the Political Parties, March–June 1933

The Enabling Law, 24 March 1933

After coordinating the states, Hitler returned to his initial objective of the destruction of the Reichstag as an effective institution, to be followed by the elimination of rival political parties, their main sphere of operation having been thereby removed. The coordination of the Reichstag was to be achieved by means of an Enabling Law which would enable the Government to introduce legislative measures independently of the legislature, including alterations to the Constitution. This idea of an Enabling Law was not an entirely new concept in German politics. Enabling Laws had been introduced during the Weimar Republic, notably those of 13 October and 8 December 1923 which dealt with the crisis caused by the inflation and the Ruhr invasion. Moreover, during the years 1930–33 laws passed by the Reichstag had increasingly been replaced by Government decrees issued by the Reich President under Article 48 of the Weimar Constitution. In 1932, for example, there were sixty emergency decrees compared with only five Reichstag laws, and in an increasing number of these emergency decrees the Government was empowered to issue supplementary regulations with the force of law.

Initially, the Enabling Law planned by the new regime was drawn up along the lines of the Weimar laws, that is to say, it was intended to permit the issuing of Government decrees with the force of law without the need for prior approval from the Reichstag or the Reich President. Some time between 15 and 20 March, however, the draft was modified to empower the Government to issue not merely 'decrees' (*Verordnungen*) but also 'laws' (*Gesetze*), and even laws which deviated from the 1919 Constitution and had therefore hitherto required a two-thirds Reichstag majority. The distinction between a 'law' and a 'decree' was not clear-cut, but the Weimar Constitution had imputed somewhat greater significance to laws than to decrees by restricting certain legislation (e.g. the taking up of loans by the Government) to laws. In the final draft of the Enabling Law the Reichstag surrendered its powers over the budget and over the taking up of loans.

Since this Enabling Law involved a change in the Constitution, a two-thirds majority in the Reichstag was necessary. The problem for the Government was therefore how to secure this majority. After the election of 5 March, the two largest parties after the NSDAP—the Social Democrats

(SPD) and the Centre Party—still possessed between them over one-third of the seats. A particular danger was that the SPD and the Centre might boycott the debate, and since a quorum of two-thirds of the Reichstag membership was necessary for changes in the Constitution this would represent an effective veto. This danger was averted by a change in the Reichstag standing orders suggested by Frick. The new regulation, accepted by all save the SPD, laid down that those members who were absent without leave or who had been excluded would count as being present, and the decision over who should be excused or not was to lie with the President of the Reichstag (Göring).

1 *The Cabinet meeting of 7 March 1933*

The Government was reconciled to the opposition of the Social Democrats; it therefore concentrated its efforts on trying to win over the Centre:

(1) *Political Situation*

The Reich Chancellor opened the meeting and stated that . . . he regarded the events of 5 March as a revolution. Ultimately Marxism would no longer exist in Germany.

What was needed was an Enabling Law passed by a two-thirds majority. He, the Reich Chancellor, was firmly convinced that the Reichstag would pass such a law. The deputies of the German Communist Party would not appear at the opening of the Reichstag because they were in jail. . . .

The Vice-Chancellor and Reich Commissioner of Prussia [Papen] expressed to the Reich Chancellor and the National Socialist Organization the thanks of the Reich Cabinet for their admirable performance in the election. . . .

With regard to the internal political situation, the Vice-Chancellor stated that yesterday (6 March) Dr Kaas[1] had been to see him. He had stated that he had come without previously consulting his party and was now prepared to let by-gones be bygones. He had, moreover, offered the cooperation of the Centre Party. . . .

Reich Minister Göring stated that the Communist deputies would not take part in the sessions of the Reichstag because they were in jail. Serious charges were also to be made against a number of Marxist deputies. Forty persons of the Iron Front had carried out united action with the German Communist Party.

He was firmly convinced that the two-thirds majority in the Reichstag would be obtained for an Enabling Law. Deputies who left the session in order to make it impossible for the two-thirds majority to be present would have to forfeit their free travel passes and allowances for the duration of the legislative period. He wished to make a change in the rules to this effect. In his opinion, the duty of the Deputy to exercise his mandate also entailed that he must not absent himself from sessions without being excused.

Grass, the chairman of the parliamentary group of the Prussian Centre Party, had been to see him even before the election. Grass had made the offer that if no further changes in personnel were made before the election, then the Centre Party

[1] Leader of the Centre Party.

would be prepared to cooperate. According to the statements made by Grass, the collaboration of the German Nationalists could then be dispensed with. It was best to tell the Centre Party that all its civil servants would be removed from office if the Centre Party did not agree to the enabling law. For the rest, the tactics to be employed towards the Centre Party would have to consist in courteously ignoring it. . . .

2 *Hitler asks the Reichstag to adopt the Enabling Bill, 23 March 1933*

The Catholic Church authorities, however, were still hostile to the Nazi Party and their influence with the Centre Party was considerable. On 19 March, Cardinal Bertram, the senior German Catholic bishop, issued a confidential statement to the Catholic bishops that 'as a result of biased announcements to the effect that the Church will revise its attitude to the National Socialists, Vice-Chancellor von Papen brought up this question during his visit yesterday. I replied that it is for the leader of the National Socialists to revise his attitude.'

To win over the Catholics and the Centre Party, Hitler promised in his Reichstag speech to respect the rights of the Catholic Church and stressed the Government's recognition of the importance of the Churches:

. . . By its determination to carry through the political and moral purging of our public life, the Government is creating and ensuring the preconditions for a truly deep and inward religious life. The political advantages derivable from compromises with atheistic organizations come nowhere near outweighing the consequences to be seen in the destruction of our common religious and moral values. The National Government sees in both Christian denominations the most important factors for the maintenance of our society. It will respect the agreements concluded between them and the states; their rights will not be touched. It expects, however, that its task of the national and moral renewal of our people will meet with similar appreciation from their side. The Government will treat all other denominations with objective justice. It can never, however, condone the idea that membership of a given denomination or race can be regarded as absolving any person from common legal obligations or as a licence to commit or tolerate crimes without punishment. The National Government will permit and guarantee to the Christian denominations the enjoyment of their due influence in schools and education.[1] Its concern will be for the sincere cooperation of Church and State. The struggle against the materialist ideology and for the establishment of a real national community is in the interests of the German nation as much as of our Christian faith. . . .

3 *'Was the Centre Party right to support the Enabling Law?'*

Besides being wooed by promises, the Centre was also intimidated by the fear of what would happen, particularly to Catholic civil servants, if they

---

[1] Significantly this sentence was omitted from the report of the speech in the *Völkischer Beobachter* and most other publications.

refused. Their uncertainty is well summed up in the reflections of the distinguished historian of the Centre Party, Karl Bachem, after the Party had voted in support of the Bill. Particularly interesting is his hope that it would be possible to cooperate with and influence the NSDAP.

Was this vote right? This may be doubted, though only future developments will make a definite judgement possible. It was certainly in the spirit of the call for unity which Kaas had sent out weeks ago on 17 October 1932 in Münster. It may also be said that the law would have been passed even if the Centre had voted against it or abstained. If the Centre had voted against it, it would, given the current mood of the National Socialists, probably have been smashed at once just like the Social Democratic Party and the Italian Partito Popolare[1]. All civil servants belonging to the Centre would probably have been dismissed. There would have been a great fracas in the Reichstag, and the Centrists would probably have been beaten up and thrown out. The parliamentary group would have made an heroic exit, but with no benefit to the Catholic cause or to the cause of the Centre Party. The links between the Centre and National Socialism would have been completely cut, all collaboration with the National Socialists and every possibility of influencing their policy would have been out of the question. Perhaps, then, it was right to make the attempt to come to an understanding and cooperate with the National Socialists, in order to be able to participate in a practical way in the reshaping of the future.

Certainly all this can be said. But what if this attempt fails? What if the National Socialist wave, true to its basic ideological beliefs, wants to engulf our Catholic organizations, our Catholic youth clubs etc., as in Italy? Will not people then say that it was the fault of the Centre for giving the Hitler Government a blank cheque for four years? Will not the Centre be so discredited with its followers that it will lose all influence on them and be unable to achieve anything?

Then again, can it be morally and politically justifiable to grant the Government, whose instincts are so completely different from what we stand for, such far-reaching, unique authority? The Centre has always been the party of the law, of the Constitution, and also of freedom. What has now happened has nothing to do with law, freedom, and the Constitution. It is true that parliamentarism and with it the democratic idea have come to a dead end. Brüning tried up to the last minute to save parliamentarism as it was part of the Constitution; but in vain. It is Hugenberg's fault. But it has really proved impossible. So was it justified to try a new way? Certainly, Hitler has inserted several points in his speech which meet our wishes, to a far greater extent than would have been thought possible, and give us a certain security. But will he be able to stick to this line since many of his colleagues—Hugenberg, Göring—are strongly opposed to Catholicism?

In any case: as in 1919 we climbed calmly and deliberately into the Social Democrat boat, so, in the same way, we were able to enter the boat of the National Socialists in 1933 and to try to lend a hand with the steering. Between 1919 and 1933 this proved quite satisfactory: the Social Democrats, since they were not able to govern without the Centre, were unable to do anything particularly antireligious or dubiously socialistic. Will it be possible to exercise a similarly sobering influence on the National Socialists now?

[1] The Catholic party in Italy.

Quod Deus bene vertat![1] It would indeed be a great thing, and if it turns out like that, everyone in our party will praise the present attitude of the parliamentary group. Just as after 1919, when the association with the Social Democrats saved us from Bolshevism. It is enough if cooperation with the National Socialists can protect us against Communists, Bolshevism and anarchy! The latter is very important now. One may say: *Prius vivere, deinde philosophari.*[2] First remove the danger of Communism; then everything will sort itself out.

In short: in this question too there is no obvious solution. As so often in politics. And in life too! The risk is great, but if one had not run it the danger would have been even greater.

Ergo: for the time being we go along with the new direction of the Centre. Whether it is right nobody can say yet. *Qui vivra, verra!*[3] All splits are dangerous now. As they were before.

4 *Pronouncement of the Fulda Conference of Bishops on National Socialism, 28 March 1933*

Hitler's Reichstag speech had satisfied not only lay Catholics but also the Church authorities, who were above all concerned to protect its various organizations:

During the last few years, the Bishops of the German dioceses, in their dutiful concern for the party of the Catholic faith and the protection of the tasks and rights of the Catholic Church, have adopted, for good reasons, towards the National Socialist movement a negative attitude, expressed through prohibitions and warnings, which were to remain in force for as long as and as far as those reasons remained valid.

It must now be recognized that public and solemn declarations have been issued by the highest representative of the Reich Government, who is simultaneously the authoritarian leader of that movement, which acknowledge the inviolability of the teachings of the Catholic faith and the immutable tasks and rights of the Church. Similarly, the full validity of the treaties concluded between the various German states and the Church is guaranteed.

Without revoking the condemnation contained in our previous statements of certain religious and ethical errors, the Episcopate nevertheless believes it can cherish the hope that those general warnings and prohibitions need no longer be regarded as necessary.

Catholic Christians, for whom the opinion of their Church is sacred, need no particular admonition to be loyal to the legally constituted authorities, to fulfil their civic duties conscientiously, and to reject absolutely any illegal or revolutionary activity.

The admonition which has so often been solemnly addressed to all Catholics, namely to stand up for peace and the social welfare of the nation, for the protection of Christian religion and morality, for the freedom and rights of the Catholic Church and the protection of the denominational school and the Catholic youth organizations, is still valid.

[1] 'May God turn this to good effect!'
[2] 'Live first, then philosophize.'
[3] 'He who lives will see!'

Furthermore, the admonition to political and similar organizations is still valid, namely that they should avoid in church and at church functions, out of respect for their sacredness, anything which might be construed as a party political demonstration.

Finally, the request, made so frequently and with such urgency, still holds good, always to encourage with far-sighted discretion the Catholic associations whose work is so full of blessings for Church, nation and fatherland, for Christian culture and social peace.

5 *A Social Democrat comment on the Reichstag debate, 23 March 1933*

The only party to vote against the Bill was the SPD and the courage this required can be judged from the following account of the atmosphere of the debate by a Bavarian SPD deputy:

... The wide square in front of the Kroll Opera House was crowded with dark masses of people. We were received with wild choruses: 'We want the Enabling Act!' Youths with swastikas on their chests eyed us insolently, blocked our way, in fact made us run the gauntlet, calling us names like 'Centre pig', 'Marxist sow'. The Kroll Opera House was crawling with armed SA and SS men. In the cloak-room we learned that Severing[1] had been arrested on entering the building. The assembly hall was decorated with swastikas and similar ornaments. The diplomats' boxes and the rows of seats for the audience were overcrowded. When we Social Democrats had taken our seats on the extreme left, SA and SS men lined up at the exits and along the walls behind us in a semicircle. Their expressions boded no good.

Hitler read out his government declaration in a surprisingly calm voice. Only in a few places did he raise it to a fanatical frenzy: when he demanded the public execution of van der Lubbe and when, at the end of his speech, he uttered dark threats of what would happen if the Reichstag did not vote the Enabling Act he was demanding. I had not seen him for a long time. He did not resemble the ideal of the Germanic hero in any way. Instead of fair curls, a black strand of hair hung down over his sallow face. His voice gushed out of his throat in dark gurgling sounds. I have never understood how this speaker could carry away thousands of people with enthusiasm.

After the government declaration, there was an interval. The former Reich Chancellor, Dr Wirth, came over and said bitterly that in his group the only question had been whether they should also give Hitler the rope to hang them with. The majority of the Centre was willing to obey Monseigneur Dr Kaas and let Hitler have his Enabling Act. If they refused, they feared the outbreak of the Nazi revolution and bloody anarchy. Only a few, among them Dr Brüning, were against any concession to Hitler.

Otto Wels read out our reply to the government declaration. It was a masterpiece in form and content, a farewell to the fading epoch of human rights and humanity.[2]

[1] An SPD Party leader and former Prussian Minister of the Interior.

[2] 'At this historic hour, we German Social Democrats pledge ourselves to the principles of humanity and justice, of freedom and Socialism. No Enabling Law can give you the power to destroy ideas which are eternal and indestructible. You yourself have declared your commitment to Socialism. The Socialist Law [of 1878] did not succeed in destroying Social Democracy. From this

In concluding, Otto Wels, with his voice half choking, gave our good wishes to the persecuted and oppressed in the country who, though innocent, were already filling the prisons and concentration camps simply on account of their political creed.

This speech made a terrifying impression on all of us. Only a few hours before, we had heard that members of the SA had taken away the 45-year-old welfare worker, Maria Janovska of Köpenick, to a National Socialist barracks, stripped her completely, bound her on a table and flogged her body with leather whips. The female members of our group were in tears, some sobbed uncontrollably.

But Hitler jumped up furiously and launched into a passionate reply. When the Social Democrats were in power the National Socialists had been outlawed. Anyone who bowed down before an International could not criticize the National Socialists. If the National Socialists had not a sense of justice, the Social Democrats would not be here in the hall. But the National Socialists had resisted the temptation to turn against those who had tormented them for fourteen years. 'You are oversensitive, gentlemen, if you talk of persecution already. By God, the National Socialists would have had the courage to deal with the Social Democrats in a different way. . . . You, gentlemen, are no longer needed. I do not even want you to vote for the Enabling Act. Germany shall become free, but not through you.'

There was no question of the National Socialists having been persecuted in the German Republic. On the contrary, the movement had frequently been furthered by the State authorities. Only when its members broke the existing laws were they punished, in most cases very mildly. The Communists were made to feel the strong arm of the law in a very different way.

We tried to dam the flood of Hitler's unjust accusations with interruptions of 'No!', 'An error!', 'False!' But that did us no good. The SA and SS people, who surrounded us in a semicircle along the walls of the hall, hissed loudly and murmured: 'Shut up!', 'Traitors!', 'You'll be strung up today.'

6 *The Enabling Law of 24 March 1933*

The Enabling Law was passed by 444 votes to the 94 votes of the Social Democrats. Its passage gave the destruction of parliamentary democracy an appearance of legality which was important for the prestige of the regime not only abroad but also among the middle class, and particularly the Civil Service, at home. From now onwards, the Reichstag became merely a sounding board for Hitler's major speeches, what one observer described as 'the most expensive male voice choir in the world'. Only seven more laws were passed by the Reichstag. Moreover, despite the statement in Article 2 that 'the powers of the President remain unaffected', in fact the signature of the President was no longer necessary for legislation or decrees. Only three more presidential decrees were issued and they had already been prepared

---

new persecution too German Social Democracy can draw new strength. We send greetings to the persecuted and the oppressed. We greet our friends in the Reich. Their steadfastness and loyalty deserve admiration. The courage with which they maintain their convictions and their unbroken confidence guarantee a brighter future.'

before the passage of the Enabling Law. From now onwards the legislation of the Third Reich took the form of 'government laws' and, increasingly, of decrees:

The Reichstag has passed the following law, which is, with the approval of the Reichsrat,[1] herewith promulgated, after it has been established that it satisfies the requirements for legislation altering the Constitution.

Article 1. In addition to the procedure for the passage of legislation outlined in the Constitution, the Reich Cabinet is also authorized to enact Laws. This applies equally to the laws referred to in Article 85, paragraph 2, and Article 87 of the Constitution.[2]

Article 2. The national laws enacted by the Reich Cabinet may deviate from the Constitution provided they do not affect the position of the Reichstag and the Reichsrat. The powers of the President remain unaffected.

Article 3. The national laws enacted by the Reich Cabinet shall be prepared by the Chancellor and published in the official gazette. They come into effect, unless otherwise specified, upon the day following their publication. Articles 68–77 of the Constitution[3] do not apply to the laws enacted by the Reich Cabinet.

Article 4. Treaties of the Reich with foreign states which concern matters of domestic legislation do not require the consent of the bodies participating in legislation. The Reich Cabinet is empowered to issue the necessary provisions for the implementing of these treaties.

Article 5. This law comes into effect on the day of its publication. It ceases to be valid on 1 April 1937: it also ceases to be valid if the present Reich Cabinet is replaced by another.[4]

The elimination of the political parties

The emasculation of the Reichstag was followed eventually by the demise of the political parties. Even the partners in the coalition, the Nationalists, came under increasing pressure, particularly since after the Enabling Law their votes were no longer necessary for legislation. Protests by their leader, Hugenberg, even at Cabinet level were treated with scarcely concealed contempt:

7 *4 April 1933 (4.0 p.m.): Session of the Reich Cabinet*

3. Outside the agenda: information from the Reich Minister of Economics, Food, and Agriculture (Dr Hugenberg):

[1] The upper house, containing the representatives of the federal states which had now all been coordinated.

[2] These concerned the authority of Parliament over taxation.

[3] These concerned the provisions for enacting new legislation.

[4] In fact the Act was renewed in 1937 for a further four years and the second part of the clause, included to reassure the German Nationalists, was ignored after Hugenberg's resignation on 27 June 1933. This was facilitated by the fact that the pressure for Hugenberg's resignation had come from the Conservatives in the Cabinet led by Neurath, who had objected to his aggressive tactics at the World Economic Conference in London earlier in June.

The Reich Minister of Economics, Food, and Agriculture pointed out that recently S A men had arrested chairmen and members of Chambers of Commerce who were listed members of the German National People's Party. These persons were removed from their positions in an unlawful way. He would no longer tolerate this state of affairs and urgently requested redress.

Reich Minister Göring explained that frequently arrests had been made solely at the request of the competent public prosecutor. Moreover, it was urgently necessary to have new elections for the Chambers of Commerce and the Chambers of Farmers as soon as possible. The structure of the Chambers no longer accorded in any way with the present political situation. It was therefore impossible for Reich Minister Göring himself to hold back the S A.

The Reich Minister of Economics, Food and Agriculture reported that he had already prepared the reorganization of the provisional Reich Economic Council and that he also wished to order the dissolution of, and new elections for, the Chambers of Commerce and of Farmers. But he had to be allowed a little time to prepare all these things. . . .

8 Goebbels notes Hitler's domination of the Cabinet

After this Goebbels had good reason to note the following in his diary:

22 April 1933

The Führer's authority is now completely in the ascendant in the Cabinet. There will be no more voting. The Führer's personality decides. All this has been achieved much more quickly than we had dared to hope. . . .

9 Pronouncement of the Catholic Teachers' Association of the German Reich, 1 April 1933

The anti-Nazi activities of S P D émigrés in Prague were used as an excuse to ban the SPD officially on 22 June. By the end of June, the two Liberal parties and the Nationalists, whose membership had by now virtually disappeared, either to join the Nazis or into what was termed 'inner emigration',[1] recognized the inevitable and disbanded themselves. They were followed on 5 July by the most powerful non-Socialist opposition party, the Catholic Centre.

The Centre had been still faced with the dilemma of whether or not to cooperate with the Nazi regime. Many of its members had already been swept away by the spirit of the 'national uprising' to which Catholics, traditionally a minority group, could be particularly vulnerable as the following document indicates:

As in the August days of 1914, a feeling of national and German emotion has seized our people. The status quo has been overthrown and new objectives have been set for a new, developing German nation and a new German state. Regrettably,

---

[1] i.e. while refraining from overt opposition to the regime, they withheld from it any cooperation as far as possible, in an attempt to keep their hands clean.

the Catholic leadership and Catholic elements have been as little involved in this change as they were in the foundation of Bismarck's Reich. Thanks to the warning summons of Adolf Hitler and his movement, and to his work, we have succeeded in breaking through the un-German spirit which prevailed in the revolution of 1918.

Now the whole German nation in all its various parts, including the Catholics, has been summoned to cooperate and to build a new order. At this critical moment, Catholicism must not once again stand aside, adopting a wait-and-see attitude. We will lend a hand to help with the construction of a new Reich and a new nation, putting our trust in the leader of the German and *völkisch* movement. If an appeal is made to the natural and true impulses and groups of our historic nationality in its totality, the Catholic element cannot be dispensed with. Over the past centuries, it has become our destiny for the nature of the German character to grow out of Catholicism and the national characteristics of the German race. After a period of decline, we now have the duty of participating in the reorientation towards a rise and a renaissance. We must—and here we agree completely with the leader of the national movement—we must first become an internally unified nation of German men and women. We must put aside everything which divides us and shake hands across the barriers which have hitherto been overemphasized, in order once more to become a nation which believes in honour, cleanliness, and loyalty. The essence of the practising Catholic population, as it has emerged in associations, status groups, and modes of life, is coming to the fore in order to consider what specific Catholic contribution can be made to the national task.

10 *Karl Bachem on the dissolution of the Centre Party, 5 July 1933*

The dilemma facing the Centre was outlined at the time by Karl Bachem. What stands out is his feeling of impotence in the face of the crisis, his sense of the inevitability of the Nazi take-over since they alone were sufficiently ruthless and determined to cope with the situation. Remarkable also is his belief that in the fight against Bolshevism there is 'no point in being fussy about legal subtleties'. The attitude revealed by this statement, made in the context of the Enabling Act and all that had happened since 30 January, goes some way towards explaining the comparative ease with which the Nazis carried out their policy of 'coordination':

So the Centre has been formally dissolved. The Centre has been dissolved by its own resolution! It is said that Brüning was strongly against. But concern for the Catholic civil servants was decisive. Brüning had wanted to wait for the Government to dissolve the Centre, which in that case would not itself have borne any responsibility. The same with the Bavarian People's Party. All political activity in the spirit of the old Centre Party is from now on impossible and 'forbidden'. It has been quite openly declared that any further attempts at such activities will be crushed by brute force.

This is indeed a terrible fate, hardly conceivable for a party with such an honourable record of more than sixty years' achievement. One can do nothing but succumb patiently and meekly to this decision of Divine Providence; even if this time it seems hard, very hard. 'Quam incomprehensibilia sunt judicia ejus, et investigabiles viae ejus', as it says in the Epistle to the Romans.[1] No wonder that particularly the younger, lively members of the Party are terribly upset and use harsh words accusing Brüning, Kaas and all the other leaders of having helped to bring about the downfall of the party through their inactivity and cowardice. But what in practical terms could Brüning and Kaas have done? Would it have been of any use to call on the Catholic population and the whole Centre Party to offer united resistance? Such resistance would have at once shown up the physical powerlessness of the party and would have been brutally suppressed; the leaders would have immediately been taken into 'protective custody', and thereby have been rendered harmless. The bishops having voted unanimously for the recognition of the new government, such resistance, no longer morally defensible, would have been impossible for us. There is nothing left to do but to follow the example of the bishops and, in spite of everything, continue to try and remain concerned for the protection of our religious interests within the National Socialist Party and in cooperation with it. Nothing else is now possible. All our large organizations have been destroyed. Even the apprentices' associations have been deprived of their independence and coordinated with the 'National Socialist workers' front'. What will happen now no one can say. In the meantime, the future before us remains extremely black. In practice, we can do nothing but continue to try and work for our religious principles within the National Socialist Party and through quiet cooperation in its organizations. National Socialists, particularly Hitler, have often declared that they want 'positive Christianity' as the basis of the State, that they regard the Catholic as well as the Protestant Confessions as 'the most important factors for the preservation of our national character'. That is something, even if it is not yet clear what this 'positive Christianity' will be like and what its effects will be. So our people must now act as 'leaven', as the 'salt of the earth', in order to help the right principles to predominate. . . .

After describing the chronic state of crisis under the Weimar Republic he concludes:

In short, no more headway could be made with the democratic form of government; there could no longer be any illusions about this. Nor with the Centre's old principle of seeking an improvement in conditions only in a constitutional way, observing the regulations and the existing law. If the nation was not to sink into poverty and the life of the state be completely ruined, a different way had to be found to get out of this appalling situation. It was clear that if this was to be done it would not always be possible to observe the letter of the law. . . .

So one could only be grateful to the new men who, with determination, took into their hands the task of saving Germany. It really was not possible to go on any further without force, without using the principle of force, and since the Centre, because of its past, could not subscribe to this principle, it could not complain if it was pushed aside. Therefore, it is right to let the new men, particularly the leaders of the National Socialists, go ahead and not put unnecessary obstacles in their way. There are a lot of dubious things in the National Socialist movement, particularly so far as principles are concerned. But that has to be put up with for the time being. Today there is no point in being fussy about legal subtleties. What matters

[1] Romans 11:33: 'How unsearchable are his judgments, and his ways past finding out!'

is first to let a strong, efficient government grow and then to support it whole-heartedly in order to suppress Bolshevism. It does seem as if Communism had already become so strong in Germany, so presumptuous, and so self-confident that it was high time to counter it with determination if it was not to result in a new Communist revolution and a terrible civil war.

But despite all this, it is hard for the Centre Party to disappear without trace after such long and honourable activity. In days to come they may say: It had ful-filled its task and could leave the stage of history. But has that task been fulfilled for the future as well? Who from now on will look after the interests of religion, the freedom and welfare of the Church? Are we not now dependent solely on the goodwill of the National Socialist Party? Will the Church keep its rights when no real political power exists to defend them? It is certain that even Catholics loyal to the Church will now join the National Socialist formations in great numbers, just as in Italy. But will their influence there become strong enough to check new animosities against the Catholic Church, especially attacks on our Catholic denominational schools and the schools of our orders etc.? There is to be a con-cordat with the Vatican. If the Pope concludes it, he will take the vital interests of the Church into account. But will such a Concordat remain permanently valid if there is no political power to support its validity? It is different in Italy. The whole country is Catholic and even the Liberals think of Catholicism as part of the national greatness. In Germany, on the other hand, denominational divisions go deep, and anything that has seemed to favour the Catholic Church has always been offensive to the Protestant section of the people. At the moment there is no evidence of any particularly hostile Protestant agitation against Catholicism. The Protestant Association has obviously lost much of its impetus. But will that remain so? Who knows? . . .

11 The Cabinet meeting of 14 July 1933

In fact, the position of the Centre had been further undermined by the negotiations between the Government, the Catholic hierarchy in Germany, and the Vatican over a Concordat. The Catholic authorities proved willing to abandon their political party in return for a Concordat guaranteeing their religious activities. Hitler, however, had no doubt that in the Concordat signed on 8 July 1933 he had a bargain:

. . . The Reich Chancellor rejected a debate on the particulars of the Reich Con-cordat. He was of the opinion that one should see only the great success here. In the Reich Concordat, Germany had been given an opening; an area of confidence had been created which was particularly significant in the urgent fight against international Jewry. Possible shortcomings in the Concordat could be rectified later when Germany's foreign relations had improved.

The Reich Chancellor saw three great advantages in the conclusion of the Reich Concordat:
  1. that the Vatican had negotiated at all, considering that they operated, especially in Austria, on the assumption that National Socialism was un-Christian and inimical to the Church;
  2. that the Vatican should have been persuaded to bring about good relations

with this purely national German State. He, the Reich Chancellor, would even a short time ago have thought it impossible that the Church would be willing to commit the bishops to the support of this State. The fact that this had now been done was certainly an unreserved recognition of the present regime;

3. that, with the Concordat, the Church should have withdrawn from activity in associations and parties, and, for instance, have abandoned even the Christian labour unions. This also he, the Reich Chancellor, would, even a few months ago, have thought impossible. Even the dissolution of the Centre could be termed final only with the conclusion of the Concordat, now that the Vatican had ordered the permanent exclusion of the clergy from party politics.

That the objective which he, the Reich Chancellor, had always been striving for, namely an agreement with the Curia, had been attained so much faster than he had imagined even on 30 January—this was such an indescribable success that, in the face of it, all critical misgivings should be withdrawn.

12 Law against the Establishment of Parties, 14 July 1933

After all the parties had dissolved themselves, the one-Party State was formally proclaimed:

Art I. The National Socialist German Workers' Party constitutes the only political party in Germany.

Art II. Whoever undertakes to maintain the organization of another political party or to form a new political party shall be punished with penal servitude of up to three years or with imprisonment of between six months and three years, unless the act is subject to a heavier penalty under other regulations.

8 The Revolution Stabilized: Conflict with the SA

Meanwhile, the SA was becoming dissatisfied with the compromises which the regime had made with established institutions. The SA contained a large number of impoverished members of the lower-middle class and a number of unemployed who were hostile to big business and wished to continue the revolution in every sphere. They took seriously the anti-capitalist aspects of the Party programme. In fact, the Government had gone some way towards conciliating the Party rank and file by insisting that old Party fighters have priority in employment, a measure which led to many SA men acquiring jobs.

1 *Ernst Röhm: The SA and the German Revolution, June 1933*

Nevertheless, the leader of the SA, Ernst Röhm, at least was not conciliated and in a newspaper article in June 1933 he expressed disillusionment at the inadequate fruits of the seizure of power and determination to continue the revolution:

... A tremendous victory has been won. But not *absolute* victory!

The new State did not have to disown the bearers of the will to revolution as the November men[1] had to with the red hordes who were the followers of their revolution, born of cowardice and high treason. In the new Germany the disciplined brown storm battalions of the German revolution stand side by side with the armed forces.

Not as part of them.

The Reichswehr has its own undisputed task: it is committed to defend the borders of the Reich, so far as its small numbers and completely inadequate armament enables it to do so.

The police have to keep down the law-breakers.

Beside these stand the SA and the SS as the third power factor of the new State with special tasks.

The Leader and Chancellor of the German people needs them for the tremendous work of German revival which still lies before him.

For the SA and the SS are the foundation pillars of the coming National Socialist State— *Their* State for which they have fought and which they will defend. The SA and SS are militant-spiritual [*kämpferisch-geistig*] bearers of the will of the German revolution.

Already here and there philistines and grumblers are daring to ask in astonishment what the SA and SS are still there for, since Hitler is now in power. We are

[1] i.e. the Social Democrats.

after all, they point out, nationalist again. Swastika flags fly over the streets. There is law and order everywhere. And if it is disturbed, the police will take care that it is restored as quickly as possible. So why the S A and S S?

The philistines and grumblers, whether they stand in the ranks of our eternal and irreconcilable adversaries, or are 'coordinated', or even wear the swastika, have not understood the meaning of the German revolution and never will understand it.

The course of events between 30 January and 21 March 1933 does not represent the sense and meaning of the German National Socialist revolution.

Anyone who wanted to be a fellow-traveller only during shining torchlight processions and impressive parades with rumbling drums and booming kettle-drums, with blaring trumpets and under waving flags, and now believes he has 'taken part' in the German revolution—can go home! He has confused the 'national uprising' with the German revolution! He has intoxicated himself with outward appearances; perhaps he has got carried away by the unheard-of mood of 'Potsdam Day', perhaps he was delighted to see millions and millions of workers march for Germany at the Festival of German Labour,[1] and for a few hours felt a breath of our spirit—*but he is not one of us*!! For the coming years of struggle he can creep back to the hearth or the desk or the pub from whence he came. The fighters in the simple brown service shirt of the S A and S S will not miss him on their path forwards to the German revolution, just as they did not meet him when, in long years marked by sacrifices and blood, they fought their passionate fight for a new Germany.

. . . The S A and S S will not tolerate the German revolution going to sleep or being betrayed at the half-way stage by non-combatants. Not for their own sake, but for Germany's sake. For the brown army is the last levy of the nation, the last bastion against Communism.

If the German revolution is wrecked by reactionary opposition, incompetence, or indolence, the German people will fall into despair and will be an easy prey for the bloodstained frenzy coming from the depths of Asia.

For this reason the fantasy in the minds of some 'coordinated' people and even some low-level dignitaries calling themselves National Socialists, that to keep calm is the first duty of a citizen, is a betrayal of the German revolution.

The people who are now everywhere 'involved' and murmur—still softly as yet—their upright-bourgeois little maxim of 'law and order' were nowhere to be seen during our long pilgrimage in search of the new Germany for which we longed. At the most they stood aside and looked on as we fought and bled for Germany. We were too undistinguished for them, too loud, too radical. We still are, as far as they are concerned. It is enough for them that the black-white-and-red colours of the Bismarck empire are flying over Germany and, as a concession to the revolution, the swastika flag. For them the degree of outward power so far acquired, in which they are allowed a share, is enough. They would have even been contented with considerably less, because they did not have to struggle; they were only the beneficiaries of our victory.

. . . If those bourgeois simpletons think it is enough that the State apparatus has received a new sign, that the 'national' revolution has already lasted too long, for once we agree with them. It is in fact high time the national revolution stopped

[1] On 1 May 1933, see below, pp. 423-4.

and became the National Socialist one. Whether they like it or not, we will continue our struggle—if they understand at last what it is about—*with* them; if they are unwilling—*without* them; and if necessary—*against* them!

2 *Party interference with the administration*

The SA were not alone at fault. All sections of the Party were guilty of arbitrary interference both in the State administration and in the business community, as the following account by an unusually responsible SA leader indicates:

The authority of the State is in danger through constant unjustified interference by political officials in the machinery of normal administration.

Every NSBO[1] functionary, NSBO local branch leader, NSBO district leader . . . , every political cell leader, political local branch leader, political district leader is giving orders which interfere with the exercise of the authority of the ministries at the lower levels, that is to say, the authority of the regional governments, the district offices, down to the smallest police station.

Everyone is arresting everyone else, avoiding the prescribed official channels, everyone is threatening everyone else with protective custody, everyone is threatening everyone else with Dachau.[2]

Businesses are being forced to dismiss any number of employees, and businesses are being compelled to take on employees without checking on their qualifications. . . .

Right down to the smallest police station, the best and most reliable officials have become uncertain about the hierarchy of authority; this clearly must have a devastating and destructive effect on the State.

I really cannot be counted among the pussyfooters, and for that very reason I must see that if the revolution is to be turned into an ordered relationship between State and people, the State apparatus must be made completely safe from all revolutionary interference from the street.

It must be left to the responsibility of the State ministries alone, both in the spheres of policy and of personnel, to embody revolutionary ideas in a form which is suitable to the community. . . .

Every little street cleaner today feels he is responsible for matters which he has never understood. . . .

No one can dispute the fact that, at the moment, two-thirds of the daily work in my area, and in all other areas I know, has to be wasted on trifles arising from Party officials' lack of discipline. . . .

The leadership principle is in grave danger from these conditions. . . . I do not mind if my giving this warning makes me appear a grumbler. I can only state that these present circumstances must inevitably lead to chaos.

Hitler had little sympathy for the disillusionment of the SA. He was concerned at the threat to the stability of the regime presented by this

[1] *Nationalsozialistische Betriebszellenorganisation*: the National Socialist Factory Cell Organization.
[2] The notorious concentration camp near Munich.

constant interference by the Party and the SA at the lower levels. Such arbitrary behaviour might alienate important groups such as the Army, industry, and the Civil Service. It could jeopardize economic recovery and so prevent the regime from gaining the popular support it needed. It could delay his main objective of mobilizing the economic resources and will of the nation for diplomatic and strategic purposes. For this a period of stability was essential.

3 *Hitler on the conclusion of the revolution, 6 July 1933*

On 6 July 1933, therefore, in a speech to the Reich Governors (*Reichsstatt-halter*), he formally ended the revolution which, he insisted, must from now on take the form of evolution. This did not mean that there were to be no more fundamental changes but that such changes must in future be initiated from above and not from below, and that tactical compromises would be necessary to ensure the stability of the regime:

The political parties have now been finally abolished. This is an historic event, the meaning and significance of which many people have not yet understood. We must now abolish the last remnants of democracy, especially the methods of election and the majority decisions still employed today in local government, in economic organizations and works committees, and the responsibility of the individual must be stressed.

The achievement of outward power must be followed by the inward education of man. We must beware of making doctrinaire decisions from one day to the next and of expecting a final solution from them. People are easily capable of bending outward form to suit their own intellectual stamp. The switch-over must not be made until suitable people have been found to carry out the switching. More revolutions have succeeded in their first assault than, once successful, have been brought to a standstill and held there. Revolution is not a permanent state, it must not develop into a lasting state. The full spate of revolution must be guided into the secure bed of evolution. In this the most important part is played by the education of the people. The present state of affairs must be improved and the people embodying it must be educated in the National Socialist conception of the State. A businessman must not therefore be dismissed if he is a good businessman even if he is not yet a good National Socialist; especially not if the National Socialist put in his place knows nothing about business. In business, ability alone must be decisive. The task of National Socialism is the safeguarding of the development of our people. But we must not keep looking round to see what next to revolutionize; rather we have the task of securing one position after another in order to hold them, and occupy them gradually in model fashion. In this we must gear our actions to a period of many years, and plan in terms of long periods of time. We do not provide bread for any worker by theoretically coordinating people. History will not judge us by the number of businessmen we dismissed or locked up, but by whether we knew how to provide work. Today we have the absolute power to succeed. But we must be able to replace those we dismiss by their betters. The businessman must be judged first on his business abilities; we must keep the economic apparatus in order. We shall not abolish unemployment with economic commissions, or with theories and blueprints of organizations. The main thing now is not programmes and ideas but the daily bread of five million people. The economy is a living organism which cannot be changed at a blow; it is constructed according to primitive laws bound up with human nature. The carriers of intellectual poison now seeking to penetrate the economy are a menace to both State and people. Practical experience must not be rejected simply because it is opposed to a particular idea.

In confronting the nation with reforms, we must show that we understand things and can cope with them. Our task is work, work, and again work! Our success in providing work will be our most powerful source of authority. Our programme is not a matter of fine gestures, but of maintaining the life of the German people.

The ideas of the programme do not demand that we act like fools and overturn everything, but that we realize our concepts wisely and carefully. In the long run, the more successful the economic underpinning of our programme, the more secure will be our political power. Reich Governors must ensure, and are responsible for seeing, that no organizations or party authorities shall claim governmental rights, dismiss people, or fill offices for which only the Reich Government and, in the field of economics, only the Reich Minister of Economics is responsible.

The Party has now become the State. All power comes under the authority of the Reich. The emphasis of German life must be prevented from shifting back into particular areas or even organizations. No longer does authority stem from any part of the Reich but only from the concept of the Germans as a nation.

4 Circular of the Reich Minister of the Interior, 6 October 1934

This statement, however, had only a limited effect on the Party activists, and above all, on the SA men, who felt disgruntled at the fact that the Nazi take-over had made so little difference to their lives, apart from giving them the satisfaction of revenge on their political opponents. This is clear from the fact that only three months later Frick felt obliged to send out the following circular:

Despite repeated announcements by the Reich Chancellor and despite my numerous circulars new infringements by subordinate leaders and members of the SA have been reported again and again during the past weeks. Above all, SA leaders and SA men have independently carried out police actions either for which they had no authority whatever or which they carried out in a way that cannot be reconciled with the existing laws and regulations of the National Socialist Government. In this way even the extra-territorial status of the ambassador of a foreign power has recently been seriously violated by unauthorized SA men, thereby involving the foreign policy of the Government.

These infringements and excesses must now cease once and for all. I make it the duty of Reich Governors, State Governments and all subordinate institutions to intervene sharply against such infringements or any attempt at unauthorized interference. Unless members of the SA are employed as auxiliary police officers or as auxiliary officials in the frontier service by the proper authorities, they have no police jurisdiction whatsoever. In future, therefore, all police activities of the SA in all circumstances must cease. Where it becomes necessary in exceptional circumstances to employ members of the SA to assist the police in particular actions, they must never act independently but only in the *presence* and *under the supervision* of the police and only in accordance with the orders of the police officer. The leader of the police force carries full responsibility for the employment and the conduct of such auxiliary SA men. Furthermore, auxiliary police officers and auxiliary border customs officers are not to carry out their work except in the company of an *official*. Only if these orders are minutely observed can *agents provocateurs* be effectively prevented from damaging the SA and the National Socialist State.

The functions of the National Socialist State administration and the police executive must not be disturbed in any way by unauthorized infringements on the part of the SA. The authorities must not submit to such interference. Punishable actions by members of the SA must be prosecuted. Officials must not have the feeling that to do so could be in any way against their interests. I consider it necessary to draw the particular attention of police and court authorities to this. In cases in which members of the SA have undoubtedly committed punishable acts, there must never again be any ground for saying that the culprits could not be found or that their prosecution was prevented, even when these were ordinary punishable acts having nothing to do with the struggle for the national uprising. Such measures are as much in the interest of the SA itself as they are essential for the maintenance of the authority of the National Socialist State, which must be safeguarded by all authorities and officials under all circumstances and against all attacks.

At the special request of the Reich Chancellor, I ask the Reich Governors to see that these principles of National Socialist State policy are observed, and to ensure that all State authorities act in accordance with them and that officials who fail to abide by them are brought to justice as well as the guilty members of the SA.

The Reich Chancellor, in his capacity as Supreme SA leader, will publish a corresponding decree to the SA which will be made known to every SA office and every SA man.

During the autumn and winter of 1933, the SA was becoming more and more a law unto itself. In addition to the interference of the SA commissars in the Government offices at various levels, the SA was also intervening in the judicial process, forcing the prosecuting authorities to drop charges against SA men and successfully asserting its right to discipline SA men who broke the law. It had even established its own police force, the *Feldjäger*, who claimed sole jurisdiction in matters involving the SA. The monthly reports prepared by the Gestapo on the political and economic situation referred to the discontent of the population at the undisciplined behaviour of the SA and their concern at the obvious inability of the authorities to do anything about it. People would refer derisively to the 'so-called Public Prosecutor'.

This resentment at the SA was not restricted to the State authorities (which included the Gestapo) or the population at large; it was even shared to some extent by the Party authorities. The feud between the SA and the political organization was one of long standing, and now the SA did not disguise its contempt for the political leadership at local and district level. According to the Gestapo, the SA men mocked the local Party officials as 'Christmas tree men' and 'Lametta stallions' because of their uniforms which the SA felt were undeserved by these Party bureaucrats. 'Political earth-worms' was another current epithet.

But much more serious from Hitler's point of view were the military ambitions of the SA. Apart from its rather vague social revolutionary aims, the SA under Röhm had a more concrete objective: it aspired to become *the* armed force of the State into which the Regular Army would be integrated. To this plan the Army leadership was totally opposed. Under the new Minister of Defence, General von Blomberg, who was a pro-Nazi, the Army had adopted a benevolent attitude towards the new regime. This was also partly dictated by the belief in the need to win Hitler's support in resisting the ambitions of the SA—a good instance of the way in which Hitler could use the Nazi organizations to put pressure on other bodies so that in effect they 'coordinated' themselves.

But by the beginning of 1934, the Army authorities were becoming increasingly concerned about the military ambitions of the SA, which by absorbing other paramilitary organizations had grown to over 2,500,000 men compared with the 100,000 or slightly more of the Army. Hitler could not afford to antagonize the Army, the one organization which had the power to remove him from office. An efficient and contented Army was also essential if he was to achieve the aims of his foreign policy. The riff-raff of the SA would be no substitute.

At a conference on 28 February 1934, attended by Army, SA and SS leaders, Hitler rejected Röhm's idea of a militia. He made Blomberg and Röhm sign an agreement by which the SA would be responsible for pre- and post-military training under the direction of the Army.

5 *The Minister of Defence to Hitler, 2 March 1934*

But two days later, Blomberg drew Hitler's attention to an instance of the growing military activity of the SA which was particularly serious in that it involved the region which had been demilitarized by the Versailles Treaty. This could cause diplomatic complications which would in turn complicate the process of rearmament:

I feel obliged to refer again to the significance of the armed staff guards of the SA. According to an order of the Chief of Staff [of the SA] every *Obergruppe* and group is to set up its own armed staff guards with a heavy machine gun company. This has already begun in certain areas. According to a report by the Commander of Military District VI, leaders of SA brigades are planning the formation of such a staff guard as well and are swearing in SA people for 1–1½ years for that purpose. Selection and training are being carried out with the aim of appearing in public. In terms of numbers this would amount to 6000–8000 men permanently armed with guns and machine guns in that military district alone. It is particularly unfortunate that the formation of these staff guards is taking place in connexion with so-called SA auxiliary labour camps which are mostly situated in the big cities. Today I received a report that a staff guard armed like this is being formed in Höchst am Main, that is to say, in the neutral zone. Such a policy nullifies all precautions by the army in the neutral zone and in the Krüger[1] camps under its control.

Since the Chief of Staff is absent from Berlin I am sending this report directly to the Chancellor.

6 Röhm's announcement of leave for the SA, June–July 1934

Tension between the Army and the SA continued to build up in the early summer. But on 7 June, following a long interview with Hitler, Röhm published the following announcement. Though it showed distinct signs of belligerence, it nevertheless seems to indicate that, despite Hitler's later allegations, Röhm had no plans for a putsch during this period.

I have decided to follow the advice of my doctors and take a cure in order to restore my energies which have been severely strained by a painful nervous complaint. My place will be taken by the Chief of the Leadership Office, Obergruppen-führer von Krausser.

1934 will require all the energies of every SA fighter. I recommend, therefore, to all SA leaders to begin organizing leave already in June.

Therefore, for a limited number of SA leaders and men, June, and for the majority of the SA, July, will be a period of complete relaxation in which they can recover their strength.

I expect the SA to return on 1 August completely rested and refreshed in order to serve in those honourable capacities which nation and fatherland expect of it. If the enemies of the SA live in hope that the SA will not return, or will return only in part, from its leave, we will allow them this brief pleasurable anticipation. They will receive the appropriate reply at the time and in the manner appearing most suitable.

The SA is and remains Germany's destiny.

7 Vice-Chancellor Franz von Papen addresses the University of Marburg, 17 June 1934

During June, the crisis was deepened by two further developments. In the first place, it became clear that the Reich President, Hindenburg, had not long to live. This raised the matter of the succession. If Hitler wished to combine the offices of Chancellor and President and avoid a new Conservative President being imposed on him, he would need the approval of the Army.

Secondly, Papen became the spokesman of conservative circles in the bureaucracy and in business who were discontented at the excesses of the

---

[1] SA Obergruppenführer Krüger ran the *Ausbildungswesen* – in charge of the pre-military training of the youth organizations.

SA and concerned about talk of a second revolution. On 17 June, Papen articulated this discontent in a speech at the University of Marburg, the reporting of which Goebbels promptly banned:

. . . The events of the past eighteen months have gripped the whole German nation and stirred it to its depths. Almost as if in a dream we have found our way out of the vale of despondency, hopelessness, hatred and division, back to the community of the German nation. . . .

The domination of a single party in place of the multiparty system, which has rightly disappeared, seems to me, historically speaking, a transitional phase, justified only so long as the revolution must be secured and until the new process of selecting personnel starts to operate. For the logic of the anti-liberal development demands the principle of an organic political development which rests on the voluntary adherence of *all* sections of the nation. Parties can be superseded only by organic bonds creating that free national community to the establishment of which this revolution must lead. . . .

There is no point in disguising the emergence of a certain hiatus between the intellectual aims and the day-to-day reality of the German revolution. . . .

It is certainly obvious that the bearers of the revolutionary principle should initially occupy also the positions of power. But once the revolution has taken place, the Government must represent the people as a whole, and must on no account be the exponent only of particular groups; otherwise it would fail in its attempt to construct the national community. We must also get away from false romantic notions which are not appropriate to the twentieth century. We cannot, for example, consider dividing the nation after the manner of the ancient Greeks into Spartans and helots. The final outcome of that development was that the Spartans had to concentrate on repressing the helots, thereby weakening the diplomatic strength of Sparta. In a state where there is a true national community, the domestic political war-cries must finally cease. There must certainly be a process of selection. But the natural criterion for the selection of people for appointments cannot be replaced by that of membership of a particular organization, so long as the motives for such membership cannot be analysed. . . .

I have defined the problems of the German revolution and my attitude towards them particularly sharply because there appears to be endless talk of a second wave which will complete the revolution. Anyone who irresponsibly toys with such ideas should not deceive himself about the fact that a second wave can easily be followed by a third, that he who threatens the guillotine is the first to come under the knife. Nor is it clear in what direction this second wave is meant to lead. It is true that there is much talk about future socialization. Have we experienced an anti-Marxist revolution in order to carry out the programme of Marxism? For any attempt to solve the social question by collectivizing property is Marxism. Will the German people become richer, will its national income grow bigger, will anybody be better off, except possibly those who smell the possibility of plunder in such a raid? There is certainly a social problem caused by economic and demographic processes. But these can be mastered only if property is once more made aware of its responsibilities, not by raising collective irresponsibility to a principle. A form of economic planning which moves further and further away from personal initiative and responsibility must not be made into a principle. For anyone who has not observed that every form of collectivism leads to ineradicable corruption has been going about the world with his eyes shut.

No nation that would survive before history can afford a permanent uprising from below. At some stage the movement must come to an end; at some point there must emerge a firm social structure held together by a legal system secure against pressure and by a State power that is unchallenged. A ceaseless dynamic creates nothing. Germany cannot be allowed to become a train hurtling into the blue with no one knowing where it will stop. History flows of its own accord, it does not need to be constantly driven forward. If, therefore, a second wave of new life is to sweep through the German revolution, then it must do so not as social revolution, but as the creative completion of work already begun. The statesman is there to create forms, his sole concern is for State and people. The State is the sole power and the final guarantee of that which every citizen can claim—iron justice. In the long run, therefore, the State cannot tolerate any dualism, and the success of the German revolution and the future of our nation will depend on the discovery of a satisfactory solution for the dualism between Party and State.

The Government is well aware of the selfishness, the lack of principle, the insincerity, the unchivalrous behaviour, the arrogance which is on the increase under the guise of the German revolution. Nor has it any illusions as to the threat to that reserve of public confidence on which the Government can draw. If it is desired to achieve an intimate and friendly relationship with the people, then their intelligence must not be underestimated, their trust must be reciprocated and there must be no continual attempt to browbeat them. The German people recognize the gravity of the situation, they feel the economic crisis, they have a keen awareness of the weak points in some of the laws that this crisis has produced, they are acutely sensitive to violence and injustice, clumsy attempts at deceiving them with false optimism merely make them smile. In the long run, no organization, no propaganda, however good, can alone retain their confidence. My interpretation, therefore, of the propaganda campaign against 'carpers' is different from that of others.[1] Confidence and willingness to cooperate will not be furthered by incitement, particularly incitement of the young, nor by threats against the defenceless classes of the community, but only by discussion based upon mutual confidence. The people know that great sacrifices are expected of them. They will shoulder them and follow the Führer with unshakeable loyalty, provided they are allowed to have a share in the making and carrying out of decisions, provided every word of criticism is not immediately interpreted as malicious, and provided that despairing patriots are not branded as traitors.

It is time to come together in brotherly love and respect for every citizen, to cease obstructing the work of those who are in earnest, and to silence doctrinaire fanatics. . . .

There was clearly a danger that the Army would combine with the conservative elements in the bureaucracy and business to veto Hitler's succession to Hindenburg, either by persuading Hindenburg before he died to nominate someone else, or by carrying out a *coup* on his death. Hitler

---

[1] On 11 May, Goebbels had launched a campaign against 'grumblers and carpers', aimed primarily at Conservatives.

might be able to counter such a *coup* with the aid of the SA, but this would make him prisoner of the SA. It would also force him into a revolution, thereby jeopardizing all his diplomatic and military objectives, to which the collaboration of business and the professional Army were essential. He needed a period of peace and quiet, in order to restore the economic situation which was dominated by a foreign exchange crisis,[1] and to avoid diplomatic complications in view of the weakness of Germany's diplomatic situation in 1934.[2] All this was threatened by the SA with its demands for a second revolution, its ambition to usurp the role of the Army, and its flagrant contempt for the disarmament provisions of the Versailles Treaty. The SA, which had been very helpful in the acquisition of power, was now a grave embarrassment under the leadership of the ambitious Röhm and his associates.

8 *Field-Marshal Ewald von Kleist on tension between SA and Army at the end of June 1934*

In the meantime, another organization had come to play an independent role in the crisis—the SS. During 1933–34, Himmler, the head of the SS, had succeeded in taking over the political police departments in every state in the Reich, including the Prussian Gestapo.[3] Nominally, the SS was still a part of the SA, and the SA with its huge membership and ambitious leadership was now the main obstacle to the ambitions of the SS. The SS therefore began to warn Hitler and the Army of the intentions of the SA. These rumours prompted the Army to take action which antagonized the SA and this in turn gave rise to more suspicion on the part of Hitler and the Army. This encouragement by the SS of mutual suspicion between Army and SA was described after the war by Field-Marshal von Kleist, from whose testimony it appears that General Reichenau, the right-hand man of Blomberg, the Minister of Defence, was also involved:

Round about 24 June 1934, I as the army commander in Silesia was warned by the Chief of the General Staff [*Heeresleitung*] that an attack by the SA on the Army was imminent and that I should unobtrusively keep my troops on the alert.

During the tense days following, I received a flood of reports and information which gave a picture of feverish preparations on the part of the SA. This information came from the most varied sources (the troops, the SA, old Stahlhelm types, SS, civilians and government authorities). Despite the very reserved attitude adopted by the troops, a dangerous state of tension developed in the garrisons between them and the local SA. Only a spark was needed to touch off the explosion.

In this situation, I considered that bloodshed could only be avoided by a man-to-man talk.

[1] For the foreign exchange crisis during 1934 see below, p. 389.
[2] For Germany's diplomatic situation during 1934 see below, pp. 512–13.
[3] See below, pp. 283–4.

On the afternoon of 28 June, therefore, I asked SA Obergruppenführer Heines[1] to come and see me; I told him to his face that I knew of his preparations and I gave him a warning.

He replied that he knew all about my measures and had thought that they were preparations for an attack on the SA. He had only put the SA on the alert in order to resist an attack. He gave me his word as an officer and SA leader that he had not planned or prepared any surprise attack upon the Army.

During the night of 28–29 June, he rang me up again. He said more or less that as far as he was concerned the situation had changed. He had just learned that not only the Army in Silesia, but from 28 June the Army throughout the Reich, was on the alert for an SA putsch. He was going to fly to Munich early on the 29th to see Röhm. Whereupon I also flew on 29 June to Berlin and reported to Colonel-General Freiherr von Fritsch and General Beck about my conversation with Heines. I added: 'I have the impression that we—Army and SA—are being egged on against each other by a third party.' By that I meant Himmler and that much of the information came from him. Thereupon, Colonel-General Freiherr von Fritsch summoned General von Reichenau and asked me to repeat to him what I had just said. Reichenau replied, 'That may be true, but it's too late now.'

9 *Arrest of SA leadership at Wiessee, Bavaria, 30 June 1934*

As the tension built up, Hitler decided to act. On 29 June he summoned a meeting of SA leaders for the following day at Wiessee in Bavaria. The Army and SS were put on the alert and Göring was given the responsibility of carrying out the action in Berlin. Then, on learning that the SA in Munich had been put on the alert, Hitler flew to Munich in the early hours of the 30th. After the war, Kempka, his chauffeur, described the events of 30 June:

... At Hangelar[2] two machines are already waiting. Hitler and Reich Minister of Propaganda Goebbels climb into a Ju 52. He is accompanied by SA leader Lutze[3] from Hanover, a frequent guest in Goebbels's house, and by the adjutants, Brückner and Schaub, Hitler's first chauffeur, Schreck, and myself. The second machine is intended for the escort squad, reinforced by SS men from the bodyguard....

It is already dawn when we land at the Munich airport, Oberwiesenfeld. During the flight, there had been a light shower and the grass at the airport is sparkling in the morning light. When Hitler jumps out of the machine, two officers of the Reichswehr report to him. He takes them aside and gives them their orders.

Outside the reception building three cars are waiting which have been ordered by wireless from the garage of the Reich Party headquarters in Munich. Some old friends of Hitler's from the early days of the Party are standing by them. Hitler goes up to the cars and orders the hoods to be raised. I am struck by the harshness

---

[1] Police-President of Breslau.
[2] The airport outside Bonn.
[3] SA Obergruppenführer Viktor Lutze, Oberpräsident of the Province of Hanover.

of his voice. His face is even more serious than during the flight. I am already at the wheel when he sits down beside me: 'Kempka, we're going to the Ministry of the Interior first.' . . .

[At the Ministry Hitler arrested the Police-President of Munich, SA Obergruppenführer August Schneidhuber.]

Hitler sits down beside me and gives the order: 'To Wiessee, as fast as possible!'

It must have been about 4.30 a.m., the sky has cleared up, it is nearly bright daylight. We meet watering carts and people on their way to work. . . . Hitler sits beside me in silence. From time to time, I hear Goebbels and Lutze talking in the back.

Just before Wiessee, Hitler suddenly breaks his silence: 'Kempka,' he says, 'drive carefully when we come to the Hotel Hanselbauer. You must drive up without making any noise. If you see an SA guard in front of the hotel, don't wait for them to report to me; drive on and stop at the hotel entrance.' Then, after a moment of deathly silence: 'Röhm wants to carry out a *coup*.'

An icy shiver runs down my back. I could have believed anything, but not a *coup* by Röhm!

I drive up carefully to the hotel entrance as Hitler had ordered. Hitler jumps out of the car, and after him Goebbels, Lutze and the adjutants. Right behind us another car stops with a squad of detectives which had been raised in Munich.

As soon as I have turned the car so that it is ready to leave in a moment, I rush into the hotel with my gun at the ready. In the hall I meet Standartenführer Uhl, the leader of Röhm's staff guard. Hitler's chauffeur, Schreck, is taking him at gunpoint down to the laundry room which for the next hour serves as the first prison for the arrested SA leaders. In passing, Schreck calls out to me: 'Quickly! Run up to the boss! He needs you!'

I run quickly up the stairs to the first floor where Hitler is just coming out of Röhm's bedroom. Two detectives come out of the room opposite. One of them reports to Hitler: 'My Führer . . . the Police-President of Breslau is refusing to get dressed!'

Taking no notice of me, Hitler enters the room where Obergruppenführer Heines is remaining. I hear him shout: 'Heines, if you are not dressed in five minutes I'll have you shot on the spot!'

I withdraw a few steps and a police officer whispers to me that Heines had been in bed with an 18-year-old SA Obertruppführer. At last Heines comes out of the room with an 18-year-old fair-haired boy mincing in front of him.

'Into the laundry room with them!' cries Schreck.

Meanwhile, Röhm comes out of his room in a blue suit and with a cigar in the corner of his mouth. Hitler glares at him but says nothing. Two detectives take Röhm to the vestibule of the hotel where he throws himself into an armchair and orders coffee from the waiter.

I stay in the corridor a little to one side and a detective tells me about Röhm's arrest.

Hitler entered Röhm's bedroom alone with a whip in his hand. Behind him were two detectives with pistols at the ready. He spat out the words: 'Röhm, you are under arrest.' Röhm looked up sleepily from his pillow: 'Heil, my Führer.' 'You are under arrest' bawled Hitler for the second time, turned on his heel and left the room.

Meanwhile, upstairs in the corridor things are getting quite lively. SA leaders are coming out of their rooms and being arrested. Hitler shouts at each one: 'Have you had anything to do with Röhm's schemes?' Naturally, they all deny it, but that doesn't help them in the least. Hitler usually knows about the individual; occasionally, he asks Goebbels or Lutze a question. And then comes the decision: 'Arrested!'

But there are others whom he lets go. Röhm's doctor SA Gruppenführer Ketterer comes out of a room and to our surprise he has his wife with him. I hear Lutze putting in a good word for him with Hitler. Then Hitler walks up to him, greets him, shakes hands with his wife and asks them to leave the hotel; it isn't a pleasant place for them to stay in, that day.

We follow Hitler into the yard and here he tells his chauffeur, Schreck, to charter a bus as quickly as possible to take the SA leaders who are in the laundry room to Munich. How slowly the minutes pass! More and more SA leaders arrive from outside and are brought into the laundry room. I stand at the hotel entrance and hear Röhm order coffee from the hotel manager for the third time.

Suddenly ... there is the sound of a car arriving! At first I thought it was the bus chartered by Schreck but instead, to my horror, a lorry full of heavily armed SA men rattles into the yard. Now there'll be some shooting, I think to myself. I can see Brückner negotiating with the Sturmführer of the SA. The man seems to be refusing. Walking backwards, he tries to get to his lorry.... At this moment Hitler goes up to him: 'Drive back to Munich immediately!' he tells the puzzled fellow. 'If you are stopped by SS on the way, you must let yourselves be disarmed without resistance.'

The Sturmführer salutes and jumps into the lorry, and the SA men leave again. No shot, no sign of resistance. All this time, Röhm is sitting unsuspectingly drinking his third cup of coffee. Only a single word from him, and the whole thing would have worked out differently.

Now the bus arrives which has been fetched by Schreck. Quickly, the SA leaders are collected from the laundry room and walk past Röhm under police guard. Röhm looks up from his coffee sadly and waves to them in a melancholy way....

At last Röhm too is led from the hotel. He walks past Hitler with his head bowed, completely apathetic. Now Hitler gives the order to leave. I sit at the wheel of the first car with Hitler beside me and our column, which in the meantime has grown to about twenty cars, starts moving.

It might be about 8 o'clock and it is a wonderful day. After St Quirin the column splits up. For security reasons, Röhm and the other prisoners are taken on a detour to Stadelheim.[1] 'Kempka,' says Hitler, when the other cars have disappeared, 'from now onwards you must stop every car we meet. We want to take a look at the SA leaders on their way to Wiessee.'

About twenty SA leaders, on leaving their cars, are arrested by Hitler in person. But now and again we do have a change. Rudolf Hess gets out of one of the cars we stop. Hitler actually asks him: 'Have you had any part in Röhm's schemes?' But Hess only smiles and Hitler shakes hands with him.... At 6 p.m. we fly back to Berlin from the Oberwiesenfeld airport. For Hitler the Munich action is over....

[1] The prison in Munich.

10 *The murder of Röhm*

After the war, the governor of the prison recorded:

... Nobody was allowed to leave the prison that night either. Next morning (Sunday 1 July 1934) two SS men asked at the reception desk to be taken to Röhm. Zink, who was at the entrance, in view of the strict instructions he had been given, refused. It was about 9.30 a.m. When the two tried to force their way in, Zink alerted the prison governor and the green police [state police], who at once occupied the corridors and prevented any intrusion. The governor ascertained that neither of the SS men had proper authorization. It therefore took hours of telephoning to check their papers; even the Reich Chancellery was rung up. When at last it became clear that they had an order from Hitler, the two murderers had to be taken to Röhm in the new building.

There they handed over a Browning to Röhm, who once again asked to speak to Hitler. They ordered him to shoot himself. If he did not comply, they would come back in ten minutes and kill him.... When the time was up, the two SS men re-entered the cell, and found Röhm standing with his chest bared. Immediately one of them from the door shot him in the throat, and Röhm collapsed on the floor. Since he was still alive, he was killed with a shot point-blank through the temple. The bullet not only penetrated his skull, but also the ceiling of the cell below....

11 *Göring's direction of the purge in Berlin*

Of the other SA leaders arrested at Wiessee, six were executed by an SS firing squad at Stadelheim Prison. The rest of the executions were carried out in the Berlin barracks of Hitler's bodyguard. In Berlin the purge was under Göring's direction. The following description by a police official gives a sense of the atmosphere of the occasion:

... Suddenly there are loud shouts in the large room next door. It is Göring's study, where the executive committee is meeting. From time to time Gestapo messengers come rushing in bringing small white pieces of paper. Through the door one can see Göring, Himmler, Heydrich and little Pilli Körner, Göring's State Secretary in the Minister-Presidency, putting their heads together. Of course it is impossible to hear what they are talking about. But things are happening devilish fast. Occasionally we hear an inarticulate sound like 'Off!' or 'Aha!' or 'Shoot!' or simply raucous laughter. In any case they don't seem in a bad mood.

Göring even exudes an air of well-fed comfort. He gives the impression of being in his element. He strides round his room. He struts to and fro, an unforgettable picture: with his flowing head of hair, his white tunic, his grey-blue military trousers, his white boots with their high flaps reaching up over the knees of this unwieldy pot-belly. A comparison springs to my mind: there goes Puss in Boots! ...

But, as I said, things suddenly begin to get very noisy within. Police Major Jakobi rushes out of the room in great haste with his helmet on and his chinstrap under his red face. Göring's hoarse voice booms after him: 'Shoot them down ... Fetch a whole company ... Shoot them down ... Shoot ... Shoot at once ... Just shoot them down ... Shoot...!' One can't begin to describe the blatant bloodthirstiness, the savage fury, the hideous vindictiveness, and yet at the same time the terror, the craven terror shown in this scene. Everyone senses, Someone has escaped who must not be allowed to escape, someone whose escape will undo the whole day's work. . . .

The man who was thought to have got away was Gregor Strasser, Hitler's old colleague and rival. But the rumour was untrue; Strasser was murdered all right. The purge was in fact used by the Nazis to pay off a number of old scores. The former Bavarian State Commissioner, Gustav von Kahr, who had thwarted Hitler at the time of the putsch in 1923, was murdered; so was General von Schleicher, who had tried to split the Nazi Party with the help of Strasser in 1932. Hitler also struck at his conservative and Catholic opponents. Papen himself was only placed under house arrest, but the author of his Marburg speech, the writer Edgar Jung, was murdered and so was his press officer, von Bose. The exact number of those murdered in the course of the purge is unknown; but it was probably not less than a hundred, and may have run into hundreds. Even Wilhelm Schmidt, the music critic of the Munich paper, *Münchener Neueste Nachrichten*, was murdered; the SS assassins mistook him for someone else.

12 *General von Blomberg's announcement to the Army, 1 July 1934*

A significant role in the affair had been played by the Army. It had not confined itself to looking on benevolently, but had actually provided arms and transport for the SS squads and had made preparations to counter any SA resistance. When it was all over, Blomberg, the Defence Minister, publicly thanked Hitler in the name of the Army:

The Führer with soldierly decision and exemplary courage has himself attacked and crushed the traitors and murderers. The Army, as the bearer of arms of the entire people, far removed from the conflicts of domestic politics, will show its gratitude through devotion and loyalty. The good relationship towards the new SA demanded by the Führer will be gladly fostered by the Army in the consciousness that the ideals of both are held in common. The state of emergency has come to an end everywhere.

13 *Hindenburg's telegram to Hitler, 2 July 1934*

The President also sent his good wishes and a similar telegram to Göring. He was no longer capable of making an independent assessment of the situation. But the fact that he was prepared to lend his prestige to the purge was of considerable help to Hitler who had the task of persuading public opinion that it had been essential for the security of the State:

I note from the reports I have received that through your decisive intervention and your courageous personal commitment you have nipped all the treasonable intrigues in the bud. You have saved the German nation from serious danger and for this I express to you my deeply felt gratitude and my sincere appreciation.

14 *Purge declared to be self-defence of the State*

The Cabinet then retroactively legalized the purge:

At the meeting of the Reich Cabinet on Tuesday 3 July, the Reich Chancellor, Adolf Hitler, began by giving a detailed account of the origin and suppression of the high treason plot. The Reich Chancellor stressed that lightning action had been necessary, otherwise many thousands of people would have been in danger of being wiped out.

Defence Minister General von Blomberg thanked the Führer in the name of the Reich Cabinet and the army for his determined and courageous action, by which he had saved the German people from civil war. The Führer had shown greatness as a statesman and soldier. This had aroused in the hearts of the members of the Cabinet and of the whole German people a vow of service, devotion, and loyalty in this grave hour.

The Reich Cabinet then approved a law on measures for the self-defence of the State. Its single paragraph reads:

'The measures taken on 30 June and 1 and 2 July to suppress the acts of high treason are legal, being necessary for the self-defence of the State.'

Reich Minister of Justice Dr Gürtner commented that measures of self-defence taken before the imminent occurrence of a treasonable action should be considered not only legal but the duty of a statesman.

15 *Hitler's report to the Reichstag, 13 July 1934*

On 13 July 1934 Hitler justified his action in the Reichstag with a fictitious story of a plot:

... Without once informing me and at a moment when I had no thought of any such action, Chief of Staff Röhm entered into relations with General Schleicher through an utterly corrupt and dishonest go-between, a certain Herr von A.[1] It was General Schleicher who spelt out the secret aims of Chief of Staff Röhm. It was he who gave concrete form to the ideas of the latter and maintained that:

1. The present regime in Germany is not to be tolerated.

2. Above all, the Army and all national associations must be united in a single band.

3. The only man to be considered for such a position is Chief of Staff Röhm.

4. Herr von Papen must be removed and he himself would be ready to take the position of Vice-Chancellor; moreover, further important changes must be made in the Cabinet of the Reich.

As usual in such cases, there began then the search for the men to form the new Government, always with the understanding that I myself should, at least for the time being, be left in the position which I now hold.

The carrying out of these proposals of General von Schleicher was bound, as soon as Point 2 was reached, to come up against my unalterable opposition. Considering either the facts or his personal character, I could never have consented to a change in the Reich Ministry of War or to the appointment of Chief of Staff Röhm to that Ministry.

[1] Werner von Alvensleben, an associate of Schleicher's.

Firstly: consider the facts. For fourteen years I have stated consistently that the fighting organizations of the Party are political institutions and have nothing to do with the Army. On the facts of the case I should consider it a disavowal of my own convictions and of my fourteen years of political life if I were now to summon the leader of the SA to the command of the Army. In November 1923 I proposed as the head of the Army not the man who was then leader of my SA, Captain Göring, but an officer.

Secondly: consider the question of human character. On this matter I could never have concurred in General von Schleicher's proposal. When these plans became known to me my view of Chief of Staff Röhm's personal worth was already such that as a man of conscience and for the sake of the Army I could then under no circumstances even think of admitting him to that post: the supreme head of the Army is none other than the Field-Marshal and President of the Reich. As Chancellor I have given my oath into his keeping. For all of us his person is inviolate. The promise I gave him that I would preserve the Army as a non-political instrument of the Reich I hold as binding, both from my innermost conviction and also from my pledged word. Furthermore, considering my personal relations with the Defence Minister of the Reich, any such act would have been impossible. Not only I myself but all of us are happy to recognize in him a man of honour from the crown of his head to the soles of his feet. He reconciled the Army with those who were once revolutionaries and has linked it up with their Government today and he has done this from his own deepest convictions. In the most genuine loyalty he has made his own the principle for which I myself will stand to my last breath.

In the State there is only one bearer of arms—the Army; there is only one bearer of the political will—the National Socialist Party. . . .

16 *Frick seeks to eliminate SA influence on administration*

In the meantime, Frick, the Reich Minister of the Interior, had seized his opportunity to eliminate the influence of the SA on the administration. This had been exercised officially through the special SA delegates (*Sonderbevollmächtigte*) who had been appointed to supervise the various levels of administration under an order issued by Röhm on 12 May 1933. On 4 July 1934 Frick wrote to the new SA Chief of Staff, Viktor Lutze:

Some time ago, the previous Chief of Staff ordered the appointment of special SA delegates and representatives to the State Governments and their subordinate offices. This institution has not proved in the least beneficial. The delegates and representatives have in many cases claimed powers to which they were not entitled and have interfered with and impeded the orderly conduct of business by the State apparatus. I therefore request that you recall the special delegates and representatives at once.

The State Governments have received a copy of this letter.

Less than a week later, on 10 July, Lutze complied by issuing an order which abolished the institution of SA delegates to the State administration.

17 The Führer raises the S S to the status of an independent organization, 20 July 1934

However, this victory of the State authorities in their battle to retain their authority and independence was to prove only temporary. A far greater threat to their power had emerged out of the Röhm 'putsch'—the SS. For Hitler now repaid his debt to the SS for their role in the affair by separating them from the now emasculated SA and granting them the status of an independent organization. The SS were to provide the regime with a much more effective weapon for social control. Whereas the SA terror had been spontaneous, arbitrary, crude and disruptive, the SS were to make use of techniques which were far more coordinated, systematic and sophisticated; in the service of the regime they were to make terror a bureaucratic weapon. Furthermore, whereas the SA had embarked on a fruitless attempt to control the State administration through the SA delegates, that is to say, from a position outside the bureaucracy, the SS had from the start adopted a policy of infiltrating the bureaucracy and taking over segments of the State apparatus, beginning with the political police.[1] This tactic was to prove itself infinitely more successful:

In view of highly meritorious service on the part of the SS, especially in connexion with the events of 30 June 1934, I elevate it to the status of an independent organization within the NSDAP. The Reichsführer SS is therefore, like the Chief of Staff [of the SA], directly subordinate to the Supreme SS Führer. The Chief of Staff and the Reichsführer SS are both invested with the Party rank of Reichsleiter.

18 Law concerning the Sovereign Head of the German Reich, 1 August 1934

On 2 August 1934 President Hindenburg died. Immediately, the following law was promulgated. The Army and the Conservatives had repaid their debt to Hitler, who had saved them from the SA. Hitler had sacrificed the 'old fighters' to his major objective—internal mobilization, to which political stability and economic recovery were essential. He was now officially Führer not only of the Party but also of the German people.

The Reich Government has enacted the following law which is hereby promulgated:
Section 1. The office of Reich President will be combined with that of Reich Chancellor. The existing authority of the Reich President will consequently be transferred to the Führer and Reich Chancellor, Adolf Hitler. He will select his deputy.
Section 2. This law is effective as of the time of the death of Reich President von Hindenburg.

[1] See below, pp. 283-4.

19 *Oath of Reich officials and German soldiers, 20 August 1934*

The absolute control which Hitler now exercised over the State was reflected in the following oaths, which were introduced within the month. Significantly, they were taken to Hitler not as Head of the State, but as 'Führer of the German Reich and people', a totally new form of authority. The first stage in the 'seizure of power' was now complete.

Article 1. The public officials and the soldiers of the armed forces must take an oath of loyalty on entering service.
Article 2.
1. The oath of loyalty of public officials will be:
   'I swear: I shall be loyal and obedient to Adolf Hitler, the Führer of the German Reich and people, respect the laws, and fulfil my official duties conscientiously, so help me God.'
2. The oath of loyalty of the soldiers of the armed forces will be:
   'I swear by God this sacred oath: I will render unconditional obedience to Adolf Hitler, the Führer of the German nation and people, Supreme Commander of the Armed Forces, and will be ready as a brave soldier to risk my life at any time for this oath.'
Article 3. Officials already in service must swear the oath without delay according to Art. 2, number 1.

20 *Hitler thanks von Blomberg, 20 August 1934*

Now, after the confirmation of the Law of 2 August by the German people, I wish to express my gratitude to you and through you to the Wehrmacht for your oath of loyalty to me as your leader and Commander-in-Chief. Just as the officers and men of the Wehrmacht pledge themselves to the new State in my person, so shall I always regard it as my highest duty to support the continued existence and inviolability of the armed forces in compliance with the testament of the late Field-Marshal [Hindenburg] and faithful to my own will to establish the Army firmly as the sole bearer of arms in the nation.

The attitude of the population to the Röhm affair varied. Some of the more educated people, particularly those with foreign sources of information, were horrified at what had happened. The propaganda of the Left in exile also made capital out of the crushing of the revolutionary wing of the Nazi movement, though Nazi propaganda cleverly emphasized the involvement of 'reactionary elements' and made it appear as if it was these which had been crushed. The majority of people seem to have been relieved by what they saw as a timely lesson to the most undisciplined section of the Nazi movement. Hitherto they had comforted themselves with the belief that the Führer was not aware of the actions of these local Nazis and would not have approved if he had been. Now Hitler's measures over the Röhm affair seemed to confirm this judgement and they hoped that he would continue the purge through other Party organizations.

21 *The Gestapo reports popular reaction to the Röhm 'putsch', 5 July 1934*

The following report of the Harburg-Wilhelmsburg Gestapo office throws light not only on the attitude of the population but even more on the attitude of the Gestapo itself and of the Government authorities in general. It is a typical instance of the way in which such reports, though offering in general a fairly objective account of events, were also used to press by indirect means a point of view which the author of the report was afraid to express bluntly. His definition of National Socialism is also a significant indication of the mentality of many officials and illustrates the virtue of the vagueness of Nazi ideology, enabling it to accommodate a range of different emphases:

In the month covered by this report the 30th of June naturally has pride of place. The measures proceeded smoothly in this area. . . . Among the population at large, confidence in the Führer has been consolidated by his energetic action. There are, however, increasing requests for further energetic measures to be taken in the various Party organizations right down to the lowest levels, and in particular there are demands for liberation from 'the local Mussolinis'. If all the [Party] formations restricted themselves to the tasks delegated to them by the Führer instead of giving orders to the governmental authorities, the whole population could long ago have been filled with the spirit of National Socialism—in particular, with a sense of responsibility, cleanliness and discipline. It is essential that the Führer's announcement regarding the purging of the SA[1] should be acted upon by all Party organizations. . . .

[1] This announcement of 2 July 1934 consisted of twelve points laid down by Hitler for the reorganization of the SA.

PART III   The Political Structure of the Third Reich

The 'seizure of power' brought two very different organizations, the Party and the Civil Service, face to face with one another. In theory the Nazi Party organization was based on the so-called *Führerprinzip* or 'principle of leadership'. This principle laid down that at all levels of the organization authority was concentrated in a single individual or leader rather than in a committee or in the membership as a whole. Furthermore, it laid down that the authority of this leader over his subordinates was absolute. Again, in theory this made for a very simple and clear-cut hierarchical structure of authority. In practice, even before 1933, the situation was much more complex and confused. For, although superficially the Party adhered to a form of hierarchy, in fact its basis of authority was not bureaucratic but charismatic. That is to say, Hitler's authority was not derived from his office as leader but from his exceptional qualities as an individual and leader in the eyes of his followers. All authority within the Party was ultimately concentrated in the hands of the leader, Hitler. It is true that some form of hierarchy was necessary for the functioning of such an elaborate organization. But those who held authority at subordinate level did so in the final analysis as Hitler's direct representatives. Hitler was never bound by the hierarchy and could go outside it whenever he chose. This is illustrated by the fact that even before 1933 the hierarchy of the political organization of the Nazi Party was undermined by the tenuous control of the headquarters in Munich over the Gauleiters, who regarded themselves as Hitler's personal representatives in their area, answerable only to him.

On coming to power in 1933, the Party found itself faced with a very different form of organization – the German Civil Service, a bureaucracy of high competence and long traditions. Until recently there has been a tendency to lay stress upon the great measure of sympathy shown to Hitler's Government by a large section of the Civil Service. This certainly was so. The German Civil Service was on the whole a highly conservative body which had regarded the Weimar Republic with some hostility. Parliamentary democracy had meant the forfeiture to party politicians of some of the power which it had exercised under the Empire, and this was resented. Many believed that an authoritarian dictatorship would free the Civil Service from 'political interference', that is to say, from party political interference. They assumed that the non-party conservative members of the Government would control the Nazis. The influence of the Civil Service had after all largely survived the revolution of 1918, and they assumed that the same would be true on this occasion.

As it became clear that the Nazis were in control, some civil servants justified to themselves their continuation in office with the argument that they were remaining 'to prevent worse things happening' under a Nazi replacement, as the Finance Minister put it in his memoirs. The danger of this attitude was that by participating in the regime they were forced more and more to compromise their principles, thereby losing their moral integrity until they were debased into becoming mere functionaries. This dilemma is starkly revealed in the attitudes of two leading diplomats to the Nazi take-over. Bernhard von Bülow, State Secretary in the German Foreign Ministry until his death in 1936 and a highly civilized diplomat, chose to stay in office in the hope of keeping German diplomacy out of the hands of the Nazis and of preventing extreme policies which might jeopardize Germany's security. Yet the result of his actions was merely to make the Nazis' task of persuading other countries to come to terms with the new regime that much easier by giving it an aura of respectability and the appearance of continuity. Shortly before his death he justified his attitude with the words: 'One can't leave one's country in the lurch because it has a bad government.'[1] The German ambassador in the United States, Friedrich von Prittwitz, on the other hand, resigned his post as early as 6 March 1933. He explained to a friend: 'One must only put oneself at the disposal of a government for which certain basic values of humanity and justice are sacred. Coming to terms with inhuman principles in order to avoid something allegedly worse leads to disaster.'[2]

Apart from the particular notion of patriotism current among the German middle class which tended to believe in 'My country, right or wrong', there was another factor involved. Crucial to an understanding of the outlook of the German Civil Service and in particular of their attitude towards the new regime is the fact that the basis of Civil Service training was extremely legalistic. Apart from those in technical fields, Civil Service recruits had invariably studied law at the university and their initial in-service training continued to have a strong legal bias. Unlike the Anglo-Saxon legal system which is based on a combination of precedent as embodied in the Common Law and statutes passed by the legislature, German law followed the Roman system and was derived almost entirely from legislation initiated by the Government. Whereas the Anglo-Saxon Common Law reflected a tradition of the defence of individual rights against the State, German law reflected the tradition of a strong state as the embodiment of the community by which individuals would be granted such rights as were considered compatible with its interests. During the nineteenth century German jurisprudence had come to be dominated by a theory which rationalized this tradition, the theory of legal positivism. The legal positivists conceived of law as a manifestation of the authority of the State. It was law because the State had decreed it to be so. In their view the sovereign State could not be bound by any prior moral order against which the justice or otherwise of the laws could be measured. In this view they were reacting against the theory of

---

[1] Peter Krüger & Erich J. C. Hahn, 'Der Loyalitätskonflikt des Staatssekretärs Bernhard Wilhelm von Bülow im Frühjahr 1933', *Vierteljahrshefte für Zeitgeschichte*, vol. 20 (1972), p. 410.
[2] ibid.

natural law which had maintained that there were certain moral precepts of natural justice which must form the basis of all law. The legal positivists considered the natural law theory to be irrational and unscientific since there would always be different views about what exactly constituted natural law. They preferred the clarity of a legal system based on legislative enactment by the State. It is important to note that, so far as the legal positivists were concerned, the nature of the regime which controlled the State or the methods by which that regime had been established were immaterial. The important fact was that it was the sovereign State. It was this fact which conferred authority on the laws which it issued.

The dominance of legal positivism in German jurisprudence during this period and the fact that the Civil Service received a predominantly legal training greatly facilitated the Nazi take-over of power. It reinforced the emphasis on conformity inherent in any bureaucracy by enabling the Civil Service to rationalize almost any action, however immoral, provided it took the form of a law or decree. It is clear that without the assistance of the Civil Service the Nazis could never have consolidated their power.

Yet ironically, it was precisely this legalistic bias of the German Civil Service which made the Nazis, and Hitler in particular, so suspicious of it. For its adherence to rational procedures and legal norms was in complete contrast to the irrational and arbitrary temper of the Nazi Party as it had developed in 'the years of struggle' before 1933. In the view of the Nazis, therefore, the Civil Service represented a serious obstacle to the arbitrary exercise of power which was their characteristic way of operating and to a limited extent this view was justified. With its insistence on 'going by the book', the Civil Service did on occasion complicate the achievement of Nazi objectives. Yet Hitler clearly needed the Civil Service to ensure the stability of his regime. This then was the context in which Party/State relations developed during the years that followed. Hitler endeavoured to solve the problem first, by using the Party and the SS as two distinct executive agencies independent of the State machine, though partially linked to it, and directly subordinate to himself through which he could both keep a check on the Civil Service and carry out measures beyond the law; and secondly, by making *ad hoc* appointments of individuals to take over responsibilities previously exercised by departments within the official hierarchy of the State, who were then encouraged to build up their own *apparat* in rivalry with the Government department traditionally responsible for that particular sphere.

9 Party and State, 1933-39

The 'coordination' of the Civil Service

During the first weeks of the 'revolution from below' in March 1933, many officials in local and regional government were forced to resign and were replaced by Party men. In this the initiative was taken by the local Party organizations with no direction from the top, except in the case of the most senior regional officials. At the same time, a large number of SA 'commissioners' moved into Government offices at various levels, with the excuse that they were making sure that the civil servants were acting in accordance with the principles of the new regime.

In the first few months, the Government did little to prevent this upheaval, partly because it favoured the purging of its political opponents from their offices, but partly because it found it difficult to control the SA and the local Party organizations. The Government was continually being confronted with local *faits accomplis*. The various Party organizations all tended to go their own way.[1]

Yet this arbitrary behaviour by the local Party organizations and the continual interference by the various 'commissars' threatened to alienate the Civil Service and to undermine the administrative effectiveness which was essential for the stabilizing of the new order. The three Government departments most concerned with this aspect were the Reich Ministry of the Interior under Frick and the Prussian Ministry of the Interior under Göring, these two being responsible for the internal administration of most of Germany, and the Ministry of Justice which was responsible for ensuring that the law was properly enforced. Göring's police was forced on occasion during these weeks to take action against excesses committed by the Nazi organizations. Frick and Göring were anxious to purge the Civil Service of those elements which were politically most objectionable, but at the same time to cause minimum disruption in doing so. In this they were able to rely on the cooperation of the bureaucracy who were very anxious to see a return to order.

1 *Law for the Re-establishment of the Professional Civil Service, 7 April 1933*

This, then, was the background to the Law for the Re-establishment of the Professional Civil Service of 7 April 1933. The law owed its title to an attempt by the Government to exploit an assertion made by the Right in the

[1] See above, p. 203.

Weimar period that the Left had filled the bureaucracy with unqualified people who carried the right party card. During the putting of the law into effect the assertion was shown to be untrue. The law provided for the purging of Jews (Art. 3) and known opponents of the regime (Art. 4) and for the retirement or transfer of officials for technical reasons (Arts. 5 and 6), which had previously been prevented by the Civil Service regulations. These last two clauses were sometimes used as a means of evading political pressure on an individual from the Party which would otherwise have required the use of Article 4. They did, however, give very wide scope for interfering with civil servants' careers; this had previously been impossible under the Civil Service regulations.

Article 1:
1. In order to re-establish a national professional Civil Service and to simplify the administration, officials may be dismissed under the following regulations, even when the necessary conditions under the relevant law do not exist.
2. The term 'officials', as used in this law, means direct [*unmittelbare*] and indirect [*mittelbare*] officials of the Reich, direct and indirect officials of the federal states, officials of local government and local government associations, officials of public corporations as well as institutions and undertakings of the same status as these public corporations. The regulations apply also to employees of agencies supplying social insurance, who have the rights and duties of officials.
3. 'Officials', as used in this law, also includes officials in temporary retirement.
4. The Reich Bank and the German State Railway are empowered to make corresponding regulations.

Article 2:
1. Officials who attained the status of officials after 9 November 1918 without possessing the requisite or usual training or other qualifications are to be dismissed from the service. Their previous salaries will be accorded to them for a period of three months after their dismissal.
2. They have no right to allowances, pensions, or dependants' pensions nor to the continued use of the official designation, the title, the official uniform and the official insignia.
3. In cases of need, a pension, revocable at any time, equivalent to a third of the normal basic salary of the last position held by them, may be granted them, especially when they are caring for dependent relatives; reinsurance according to the provisions of the Reich social insurance law will not occur.
4. The provisions in Sections 2 and 3 will be applied in the case of persons who come under the provisions of Section 1 and who had already been retired before this law came into effect.

Article 3:
1. Officials who are of non-Aryan descent are to be retired;[1] honorary officials are to be dismissed from office.
2. Section 1 does not apply to officials who were already in service on 1 August

[1] On 11 April 1933 'non-Aryan' was defined to include persons with only one non-Aryan grandparent; and on 30 June this provision was extended to those married to non-Aryans.

1914, or who fought in the world war at the front for the German Reich, or who fought for its allies, or whose fathers or sons were killed in the world war. The Reich Minister of the Interior, with the agreement of the competent departmental minister, or of the highest authorities of the federal states, may permit further exceptions in the case of officials who are abroad.

Article 4:
Officials who because of their previous political activity do not offer security that they will act at all times and without reservation in the interests of the national state can be dismissed from the service.[1] They are to be accorded their previous salary for a period of three months after dismissal. From then on, they will receive three-quarters of their pension and corresponding dependants' benefits.

Article 5:
1. Every official must allow himself to be transferred to another office in the same or equivalent career, even to one carrying a lower rank or regular salary—reimbursement for the prescribed costs of transfer will be given if the needs of the service require it. If the official is transferred to an office of lower rank and regular salary he retains his previous official title and the official income of his former position.
2. In place of transfer to an office of lower rank and regular income, the official can request to be retired.

Article 6:
Officials can be retired for the purpose of rationalizing the administration even if they are not yet unfit for service. If officials are retired for this reason, their places may not be filled again.

Article 7:
1. Dismissal from office, transfer to another office and retirement will be ordered by the highest Reich or federal state agency which will make the final decision without right of appeal against it.
2. The dispositions according to Articles 2–6 must be made known to those affected by 30 September 1933 at the latest. The time may be shortened by agreement with the Reich Minister of the Interior, if the relevant Reich or federal state agency declares that the measures authorized in this law have been carried out.

Article 8:
A pension will not be granted to the officials dismissed or retired in accordance with Articles 3 and 4, if they have not completed a term of service of at least ten years: this applies also to the cases in which, according to the existing regulation, a pension is accorded after a shorter term of service. . . .

2 *The implementing of the Civil Service Law of 7 April 1933*
The desire to cause minimum disruption in the administration appears from the official instructions for the carrying out of the provisions of the law. In fact, the effects of the law were comparatively small, though greater in Prussia than elsewhere. At the higher level, 12·5 per cent of civil servants in

---

[1] A supplementary law of 20 July 1933 ruled that civil servants who belonged to any party or organization which furthered the aims of Communism, Marxism or Social Democracy were to be dismissed.

Prussia were affected by Sections 2-4 and 15·5 per cent by Sections 5-6. This does not, however, give a complete picture of the situation in Prussia. Many of the Socialist and Democrat officials in Prussia had already been dismissed before the Nazis came to power under the regime of Dr Bracht, who had been appointed State Commissioner in Prussia on 20 July 1932 by the then Reich Chancellor, Papen. In the other states 4·5 per cent of higher civil servants were affected by Sections 2-4 and 5 per cent by Sections 5-6. An even smaller percentage of middle- and lower-ranking civil servants were affected.

A record of the ministerial discussion of 25 April 1933 concerning the implementing of the Professional Civil Service Law made by State Councillor Dr Schultz (Hamburg) on 27 April

... The Prussian Minister-President[1] Göring in very forceful and impressive words said roughly as follows: The Reich Chancellor had asked him to draw up certain guidelines. It was an unusual and extremely important law, therefore only the Minister could make the final decisions. Half a year was hardly enough time to carry out a purge of the administration in Prussia. The Fascist purge law had had a duration of two years.

There was no question of justice being in acute danger. It did not say much for the judges if they felt concerned about such a law. Civil servants who somewhere some time had made some human error were not to be touched by the law.

He particularly wished to point out the dangers to which the law could lead under confined local circumstances where everyone more or less knew everyone else. A strong personality must be able to overcome any personal hostility he may have or possible feelings of revenge. 'Someone who has grumbled at us some time somewhere' may be a very capable civil servant and need not be damned just like that.

The carrying out of the law in the states was the responsibility of the governments there. The question of how far the parties could be involved depended on the circumstances. But it was very important that only such people should take part in the preparations for the decisions who were absolutely decent characters and not themselves aspirants for the new vacancies. National Socialists were not immune from human weakness. A law was being passed for Prussia that every informer who could not absolutely prove the truth of his statements should be punished with the full force of the law.

Civil servants carrying a Party card should be dismissed. So one should not simultaneously create new Party-card-carrying civil servants. That did not of course exclude isolated cases of people being made civil servants who did not have full training, if this lack of a general Civil Service training was made up for by a clear eye for the political situation and a decent character. In this context, the Minister-President sharply attacked time-servers who often seemed to be more papal than the Pope. It had riled him to see how in his ministry, in which it was notorious that 60 per cent of the civil servants had been followers of Severing, within a few days the swastika badges had popped up out of the ground like mushrooms and after only four days the clicking of heels and raising of hands had

[1] On 11 April Hitler had appointed Göring Minister-President (Prime Minister) in Prussia.

become a common sight in the corridors. The Minister-President gave his full approval to those civil servants who because of their character and sense of decency had certain inhibitions about joining the Party at this particular moment and who, because of this, were especially exposed to the pressure and enmity of those who had already climbed on the bandwagon. Such civil servants were 'the most valuable workers' for the new government as well.

'The army of commissars' threatened gradually to undermine and shatter the authority of the State. Yesterday he had abolished these commissars in Prussia. They produced great confusion. They created considerable disruption in private firms. In practice, they had often turned out to be aspirants for directorships, insisting on creating vacancies for themselves: the director sat outside, while 'a little man' ran the business. The commissars had become a public menace. In one case a commissar, who had declared a director intolerable because of certain grandiose habits, was himself a few days later driving the dismissed director's car and had granted himself his salary of 60,000 RM. In such a state of affairs the Minister had to intervene and protect his civil servants. Attacks by the Government press on civil servants should not be allowed.

There should be no dismissals on trivial pretexts. If a mayor installed a bathroom in 1927, even if he overdrew the budget, or if he had given his aunt a lift in his official car, the matter should now be dropped. Neither should an individual official be held responsible for decisions made by corporations. Where an individual has himself acted corruptly, the prosecutor must intervene. Criminal matters must be passed on to the Public Prosecutor at once. Hardly a single large enterprise can be found in which over some decades irregularities have not occurred. There is no point in dragging this into the open; by doing so our prestige abroad may be harmed.

The Reich Chancellor had pointed out emphatically that there were two things which must not be overlooked in carrying out the law: 1. The Reich President; 2. Foreign countries.

1. The Reich President and Reich Chancellor both wished that, in particular, the withdrawal of pensions should be handled carefully and with a certain generosity. A petty attitude only created hotbeds of hatred and embitterment. Such imponderables should not be weighed lightly ... Political activity from personal initiative must be distinguished from political activity under official instructions. Swamping the Reich President with complaints about the effects of the law must be avoided at all costs.

2. Germany could not simply say we shall do what we like. The isolation of Germany was unique. The Jews were working extremely hard to aggravate it. Therefore we must hit the Jews hard, but we must not give them a chance to malign us as barbarians in places where it could be interpreted in the wrong way. A Jew who had contributed something scientifically important for humanity must not be removed; the world would not understand that. The Reich President would examine again the question whether such scientific experts were not in the same category as soldiers.

In conclusion, the Minister-President made the following point with great gravity: 'I remind you of the seriousness of the law, you must bear in mind that your signature is often equivalent to a death sentence. This you must settle with your conscience. The Führer is responsible to history for your decisions. The dismissal, the assessment and the weeding out of individuals must therefore lie only in the hands of men of character.'

Party/State relations at the centre

3   *Law to ensure the unity of Party and State, 1 December 1933*

Hitler was fully aware of the danger of the Party and the SA getting out of hand and, during the summer and autumn of 1933, he increasingly began to emphasize the importance of the State in relation to the Party organizations. One suggestion mooted for the regulation of Party/State relations was that the Party should be merged into the State. This idea found expression in the Law to ensure the Unity of Party and State.

1. After the victory of the National Socialist revolution, the National Socialist German Workers' Party is the bearer of the concept of the German State and is inseparably linked with the State.

It is a corporation under public law.

2. The deputy of the Führer and the Chief of Staff of the SA will become members of the Reich Government in order to ensure close cooperation of the offices of the Party and the SA with the public authorities.

3. The members of the National Socialist German Workers' Party and the SA (including their subordinate organizations) as the leading and driving force of the National Socialist State will carry greater responsibilities towards Führer, people and State.

In the case of violation of these duties, they will be subject to special jurisdiction by Party and State.

The Führer may extend these regulations to include members of other organizations.

4. Every action, or failure to carry out an action, on the part of members of the SA (including their subordinate organizations), which threatens the existence, organization, activity or reputation of the National Socialist German Workers' Party, in particular any infringement of discipline and order, will be regarded as a dereliction of duty.

5. Custody and detention may be imposed in addition to the usual penalties.

6. The public authorities are bound to grant legal and administrative assistance to the offices of the Party and the SA, which are entrusted with the exercise of jurisdiction over the Party and the SA.

7. The law of 28 April 1933 regarding the authority to inflict penalties on members of the SA and SS is revoked.

8. The Reich Chancellor, as Führer of the National Socialist German Workers' Party and as supreme commander of the SA, will issue the regulations required for the execution and augmentation of this law, particularly with regard to the juridical organization and procedure of the Party and the SA. He will determine the date on which the regulations concerning this jurisdiction will become effective.

This law proved to be highly ambiguous and completely failed to define and regulate Party/State relations satisfactorily. It is significant, for example, that neither the Party nor the State could claim superiority to the other. For, while the Party is considered to be 'the bearer of the concept of the German State', this is never defined in legal or institutional terms. In addition, by being made a corporation under public law, and through the appointment of the deputy Führer (Hess) and the Chief of Staff of the SA as Ministers, the integration of the Party into the State appeared to take the form of its subordination to the State, though this was by no means so, as will become clear. The only unqualified gain for the Party was its right as a public corporation to claim money now from the State, though even here its demands had to be granted by the Reich Finance Minister. In practice, however, the non-Nazi Reich Minister of Finance, Schwerin von Krosigk, dared not exercise more than a very limited supervision.

4 Hitler on the tasks of the Party

At a conference of Gauleiters on 2 February 1934, Hitler defined the tasks of the Party in limited terms. It was to be used primarily for propaganda and indoctrination as well as to perform auxiliary functions for the State:

The Führer stressed:
The most essential tasks of the Party were:
1. to make the people receptive for the measures intended by the Government;
2. to help to carry out the measures which have been ordered by the Government in the nation at large;
3. to support the Government in every way.
Furthermore, the Führer stressed that those people who maintained that the revolution was not finished were fools; they did this only with the intention of getting particular jobs for themselves. The Führer described what difficulty he had had in filling all the posts with the right people and went on to say that we had people in the movement whose conception of revolution was nothing but a permanent state of chaos. But we needed an administrative apparatus in every sphere which would enable us to realize National Socialist ideas at once. And to achieve this, the principle must remain valid that more orders must not be given, and more plans must not be discussed, than the apparatus could digest; there must be no orders and plans beyond what could be put across to the people and actually carried into effect. The question of the amalgamation of Party and State was of fundamental importance; upon it Germany's future essentially depended.

The Führer described our main immediate task as the selection of people who were on the one hand able, and on the other hand willing, to carry out the Government's measures with blind obedience. The Party must bring about the stability on which Germany's whole future depended. It must secure this stability; this could not be done by some monarchy or other. The first Führer has been chosen by fate; the second must have right from the start a faithful, sworn community behind him. Nobody with his own power base must be chosen! What is vital is that he should have everyone completely behind him from the outset. This fact must be well known, and it will then be clear that there is no point in trying to assassinate him.

Apart from this: Only one person at a time can be Führer; who it is, is not so important; the important thing is that everybody should back up the second and all subsequent leaders. An organization with such inner solidity and strength will last for ever; nothing can overthrow it. The sense of community within the movement must be inconceivably intense. We must have no fighting among ourselves; no differences must be visible to outsiders! The people cannot trust us blindly if we ourselves destroy this trust. If we destroy other people's trust in us, we destroy our own trust in ourselves.

Even the consequences of wrong decisions must be mitigated by absolute unity. One authority must never be played off against another. There must be only *one* view, that of the movement.

To work against someone in an official position, who embodies part of this authority, is to destroy all authority and trust completely.

There must therefore be no superfluous discussions! Problems not yet decided by individual officials must under no circumstances be discussed in public. Otherwise, this will mean passing the decision on to the mass of the people. That was the crazy idea behind democracy. By doing that, the value of any leadership is squandered. The man who has to make the decisions must make them himself and everyone else must back him up. The authority of even the most junior leader is the sum of the authority of all leaders and vice versa.

Apart from this we must carry on only one fight at a time. The saying, 'Many enemies, much honour' should really run: 'Many enemies, much stupidity'. In any case, the whole nation cannot engage in twelve campaigns at the same time and understand what is involved. For this reason, we must always instil the whole nation with only one idea, concentrate its attention on *one* idea. In questions of foreign policy it is particularly necessary to have the whole nation behind one as if hypnotized. The whole nation must be involved in the struggle as if they were passionate participants in a sports contest. This is necessary because, if the whole nation takes part in the struggle, they also will be losers. If they are not involved, only the leadership loses. In the one case the wrath of the nation will rise against the opponent, in the other against their leaders.

5 *Party resentment at the inadequacy of Nazi control over the Civil Service*

An important element in the strength of the State in relation to the Party and the SA was the fact that, as shown above, the Civil Service Law of April 1933 had had comparatively little impact on the Civil Service. In fact, the bureaucracy carried out the policies of the Government loyally, but it continued to resist arbitrary interference by the Party authorities. The resentment felt by Party militants at this attitude on the part of the Civil Service is shown in the following memorandum by a Nazi activist in the Civil Service:

Memorandum of Oberregierungsrat and SA-Obersturmbannführer Hans von Helms of 26 May 1934 on 'National Socialist appointments policy in the central administration in relation to "Party and State"'

Among the most difficult tasks which the National Socialist State still has to solve during the next few years is the question of 'Party and State'. Although the identity of Party and State must be our ultimate aim, the realization of this aim is at the moment a long way off. Anyone who has had the opportunity, on the one hand, of closely following the organization of the Party through all the phases of its development from its beginnings to the seizure of power by the Führer and of playing an active part in its success, and on the other hand of working in the State apparatus of the new Reich, must unfortunately admit that the influence of the Party on the State and the permeation of the State with National Socialist ideas does not correspond with the sacrifices made by the movement. The last few months in particular show a considerable decrease in the rate of the growth of National Socialist influence upon the State.

The State apparatus, whose character, and particularly its methods of administration and bureaucracy, represents in itself a certain element of danger for a National Socialist Government with different methods, is still far from making National Socialist ideas its most important tools. This is most strongly pronounced in the behaviour of a large section of the representatives of our State, the civil servants. The best gauge for the permeation of a State by an idea is still the appointments policy pursued by that State. Since everyone knows that 'men make history' one will be able to tell by the faces of people employed in decisive positions whether they are willing to pull their weight for the new State or whether they have no comprehension of, or sympathy for, National Socialism. It is for this reason that many civil servants in our State attempt, partly consciously, partly unconsciously, by using exaggeratedly bureaucratic means to carry out things which they would be unable to realize in any other way. Once again people are beginning to value a person's knowledge more highly than his character. Once again people are daring to defame old experienced fighters in our movement who have been taken into the administration for political reasons in order to form a counterweight to old, burnt-out, unreliable hangers-on. They are reproached with lack of knowledge and recommended to learn administrative techniques, whereas in fact these officials are the best guarantee of the thorough permeation of the State by National Socialism. Every day one can find similar attitudes and modes of operation in the State apparatus. Many contemporaries who have so far missed joining the Party are already glad not to have taken this step and believe they are on top. Unfortunately, the top people in government offices, in the administration and the like are unable to keep a constant eye on this situation because, owing to overwork, to those around them, to the wrong advisers and so forth, they have no opportunity of dealing with these things. Also, these compatriots know how to win the favour of the administrative chiefs by using the most remarkable methods. Very often it would be better if the administrative bosses used the old Party warriors instead of falling for those who joined the Party after the March 1933 election [*Märzgefallene*]. In part, this is the result of fundamental errors made during the first months in the form of compromises which were probably unavoidable because National Socialism had not yet acquired total control over the State. So now also unfortunate compromises have to be put up with in the filling of posts. But even now there would be time to improve things if a consistent appointments policy were pursued, a policy which would prove particularly productive in the central administration. It must be self-evident for the National Socialist State that the head of a personnel department and the official in charge of personnel in the central administration, who in their turn have to be entrusted with the personnel files of their subordinate offices, should be trusted agents of the Party, men who have proved themselves as old Party fighters before the seizure of power. A responsible task is placed in their hands which they are able to solve more easily, the more fanatically they strive as National Socialists for the purity of the movement and of the State.

Circumstances have brought it about that people often fill decisive positions in the State apparatus who are either not National Socialists or who, even as National Socialists, have been infected by other ideologies in such a way that they no longer detect a policy that is disloyal to National Socialism. It is therefore particularly important that measures taken by the central authorities, among them their appointments policy, are examined to see whether they are correct from a National Socialist point of view.

Is it possible for a Party member or the representative of the Party within the administration (the Federation[1]) to report any abuses to the Party leadership and thus act as the eyes and ears of the Party? Unfortunately the answer is No!

As can be seen from the enclosed decree of the Prussian Minister-President of 4 October 1933 and the Prussian Minister of the Interior of 4 August 1933, the Federation is even forbidden to report un-National Socialist behaviour to the Party or to disclose abuses unless the person reporting wishes to expose himself to the risk of disciplinary action.

For instance, if the Party were now to ask an agent for a list of the officials in a ministry arranged according to departments and stating what party they had belonged to before the seizure of power, and if the contents of that list, as far as some ministries are concerned, were shattering for the Party, that person would officially be liable to punishment. This state of affairs is completely intolerable since the Party has no means of control over the execution of National Socialist ideas.

Of course the authority of the head of the ministry must be recognized. But because of the amount of work involved, it is absolutely impossible for him to be informed about all matters, especially if he is surrounded by the wrong advisers who perhaps assume they are National Socialists but are far from being so. . . .

There is a great danger that in the near future even National Socialist ministerial chiefs will have only a bureaucratic apparatus behind them whose representatives lack true National Socialist principles. The pillars of the Party in times of need were always the old Party fighters. This must not be underestimated!!

6 *Hess to take part in preparing legislation*

Hitler was, however, aware of this danger. Despite his speech to the Gauleiters which apparently relegated the Party to being merely a propaganda organization, he took steps to ensure that the Party acquired some powers of supervision over central State authorities. This was achieved by means of the 'Office of the Deputy Führer'. On 27 April 1933, Hitler had appointed Hess as his deputy and given him authority 'to take the decisions in my name in all matters concerning the leadership of the Party'. This appointment was probably intended initially to keep a check on the independence of the Gauleiters, while ensuring that the responsibility for the

[1] The *NS Beamtenbund*, the Nazi Civil Service organization.

inevitable confrontations with them did not fall upon Hitler himself. By appointing Hess, a weak figure, to a new office, Hitler probably hoped to make certain that the Party would not build up too strong a central authority. Hess's office never in fact acquired much authority over the Gauleiters. But, thanks largely to the ruthlessness and energy of Hess's deputy, Martin Bormann, the Office of the Deputy Führer acquired more and more influence over the ministerial bureaucracy. In June 1933 Hess was permitted to attend Cabinet meetings, in December he became a Minister, and the following decree was issued by Hitler on 27 July 1934:

I decree that the Deputy of the Führer, Reich Minister Hess, will have the status of participating Reich Minister in connection with the preparation of drafts for laws in all Reich Government departments. All legislative work is to be sent to him when it is received by the other Reich Ministers concerned. This also applies in cases where no one else participates except the Reich Minister making the draft. Reich Minister Hess will be given the opportunity of commenting on drafts suggested by the civil servants concerned.

This order will apply in the same sense to legislative ordinances. The Deputy of the Führer in his capacity as Reich Minister can send an expert on his staff as his representative. These experts are entitled to make statements to the Reich Ministers on his behalf.

7 *Hess is given a share in the appointment of officials, 24 September 1935*

This decree, which was extended on 6 April 1935 to cover executive regulations also, provided the Party with a means of blocking or modifying legislation of which it disapproved. Hitler did not, however, always back Hess against his ministers.

Even more important than the participation of Hess's office in the preparation of legislation were the powers granted by the following decree of 24 September 1935, which gave the Deputy Führer a share in the appointment of officials:

I

The Deputy Führer must participate in the appointment of officials who are appointed personally by the Führer and Reich Chancellor. . . .

II

The participation of the Deputy Führer will take the form of his receiving a copy of the recommendation for promotion which must contain more detailed information about the official to be promoted. The Deputy Führer must be given reasonable time to express his opinion.

This decree gave the Party, through Hess's office, a veto over the appointment and promotion of all civil servants of any importance. What generally happened was that on receiving details of a proposed appointment, Hess's office would make inquiries of the Gauleiter of the area in which the civil servant lived, to make sure he was politically reliable. This, of course, also gave considerable influence to the Gauleiter. In addition, in 1936 the Party established indoctrination camps for administrative branch civil servants, who were given a three-week course before joining.

Party/State relations at regional and local level

It was, however, at regional and local level that tension between Party and State was most acute because it was in the regions and localities that the main power of the Party organization lay. The essence of the conflict was, on the one hand, a growing centralization of the State authorities, with, on the other hand, a determination by the Gauleiters and the district and local Party leaders to hang on to the authority which they had won for themselves in the first months of 1933, and which they believed was theirs by right of conquest owing to their Führer's role as Head of State.

At regional level, Party/State relations took the form of a conflict between the Reich Governors (*Reichsstatthalter*) and the Gauleiters on one side, and the *Regierungspräsidenten* (of Prussia) and the Minister-Presidents (of the other states), that is, the heads of the regional state authorities, on the other. A distinction must be made between Prussia and the other states. In many of the Prussian provinces, particularly in the east, the Gauleiter had taken over the senior administrative post of *Oberpräsident*. But although this concentration of Party and State power was considerable, it did not ensure supreme authority within the province because the post of *Oberpräsident* had only a supervisory function over the real centres of Prussian state authority in the province, which were the *Regierungspräsidenten*. The *Regierungspräsidenten* tended to resist the supervisory authority of the *Oberpräsident*, so that the Ministry of the Interior in Berlin could use the *Regierungspräsidenten* as a centripetal force to counter the centrifugal tendencies of the *Gauleiter-Oberpräsidenten*.

8 *Second Law for the Coordination of the Federal States under the Reich, 7 April 1933*

In the other states the situation was defined by the following law:

The Reich Government has passed the following law which is published herewith:

I

1. In the German states with the exception of Prussia, the Reich President, at the suggestion of the Reich Chancellor, shall appoint a Reich Governor [*Reichsstatthalter*]. The Reich Governor shall require the observance of the general policy laid down by the Reich Chancellor. The following powers of state authority belong to him:

(i) Appointment and removal of the head of the state government, and at his suggestion, the other members of the state government.

(ii) Dissolution of the legislature and the calling of new elections, subject to the rule of Section 8 of the Preliminary Law of 31 March 1933 for the Coordination of the Federal States under the Reich.

(iii) Preparation and publication of state laws, including those determined by the state government, according to Section 1 of the Provisional Law of 31 March 1933 for the Coordination of the Federal States with the Reich. Article 70 of the Constitution of 11 August 1919 applies accordingly.

(iv) The appointment and dismissal of the high state officials and judges at the suggestion of the state government, in so far as this was formerly accomplished by the highest state officials.

(v) The power of pardon.

(vi) The Reich Governor may preside over the meetings of the state government.

(vii) Article 63 of the German Constitution of 11 August 1919 remains unaltered. . . .

II

1. A Reich Governor may not simultaneously be a member of a state government. He shall belong to the state whose sovereign powers he exercises. His official residence is at the seat of the state government.

2. For several states, in each of which there are less than two million inhabitants, a common Governor, who must be a resident of one of these states, may be appointed. The Reich President shall designate the Governor's official residence.

III

1. The Reich Governor is appointed for the duration of a state legislative period. He can be recalled at any time by the Reich President at the suggestion of the Reich Chancellor. . . .

IV

Votes of no confidence of the state legislature against the head and members of the state government are not permissible. . . .

9 *Party and State authorities conflict at regional level*

This law created the post of Reich Governor (*Reichsstatthalter*) of which there were ten in all. In most cases the senior Gauleiter in each state was appointed. The Reich Governors had the function of supervising the carrying out in the states of the political guidelines laid down by the Reich Chancellor. It appears to have been Hitler's intention to use the Reich Governors to avert the centrifugal tendencies which had resulted from the seizure of power by the Party in the states, presumably on the principle of using poachers as gamekeepers, that is to say, the Reich Governors were to act as representatives of the Reich in the states. In practice, this measure produced intense rivalry between the new Reich Governors and the Minister-Presidents of the states. A typical instance was the following confrontation in August 1933 between Professor Werner, the Minister-President of Hesse, and Jacob Sprenger, the Reich Governor/Gauleiter of Hesse, over their respective claims to authority:

Werner: These things have unfortunately not been settled in detail. Because of this it was possible for the State Secretary, when going away on holiday, to tell me that he had appointed Herr Ringshausen as his deputy. That is preposterous. I am the only person who can be deputy and when I go on holiday the State Secretary deputizes for me. Thus the whole thing is fluid and gives rise to mis-understandings which must be removed. Clear lines of demarcation are best: clear lines of demarcation as to the position of the state government in relation to the representative of the Führer, the Reich Governor, and clear lines of demarca-tion between the Minister-President and the State Secretary, and between him and the Government. I once told the Führer in a conference: Transfer all authority to the Reich Governor. Since he rejected this and declared that it did not correspond to the intentions of the Reich Governors' Law, a separate head became necessary for the Government. This entailed a demarcation of areas of authority. How far does the power of the Reich Governor reach into the state government? A com-mentary is needed for the Reich Governors' Law and for the state governments. The governments are not simply organs of administration. That is clear from the fact that they have the right of nominating civil servants. In fact, generally speak-ing, I complied with all requests regarding personnel. In one or two cases I was unable to do so and have freely expressed my opinion on this, as you have repeatedly asked me to do.

Sprenger: Everything that you regard as unsettled, I now regard as settled. From a formal point of view the letter of the law prevails; beyond this the unwritten law of evolution. The Chancellor has declared: 'Revolution is dead, evolution has begun.' I remind you of the speech of the Führer in Berchtesgaden and at the Nuremberg Party Rally. In both speeches the theory of evolution is expressed entirely unambiguously. The Chancellor made a quite definite decision during the Berlin discussion. He refused to be regarded as a court for dealing with complaints and, as you, Herr Minister-President, will remember, he named me, the Reich Governor, as your superior. All the things you mention here, based on past legis-lation, must evolve in this direction. The Party takes precedence and is responsible for political questions. The Government is there to administer. The Gauleiter has determined political questions since the Party began. This principle was explicitly mentioned by the Führer at the time we took over power. The Gauleiters were the holders of power and as things have developed the Government has also been determined by the Gauleiters. Let me repeat, not for the first time, everybody can express his view like a man. I have never been biased. But if differences of opinion occur, only one person can decide: namely, myself as Gauleiter. And when I have made my decision, there must be no further speculation. Contact with Reich Government offices or the Chancellor is allowed only after consultation with and with the permission of the Gauleiter and Reich Governor, not otherwise. For those bodies have no authority over this....

From this particular confrontation Sprenger emerged victorious. He succeeded in removing the Minister-President and eventually in combining the Minister-Presidency with the position of Reich Governor. But other Reich Governors were less successful.

In effect, by dividing the authority between the Reich Governors and the state governments, Hitler ensured that they would keep each other in check and thereby prevent the emergence of strong concentrations of power at regional level.

10 *Law for the Reconstruction of the Reich*

At the beginning of 1934 a new law was introduced which strengthened the hand of regional state authorities against the Party through the abolition of the federal system. Hitler had no use for the historic federal structure of Germany and by the Law for the Reconstruction of the Reich, dated 30 January 1934, it was officially abolished. The state governments remained in existence but were subordinated to the Reich authorities:

The referendum and the Reichstag election of 12 November 1933 have demonstrated that the German people have attained an indestructible internal unity superior to all internal subdivisions and conflicts of a political character.

Consequently, the Reichstag has enacted the following law which is hereby promulgated with the unanimous vote of the Reichstag after ascertaining that the requirements of the Reich Constitution have been met:

Article 1. Popular assemblies of the Federal States shall be abolished.

Article 2. (a) The sovereign powers of the Federal States are transferred to the Reich.

(b) The Federal State governments are subordinated to the Reich Government.

Article 3. The Reich Governors are placed under the administrative supervision of the Reich Minister of the Interior.

Article 4. The Reich Government may issue new constitutional laws.

Article 5. The Reich Minister of the Interior issues the necessary legal and administrative regulations for the execution of the law.

Article 6. This law becomes effective on the day of its promulgation.

11 *A Reich Governor complains that his position is unclear*

The abolition of the federal structure made the position of Reich Governor superfluous because the Minister-Presidents were now directly subordinate to the Reich Ministry of the Interior, that is to say, there was no longer any need to have a representative of the Reich Chancellor supervising the putting into effect of Reich policy in the states. It was, however, characteristic of Hitler's style that the post of Reich Governor was not abolished, as the principles of good administrative order required, but left in continuing rivalry with that of Minister-President. But the Law did subordinate the Reich Governors to the Reich Minister of the Interior (Art. 3), and this was something which senior Gauleiters were not prepared to tolerate, as is shown by the following letter of 9 April 1934 from the Reich Governor of Brunswick and Anhalt, Wilhelm Loeper, to State Secretary Lammers at the Reich Chancellery:

I am taking the liberty below of asking you for your opinion on the following matter:

The position of Reich Governors seems to me unclear at the moment. Whereas, on the one hand, the Reich Governor has been appointed by the Reich President and sworn in by him personally, and whereas, as regards salary, he is also on the same level as the Reich Ministers, on the other hand he is subject to instructions from the Reich Ministry of the Interior. With this new law[1] it is now not quite clear whether the Reich Governor has retained his old position or whether he has become an authority subordinate to the Reich Ministry of the Interior. Owing to this lack of clarity, there is uncertainty about the actions of the Reich Governor. One is often in the position of not knowing whether one is allowed to act independently in accordance with the policy of the Führer, or whether one is merely an executive organ of the Reich Ministry of the Interior. If the old position of the Reich Governor is to be retained, the subordination to the instructions of the Reich Ministry of the Interior must be of a purely general character and this fact should be manifest in externals as well. Just as one Reich Ministry cannot give orders to and make requests of another but must *invite* it to do something, the same practice should be observed towards the Reich Governor. But in fact the practice has developed of the Reich Governor himself (not only his office) receiving requests signed by some *Ministerialrat* and certified by some Chancellery secretary. The Reich Minister of the Interior is of the opinion that this is of no importance and is part of official business. I am of the humble opinion that that is not so. Either I am the subordinate of the Reich Ministry of the Interior and represent a subordinate office, in which case, of course, I must accept correspondence in this form, or the position of Reich Governor is to be the old one, in which case this should find expression at least in the form in which letters are addressed to the Reich Governor and not to his office. If possible, they should be signed by the State Secretary himself. I hope my comments will not be regarded as excessive pedantry, but I do like clarity in all things. It is in such external matters that one's position is defined for officialdom and for the public. I can very well imagine that the professional bureaucracy is happy to make use of the opportunity of reducing the position of the Reich Governor below that intended by the Führer. But I also recall the words of the Führer during a conference of Reich Governors when he declared: 'You are the first Reich Governors and what you make of this position will determine what it will be in the future.' This comment by the Führer gives me the right to make this inquiry.

12 *Who has final authority over the Reich Governors?*

The Reich Governors insisted on their right to appeal to Hitler direct. But Frick, the Minister of the Interior, resented this attempt to go over his head and appealed to Hitler. Hitler's reply made it clear that he wished to keep important decisions in his own hands:

Reich Minister of the Interior Frick to the Reich Chancellery, 4 June 1934:

If we are to stick to the idea of a central and unified leadership of the Reich through the Reich Chancellor and the departmental ministers assisting him, who

[1] Law for the Reconstruction of the Reich, of 30 January 1934; see p. 242, above.

corporately together with the Reich Chancellor form the Reich Government, then it is impossible to leave differences of opinion between a departmental minister on the one hand and a governor on the other ... to be decided by the Reich Chancellor. On the contrary, the decision of the Reich Minister who represents the Reich Government in his area of responsibility must be accepted by the Reich Governor without allowing him a form of legal redress against the decision of the Reich Minister in the field of legislation.

State Secretary Lammers to Frick, 27 February 1934:
The Reich Chancellor agrees that, generally speaking, differences of opinion between a departmental minister and a Reich Governor on the legality or expediency of a state law cannot be left to his decision. In the Chancellor's view an exception must be made for those cases which are concerned with questions of special political importance. In the view of the Reich Chancellor such a regulation is consistent with his position of leadership.

13 *Party resentment at the growing centralization of authority by the Reich Government*

The regional state authorities could not afford to ignore the wishes of the Gauleiter-Reich Governors and Gauleiter-*Oberpräsidenten*, but during the period 1935–39 they could usually bring the authority of the Reich Ministry of the Interior into play to maintain much independence of action and they possessed greater skill as professional civil servants. The Reich Governor and Gauleiter of Thuringia, Fritz Sauckel, for example, complained about the growing centralization of the state authorities which was reducing the position of the Reich Governor to that of a figurehead. After an interview in January with Hitler, attended also by Hess and Frick, Sauckel wrote the following thirty-six-page memorandum which he then passed to Hitler at lunch in the Reich Chancellery. According to Sauckel, Hitler had 'expressed strong agreement with my views' at the January interview, but then, typically, had not acted on the memorandum. Sauckel was obliged therefore to write to the head of the Reich Chancellery, Dr Lammers, to ask him to place the memorandum before Hitler again. Once again there was apparently no result:

Excerpts from the Memorandum of Reich Governor and Gauleiter Fritz Sauckel of Thuringia: 'On the Transfer of Spheres of Authority and Responsibility from the States and Regional Offices to the Government Departments in Berlin and the Political and Administrative Consequences', 27 January 1936

I
The influence of the leading men in the Party in the regions [Aussenbezirken] *is in danger of being absorbed back into the Reich administration.*
... 2. Often the members of the state governments are not even notified of the plans of the Reich Government departments and of the drafts of laws and decrees which affect their sphere of operations and indeed the very existence of their offices and subordinate offices. ... Thus a directive from the Reich and Prussian

Minister of Education of 23 February 1935 to the Education Departments of the states, following on the Law on University Teachers of 21 January 1935 and the 2nd Reich Governors' Law of 1 February 1935, subordinated the appointment of university teachers to 'Office W' in the Reich and Prussian Ministry of Education. ... In this way, bit by bit the powers of those people in the regions who have the confidence of the movement are being absorbed into the central authorities in Berlin. There the Ministers of the states often have to see a bunch of desk officials to get permission for the most trifling matters which were previously within their own discretion.

In many cases which could be dealt with by the state Ministries without any difficulty, the red tape and waste of time involved in the relations between the state and Reich authorities reaches grotesque proportions. The initiative of the Reich field administration is often restricted because the individual Reich Government departments in the various spheres declare that a Reich regulation is to be issued. It then often appears that they have only just begun formulating these Reich regulations or that their formulation has been shelved. And yet, all this while, measures urgently necessary for local reasons are not introduced in the states and so damage is done both to the movement and to the state.

The progressive restriction of the sphere of activity at the level of both state and *Gau* has occasionally led to irritability even between leading Party members, indeed to friction and tensions. This is particularly apt to happen since these personalities are forceful and independent, refractory and self-willed, shaped by struggle rather than smooth administration....

3. *The position of the Reich Governors has in reality even less substance than that of the state Ministers.* The Reich Governors have hardly any direct legal responsibilities in the day-to-day affairs of state.... [After describing their legal responsibilities Sauckel continued:] It is not true that the activities of a Reich Governor need be restricted to these paltry legal responsibilities. He can act as the official representative of the Reich Government which he is officially declared to be. He can hurry from rallies to receptions, from public addresses to serious accidents, from dedication ceremonies to meetings—but he can give no orders. He is by no means without influence; he can get somewhere by diplomacy, by persuasion, by threats, or through the Party—but he can give no orders. He can make suggestions, he can request information, he can make inquiries and complaints—but he can give no orders. To make a comparison, he has a similar position in his district to that of the English king in England. He can make quite a lot of his position through his energy and skill but largely outside the legal limits. There can be differing opinions about the expediency of having such representative figures in the regions; but whether the most combative and active personalities in the movement are the most suitable people for such a purely representative role is questionable, except perhaps when they are near retirement.

The Reich Governors, who have after all been officially declared to be the representatives of the Reich Government and the men responsible for seeing to the carrying out of its policies and are intended to be particularly well-informed agents and interpreters of its plans and intentions, are usually even less well informed than the state Ministers about its legislative and administrative plans....

4. The constitutional position of the Prussian *Oberpräsidenten* is equally weak. The administrative responsibilities attached to them are limited and fairly remote

from politics. Their real function is almost entirely informatory and representative in character. As is well known, the *Regierungspräsidenten* are not subordinate to the *Oberpräsidenten*. Under Prussian law the *Regierungspräsidenten* and the Ministry can work together with one another, by-passing the *Oberpräsidenten*, and to my knowledge they make full use of this. The *Oberpräsidenten* hang, as it were, in the air.

5. As a result the leading personalities in the movement in the provinces who occupy such positions appear in the eyes of the people as the most senior exponents of a political development over which they basically have hardly any influence. . . .

II

The shift in the seat of power as a result of the centralization in the hands of the Reich does not benefit the Führer and Reich Chancellor or the Reich Ministers as individuals so much as mainly the anonymous central bureaucracy. . . .

III

Overcentralization does not bring unity but rather inflates the administration, makes it cumbersome and difficult to supervise; it breeds departmental particularism and splits up the authority of the State. . . .

The Reich Government departments clearly desire—and all of them are more or less forced by one another's actions to follow suit—to establish for themselves their own self-contained field organizations with a separate identity, imposing sharper and sharper lines of demarcation from the other administrative bodies and seeking to achieve independence of them. These huge administrative bodies are therefore bound in the long run to diverge more and more from one another; each one creates a state within the State. Instead of seventeen Federal States there will be in the end fourteen departmental bodies which at their middle and lower levels are cutting themselves off more and more from one another. It only requires the shock of a crisis to bring about open chaos.

Instead of state particularism we are getting departmental particularism. . . .

This centralism and the departmental point of view are leading to the complete disintegration of the field administration. And the main point is that the Party men, whether Reich Governors, Minister-Presidents or state ministers, are being more and more excluded from the administration. The whole process shows the infinitely subtle, secret and persistent endeavours of particular Civil Service cliques to acquire sole authority and to neutralize the influence of the Party representatives. . . .

14 Relations between Party and State at local government level

It was at district and local level that Party interference in the administration tended to be most prevalent and it was here that the Gauleiters exercised greatest influence. They had in most cases been responsible for building up the Party *apparat* in their region from the earliest times after the refounding of the Party in 1925. They were usually local men who had over the years built up a clique of loyal supporters, particularly at district level the district leaders or *Kreisleiter*. This gave the Gauleiters considerable independence of the central Party organization. This independence was increased by the serious blow which the attempt to create a powerful central organization in the years 1930-32 had suffered in the resignation of Gregor Strasser. After 1933, Hitler characteristically divided the central authority of the Party between, on the one hand, the Office of Deputy Führer under Rudolf Hess and his deputy Martin Bormann, and on the other, the so-called Political Organization under Dr Robert Ley. In the inevitable conflict between these two organizations, the Office of the Deputy Führer came out on top as Ley concentrated his attentions on trying to build up the German Labour Front as a rival to the Party.[1] But Hess and Bormann continued to find difficulty in exercising control over the Gauleiters, who were deeply rooted in their areas. The central Party agency which was most successful in exerting control over the Gauleiters was the Treasury under Franz Schwarz, but this in turn was a semi-independent authority.

The control of the Gauleiters over the district and local Party *apparats* also gave them a large measure of influence over local government, since the district and local branch leaders were determined to dominate the state and local government officials in their district. The Party had won considerable influence over local government at the time of the seizure of power by packing the local councils and in some cases by taking over the office of mayor. But, as in most other spheres, this influence was then given legal expression although it was also delimited by legislation, in the form of the Prussian Local Government Law of 15 December 1933 and the Reich Local Government Law of 30 January 1935. The Prussian Law laid down, first, that the mayors were in future to be nominated (to serve for twelve years) rather than elected: in large cities by the Minister of the Interior (Göring); in towns by the *Regierungspräsident* 'in consultation' with the Gauleiter. Secondly, it laid down that, subject to the general supervision of the Ministry of the Interior, the mayor was to have absolute authority in his town. In some cases, the mayor was at the same time local branch leader of the Party. But in many cases this law actually had the effect of strengthening a non-Nazi or nominal Nazi mayor against the Nazi-dominated town council which had been reduced to a mere advisory body. As a result, the law met with considerable opposition from the Party.

This opposition was taken account of to some extent in the Reich Local Government Law of 30 January 1935. This law also gave the mayor dictatorial powers but introduced a so-called 'Delegate of the NSDAP in the Municipality'. This Nazi delegate had the right of participation in the appointment and dismissal of the mayor and his deputies, in the appointment and dismissal of the local councillors, and in the drawing up of the bye-laws. The district Party leaders (*Kreisleiter*) were appointed to this post, which meant that any local branch leader was officially excluded from effective influence on local government unless he happened to be mayor. Furthermore, the powers of supervision over local government remained with the Ministry of the Interior acting through the district and regional

[1] See below, pp. 435ff.

state authorities—the *Landräte* and the *Regierungspräsident* or Minister-President. These laws operating against the background of ambitious local Party leaders created patterns of conflict within local government. Thus the mayor, unless he was simultaneously local branch leader, would have to face interference both from the district leader in his capacity as 'Delegate of the NSDAP' and from the local branch leader who resented the mayor's role. The mayor could to some extent call on the support of the supervisory state authorities to help him to resist interference by the Party, but the *Landräte* and the *Regierungspräsidenten* were also having to fight off interference from the district Party leaders and the Gauleiters. The result was a constantly fluctuating power relationship within the localities. The following account of the *Landrat* of Kreuznach in the Rhineland for December 1935 indicates the extent of Party interference at district and local level:

I have often reported that the subordinate Party posts are still frequently filled with unsuitable persons and this is still so today. It is true that I was told by the mayors and police officers at the last official meetings that cooperation had improved between the offices of the Party and those of the administration. But against that is the statement from a reliable source that the Party itself does not find cooperation with the administration satisfactory because the offices of the administration are not sufficiently 'obedient'. In my opinion, the relationship

---

Note and footnotes to diagram on facing page:

Perhaps the most outstanding characteristic of the political system of the Third Reich was its lack of formal structure. This diagram, therefore, should be regarded as no more than a rough indication of the position of the various State and Party offices and their relationship to one another. It was difficult to get agreement on policy at ministerial level except in the comparatively rare event of Hitler issuing a clear-cut Führer order. But because of the lack of an effective hierarchy it was equally difficult to ensure a uniform and comprehensive implementation of policy at the lower levels.

[1] On 11 April 1933, Hitler appointed Göring Prussian Minister-President in addition to his post as Minister of the Interior. On 1 May 1934, however, Hitler, at Göring's request, transferred the Prussian Ministry of the Interior to Frick, who then became Reich and Prussian Minister of the Interior, though the Prussian administrative apparatus as such remained intact.

[2] After 1928 the *Gaue* came to correspond, broadly speaking, with the electoral districts (see map on p. 115). Over the years, however, there were a number of amalgamations and subdivisions as well as the addition of the annexed territories after 1938, so that during the years 1928–45 the *Gaue* varied in number between thirty and forty. The area of the individual *Gaue* varied considerably. Some, such as East Prussia or Baden, corresponded to a Prussian province or a large federal state; others were smaller – Hanover-East, for example, embraced two *Regierungsbezirke* and was less than half the size of the Province of Hanover. The importance of the individual Gauleiter was, however, related more to his length in office and his relations with Hitler than to the size of his *Gau*.

[3] In large cities such as Leipzig or Cologne the Oberbürgermeister had traditionally been sufficiently important to have a direct line to the Ministry of the Interior.

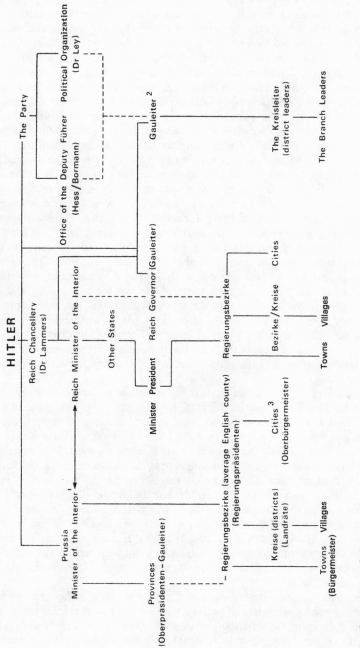

HITLER

Reich Chancellery
(Dr Lammers)

The Party

Prussia
Minister of the Interior

← Reich Minister of the Interior →

Office of the Deputy Führer
(Hess/Bormann)

Political Organization
(Dr Ley)

Other States

Reich Governor (Gauleiter)

Gauleiter [2]

Provinces
(Oberpräsidenten – Gauleiter)

Minister President

Regierungsbezirke (average English county)
(Regierungspräsidenten)

Regierungsbezirke

The Kreisleiter
(district leaders)

Regierungsbezirke (district)
(Landräte)

Cities [3]
(Oberbürgermeister)

Bezirke/Kreise   Cities

The Branch Leaders

Towns   Villages

Towns   Villages

For footnotes see facing page.

Party/State Relationships in the Third Reich

between Party and administration can be described as follows: the heads of the administration, especially of the public administration, have gradually got so used to constant interference by political leaders in purely administrative matters that they have come to regard this state of affairs as tolerable only so long as these conflicts do not become too violent. But it is an unhealthy state of affairs if, in the interests of cooperation and their public image, the authorities are invariably lenient, often to the detriment of the cause. After nearly three years' service in the district, I feel obliged to say again clearly that the duplication in the work of the Party and of the authorities in administrative matters is intolerable in the long run and tends to jeopardize constructive work. This is not only my view but that of old Party comrades who have for many years occupied leading posts as administrative officials. It is they particularly who complain to me that the subordinate Party officers, obviously because of their training by their superiors, are convinced that the authorities are nothing more than their executive organs. In fact, the local district leader [of the Party] is of the opinion that in the district of Kreuznach there can be no other will but his. This principle is of course employed even more rigidly by the subordinate local Party leaders. They are often on the look-out for cases of complaint and possibilities of interference, in order to keep the authorities aware of Party supervision. Having no competently trained apparatus at their command, Party offices deal with administrative matters and prejudge questions which either have already been officially dealt with by the authorities or are undecided and in the end have to be left to the authorities for examination and final decision on their own responsibility. But by then much work has been duplicated and time and energy wasted. I get the impression that the main cause of all this is the personal ambition of the political leaders. They seek to claim success for administrative work and exploit it with the public and in the press, while their failures are blamed on the authorities which in any case have to bear the responsibility.

The remark of the district leader that his will alone is decisive expressed itself clearly in his function as district delegate [*Kreisbeauftragter*]. This position functions in effect as a second local government supervisory office over local government and, judging by experience to date, I cannot describe it as a satisfactory solution.... Consequently there is discontent in many places at the district delegate's failure to consult mayors before appointing parish councillors, as prescribed, or to consult parish councillors as to his suggestions for the appointment of the mayor. In this connexion it is remarkable that the district delegate himself sent letters summoning the councillors before I had a chance to do so, probably out of self-importance and the desire to steal a march on the authorities. When his attention was drawn to this breach of the law, he replied that his letter was intended to announce the summons by the authorities. I cannot help feeling that these and similar interferences with administrative matters are intended to emphasize publicly his personal ascendancy.

Furthermore, the decisive influence of Party membership rather than personal suitability on the appointment of parish councillors and mayors leads one to suppose that right from the start the intention has been to make the parish organs dependent on the Party offices. In actual fact, mayors and parish councillors usually feel more subordinate to the Party than to their official superior. This has not only caused discontent among a large section of the population but has the further consequence that the parish organs frequently meet with resistance and rejection, thereby damaging the National Socialist movement.

The endeavour of the political leaders to fill civil servants' and employees' posts in Government offices solely on the ground of length of Party membership often reaches the point of excluding non-Party members and those Party members who joined the Party after 30 January 1933, even if they have far more skill and higher moral qualities. A particularly striking case was one in which other suitable applicants were turned down for the post of district welfare leader here, and the district committee proceeded to elect a civil servant who was an old Party member but who was not suited either by character or technical qualifications and whom meanwhile the police had to arrest for embezzlement in his previous post. No wonder, then, that the view is often expressed among people that the Party is pursuing the policy of getting Party members into public appointments regardless of their suitability, and is thereby doing exactly what it fought against in the old system.

Old Party members also confirm this view. But they are usually those who refrain on principle from turning their Party membership to any personal advantage.

It appears urgently necessary, in the interests both of the authority of the state and of constructive progress, to clear up the unsatisfactory situation I have described. Responsibilities for actual Party tasks must be clearly defined. I can see no solution in the linking up of Party offices with the state offices, whether with the district administration or with the local authorities. Moreover, the responsibility of the political leaders must, in my opinion, not only be a moral responsibility, but it must be emphasized by legal regulations.

15 Popular discontent with Party officials' behaviour at local level

In their monthly reports on the political situation the *Regierungspräsidenten* frequently referred to local discontent at the behaviour of the officials of the various Party organizations, notably the Hitler Youth. This reflected to some extent their resentment at Party interference in the state administration, but their evidence is often confirmed by the reports of the regional Gestapo offices:

Report of the Regierungspräsident of Hanover to the Reich and Prussian Minister of the Interior of 5 February 1935 concerning the NSDAP and its organizations

There are repeated complaints from the public that they have no respect for many of the subordinate leaders of the movement. Arrogance, presumption, particularly on the part of the Hitler Youth, morally objectionable conduct, and alcoholic excesses are the reasons for this attitude, with embezzlement added. During the period covered by this report there have been in my region a number of incidents which, by their nature and frequency, are calculated to lead to a deterioration in the attitude of the public and to undermine confidence in the state and the Party.

Some people in authority mistakenly believe themselves to be outside the normal jurisdiction of the police, and that, since they are representatives of the movement, no action, even should they commit offences or crimes, can be taken against them by police officials. This attitude was adopted recently by a branch leader when a police officer began to investigate a secretary of the NSV[1] suspected of embezzling or misusing funds of the Winter Aid Programme.

Cooperation between the Party and state and local government officials is sometimes complicated or even wholly frustrated by unsuitable or incompetent Party officials. Thus the *Landrat* in Hamelin reported to me that there could be no satisfactory relationship between the National Socialist organizations and the administrative authorities in Bad Pyrmont until a new branch leader had been appointed. The German Labour Front also frequently lacks suitable officials. That cooperation which is desirable, and indeed in the interests of the Party essential, between the separate organizations of the Party and the subordinate leaders and officials of these organizations is by no means everywhere to be found. On the contrary, in some places there have been unpleasant altercations of which the public has not been unaware. In a certain branch in the district of Hanover there has been dissatisfaction and hostility among the members over financial matters—a situation which is obviously the cause of the incident on 3 January 1935 when the district leader of the German Labour Front, his adjutant, and another Party comrade beat up another comrade so severely that his recovery is still doubtful; the injured man had several ribs on his right side smashed in, causing penetration of his lungs. Those responsible have been arrested. In another village a Troop leader of the SA when drunk hit two members of the SA Reserve I over the head with a steel pipe without any provocation. It was only the Storm Leader's energetic and sensible intervention that prevented a greater disturbance. . . .

The Hitler Youth leadership is unsatisfactory. It often sets no example to young people, it does not achieve a proper relationship with the teachers, and shows no aptitude for making the State Youth Day[2] into an occasion which will help the young. In the country districts parents will have nothing to do with the State Youth Day; they prefer their children to go to school. . . .

At each level of administration, therefore, the state authorities, frequently headed by nominal Nazis, had to fight off interference by the Party organization at their level. How successful they were in doing so was partly a matter of personality, depending on how good the connexions of the respective combatants were with those at the top and particularly with the Führer, and also on how good they were at this kind of political in-fighting. The state authorities tried to insist that since the State was now a Nazi State with a Nazi Head of State and Nazi ministers, they must be allowed to carry out the decisions and policies of the Government in accordance with official procedures and without interference by the Party, which would introduce an entirely arbitrary element. This attitude on the part of the Civil Service received the support of the Government ministers, even of Frick and Göring, Nazi leaders of long standing. The Nazi Party officials, on the other

[1] *Nationalsozialistische Volkswohlfahrt*: the Nazi Welfare Organization, which organized semi-compulsory collections.
[2] The Government had turned Saturday into a State Youth Day in which children could take part in Hitler Youth activities instead of going to school.

hand, were determined not to allow themselves to be ordered about by the state authorities. They claimed, as the true representatives of the will of the Führer, to be fighting a reactionary and formalistic bureaucracy which was always blocking the putting into effect of Nazi policy on the grounds that it was 'against regulations'.

Hitler's role and attitudes

Hitler's attitude to this struggle between Party and state authorities was ambivalent. During the seizure of power, Party members had seized power at various levels in the administration and the Party began showing signs of independence. Accordingly, in the first few years after 1933 Hitler tended to back the administration against interference from the Party. He needed stability to consolidate the regime, internally and externally. During this period, in fact, the power of the individual Government departments actually increased, up to a point. This was because of the virtual elimination of the federal structure, which gave the Reich ministries far more control over the lower levels of the administration than they had ever possessed before. The administration was increasingly centralized in the hands of the Reich ministries in Berlin. In addition, because of the reduced importance of Parliament, the ministries now had the power of issuing decrees without recourse to parliamentary approval. But, on the other hand, the ministries had increasingly to suffer the growth of competing organizations led by individuals to whom Hitler had given authority – organizations such as the Four-Year Plan which drained authority from the Ministry of Economics.[1] Also, while the individual Government departments were being strengthened, the corporate structure of the Government was being weakened by the decline of the Cabinet. After 1934, the Cabinet met less and less often and was replaced by personal contacts between Hitler and his individual ministers. Hitler did not like the idea of a corporate body which might limit his freedom of manoeuvre, and therefore the Government disintegrated into its departmental components with less and less coordination between them. The only official coordination was provided by the Reich Chancellery under its State Secretary, Dr Lammers, a colourless civil servant. But ultimately, since all authority was concentrated in Hitler's hands, the power to make the decisions between competing individuals and policies was his alone. Significantly, this position of absolute power was justified not so much in terms of his constitutional position as Reich Chancellor and Head of State, which would have imposed constitutional limitations on his authority, as in terms of his charismatic role as Leader of the German people. This is made clear in a speech by Hans Frank, the head of the Nazi Association of Lawyers, in 1938:

[1] See below, p. 441.

16 *The Constitution of the Third Reich*

... Even if no further decisions or legal formulations were added to the present laws of the Third Reich governing its legal structure, as a result of five years' government by the Führer there can be no juridical doubts about the following absolutely clear principles of the Reich:

1. At the head of the Reich stands the leader of the NSDAP as leader of the German Reich for life.

2. He is, on the strength of his being leader of the NSDAP, leader and Chancellor of the Reich. As such he embodies simultaneously, as Head of State, supreme State power and, as chief of the Government, the central functions of the whole Reich administration. He is Head of State and chief of the Government in one person. He is Commander-in-Chief of all the armed forces of the Reich.

3. The Führer and Reich Chancellor is the constituent delegate [*verfassung-gebende Abgeordnete*] of the German people, who without regard for formal preconditions decides the outward form of the Reich, its structure and general policy.

4. The Führer is supreme judge of the nation. . . . There is no position in the area of constitutional law in the Third Reich independent of this elemental will of the Führer.

The real characteristic of constitutional law in the Third Reich is that it does not represent a system of competencies but the relation of the whole German people to a personality who is engaged in shaping history. We are in a juridical period founded on the Führer's name, and shaped by him. The Führer is not backed by constitutional clauses, but by outstanding achievements which are based on the combination of a calling and of his devotion to the people. The Führer does not put into effect a constitution according to legal guidelines laid before him but by historic achievements which serve the future of his people. Through this, German Constitutional Law has produced the highest organic viewpoint which legal history has to offer. Constitutional Law in the Third Reich is the legal formulation of the historic will of the Führer, but the historic will of the Führer is not the fulfilment of legal preconditions for his activity. Whether the Führer governs according to a formal written Constitution is not a legal question of the first importance. The legal question is only whether through his activity the Führer guarantees the existence of his people.

On the whole Hitler was loath to arbitrate in conflicts between competing individuals unless a vital issue was at stake. He preferred the combatants to settle the matter between themselves with the stronger or the more ruthless personality coming out on top or else the establishment of an uneasy stalemate. This unwillingness of Hitler to make decisions tends to give an impression of weak leadership. What is certainly true is that Hitler had particular areas of interest, such as foreign policy and architecture, on which he concentrated his attention and he preferred to leave other matters to his subordinates who were given a free hand to expand their authority as much as they could. The fact that there were competing individuals and organizations in every sphere ensured that no single individual or organization acquired too much power and that the ultimate power of decision remained in his own hands should he care to use it. The prestige of an individual and his organization depended entirely on his relationship with the Führer. By withdrawing his favour from an individual, Hitler could always encourage rivals to undermine that individual's position. The implications of Hitler's position of absolute power and his monopoly of final decisions are described in the following documents from Carl Schmitt, a leading constitutional lawyer, and von Weizsäcker, State Secretary in the Foreign Ministry, respectively:

17 *The constitutional effects of Hitler's personal dictatorship*

Such a concentration of total power in the hands of a single human individual, who claimed to rule a modern industrial state of 70 million people right down to every detail and to conduct a modern total war personally right down to orders to the individual surpasses all known examples of a 'personal regime'. . . . Correspondingly, the importance of those around Hitler surpasses the analogous phenomena of the other cases mentioned (e.g. William II).

Hitler's chauffeurs became high dignitaries of the regime. They received the rank of *Gruppenführer*, i.e. a general's rank. . . . A *Gau* leader who had access to Hitler was politically more important than a Reich Minister who did not see his Head of State for years. Thus, all concepts of a regulated and calculable distribution of responsibilities cease to be applicable.

Hitler's personal position of power involved an immense claim to omnipotence but also the claim to omniscience. His omnipotence existed to a large extent in fact and was highly effective. His omniscience, however, was purely fictitious. The first practical question therefore was who conveyed to the omnipotent Führer the material on which his decisions were based and who selected from the mass of mail which arrived and decided what was or was not to be shown him. The second question concerned the other aspect of dealing with things, the passing on of orders and decisions to the executive, a question of special importance because there were no clearly defined forms for the so-called Führer orders and the orders were often brief and abrupt. . . .

The higher Hitler climbed, and with him everyone who had access to him and who was in personal contact with him, the lower the Reich ministers who did not belong to these privileged people (e.g. Reich Minister of the Interior Frick) sank to the level of mere civil servants. The Reich Cabinet did not meet after 1937. Between the top level of political power and the previous highest posts which were sinking, a vacuum developed that had to be filled by new 'superministerial' structures corresponding to the extremely personal character of this kind of power and use of power. They could not be authorities in the sense of a rationally and functionally developed hierarchy, but could only be a highly personal staff regardless of any name under which they were registered. The usual, and in a certain sense typical, term which emerged to describe them was 'Chancellery' [*Kanzlei*]. . . .

18 *Von Weizsäcker on the difficulties of access to Hitler*

Hitler did not love Berlin. Mostly he was in Berchtesgaden in the Berghof. There was no such thing as a Government with Cabinet meetings. Ministers in charge of departments might for months on end, and even for years, have no opportunity of speaking to Hitler. As early as 1938 there was, as it were, a Supreme Head-quarters. Anything that could not be settled between departments on their own account was referred there, in order that it might be brought to Hitler's attention by the Head of the Chancellery; or else the matter was simply put on one side as 'pending'. Ministerial skill consisted in making the most of a favourable hour or minute when Hitler made a decision, this often taking the form of a remark thrown out casually, which then went its way as an 'Order of the Führer'. . . .

In order to keep oneself informed of Hitler's opinion at any time, it was desirable to have one's own representative on his staff. The Army and Navy had their permanent adjutants there. Göring had a General Bodenschatz stationed there. Goebbels often visited Hitler's quarters personally. Ribbentrop, who had made the handling of Hitler a special study, posted his own *homme de confiance*, Hewel, later an ambassador, in Hitler's inmost circle. But apart from this, Ribbentrop, whenever he could do so, followed Supreme Headquarters from place to place. He then used to settle down somewhere half an hour or an hour away from where Hitler was, since the latter did not always want to have him around, and there he used to stay, on his toes, so to speak, and ready to appear on the scene at any moment. And so it came about that I was often alone in Berlin with the foreign ambassadors and envoys, reduced to guessing what had been planned in our foreign policy, or constrained to intercept rude aphorisms from Supreme Headquarters. Up to autumn 1938 I had not abandoned the attempt to influence political developments through the normal channel, by way of the Foreign Minister. From winter 1938/39 onwards, my notes of such efforts became ever rarer. . . .

19　*Hitler's attitude to the bureaucracy*

Although Hitler prevented the Party from dominating the State administration, there is no doubt that he was highly suspicious of the traditional bureaucracy. It was not suited to his style of leadership as it had evolved during the pre-1933 'time of struggle'. The following comment by Hans Frank makes this clear:

Hitler had been a Party man. As such he had come to power and he remained one as a statesman: he always kept the position of supreme leader of the NSDAP as well as his Reich positions. On 30 January 1933 the investiture of this function in his person was clarified and consolidated. It was also formally secured. His will was Party law. He was the absolute autocrat of the NSDAP. The Reich, however, especially the State apparatus bound by formal lines of jurisdiction and a hierarchy of command, was unfamiliar and strange to him. On 30 January 1933 his will alone was not yet 'law' in this area. Therefore he felt insecure and inhibited towards it. But since he believed he had been victorious in pushing through his concept of the Party, he saw the organizational form of the NSDAP as suiting him best: instead of transferring to the Party the traditional form of a legally ordered, expertly supervised, formally interdependent, juridically controlled State executive, his whole aim was to transfer the independent position he had in the NSDAP and its inner structure to the State. On 30 January 1933 he brought this aim with him.

20 *Hitler on the functions of the State (in 1935)*

Above all, Hitler was determined to ensure that the State bureaucracy should not restrict his freedom of manoeuvre, as he made clear in his proclamation to the Nuremberg rally in 1935:

We have given you [Marxists], perhaps with too much generosity, the chance of becoming in course of time forgotten if you show a sensible reserve. We have the feeling that our forbearance has been misunderstood. The consequences could not fail to appear, as they have appeared. The National Socialist State will now pursue its way still further in order to overcome these dangers. I should like to make it quite clear that the fight against foes within the nation will never be defeated by the inadequacy of a formal bureaucracy; wherever the formal bureaucracy of the State proves itself unfitted to solve a problem, there the German nation will bring into play its own more living organization in order to clear the way for the realization of its vital necessities. It is a great mistake to suppose that the nation exists to defend any formal institution [*Erscheinung*], or that, if an institution is incapable of solving the problems set it, the nation must therefore capitulate before these problems. On the contrary, whatever can be solved by the State will be solved through the State, but any problem which the State through its essential character is unable to solve will be solved by means of the Movement. For the State itself is but one of the forms of the organization of the *völkisch* life; it is set in motion and dominated by the immediate expression of the *völkisch* vital will [*Lebenswillens*], the Party, the National Socialist Movement. . . . Party, State, Army, Economics, Administration are all but means to the end, and that end is the safeguarding of the nation. That is a fundamental principle of National Socialist theory. What is obviously damaging to the safeguarding of the nation must be removed. If an institution proves unfitted to undertake this task, then another institution must undertake the task and carry it out. All of us, my comrades, and especially you who hold positions of leadership in the State and the Movement, will not be judged by your observance of forms [*nach Ihrem formalen Verhalten*] but by your successful realization of our programme, i.e. by the measure in which you defend our *völkisch* life. And especially one principle must be maintained with fanatical obstinacy: an enemy of the National Socialist State—it matters not whether he be a domestic or a foreign foe—must never know of, must never find, any authority [*Stelle*] which will meet him with understanding or with assistance. We live in the midst of a world which is in ferment. Only iron principles and their ruthless application will make us strong so that Germany may not sink into Bolshevist chaos. . . .

This resolute determination under any conditions to nip certain dangers in the bud will never hesitate, should the need arise, to hand over, through legislation, functions for which the State is obviously unfitted (since they are alien to its essential character) to institutions which appear better fitted to solve such problems. But on that point the will of the leadership alone decides, not the will of the individual. Our strength lies in our discipline.

Criticisms of the system

21 *Civil servants' resentment at Party interference*

Continual denigration by the Party, with Hitler's barely concealed connivance, inevitably undermined the morale of the Civil Service and thereby
made it all the more vulnerable to pressure from the Party. The growing
attitude of disillusionment shared by many civil servants found expression
in this memorandum written in September 1937 by Fritz-Dietlof von der
Schulenburg:

The crisis of the Civil Service

1. *The Civil Service—the main pillar of the State*. In the Reich Civil Service Law
the Civil Service is termed the main pillar of the State. And this is really what it is.
However the bureaucracy may be abused, every responsible statesman in his
political calculations counts on the work of the Civil Service.

Without a stable Civil Service no work can be achieved, no economy, especially
in its financial aspects, can be run, but *above all no Four-Year Plan can be carried out,
no war can be won. It is an appalling error for other institutions to think that there is no
need of a creative Civil Service*, that it will be sufficient to replace its work or steer it
from outside. For, in the first case, they would themselves ossify into complete
bureaucracies. In the second case, the heavy weight of a stagnating bureaucracy
would drag down anyone, even the highest flier. *Therefore, the only way left is to put
the Civil Service itself into shape*.

2. *Situation*. The Civil Service, however, especially at the top levels, finds itself
in a *situation which is beginning to destroy the prerequisites of creative work*.

(a) *The clear objective task* of the Civil Service and of the individual official *is
more and more lost to sight* since the formerly unified State power has been split into
a number of separate authorities; Party and professional organizations work in the
same areas and overlap with no clear divisions of responsibility, while the whole is
not always given priority over the particular aim, nor the cause over the individual.
The Civil Service, as well as the individual official, lacks both clear directives from
the State as well as objective backing when acting according to its laws. The civil
servant too often stands alone and unprotected.

(b) *Politically* the Civil Service has already been purged for four years since 1933.
Of 1600 administrative grade civil servants of the Prussian interior administration
about 400 have left. Moreover, about 750 young referendars[1] and assessors were
taken on, of whom up to 75 per cent were old Party members, to a great extent
pre-1930. *Despite all this* the Civil Service is still *exposed to political discrimination*.
Although it has considerable achievements to its credit since the take-over of
power, it is publicly *ridiculed* as a 'bureaucracy', devalued as a mere piece of
machinery, given no part to play or authority either by the Führer or by the community and decried as alien to the people, even as disloyal, without anyone being
prepared to reject officially this disparagement of a class on which the State
depends. Civil servants, especially leading ones, are *exposed to attacks* on their
work, *which in fact are directed against the State as such*; if the matter comes to an

---

[1] Junior civil servants or lawyers who have not yet passed the final examination.

argument they are never protected politically, but are let down even if they are doing no more than their duty. Despite the purge and the new recruitment of staff, they are under *special political control*. Through the *declaration of political reliability* they are judged by outsiders who, without a feeling for the State and authority, often cannot appreciate the nature and value of their work.

But, short of respect and appreciation, the historic achievements of the Civil Service, which the Führer himself has expressly acknowledged, are unthinkable. If the *honour of the Civil Service is no longer protected, results cannot be expected.* Furthermore, achievement must be recognized by a post corresponding to it: the highest post for the highest achievement. *What is given to all other great institutions is denied to the State: no young civil servant today carries 'the field-marshal's baton in his knapsack',* since the highest posts are filled from outside.

The consequences of this treatment of the Civil Service are that the Civil Service feels increasingly *defamed, without honour, and in some degree of despair. New recruitment is beginning to dry up.* Whereas in 1933 applications exceeded vacancies by 4–5 times, now vacant Civil Service posts can no longer be filled. Young law students who, for all the interest they showed in the State and administration, did not become civil servants openly give as their reason that there is no protection of professional honour nor any promotion on the basis of merit. For the same reasons able people are now already resigning and a growing number are about to do so. The Army, business, and the Party administration increasingly attract the best material. The only people who remain in the State and independent sector are those who become civil servants for the sake of the pension or the rank. This will mean the end of a true Civil Service and the emergence of a subservient bureaucracy.

(c) The Civil Service is largely reduced to the economic status of the proletariat. Its loss of capital is a consequence of war and inflation which it willingly bears together with large sections of the population. Financial stringency and reductions in salary, however, exceed what is bearable, and bring constant financial worries, distress and debts, especially to those who have many children or are sick; they close educational opportunities and do not allow the necessary freedom and sense of independence. By comparison, business offers many times the salary and attracts able civil servants whom the State needs (namely, in the Ministry of Economics) in order to control business.

The position is clear: because of all these stringent conditions the Civil Service is in a crisis which is dangerously sapping its substance, something which even the 'period of the system' [Weimar] was unable to destroy. Another few years and the substance will disintegrate; and that which it took generations to build up, it will take generations to rebuild. ...

22 *A Gauleiter criticizes the political structure*

The following excerpts from a long unsigned memorandum written in 1942, probably by Carl Röver, Gauleiter of Weser-Ems, sum up from the point of view of the Party and in a highly illuminating fashion many of the problems involved in Party/State relations. They provide a fascinating insight into the nature of the Party. The memorandum was written at a time when, owing to the war emergency, the Party was about to acquire more and more power from the State administration:

1. . . . The present laws prescribe that public corporations must be supervised by the State. If in practice this does not happen in the case of the Party at present, in my opinion one must not forget that in future generations when the leadership of the Reich may be weaker, which is possible even in our system, someone might have the idea of supervising the Party on the basis of its legal position as a public corporation.[1] The authority of the Party today is based on—to put it in plain terms—'bawling-out' [Schnauze], on old Party men who know how to get what they want, and also on officials who think it will be to their disadvantage if they make difficulties.

The NSDAP is a unique phenomenon; it has no precursors or models. Its legal position as a public corporation is unsatisfactory and undignified because it is derived from the legislation of the State and therefore incompatible with the sovereign position of the Party. The Party has fought for its position and conquered the State. For this reason, it cannot be a public corporation but must, in accordance with its leading and special position, have its own position within the law.

For the same reason, I consider it wrong that the influence of the Party on legislation is made dependent on any appointment to the position of Reich Minister, as it was earlier on, or on the conferring on the head of the Party chancellery the status of Reich Minister, as it is now. This right must be given to the Party by virtue of its position and its entitlement to leadership and must be granted by the Führer for the future.

In my opinion the 'Law on the Winter Emergency Programme of the German Nation' is a classic example of how not to do things. The Winter Emergency. Programme has always been a purely Party matter and it is by no means clear why the State had to pass a law on this. If the cooperation of the State was necessary in this or in some other case, the Party, by virtue of its position as granted by the Führer, should be able to require the State to carry out the necessary measures.

In any case, I regard the type of participation in legislation as carried out by the head of the Party chancellery and in the Law on the Winter Emergency Programme, which I chose as an example, as a concession to the State. This right must exist on the strength of the position of the Party. Otherwise the impression will undoubtedly arise that the offices conferred by the State are more important than the Party offices. Quite apart from that, and this is my main worry, the position of the Party could in the future be undermined, to say the least.

For the same reason, the endeavour of so many high-ranking Party members to have their Party apparatus legally consolidated by the State must be rejected. The result so far has always been an advantage for the State and a disadvantage for the Party. This is quite natural if one takes account of the greater powers of endurance which the State will always possess. It is indeed very easy and tempting to be able simply to use the State executive to carry out one's own measures. The leading Party members who seek their salvation in the State will in most cases forget the infinitely more important Party work involved with the people and, in their State posts, will either become more bureaucratic, that is to say, move away from the people, or pursue the quiet life of an official.

I must therefore reject the attempt to achieve the aim of controlling the State

[1] Under Paragraph 1 of the Law to ensure the Unity of Party and State of 1 December 1934. See above, p. 233.

executive by establishing a personal union between Party and State offices. The supporters of this view always argue that if this was carried out, all quarrels, controversies and other negative manifestations would be avoided. But against this it is arguable that, although the Party is in a leading position, it does not have to fulfil any executive tasks and that the objective airing of differences of opinion can only be advantageous for a cause. The Party has become great through struggle, and only continual struggle with problems and close contact with the people, such as the Party has, but which the State, of its inherent nature, can never have, will guarantee that our senses remain sharp and alert and that the dynamic and elasticity of the movement are maintained.

Thus I regard any unfounded personal union of Party and State offices as the surrender of a Party position and a retreat into the State. The holders of offices at *Gau* level are an exception, because their functions are conceived from totally different considerations. On the strength of their Party office, they are leaders of large areas and because of their important tasks of leadership must always be able to affect State measures directly. To extend these exceptions to the district level or even further would, I think, be wrong for the reasons given above and I would advise strongly against it.

I am convinced that the bad developments described above would have been avoided if the legal position of the Party had given it a different basis from the start.

A demand should therefore be made for a Führer decree to give the Party a legal status, perhaps in connexion with the Senate announced by the Führer at the Party Congress, corresponding to its struggle, its importance, and its mission of leadership, so that it may be in a position to demand from the executive authorities of the State the carrying out of certain measures for the fulfilment of its tasks, and to give them binding instructions in specific areas. This Führer decree, as the bequest of the creator of the movement, should secure the claim to leadership and the basic rights of the movement for all time.

2. *Fighting things out or defining spheres of responsibility.* The principle of letting things develop until the strongest has won is certainly the secret of the really remarkable development and achievements of the movement. But this principle too must be looked at from both sides. If both partners have the same character traits, the principle is right. If, however, one of the partners possesses character but the other one because of the weakness of his character operates the more craftily and slyly, the latter will usually be the winner.

As I said, the tremendous achievements and the rapid development of the Party are largely due to the system described above, and one must admit that this was certainly useful during the period when the Party was being built up. But now that the Party's position and tasks have acquired firmer outlines, now that it must be regarded as having attained full growth, the position here also must be consolidated; that is to say, a clear conception must be gained of its organizational structure, and spheres of competence must be precisely defined. Otherwise, conflicts over the boundaries of power and authority will be carried into the local branches, some of them possibly lasting for years, and we should not be blind to the damage that will be done. The flexibility and adaptibility needed to counteract the establishment of a bureaucracy can be achieved in a different way. We must ensure a rapid consolidation of the position in this respect, for it cannot be denied that in many spheres of Party activity several offices are dealing with the same task: two or more seize upon the same task without as yet the intervention of any authority. Some outstanding personality may perhaps be able to assert himself through his superior abilities and thereby in time unite the various spheres in his control unless he is brought down by intrigue. But if all these men are more or less on the same level, they will continue to simmer in a permanent quarrel about spheres of authority, or else anyone who can will elbow his way forward and grab everything, and damage will be done to the cause. The number of different competencies means that many people are employed unproductively and unprofitably in continual disputes about authority, with a considerable wastage of resources. The success of the work is jeopardized and, in the end, the subordinate offices no longer know whom to follow. They become indifferent and in some instances they cannot even carry out the contradictory instructions they receive. The result is that important matters are treated in exactly the same way as unimportant matters; that is to say, important matters remain just as neglected and unfinished as unimportant ones. Moreover, it is not surprising that all this undermines respect for superiors. It is no secret that the higher the office, the more muddled is the demarcation of tasks within it. The block, the cell, and the local branch are spheres of authority in which problems of competency are unknown. It is true that plenty of orders reach the local branch, but in the local branch things are arranged in such a way that the local branch leader has all the reins in his hand. In the district organizations confusion is more noticeable, but the district leaders through their personality know how to maintain uniformity. In the *Gaue*, on the other hand, confusion stares one in the face.

Thus a clear demarcation of tasks is urgently necessary in order to stop the considerable waste of energies caused by continuous disputes over competencies. Ways and means must be found, on the one hand, of letting the personality develop fully and thereby achieve its potential, and on the other, of securing a clear demarcation of tasks without transferring to the Party the bureaucratic system which exists in the State administration with all its adverse consequences in terms of restrictions. For it corresponds with the character and aims of the Party for the Party leader to be able to develop as freely as possible and independently of regulations and other obstacles. It must not be forgotten that in the administrative apparatus of the State a certain bureaucratic element is necessary and will be indispensable also in the future. But the task of leadership which has been given to the Party necessitates other methods in the work itself and in the demarcation of tasks, namely those outlined above.

3. *The Leader Principle.* The leader principle depends absolutely on the personality of the leader. The advantages of the leader principle itself have been sufficiently proved by the historical events of the past and the present, especially since the coming into existence of the National Socialist German Workers' Party, so that further discussion of it is unnecessary. But one cannot help recognizing the disadvantages of the leader principle, so that one can take suitable steps to eliminate the danger resulting from this as far as possible.

As already mentioned, the leader principle depends absolutely on the personality of the person entrusted with the office of leadership. This is true at a low level just as much as at a high one. The only difference is that the higher the authority, the more far-reaching are the effects whether positive or negative.

In the first place, the good leader excels through his achievements and, secondly, he tends to choose suitable people and experts as his assistants. These assistants grow in stature through the tasks given to them, adapt themselves to their leader and can take his place at any time. Through this process the succession to the leadership is automatically guaranteed and it is even possible to provide good people for other purposes. When the holder of a leading post is not a good leader and, in addition, has weaknesses of character, the position is usually completely reversed: to start with, there are no actual achievements; secondly, he usually chooses fools and blockheads as his assistants who also have defects of character and act accordingly so that no results are achieved and, what is even worse, all the power lies in the hands of incompetents and people with defects of character. A change in the situation appears impossible since, on the basis of the leader principle, people of the same kind jealously see to it that they stay in power unless a superior authority intervenes. It is in the nature of stupid people who have been entrusted with an office on the basis of the leader principle to try to disguise their stupidity, put obstacles in the way of all progressive measures, and endeavour to consolidate their position by selecting assistants with a similar outlook; by the masterly staging of intrigue they usually succeed.

It is all very well to reward people's merits, but the welfare of the nation must come first. It will not always be necessary to dismiss weak leaders who have performed meritorious service in the cause of the movement but who do not possess the requisite qualities for a leader. In most cases, if the faults which have been detected permit this, one will be able to give them other tasks where it will be impossible for them to do any damage. Certainly, loyalty is one of the noblest of virtues, but it cannot be used one-sidedly; that is to say, if a leader repays the loyalty shown him with neglect of duty, unprincipled actions or similar behaviour, the necessary conclusions must be drawn.

We must therefore demand that leaders who do not possess the prerequisites of ability, character, and ideological reliability be replaced by better ones; for the damaging effect upon the nation and the State resulting in many fields from the silent toleration of such leaders must not be ignored.

The correct selection and choice of leaders and the building in of safety valves are of decisive importance for the removal of the faults which have been described. . . .

We have approximately six million Party members in the Reich. There is no question of their forming a unified combat group. One day, the Party will certainly be an elite order of the Führer; it is not so yet because the principles governing admission to it have obviously been influenced by the financial needs of the Party. Many have been admitted who merely needed Party membership to consolidate their social position or who wanted to gain professional or economic advantages through it. It must not be forgotten that, if the movement was to be able to master its various tasks, especially in those areas which from the Party's point of view could only be called backward, many ideologically immature citizens had to be admitted, if only to enable the Party organization to be built up since the required number of ideologically mature citizens were simply not there, particularly in the so-called black [i.e. Roman Catholic] areas. The Party accepted these citizens in

order, as I said, to be able to carry out the necessary work. Through the opportunities which the Party has gained for influencing such citizens, some have meanwhile become reliable National Socialists, but by no means the majority.

This development is regrettable. It will be necessary to overhaul the whole
Party apparatus and to investigate every individual Party member, especially his
ideological attitude and his sense of commitment. During the coming ideological
conflicts we must be able to rely on the Party members in all circumstances. But we
should have no illusions about the fact that this is by no means possible at
present....

We must expect of the *Reichsleiter* [Reich Party leaders] that they do not carry
differences of opinion down to the lower levels on the principle of whose elbows
are the strongest. They must dispute among themselves until they have come to an
agreement....

Since 1933 there has been no continuous unified concentration of the higher
Party leadership corps. The result is that everybody has more or less set himself
up on his own ... that in the *Gaue* everybody rules in his own way and that
opinions on basic questions are not formed in a unified manner....

23 *Statistics on the Nazi Party as of 1 January 1935*

Total Membership = 2,493,890
Percentage of population over 18 = 5·1
Percentage of male population over 18 = 10·2
Percentage of female population over 18 = 0·5
Percentage of male Party members = 94·5
Percentage of active[1] Party members = 57·2
Percentage of members who took part in the war = 40·5
Percentage of members who joined before 30.i.33 who took part in the war = 29·7
Percentage of members who joined before 14.ix.30 = 5·2
Percentage of members who joined between 15.ix.30 and 30.i.33 = 28·8
Percentage of members who joined after 30.i.33 = 66

[1] Who attended Party meetings regularly.

10 Law and Order

Clearly two of the most crucial areas of State authority which the Nazis needed to coordinate were those of the legal system and the police. Both Hitler personally and Nazism as an ideology and as a movement were fundamentally hostile to legal processes. Since the 'Führer' regarded himself and was so regarded by his movement as a man of destiny, chosen to lead Germany and expressing the will of the nation, any body of laws was viewed with suspicion as a restriction on his freedom of action, particularly since their enforcement was the responsibility of a legal profession which was considered pedantic and tainted with liberalism. Point 19 of the Nazi Party programme of 1920 had demanded 'that Roman Law, which serves a materialistic world order, be replaced by a German common law'. In fact, however, just as Hitler had avoided introducing a new constitution, preferring to leave the Weimar Constitution as a façade while undermining its substance, similarly attempts to formulate a new comprehensive corpus of National Socialist law came to naught. Thus, the attempt to replace the Civil Law Code with a so-called People's Law Code and, more important, the elaborate discussions about a new Nazi penal code were all eventually shelved by Hitler. As in the constitutional sphere, this policy of adapting the legal system to suit the requirements of the regime, by a series of *ad hoc* measures over a period of years rather than by speedy and systematic reform, reflected the nature of the Nazi take-over of power with its quasi-legal emphasis on continuity, its anxiety to avoid serious economic or social disruption, and also its total lack of forward planning springing from the Party's concern with immediate questions of power rather than with formal structures. Above all, however, it had the advantage of leaving the Nazis free to criticize the existing laws as products of a liberal era without at the same time binding them to new ones which would have had the authority of the regime behind them.

In place of a systematic reconstruction several methods were used to coordinate the legal system. During 1933, the professional associations of judges, lawyers, and other legal officials of various kinds were forced to dissolve themselves and to merge with the Nazi Association of German Lawyers to form a massive new organization, the National Socialist League for the Maintenance of the Law (*Nationalsozialistischer Rechtswahrerbund*) under the leadership of Dr Hans Frank who became 'Reich Law Leader'. Measures were also passed to ensure a tight control over the appointment of judges and the admission of lawyers. Finally, sensitive areas of particular concern to the regime such as political offences, the Party and its various offshoot organizations, various occupations such as agriculture, and hereditary disabilities, were removed from the jurisdiction of the ordinary courts and transferred to special courts which could be more easily packed with loyal Nazis.

More fundamental than these specific measures, however, was the way in which the regime undermined the basic principles which had hitherto governed German law. The Nazis criticized the existing legal system as 'liberal' and 'formalistic'. In particular, they objected to principles such as equality before the law, or that no action should be treated as a crime unless it had been declared such by a law. Although it is true that the legal positivist approach of the judiciary enabled the new Government to implement its will as law, this approach defined the will of the regime far too rigidly and narrowly for the purposes of Hitler and his movement. As a result, the regime increasingly insisted that formal law must no longer be regarded as the sole criterion for judging whether an action was right or wrong. Instead of the strict adherence to the letter of the law characteristic of the legal positivist approach, more scope must be given to the interpretation of the law in the light of wider values. In place of the principles of natural justice the Nazis substituted 'healthy popular feeling', 'the welfare of the national community', 'National Socialist ideology' or, most crucial of all, 'the will of the Führer', as the criteria which should influence the judiciary in its interpretation of the law. This new theory was advocated by a group of mostly younger academics, the majority of them in their early thirties, who were able to express their views unchallenged since the legal journals were now controlled by the regime. Thus, in place of the admittedly rather rigid but at least relatively clear-cut and objective approach of legal positivism, there developed a highly subjective, arbitrary, and confused system, dominated by political considerations which, when combined with a judiciary largely subservient to the regime, resulted in the progressive undermining and perversion of the law.

Initially, the process of coordination concentrated on the political sphere. But it was of the nature of Nazism as a totalitarian movement that it should seek the broadest possible definition of political offences; indeed, with the increased politicizing of life in the Third Reich, more and more spheres of activity were brought within the scope of coercion. Even criminal matters, particularly during the war, came in greater degree to be regarded as quasi-political offences, since they were considered to be directed against the national community in its struggle for survival. Only in parts of the civil and commercial spheres did the legal system continue to retain a degree of independence and objectivity. Clearly the regime could not afford to dispense completely with a legal system for the regulation of social and economic activity on a rational basis.

Despite the extent of its coordination, however, Hitler never came to terms with the legal system and preferred to rely on the SS. The years 1933–36 saw the gradual absorption of the police by the SS. With its powers of 'protective custody' for political offences, under the decree of 28 February 1933, and of 'preventive custody' in the criminal and 'anti-social' spheres under an edict of the Ministry of the Interior dated 14 December 1937, and with the establishment of its own independent prison network, the concentration camps, the SS developed a penal system parallel to the official system. Moreover, increasingly, the SS-police began to interfere in the judicial process itself, ignoring verdicts or intervening to have them changed. The two systems continued to coexist side by side, just as the State administration continued to coexist side by side with the Party administration. The peculiarity of the Third Reich lay precisely in this coexistence of the two systems – on the one hand, the civil servants trained to adhere to rational and legal norms, some indeed trying to retain some sort of rationality in the regime and thereby in effect helping to stabilize it; on the other hand, the representatives of arbitrary Führer authority who resisted any attempt to limit the exercise of this authority on legal or procedural grounds. Well before the end of the war it had become only too clear which of the two had achieved dominance.

The legal system

1 *The Cabinet discusses the punishment of van der Lubbe, 7 March 1933*

When appointing Hitler as Chancellor, President Hindenburg had insisted on retaining the Minister of Justice, Franz Gürtner. Gürtner, formerly Minister of Justice in Bavaria, had indeed helped the Nazis in the early days in Munich, but he was a Nationalist, not a Nazi. Instead of providing a barrier against Nazi illegality, however, Gürtner's position merely served to camouflage the coordination of political justice which was taking place. At an early stage, Hitler made it clear that he was not prepared to let legal niceties stand in his way. Thus, on 7 March he expressed his determination to bend the law in the case of van der Lubbe, who had set fire to the Reichstag. The attitude of the officials of the Ministry of Justice was ambivalent. They felt obliged to point out the impropriety of such a step; they also showed themselves anxious to meet Hitler's wishes as far as possible:

The Reich Minister of the Interior spoke about the Reichstag fire and the punishment of the culprits, and stated that it was urgently necessary to hang van der Lubbe at once – and, moreover, in the Königsplatz. To be sure, the law on arson provided for no more than a prison sentence, but it must be possible to impose, with retroactive effect, the penalty of death by hanging for such a heinous crime. The principle of *nulla poena sine lege*[1] should not have an unqualified

[1] The principle that no one should be tried for an act which was not a crime at the time he committed it or be given a punishment which was not stipulated for the act at the time he committed it.

application. Professor Dr Nagler (Breslau), Professor Dr von Weber (Jena), and Professor Dr Öttler (Würzburg) had delivered opinions in this sense.

The Reich Minister of Interior then reported on the substance of the opinions as enclosed.

The Chancellor stated emphatically that he also believed it to be urgently necessary to hang van der Lubbe. The German public demanded it. He could not recognize the doctrine that 'the law must be observed', if this constituted a threat to the life of the whole nation. . . .

State Secretary Schlegelberger[1] stated that he agreed entirely with the view of the Reich Chancellor that the law must be adjusted to the circumstances. A preliminary investigation of van der Lubbe on charges of high treason and arson had been opened that day (7 March). He must strongly emphasize the doctrine of *nulla poena sine lege*. Only in Russia, China, and some of the minor Swiss cantons did that doctrine not apply. He would again study carefully the opinions mentioned by the Reich Minister of Interior. The Reich Ministry of Justice would itself then formulate an opinion and send both opinions to the Reich Ministers for their information.

State Secretary Dr Meissner stated that the arguments of the Chancellor were politically quite correct. The public was right in demanding a severe penalty for van der Lubbe.

The Reich President might, however, suffer severe twofold qualms of conscience, namely, if he were to sign an order prescribing the death penalty and so forth, and then later to decide on a petition for pardon of the condemned man. He asked that the Reich Chancellor, the Reich Minister of the Interior, and the Reich Ministry of Justice should submit the matter to the President before the Cabinet reached a final decision.

Reich Commissioner Dr Popitz[2] stated that he feared the Reich Supreme Court would not recognize the retroactive effect of an order prescribing the death penalty.

The Chancellor stated that he would get in touch with the President of the Reich Supreme Court about this.

It was expected that the Chancellor would first speak alone with the President on the matter. . . .

In fact a law introducing the death penalty for arson—a 'lex Lubbe'—was passed on 29 March 1933.

2 *Decree of the Reich President for the protection of the Nationalist movement against malicious attacks upon the Government, 21 March 1933*

As the 'revolution from below' developed during March, the legal authorities became increasingly conscious of their helplessness in the face of the SA and SS terror. On the one hand, they were under pressure to conform exerted by the atmosphere of 'national uprising'. On the other hand, they were anxious to restore some sort of order to the situation. Their position was similar to that of the State administration and their way out of the dilemma also was similar. They compromised with the regime by producing laws which systematized, and therefore promised to establish

[1] Of the Ministry of Justice.
[2] Dr Johannes Popitz was Prussian Minister of Finance.

some sort of control over, political discrimination. Whereas the State administration produced the Law for the Re-establishment of the Professional Civil Service, the legal authorities produced new measures regulating the application of the law to political activity:

...

Paragraph 3

1. Whoever purposely makes or circulates a statement of a factual nature which is untrue or grossly exaggerated or which may seriously harm the welfare of the Reich or of a state, or the reputation of the National Government or of a state government or of the parties or organizations supporting these governments, is to be punished, provided that no more severe punishment is decreed in other regulations, with imprisonment of up to two years and, if he makes or spreads the statement publicly, with imprisonment of not less than three months.

2. If serious damage to the Reich or a state has resulted from this deed, penal servitude may be imposed.

3. Whoever commits an act through negligence will be punished with imprisonment of up to three months, or by a fine. . . .

On 20 December 1934, this decree was turned into a law and was broadened to include any criticism which was 'malicious' of any 'leading personality' of the Party or State. This law was to provide one of the main 'legal' bases for the activities of the Gestapo.

On the same day as this decree (21 March 1933), another decree was issued setting up special courts with jurisdiction over political crimes, except for cases of high treason, which remained within the jurisdiction of the Supreme Court in Leipzig. These courts were staffed with loyal Nazi judges and there was no right of appeal from them. They were to be greatly expanded during the following years.

3 Hitler defines what is required of the legal system

Two days later, though paying token respect to the principles of equality before the law and the irremovability of judges, Hitler disclosed his real attitude to the law in his speech to the Reichstag on the occasion of the passage of the Enabling Law:

. . . The Government of the national revolution regards it as its duty on principle, in accordance with the nation's vote of confidence, to keep those elements from influencing the nation which consciously and intentionally act against its interests. The theory of equality before the law cannot be allowed to lead to the granting of equality to those who, on principle, treat the law with contempt, let alone to the surrendering of the freedom of the nation to these people on the grounds of democratic principles. But the Government will grant equality before the law to all those who, by taking part in the formation of a national front against this danger, back the national interest and do not fail to support the Government. . . .

Our legal system must, in the first place, serve to maintain this national community. The irremovability of the judges must, in the interests of society, be paralleled by an elasticity in sentencing. The nation rather than the individual must be regarded as the centre of legal concern. High treason must in future be ruthlessly exterminated. The basis of the existence of the judicial system cannot be other than the basis of the nation's existence. It should therefore always consider the difficult decisions which face those who, under the hard pressure of reality, are responsible for shaping the life of the nation. . . .

4 *Law to change the rules of criminal law and criminal procedure, 24 April 1934*

The fact that cases of high treason did not come under the special courts but were still tried by the Supreme Court proved to be a loophole, for the Reichstag Fire trial ended with the acquittal of most of the alleged Communist accomplices of van der Lubbe. On 24 April, therefore, the following law was passed, establishing a so-called 'People's Court' to try all cases of treason. It consisted of two professional judges, carefully selected for their loyalty to the regime, and five Party officials as lay judges.

. . .

CHAPTER III

1. A People's Court shall be formed to try cases of high treason. When the People's Court sits for a trial, the judgements are to be made by five members, otherwise by three members, including the President. The President and one other member must be qualified judges. Several senates may be formed. The Supreme Reich Prosecutor is the prosecuting authority.

2. The Reich Chancellor appoints the members of the People's Court and their deputies for a period of five years, on the proposal of the Reich Minister of Justice. . . .

5. There is no appeal from the decisions of the People's Court. . . .

CHAPTER IV

3. The appointment of defence council must be approved by the President of the People's Court. . . .

The willingness of the authorities to ignore the principle of *nulla poena sine lege* which had been shown in the van der Lubbe case was confirmed in July 1934 when the murders at the time of the Röhm 'putsch' were retroactively legalized on the grounds that they were 'necessary for the self-defence of the State'.[1] Once more, the Minister of Justice could rationalize his action with the belief that the taming of the SA would mean a return to a more orderly situation.

5 *Law to change the Penal Code, 28 June 1935*

This attitude, which had hitherto found expression in the treatment of

[1] See above, p. 217.

specific instances, was finally enshrined in the Law to Change the Penal Code, passed on 28 June 1935 and given an official interpretation by Gürtner. From now onwards, judges were obliged to take into account not merely the law as written, but also the 'concept of justice behind it' and 'healthy popular emotions':

. . .

Article 1, Section 2. Any person who commits an act which the law declares to be punishable or which is deserving of punishment according to the idea of a penal law and healthy popular feeling, shall be punished. If there is no penal law directly covering an act it shall be punished under that law the basic idea of which fits it best. . . .

6 *The Reich Minister of Justice on the principle of* nulla poena sine lege, *1935*

A law which originates from the rule *'nulla poena sine lege'* regards as illegal only such action as violates an existing clause of a penal law. Whatever is not forbidden and threatened with punishment is considered to be permissible. Such a law follows from the conception of formal wrongdoing. National Socialism substitutes for the conception of formal wrong the idea of factual wrong: it considers every attack on the welfare of the national community, every violation of the requirements of the life of a nation as wrong. In future, therefore, wrong may be committed in Germany even in cases where there is no law against what is being done. Even without the threat of punishment, every violation of the goals towards which the community is striving is wrong *per se*. As a result, the law gives up all claim to be the sole source for determining right and wrong. What is right may be learned not only from the law but also from the concept of justice which lies behind the law and may not have found perfect expression in the law. The law certainly continues to be the most important source for the determination of right and wrong because the leaders of a nation express their will in the law. But the legislator is aware of the fact that he cannot give exhaustive regulations covering all the situations which may occur in life; he therefore entrusts the judge with filling in the remaining gaps. . . .

The Nazis also endeavoured to mould the legal system to suit their ends by pressure on the judges who administered the law. In their coordination of the legal system they were assisted by the fact that during the Weimar Republic the judiciary had remained a bastion of the Right. Its sentencing policy was notoriously biased in favour of extremists of the Right and against those of the Left. But there are also other factors which help to account for the relative ease with which the legal system was coordinated. The vast majority of judges were initially Nationalists rather than Nazis and it is doubtful whether the judiciary, despite its right-wing bias, would have proved so vulnerable, had its position not already been relatively weak.

In the first place, the status of the judiciary in Weimar Germany was not particularly high. The position of a judge did not carry the great prestige associated with that office in Britain. Apart from anything else there were far more of them—between 8,000 and 10,000. In other words, the range of activity of the German judiciary embraced far lower courts than in Britain, where laymen have a more important role to play as magistrates. But more significant in their relative lack of prestige was the fact that they did not appear to have the same degree of independence. Judges were career civil servants. Furthermore, the judicial branch of the Civil Service was considered inferior to the administrative branch. The salary was modest and, for the majority, prospects of promotion were poor. The ablest law students therefore tended to go into the administrative branch or to become private lawyers. The fact that, unlike its British counterpart, the German judiciary did not form a powerful independent professional body with long traditions, highly conscious of its role as the guardian of the law, if necessary, against governments, and supported by the respect of the population, undoubtedly weakened its powers of resistance to Nazism.

Secondly, there was the fact that the doctrine of legal positivism tended to degrade the judge into a mere agent of the State in the sense that he was reduced to implementing the law with his freedom to interpret it restricted within the very narrow limits of the particular law or body of law. In short, he lacked a creative role and, as far as the general public was concerned, tended to appear as just one more civil servant rather than as the guardian of the rights of the individual and as someone who could be relied upon to interpret the law with a sense of justice.

Thus the judiciary could not rely on the support of public opinion for a defence of its independence. In fact before 1933 this independence was very real. For, although judges were civil servants, it would be wrong to suggest that German judges before 1933 allowed themselves to be influenced in reaching their decisions by any political pressures. Judicial independence was respected by the Government and backed by the law. Judges were appointed for life and could not be dismissed or transferred against their will except in very narrowly defined circumstances. This independence of the judiciary clearly represented a barrier which the new regime would have to remove or by-pass if it was to establish total political control. This point was soon underlined by the judgement of the Supreme Court in the Reichstag Fire trial, in which the charges against the majority of the Communist defendants were dismissed.

In the first place, the judiciary were subject to the Law Concerning the Reconstruction of the Professional Civil Service of 7 April 1933, which abolished the principle that judges could not be dismissed or demoted for political reasons and thus undermined the principle of the independence of the judiciary. But this law affected relatively few judges since the vast majority were right-wing. More important were other measures affecting the Civil Service in general. The 1935 decree involving the Party, through the Office of the Deputy Führer, in the appointment of civil servants also applied to judges. Finally, Paragraph 71 of the German Civil Service Law of

26 January 1937 laid down that civil servants could be compulsorily retired if they 'could not be relied upon to support the National Socialist State at all times'. Although Hitler was persuaded to agree to a qualification in Paragraph 171 by which Paragraph 71 did not apply to a judgement in court, he removed it a year later in a confidential memorandum from Dr Lammers to the Reich Minister of Justice dated 12 July 1938.

7 *The position of judges in the National Socialist State*

The judges were also reminded of what the regime expected of them in statements issued by persons in authority such as the following statement formulated by Professor Karl Eckhardt, the editor of a legal journal, but issued on 14 January 1936 under the name of Dr Hans Frank. Point 5 of this declaration was not in fact in line with Hitler's views or with those of other Party officials. It was presumably included as a gesture of reassurance to the judges, though it also reflected the views of Frank himself:

1. The judge is not placed over the citizen as a representative of the State authority, but is a member of the living community of the German people. It is not his duty to help to enforce a law superior to the national community or to impose a system of universal values. His role is to safeguard the concrete order of the racial community, to eliminate dangerous elements, to prosecute all acts harmful to the community, and to arbitrate in disagreements between members of the community.
2. The National Socialist ideology, especially as expressed in the Party programme and in the speeches of our Führer, is the basis for interpreting legal sources.
3. The judge has no right to scrutinize decisions made by the Führer and issued in the form of a law or a decree. The judge is also bound by any other decisions of the Führer which clearly express the intention of establishing law.
4. Legal decrees issued before the National Socialist revolution are not to be applied if their application would violate the present healthy feelings of the people. In the event of a judge suspending some legal regulation on these grounds, the decision of the highest court must be sought.
5. To carry out his duties effectively within the national community, the judge must be independent. He is not bound by instructions. The independence and dignity of the judge make it necessary to give him adequate protection against any attempt to influence him or against any unjustified attacks.

8 *Decree on the Qualifications for the Offices of Judge, Public Prosecutor, Notary Public and Lawyer, 4 January 1939*

Thirdly, the training of judges was designed to include a generous dose of Nazi ideology as is indicated by the following decree:

1. A thorough, conscientious specialized training should be at the centre of the course of studies.
2. But it is desirable that the course should not be restricted to this. On the contrary, the candidate should as a student acquire such a general picture of the whole intellectual background of the nation as would be expected of an educated German.

This should include a knowledge of German history and of the history of those nations which have had a positive influence on the cultural development of the German people, above all the Greeks and the Romans. Furthermore, it must include a serious study of National Socialism and its ideological foundations, of the idea of the relationship between blood and soil and between race and nationality, of German community life and of the great men which the German nation has produced.

Lawyers too were strictly controlled. Before 1933 German lawyers had been members of a free profession. Having passed their examinations, they were free to practise in a court and were not subordinate to the State in any way. After 1933 their independence was rapidly eroded. The provisions of the Civil Service Law of 7 April 1933 were applied to lawyers in a Law Concerning the Admission of Lawyers of the same date. Even more significant was a law of 13 December 1935, which established probationary periods for new lawyers and gave the Ministry of Justice authority over the admission of lawyers to practise. Decisions over admissions were to be made in consultation with the Reich Law Leader, Dr Hans Frank. In addition lawyers were required to swear an oath of loyalty to Hitler.

9 *The Court of Honour of the Reich Chamber of Lawyers on the refusal of a lawyer to give the Nazi salute, 1 November 1937*

Before 1933 discipline within the profession had been exercised through district chambers which were self-governing bodies. In 1933 a new Reich Chamber of Lawyers was established whose officials were nominated by the Reich Minister of Justice in consultation with the Reich Law Leader and membership of which was compulsory. The new Chamber concentrated on ensuring that lawyers conducted themselves in the way expected of them by the National Socialist State and maintained discipline through a Court of Honour:

The Court of Honour regards the refusal to give the German salute as a breach of professional etiquette which deserves severe punishment. The Appeal Court of Honour cannot share the assumption of the previous court that the accused acted from understandable indifference and not on purpose. Both the behaviour of the accused and the observations of the witness make it clear that the accused frequently failed to give or return the German salute on purpose. This evidence and the fact that the behaviour of the accused caused annoyance and tended to degrade the German legal profession in the eyes of other citizens were bound to result in an increase in the sentence imposed by the lower Court of Honour. The sentence of reprimand seems an appropriate punishment, taking into account the extenuating circumstances already mentioned by the Court of Honour.

10 *Two examples of courage in the courts*

It was not entirely impossible for lawyers and judges to resist pressure, but, in view of the atmosphere of the time and the possible penalties, exceptional courage was required such as was shown in the following examples both of a lawyer and of a judge:

On the day of the trial the cross examination of the defendants took an unusually long time. . . . Appeal Judge —, who presided over the provincial Court of Appeal, had obviously already lost patience and only asked my defendant whether he wanted to plead guilty or not guilty. My client replied briefly that he denied the crime of which he was accused. Then Appeal Judge — said: 'In that case we can begin with the hearing of the evidence.' At that moment I intervened and asked permission to question the defendant, before the hearing of evidence, about the circumstances in which he had signed the statement quoted above,[1] and in particular as to whether he had been beaten by the officers of the Secret State Police in connexion with the signing of these statements.

I had hardly finished the question when the State prosecutor jumped up excitedly and asked the president of the court to protect the officers of the Secret State Police against such attacks by the defence.

Appeal Judge — rose from his chair, leant on his hands on the court table and said to me: 'Council for the defence, I must draw your attention to the fact that even though the trial here is conducted *in camera* a question such as you have asked can lead to your being arrested in the courtroom and taken into custody. Do you wish to sustain the question or not?'

These details are still fresh in my memory because they made an extraordinary impression on me. Also, subsequently I have repeatedly discussed this case because it seemed to me typical of National Socialist justice.

Suddenly, into the dead silence which followed the Appeal Judge's question came the words of the assistant judge, Dr —. I remember these words very clearly; they were: 'The defence need not sustain this question, I will take it over on behalf of the court.'

I do not know if I would personally have had the courage to stick to my question under the pressure of the situation and as a recently admitted lawyer. Dr — saved me this decision. I wholeheartedly admired such courage from a German judge. I also got the impression that only a judge who had been badly wounded in the 1914–18 war could get away with such courage.

In the course of the trial the question raised by me and taken over by Dr — was thoroughly examined. The trial lasted from 9 a.m. to 7.30 p.m. The cross-examination alone took about two hours. My client was released for lack of evidence.

With the outbreak of war, however, the possibility of passing just verdicts and sentences was reduced still further as the legal system became increasingly subjected both to interference from outside influences and to growing supervision from within.

11 *Hitler's interference in the judicial process*

Perhaps the most striking example of interference from outside was Hitler's new practice of intervening personally to 'correct' sentences which in his

---

[1] The defendant had signed a statement confessing his guilt after interrogation by the Gestapo.

view were too lenient. During the years 1939–42 there were some twenty-five to thirty cases in which Hitler imposed the death sentence in place of some lesser penalty passed by the courts. After such an intervention by the Führer, the prisoner was invariably handed over to the SS for execution. Hitler reached his decisions on the basis of an emotional reaction to newspaper cuttings or to hearsay passed through Party channels and then via his adjutant, Julius Schaub, or Martin Bormann, rather than through any rational consideration of all the circumstances which led the judges to pass that particular sentence. The following case in which a Jew was convicted of hoarding a large quantity of eggs illustrates the process. The inconsistent spelling of the name of the accused and the naming of two different towns as the place of the court where he was sentenced shows the carelessness with which these cases were handled:

(a) Reich Minister and Head of the Reich Chancellery [Dr Lammers] to State Secretary Schlegelberger, Acting Minister of Justice, 25.x.1941:
   The Führer has been shown the enclosed press cutting concerning the sentencing of the Jew, Markus Luftgas, to 2½ years' imprisonment by the Special Court at Bielitz.
   The Führer desires that Luftgas should be sentenced to death. I would be obliged if you would make the necessary arrangements as soon as possible and report to the Führer through me on the measures you have taken.

(b) Lammers to SS Gruppenführer Julius Schaub:
On receiving your letter of 22 October 1941 I contacted the Reich Minister of Justice and requested him to make the necessary arrangements.

(c) Schlegelberger to Lammers, 29.x.41:
On receiving the Führer command passed on to me by the Minister of State and Head of the Chancellery I handed over the Jew, Markus Luftglass, who was sentenced by the Special Court at Kattowitz to 2½ years' imprisonment, to the Secret State Police for execution.

But apart from these sporadic instances of personal intervention by Hitler, the war also saw the emergence of more formal controls which still further undermined the independence of the judiciary. This trend accelerated after the death of Franz Gürtner in January 1941. Despite his connivance in the regime since 1933, Gürtner had remained at heart a Nationalist and had had as his personal assistant Hans von Dohnanyi, a leading member of the opposition to Hitler. After an interim period under a bureaucrat, State Secretary Franz Schlegelberger, as acting Minister, Hitler, on 20 August 1942, gave the Ministry of Justice to a hard-line Naxi, Otto Thierack.

12 Judges' Letters

Shortly after coming into office, Thierack responded to complaints about a number of sentences which were regarded as too lenient by instituting on

7 September 1942 the practice of circulating to the judiciary so-called 'Judges' Letters'. These letters commented on what he as Minister regarded as good and bad examples of sentencing. They did not actually name the judges involved, but they did name the courts and therefore in fact exerted pressure on the judges while preserving the fiction of judicial independence:

I do not wish to, cannot, and must not, tell a judge who has been given a case how he is to decide in an individual instance. The judge must remain free to carry the responsibility for his decisions. I cannot order him, therefore, to follow a particular interpretation of the law but can only convince him of the way in which a judge must help the community in order to regulate behaviour which has become disordered or requires ordering with the help of the law.

To this extent the profession of the judge is related to that of the doctor who also has to bring help to his fellow citizen who asks for it or to protect the community from injury. In the same way, a judge must, like a doctor, eradicate centres of infection or be able to carry out the operations of a surgeon.

This concept of the field of law has now been widely accepted among German lawyers. But its practical effects on the administration of justice have not yet been realized.

In order to help the judge to fulfil his high office in the life of our people, I have decided to publish 'Judges' Letters' which are to be sent to all German judges and public prosecutors. These Judges' Letters are not meant to create a new casuistry which would lead to increased rigidity in the administration of justice and would put the judges under tutelage. They are intended merely to illustrate how the judicial leadership envisages a National Socialist application of the law and in this way to give the judge the inner security and freedom to make the right decision.

The contents of the letters are confidential; the official in charge must look after them personally and hand them out to judges and prosecutors in return for a receipt.

The cooperation of all judges and prosecutors is needed for the publication of the Judges' Letters. I expect to be given suitable verdicts from all fields of law for publication. In making use of these neither the judge nor the relevant court will be mentioned by name.

I am convinced that the Judges' Letters will contribute greatly to a uniform alignment of justice in the National Socialist spirit.

The following is an example of these Letters:

13 *Judges' Letter No. 14*

Refusal of the German Salute by a child of school age. Guardianship Court judgement of 21 September 1940:

An eleven-year-old girl has been noticed at school continually refusing to give the German salute. She gives her religious convictions as the reason and quotes several passages from the Bible. At school she shows a complete lack of interest in matters concerning the Führer.

The parents who have another daughter of six approve of this attitude and stubbornly refuse to influence the child in the contrary direction. They also refuse to give the German salute referring to the biblical passage: 'Do nothing with a raised hand for this displeases the Lord.' They stick to this despite instructions from the court and from the headmaster of the school. The mother utterly refuses to speak to the child about it. The father is willing to do so but says the child must decide for herself. The parents show themselves to be opponents of the National Socialist State in other ways. They do not possess a swastika flag. They have not put down their child for the Hitler Youth. They are excluded from the NSV because they have not joined in contributing although the father could afford it. Nevertheless they deny being opponents of the movement.

Because of their attitude the Youth Office has proposed the removal of both children from the care of their parents. The Guardianship Court has turned this down and has only ordered supervision, arguing in the judgement that it has not been proved that the parents are opponents of the National Socialist movement or have even fought against it; they simply do not 'regard the movement sympathetically and are not inclined to further it'. The judgement goes on to say: 'The parents are responsible for their personal attitude towards the National Socialist movement only in so far as they break laws that relate to the movement.' The parents have to agree that the children must be brought up in the National Socialist spirit and that the school is bound to give this education. If the parents do not want to bring their children up in this spirit themselves or, from religious convictions, think it impossible for them to do so, they must be asked at least not to counteract the National Socialist education given by the school. Since the child is otherwise well brought up and the parents give the impression of having 'reliable characters' it may be assumed that they will make no further difficulties for the school in future.

The Court of Appeal has revised the verdict of the Guardianship Court and removed the guardianship of both children from the parents because they are unsuitable to bring them up.

Comment by the Reich Minister of Justice:

The verdict of the judge of the Guardianship Court shows a misunderstanding of the principles of National Socialist youth education.

Those responsible for the education of German youth today are the parents, the school and the Hitler Youth (Law on the Hitler Youth of 1 December 1936). Working together, each in his own sphere, these fulfil the educational mission given to them by the community. The aim of the communal work of education is to educate youth physically, mentally and morally in the spirit of National Socialism for the service of the people and of the community. This aim can be achieved only through cooperation between parents, school and Hitler Youth. Every conflict and deviation in education endangers the common aim. Parents have been given a decisive role in education and a special responsibility. They are connected with the child by ties of blood. The child lives near them and continuously watches his parents' habits and example. Educating means guiding. Guiding means setting an example by their way of life. The child shapes his life according to his parents' example. What he hears and sees there, especially in early youth, he gradually adopts as a habit and a standard for his life. Therefore, the educational aim of the National Socialist State can be achieved only if parents are conscientious and responsible in thought and action and give the child a model example of how to behave in the communal life of our people. Part of the education of the German

man or woman is the early conveying of respect and reverence for the symbols of the State and the movement. Here also the community expects active cooperation on the parents' part. Reserved neutrality here is just as damaging as combating the National Socialist idea. Indifference towards education in patriotic citizenship, therefore, means a neglect by the parents of their duties and endangers the education of the child even if this is not immediately apparent. Accordingly, it is not sufficient for the parents in this case not to oppose the child's future education by the school; they must take an active part in the communal education. The parents' educational responsibility, then, does not begin only at the point at which their violation of it is punishable. The danger for the child becomes apparent when the parents openly oppose education through the community. This was so here. Those who stubbornly refuse the German salute because of wrong doctrine, who exclude themselves for no reason from the socially constructive work of the NSV, purposely keep their children away from the Hitler Youth and are inaccessible to all advice, can no longer be said only to be 'not sympathetically disposed' towards the movement or not to be furthering it. Through their resistance they are fighting it and are its enemies. This is shown by their attitude and inclination.

The guardianship judge should therefore have deprived them of their guardianship with the simple explanation that parents who openly profess the ideas of the Jehovah's Witnesses are not suited for the education of their children in the National Socialist spirit.

Thierack also instituted a system of so-called preliminary hearings and post-mortems (*Vor- und Nachschau*) for offences of a political nature. Under this system judges were obliged before the trial to consult with their superiors, and often with the prosecutor as well, about what verdict and sentence they were proposing to pass, and then after the trial to justify their verdict and sentence. Perhaps most significant of all, however, was Thierack's willingness to surrender more and more jurisdiction to the SS. This was indeed the underlying trend throughout the period, a trend which had been greatly accelerated by the emergency situation created by the war. What, then, was the background to this enormous growth in influence of the SS?

The SS-police state

However much the legal system was subservient to the regime, Hitler continued to regard it with great suspicion. He needed an organization which would not feel restrained by legal paragraphs or bureaucratic qualms, which would act with utter ruthlessness, and which would be dedicated to expressing his will and the ideology of the Nazi movement. He found what he needed in the SS. The SS established a separate organizational framework for the enforcement of the will of the regime. This organization was independent of the State and yet, through its control over the police, it was linked with the State. It could therefore operate either outside the legal system or in association with it, depending on circumstances. The characteristic political

and administrative development in the Third Reich was for the traditional
State authorities to become increasingly a façade, the substance of which was
progressively being eaten away by the cancerous growth of new organizations under individuals appointed by Hitler. The old authorities were not
abolished; they were left still in apparent control. But in reality, their power
was being drained away to the new organizations which were untrammelled
by traditional norms and bureaucratic procedures, and whose leaders were
directly dependent on Hitler. This development was reflected in the
relationship between the SS and the police and legal system.

14 The character of Himmler

The SS began as an elite bodyguard for the Party leaders, and it was only in
1929, after it had been taken over by Heinrich Himmler, that it acquired its
characteristic features. The SS was a paradox and in this it reflected the
personality of its leader. Himmler was a bizarre combination of naive crank,
pedantic schoolmaster, and coldly efficient bureaucrat, a master at accumulating power in the administrative jungle of the Third Reich. The following
documents signed by him illustrate the various aspects of his personality:

(a) *How to make sure a boy is born*

SS Obersturmbannführer Dr Brandt to SS Standartenführer Max Sollmann,
Head of the *Lebensborn*[1], 14.ii.44:

I enclose a copy of the letter of a certain Artur Dombeck of Hamburg. I also add a
minute dictated by the Reichsführer SS. The Reichsführer SS wishes the
Lebensborn to start a research project on 'The question of the procreation of girls
or boys'.

Enclosure: 12.ii.44 Minute of RF:
SS Obergruppenführer Berger told me recently, when we were talking about the
procreation of girls or boys, that it is the custom where he comes from in the
Swabian Alps that if a family wants to have a boy at last they do the following:
    The man, after keeping off alcohol for a week like his wife, sets off from home at
12 o'clock noon and walks the 20 kilometres to Ulm and back. He must not stop at
an inn on the way. The wife does no work in the preceding week, eats very well,
sleeps a lot, and does not exert herself in any way. After the man's return intercourse takes place. The result is said to be always the birth of a boy.

(b) *Himmler imposes a ban on smoking*

Himmler to SS Sturmbannführer Count Adalbert Kottulinsky, 16.ix.38:

You have been very ill and have had a lot of trouble with your heart. In the interests
of your health I am imposing on you a total ban on smoking for two years.

[1] The *Lebensborn* (lit. 'Lifespring') was an SS organization for the care of illegitimate children
who were 'of good racial stock'.

Will you please provide a doctor's health certificate at the end of these two years. I will then decide whether the ban should be lifted or maintained.

(c) '*All agreements with the Army High Command require my personal approval*'

Reichsführer SS Himmler to SS Obergruppenführer August Heissmeyer, Inspector of the National Political Educational Establishments,[1] 7.v.40:

I have received your report of 29 April 1940 concerning the expansion of the National Political Educational Establishments. There can be no question of a division of responsibilities. I told Colonel Friessner this personally before the start of the parade of the 6000 officer cadets in front of the Führer.

Colonel Friessner's suggestion would result in the National Political Educational Establishments being entirely subordinated to the Army Cadet Corps and all their pupils would go into the Army.

In addition, I strongly object to the particular emphasis placed on officer-type attitudes and behaviour in accordance with normal Army principles. I would be obliged if you would tell the gentlemen during your next discussion politely but firmly that I am the one who lays down the lines of policy on education for the National Political Education Establishments and not the Army.

All agreements with the Army High Command require my personal approval.

The SS reflected its leader's personality. On the one hand, it was the exponent and instrument of the most extreme ideological views of the Nazi movement. On the other hand, many of its officers—men such as Walter Schellenberg, the head of its foreign security service—tended to be the most unideological of men. They were often career men, young graduates who would today be business executives or bright young civil servants, men for whom administrative efficiency was the main criterion.

15 *The SS Marriage Order*

When he took over the SS in 1929, Himmler was determined to turn it into the elite order of National Socialism. To achieve this he insisted that even the wives of SS men should be racially pure:

1. The SS is a band of definitely Nordic German men selected according to certain principles.
2. In accordance with the National Socialist ideology and with the realization that the future of our nation rests on the preservation of the race through selection and on the inheritance of good blood, I hereby institute from 1 January 1932 the 'Marriage Certificate' for all unmarried members of the SS.
3. The aim is to create a hereditarily healthy clan of a definitely Nordic German type.

[1] The *Nationalpolitische Erziehungsanstalten* (popularly known as Napolas) were Nazi boarding schools. Originally established by the Ministry of Education, they were gradually taken over more and more by the SS in a typical accretion of power by Himmler. Yet their tradition had always tended to be that of an officer cadet school and most of their pupils became officers. This was resented by Himmler who wished to ensure that a greater proportion went to the SS.

4. The marriage certificate will be awarded or refused solely on the basis of racial health and heredity.

5. Every SS man intending to get married must procure for this purpose the marriage certificate of the Reichsführer SS.

6. SS members who marry despite having been denied marriage certificates will be removed from the SS; they will be given the chance of resignation.

7. It is the task of the SS 'Race Office' to work out the details of marriage petitions.

8. The SS Race Office is in charge of the 'Clan Book of the SS' in which the families of SS members will be entered after being awarded the marriage certificate or after acceptance of the petition to enter into marriage.

9. The Reichsführer SS, the director of the Race Office, and the specialists of this office are pledged to secrecy on their word of honour.

10. The SS is convinced that with this order it has taken a step of great significance. Derision, scorn, and incomprehension will not move us; the future is ours!

In fact, however, marriage certificate statistics for 1932–40 show that only 958 applicants out of 106,304 were turned down; but only 7,518 satisfied every requirement.[1]

16 *Description of an SS wedding*

The central point in the ceremonial was represented by the wedding table decorated by two conjoined runic[2] figures. On the table lay a yellow sun disc made of flowers on a blue background; to the left and right stood torchbearers and behind the table a bowl, containing fire, and the pulpit. The choir opened the ceremony with a chorus from *Lohengrin*. A representative of the new usage, SS Comrade Elling, gave the dedication—an address based upon the song from the Edda Helga and Sigrun. The choir chanted both before and after the address. Then the bridal pair were offered bread (representing the germinating force of earth) and salt (the symbol of purity) on silver vessels. Finally, the pair thus married according to German custom received their wedding rings.

17 *How the SS introduced a new spirit into the police*

In March 1933 Himmler was appointed to the rather modest post of Police-President of Munich. He later described the state of the police as he found it and the way in which he introduced a new spirit:

Excerpt from a speech by Reichsführer SS Heinrich Himmler in the Constituent Session of the Committee for Police Law of the Academy of German Law, 11.x.36

... When we, the National Socialists, came to power in 1933, some of us were given the task of taking over the police. I can speak here from personal experience: in March 1933 I took over the post of Police-President of Munich, and later of Munich and Nuremberg. We National Socialists found a police force which had originally been formed as an instrument of power, blindly obedient to an absolutist State; its main and most important legacy from that period, however, was the dislike, indeed the hatred, of the population for it; yet it had lost the absolute power

[1] H. P. Bleuel, *Strength through Joy. Sex and Society in Nazi Germany* (London 1973), p. 199.
[2] Symbols in German mythology.

which distinguishes the police of an absolutist State. It was still called 'a power structure' but in reality it was not; it was a helpless organization, tied hand and foot. Whenever police officers arrested a criminal they had to watch out that they did not get into trouble themselves while the criminal got away scotfree. We National Socialists then set to work—it may sound odd that I should say this in the Academy of German Law but you will understand what I mean—not without justice behind us since we had that within ourselves, but possibly outside the law. Right from the start I took the view that it did not matter in the least if our actions were contrary to some paragraph in the law; in my work for the Führer and the nation, I do what my conscience and common sense tells me is right. During those months and years when the life and death of the German people were at stake, I was completely indifferent about the fact that others were bemoaning 'violations of the law'. There was of course talk abroad—to a large extent inspired by elements within Germany—about the police, and therefore the State, being in a condition of lawlessness. They called it lawless because it did not correspond to their conception of law. It was in reality through our work that we laid the foundations for a new code of law, the law governing the life of the German people. . . .

18 *The ambitions of the SS*

Himmler soon took over the political police throughout Bavaria. But he and his ruthless deputy, Reinhard Heydrich, were not content with this. Their ambitions went much further and during the course of 1933 they succeeded in taking over the political police departments in all the States except for by far the most important one, Prussia. In Prussia Göring had taken the department I A in the Berlin police department which had handled political matters, and turned it into a Secret State Police Office (Gestapa). In November 1933, this office was removed from the administrative apparatus of the Ministry of the Interior and subordinated directly to Göring as Minister-President. But essentially these measures did no more than legalize the existing situation. The Gestapo in fact, if not yet in name, was already in action by February 1933. It was responsible for the use of 'protective custody' after the Reichstag Fire decree and was already acting independently of the rest of the administrative apparatus, taking its orders direct from Göring. Himmler was determined to take over this powerful new organization, as Rudolf Diels, Gestapo chief at the time, recalls in his memoirs:

The SS prepared their *coups* long in advance and in a more consistent way than the careless SA. The net of the Security Service[1] of the SS led by Heydrich from Munich had already been thrown across Prussia. In the areas ruled by the SA the SD confined itself to the completion of their card files of Jews, Freemasons, 'Catholic Action' and Communists. The SS, in the states in which their leaders had taken charge, were already putting into practice their slogan against the 'cosmopolitical powers'.[2] In Prussia they gave a hint of their future development in only

[1] *Sicherheitsdienst* (SD).
[2] The Nazi term for Jews, Freemasons and Catholics.

a few areas. Their concentration camps in Papenburg, Esterwegen and Stettin were, following the example of Dachau, no longer haphazard *ad hoc* foundations, they were already organized systematically. When Heydrich had been careless enough to make Göring even more suspicious of SS competition by arresting people in Bavaria who were close to him, I was able to counter Himmler's vanguard in Berlin. I forbade the SD 'actions' which had been directed almost exclusively against the lodges, particularly the Jewish ones, and against Catholic Action. When Göring told me one day to arrest Heydrich when he next entered Berlin, I replied that I could not carry out an order which I knew would be cancelled an hour later by pressure from Himmler; but at that moment of anger he had really made up his mind to put him out of business. I told him I knew that he would not protect me from Himmler's revenge once Heydrich had finally taken over the Berlin political police despite his resistance. At that time he still replied cuttingly and with determination, 'Himmler and Heydrich will never come to Berlin.' Yet with this vain man there was always a restless insecurity undermining his lust for power. He was by no means stupid. He knew Hitler and the upstarts seeking his favour. 'Everything is like cottonwool', he once said to me when he talked about the future, the State and his aims.

Looking for an ally against the growing threat from the SA, on 20 April 1934, Göring allowed Himmler to replace Diels as head of the Gestapo, who put the day-to-day running of the organization in the hands of Reinhard Heydrich. Nominally Himmler was still subordinate to Göring as Minister-President of Prussia, but in practice he was independent.

19 *The regulations at Dachau concentration camp*

The SS like the SA used the Reichstag Fire decree of 28 February 1933, and the technique of 'protective custody' which followed from it, to justify the establishment of concentration camps. The most important of these SS camps was the one established in a former factory in Dachau near Munich. Dachau, under its commandant, Theodor Eicke, became the model for the other concentration camps. Eicke was appointed 'Inspector of Concentration Camps' in July 1934 and he replaced the haphazard brutality of the SA with systematic principles of terror:

I.X.33

Disciplinary and Punitive Regulations
for the Internment Camp

Introduction. The following regulations on punishment are issued for the maintenance of discipline and order within the area of the Dachau Concentration Camp as part of the existing camp regulations.

All internees of the Dachau Concentration Camp are subject to these regulations from the time of their imprisonment to the hour of their release.

Authority for ordering punishments lies in the hands of the camp commander, who is personally responsible to the political police commander for the carrying out of the camp regulations.

Tolerance means weakness. In the light of this conception, punishment will be mercilessly handed out whenever the interests of the fatherland warrant it. The fellow countryman who is decent but misled will never be affected by these regulations. But let it be a warning both to the inciting politicians and to intellectual agitators, no matter which: watch out that you are not caught, for otherwise it will be your neck and you will be dealt with according to your own methods.

* * *

Article 6. The following are punishable with eight days' solitary confinement, and twenty-five strokes to be administered before and after the serving of the sentence:

1. Anyone making depreciatory or ironical remarks to a member of the SS, deliberately omitting the prescribed marks of respect, or in any other way demonstrating unwillingness to submit himself to disciplinary measures.

2. Prisoner-sergeants and prisoner squad leaders or foremen who exceed their authority as orderlies, assume the privileges of a superior over other prisoners, accord likeminded prisoners special privileges in work or in any other way, tyrannize over fellow prisoners who have political views different from their own, make false reports on them, or prejudice them in any other way.

Article 7. The following are punishable with two weeks' solitary confinement:

1. Anyone exchanging by his own volition, without being authorized by the company commander, the quarters to which he is assigned, or instigating or inducing his fellow prisoners to do so.

2. Anyone enclosing or hiding forbidden articles or articles produced in the camp in outgoing laundry bundles, or sewing them into pieces of laundry, etc.

3. Anyone entering or leaving barracks, shelters, or other buildings by other than authorized entrances, or creeping through windows or other openings.

4. Anyone smoking in shelters, toilets and places which are fire hazards, or keeping or depositing inflammable objects in such places. If a fire results from neglect of this prohibition, it will be considered as an act of sabotage.

Article 8. The following are punishable with two weeks' solitary confinement and twenty-five strokes to be administered before and after the serving of the sentence:

1. Anyone leaving or entering the internment camp without an escort or who joins an outgoing work detail without proper authority.

2. Anyone making depreciatory remarks in letters or other documents about National Socialist leaders, the State and Government, authorities and institutions, glorifying Marxist or liberal leaders or November [Weimar] parties, or reporting on occurrences in the concentration camp.

3. Anyone keeping forbidden articles, tools, or weapons in his quarters or in palliasses. . . .

Article 11. In accordance with the law on revolutionaries, the following offenders, considered as agitators, will be hanged. Anyone who, for the purpose of agitating, does the following in the camp, at work, in the sleeping quarters, in the kitchens and workshops, toilets and places of rest: discusses politics, carries on controversial talks and meetings, forms cliques, loiters around with others; who, for the purpose of supplying the propaganda of the opposition with atrocity stories, collects true or false information about the concentration camp; receives such information, buries it, talks about it to others, smuggles it out of the camp into the hands of foreign visitors or others by clandestine or other means, passes it on in writing or by word of month to released prisoners or prisoners who are placed over them, conceals it in clothing or other articles, throws stones and other objects over the camp wall containing such information; or produces secret documents; or, for the purpose of agitating, climbs on barrack roofs or trees, seeks contact with the outside world by giving light or other signals, or induces others to escape or commit a crime, gives them advice to that effect or supports such undertakings in any way whatsoever.

Article 19. Confinement will be in a cell, with a hard bed, and with bread and water. The prisoner will receive warm food every four days. Punitive work consists of severe physical or particularly dirty work, performed under close supervision. Incidental punishments are: drilling, beatings, withholding of mail and food, hard rest, tying to stakes, reprimands and warnings.

All punishments will be recorded on files.

Confinement and punitive labour prolong the term of internment by at least eight weeks, an incidental punishment by four weeks. Prisoners in solitary confinement will not be released for a considerable time.

I.X.33

Service Regulations for Prisoner
Escorts and Guards

Anyone letting a prisoner escape will be arrested and handed over to the Bavarian Political Police for liberating prisoners through negligence.

If a prisoner attempts to escape, he is to be shot without warning. The guard who has shot an escaping prisoner in the line of duty will not be punished.

If a prisoner attacks a guard, the latter is to resist the attack not by physical force but by the use of his weapons. A guard disregarding this regulation must expect his immediate dismissal. In any case anyone who keeps his back covered will seldom have to worry about an attack.

If a unit of prisoners mutinies or revolts, it is to be shot at by all supervising guards. Warning shots are forbidden on principle.

The work time is determined by the camp commander. A guard who brings his prisoners back too early is guilty of serious dereliction of duty and can be dismissed.

Should a work detachment be obliged to stop its work prematurely for some reason or other, then the work detachment leader must have the reason certified on the back of the work service slip [*Arbeitsdienstzettel*] by either the construction division or the requisitioning office.

20 *The loss of control over the police to the SS, on the part of the Reich Ministry of the Interior*

The control of the SS over the political police throughout the Reich and over its own concentration camp network, which was expanded in July 1934 to include those previously controlled by the SA, gave the SS considerable freedom of action. The Reich Ministry of Justice, and the Reich Ministry of the Interior, to which in theory the whole police force was still subordinate, found it increasingly difficult to exercise any influence over the activities of the SS and the Gestapo. Between October 1935 and May 1936, for example, the Gestapo took into protective custody 7266 people 'on account of activity in support of the Communist and Socialist parties'. The situation is described in the following undated memorandum of Frick, Reich Minister of the Interior during 1935–36:

As head of the police department in the Reich and Prussian Ministry of the Interior, I have noticed recently an increase in tension in domestic politics which clearly requires, as a matter of urgency, the clarification of authority both as regards the general police and, more especially, the political police.

1. *The Fight against the Church.* The Reich Minister of the Interior is the competent authority for general regulations on denominational policy. The leaders of the various denominational groups therefore address their petitions to our office. Recently, half the political police reports have concerned religious matters. We have no end of petitions from all sorts of cardinals, bishops, and dignitaries of the Church. Most of these complaints concern matters under the jurisdiction of the Reich Ministry of the Interior, although the relevant regulations were not drawn up by it. Frequently, in our capacity as a court of appeal, we have to settle incidents about which we know nothing at all until we receive the complaint. There no longer appears to be any coordination between our principles regarding matters of ecclesiastical politics and the way in which these are carried out in the states. It is an inexcusable state of affairs that advice should be given to complainants and promises made to ecclesiastical leaders without there being any guarantee that they will be carried out in the states. I regard it, therefore, as absolutely essential that this matter should be fully clarified, not only as regards the *principles but also the way in which they are to be enforced.*

I should like to point out that, in my opinion, when these principles are being considered and carried out, account should be taken not only of domestic but also of foreign policy. I enclose a papal encyclical which was submitted to me today. In this instance, the question arises as to whether the treatment meted out to young Catholics returning to Germany in front of Swiss Customs guards has something to do with the unfavourable foreign reactions evoked by this action on the part of the political police.

This concerns not only the political police; the whole police force as such will be involved in the consequences resulting from the political struggle. The number of blatant disturbances of congregations has recently been greatly on the increase, often necessitating the intervention of the emergency squad. I cannot carry the responsibility in the long run; officials will become involved and will be compelled to support one party or the other. The struggle for power is so recent that we know from our own experience that in the end the police official will quite often be blamed for everything by both warring parties. Now that the rubber truncheon has been discarded, it is intolerable that police officials should be exposed to situations in which, during the disturbance of meetings, they may be forced to use cold steel.

In my opinion, everything must be done to prevent an uncalled-for religious struggle exhausting the police force as well as general State authority.

Nor do I believe it is desirable for the lower ranks of the police to handle and report on these religious matters in a somewhat one-sided manner.

2. There has been of late a marked increase in cases of protective custody. I urgently demand that in this matter also final directives be given concerning *methods, proof, length of time*, and manner of *execution*. The decree on protective custody issued by the Reich Ministry of the Interior[1] has long ago been rendered invalid by the actions of the political police. It is almost impossible to get an adequate report on a case of protective custody. The petitions addressed to us on this matter all stress the same point, which I too regard as important. The persons concerned and their relatives accept the fact of protective custody, but not the utter uncertainty of the principles and methods of its imposition. This definite *lawlessness* fosters unrest and antagonism. It is intolerable for the Reich Ministry of the Interior that any uniform application of the law should be prevented by the variety of its interpretation and application in the various states. The question must also be settled whether, in cases of protective custody a person is to be allowed a lawyer, as approved by the NS Lawyers' Association in conjunction with the Reich Ministry of Justice, or, following the present practice of the Gestapo, to be refused one. I refer in this connexion to the case of the lawyer, Pünder. He was confined in protective custody with his colleagues for bringing an action, being obliged to do this by a Reich law, after duly informing the Reich Ministry of Justice and our Ministry. This complaint could not involve any complications, since the legal proceedings could be immediately quashed by us.

3. *For official political reasons*, I must object on principle to the fact that once again recently, and without the previous knowledge of their superiors, civil servants have been taken into protective custody or have been subjected to Gestapo investigations. I can cite here the case of my teacher, who is the *Kreisleiter* at Esterwegen, and who was kept in custody for eight days, because he had sent a report, proved afterwards to be correct, to his district councillor on abuses by the SS. I recall the investigations by detectives of the Gestapo in Kottbus which lasted two weeks, on the chief of police who was, by the way, an SS *Brigadeführer*. Likewise, I have already presented today a complaint by *Oberpräsident* Lohse[2] concerning the order, given by officers of the political police to an official of the gendarmerie, to spy on superior officials.

It is intolerable from the point of view of the National Socialist authoritarian form of State leadership that subordinate offices should procure information on officials in this manner over the heads of a superior office. This will create a great deal of trouble quite apart from the fact that information thus obtained must be prejudiced and very often even actually false.

4. Abductions by officers of the political police on *foreign territory* have lately created serious incidents in the sphere of foreign affairs. I cite the cases of Berthold Jakob (Switzerland), Gutzeit (Holland) and the latest incident at the Czech frontier. In my opinion, in view of possible diplomatic complications, the police office should receive orders for such measures only from the Reich officer responsible, and not from subordinate offices.

5. On several occasions the Reich Ministry of Economics has pointed out to me the disturbing effect on the economy which must result from the various political incidents caused by the police, the atmosphere of insecurity caused by cases of

---

[1] 11 March 1934.
[2] Oberpräsident and Gauleiter of Schleswig-Holstein.

protective custody (particularly in the case of leading businessmen), and also in the latest cases of a boycott of the Jews (Cologne, Düsseldorf).

6. I can only undertake the protection of the Führer through my police department if I am entirely responsible for the officials working there, their service, capabilities, and their cooperation with the other sections of the Crime Department.

7. I propose that it be settled once and for all, not only who is to carry the responsibility for orders, but also who shall bear the responsibility for the execution of those orders in all matters that concern the political police.

Either this responsibility rests with the Reich Minister of the Interior, in which case he must be vested with altogether different powers to give orders in political matters concerning the police;

or this responsibility with all its implications rests with the Reichsführer SS, who is already actually claiming the control of the political police in the Reich. In that case I would propose that the law proposed for Prussia by Reichsführer SS Himmler becomes a Reich law immediately, elevating the Office of the Secret State Police [Gestapa] to the status of a ministry and enabling the Chief of the Office of the Secret State Police to undertake the tasks which he, in the words of the draft law, 'determines'.

21 *The Prussian Law on the Secret State Police (Gestapo), 10 February 1936*

This and similar complaints from the Ministry of the Interior and its regional authorities, the *Oberpräsidenten* and *Regierungspräsidenten*, eventually obliged Himmler and Heydrich to agree to a new Gestapo law. This law of 10 February 1936 represented merely a token concession on the part of the SS, for it did not give the Ministry of the Interior effective control of the Gestapo. For whereas Paragraph 5 subordinated the regional offices of the Gestapo (*Stapostellen*) to the regional offices of the Ministry of the Interior (*Regierungspräsidenten*), Paragraph 3 laid down that the Gestapo head office in Berlin (Gestapa) was the highest Gestapo authority, to which the *Stapostellen* were therefore also subordinate. No provision was made by the law for dealing with conflicting orders from the two authorities and in fact the Gestapo continued to go its own way regardless of the Ministry of the Interior. Moreover, Paragraph 7 confirmed the independence of the Gestapo by freeing its actions from review by the administrative courts. This was important because it meant that there was no possibility of appeal against actions of the Gestapo except to a higher authority within the Gestapo itself:

The State Ministry has determined on the following law:

1(i). The task of the Gestapo is to investigate and combat all activity throughout Prussia which poses a threat to the State, to collect and assess the results of these investigations, to keep the State government informed, to keep other authorities posted about any conclusions that concern them and to make suggestions. The Chief of the Gestapo, in agreement with the Minister of the Interior, will decide in detail what duties are to be transferred to the Gestapo.

1(ii). The responsibilities of the constituted legal authorities remain unaffected.

2(i). The Chief of the Gestapo is the Minister-President.

2(ii). Current business will be transacted on his behalf by a Deputy Chief of Gestapo nominated by him.

3(i). The highest Gestapo authority in the *Land* is the Gestapa. It has the prerogatives of a *Land* Police authority.

3(ii). The Gestapa is located in Berlin.

4. The functions of the Gestapo will be carried out at intermediate level by *Stapostellen* in the individual *Land* Police districts [*Landespolizeibezirke*]. Gestapo duties on the frontier will be the responsibility of special frontier commissions. Apart from this, Gestapo duties will be carried out by the *Kreis* [district] and *Ort* [local] Police authorities acting as agents for the *Stapostellen*.

5. *Stapostellen* are at the same time subordinate to the competent *Regierungspräsident*, will follow his instructions and will keep him informed of all political police matters. The Head of the *Stapostelle* is at the same time the *Regierungspräsident*'s expert political adviser.

6. The appointment and dismissal of Gestapo officials will be the responsibility of the Chief of the Gestapo in agreement with the Minister of the Interior in accordance with the general legal provisions of the Reich concerning the appointment and dismissal of *Land* officials.

7. Neither the instructions nor the affairs of the Gestapo will be open to review by the administrative courts.

8. The Chief of the Gestapo will issue executive instructions for the present law in agreement with the Minister of the Interior. . . .

22 Decree on the appointment of a Chief of the German Police within the Reich Ministry of the Interior, 17 June 1936

Finally, on 17 June 1936, Hitler at last went some way towards answering Frick's plea for a regulation on who was to control the police. But he did not decide in favour of the Ministry of the Interior. Instead, he unified all police powers in the hands of Himmler, who was made Chief of the German Police. Himmler was still nominally subordinate to Frick as Reich Minister of the Interior, but in practice he now exercised sole authority over the police forces throughout Germany. In fact, the uniformed police were still within the administrative hierarchy of the State and yet subordinate to Himmler, a situation producing confusion at regional and local level.

I

To unify the control of police duties in the Reich, a chief of the German Police shall be appointed within the German Ministry of the Interior, to whom is assigned the direction and executive authority for all police matters within the jurisdiction of the Reich and Prussian Ministries of the Interior.

II

1. The Deputy Chief of the Prussian Gestapo, Reichsführer SS Himmler, is hereby nominated Chief of the German Police in the Reich Ministry of the Interior.

2. He is personally and directly subordinate to the Reich and Prussian Ministers of the Interior.

3. For matters within his jurisdiction he represents the Reich and Prussian Ministers of the Interior in the absence of the latter.

4. He carries the service title: Reichsführer SS and Chief of the German Police within the Reich Ministry of the Interior.

III

The Chief of the German Police in the Reich Ministry of the Interior will take part in the meetings of the Reich Cabinet in so far as matters within his jurisdiction are concerned.

IV

I hereby charge the Reich and the Prussian Ministers of the Interior with the execution of this decree.

23 *'Protective Custody is the best method of dealing with troublemakers'*

On 26 June 1936, following on from this law, Himmler combined the Gestapo and the Criminal Police to form separate sections of a new Security Police (*Sicherheitspolizei*) which was placed under the command of Heydrich, who also continued to direct the Security Service (SD) of the SS. From now onwards, the police was increasingly infiltrated by members of the SS or, in many cases, police officers joined the SS. In the meantime, a network of informers had spread throughout Germany and, even where there was no informer, fear made everybody suspicious of one another, thereby reinforcing the security system.

. . .

1. *Opponents of the State and the movement*

There have been repeated reports of derogatory remarks being made about the State, the movement, or leading personalities. In some cases I have imposed protective custody which, I have just been assured by the rural districts, is the most appropriate method for deterring persistent troublemakers. . . .

24 *A message to all Gestapo Offices and to the Political Police of the State*

No. 33590   *Berlin, 22 April 1936*

Re: Prominent personalities of the Weimar period [Systemzeit]

A list must be sent in by return of post of those people in your area who were prominent in opposing and slandering the National Socialist movement before the take-over of power. The following details are requested concerning the prominent leaders in politics and business from the camp of the former DNVP,[1] DVP,[2] and Democratic Party [*Staatspartei*]:[3] the first name and surname, the date and place of birth, whether or not a Jew, present domicile, profession, including all offices held by the, person concerned, whether the person is in receipt of a pension etc. and whether the person had his citizenship revoked or whether an application has been made for the revocation of his citizenship. Furthermore, his present occupation must be reported. At the same time, a detailed report must be made about the

---

[1] *Deutschnationale Volkspartei*: the German National People's Party.

[2] *Deutsche Volkspartei*: the German People's Party.

[3] The *Deutsche Demokratische Partei* (DDP) adopted the title of '*Staatspartei*' in 1930 after merging with another organization, the *Jungdeutscher Orden*.

incidents in which the individual was involved, particularly hostile activity towards the NSDAP, and whether or not the person in question is still a clandestine opponent of the National Socialist State or has drawn attention to himself by acting in a hostile way towards the State and the Party.

25 *Gestapo supervision of released prisoners*

Even if a person was fortunate enough to be let out of a concentration camp, he was still subjected to further police supervision:

Naumburg (Saale), 5.ix.36

Walther P., commercial traveller, formerly in protective custody, now of no fixed address, appears voluntarily and makes the following statement:

I hereby submit my certificate of release from Lichtenburg concentration camp and report to the competent local police authority.

I am bound to report to the local police authority, criminal department, room 114, every Wednesday and Saturday at 11 o'clock. I shall fulfil this obligation punctually.

Naumburg (Saale), 28.iv.37

Walther P. has punctually obeyed the police order to report twice a week. P. finds this measure extremely unpleasant and embarrassing. He has repeatedly expressed the wish to be released from this obligation to report. P. performs his job regularly and lives a very secluded life. He has no contact with people who are suspected of an attitude hostile to the State. P. is a member of the German Labour Front and is obviously trying to integrate himself into the national community. Further strict observation of P. no longer appears necessary.

26 *Police supervision of plebiscites*

Subject: *Plebiscite of 10 April 1938*

Copy of a schedule is attached herewith enumerating the persons who cast 'No' votes or invalid votes at Kappel, district of Simmern. The invalid votes are listed first, ending with ——; thereafter come the 'No' votes.

The control was effected in the following way: some members of the election committee marked all the ballot papers with numbers. During the ballot itself, a voters' list was made up. The ballot papers were handed out in numerical order, therefore it was possible afterwards with the aid of this list to find out the persons who cast 'No' votes or invalid votes. One sample of these marked ballot papers is enclosed. The marking was done on the back of the ballot papers with skimmed milk.

The ballot cast by the Protestant parson Alfred Wolferts is also enclosed.

The identification of two persons was impossible because there are several persons of the same name in the village and it was impossible to ascertain the actual voter.

27 *The legal system is concerned merely to preserve appearances*

Thereafter the Gestapo acted with increasing contempt for the law. Even where an individual had been tried by a court of law and had been found innocent, or had served his sentence, he was still not immune from the Gestapo. The following circular to the Gestapo offices by the Gestapo chief, Heinrich Müller, dated 5 August 1937, indicates the sense of powerlessness felt by the legal system in regard to the Gestapo. They were now merely concerned to preserve appearances:

Reference: Protective Custody for Jehovah's Witnesses

The Reich Minister of Justice has informed me that he does not share the opinion expressed by subordinate departments on various occasions, according to which the arrest of Jehovah's Witnesses after they have served a sentence is supposed to jeopardize the authority of the Law Courts. He is fully aware of the necessity for measures by the Gestapo after the sentence has been served. He requests, however, that Jehovah's Witnesses should not be taken into protective custody under circumstances that may harm the reputation of the Law Courts.

The Reich Minister of Justice has instructed his subordinate departments in this connexion that protective custody for Jehovah's Witnesses, when this has been decreed after the serving of sentence or after the cancellation of an order of arrest, will no longer be carried out in convict prisons under the administration of the courts. At the same time, at my suggestion he has instructed the departments concerned with the carrying out of the sentences to notify the appropriate Gestapo department of the impending discharge of Jehovah's Witnesses one month before they are discharged.

Accordingly, I order:

1. If a Jehovah's Witness has been acquitted as the result of a trial, or if part of the sentence is remitted because of the period spent in remand, an arrest in court under my circular decree dated 22 April 1937 will not, for the time being, be carried out.

2. If information regarding the impending release of a Jehovah's Witness from arrest is received from the authorities carrying out the sentence, my decision regarding the ordering of measures by the State Police shall be requested in accordance with my circular decree dated 22 April 1937, so that transfer to a concentration camp can take place immediately after the sentence has been served. If it is impossible to transfer Jehovah's Witnesses to a concentration camp immediately after the serving of the sentence, they will be detained in police prisons.

In each case an immediate report must be made.

28 Dr Werner Best on the police and the law

The relationship between the police and the law was defined by Dr Werner Best, a leading Gestapo official, as follows:

... The police never act in a lawless or illegal manner so long as they act in accordance with the rules laid down by their superiors — up to the highest authority. The High Administrative Court of Hamburg rightly states in its judgement of 19 November 1937:

It is the function of the police to deal only with what the Government wishes to have dealt with.

What the Government wants to be dealt with by the police is the essence of police law and is what guides and restricts the actions of the police. So long as the police carries out the will of the Government, it is acting legally; should it over-step the will of the Government, then it is no longer a case of police action, but a breach of duty by a member of the police.

Whether the will of the Government is 'right', i.e. whether it lays down rules that are practical and needed for police action, is no longer a question of law, but one of destiny. If the leadership of the nation misuses the 'right to lay down the law' (through excess either of severity or of weakness) it will be punished more inexorably by fate, because of its violation of the 'laws of existence', than by any State court. It will be punished with disaster, upheaval and ruin. . . .

29 *Interference in the course of justice*

During the war, the influence of the Gestapo over the legal system increased. This was expressed in growing interference in the judicial process. This interference occurred even in criminal cases in which the police did not consider the sentence sufficiently severe, as is clear from this letter from a prosecutor to the Reich Minister of Justice dated 28 April 1942:

The defendant Paul Krüger was condemned to fifteen years' imprisonment by the special court here in its session of 4 March 1942; furthermore this was to be in the form of protective custody. I demanded a sentence of death. I enclose the file containing the sentence.

I have heard today from the head of the local criminal police office that the local police in a report sent to several State authorities have expressed their regret that Krüger was not sentenced to death. He recommends me to try to influence the Reich Minister of Justice to change the judgement into a sentence of death by plea of nullity; *otherwise another authority might possibly intervene.*

As things are, I recommend that a plea of nullity should be arranged with the Reich Prosecutor, particularly since sentences of over ten years are regarded as undesirable according to the latest guidelines.

30 *Treatment of various categories of prisoner*

The culmination of the gradual capitulation of the legal system to the SS was the following agreement between Thierack and Himmler which consigned certain 'anti-social' elements *in toto* to the SS:

Discussion with Reichsführer SS Himmler on 18.ix.42 in his Field Headquarters in the presence of State Secretary Dr Rothenberger, SS *Gruppenführer* Streckenbach and SS *Obersturmbannführer* Bender.
1. Correction by special treatment[1] at the hands of the police in cases where judicial sentences are not severe enough. At the suggestion of Reichsleiter Bormann, the following agreement was reached between the Reichsführer SS and myself:
(a) As a rule the Führer's time is no longer to be burdened with these matters.
(b) The Reich Minister of Justice will decide whether and when special treatment at the hands of the police is to be applied.

[1] A Nazi euphemism for execution.

(c) The Reichsführer SS will send the reports, which hitherto he has sent to Reichsleiter Bormann, to the Reich Minister of Justice.

(d) If the views of the Reichsführer SS and those of the Reich Minister of Justice coincide, the final decision on the case will rest with them.

(e) If their views are not in agreement, the opinion of Reichsleiter Bormann will be sought on the case, and he may inform the Führer.

(f) In cases where the Führer's decision on a mild sentence is sought through other channels (such as by a letter from a Gauleiter) Reichsleiter Bormann will forward the report to the Reich Minister of Justice.

The case will then be decided as already described by the Reichsführer SS and the Reich Minister of Justice.

2. The following anti-social elements are to be transferred from the prison where they are serving their sentence to the Reichsführer SS to be worked to death: persons under protective arrest, Jews, gypsies, Russians and Ukrainians, Poles with sentences of more than three years, Czechs and Germans with sentences of more than eight years, according to the decision of the Reich Minister of Justice. First of all, the worst anti-social elements amongst those just mentioned are to be handed over. I shall inform the Führer of this through Reichsleiter Bormann. . . .

14. It is agreed that, in view of the plans of the Government for settling the eastern problems, in future Jews, Poles, gypsies, Russians and Ukrainians are no longer to be judged by the ordinary courts, so far as punishable offences are concerned, but are to be dealt with by the Reichsführer SS. This does not apply to civil lawsuits, nor to Poles whose names are announced or entered in the German Racial Lists.[1]

[1] i.e. Poles who were racially acceptable.

11 Opposition

The German Resistance took many forms – illegal underground activities, the infiltration of economic organizations, plans for post-Hitler Germany, open protest, conspiracy and attempted *coups d'état* – and originated in different circles, left-wing, ecclesiastical, military, academic and aristocratic; but it was never a mass movement. The Nazi State, with its control of the mass media and its use of terror through the ever-watchful secret police, confined opposition to restricted groups, which had to operate in secret. Unlike the Resistance in the occupied countries, the German Opposition had no recognized claim to be a patriotic force relying on the support of the mass of the population. Hitler's successes in economic and foreign policy in the middle and later 1930s won the approval of the majority of the nation, while his early wartime victories made effective opposition unlikely, with the added problem that from September 1939 the German Resistance was open to charges of national betrayal. The German Opposition by the nature of its clandestine activities is difficult to document, especially in the case of the left-wing underground movements which unlike the conservative circles did not compose numerous memoranda about the shape of the future Germany. The Communist and Social Democratic opposition groups were less concerned with the moral questions raised by the character of National Socialism and concentrated chiefly on preparing for the overthrow of the Nazi regime; but they had serious weaknesses. They failed to unite even after 1933. The Communists still associated the SPD with the 'Fascist' system of Weimar and saw the Nazi regime as an outcome of that system. By the time they discovered that the Nazi regime was not going to crumble automatically, it was too late, for their leaders had been arrested early in 1933. The Social Democrats maintained a suspicious attitude towards the Communists, as any cooperation in a united anti-Fascist front would ultimately be hampered by the implied conflict between their aims – on the one side, the totalitarian form of State as practised in Russia, and on the other the SPD's preference for a Western type of democracy. Even temporary cooperation for tactical reasons proved difficult. The Social Democrats at first swung more to the extreme left and advocated revolutionary solutions, but this led to divisions among their leaders over the use of illegal methods. The Communists were less plagued by differences in their ranks but they were equally decimated by the waves of arrests by the Gestapo and the emigration of many of their members. These and other smaller left-wing groups were eventually reduced to underground activities of a less ambitious kind, such as the formation of smaller groups to limit their detection by informers and the greater reliance on personal contacts to replace the distribution of clandestine literature. They relied more on their *émigré* organizations for the provision of such material by means of frontier-based agencies.

1 *Underground activities of the Communists and Social Democrats*

The only documentary source of information on the activities of the left-wing underground groups is official reports, which are suspect because of the reluctance of those arrested to give a full picture of the operations in which they had been engaged. The following report by the Gestapo office in Düsseldorf for the year 1937 refers to the changes in methods used by the Communists and the network of contacts built up by the Social Democrats:

A. The Communist movement

During the first years after the take-over of power, until about 1936, the Communists tried to expand their party and its various subsidiary organizations. But later they saw clearly that they only endangered those members illegally active inside the country and made it easy for the police to break up the illegal organizations, particularly since the distribution route of a pamphlet could be followed and traced fairly easily. In the high treason trials carried out in recent years it has already been noted that those engaged in illegal activities refused to distribute literature because of the danger involved in it. So this may have been one of the reasons that prompted the Central Committee of the Communist Party of Germany based in Paris under the leadership of the former Communist Reichstag deputy, Wilhelm Pieck, to publish new guidelines for illegal activity in Germany at the beginning of 1937. Whereas until 1936 the main propaganda emphasis was on distributing lots of pamphlets, at the beginning of 1936 they switched to propaganda by word of mouth, setting up bases in factories, and advocated the so-called Popular Front on the French pattern. . . .

It became apparent that the Communist propaganda described above was already having some success in various factories. After factory meetings at which speakers of the Labour Front had spoken, some of whom were in fact rather clumsy in their statements, the mood of discontent among the workers was apparent in subsequent discussions. In one fairly large factory the speaker from the Labour Front greeted the workers with the German [Nazi] salute: but in reply the workers only mumbled. When the speaker ended the factory parade with the German salute, it was returned loudly and clearly, but they made it clear that they had only used the German salute because it brought the factory parade to an end. The shifting about of workers within the various factories, necessitated by the scarceness of raw materials, creates more fertile soil for the subversion of the workers by the KPD. Furthermore, the transfer of workers who were shortly due for leave to a different factory with the result that the leave due to them was cancelled contributes to the discontent of the workers. The Christmas bonuses produced more discontent among the workers. Some factories paid Christmas bonuses to their workers with the result that workers from other factories who received nothing were annoyed. Here too a uniform method would help to remove fertile soil for KPD propaganda.

The 'Rote Hilfe' ['Red Help'] must be regarded by now as the only subsidiary organization of the KPD still in existence. Political prisoners and their families are still supported by the Rote Hilfe to a considerable extent. It has been noted that money collections and food parcels have arrived at the relevant departments of the courts, the senders of which could not be traced. Grocery parcels have also been sent from Holland to families of political prisoners by the Communist Party. These parcels are sometimes handed over to the State police by the recipients and transferred to the NSV. . . .

C. Social Democratic Party

In the period covered by the report the SPD has worked mainly by means of the dissemination of news. The information that reaches the leadership of the illegal SPD from their news service in Germany is collected there and distributed as information material in Gothic type. The information material that is smuggled into Germany is produced in postcard size editions in small print. The articles appearing in these information leaflets are biased criticisms of Government measures. They are sent only to reliable old SPD people. . . .

Apart from this, the illegal activity of the SPD is the same as that outlined in the newly published guidelines for the conspiratorial work of the KPD: the setting up of cells in factories, sports clubs and other organizations. Since the former SPD members carry on propaganda only by word of mouth, it is very difficult to get hold of proof of their illegal activities which would be usable in court.

One thing, however, appears to be certain: Even if former members of the SPD and its subsidiary organizations have always more or less refused to form organizations, or to distribute leaflets in larger numbers etc., the solidarity among them appears even now to be extremely strong owing to the fact that most of them have known each other for years, if not decades. They are too clever and have been trained for too long to be proved guilty of illegal activity.

Before the take-over of power the works' councils consisted mainly of old officials of the SPD workers' movement. These people who were removed or dismissed from their functions in the factories have been largely accommodated in other factories. As old and trained officials, they are well known in the workers' movement and are well versed in the workers' fight against the employers over questions of wages, hours of work, etc.

It is often noticed that workers, instead of approaching the representatives of the Labour Front with wage questions, go instead to trained people who are known to them and ask them for their advice. Not infrequently these people have been re-elected to the works council. Then through their skilful propaganda they get their former comrades on to the works council and into leading positions in the factories. The illegal SPD leadership places the greatest emphasis on these people and relies on them to stand up for their former ideals at the right moment and to influence the workers by their own spirit.

On 10.xi.37 we succeeded in arresting a Dutch sailor called Gert Dooyes from Rotterdam. . . . Dooyes admits to having smuggled pamphlets into Germany for two Dutchmen who were members of the SPD centre in Amsterdam and to having passed them on to SPD officials in Duisburg and Oberhausen. Furthermore, Dooyes has confessed to importing nearly thirty food parcels into Germany by water between 1936 and his arrest in November 1937 and to passing these on to SPD functionaries who sent the parcels on to the families of political prisoners. . . . During the course of these investigations another thirty-four people were arrested who were under strong suspicion of working for the illegal SPD. . . .

The top brain and leading official in the SPD is the *émigré* Ernst Schumacher. He works in accordance with the instructions of the SPD leadership in Prague.[1] At Schumacher's request reading circles were formed in Duisburg and Oberhausen in which the material referred to above was passed on from hand to hand. It was hoped to increase the number of supporters through these reading circles. The people who have been arrested also belonged to the news service described above. . . .

In 1938 we will have to devote particular attention to illegal activity in the factories. Trusted agents have been infiltrated into several big factories in my district who have already provided proof that the KPD and the SPD are carrying out conspiratorial work jointly. In one factory the KPD, KPO[2] and SPD work hand in hand. In another factory the KPD is deviating from its prescribed rules and is forming a factory group according to previous guidelines of the RGO.[3] Here too it is noticeable that no pamphlets whatsoever are distributed; information is only passed on orally.

2 The use of cooperatives as a front for opposition

This report called special attention to the strong foothold maintained by the left-wing underground groups in the factories. At a conference near Moscow in October 1935 the KPD had decided to concentrate on a policy of subversion giving emphasis to the creation of illegal factory cells and the infiltration of Nazi occupational organizations. The Communists were better prepared than the Social Democrats for such clandestine activities by the disciplined nature of their organization and through their experience in such work before 1933. In spite of these Communist advantages, the police kept themselves well informed of Communist activities through their system of spies. Sometimes SA squads were sent as observers. One SA leader reported on a meeting of the Consumer Cooperative Society in Homberg on 2 January 1935:

From 31 December 1934 to 1 January 1935 the local consumer co-op held a meeting of members in the hall of the Walter Inn. Towards 8 o'clock at night this was opened by a Herr Brenne. Since there were obviously crowds of people from outside and the hall was going to be full, I became interested in this celebration and investigated how full the hall was. I had a chance to get on to the platform unnoticed to listen to Herr Brenne's speech. Brenne's words struck me deeply since neither our present Government nor our honoured leader was mentioned, but again and again one heard such words as 'comrades, we must stick together', 'it is no good all the comrades being there for a celebration', 'I must ask all comrades

---

[1] The SPD *émigré* organization was centred in Prague until late 1937, when it moved to Paris.
[2] *Kommunistische Partei Deutschlands-Opposition*, a Communist splinter group.
[3] *Revolutionäre Gewerkschafts-Opposition*, a Communist trade-union organization.

to come at least once a week to our sales centres and buy there'. Furthermore, '400 RM' were mentioned which I did not quite understand, so I assumed that in the year 1934 a surplus of 400 RM was made which was to be increased in the year 1935 through more customers. Otherwise they just talked of 'comrades', of 'sticking together', but there was no mention of the Government, even after the generous winter aid scheme through which many of the people present must have been helped. My first impression while observing the hall which was very full (about 600 people) was that the visitors were former Marxists. Furthermore, the speech was somewhat ambiguous, the talk was always of 'comrades' and 'standing together'. This standing together probably refers to the consumer co-op because a great number of non-members were present in the hall as well.

I went away to my flat. Towards 1.45 I was called back into the hall by Oberscharführer M.

There I noted the following: I had arranged an S A patrol for the holidays, particularly for New Year's Eve. This had the task of intervening in any incidents. It also went into the Walter Inn where the above-mentioned celebration was taking place. Immediately Oberscharführer K. entered the hall in uniform he was met with: 'You are in your brown shirt, we can't stand seeing the brown shirt tonight.' M.,who was accompanying K.,was abused by the former Communist M. (who still is one). When the S A men objected to this they were shouted at. At the same moment, the police sergeant D. entered the inn and it was only through his intervention that an attack on them was avoided.

After Brenne's speech I felt deeply shocked for the rest of the evening and when I went back to the hall I saw the result. It reminded me of a 1928 Communist meeting. The police officer and the S A men were surrounded and at any moment an attack on them could be expected. The whole audience was in a turmoil and rushed towards the police officer and the S A. After Obertruppf. H. was attacked by one of the audience, I formed a line together with my companions to protect the S A patrol and the police officer. The police sergeant ordered the closure of the meeting, the bar was closed and people were asked to leave. Now the turmoil really started; when they realized they couldn't get at the police officer and the S A men, they started arguing among themselves, so that it was only with great difficulty that the hall could be cleared. Outside the door the resistance continued and people shouted to us: 'We'll teach you National Socialism'. From this too it can be seen to which camp these people belong.

From the above report it can be deduced that the consumer co-op is only a means to an end, that only Marxist and Communist elements gather in it in order to keep up their old contacts. Because the consumer cooperative in its present form represents a danger to the State its dissolution appears to be urgently necessary.

3 Passive resistance from Social Democrats

Even the Communist penetration of factories was severely weakened by wholesale arrests made by the Gestapo. As soon as such groups began to widen the scope of their activities, the Gestapo tracked them down. One left-wing group called 'New Beginning' (Neu Beginnen), which included dissident Social Democrats and Communists, was virtually wiped out in Berlin by the autumn of 1938. Earlier, the main body of Social Democrats had realized the futility of their opposition methods and resigned themselves to the situation. Social Democratic opposition now took rather the form of passive resistance to maintain a feeling of solidarity. According to the Gestapo:

... the expected change will come from outside. But preparations have to be made for this event so that past activities can be resumed in a pre-arranged form. This inner conviction and the wish of the SPD leaders that there should be no rigid organizations is reflected in the behaviour and solidarity of the country's illegal workers. After work they join each other over a glass of beer, meet former kindred spirits near their homes, or keep in touch by means of family visits; they avoid all forms of organization, and seek in the manner described to help their friends remain steadfast. During these meetings, of course, there is talk about the political situation and news is exchanged. They promote energetically the so-called whispering campaign which, for the time being, represents the most effective illegal work against the State, against its institutions and activities, and against the Party. The main subjects of discussion are price increases, low wages, economic exploitation of the people, freedom, shortage of raw materials, corruption, nepotism, gifts at the nation's expense and so on. Since many former SPD and trade union officials are now commercial representatives and travelling salesmen, such catchwords will spread comparatively quickly into the furthest parts of the Reich. Despite the extent of these subversive activities it has not yet been possible to catch a single one of these persons in the act and bring him to trial.

4 *Opposition within the Army to Hitler's Czech policy*

Increasingly, it became clear that opposition within a totalitarian dictatorship was most effectively carried out by military *coup d'état*. The Army had been attracted by Hitler's policy of rearmament, but discontent among its leaders appeared with Hitler's arbitrary methods and his assumption of control over military decisions, which culminated in his take-over of the Supreme Command of the Armed Forces in February 1938. Hitler took the opportunity to appoint more pliable leaders in the Army. Other generals with their traditional outlook were hamstrung by the fact that Hitler's Government had originally been legally constituted. In the summer of 1938 some officers took the initiative in planning the first major attempt at Hitler's removal. A leading figure in the conspiracy was General Ludwig Beck, Chief of the General Staff, who produced three memoranda arguing that a German war against Czechoslovakia would soon broaden into a major conflict and have disastrous consequences for Germany. In the third of his memoranda, presented on 16 July, Beck wrote:

... So we are faced with the fact that military action by Germany against Czechoslovakia will automatically lead to a European or a world war. I need not enlarge upon the fact that such a war will in all probability end not only in a military but also in a general catastrophe for Germany.

... On the basis of my preceding account, I now find myself obliged – conscious of the significance of such a step but in view of the responsibility laid upon me by my official instructions for the preparations and carrying out of war – to request urgently that the Commander-in-Chief of the Armed Forces should stop the preparations for war ordered by him and postpone the plan to solve the Czech question by force until the military situation has fundamentally changed. For the time being I regard it as hopeless, and this opinion is shared by all subordinate quartermaster-generals and departmental chiefs on the general staff who are involved in the preparation and carrying out of the war against Czechoslovakia. ...

Final decisions involving the existence of the nation are at stake here. History will charge our present leaders with having committed a capital crime if they do not act according to their professional and political knowledge and consciences. Their obedience as soldiers has a limit at which their knowledge, their consciences and their sense of responsibility forbid the carrying out of an order.

If their advice and warnings are not heeded in such a situation they have the right and the duty to their people and to history to resign their commands. If they all act in unison, it will be impossible to carry out an act of war. They will thereby have preserved their fatherland from the worst that could happen – its downfall.

It shows a lack of greatness and of awareness of the task in hand if a soldier holding a senior position in such times sees his duties and tasks purely in the limited context of his military orders without being conscious of his supreme responsibility to the whole people. Exceptional times demand exceptional actions. ...

Beck failed to convince General Brauchitsch, Hitler's newly appointed Commander-in-Chief of the Army, of the need to resist Hitler's aims and resigned his post in August 1938. The conspiracy failed to materialize as Hitler's plan to attack Czechoslovakia was foiled by the Munich Conference. The outbreak of war a year later had important repercussions on the German Opposition. For the Communists the Nazi pact with the USSR presented an embarrassing problem and brought them a loss of support, although the KPD continued the policy of subversion while officially toeing the new Moscow line. The conclusion of this treaty confirmed certain assumptions among conservative opposition circles, which after their initial flirtation with the Nazis came to the conclusion that National Socialism was the forerunner of Bolshevism. Adam von Trott, one of the younger members of these predominantly upper-class circles, once remarked that 'what in Germany is dirty brown slush is invested in Moscow with harsh Asiatic brutality'. These groups were characterized by a certain social solidarity through a network of contacts and had supporters in most branches of the Establishment, especially the diplomatic corps which was less Nazified than most other sections of the Civil Service and had easier access to contacts abroad.

5 Problems of the Opposition at the outbreak of the war

Ulrich von Hassell, who after his resignation as ambassador to Italy in 1937 became a leading figure in the conservative Resistance, revealed in his diary on 19 October 1939 a typical contempt for the Nazi rulers and also a feeling of moral objection to their extermination policy:

Among well-informed people in Berlin I noticed a good deal of despair. In wide circles there is still rejoicing over the 'inspired chess move of the pact with Russia', over the victories in Poland, and over the performance of the submarines and the Air Corps against England. But among informed people there is growing awareness of our impending disaster.

The principal sentiments are: the conviction that the war cannot be won by military means; a realization of the highly dangerous economic situation; the feeling of being led by criminal adventurers; and the disgrace that has sullied the German name through the conduct of the war in Poland, namely, the brutal use of air power and the shocking bestialities of the SS, especially towards the Jews. The cruelties of the Poles against the German minority are also a fact, but somehow psychologically excusable. When people use their revolvers to shoot down a group of Jews herded into a synagogue one is filled with shame. A light court-martial sentence pronounced against some of these criminals was set aside by Brauchitsch; a second sentence, also light, was voided by the disgraceful general amnesty for such deeds. And all this time a man like Niemöller[1] has been sitting for years in a concentration camp!

I hear that Blaskowitz, as an Army commander, wanted to prosecute two SS leaders, including that rowdy, Sepp Dietrich,[2] for looting and murder. But in vain. Those who saw Warsaw, with its devastation and the many thousands of dead bodies lying around, came away appalled. Of course the commander of the city should not have permitted this to happen, but the Nazi determination to bring the war to a quick end was primarily responsible. . . .

Now that Germany is in the midst of a great war, the situation of most politically clear-headed and reasonably well-informed people today is indeed tragic. They love their country. They think patriotically as well as socially. They cannot wish for victory, even less can they wish for a crushing defeat. They dread a long war, and yet they see no possible way out: simply because there is no confidence that the military leadership possesses enough insight or willpower to assert itself at the decisive moment.

Brauchitsch is said to have some understanding but no determination; moreover, he seems to be suffering from some stomach ailment. Halder is more reasonable but has less power; physically he is not at his best—a matter of nerves. No one expects anything of Raeder, and I have spoken often enough about Göring in these pages. Among the Army leaders there are excellent people: Rundstedt, Blaskowitz, Bock, Leeb, Witzleben, List. But in their local commands they are not near enough to the helm. Hammerstein, who had commanded an Army group in Cologne, was ordered first to a less important command and has now been put on the shelf altogether.

On *Monday the sixteenth*, in the afternoon, I went to see Beck. He saw no great chance of success either in a breakthrough on the Maginot Line or in Belgium and

---

[1] Martin Niemöller, Protestant pastor and leader of the Confessional Church opposition, had been interned in a concentration camp since 1937.

[2] Sepp Dietrich, a notorious SS leader and friend of Himmler, played an important part in crushing civilian resistance during the Polish campaign.

Holland. His opinion of the top people is of the very worst; that goes for Göring too. . . .

The war made the task of the Opposition groups more difficult; not only could they now be accused of treason, but wartime conditions imposed even stricter limitations on their activities. The Communists were most vulnerable because of their links with Moscow, and were severely dealt with by the Gestapo. Such was the fate of the 'Rote Kapelle', a Soviet-controlled espionage organization formed in 1940, which was eliminated two years later. The conservative groups were in a more advantageous position since they could claim to be reasserting German tradition against the 'unnatural' phenomenon of National Socialism—it was a favourite theme of Carl Goerdeler, one of their principal leaders, that since Bismarck Germany had had no leadership. But their success depended on exploiting the weaknesses of the Nazi regime. In the autumn of 1939 von Hassell had had the forlorn hope that the generals would act before Hitler carried out his plan for the invasion of the Low Countries—a hope that was dashed by the German military successes of 1940. In August 1941 a military plan for the assassination of Hitler was dropped because Nazi security precautions were too strict.

6 *Conversation with Fabian von Schlabrendorff*

Two months later von Hassell reported in his diary (4 October) on a conversation he had had with Fabian von Schlabrendorff, an officer on the staff of Major-General von Tresckow on the Russian front:

On the day before yesterday I had a long talk with Popitz and General Thomas[1] at Popitz's home about further action. Both were alert, judicious, and discreet, although Thomas is not entirely immune to propaganda. In any event they both see things as they are; they are not reactionary but wish to move forward. A great problem, till now insoluble, is where we can find names that carry weight with the workers. In this respect everything is smashed to pieces. It is becoming ever clearer what great destroyers the Nazis are in matters political and ethical.

The generals seem to be recognizing this gradually. A few days ago Fabian von Schlabrendorff, a reserve lieutenant and a lawyer by profession, turned up. He had been sent by General von Kluge in order to find out whether opposition was crystallizing at home, and to assure opposition groups that 'one' was ready to act. He came to me through Guttenberg[2] to get some information on foreign affairs. A very sensible man, but his comments revealed with what *naïveté* the generals approach this problem. Among other things he asked whether there was any guarantee that England would make peace soon after a change of regime was effected. I told him there were no such guarantees and that there could be none.

---

[1] General Thomas was head of the armaments division of the Ministry of War. Both he and Popitz were arrested in 1944 in connexion with the July Plot.

[2] Baron Karl Ludwig von Guttenberg, a landowner, worked for Military Intelligence and was editor of *Weisse Blätter*, a periodical he published in Neustadt an der Saale.

Were it otherwise, any cobbler's apprentice could overthrow the regime. But I could guarantee him something else:

(1) That unless England and America were completely knocked out Hitler could get no peace.

(2) That a respectable Germany, on the other hand, would always have a very considerable chance to get peace, and an acceptable peace at that. However, a change in regime was our own affair—a question which we alone could decide, not our opponents.

He seemed to think that we would have to make peace immediately after the change. I had to explain to him that although peace was, of course, our goal, we would have to proclaim our preparedness to continue the war, at the same time emphasizing our readiness to conclude an acceptable peace. What else had to be done was another question. We agreed that immediately after the end of the pending offensive in Russia his general should send a suitable high-ranking man here for further discussion.

The whole incident is gratifying because, for the first time, some kind of initiative comes from that source. But I had to make clear to Schlabrendorff that there was no way to avoid the unpleasant reality that there would be a period in which disillusioned people might declare that Hitler had been robbed of a victory within his grasp and that the new rulers wouldn't be able to achieve peace either. It is the old dilemma. If we wait until the impossibility of victory becomes clear to the whole world we shall have lost the chance for a reasonable peace. But we must not wait. Whatever the outcome, our inheritance will be a bad one.

7 *Bishop Galen of Münster protests against euthanasia, August 1941*

The revelation during the war of the full extent of the racial policies of the Nazis provided a moral justification for the opposition of conservative groups, already offended by Hitler's contempt for the constitutional order of the State. This was particularly true of the opposition of the Churches. The Roman Catholic Church had initially concentrated on guarding against any infringements of its rights as defined by the Concordat of 1933, which had forbidden priests to participate in politics. The Concordat had virtually crippled Catholic opposition until it became evident that the Nazis had little respect for the terms of the agreement. On the Evangelical side, the Confessional Church, which resented the establishment of the Nazi-controlled organization of 'German Christians', had already issued in 1934 its Barmen Declaration protesting against the interference of the State in religious matters. Popular feeling seemed to be aroused especially in strong Catholic areas, such as in 1936 when the Catholics in Oldenburg successfully demanded the restoring of the crucifixes to their schools. The Catholic Church leaders in Germany were torn between the offence given them by the behaviour of the authorities on religious questions and the attraction they felt for other aspects of Nazi policy, especially anti-Communism. Individual bishops like Bertram of Breslau, Preysing of Berlin and Galen of Münster took a more independent stand than the official body of bishops. In June 1941 Cardinal Bertram protested to the Reich Ministry of Justice about the killing of insane persons.[1] Cardinal von Galen followed on 13 and 20 July and 3 August with a series of sermons in Münster. The first of these sermons attacked the brutal and arbitrary methods of the Gestapo, the violation of personal freedoms and the 'lawlessness' detrimental to 'the German *Volksgemeinschaft*' and referred to his duty as a bishop to intervene on behalf of the moral order. Galen followed an exhortation on Christian duty even at the cost of life with his renowned sermon in the St Lamberti Church on 3 August attacking the euthanasia policy of the Nazis:

... Catholic Christians! In the joint pastoral letter to the German bishops of 26 June which was read in all Catholic churches throughout Germany on 6 July of this year it is said among other things: 'It is true that there are positive commandments which, according to Catholic moral teaching, are no longer obligatory if their fulfilment involves too great difficulties or dangers. But there are also obligations of conscience from which nobody can free us and which we must fulfil even if it costs us our lives. Never, and under no circumstances apart from war and justified self-defence, is a human being allowed to kill another innocent human being.' Already on 6 July I had occasion to add the following commentary to these words of the pastoral letter: 'For several months we have been hearing reports that patients in clinics and nursing homes for the mentally ill, who have been ill for some time and may seem incurable, are being forcibly removed on orders from Berlin.' Then usually, after a short time, the relatives receive notification that the patient has died, that the corpse has been burnt and that the ashes can be delivered. There is a general suspicion, bordering upon certainty, that these numerous unexpected deaths of mental patients do not occur of themselves but are deliberately induced, and that in this matter the doctrine is being followed which maintains that one may destroy so-called 'lives which are not worth living', that is to say, one may kill innocent people if their lives are regarded as worthless to the nation or the State – a shocking doctrine which sets out to justify the murder of innocent people, that licenses the compulsory killing of invalids, cripples, the incurably sick, and the old who are unable to work. In the face of this, the German bishops declare: Never, and under no circumstances, must a human being kill an innocent human being apart from war and justified self-defence. I have heard according to reliable information that lists are being drawn up in the clinics and nursing homes of the province of Westphalia as well, of such patients as are to be sent away as so-called 'unproductive citizens' and are shortly to be killed. The first transport left last week from the institution at Marienthal near Münster.

German men and women! Paragraph 211 of the Reich Criminal Code is still valid. It states: 'Anyone who wilfully kills another person shall, if the killing is premeditated, be punished by death for murder.' Probably in order to protect those who deliberately kill these poor sick people, members of our families, from this legal punishment, the patients selected to be killed are taken from near their homes to a distant institution. Some illness is then given as the cause of death. Since the corpse is burned straightaway, the relatives and the police are unable to find out whether the illness really occurred and what was the actual cause of death. But I have been assured that in the Reich Ministry of the Interior and in the office

---

[1] For Hitler's 'Euthanasia Order' see below, p. 614.

of the Reich Physicians' Leader, Dr Conti, little effort was made to hide the fact that a large number of mental patients had been deliberately killed in Germany and that more were to be killed in the future. Paragraph 139 of the Reich Criminal Code states: 'Anyone who has definite knowledge of an intended crime against life . . .[1] and refrains from informing the authorities or the person threatened at the proper time will be punished.' When I heard of the plan to remove patients from Marienthal in order that they should be killed, I reported this on 28 July to the Public Prosecutor's Office at the district court of Münster and to the Police-President in Münster in a registered letter as follows: 'According to information I have received, during this coming week (the 31 July is mentioned) it is intended to move a large number of patients from the Provincial Mental Hospital of Marienthal near Münster to the Eichberg Hospital, in order that they should be premeditatedly put to death as so-called unproductive citizens. It is the general belief that this has occurred with the members of similar transports from other institutions. Since such an action not only violates divine and natural law, but is also punishable by death according to Paragraph 211 of the Reich Criminal Code, I hereby prefer charges as I am obligated to according to Paragraph 139 of the Criminal Code and I request that the citizens threatened in this way shall be protected by action taken against the authorities intending their removal and murder and that I shall be notified of such action taken.'

On 26 July I had already made a serious protest to the provincial administration of the Province of Westphalia which is responsible for these institutions caring for these sick people. It was in vain. The first transport of innocent people who have been condemned to death has left Marienthal. And I have heard that 800 sick people have already been removed from the provincial mental hospital of Warstein.

So we have to be prepared for these poor, helpless, sick people to be prematurely killed. Why? Not because they have committed a crime deserving death. Not because they have attacked their nurses so that the nurses could not help fighting off their attackers in order to preserve their own lives in justified self-defence. No, it is not for such reasons that those unfortunate sick people must die. It is because, in the opinion of some doctor or committee, they do not deserve to live, being, according to the testimony of these doctors, 'unproductive citizens'. It is argued: they can no longer produce goods; they are like an old machine that no longer works; they are like an old horse that has become incurably lame; they are like a cow that no longer gives milk. What does one do with such an old machine? It is scrapped. What does one do with such a lame horse? With such an unproductive animal? No, I do not want to finish the comparison, however frighteningly justified and striking it is! For here we are not dealing with machines nor with horses or cows whose sole function it is to serve man, to produce goods for men. They may be scrapped; they may be killed as soon as they no longer fulfil their purpose. No, here we are dealing with people, with our fellow human beings, with our brothers and sisters! With poor people, sick people, unproductive people if you like! But have they lost their right to live because of that? Have you, have I, the right to live only so long as we are productive, so long as we are recognized by others as productive? If you put forward and apply the maxim that unproductive human beings may be killed, then woe to us all when we become old and weak! If people are allowed to kill unproductive human beings then woe to the invalids who

[1] Ellipsis in original.

have used, sacrificed and lost their strength, their healthy limbs in the productive process! If people are allowed to remove unproductive fellow citizens by force then woe to our good soldiers who return home seriously disabled by war, cripples, invalids!

Once it is admitted that people have the right to kill unproductive human beings, even if it now affects only poor, defenceless, mentally sick persons, then a principle will have been established which will license the murder of all unproductive people, that is to say, the incurably sick, people incapable of work, cripples, people who have become invalids through work or through the war, a principle which will license the murder of all of us when we become senile and unproductive. Then only some secret decree will be needed to extend the procedure tried out on the mentally sick to other unproductive people, to incurable lung patients, to senile people who have become invalids through their work, to soldiers seriously disabled by war. After that no one will again feel sure of his life. Some committee or other will be able to put him on the list of unproductive people who in their judgement are no longer worth keeping alive; and he will get no protection from the police; and no court of law will revenge his murder and give his murderer the punishment he deserves. Who will then still be able to trust his doctor? He may report his patient as unproductive and receive the order to kill him. It is impossible to imagine the moral deterioration which will result; the general sense of mutual mistrust will spread even through families, if this doctrine is tolerated, accepted and followed. Woe to mankind, woe to our German people, not only if God's holy commandment, Thou shalt not kill, which the Lord pronounced on Sinai amidst thunder and lightning, which God our creator from the very beginning wrote into man's conscience—if this commandment is broken, but if this transgression is actually tolerated and carried out unpunished. . . .

8 Goebbels on policy toward Church resistance

Galen's public protests were too great a provocation for the Nazis to ignore, particularly as news of them soon spread abroad, but Count von Galen, a Westphalian aristocrat, was one of those few individuals who enjoyed a public following which saved him from arrest. Hitler preferred to wait until the successful conclusion of the war before settling the position of the Churches in the Third Reich. Goebbels defined the Government's policy towards the Church in answer to a suggestion from Tiessler, a member of his staff, that Galen should be hanged. According to a secret memorandum by Tiessler (13 August):

Concerning: Sermon of the Bishop of Münster
After the conference of Ministers, Dr Goebbels discussed with me the sermon of the Bishop of Münster. He could not say what effective measures could be taken at the moment.
I explained to him that in my opinion there could be only one effective measure, namely, to hang the Bishop, and that I already had informed Reichsleiter Bormann accordingly.
Dr Goebbels thereupon said that this was a measure on which the Führer alone

could decide. He feared, however, that, if anything were done against the Bishop, the population of Münster could be regarded as lost to the war effort, and the same could confidently be said of the whole of Westphalia.

I pointed out to him that it would only be necessary to show up properly that brazen lie through propaganda channels. By that means it should be possible not only to bring the population there to an understanding of that measure but to foster among them rebellion against the Bishop.

To that Dr Goebbels again replied that the Führer himself would certainly come to a decision on that question.

He went on to observe that it would be wiser, in his opinion, not to challenge the Church during the war but only to try to steer it as far as possible in the direction of our interests. For that reason he had ordered the interview with Party Comrade Gutterer.[1] But in that case he had not followed up the matter in this way because the Party Chancellery had taken the line of uncompromising refusal and an open breach. Although it was easy for him, in contrast to other Reich Leaders, to gag the Church press, because in that connexion he had the proof and the justification for doing so, yet he maintained that it would be better during the war to preserve appearances where the Church was concerned. To attack an opponent is permissible, always provided that one is in a position to reply adequately to the opponent's decisive counterattack. But in the case of the Church's counterattack in wartime this was extraordinarily difficult, indeed, next to impossible. Revenge should not be indulged in with heat but taken coldly. In politics one should know how to wait.

9 *A case of euthanasia*

Religious opposition became political because the Church's involvement with questions of human rights led it to criticize methods used by the Nazi regime (e.g. concentration camps and forced foreign labour as well as euthanasia). The euthanasia programme was officially halted after the public disturbance caused by Galen's sermon, although euthanasia continued under the greatest secrecy. Galen's public protest had caused the Government much embarrassment, as copies of his sermon had been distributed in pamphlet form throughout the country and even reached soldiers at the front. On 13 August, Bishop Hilfrich of Limburg wrote to the Reich Minister of Justice referring to a specific case of euthanasia in his diocese. In his letter Hilfrich, presumably with the intention of putting pressure on the authorities, mentioned the fact that news of this case had reached the ears of the surrounding population.

Regarding the report submitted on 16 July by Cardinal Dr Bertram, Chairman of the Fulda Bishops' Conference, I consider it my duty to present the following as a concrete illustration of the destruction of so-called 'useless life'.

About eight kilometres from Limburg, in the little town of Hadamar, on a hill overlooking the town, there is an institution which had formerly served various purposes and of late had been used as a nursing home; this institution was renovated

[1] A State Secretary in the Propaganda Ministry.

and furnished as a place in which, by consensus of opinion, the above-mentioned euthanasia has been systematically practised for months—approximately since February 1941. The fact has become known beyond the administrative district of Wiesbaden, because death certificates from the Hadamar–Mönchberg Registry are sent to the home communities. (Mönchberg is the name of this institution because it had been a Franciscan monastery before its secularization in 1803.)

Several times a week buses arrive in Hadamar with a considerable number of victims. School children of the neighbourhood know the vehicle and say: 'There comes the murder-box again.' After the arrival of the vehicle, the citizens of Hadamar watch the smoke rising from the chimney and are tormented by the constant thought of the miserable victims, especially when they are sickened by repulsive smells, depending on the direction of the wind.

The effects of the whole operation here are these: Children call one another names and say 'You're loony, you'll be sent to the baking oven in Hadamar.' Those who don't want to marry, or haven't the chance, say, 'Marry? Never! Bring children into the world so they can be put into pickle?' You hear old folks say, 'Don't send me to a State hospital! After the feeble-minded have been finished off, it'll be the turn of the next lot who eat more than they're worth—the old people.'

All God-fearing men regard this extermination of helpless creatures as gross injustice. And if anybody says that if there's still a just God, then Germany cannot win the war, these expressions are proof, not of any lack of love of the fatherland, but of deep concern for our own people. The population cannot grasp that actions are systematically being carried out which, according to Paragraph 211 of the German Criminal Code, are punishable with death. The result of these happenings is that the moral concept of supreme authority has suffered a severe shock. The official notice that So-and-so has died of a contagious disease and that for that reason his body has had to be burned, is now met with plain disbelief, and this disbelief of such official notices has further undermined the ethical value of the concept of authority.

Officials of the Secret State Police, it is said, are using severe threats in their attempt to suppress any discussion of the Hadamar occurrences. In the interest of public peace, this may have good motives. But it does not change the conviction and indignation of the people at what they know of; their conviction will only be increased by their bitter realization that discussion may be forbidden under threat while the actions themselves remain unprosecuted under penal law.

Facta loquuntur.

I beg you most humbly, Herr Reich Minister, in the sense of the report of the Bishops of 16 July of this year, to prevent further transgressions of the Fifth Commandment of God.

10 *The Bishop of Chichester's meeting with Bonhoeffer and Schönfeld*

One problem, referred to in von Hassell's conversation with von Schlabrendorff, which concerned Opposition leaders was the likely reaction of the Allied Powers to any approaches they made. How seriously would the Allies take peace moves by the Opposition? Would total war exclude any consideration of anti-Hitler groups in Germany? With these questions in mind two Evangelical pastors visited Dr George Bell, Bishop of Chichester, who had several contacts with German Resistance leaders, in Stockholm. They were Dietrich Bonhoeffer, a leading figure in the Confessional Church opposition, and Hans Schönfeld from the foreign relations office of the Evangelical Churches. Their aim was to impress the British through the mediation of Dr Bell of the strength and sincerity of the German Opposition. Dr Bell's memorandum on his meetings with Bonhoeffer and Schönfeld in May 1942 refers to the peace terms they suggested in the event of Hitler's overthrow and throws some light on the intentions of the different opposition groups in Germany at this time:

I. Towards the end of May 1942 two German pastors came from Berlin to Stockholm in order to meet the Bishop of Chichester there. They arrived independently of one another and one of them only stayed for forty-eight hours. The Bishop spoke to them separately as well as together on four different days. Both men are well known to the Bishop and have worked together with him for many years in connexion with the ecumenical movement and the World Council of Churches and at various stages in the German church struggle [Kirchenkampf]. One of them lives in Switzerland but visits Germany frequently. The other lives in Berlin and is one of the leaders of the Confessional Church; he has been banned from speaking and preaching by the Gestapo. Their intention was:

A. To give information about a strong, organized resistance movement within Germany which had prepared plans for the destruction of the whole Hitler regime (including that of Himmler, Göring, Goebbels, and the chief leaders of the Gestapo, SS and SA) and for the foundation of a new German Government, consisting of:

1. Representatives of strongly anti-National Socialist forces in the Army and central State administration;

2. Former trade-union leaders;

3. Representatives of the Protestant and Catholic Churches.

They commit themselves to the following policy:

(a) The abandonment of offensive operations;

(b) The immediate suspension of the Nuremberg laws;[1]

(c) The gradual withdrawal of German troops from countries which have been occupied and attacked;

(d) The withdrawing of support from Japan, and the supporting of the Allies in order to end the war in the Far East;

(e) Collaboration with the Allies in order to rebuild the areas destroyed or damaged by the war.

B. To ask whether the Allies would be prepared, provided the whole Hitler regime had been destroyed, to negotiate with such a new German Government a peace settlement which would provide for the following:

1. The institution of a system of law and social justice in Germany combined with a far-reaching distribution of tasks to single States;

2. The creation of mutual economic dependence between the various nations of Europe which would be justified in itself as well as the most efficient guarantee against militarism;

[1] See below, pp. 463ff.

3. The foundation of a representative federation of free nations or States which would include a free Polish and a free Czech nation;

4. The setting up of a European army for the control of Europe under central direction in which the German army could participate.

II. Structure of the opposition:

The opposition had been developing for some time and was already in existence before the war. The war now gives it a chance which is only waiting to be seized. The opposition crystallized in the autumn of 1941 and could have seized an opportunity when many officers refused to continue fighting in Russia. But nobody took on the leadership. Hitler's most recent speech in which he claimed quite openly to stand above the law has shown the German people more clearly than ever the complete lawlessness of the regime. The opposition has complete confidence in the struggle of the German army and is prepared to fight the war to the bitter end if the Allies should refuse to negotiate with the new Government of a Germany freed from Hitler after the overthrow of the whole Hitler regime, but it also believes that the continuation of the war on its present or even on a bigger scale would condemn further millions to destruction especially in the occupied countries. It also believes that to fight until a decision had been reached would be suicidal for Europe. From this springs the wish to destroy Hitler and his regime first and then reach a peace settlement by which all European nations are to become economically interdependent, are to be defended against aggression through the possession of adequate European military forces, and are in some way to be allied with one another. Although the opposition has some doubts with regard to Russia, none the less, relying on impressions made on German officers by some of the higher Russian officers, it hopes that it may be possible to reach an agreement.

III. Organization of the opposition:

The opposition is based on members of the State administration, the State police, former trade-union leaders and high-ranking officers of the Army. It has contacts in every ministry, military officials in all the big cities, commanding generals in all armies. It has contact men in the wireless stations, in the big factories, in the main offices of the army depots and in the gas distribution network. It is impossible to give the numbers of the opposition. The main thing is that key positions everywhere are in the hands of the opposition and that key positions are of the greatest importance in Germany.

The following names were given of men thought to be closely connected with the resistance movement:

Colonel-General Beck: Chief of the General Staff before the Czechoslovakian crisis in 1938, 60 years old.

Colonel-General von Hammerstein: Chief of the General Staff before Beck.

Goerdeler: Formerly Price Commissar, Lord Mayor of Leipzig, director of the Civil Front.

Leuschner: Former President of the United Trade Union.

Kaiser: Head of the Catholic Trade Union.

All those mentioned above are said to be convinced Christians, the most important of them are Beck and Goerdeler.

Certain other people of less pronounced Christian character would be available, such as Schacht, for example. Most of the Field-Marshals can be relied on, especially von Kluge, von Bock, Küchler and possibly Witzleben. The question was put whether England would recommend a monarchy in Germany, in which case Prince Louis Ferdinand was eligible. But it was not stated whether he was a member of the opposition or not. He had been brought back from the United States by Hitler after the heroic death of the Crown Prince's eldest son. He had had a job as a worker in the Ford factory and now lives on an estate in East Prussia. He is a Christian, shows a genuine social conscience and is known to one of the two German pastors. The leaders of the Protestant and Catholic Churches also are closely connected with the whole resistance movement, especially Bishop Wurm of Württemberg (Protestant) and Bishop von Preysing who acts as spokesman of the Catholic bishops. (At the same time it should be mentioned that many members of the opposition are not only filled with deep remorse for the crimes committed in the name of Germany but even say: 'Christians do not want to shirk any penance or disaster if God's will places it upon us.')

IV. Course of action of the opposition:

The opposition knows of the rebellion against Hitler by Himmler and his associates which is threatening within the Nazi Party; but while a successful *coup d'état* by Himmler could be useful to the opposition, the complete extermination of Hitler, Himmler and the whole regime is indispensable. The plan of the opposition consists of a cleansing action which would have to be carried out as simultaneously as possible in the fatherland and in the occupied countries. After that a new Government would be set up. The opposition is aware of the necessity for an effective police control everywhere, in Germany and in the countries which have been occupied and attacked, in order to secure the new Government, and it seems as if the help of the Allied army as a means of maintaining order would be necessary and welcome, the more so if it was possible to combine the army of a neutral power with the Allied army to maintain order.

V. Questions put by the opposition to the Governments of the Allies:

After the course of action and plans of the opposition have been explained, the question arises of what support can be given to their leaders to start the operation, and to meet all the dangers connected with it. The following questions are put as examples of means for promoting it:

1. Would the Allied Governments be prepared to enter bona fide negotiations with a new German Government constructed according to the guidelines of Paragraph I,A, for a peace settlement as described in Paragraph I,B. (The reply to this could be sent privately to a representative of the opposition through a neutral country.)

2. Could the Allies announce to the world now and in the clearest terms that, if Hitler and the whole regime were overthrown, they would be ready to negotiate with a new Government with regard to a peace settlement of the kind described in Paragraph I,B, which renounced all aggression and committed itself to a course of action as described in Paragraph I,A? . . .

11 *Goerdeler's Declaration on the Atlantic Charter, 13 December 1942*

Dr Bell reported his meetings to the Foreign Office in London but Eden's reaction was negative. Reservations about the aims of the German Opposition were understandable in those who saw the only alternative in Germany to the Nazi system as a Western-type democracy. Carl Goerdeler, the former mayor of Leipzig and perhaps the principal figure in the conservative Opposition, was anything but a democrat. Goerdeler had had no sympathy for the Weimar Republic and in a number of peace plans outlined during 1941–42 he showed a deep contempt for political parties, and a preference for an oligarchy of local notables over a parliamentary democracy. Goerdeler, whose outlook was fundamentally 19th-century, emphasized traditional elements in society such as the family and the importance of Christianity. He showed an extraordinary lack of realism in that he did not realize that the course of the war might lead to severe terms for Germany after an Allied victory. In August 1941 Roosevelt and Churchill had issued their Atlantic Charter containing Allied principles for a postwar settlement. It became increasingly clear that the Allies were determined to prevent any repetition of German aggression and at the Casablanca Conference in January 1943 issued their demand for Germany's 'unconditional surrender'. A month earlier, on 13 December 1942, Goerdeler's declaration on the Atlantic Charter envisaged a 'gentlemanly' arrangement for postwar Europe with Germany's retention of her sovereignty, a fair settlement of national frontiers (including the granting to Germany of her frontiers of 1914) and European economic cooperation:

The peace must be a lasting one. It can only be that if it leaves the nations their independence and honour and enables them to repair the war damage, to repay debts through their work, and then to rebuild prosperity by means of their productive efficiency. To achieve this it must let the spiritual, mental and material powers of man develop harmoniously. The indispensable basis is cooperation in Christian solidarity.

Special points:

1. Law and decency must be restored in Germany. All those who have committed crimes and offences will be held responsible by the German people in accordance with the law. Unfortunately, much of what has happened cannot be expiated. The German people have been kept ignorant of it. When it learns the whole story, it will see the mitigation of suffering as its clear duty. It will have to bear through history the pain of seeing its name weighed down for ever by the burden of terrible events, of the perversion of noble feelings. A combination of toughness and patience will be needed to restore to the German people, despite this burden, a measure of self-respect and decency.

2. The damage caused by war will have to be borne by each nation itself as a matter of principle. But Germany will agree to any suggestion for communal reconstruction and will make its resources available for special efforts so long as the great goal is a real lasting peace and permanent cooperation.

3. The national economies must as far as possible be freed from all restrictions. That cannot happen overnight. The economies which are planned and controlled by the State can only be decontrolled gradually until the scarcity of food and raw materials has been overcome with the corresponding progress of demobilization.

4. In Germany the State will withdraw completely from active engagement in the economy and will leave the economy to the people, to their will to live and to their enterprise. The State will give the people's economic activity a secure basis simply by the protection of the law, by the prevention of dishonest competition, by the cultivation of decency and last but not least by securing as quickly as possible a genuine balance between income and expenditure in the public finances. This last measure is the decisive contribution which the State can make to the economy of its own nation and to economic cooperation with other nations. Without this balance stable currencies are impossible. For this reason too the States of Europe must be restored to complete independence as they existed at the outbreak of war with the following exceptions: . . .

(f) Germany will receive approximately the frontiers of 1914 in the east. Poland and Lithuania will be united as a federal state but with internal autonomy and common access to the sea.

(g)The frontiers between France and Germany will be settled along the language line in Alsace-Lorraine. Thus the larger part of Alsace would come to Germany, an insignificant part of Lorraine to France. If necessary this settlement can be subjected to a plebiscite after ten years.

(h) Where changes of frontiers take place, the inhabitants of the area concerned will have the liberty to move into the area of a different State within a period of ten years. They must be fully compensated. There is to be absolute freedom of decision. The procedure must be as generous and decent as possible. There is no objection to international control of the procedure. But if the peace is a really just one, the frontiers after ten years will no longer be considered oppressive, for the nations of Europe will strive towards one another and will have learned to live together.

(i) The principle of independence is particularly valid for Poland and Czechoslovakia. They shall decide completely freely whether they want to establish economic links with any other countries. After what happened the Germans will volunteer to help the Poles rebuild their country and take this willingness to help very seriously. This is the only possible way of making amends for the degree of human injustice that happened there over and above the necessities of war.

(k) Italy will cede the purely German South Tyrol to Germany up to about the line linking Bolzano and Merano.

(l) At the moment no particular suggestions can be made for dealing with the colonial question. This must be discussed calmly round the table and in the meantime one can only state that it is not wise to exclude Germany from all colonial activities. If the idea of transferring colonies to individual European powers were maintained one would have to examine where such participation would be possible. Japan must leave the colonial territories it has already occupied. On the other hand, it will be necessary to give Japan some possibility for peaceful activity in East Asia if renewed tension is to be avoided.

5. The European States reconstituted in this way will have full sovereignty. Germany will voluntarily create this state of affairs as quickly as possible by first of all removing everything non-military from the occupied territories. At the same time, the occupied territories will be asked to reinstate their national governments. Then negotiations will take place with them as to how quickly the reconstruction of the administration and the evacuation of the territories by the German

troops should take place. It is a prerequisite for this that the Anglo-Saxon great powers undertake no military operations during this period.

The next task of the State is to put its public finances in order again. For this too cooperation is necessary.

6. No detailed plan can be given for this cooperation. The Paris Conference in 1919 was based mainly on French plans. Only a state of affairs that develops organically will last. It is therefore suggested that an arbitration treaty be signed at once and that a European Economic Council be formed which would remain in permanent session. It may have various departments for various spheres of activity. The main thing is that it should remain in session. Its headquarters, containing office rooms and archives, will have to be permanent. Individual sessions can be held in various places. The presidency can be easily agreed upon. As far as Germany is concerned, questions of prestige must not count in this matter.

This Economic Council will have the following tasks:

(a) To reduce the difficulties involved in travel between the individual countries as quickly as possible and in particular to simplify regulations. The aim must be the ability to travel throughout Europe again without a passport and as soon as possible.

(b) To abolish customs barriers gradually. It is impossible to abolish customs barriers at once without serious economic damage to nearly every country.

(c) To prepare uniform regulations for communications on the basis of the World Postal Union and agreements for railways, shipping etc.

(d) To make uniform as far as possible the trade laws, exchange laws, and finally civil laws of the various countries.

(e) To support the coordination of all efforts helping to bring countries together spiritually, economically and culturally, by making use of existing national organizations rather than by creating new ones.

(f) In this way the Economic Council in permanent session will gradually achieve what cannot be planned in advance. A European Federation could be the end-product of this development in which successful economic cooperation will create the basis for political cooperation. It cannot be said what this political federation will one day look like; it will hardly equal the United States because of the lack of a common language and because the phases of the historical development of individual States are too diverse. But we do not want to set here an ideological limit for their unification. . . .

After describing the need for the creation of a League of Nations, he emphasized that to be successful it would need to be strengthened by a strong 'moral sense'.

This moral sense can only be recreated if every nation restores religious ties as the basis for moral attitudes and if these moral ties are respected and felt to be indispensable for international politics as well. We must take the big step of abandoning double moral standards which permit one morality for national use and one for international to exist side by side. This is the demand God makes of us after the fearful experiences of these recent decades and particularly of the decade just past.

It depends more on this and on a new spirit than on individual plans. Only in this way will healthy organic developments come about and make progress; only in this way can the danger of ossification and senility and therefore of new wars be forestalled.

12 Von Hassell on the Resistance leaders

Goerdeler's plans and those of other conservative Opposition leaders were noted for their emphasis on moral values and were characterized more by the principles for any postwar settlement than by an awareness of the practical difficulties of achieving a settlement. This was inevitable so long as there was uncertainty about the outcome of the war. Goerdeler was frequently criticized for his persistent optimism and his many illusions by other Opposition leaders, including von Hassell, who in his diary entry of 21 December 1941 referred to Goerdeler's disagreements with younger Resistance leaders, the general lack of political sophistication among them, and the absence of any widely-accepted central figure in the Opposition.

What has engrossed and disquieted me most during the past weeks has been the numerous conferences on questions concerning a change of the regime. One major difficulty is Goerdeler. He is too sanguine, always sees things as he wishes to see them, and in many ways is a real reactionary, though otherwise he has splendid qualities. Nevertheless, we finally agreed on the main issues. We also agreed, despite all doubts about his position, that the Crown Prince must come to the fore. Beck assented, although through past connexions he knows the Crown Prince well.

The principal difficulty with Beck is that he is very theoretical. As Popitz says, a man of tactics but little willpower, whereas Goerdeler has great willpower but no tact(ics). Popitz himself often displays a slightly professorial manner, the somewhat abstract views of an administrator. Nevertheless all three are capital men.

I have always feared that we have too little contact with younger circles. This fear has now been demonstrated, but only to reveal new and formidable difficulties. First of all, I had a long talk with Trott during which he passionately contended for the avoidance, within as well as outside the country, of any semblance of 'reaction', of a 'gentlemen's club', or of 'militarism'. Therefore, though he also is a monarchist, we must under no circumstances have a monarchy now, for a monarchy would not win the support of the people or win confidence abroad. 'Converted' Social Democrats, that is, Christian Social Democrats, one of whom (a former Reichstag deputy) he named, would never go along with us on the monarchy and would wait for the next group.

To these negative points he added the single positive thought, that Niemöller should be made Chancellor of the Reich. He was, on the one hand, the strongest internationally recognized exponent of anti-Hitlerism, and, on the other hand, the most popular reformer here and the one most likely to appeal to the Anglo-Saxon world.

Afterwards I met the alert, cultured Peter Yorck,[1] a true scion of a family of high intellect, though sometimes too inclined to theorizing. He expressed similar

[1] Count Peter Yorck von Wartenburg, executed in August 1944, was a member of the staff of the Reich Price Commissioner.

sentiments. Finally, at Yorck's own request, I went to see him again. There I met Moltke,[1] Trott, and Guttenberg. All four, under the leadership of Trott, set to work on me furiously.

On the day of my departure, at Popitz's, Fritzi Schulenburg[2] hammered away at the same theme. Of the five young men he was easily the most sober-minded, the most politically conscious, but, on the other hand, the most prejudiced against the Crown Prince, since his father had absolutely enjoined him to oppose any such possibility because of the stand taken by the Crown Prince in the crisis of 1918. So far as Prince Louis Ferdinand[3] is concerned, he apparently considers himself the man of the hour, though he lacks many essential qualities. He seems to have got along without them by insisting that they are part of his inheritance.

Goerdeler takes an almost completely unsympathetic attitude towards the ideas of these young men, who for their part disapprove of him. He maintains that he himself has good relations with the Social Democrats. In the matter of the Crown Prince his views are less positive.

Beck firmly supports Goerdeler in this as in most questions. Popitz, more than anyone, favours the Crown Prince as an immediate solution. All three emphasize that we should not permit ourselves to be unduly influenced by the passing moods of the populace; but Goerdeler, of course, overestimates the degree to which people in general resent the present system and long for a move towards liberation.

I am trying to find some sort of connecting link with the younger men by arguing somewhat as follows: The premiss, 'No reaction, but attempt to get popular support', was correct. Therefore it is most earnestly to be desired that we find, to head the government, a man whose name will stand both for liberation and for a policy. This is important also, even if only to a limited degree, in the interest of foreign policy. This interest is necessary because the national character of this change, rising out of the peculiar will and needs of our people, can be maintained only if we do not look over our shoulder at other countries; also because the Christian-pacifist circles among the Anglo-Saxon peoples, on whom Trott counts most heavily, are entirely useless as a dependable political factor.

In general I am against Trott's theoretical and visionary outlook. Unfortunately the kind of personality we are hoping for is not to be found. I am convinced that the man whom Trott has proposed (Niemöller) has some unsuitable characteristics. He is somewhat unbending, non-political, and not a good strategist. Aside from all this, I think that, after the first effect had worn off, he would not be a successful symbol. On the contrary, he might even create opposition.

In this state of affairs there is nothing left but to act without such a popular personality—for act we must, and that very soon. It is clear that the situation has reached such a pitch that the role of any new government will be an utterly thankless one, taken on in the middle of a mess—indeed, the role of a kind of liquidator.

We must bear in mind that we may be used only to clean up and will then be

[1] Helmut James Count von Moltke, a landowner, was leader of the Kreisau Circle (see below, pp. 320-1) and worked on the staff of the High Command of the Armed Forces. He was executed in January 1945.
[2] Fritz-Dietlof Count von der Schulenburg, deputy Police-President of Berlin, was executed in August 1944.
[3] Prince Louis Ferdinand was a grandson of the last Kaiser, William II.

replaced by others, or that we may fail altogether. The task is to manage this as well as humanly possible. Moreover, we shall have to assemble a government as free as possible of any whiff of reaction, militarism, or the like. Action, however, is now the main thing!

So far as the Hohenzollern family is concerned, the situation is serious enough. Nevertheless, in spite of all doubts, this is the one way which still offers the greatest hope of coordinated action. The decision will have to be made according to the situation of the moment; and the one who swings into action first will have the most to say.

Trott asked me whether I would back out if Brauchitsch accepted the Niemöller solution. I countered by asking whether he, Trott, wanted to influence Brauchitsch in this sense.

13 *The Manifesto of the Munich students, February 1943*

The prospect of national defeat together with the mounting bombing of German cities provided further justification for opposition but the exploitation of popular discontent still remained virtually impossible with the Gestapo's swift method of tracking down Resistance groups. This was the fate of the 'White Rose' movement, a group of students at Munich University, inspired by religious and moral idealism. They were led by Hans and Sophie Scholl, medical and philosophy students, and had the backing of their teacher, Professor Kurt Huber. From the middle of 1942 they began distributing anti-Nazi leaflets which attempted to draw attention to the moral degradation caused by Nazism and advocated passive resistance to the Nazis. The last of their leaflets appeared on 18 February, shortly after the German surrender at Stalingrad. The Scholls chose to make a public demonstration. Instead of following their earlier practice of circulating the leaflets, they displayed them all over the university buildings. This last declaration by the Munich students demanded the restoration of personal and political freedom and attacked the Nazi Party defiantly:

Fellow Students!

The nation is profoundly shaken by the defeat of our troops at Stalingrad. Three hundred and thirty thousand Germans have been senselessly and irresponsibly led to death and destruction through the cunning strategy of a corporal from World War I. Our Führer, we thank you! The German people are growing restive. Are we to go on handing over the fate of our armies to an amateur? Are we to offer up what is left of German youth to the base instincts of the Party clique? Never. The time is coming for the youth of Germany to settle accounts with the most loathsome tyranny ever to be visited upon our people. In the name of German youth we demand from this Adolf Hitler Government the return of our personal freedom, our most treasured possession, which he has filched from us in the most despicable way.

We have grown up in a state which has ruthlessly muzzled every free expression of opinion. During the critical years of our development the Hitler Youth, the SA, and the SS have tried to regiment us, to revolutionize us, to dope us. 'Ideological education' [*Weltanschauliche Schulung*] is the name they give to their contemptible method of drowning in a flood of empty phrases every attempt we make to think for ourselves. The pick of their leaders [*Führerauslese*] are being groomed in Nazi camps by the present Party bosses who are educating them to be the godless, shameless, unscrupulous exploiters and murderous leaders of the next generation. Those of us who work with our minds will of course be expected to twist everything into the service of this new race of masters. Front-line troops will be ordered about by student leaders and *Gauleiteraspiranten* as if they were nothing but schoolboys. Gauleiters are free to make a shameless mockery of the honour of our women students. German women studying at the University of Munich gave the right answer to that sort of smearing of their honour; indeed, German students have stood up in defence of their colleagues.[1]

That is the beginning of the struggle for our right of self-determination, without which any really creative work is impossible. We all owe a vote of thanks to our brave comrades who have set us such a shining example!

For us there can be only one cry. Fight against the Party! Give up your membership of Party organizations in which all political expression has been muzzled. Quit those courses offered by SS leaders or other Party stool-pigeons! This is just as important a matter as objective truth or academic freedom! And we will not be terrified by any threats, no, not even by the threat to close the universities. This is something which concerns every single one of us now and in the future: our freedom and honour as members of a morally responsible nation.

Freedom and honour! For ten long years Hitler and his mob have perverted, degraded and twisted those two fine German words beyond recognition as indeed only a playboy could, taking the most prized possessions of a nation and casting them before swine. Just what freedom and honour means to them they have shown in these ten years, a period during which they have destroyed all material and intellectual freedom as well as blotted out every trace of morality from the German people. Surely the stupidest of our countrymen has had his eyes opened by this horrible blood bath which has drenched the whole of Europe and is now continuing that process day after day, all in the name of national freedom and honour. The name of Germany will be tainted for ever unless youth arises, seeking at the same time vengeance and expiation by annihilating these torturers and so help in the building of a new spiritual Europe. Fellow students! The German people look to us! As in 1813 the people looked to us to destroy the Napoleonic terror, so today in 1943 they look to us to destroy the terror of National Socialism. Beresina and Stalingrad are burning in the east; the dead of Stalingrad adjure us.

'Rise up my people; the signal fires are ablaze!'

Our people are ready to revolt against the enslavement of Europe by the Nazis and look to the triumph of a new faith in freedom and honour.

14 *The Programme of the Kreisau Circle, 9 August 1943*

Christianity formed the basis of the ideas of the Kreisau Circle, a group of mainly young conservative aristocratic intellectuals, meeting at von Moltke's estate at Kreisau (Silesia) to discuss Germany's postwar rehabilita-

[1] A reference to the indecent suggestion recently made to students in Munich by Paul Giesler, a Gauleiter in Bavaria, that girl students should contribute to the national cause by giving birth to a son once a year. The student audience responded by jeering.

tion. The group, which began to meet in 1940, included Adam von Trott zu Solz, the diplomat and philosopher, and Count Peter Yorck von Wartenburg, but some liberals and even Socialists joined it later (such as Julius Leber, the Social Democrat, Jakob Kaiser of the Christian Trade Unions and Eugen Gerstenmaier, the Evangelical pastor). The Kreisau Circle held several conferences during 1942–43 to discuss the nature of postwar Germany and Europe. It provided the intellectual inspiration for the German Opposition, but its proposals were highly utopian and implied a return to the universal society of the Middle Ages with its rejection of much of modern industrial society. Its members emphasized the importance of a 'new beginning'. Many of their ideas were incorporated in the programme of the Kreisau Circle, called 'Principles for the New Order of Germany':

The Government of the German Reich sees in Christianity the basis for the moral and religious revival of our people, for the overcoming of hatred and lies, for the reconstruction of the European community of nations.

The starting point is man's commitment to the divine order on which his inner and outer existence depends. Only when one has succeeded in making this order the criterion for relations between people and nations can the disorder of our time be overcome and a genuine state of peace be created. The internal reorganization of the Reich is the basis for the achievement of a just and lasting peace.

In view of the collapse of a power structure which no longer feels any obligations and which is based solely on its command of technology, European humanity is faced above all with this task. The way to its solution lies in the determined and active realization of Christian values. The Reich Government is therefore determined to realize the following indispensable requirements, which cannot be renounced inwardly or outwardly, with all available means:

1. Justice which has been trampled under foot must be raised again and made predominant over all areas of human life. Under the protection of conscientious, independent judges free from fear of men, it is the foundation for all future plans for peace.

2. Freedom of faith and of conscience will be safeguarded. Existing laws and regulations which violate these principles will be repealed at once.

3. Totalitarian moral constraint must be broken and inviolable dignity of the human person must be recognized as the basis for the order of justice and peace which is to be striven for. Everybody will partake in the responsibility for the various social, political and international spheres of life. The right to work and to hold property will be under public protection, irrespective of race, nationality or faith.

4. The basic unit of peaceful social life is the family. It will be under public protection which, apart from education, will also secure its material needs: food, clothing, dwelling, garden and health.

5. Work must be organized in such a way that it promotes personal responsibility and does not let it wither. Apart from creating the material conditions of work and further professional training this requires everyone's effective co-responsibility in the factory and further in the general economic context to which his work

contributes. Through this he will contribute to the growth of a healthy and durable structure of life in which the individual, his family, and the community can achieve organic development in a balanced economic system. Those who manage the economy must safeguard these basic requirements.

6. The political responsibility of every individual demands his cooperation in the self-government of small communities which are to be revived. Rooted and tested in these, his co-determination in the State and in the community of nations must be secured by elected representatives and in this way he must be convinced of his co-responsibility for political events.

7. The special responsibility and loyalty due from every individual to his national origin, to his language and to the intellectual and historical traditions of his people must be guarded and respected. But it must not be misused for the concentration of political power or for the degrading, persecution, or suppression of foreign races. The free and peaceful development of national culture can no longer be reconciled with the claim to absolute sovereignty of individual States. Peace requires the creation of an arrangement comprising individual States. As soon as the free agreement of all nations concerned is guaranteed, those responsible for this arrangement must have the right to demand obedience, reverence, if necessary even the risking of life and property for the highest political authority of the community of nations. . . .

15 The July Plot: the scene in the War Ministry

The Kreisau Circle provided a stimulus to the Opposition, but it was not conspiratorial in the sense of actively plotting to overthrow Hitler. In March 1943 Schlabrendorff's attempt to kill Hitler by blowing up his aircraft had failed. During 1943–44 the Opposition suffered many losses through arrests by the Gestapo, including most leaders of the Kreisau Circle. Admiral Canaris and Major-General Hans Oster, who had both used their high positions in the Counter-Intelligence Service to acquire information for the Opposition, were sacked. The main impetus behind plans to assassinate Hitler was now provided by the 36-year-old Count Claus Schenk von Stauffenberg, who had been posted to Berlin in the autumn of 1943 as Chief of Staff to General Olbricht in the Ministry of War. Stauffenberg differed from Goerdeler and other older conservative leaders of the Opposition and pressed for radical action against the Nazi regime. The outcome of these plans was the plot to kill Hitler and other leading Nazis at Hitler's headquarters at Rastenburg in East Prussia on 20 July 1944. Stauffenberg himself deposited the bomb there during one of Hitler's conferences and left before it exploded. Assuming that Hitler had been assassinated, he at once left for Berlin. Hitler had in fact not been killed, but news of his survival was delayed because of the confusion. Delays in setting in motion the plan for seizing power further contributed to the disaster of the July Plot. Stauffenberg arrived just before five o'clock at the Ministry of War in the Bendlerstrasse and started contacting others involved in the conspiracy. But the SS were alerted and a broadcast at nine o'clock announced to the country that Hitler was alive and would make an address later that night. Otto John, an official of the Lufthansa company who had worked for the Resistance, described what happened in the Ministry of War that day:

On 20 July between five and six o'clock in the afternoon Haeften telephoned and told me to come at once. 'We're taking over,' he said. Colonel Fritz Jaeger met me at the second-floor entrance in the Bendlerstrasse. My first impression was that he had been arrested; just behind him to the left and right stood two soldiers with steel helmets and bayonets. Next to them was an SS colonel with cap and pistol, while Jaeger, wearing no cap and carrying no arms, stood between the men, looking as if he were about to be led away. But it was an illusion. Jaeger came up and saluted me in the most friendly manner. He directed me to Fromm's ante-room. 'I can't leave here for the moment,' he said. And winking in the direction of the SS officer, he made me understand that the man was his prisoner. It was of course Piffraeder.

I had expected to find Hansen in Fromm's ante-room, but he was not there, and no one could tell me where he was. However, Stauffenberg was next door busily telephoning in the chief's office. He waved to me through the half-open glass door. Having nothing else to do, I watched what was going on. My idea of the General Staff in action had been rather different from the truth, probably because I had never been a soldier myself. Generals and other senior officers were simply hanging around, none of them apparently knowing what he was supposed to do. Count Schwerin gave me an account of the situation; he said that although Hitler was dead, the Deutschlandsender, the main radio station, was spreading a report asserting that the Führer had been only slightly wounded. Schwerin concluded by saying, 'Anyhow, Beck is absolutely determined to see the thing through. If only the occupation of Broadcasting House had come off properly!' . . .

For the time being there was nothing I could do except hang around and observe. In spite of the apparent turmoil, all I heard and saw, particularly snatches of Stauffenberg's telephone calls, gave me the impression that the whole Army was up in arms against the Nazis. It never occurred to me at that moment that they could reverse the process and stop everything. I was very impressed by Stauffenberg when he came into the ante-room and, taking a receiver from one of the girls, began to issue instructions: 'Stauffenberg speaking. Jawohl. Ja. All orders . . . Yes, as I said, all orders are to be executed at once . . . all radio and news agencies to be occupied . . . all resistance to be crushed. You'll probably get counter-orders from the Führer's headquarters, but they're not, do you understand, not valid. The Army has taken over power. No one except us is authorized to give orders. As always in hours of extreme emergency, the soldier has to take over. Yes, Witzleben has been appointed supreme commander—it's purely a formal appointment. Now go ahead and occupy all the news agencies. You understand. Heil!'

This conversation gave me confidence that the Army was determined to see the emergency through. Soon I heard Haeften, acting on instructions from Stauffenberg, order an elderly major to prepare a suitable room for the custody overnight of certain 'doubtful characters'. So I believed our cause was really won. I had little doubt that Himmler would try to put up some resistance through the SS, but I was sure Hitler was dead and that I could trust the resolution of the generals and the loyalty of their officers and men.

Having no part in this military action, I told Schwerin that I thought I had better go and see if some understanding could be reached between Popitz and Leber. Schwerin agreed this was a good idea and said that I should go and see Popitz at once. He promised to telephone me if there should be any further developments. So I told Haeften that as there was nothing further I could do at the Bendlerstrasse, I would go, but that I would telephone him the following morning at eight o'clock. 'By then we'll either have done it, or we'll be strung up,' said Haeften. I gave him a questioning look, but he shook my hand and said with a smile, 'Till tomorrow then. Auf Wiedersehen!'

I left the Bendlerstrasse about 8.45; strangely enough I remember looking at the clock in the near-by Underground station and noting that it was exactly 8.53.

Popitz's house was at Dahlem, near my own house which I shared with my brother. I had an arrangement with Popitz that I might call to see him at any time — even at night provided I could see a faint strip of light at his window, which was the sign that he had not gone to bed, or that it would not be dangerous to call.

You must remember I still believed Hitler was dead, and that the radio announcements to the contrary were false. I was delighted that we had succeeded at last, and I was anxious to tell Popitz the good news. But by the time I had reached Dahlem there was no sign of light at his window, and I did not dare to break our arrangement. I could tell him in the morning. So I went home to tell my brother what I believed had happened at Rastenburg.

When I got there, I found my brother with Claus Bonhoeffer. We opened a bottle of champagne to drink to the glorious future. We were too excited to sleep, and stayed up drinking champagne. We had the radio on, waiting for further news. The continuous recital of military music which had been going on all evening worried me slightly; I wondered why it was we had not yet taken over the broadcasting stations. Then, around one o'clock, Hitler spoke. It was unmistakably his voice. All our high hopes vanished; we listened, breathless with sudden anxiety and bitter disappointment. What would happen now? I telephoned the Bendlerstrasse, using the secret extension number that connected up to Stauffenberg's office—I seem to remember it was 1293. But there was no reply. I realized that they must have arrested Stauffenberg. . . .

16 *Organized demonstrations in support of Hitler*

The Propaganda Ministry had acted swiftly in turning the tables on the conspirators, who had neglected to seize control of the radio stations. Goebbels, who had remained in Berlin, took charge of operations there until Hitler arrived. Goebbels was concerned that the shock of the July Plot should not damage public morale. On 23 July his Ministry sent this order to Propaganda Offices throughout the Reich to organize demonstrations in support of Hitler:

HIGHLY CONFIDENTIAL

Over the next few days a wave of demonstrations of loyalty to the Führer must be organized in all *Gaue* and districts of the Reich as a spontaneous reaction of our people to the nefarious assassination attempt on the Führer. Full participation of local military units must be secured through collaboration with the appropriate military headquarters. Apart from these demonstrations of loyalty, factory meetings must be held, with the cooperation of the *Gau* leaders of the German Labour Front, at which the workpeople will express their National Socialist loyalty in congratulatory addresses to the Führer. . . .

The German press will receive daily instructions to provide effective publicity for the demonstrations and factory meetings as well as for the handing over and sending off of the congratulatory addresses in the various *Gaue*.

The speakers at the demonstrations must emphasize the following points in particular: . . .

    1. Only a small group of reactionary traitors are behind the assassination attempt and putsch. . . .

    3. It was this camarilla which from hatred against the movement and snobbish class spirit has always tried to prevent the conversion of the Army to National Socialism; the same clique always opposed the giving of leading posts in the Army to convinced National Socialist officers who had distinguished themselves at the front. It opposed the giving of the highest awards like the Knight's Cross to N.C.O.s and men from the ranks and it opposed making officers of soldiers from the ranks.

    4. The Army, tested again and again in the most difficult situations at the front, emerges without a blemish from the attempted putsch.

The most experienced speakers must be employed so as to guarantee the decisive success of the wave of demonstrations which have been ordered. Press and pictorial reports of the most impressive events must be sent without delay to the Propaganda Department of the Ministry for Enlightenment and Propaganda for further evaluation.

17 *General Oster on the outlook of Army officers*

Stauffenberg and the other main conspirators were arrested and executed within a few hours of the plot collapsing. The July Plot was used by the Nazis to round up scores of people who had been involved, or were suspected of involvement, in the Opposition. Some like General Beck and Field-Marshal Rommel committed suicide; others like Goerdeler and Witzleben faced trial and were executed. The trial before the People's Court was noted for the brutal questioning of Roland Freisler, its President. General Oster, himself one of those executed, gave evidence on the outlook of officers in the Army and this was summed up in a report prepared for the Security Chief, Kaltenbrunner:

Hans Oster spoke with greater clarity than any of the others involved about the intellectual and political outlook of the older, professional officers. What governed their attitude, he said, and made it exceptionally complicated, was the fact that in the space of thirty years (1914–44), i.e. barely a generation, they had served three entirely different political systems, namely, first the monarchy, then every sort of government under the 'System',[1] and lastly the National Socialist State. In a statement on the officers' attitude, Oster says:

'Under the monarchy it was really a sort of boyish enthusiasm for soldiering

[1] 'The System' was the standard Nazi term of abuse for parliamentary democracy as practised under the Weimar Republic.

that sent us into the Army. It never even crossed our minds that one day the whole regime might collapse. Politics meant nothing to us. We were in uniform and that was all that mattered. It was "not done" to read the *Berliner Tageblatt* or the *Frankfurter Zeitung* in the "Kasino".'

The collapse of the monarchy as the result of the revolution in 1918 had been a fearful shock and surprise to the officers, for they were all monarchists at heart.

'It was like being hit on the head with a hammer—the collapse in 1918 and the way the monarchy ended in a rickety affair of political parties.'

The State that emerged then faced the older officers with a fresh decision. 'After the gravest struggle with ourselves we finally decided, against our inclinations, to serve the Socialist Republic and under a new flag. What we hoped and intended was to help the country get over the worst of it.'

General von Seeckt, he said, had forbidden the Reichswehr of the day to engage in any political activities whatever. Even under the monarchy the officers had deliberately paid no attention to current politics or political movements, but now they were ordered to ignore current politics by the law itself, so to speak.

'When the Army was only 100,000 strong the system of training made us into non-political soldiers in the crucial years of our military development, and we learned that we were to obey the Head of the State.'

In his written statement Oster says:

'We were all quite sure that under the political conditions of the times this was the only road to our objective, namely, getting the troops under discipline again, and making them the foundation and preparation for building up the Army later on into the Wehrmacht of today. The words "party" and "playing politics" had an unpleasant ring for us.'

With the upheaval [*Umbruch*] of 1933, says Oster, the soldiers felt released from the strain which the 'System' had laid on their consciences. The return to a vigorous patriotic policy, the rearmament, the re-introduction of universal military service—to the officers all this meant a return to older traditions. Under the 'System' soldiers had done their work because it was their duty: but these features of the National Socialist work of reconstruction had warmed their hearts. 'All the same, as professional soldiers, we too had to come to terms with this upheaval. Some managed it quicker than others.

'Not everyone, for example, understood the identification of "Party" and "State". After all, we had never had any use for the word "party".

'We had to swallow a good deal, too—some things that really stuck in our throats—the "Stormtroopers" Song—reaction—shootings. The Röhm putsch—Schleicher—Bredow—the Blomberg affair—the Fritsch trial—the Waffen-SS being made the elite of the Wehrmacht. In my opinion the Blomberg business was the worst of all because it did terrible damage to the reputation of the corps of officers. Putting up with all that was pretty hard for some of us.'

Ever since 1933, in Oster's opinion, certain sections of the corps of officers had remained totally impervious to National Socialism as a *Weltanschauung* that embraced the whole of life. There were still men here and there in the corps of officers who had never grasped, or had already forgotten, the fact that National Socialism had brought forth a revolution in the true sense of the word—a revolution entailing reforms that had become necessary, painful adjustments and the renunciation of much that used to be dear.

At the end of his statement Oster makes this admission:

'We were not born into the world of politics; we are not political fanatics fighting to get power in the State for one party. That is not what we were taught to do. In November 1923 we did not march in a solid mass to the *Feldherrnhalle*: on the contrary, my general gave me the unwelcome job of disbanding a brigade of the Reichswehr that was among the units that had joined Kapp.'

The foregoing amounts to an admission on Oster's part that to some extent he still subscribes to the ideal of the non-political officer (see also the report dated 20 August 1944). The account he gives is true of a whole section of the older officers, and it shows that in fighting the ideological battle and carrying out a Socialist revolution, the National Socialist Reich was obliged to use a certain number of officers who so far from realizing the historic nature of the revolution were politically more inclined to watch and wait, or else would really rather have sided with our opponents.

• • •

PART IV

The New Social Order: Idea and Reality

The Nazi 'seizure of power' in 1933 was more than just a change of government. The Nazi movement had always claimed that it would substitute for the political and social divisions which had bedevilled Weimar Germany a new 'national community' in which class conflict and ideological cleavages would disappear and be replaced by a sense of national solidarity and by a commitment on the part of every individual to put the interests of the nation before self. The Nazis believed that it was possible to shape social reality in accordance with ideology. They thought this could be achieved by means of propaganda and indoctrination. Propaganda, therefore, was not confined to the conventional political fields though here its role was greater than ever before. Indeed Goebbels believed that 'while in a democratic state public opinion largely determines the nation's political course, in the authoritarian state the state guides public opinion towards its goals and determines its own policy'. But Nazi ideology tried to claim the whole man — in his political, economic, social and even private life. Propaganda therefore had the function of creating a 'new' man and a 'new' society.

Yet this aim was fruitless and for two reasons. In the first place, the ideology which the Party wished to impose was itself contradictory. It was a product of the unresolved tensions created by the process of modernization which occurred in Germany unusually late and with exceptional speed. It reflected the dream, which had haunted the German Right for the past sixty years, of a return to the age before modern capitalism and industrialization had disrupted the traditional patterns of the old society. It was therefore anti-capitalist, anti-industrial, anti-urban. And yet, on the other hand, it was also a product of this process of modernization in its hostility to the old social hierarchy, in its determination to create a society which would be in theory classless, but in fact divided into a new elite on the one side and an undifferentiated mass on the other. Thus, in its attempt to replace traditional social and family ties by the one tie of personal subordination to the regime, it worked in direct conflict with those archaic *Gemeinschaft* values which it claimed to uphold.

The second reason why the Nazi objective of transforming society in accordance with its ideology was in vain was because its anti-capitalist, anti-industrial and anti-urban goals conflicted with the dynamic and aggressive nature of the movement and with the requirements imposed by the major objective of its leader — territorial expansion. Rearmament and war required maximum industrial output and therefore an expansion both of the industrial and urban sector at the expense of agriculture and rural society, and of the big firms at the expense of the small man whom Nazi ideology was committed to encourage. There was no way out of this conflict between ideological theory and economic reality, despite the efforts of

331

propaganda to persuade people to accept an alternative reality to the one that actually faced them. The Nazis therefore, who came to power as the champions of the socially and economically most backward elements in the community, ended by taking Germany further forward on the path towards modernization, and in a shorter space of time, than any of their predecessors.

There was only one field in which idea and reality increasingly came to coincide and this was the role of the Jews in German society. Among the medley of National Socialist ideas, certain ideas were paramount. One of Hitler's consistent themes from his early days in politics until the defeat of Germany was his determination to settle the 'Jewish question'. And while initially he was forced to rein in his more enthusiastic supporters in the interests of economic stability, his determination remained to remove the Jews from German society. As soon as the regime had consolidated itself internally and externally, he intensified the pressure on the Jews along with his intensification of diplomatic pressure. In the shadow of the Czech crisis social and economic restrictions on the Jews increased month by month. Finally, the war, for which he claimed that the Jews were responsible, gave him the opportunity and the excuse for the most radical policy of all — extermination.

12 Ideology and Society

1 Hitler on the ideological aims of National Socialism

Speaking to the Party faithful in September 1933, at the first NSDAP Rally at Nuremberg after the 'seizure of power', Hitler distinguished between the political and the ideological revolution:

. . . On 30 January 1933 the National Socialist Party was entrusted with the political leadership of the Reich. At the end of March, the National Socialist revolution was completed on the external plane, completed so far as regards the entire take-over of political power. But only those who have not fully comprehended the character of this tremendous struggle can believe that the struggle between ideologies [*Weltanschauungen*] has thereby come to an end. This would be so if the National Socialist movement wanted nothing other than the ordinary parties. These do indeed seem to reach the peak of their ambition and therefore of their existence on the day of the take-over of political power. Ideologies, however, see in the achievement of political power only the prerequisite for the beginning of the fulfilment of their real mission. The word 'ideology' already contains the solemn proclamation of the decision to base all actions upon a particular initial position and therefore a clear orientation. Such an attitude may be right or wrong: it is the basis for the attitude to be adopted towards all the phenomena and processes of life and therefore is a law which binds and determines all action. . . .

Propaganda

2 The tasks of the Ministry of Propaganda

The Ministry for People's Enlightenment and Propaganda was established in March 1933 under Dr Joseph Goebbels, the propaganda chief of the NSDAP. As a new creation, it was from the beginning more fully staffed with Nazis than the older ministries. Most of the high positions in the Ministry were held by officials from the Propaganda Department of the NSDAP. Like Goebbels himself, they held positions in both Party and State. The new ministry took over many functions from other ministries: propaganda abroad from the Foreign Ministry; the supervision of press, radio and cultural activities from the Ministry of the Interior; commercial advertising from the Ministry of Economics; tourism from the Ministry of Transport. Goebbels was very ambitious for his new ministry. He saw its creation as 'revolutionary', since it represented the new 'union between Government and people'. In a speech on 15 March he explained the aims of the Ministry:

The most important tasks of this Ministry must be the following. Firstly, all propaganda ventures and all institutions for the enlightenment of the people throughout the Reich and the states must be centralized in one hand. Furthermore, it must be our task to instil into these propaganda facilities a modern feeling and bring them up to date. Technology must not be allowed to proceed ahead of the Reich; the Reich must go along with technology. Only the most modern things are good enough. We are living now in an age when the masses must support policies. . . . It is the task of State propaganda so to simplify complicated ways of thinking that even the smallest man in the street may understand.

3 *The Government Press Conference*

Consistent with Goebbels's idea that the purpose of the press was not only to inform but also to instruct, the daily press conferences, which had been a regular feature since the beginning of the Weimar Republic, changed their function. The press conferences were now organized by the Press Department of the Propaganda Ministry, which controlled attendance at them and issued instructions on the handling of news. The proceedings of these conferences were secret. Fritz Sänger, who represented the *Frankfurter Zeitung* at them for eight years, commented:

The press conference *with* the Reich Government founded in 1917 was changed by the National Socialists on their seizure of political power in Germany in 1933 into a 'press conference *of* the Reich Government'. So it was now an institution of the Government. There it gave directives, laid down language regulations, and there were daily opportunities to give directives to the press 'to bring it into line' (a phrase in fashion then) and to inform it so far as seemed advisable. Before 1933, these press conferences were run by journalists and the Government was their guest; after 1933 they were run by the Government.

Every German paper was anxious to have a representative at the Reich Press Conference. Some papers (the big ones like the *Frankfurter Zeitung* of whose Berlin editorial office I was a member) had several representatives there, and some who attended the press conference represented several papers. Every representative in the press conference became a 'member' there, that is, he was admitted or accredited. Previously, the board of the press conference was responsible for admissions; after 1933 it was in the hands of the Reich Ministry for People's Enlightenment and Propaganda—its German Press Department.

Several of the Berlin editors of the *Frankfurter Zeitung* were members, including myself. The Reich press conference took place at 12 noon on weekdays; later on, in the war years, at a second time, usually at 5 p.m., but occasionally also late in the evening and even during the night or very early in the morning. The summons came by telephone or telegram if it was not the daily noon or evening conference.

In these conferences there was no discussion, we were simply spoken to somewhat one-sidedly (by the Government) and at the most the press asked questions.

4 *Press directives of the Ministry of Propaganda*

The instructions covered multifarious subjects from the suppression of unwelcome news from abroad and emphasis on events favourable to the

Government to a silence about the arrest of notable opponents of the Nazis and the treatment of news items about the Nazi leaders. Hitler, who was a voracious reader of newspapers, was particularly concerned about news on his whereabouts—plans of his visits around the country were rarely disclosed beforehand—and his living habits. Unlike certain other Nazi leaders, Hitler was abstemious; he was a vegetarian and neither smoked nor drank. He wished to maintain an image of modesty and simplicity. A lack of sense of humour may be detected in the following selection of directives of the Propaganda Ministry:

6.vii.33: The Propaganda Ministry once again points out that announcements about future journeys and visits of the Reich Chancellor must not be published under any circumstances, not even if local National Socialist offices give out these announcements. The *Dortmunder Generalanzeiger* yesterday publicized the fact that the Reich Chancellor was to speak at a big SA rally in Dortmund. Following this, the paper (although it is an official Party organ of the NSDAP *Gau* Düsseldorf) got a message from the Propaganda Ministry in which the behaviour of the *Dortmunder Generalanzeiger* was sharply criticized and disapproved of. National Socialist Party sources comment that the paper would have been banned for an indefinite period if it had been a bourgeois paper and not a Party organ. This measure shows clearly the necessity of watching out for and checking announcements of future visits by the Chancellor.

12.xi.33: Reports on the protective custody of Duke Albrecht of Württemberg must not be published under any circumstances. Purely for your information, Duke Albrecht this morning refused to take part in the election. This came to the notice of the public, which assembled in a great crowd in front of his flat. Duke Albrecht then made derogatory remarks to the crowd about the Reich Government and the new State. He had to be taken into protective custody because of pressure from the crowd.

6.iv.35: The Propaganda Ministry asks us to put to editors-in-chief the following requests, which must be observed in future with particular care:
    Photos showing members of the Reich Government at dining tables in front of rows of bottles must not be published in future, particularly since it is known that a large number of the Cabinet are abstemious. Ministers take part in social events for reasons of international etiquette and for strictly official purposes, which they regard merely as a duty and not as a pleasure. Recently, because of a great number of photos, the utterly absurd impression has been created among the public that members of the Government are living it up. News pictures must therefore change in this respect.

10.xi.38: With regard to last night's events throughout the Reich[1], Bareckow declared that papers could publish their own reports on the events following the DNB[2] report issued that morning, that is, they could state that here and there

---

[1] The *Kristallnacht*; see pp. 427ff.
[2] The *Deutsche Nachrichten-Büro*—the German Press Agency.

windows had been broken and that synagogues had gone up in flames. He requested that the reports should not be exaggerated—above all, no front page headlines. He also asked that no photos should be published yet. Nor should collective reports from the Reich appear. Of course the papers could mention in their reports that there had been understandable indignation and corresponding actions by the population in other parts of the country.

16.vi.39: Tomorrow, on Saturday evening, there will be an important political event, namely a great rally with a speech by Dr Goebbels in which the minister will make a strong demand for the reintegration of Danzig into the Reich. The papers may be given an excerpt of the Goebbels speech by the Berlin bureau during Saturday. It is a kite to test the international atmosphere for the regulation of the Danzig question, etc.

5 *Editorial Law, 4 October 1933*

The erosion of the independence of the press was only gradual. In 1933 Nazi newspapers accounted for only 2·5 per cent of the total German press. Party newspapers were poor in quality and before the 'seizure of power' had suffered from continual financial difficulties. By 1944, Max Amann, head of the Nazi Eher publishing house, controlled 82 per cent of the 977 papers which remained in Germany. Different methods were employed to bring the press into line with the Government. Left-wing papers were banned soon after Hitler became Chancellor. Exceptional papers such as the highly respected liberal *Frankfurter Zeitung* retained some independence for the purposes of propaganda, but this was slowly whittled down until the paper's final prohibition in 1943. Generally, the press was controlled through the Editorial Law of October 1933. This served in place of an official censorship. Editors were required to follow the dictates of the Government, otherwise they would face the threat of dismissal or imprisonment and the closure of their papers. The ideal editor, in the words of Wilhelm Weiss who edited the *Völkischer Beobachter*, was 'never a journalist exclusively but always and foremost a propagandist, very often a newspaperman, a Party speaker and a Stormtrooper in one person'.

The Reich Government has resolved upon the following law, which is hereby promulgated:

PART I. THE EDITORIAL PROFESSION

Section 1

Participation in the shaping of the intellectual content of the newspapers or political periodicals published within the area of the Reich, whether by written word or by dissemination of news and pictures, and whether carried out as a main employment or based on an appointment to the position of editor-in-chief, is a public task, of which the professional duties and rights are regulated by the State through this law.

Section 2

1. Newspapers and periodicals are printed matter, appearing in regular sequence

at intervals of at most three months, not limiting its circulation to a certain group of persons.

2. All reproductions of writings or illustrations, destined for dissemination, which are produced by means of a mass reproduction process, are to be considered as printed matter.

Section 3

1. The provisions of this law relating to newspapers are also valid for political periodicals.

2. This law does not apply to newspapers and periodicals published by official order.

3. The Reich Minister for People's Enlightenment and Propaganda will determine which periodicals are to be considered as political within the meaning of the law. In case the periodical affects a specific vocational field, he will make the decision in consultation with the highest Reich or state agency concerned.

Section 4

Participation in the shaping of the intellectual content of the German newspapers is also considered as such, even if it does not take place in the management of a newspaper, but in an establishment which is to supply newspapers with intellectual content (the written word, news, or pictures).

PART II. ADMISSION TO THE PROFESSION OF EDITOR

Section 5

Only those persons can be editors who:

1. possess German citizenship;

2. have not lost their civic rights and the qualification for the tenure of public office;

3. are of Aryan descent, and are not married to a person of non-Aryan descent;

4. have completed their 21st year;

5. are competent at business;

6. have been trained in the profession;

7. have the qualities which the task of exerting intellectual influence on the public requires. . . .

Section 22

The editorial group as a whole will watch over their individual professional colleagues' fulfilment of their duty and will look after their rights and their welfare.

Section 23

Editors are legally combined in the Reich Association of the German Press. Every editor belongs to it by virtue of his registration on the professional roster. By virtue of this law the Reich Association becomes a public corporation. It has its headquarters in Berlin.

Section 24

1. The Reich Minister for People's Enlightenment and Propaganda will appoint the head of the Reich Association who will issue a charter for the Reich Association,

which will require the approval of the Minister. The head of the Reich Association
will appoint an advisory council. . . .

Section 36
Whoever works as an editor· despite the fact that he is not registered in the professional rosters, or despite the fact that he has been temporarily prohibited from
exercising his profession, will be punished with imprisonment of up to one year,
or fined. . . .

Control over the press by the Ministry of Propaganda was not absolute.
In February 1934, Hitler appointed Dr Otto Dietrich, a young journalist, to
be Reich Press Chief of the Party with the function of supervising editors and
journalists of Party papers. His appointment can be seen as a move by
Hitler to check Goebbels on the principle of 'Divide and rule', especially
when he made Dietrich a State Secretary in the Propaganda Ministry in 1938
(at a time when Goebbels was out of favour with Hitler because of his affair
with the Czech actress Lydia Barova).

6 *Law relating to the Reich Chamber of Culture, 22 September 1933*
The rivalry of Goebbels and Dietrich and the competition of different
authorities for control of the press (the Foreign Ministry and Party organizations as well as the Propaganda Ministry) was confusing to newspaper editors,
who were required to avoid offending any of them. The influence of Goebbels
and Dietrich was restricted by Max Amann, who in addition to being the
main Nazi publisher had become President of the Reich Press Chamber.
This was one of six chambers of the new Reich Chamber of Culture set up
by Goebbels to centralize control over the whole range of cultural activities.
These chambers acted through the various professional associations as
patronage bodies and could withdraw financial support and recognition from
those artists who incurred the disfavour of the regime. As the law establishing
the Chamber of Culture made clear, it was little more than a subordinate
body of the Ministry of Propaganda (Goebbels was himself President of the
Chamber):

The Reich Government has decreed the following law which is hereby promulgated:
Section 1
The Reich Minister for People's Enlightenment and Propaganda is ordered and
authorized to organize the functions under his jurisdiction into public corporations.
Section 2
Pursuant to Section 1, the following chambers are established:
  1. a Reich Chamber of Archives
  2. a Reich Press Chamber
  3. a Reich Radio Chamber
  4. a Reich Theatre Chamber
  5. a Reich Music Chamber
  6. a Reich Chamber of the Creative Arts. . . .

Section 5
The corporate bodies in Section 2, together with the Provisional Film Chamber,[1] referred to as the Reich Film Chamber, are combined in a Reich Chamber of Culture. The Reich Chamber of Culture is under the supervision of the Reich Minister for People's Enlightenment and Propaganda. It has its headquarters in Berlin. . . .

Section 7
The Reich Minister for People's Enlightenment and Propaganda is authorized to decree laws and general administrative regulations as well as amendments for the purpose of enforcing this law. The laws and general administrative regulations affecting the financial or trade interests of the Reich require the consent of the Reich Minister of Finance, in agreement with the Reich Minister of Economics.

7 *The supervision of station booksellers, May 1942*
One of the professional organizations under the direction of the Reich Press Chamber was the Reich Association of German Station Booksellers. Its function was to vet those who worked in railway bookshops:

Re: Karl Friedrich Menzel, Berlin-Wilmersdorf, Hildegardstr. 4. Born 30.x.96.
    It follows from Section 10 of the first executive regulation of the Reich Chamber of Culture, Law of 1 November 1933, that the admission of a station bookseller to the Reich Press Chamber and to the Reich Association of German Station Booksellers can be refused if facts are available which show that the station bookseller in question does not show the political and moral reliability necessary for carrying out his activity.
    We therefore ask you to send us a short statement on the political, ideological, and denominational attitude and activities of the above mentioned, via the appropriate Reich Propaganda Office.
    When writing this report it is necessary to start from the basic question of whether in your opinion it is justifiable and advisable for Herr Menzel to continue with his occupation as a station bookseller in the context of the reconstruction of the German press in the National Socialist State.

8 *The duty of station booksellers*
Evasion of official regulations usually came to the attention of the authorities. Railway stations were often important as meeting-places in the larger German cities, and station booksellers were under particular supervision since there had been complaints about the sale of foreign newspapers:

The main administration of the Reich railways has been informed that station bookshops have been offering travellers foreign papers even though they had not been asked for. Such a promotion of foreign papers is not approved by the Reich railways as it is laid down in a decree that it must be the first duty of station booksellers to spread German ideas. The leaseholders of station bookshops must be

[1] Established on 14 July 1933.

instructed to desist from everything that could promote the distribution of foreign papers. In the case of serious offences, the lease will be cancelled without notice.

Control over the radio proved easier than control over the press because radio was an innovation in mass communications and therefore less bound by tradition. The broadcasting system was already State-run in 1933, but listening to the radio was still the privilege of a restricted number. Although the NSDAP had not been permitted to make use of the radio before 1933, Goebbels was quick to recognize the importance of broadcasting in view of the Nazis' emphasis on the spoken word. Opening a radio exhibition in Berlin in August 1933, Goebbels referred to the radio as 'the eighth great power': 'What the press was for the nineteenth century, wireless will be for the twentieth.' Hitler in fact made few live broadcasts – his fifty 'political broadcasts' in 1933 were nearly all recordings – as he depended on the response of his audience. The Nazis popularized broadcasting by making cheap sets available to every household. The 'People's Receiver' was put on the market in 1933 at a very reasonable price, so that by 1939 Germany had the highest percentage of radio owners in the world (70 per cent of all households). In addition, the Ministry encouraged community listening, both in factories with the 'Labour Front Receiver' and in community halls.

9 *The technique of Nazi film-making: the celebration of Hitler's fiftieth birthday*

Goebbels's special interest was in the production of films, on which he considered himself an authority. He saw in films a means of reaching an audience of millions (rather than the thousands who attended Party rallies and parades) and was notorious for his frequent interference in the making of them. Unlike broadcasting, the film industry was not already nationalized. It took the Ministry of Propaganda about five years to establish a monopoly, although the industry was not fully nationalized until 1943. Goebbels soon faced the risk of boring his audiences as too many monotonous and tendentious films led to a fall in cinema attendance (because most people went to the cinema for amusement and escape rather than extra instruction in their duties to the fatherland). Straightforward propaganda films – like *Jew Süss* (antisemitic), *Ohm Krüger* (anti-British), and *Hitler Youth Quex* (the glorification of the youthful heroism of a Hitler Youth member) – were few and usually poor in artistic quality. The films of Leni Riefenstahl, on the other hand, demonstrated exceptional technical skill, e.g. the films of the Berlin Olympic Games of 1936 and the Nuremberg Party Rally of 1934 ('*Triumph of the Will*'). Goebbels was best at the production of documentaries, which often succeeded in retaining something of the mood of the occasion. A special film was made of the celebration of Hitler's fiftieth birthday in 1939 for the weekly newsreel, the *Wochenschau*. An official report revealed some of the techniques of Nazi documentaries:

The Führer's fiftieth birthday. Berlin puts on its finery, makes the last preparations for this twentieth of April, 1939, which is to become a unique day of thanksgiving.

The *Filmwochenschau* has a specific assignment in this. Transcending the present, it must create an historic document for the future, to capture in pictures the greatness of this day for all the future to see. This parade must become a paradigm of film reporting. It is not simply a matter of outward form—the spirit of the hour must be captured also, the whole atmosphere of discipline and of concentrated power. Every second of the action must be captured as it occurs. If something is missed, it cannot be repeated and is lost for ever.

The programme begins. The Führer drives between lines of troops from the park [*Lustgarten*] to the parade ground. Immediately on his arrival the march past begins. But in the meantime, unseen by most of the people despite the variety of events, the formation of the units of the parade takes place. Each unit, after first lining the street, is wheeled into a marching column; men on foot and men in vehicles are skilfully interspersed in a colourful order. A broad street, many kilometres long, is completely filled by soldiers of all the armed forces, which must now be ordered into a regular formation for the great moment when they are to march past Adolf Hitler. The twelve pairs of eyes of the twelve cameramen must see more than all the hundreds of thousands of onlookers. And so they do, as the success of this *Wochenschau* demonstrates. . . .

Under a bright, shining sky the birthday itself begins. Cheerful marching tunes resound: the SS *Leibstandarte*[1] give Hitler a birthday serenade. Surrounded by some of his co-workers, among whom Himmler stands out, Hitler receives the homage. The camera lingers lovingly on the Goebbels children, all clothed in white, who stand, curious but well behaved, next to Hitler, thus strengthening his reputation as a true lover of children—a special shot for the women in the audience. Now the picture turns to the crowd. A gigantic chorus in front of the Reich Chancellery swells in a song of jubilation for Hitler. Now Hitler appears on the balcony before the crowd, which breaks out into a repeated ovation.

In the second half of the film the scene shifts finally from the preparations to familiar close-ups, to mass demonstrations, and then at last to the sphere of the official, political, and military. With screaming engines the great automobiles leave the Wilhelmstrasse; Hitler and his entourage depart for the parade. Military orders and marching tunes introduce the second act of the spectacle. Jubilation breaks out: the film is focused, sight and sound, on the exact moment when Hitler passes the Brandenburg Gate between the troops. The Hitler who now, erect and poised, climbs the steps to the canopied platform and takes his place on a 'throne' (already significantly picked out by the camera) to await the parade—this Hitler is not only a 'statesman' but also clearly a field-commander-to-be, who intends to review his armed forces. This is the way the film has it.

The Arts

10 *Correspondence between Furtwängler and Goebbels*

Since the Nazis aimed at transforming society along the lines of their ideology, it was not surprising that their propaganda concerned itself with

[1] Hitler's personal bodyguard.

questions of culture. Early in 1933 Jewish artists were being persecuted, their theatre performances and concert appearances banned, so that many of them emigrated from Germany. The Reich Chamber of Culture and its sub-organizations (see above) provided an official means of controlling artistic activities and succeeded in establishing a certain conformity to the regime. Members of the Prussian Academy of Arts, for instance, were required to sign a declaration that they would not engage in public opposition to the Government 'in view of the changed historical situation'. Total control would have meant the destruction of creative art, which depended on a feeling of independence of political events. Goebbels was willing at first to grant distinguished artists some freedom as he wished to use their prestige. Wilhelm Furtwängler, the conductor, was one of those who chose to remain in Nazi Germany, even though this involved more and more concessions to the Government. He hoped, perhaps naively, to maintain a boundary between the worlds of art and of politics. On 12 April 1933 Furtwängler wrote to Goebbels that the only true criterion was the quality of art. Goebbels in his reply implied that art had a duty to serve the interests of the community:

Dear Reich Minister,
In view of my work over many years with the German public and my inner bond with German music I take the liberty of drawing your attention to events within the world of music which in my opinion need not necessarily follow from the restoration of our national dignity which we all welcome with joy and gratitude. My feelings in this are purely those of an artist. The function of art and artists is to bring together, not to separate. In the final analysis, I recognize only one line of division—that between good and bad art. But while the line of division between Jews and non-Jews is being drawn with a relentless, even a doctrinaire, sharpness, even where the political attitude of the person concerned gives no grounds for complaint, the other line of division, extremely important, if not decisive, in the long run – that between good and bad – is being far too much neglected.
Musical life today, weakened anyway by the world crisis, radio, etc., cannot take any more experiments. One cannot fix the quota for music as with other things necessary for life like potatoes and bread. If nothing is offered in concerts, nobody goes to them. So that for music the question of quality is not simply an idealistic one, but a question of life and death. If the fight against Jews is mainly directed against those artists who, lacking roots themselves and being destructive, try to achieve an effect through kitsch, dry virtuosity and similar things, then this is quite all right. The fight against them and the spirit they embody cannot be pursued emphatically and consistently enough. But if this fight is directed against *real* artists as well, this will not be in the interests of cultural life, particularly because artists anywhere are much too rare for any country to be able to dispense with their work without loss to culture.
It should therefore be stated clearly that men like Walter, Klemperer, Reinhardt, etc. must be allowed in future to express their art in Germany.
Once again, then, let our fight be directed against the rootless, subversive,

levelling, *destructive* spirit, but not against the real artist who is always creative and therefore constructive, however one may judge his art.

In this sense I appeal to you in the name of German art to prevent things from happening which it may not be possible to put right again.

Very respectfully yours,
[signed] WILHELM FURTWÄNGLER

Goebbels replied:

I am grateful for the opportunity given me by your letter to enlighten you about the attitude of the nationally-inclined forces in German life to art in general and to music in particular. In this connexion, I am particularly pleased that, right at the beginning of your letter, you emphasize in the name of German artists that you gladly and gratefully welcome the restoration of our national dignity.

I never assumed that this could be anything other than the case, for I believe that the struggle we wage for Germany's reconstruction concerns the German artist not only in a passive but in an active way. I refer to something the Reich Chancellor said publicly three years ago, before our seizure of power: 'If German artists knew what we shall do for them one day, they would not fight against us but with us.'

It is your right to feel as an artist and to see things from an artist's point of view. But that need not mean that you regard the whole development in Germany in an unpolitical way. Politics too is an art, perhaps the highest and most comprehensive there is, and we who shape modern German policy feel ourselves in this to be artists who have been given the responsible task of forming, out of the raw material of the mass, the firm concrete structure of a people. It is not only the task of art and the artist to bring together, but beyond this it is their task to form, to give shape, to remove the diseased and create freedom for the healthy. Thus, as a German politician, I am unable to recognize only the single line of division which you see— that between good and bad art. Art must not only be good, it must also appear to be connected with the people, or rather, only an art which draws on the people itself can in the final analysis be good and mean something to the people for whom it is created.

There must be no art in the absolute sense as known by liberal democracy. The attempt to serve it would result in the people no longer having any inner relationship to art and in the artist himself isolating and cutting himself off from the driving forces of the time in the vacuum of the '*l'art pour l'art*' point of view. Art must be good; but beyond this it must be responsible, professional, popular [*volksnah*] and aggressive. I readily admit that it cannot take any more experiments. But it would have been more suitable to protest against artistic experiments at a time when the whole world of German art was almost exclusively dominated by the love of experiments on the part of elements alien to the people and of the race who tainted and compromised the reputation of German art.

I am sure you are quite right to say that for music quality is not only an idealistic question but a matter of life and death. You are even more right to join our struggle against the rootlessly destructive artistic style, corrupted by kitsch and dry virtuosity. I readily admit that even Germanic representatives took part in these evil goings-on, but that only proves how deeply the roots of these dangers had penetrated into the German people and how necessary it has seemed, therefore, to oppose them. Real artists are rare. Accordingly they must be promoted and supported. But in that case they must be real artists.

You will always be able to express your art in Germany—in the future too. To complain about the fact that now and then men like Walter, Klemperer, Reinhardt etc. have had to cancel concerts seems to me to be particularly inappropriate at the moment, since on many occasions real German artists were condemned to silence during the past fourteen years; and the events of the past weeks, not approved of by us either, represent only a natural reaction to those facts. At any rate, I am of the opinion that *every real artist* should be given room for free creativity. But in that case, he must, as you say yourself, be a *constructive creative person* and must not be on the side of the rootlessly subversive, levelling, in most cases purely technical professionals whom you rightly criticize. . . .

11 'The Burning of the Books', 10 May 1933

The Nazi attitude to the arts was xenophobic, combined with a belief that culture during Weimar times had had a corrupting influence on society (for instance, their attack on 'modernists'). A censorship was imposed on foreign publications and soon after the 'seizure of power' action was taken against all 'Communist' literature, including the works of Marx, Engels, Liebknecht, Rosa Luxemburg and all books published in the Soviet Union since 1917. In May 1933, the political police in Berlin reported that they had seized about 500 tons of books and periodicals. On 10 May, the Nazis, with the support of students, instigated a symbolic 'act against the un-German spirit' by burning the works of twenty-four 'undesirable' writers in Berlin and other university towns. Louis P. Lochner, head of the Associated Press Bureau in Berlin, described the scene there:

The whole civilized world was shocked when on the evening of 10 May 1933 the books of authors displeasing to the Nazis, including even those of our own Helen Keller, were solemnly burned on the immense Franz Josef Platz between the University of Berlin and the State Opera on Unter den Linden. I was a witness to the scene.

All afternoon Nazi raiding parties had gone into public and private libraries, throwing on to the streets such books as Dr Goebbels in his supreme wisdom had decided were unfit for Nazi Germany.[1] From the streets Nazi columns of beer-hall fighters had picked up these discarded volumes and taken them to the square above referred to.

Here the heap grew higher and higher, and every few minutes another howling mob arrived, adding more books to the impressive pyre. Then, as night fell, students from the university, mobilized by the little doctor, performed veritable Indian dances and incantations as the flames began to soar skyward. When the orgy was at its height, a cavalcade of cars hove into sight. It was the Propaganda Minister himself, accompanied by his bodyguard and a number of fellow torch-

[1] They included works by Freud, Marx, Heinrich Mann, Stefan Zweig and Erich Kästner.

bearers of the new Nazi *Kultur*. 'Fellow students, German men and women!' he cried as he stepped before a microphone for all Germany to hear him. 'The age of extreme Jewish intellectualism has now ended, and the success of the German revolution has again given the right of way to the German spirit. . . . You are doing the right thing in committing the evil spirit of the past to the flames at this late hour of the night. It is a strong, great and symbolic act, an act that is to bear witness before all the world to the fact that the spiritual foundation of the November Republic has disappeared. From these ashes there will arise the phoenix of a new spirit. . . . The past is lying in flames. The future will rise from the flames within our own hearts. . . . Brightened by these flames our vow shall be: The Reich and the Nation and our Führer Adolf Hitler: Heil! Heil! Heil!

12 The nature and functions of the Reich Chamber of Literature

The job of censorship was carried out by the Reich Office of Literature, an agency of the Ministry of Propaganda, while the Reich Chamber of Literature issued official indexes of prohibited publications. Under its Presidents, Hans Friedrich Blunck and Hanns Johst, the Chamber also attempted to introduce a new brand of literature known as 'Blood and Soil'. Among the most widely read examples of this ideological fiction were the books of Josefa Berens-Totenohl, whose novels eulogized peasant life for its simplicity and attachment to nature.

The Reich Chamber of Literature comprises as members all persons who are connected with German literature, whether they are the authors of the original literature or just commercial dealers. It keeps the profession free from undesirable elements and the book market free from un-German books. The Chamber safeguards the ethical standards of the profession and ensures economically and socially sound foundations for its work. The primary aim, however, is for authors once more to become national in character, and for literature to be no longer the prerogative of a privileged class of people but the possession of the entire nation.

It is the function of the Reich Ministry for People's Enlightenment and Propaganda (Department VIII) to exert political influence on German literature and especially to influence the policy of libraries. To solve this problem it makes use of the Reich Office of Literature established in the Ministry. The Reich Office of Literature is headed by Edgar Diehl, Berlin W8, Mohrenstrasse 65, tel. 1126 46. Its function, which is one that is deliberately eschewed by the Chamber, is the critical assessment and promotion of literature recognized to be valuable. (Like the Reich Chamber of Literature, the Reich Chambers of Theatres, of Films and of Creative Arts have conferred the function of critical assessment upon special authorities created within the Ministry, i.e. the Reich Dramaturgist, the Reich Dramaturgist for Films, and the Reich Commissioner for Artistic Creations, respectively.) (*Manual of the Reich Chamber of Culture*, 1937)

13 Purge of the libraries

The Gestapo was responsible for purging libraries and bookshops, as the following Gestapo report of 15 February 1937 from Düsseldorf illustrates:

Re: Raids on bookshops
Decree of 19.viii.36

On the basis of the above-mentioned decree all bookshops and libraries in the district of Düsseldorf were subjected to examination between 8.ix and 14.xi.36 with reference to the list of harmful and undesirable literature. The SD West region [*Oberabschnitt*] was heavily involved in these actions. . . .

In the district of Düsseldorf thirty-eight searches for forbidden literature took place during the period of the report during which 898 firms in forty-two places were searched and 37,040 volumes confiscated.

All literature found in these actions was handed over to the SD West region responsible for the Düsseldorf district, which will pass on the books, after the sorting which is still going on, to the security office in Berlin. The sorted literature will then be pulped under the supervision of the State police.

14 *Hitler on art as an expression of the German race*

The main criterion of the Nazis in their attitude to art was its relevance to their ideology—or, in the words of the Propaganda Ministry's declaration on the Theatre Law of 1934, 'art is for the National Socialist State a public exercise; it is not only aesthetic, but also of a moral nature and the public interest demands not only police supervision but also guidance'. The Government claimed the right to intervene in cultural matters and dismissed directors of art galleries who did not conform to their wishes. One of those concerned with artistic activities was Alfred Rosenberg, the Nazi ideologist, who received in 1934 the highfalutin title of the 'Führer's Commissioner for the Control of the Entire Intellectual and Ideological Training and Education of the Party and of All its Affiliated Bodies'. The official aim was vague—the creation of 'a German artistic type'. Hitler, who considered himself an artist *manqué*, continued to pursue in private a passion for art and architecture. In his speech opening the House of German Art (*Haus der Deutschen Kunst*) in Munich in July 1937, Hitler revealed some of his ideas on the subject:

. . . But the House is not enough: it must house an exhibition, and if now I venture to speak of art I can claim a title to do so from the contribution which I myself have made to the restoration of German art. For our modern German State, which I with my associates have created, has alone brought into existence the conditions for a new and vigorous flowering of art. It is not Bolshevist art collectors or their henchmen who have laid the foundations, for we have provided vast sums for the encouragement of art and have set before art itself great, new tasks. As in politics, so in German art-life, we are determined to make a clean sweep of empty phrases. Ability is the necessary qualification if an artist wishes his work to be exhibited here. People have attempted to recommend modern art by saying that it is the expression of a new age; but art does not create a new age, it is the general life of peoples which fashions itself anew and often looks for a new expression. . . . A new epoch is not created by *littérateurs* but by the fighters, those who really fashion and lead peoples, and thus make history. . . . It is either impudent effrontery or an almost inconceivable stupidity to exhibit to people of today works which perhaps ten or twenty thousand years ago might have been made by a man of the Stone Age. They talk of primitive art, but they forget that it is not the function of art to retreat backwards from the development of a people: its sole function must be to symbolize that living development.

The new age of today is at work on a new human type. Men and women are to be healthier and stronger. There is a new feeling of life, a new joy in life. Never was humanity in its external appearance and in its frame of mind nearer to the ancient world than it is today.... This, my good prehistoric art stutterers, is the type of the new age, but what do you manufacture? Misformed cripples and cretins, women who inspire only disgust, men who are more like wild beasts, children who, were they alive, must be regarded as under God's curse. And let no one tell me that that is how these artists see things. From the pictures sent in for exhibition it is clear that the eye of some men portrays things otherwise than as they are, that there really are men who on principle feel meadows to be blue, the heaven green, clouds sulphur-yellow, or, as perhaps they prefer to say, 'experience' them thus. I need not ask whether they really do see or feel things in this way, but in the name of the German people I have only to prevent these miserable unfortunates, who clearly suffer from defects of vision, attempting with violence to persuade contemporaries by their chatter that these faults of observation are indeed realities or from presenting them as 'art'. There are only two possibilities here. Either these 'artists' do really see things in this way and believe in what they represent. Then one has only to ask how the defect in vision arose, and if it is hereditary the Minister for the Interior will have to see to it that so ghastly a defect of vision shall not be allowed to perpetuate itself. Or if they do *not* believe in the reality of such impressions but seek on other grounds to burden the nation with this humbug, then it is a matter for a criminal court. There is no place for such works in this building. The industry of architects and workmen has not been employed to house canvases daubed over in five hours, the painters being assured that the boldness of the pricing could not fail to produce its effect, that the canvas would be hailed as the most brilliant lightning creation of a genius. No, they can be left to cackle over each other's eggs!

The artist does not create for the artist. He creates for the people, and we will see to it that the people in future will be called in to judge his art. No one must say that the people has no understanding for a really valuable enrichment of its cultural life. Before the critics did justice to the genius of a Richard Wagner, he had the people on his side, whereas the people has had nothing to do with so-called 'modern art'. The people has regarded this art as the outcome of an impudent and shameless arrogance or of a simply deplorable lack of skill. It has felt that this art stammer, these achievements which might have been produced by untalented children of eight to ten years old, could never be considered an expression of our own times or of the German future. When we know today that the development of millions of years, compressed into a few decades, repeats itself in every individual, then this art, we realize, is not 'modern'. It is on the contrary to the highest degree 'archaic', far older probably than the Stone Age. The people in passing through these galleries will recognize in me its own spokesman and counsellor. It will draw a sigh of relief and gladly express its agreement with this purification of art. And that is. decisive: an art which cannot count on the readiest and most intimate agreement of the great mass of the people, an art which must rely upon the support of small cliques, is intolerable. Such an art only tries to confuse, instead of gladly reinforcing, the sure and healthy instinct of a people. The artist cannot stand aloof from his people. This exhibition is only a beginning, but the end of Germany's artistic stultification has begun. Now is the opportunity for youth to start its industrious apprenticeship, and when a sacred conscientiousness has at last come into its own, then I have no doubt that the Almighty from the mass of these decent creators of art will once more raise up individuals to the eternal starry heaven of the imperishable God-favoured artists of the great periods. We believe that especially today, when in so many spheres the highest individual achievements are being manifested, in art also the highest value of personality will once again assert itself.

Exhibitions of 'degenerate art' were organized by Adolf Ziegler, President of the Reich Chamber of Creative Arts, to demonstrate to the public the kind of art which was regarded as harmful to the community. Much to the embarrassment of the Government, these exhibitions held in Munich and other cities drew large crowds out of curiosity and had to be closed.

Many artists chose to leave the country, including architects such as Walther Gropius and Mies van der Rohe, painters such as Käthe Kollwitz and Kandinsky. Others were less fortunate. Carl von Ossietzky, the writer and pacifist, was awarded the Nobel Peace Prize by Norway in 1936. The Government took this as a provocation and forbade all German citizens to accept this prize in future. Ossietzky was sent to a concentration camp, and a National Prize was introduced (one of the recipients of which was none other than Alfred Rosenberg). The Nazis attempted to isolate German culture from its international links and introduced the criterion of race in art. In November 1936, Goebbels officially banned art criticism because it had 'typically Jewish traits of character'.

15 'German Physics'

The criterion of race was also applied to the field of science. One of the most distinguished scientists to emigrate was Albert Einstein, whose theory of relativity was dismissed as 'Jewish speculation'. A foremost exponent of the official view of science was the Nobel prizewinner Professor Philipp Lenard, whose book *German Physics* (1936) stressed the connexion between science and politics. In another publication the same year, Lenard wrote:

'*German* physics?' you will ask. I could have said 'Aryan physics' or 'physics of the Nordic type', physics of the explorers of reality, the truth-seekers, physics of those who founded scientific research. You will want to object: 'Science is international and always will be!' But that is based on an error. In reality, science like everything that people produce is racially conditioned. It can present an appearance of being international when from the general validity of the results of science one wrongly assumes their common origin or fails to see that the peoples of different countries who have produced science of the same or of a kindred nature to that of the German people could do so only because they also are or were of predominantly Nordic race. Nations of another racial composition have a different way of carrying out science.

Education

In view of the Nazis' wish to impose their ideology on German culture, it was not surprising that they should have allotted a major role in their State to education. Nazi education policy combined an anti-intellectual approach with an emphasis on those subjects and activities which would train the new generation in loyalty to the Nazi State. In the universities, the NSDAP had found little support among the teaching body before 1933, although the Nazi student organization[1] did win a majority in the AStA[2] elections at most universities in 1931–32. The 'seizure of power' had aroused much enthusiasm among students, who already had little sympathy for the traditional liberal values of the university. In many cases, the NSDStB provoked demonstrations against those professors suspected of lukewarmness towards the aims of the Nazi regime. At Marburg University a professor of law was humiliated by students when during a lecture on Roman law he expressed the view that Nazi policy had non-German roots. Many professors found the conflict between their academic consciences and the required compliance with Nazi policy unbearable and resigned. By 1935 over 300 university teachers had left their posts and during 1933–38 the number of professors declined to 71 per cent of its 1931–32 level.

16 The new role of the universities

In a speech at Berlin University in May 1933, Bernhard Rust, the Prussian Minister of Education (and later head of the new Reich Ministry of Education created in May 1933), told the assembled professors that the universities had a purpose other than scholarship:

... The German university has two tasks, which must be seen quite clearly. The university is not only the place of research, but also the place of education. We cannot measure the value of a German university only by the number of academic publications; we must also consider it from another standpoint. Gentlemen, during those years when this un-German State and its un-German leadership barred the way to German youth, you, in your professional solitude and devotion to your great work of research, overlooked the fact that youth looked to you to lead the future of the German nation. Youth was marching while you, gentlemen, were not out in front. ...

Rust's aim was to 'reorganize the teaching body so that it can fulfil its task running parallel with the will of the nation'. The Government assumed formal control over the universities through its appointment of the rectors, who were given full responsibility for administration. Academic senates and other autonomous bodies lost their power. An emphasis was put on subjects

---

[1] *Nationalsozialistischer Deutscher Studentenbund* (NSDStB).
[2] *Allgemeiner Studentenausschuss*: the General Student Committee.

which the authorities preferred. New chairs were established for military and racial science, and the qualification for university teaching (the *Habilitation*, an advanced dissertation) now included training in field sports and labour camps. Official attitudes were influenced by the views of Party militants, who had little respect for academic distinction – in a speech in Berlin in 1938 Streicher asked rhetorically: 'If one put the brains of all university professors into one side of a pair of scales, and the brain of the Führer into the other, which side do you think would sink?' Nazi lecturers were of course preferred, to fill the vacancies left by the many professors who had resigned, but their quality as academics was not always high. As Professor Paul Kahle of Bonn University wrote,

17 *The promotion of Nazi professors*

Among the *Privatdozenten*[1] there were several who became Nazis in the hope of getting a professorship which they were otherwise doubtful of obtaining. Many of them had been pronounced, not convinced, Catholics so long as it was profitable, but as soon as advantages were no longer to be seen there, they turned to Nazism. Amongst them was Karl Schmidt. . . .

Karl Schmidt had been *Privatdozent* and assistant in the clinic of Ophthalmology, which he had to manage for some time during the illness of the able Professor Römer. He was a fairly good physician but no scholar, and he doubted whether he would be promoted to a professorship on merit alone. I remember a long conversation with him shortly before the Nazis came to power. He complained then about the policy of the Centre Party which he held responsible for his non-promotion. He had secretly turned to Nazism in good time and had some connexion with Reich Doctors' Leader Wagner in Munich, an influential man in Germany during the first period of Nazi rule. So in 1935 he became Professor Römer's successor, and as he turned more and more to active Nazism, he became Rector of the University in 1937 and still held his post in 1939 when I left Bonn. Schmidt had been given the nickname 'Beer Schmidt', of which he knew and was proud. At a social gathering of the staff of the University with their families in 1938, he let us see a film representing him and his companions performing gymnastic exercises – gymnastics were somewhat over-estimated under the Nazis. He was a fat man, and for recreation he drank down in long draughts, one after another, seven big jugs of beer which stood before him.

18 *Dismissal of Professor Kahle*

Kahle was one of those who managed to retain their posts despite their reluctance or refusal to conform to political requirements. A full Nazification of the universities proved impossible because wholesale dismissals would have created an enormous gap in the staff, which could only have been filled by those who had little experience or few qualifications for the work. Kahle was himself dismissed because of an indiscretion by members of his family:

[1] Unestablished and unsalaried university lecturers.

But my whole activity came to a sudden end in November 1938. The fact that I had an influential position without being a Nazi, that I was in contact with many more Nazi authorities than most of my colleagues in Bonn, especially those who regarded themselves as good Nazis, the fact that, thanks to my position, it was not necessary for me to make any compromise with Nazi ideology, to go to any meeting arranged by the Nazis, to send any of my sons to the Hitler Youth, may have alarmed some of the Nazis in Bonn, inside and outside the university. Already during my negotiations with the Ministry in 1935 I had been told by the official of the Ministry with whom I dealt of denunciations of me sent to the Ministry at regular intervals by Anton Baumstark, who had been Professor in Münster University and had been dismissed there on moral grounds in spite of his being an outspoken Nazi and Dean of the Philosophical Faculty in Münster. Since 1934 he had been living in Bonn again, where he had been before he was called to Münster in 1930. He was a Nazi spy and a most suspicious hypocrite. . . .

My wife had paid a five minutes' visit to a Jewish shop which had been destroyed by the Nazis on 10 November 1938. My eldest son, a student at Bonn University, had accompanied her. A policeman had seen them in the shop and had noted their names. The Nazis prepared a long and very abusive article against my wife and son for the *Westdeutscher Beobachter*. I was informed about the 'crime' committed by members of my family for whose actions I was held responsible by the Rector, who told me the news by telephone. He knew about the article, but did nothing to prevent it. When the article—four columns!—appeared in the paper two days later, I was suspended from my post in the university, my son was expelled from the university, my wife was condemned by the secret Nazi court, and in consequence of this we were outlawed. The Ministry in Berlin was completely powerless against the local Nazi authorities. We succeeded in leaving Germany quite secretly in March 1939. It was only at the end of May that the Nazi officials, the Gestapo, came to my house in Bonn. They were greatly surprised to hear that the whole family had disappeared and had been safely in England for nearly two months. . . .

Academic work suffered because of the wide range of duties demanded of students. They were required to pursue many extra-curricular activities such as working on farms as well as frequent sport, on the principle that they should not regard themselves as an intellectual elite but should serve the community (the heroism of Spartan youth was held up as a model). The Ten Commandments of Student Education (September 1937) urged students to do their duty towards the German people, to live in order and discipline, to be comradely, chivalrous and modest and to 'live up to the Führer'.

19 *Guidelines for school regulations*

Similar considerations, the emphasis being on character rather than intellectual ability and on dedication to the community (*Volksgemeinschaft*), determined the policy on schools. Wilhelm Frick, Minister of the Interior, announced in his decree of 18 December 1934 that 'the principal task of the school is the education of youth in the service of nationhood and State in the

National Socialist spirit'. In the same decree he ordered the use of the Hitler salute in schools:

Teachers and pupils are to give one another the German salute [the Hitler salute] within and outside the school.

At the beginning of each lesson the teacher goes in front of the class, which is standing, and greets it by raising his right arm and with the words 'Heil Hitler'; the class returns the salute by raising their right arms and with the words 'Heil Hitler'. The teacher closes the lesson after the pupils have risen by raising his right arm and with the words 'Heil Hitler'; the pupils reply in the same way.

Apart from this, the pupils greet the members of staff by raising their right arms in the appropriate posture within the boundaries of the school.

Where hitherto Catholic religious instruction began and ended with the verse and response: 'Praised be Jesus Christ.' 'For ever and ever, Amen.', the German salute is to be given *before* this at the beginning of the lesson and *after* it at the end of the lesson.

The non-Aryan pupils are given the choice of whether or not they want to give the German salute. . . .

20 *The importance of the 'New Education'*

The hoisting of flags and such ceremonies were calculated to induce a spirit of conformity. The Nazis hoped through the introduction of ideological training at the impressionable stage to mould the younger generation into a more acquiescent body than their elders, whose ideas had been mainly formed during the days of Imperial Germany. Understandably, the authorities paid special attention to school curricula. A preference was given for those subjects which contained a strong ideological element, such as German history and literature. In a speech on 'the new education' to a conference of ministers of state governments (May 1933), Frick proclaimed:

Our mother tongue, of the harmony, power and flexibility of which we can be proud, belongs to the noblest values, whose preservation lies close to our hearts. Unfortunately, its purity is not always cared for as much as is desirable. Even government offices frequently employ superfluous foreign words, which plainly endanger the comprehension of language among wide sections of the people. The school has in this respect important tasks to fulfil so that we can hand down the precious treasure of the German language pure and unadulterated. We also include here the German script, which should never lose its unquestionable superiority over the Latin script. With reference to the general aim of education, which I have indicated, it follows that history stands in the foremost place among school subjects. Therefore, special attention should be given to the development of the teaching of history and the selection or production of new history books. . . .

The Nazi version of German history emphasized such themes as the existence of Germans outside the borders of the Reich, the superiority and heroic nature of the German race and the line of continuity from Charlemagne through Frederick the Great to Hitler. But the remodelling of history textbooks was not handled in any coordinated fashion until the introduction of a general censorship in 1938. The uniformity of education policy suffered from the conflicts of the different authorities which had an interest in education. Rust was formally Education Minister, but Frick (as Minister of the Interior) and Goebbels (with his claim to supervise the cultural health of the nation) also had a hand in educational matters, not to mention such Party leaders as Rosenberg (concerned with the ideological relevance of education), Bouhler (who controlled the production of school-books) and, of course, Baldur von Schirach (who as Hitler Youth Leader wished to restrict the influence of traditional schools).

The ultimate aim of the proponents of a radical educational policy—like Baldur von Schirach and Robert Ley, leader of the German Labour Front— was the creation of a special school system under Party control, which would train the Nazi elite for future generations. The establishment of a completely new system separate from the State was based on the wish to implement the 'revolutionary' ideological aims of the NSDAP. Hitler gave his approval to this idea and thereby enabled the Party to by-pass Rust, the Minister of Education, whose policy was considered too slow by the radicals. The new system consisted of three stages: the Adolf Hitler Schools (initiated in 1936), which the selected pupil would enter at the age of 12; the so-called *Ordens- burgen* (the name was borrowed from Teutonic Knights); and finally, the Party High Schools in place of universities. Of these the first two stages were completed. The Adolf Hitler Schools, founded in 1936–37, were under the control of the local Gauleiter and boys were selected who had excelled in the *Jungvolk*. Four *Ordensburgen* were established in castles throughout the Reich under the authority of Robert Ley, as head of the Party organization.

These institutions illustrated the aim of the Third Reich to create on the one hand a classless society, and on the other a new elite to lead that society. The Nazis intended to form a new elite based not on social class but on equality of opportunity, where the criterion for selection was the degree of devotion to National Socialism. But these new institutions failed to establish themselves satisfactorily because of the lack of sufficient and suitable applicants and because of competition from the traditional institutions of education, which remained relatively strong despite the Government measures.

Youth

An increasingly serious competitor for control over education was the Hitler Youth, the youth branch of the Party. Its leader, Baldur von Schirach, who sought to exclude the influence of school and home on the minds of the young, was ambitious that his organization should with its educational and semi-military activities provide the basis for training future generations. According to Schirach, 'the Hitler Youth is an ideological community of education—he who marches in the Hitler Youth is not one among millions but a soldier of an idea'. It was a frequent theme of Nazi ideology that youth had a major role to play in 'the new Germany'.

21 *Hitler's views on Youth*

Hitler took up this theme when he spoke to the Hitler Youth at the Nuremberg Party Rally in September 1935:

German Youth!

You are assembled here on parade for the third time. Over 54,000 representatives of a community which is getting larger year by year. The weight of those whom you represent here every year is becoming heavier and heavier. Not only numerically speaking; no, we see it in terms of quality. When I think back to that first parade and to the second and compare them with this one today, I see the same development which we can see in the whole of the rest of German life. Our people are becoming noticeably more sturdy and disciplined and youth is beginning to do the same.

The ideal of manhood has not always been the same even for our own people. There were times which now seem to us very far off and almost incomprehensible when the ideal of the young man was the chap who could hold his beer and was good for a drink. But now his day is past and we like to see not the man who can hold his drink, but the young man who can stand all weathers, the hardened young man. Because what matters is not how many glasses of beer he can drink, but how many blows he can stand; not how many nights he can spend on the spree, but how many kilometres he can march. We no longer see in the boorish beer-drinker the ideal of the German people: we find it in men and girls who are sound to the core, and sturdy.

What we look for from our German youth is different from what people wanted in the past. In our eyes the German youth of the future must be slim and slender, swift as the greyhound, tough as leather, and hard as Krupp steel. We must educate a new type of man so that our people is not ruined by the symptoms of degeneracy of our day. . . .

22 *Membership of the Hitler Youth*

Hitler envisaged a process whereby a German youth would enter the Party youth organization at the age of 10 and in his late teens pass on to the SA and SS and later the armed forces. At the beginning of 1933, the Hitler Youth had been a relatively small organization, containing no more than 1 per cent of the total membership of youth organizations in the country. Its leader, von Schirach, used the new authority enjoyed by the Nazis through Hitler's appointment as Chancellor to put pressure on the other youth organizations, some of which rapidly dissolved themselves and joined the Hitler Youth. But the establishment of a monopoly over German youth took longer than expected because of strong resistance from conservative groups and especially from the Catholic associations. The following statistics illustrate the rate of increase in membership:

	HJ (boys aged 14–18)	DJ (boys aged 10–14)	BDM (girls aged 14–18)	JM (girls aged 10–14)	Total
End 1932	55,365	28,691	19,244	4,656	107,956
End 1933	568,288	1,130,521	243,750	349,482	2,292,041
End 1934	786,000	1,457,304	471,944	862,317	3,577,565
End 1935	829,361	1,498,209	569,599	1,046,134	3,943,303
End 1936	1,168,734	1,785,424	873,127	1,610,316	5,437,601
End 1937	1,237,078	1,884,883	1,035,804	1,722,190	5,879,955
End 1938	1,663,305	2,064,538	1,448,264	1,855,119	7,031,226
Beg. 1939	1,723,886	2,137,594	1,502,571	1,923,419	7,287,470

and the BDM Werk (girls aged 18–21): 440,189

ABBREVIATIONS. HJ, Hitler-Jugend (Hitler Youth); DJ, Deutsches Jungvolk (German Young People); BDM, Bund Deutscher Mädel (League of German Girls); JM, Jungmädelbund (League of Young Girls).

23 Members of a Catholic Youth Club forced to join the Hitler Youth

The degree of the enrolment in the Hitler Youth was lowest in Catholic areas, where the Hitler Youth faced strong competition from the well-established confessional youth groups. A case of pressure being applied by a teacher was recorded in Trier early in 1934. A local Catholic priest wrote to the Party district leader on 14 February 1934 complaining:

In the 5th Class which is taught by teacher A there are 10 members of the Youth Club W. These boys have been youth club members for years and remained when the Hitler Youth was founded. Because of this latter fact they have had to endure a good deal of chicanery from their teacher. Despite the fact that there is a Reich Concordat, despite the fact that the Supreme Youth Leadership of the Reich stresses again and again that no boy is to be forced into the Hitler Youth, teacher A exerts such pressure on the members of the Youth Club that it is almost unbearable for the boys. For example: last Saturday he set those boys concerned the essay: 'Why am I not in the Hitler Youth?', while all the other children in the class had no homework. On setting the essay he added: 'If you don't write the essay I shall beat you until you can't sit down.' Another case: a member of the HJ had come back to the Catholic Youth Club. When Mr A heard of this he threatened he would set him forty sums every time he stayed away from the HJ parade. This was made even worse by his threat of a beating as well. After this, the boy who had voluntarily wanted to come back to us stayed in the Hitler Youth. The teacher's pressure on the Youth Club members even goes so far as to threaten the boys that he would 'muck up' their reports at Easter and would not move them up, and so on. When Mr A was asked why he often punished only the members of the Youth Club, he said: 'It goes against the grain to beat a boy wearing the brown shirt of honour.'

From this one can figure out how unbearable the pressure of the teacher is on members of the Catholic Youth Club. It would be in the interest of the boys and of the whole class if this situation was changed and the Youth Club members were given the same freedom and just treatment as the other members of the class.

24 *Letter of the Party district leader to the district leader of the NS Teachers'*
League, 2 March 1934

The reply from the Party district leader makes it clear that, at this stage at
least, the Party wished to avoid too much controversy by precipitate action.

I send the enclosed report of the Chaplain of W re treatment of the Catholic Youth
Club of W in the primary school by Mr A for your information. It is advisable to
suggest to the teacher concerned that he proceed more wisely, cautiously, and
inconspicuously so that the other side has no occasion for complaint.

25 *Law on the Hitler Youth, 1 December 1936*

During the first two years of the regime, while Hitler was consolidating
his position, he was anxious not to give unnecessary offence to the Catholic
Church. The Church had resented the aggressive and precipitate manner in
which von Schirach had attempted to 'coordinate' Catholic youth clubs
during the first months of the regime. In June 1933, therefore, Hitler
endeavoured to establish greater control over the youth movement by
placing Schirach, as Reich Youth Leader, under the authority of the Reich
Minister of the Interior. As the regime consolidated itself, however, the
Hitler Youth began to acquire greater scope to assert itself. Teachers came
under growing pressure from the authorities to persuade their pupils to join,
and in November 1935 the Ministry of the Interior decreed that future
applicants for posts in the Civil Service should show evidence of 'successful
activity' in the Hitler Youth. Finally, a law of 1 December 1936 declared the
Hitler Youth to be the State youth organization of which membership was
compulsory:

The future of the German nation depends upon its youth and German youth must
therefore be prepared for its future duties. The Reich Government has accordingly
decided on the following law which is published herewith:
1. The whole of German youth within the borders of the Reich is organized in
the Hitler Youth.
2. All German young people, apart from being educated at home and at school,
will be educated in the Hitler Youth physically, intellectually, and morally in the
spirit of National Socialism to serve the nation and the community.
3. The task of educating German youth in the Hitler Youth is being entrusted
to the Reich Leader of German Youth in the NSDAP. He therefore becomes the
'Youth Leader of the German Reich'. His office shall rank as a Supreme Governmental Agency with its headquarters in Berlin and he will be directly responsible to
the Führer and Chancellor of the Reich.
4. All regulations necessary to execute and supplement this decree will be issued
by the Führer and Reich Chancellor.

Most activities outside school were taken over by the Hitler Youth, such
as scouting, hiking, camping and, of course, all sporting activities, some of

which, like shooting, had a military emphasis. In 1934, the State Youth Day had been instituted, when such outdoor activities replaced all school instruction (it took place on a Saturday).

26 *Ceremony of admission into the Cubs of the* Deutsches Jungvolk

Members of the Hitler Youth were required to swear an oath to the Führer. The following ceremony for admission to the junior male branch of the HJ was laid down on instructions of the Trier section of the Hitler Youth (dated April 1940):

It is of the greatest importance that the admissions are arranged in a solemn way. For everybody the hour of his induction must be a great experience. The cub [*Pimpf*] and young lass [*Jungmädel*] must regard this hour of their first vow to the Führer as the holiest of their whole life.

Text of the speech of the DJ leader, to be read in all branches:
Dear boy!/Dear girl!

This hour in which you are to be received into the great community of the Hitler Youth is a very happy one and at the same time will introduce you into a new period of your lives. Today for the first time you swear allegiance to the Führer which will bind you to him for all time.

And every one of you, my young comrades, enters at this moment into the community of all German boys and girls. With your vow and your commitment you now become a bearer of German spirit and German honour. Every one, every single one, now becomes the foundation for an eternal Reich of all Germans.

When you too now march in step with the youngest soldiers, then bear in mind that this march is to train you to be a National Socialist conscious of the future and faithful to his duty.

And the Führer demands of you and of us all that we train ourselves to a life of service and duty, of loyalty and comradeship. You, ten-year-old cub, and you, lass, are not too young nor too small to practise obedience and discipline, to integrate yourself into the community and show yourself to be a comrade. Like you, millions of young Germans are today swearing allegiance to the Führer and it is a proud picture of unity which German youth today presents to the whole world. So today you make a vow to your Führer and here, before your parents, the Party and your comrades, we now receive you into our great community of loyalty. Your motto will always be:

'Führer, command—we follow!'

(*The cubs are asked to rise.*) Now say after me: 'I promise always to do my duty in the Hitler Youth in love and loyalty to the Führer and to our flag.'

27 *Poem for a Hitler Youth ceremony in 1941*

Such ceremonies took on an almost religious character. New members had to recite set poems, which expressed dedication to the Führer. The following may serve as an example of the sort of kitsch which typified them:

Vow

You, Führer, are our commander!
We stand in your name.
The Reich is the object of our struggle,
It is the beginning and the Amen.

Your word is the heartbeat of our deeds;
Your faith builds cathedrals for us.
And even when death reaps the last harvest
The crown of the Reich never falls.

We are ready, your silent spell
Welds our ranks like iron,
Like a chain, man beside man,
Into a wall of loyalty round you.

You, Führer, are our commander!
We stand in your name.
The Reich is the object of our struggle,
It is the beginning and the Amen.

It was the Nazi belief that 'youth must be led by youth'; namely, that leaders of the youth organizations should be chosen from the members themselves, and not, as had often been the case with other youth organizations, by senior instructors (in the case of Catholic groups, the clergy had played an important part). This required that youth leaders should follow uniform instructions and undergo a disciplined training course. The typical three-week course for HJ leaders comprised 105 hours out of the total of 170 hours for physical training and the remaining 65 hours devoted to ideological instruction (mainly political indoctrination). Regulations for the test for members of the cub organization gave priority to military-type qualities like self-discipline, the mastery of weaknesses and physical achievement.

28   *Plan for a fortnight's camp*

The following plan for a fortnight's camp, outlined by the office of culture of the Reich Youth Leadership (1937 Handbook), underlined the need to instil feelings of duty, unity, patriotism and a fighting spirit into those who took part, even through the use of selected passwords:

What is outlined below is only to be regarded as an example of how various material should be evenly distributed. The 9th of July is used as the day of arrival, the 23rd of July as the day of departure.

Friday 10 July:
Password: Adolf Hitler
Motto for the day: Hitler is Germany and Germany is Hitler.
Words: We owe to our leader Adolf Hitler the fact that we can open our camp
   today.

Song: Onward, onward ...
Community hour: is omitted since the group is still very tired.

Saturday 11 July:
Password: Baldur von Schirach
Motto for the day: Anything that undermines our unity must go on the pyre!
Song: We are no civilian, peasant, workman ...
Community hour: What do I want in the Hitler Youth? (Reich Youth Leadership
   folder)

Sunday 12 July:
Password: Germany
Motto for the day: Germany, Germany above all!
Words for the morning celebration: We are not in the Hitler Youth to be provided
   for life, to receive perhaps a position or office later on, but we want to serve
   Germany unselfishly, as is spoken of in the song: 'We carry in our beating hearts
   faith in Germany.'
Song: On, raise our flags ...
Community hour: is omitted on account of Sunday duties, i.e. sports contests etc.

Monday 13 July:
Password: Widukind[1]
Motto for the day: To be one nation is the religion of our time.
Words: If we fight to create a united youth organization and for all young men to be
   in it, we serve our nation, because the youth of today will become the nation of
   tomorrow.
Song: Holy fatherland ...
Community hour: We commit ourselves to the ideal of our ancestors. (Reich Youth
   Leadership folder)

Tuesday 14 July:
Password: Frederick the Great
Motto for the day: It is not necessary for me to live, but certainly necessary for me
   to do my duty!
Words: We speak of the principle of volunteering, on which basis we have met.
Song: The marching of the column sounds ...
Community hour: Prussianism, our ideal.

Wednesday 15 July:
Password: Schill[2]
Motto for the day: Germany's defence—Germany's honour.
Words: Schill revolted against a Prussia without defences and therefore without
   honour. Adolf Hitler restored honour to Germany when he gave the German
   nation back her weapons. We want to make ourselves strong so that we never
   again lose our honour.
Song: Now we must march ...
Community hour: The soldier protects German work. (Reich Youth Leadership
   folder)

[1] Leader of the Saxons against Charlemagne.
[2] Ferdinand von Schill was a Prussian Officer in the War of Liberation against Napoleon,
killed in 1809.

Thursday 16 July:
Password: Langemarck[1]
Motto of the day: You have not fallen in vain!
Words: The camp leader speaks of the respect the whole youth should have for
the two million dead who were killed in the world war. They died for Germany;
we strengthen ourselves also for Germany. Therefore we are the heirs of the
front. Once the soldiers of the Great War were dragged through the dirt (they
were called murderers!); today the whole of German youth goes on a pilgrimage
to the places where they were killed and lowers its flags in memory of their holy
sacrifice.
Song: Wild geese rush through the night . . .
Community hour: Out of the World War grew the Third Reich. (Reich Youth
Leadership folder)

Friday 17 July:
Password: Richthofen[2]
Motto for the day: Nation, fly again!
Words: The camp leader tells about the determined sacrifice which the few German
combat aviators had to make during the world war. Names like Immelmann,
Boelcke, Richthofen are not forgotten. Today we possess a strong air fleet
which has continued the tradition of those few who accomplished the impossible
with technically imperfect planes.
Song: Soldiers carry rifles . . .
Community hour: Letters and some excerpts are read from the numerous good
books about aviation.

Saturday 18 July:
Password: Schlageter[3]
Motto for the day: Let struggle be the highest aim of youth!
Words: The camp leader speaks about the fact that we all have to become fighters,
that we have to accept as slogans for our life everything which requires from us a
manly, heroic attitude: That which does not kill me makes me only the stronger!
One does not beg for a right, one fights for it! What is good?—To be brave is
good! He who fights has right on his side; he who does not fight has lost all
rights! What we can do ourselves, we must not leave to God. . . . Therefore pray,
when we have to pray: Lord, let us never be cowardly!
Song: Unroll the blood-red flags . . .
Community hour: Germans in the world—Versailles is a burden on us. (Reich
Youth Leadership folders)

Sunday 19 July:
Password: Herbert Norkus[4]

[1] The site of a battle in the First World War in which a company of German students marched
straight at British machine-gun posts, allegedly singing 'Deutschland, Deutschland über alles'.
[2] Manfred Baron von Richthofen was a German aviator in the First World War, credited with
shooting down 80 aircraft.
[3] Albert Leo Schlageter, officer in the First World War and later member of the NSDAP, was
shot for sabotage by the French during their reoccupation of the Ruhr in 1923. The Nazis made
him one of their 'martyrs'.
[4] Herbert Norkus was a member of the Hitler Youth killed by Communists in 1932. He also
became a Party 'martyr' and was held up as a hero to members of the HJ.

Motto for the day: Our service to Germany is divine service!

Song: Now let the flags fly . . .

Morning celebration: On this morning a bigger morning celebration takes place.

Fundamental thought: We cannot be called heretics and pagans, if we have made a Herbert Norkus's readiness for sacrifice the motto of our lives.

Community hour: is omitted because of Sunday duties, i.e. parents' day, contests, etc.

Monday 20 July:

Password: Blood

Motto for the day: To remain pure and become mature.

Words: The camp leader talks about this motto by Walter Flex and demands from the boys clean, decent thinking and action. The sentence, 'Service is service and liquor is liquor' is not valid for us; but: 'All or nothing!'

Song: Young nation, step forward, for your hour has come . . .

Community hour: Ideological examination for the Hitler Youth and German Young People efficiency medal.

Tuesday 21 July:

Password: Honour

Motto of the day: For a member of the youth organization his honour is the greatest thing!

Words: The camp leader speaks about this motto.

Song: Behind the flag we march . . .

Community hour: see 20 July.

Wednesday 22 July:

Password: Old Guard

Motto of the day: Germany must live, even if we have to die!

Song: Through Greater-Berlin we march . . .

Final celebration: On this evening the final celebration takes place, at which the camp leader speaks for the last time. Adolf Hitler, Baldur von Schirach, Widukind, Frederick the Great, Schill, Langemarck, Richthofen, Schlageter, Herbert Norkus, Blood, Honour, Old Guard have been the passwords. All commit themselves to the one word 'Germany' which shall also prevail over the whole life of the Cub [*Pimpf*].

29 *The camp community a model of the national community*

The feeling of participation was important to someone like Melita Maschmann, the BDM leader, who saw in the camp community a microcosm of the kind of society the Nazis aimed to create. She emphasized the fact that class distinctions no longer appeared significant:

Our camp community was a model in miniature of what I imagined the National Community to be. It was a completely successful model. Never before or since have I known such a good community, even where the composition was more homogeneous in every respect. Amongst us there were peasant girls, students, factory girls, hairdressers, schoolgirls, office workers and so on. The camp was run by the daughter of an East Prussian farmer, who had not overcome the narrowness of her background. But although she could hardly pronounce a single foreign word correctly, it would not have occurred to anyone to make fun of her. She brought us to the point at which we each recognized one another's particular value, after having come to know one another's weak and strong points, and everyone strove to be willing and reliable.

The knowledge that this model of a National Community had afforded me such intense happiness gave birth to an optimism to which I clung obstinately until 1945. Upheld by this experience, I believed, despite all the evidence to the contrary, that the pattern of our camp would one day be magnified on an infinite scale—if not in the next, then in future generations.

The feeling of comradeship based on common membership of the German nation was largely a state of mind and did not reflect the real nature of German society, only an attitude towards it. It was based on a belief about Nazi society—that people were first of all Germans rather than Catholics or Protestants, workers or members of the bourgeoisie. It was superficial to the extent that it usually produced an outward conformity. Students were warned not to get out of touch with the ordinary man in the street because of any feeling of intellectual superiority. Hitler himself, as 'the People's Chancellor', made concessions to this attitude by sitting on the front seat (of his Mercedes) beside his chauffeur and by officially refusing an honorary doctorate (symbol of bourgeois class status).

30 *Melita Maschmann's criticisms of the Hitler Youth*

Melita Maschmann later contrasted the Hitler Youth with other youth organizations and referred in particular to its regimentation and its being transformed into an institution, the culmination of which she saw in the organized mass extermination of people by the Nazis:

Apart from its beginnings during the 'years of struggle', the Hitler Youth was not a youth movement at all: it became more and more the 'State youth organization', that is to say, it became more and more institutionalized, and finally became the instrument used by the National Socialist regime to run its ideological training of young people and the war work for certain age groups.

The reasons for this development can be found in the external pressure of events, since the increased membership which the Hitler Youth had to absorb after 1935 was such that any healthy growth was impossible. . . .

And yet the Hitler Youth was a youth organization. Its members may have allowed themselves to be dressed in uniforms and regimented, but they were still young people and they behaved like young people. Their characteristic surplus of energy and thirst for action found great scope in their programme of activities, which constantly required great feats to be performed. It was part of the method of the National Socialist Youth leadership to arrange almost everything in the form of competitions. It was not only in sport and one's profession that one competed. Every unit wanted to have the best group 'home', the most interesting expedition log, the biggest collection for the Winter Relief Fund, and so forth—or at least they were supposed to want it. In the musical competitions Hitler Youth choirs, fife and drum bands, chamber orchestras and amateur theatrical groups competed as did young singers, instrumentalists, sculptors, painters and poets for the glory of the most brilliant performance. There were even story-telling competitions to see which boys and girls out of all their contemporaries were best at telling folk stories.

This constant competition introduced an element of unrest and forced activity into the life of the groups even in peacetime. It did not merely channel young people's drive for action; it also inflamed it, where it would have been wiser and better to give the individual within the group and the group as a whole periods when they could mature and develop in tranquillity.

There was certainly a great deal of good and ambitious education in the Hitler Youth. There were groups who learned to act in a masterly way. People told stories, danced and practised handicrafts, and in these fields the regimentation was fortunately often less strict. But the idea of a competition (behind which lay the glorification of the fighter and the heroic) often enough banished the element of meditation even from musical activities, and the playful development of the creative imagination, free of any purpose, was sadly stunted.

The leaders of a youth movement so drilled to activity and performance gradually created a style of their own as 'managers'. They were themselves driven from one activity to the next, and so they drove their charges on in the same manner. Even the young men and women in the Reich Youth Leadership who initiated all this activity were subject to the same restless compulsive drive. The constantly turning wheel of incessant activity continually created a fresh momentum and carried along everyone who came within its sphere of influence....

Women

31 Hitler's views on the role of women

Nazi ideology was solidly conservative on the question of the role of women and attacked female emancipation as part of its more general attack on liberal democracy – the Weimar Constitution had both given women the vote and proclaimed their equality of rights with men. The Nazis held up a certain ideal of womanhood, according to which women should confine themselves to their allotted functions in society – as the familiar saying had it, to bear children, go to church and work in the kitchen – and above all to be submissive to men, who were by nature superior. In the words of Goebbels, 'The mission of woman is to be beautiful and to bring children into the world ... the female prettifies herself for her mate and hatches the eggs for him.' Politics was, in the Nazis' view, a male preserve, confirmed by the fact that before 1933 women formed a minimal proportion of the membership of the NSDAP (about 6 per cent of the total membership in January 1933) and women were excluded from high positions in the Party (all NSDAP Reichstag deputies were male, despite the fact that during the 1920s Germany had for a western country a record number of female parliamentary deputies). Hitler, speaking to the National Socialist Women's Organization in September 1934, elaborated the official attitude towards women:

... The slogan 'Emancipation of women' was invented by Jewish intellectuals and its content was formed by the same spirit. In the really good times of German life the German woman had no need to emancipate herself. She possessed exactly what nature had necessarily given her to administer and preserve; just as the man in his good times had no need to fear that he would be ousted from his position in relation to the woman.

In fact the woman was least likely to challenge his position. Only when he was not absolutely certain in his knowledge of his task did the eternal instinct of self- and race-preservation begin to rebel in woman. There then grew from this rebellion a state of affairs which was unnatural and which lasted until both sexes returned to the respective spheres which an eternally wise providence has preordained for them.

If the man's world is said to be the State, his struggle, his readiness to devote his powers to the service of the community, then it may perhaps be said that the woman's is a smaller world. For her world is her husband, her family, her children, and her home. But what would become of the greater world if there were no one to tend and care for the smaller one? How could the greater world survive if there were no one to make the cares of the smaller world the content of their lives? No, the greater world is built on the foundation of this smaller world. This great world cannot survive if the smaller world is not stable. Providence has entrusted to the woman the cares of that world which is her very own, and only on the basis of this smaller world can the man's world be formed and built up. The two worlds are not antagonistic. They complement each other, they belong together just as man and woman belong together.

We do not consider it correct for the woman to interfere in the world of the man, in his main sphere. We consider it natural if these two worlds remain distinct. To the one belongs the strength of feeling, the strength of the soul. To the other belongs the strength of vision, of toughness, of decision, and of the willingness to act. In the one case this strength demands the willingness of the woman to risk her life to preserve this important cell and to multiply it, and in the other case it demands from the man the readiness to safeguard life.

The sacrifices which the man makes in the struggle of his nation, the woman makes in the preservation of that nation in individual cases. What the man gives in courage on the battlefield, the woman gives in eternal self-sacrifice, in eternal pain and suffering. Every child that a woman brings into the world is a battle, a battle waged for the existence of her people.   And both must therefore mutually value and respect each other when they see that each performs the task that Nature and Providence have ordained. And this mutual respect will necessarily result from this separation of the functions of each.

It is not true, as Jewish intellectuals assert, that respect depends on the overlapping of the spheres of activity of the sexes; this respect demands that neither sex should try to do that which belongs to the sphere of the other. It lies in the last resort in the fact that each knows that the other is doing everything necessary to maintain the whole community. . . .

So our women's movement is for us not something which inscribes on its banner as its programme the fight against man, but something which has as its programme the common fight together with man. For the new National Socialist national community acquires a firm basis precisely because we have gained the trust of millions of women as fanatical fellow-combatants, women who have fought for the common life in the service of the common task of preserving life, who in that combat did not set their sights on the rights which a Jewish intellectualism put before their eyes, but rather on the duties imposed by nature on all of us in common.

Whereas previously the programmes of the liberal, intellectualist women's movements contained many points, the programme of our National Socialist Women's movement has in reality but one single point, and that point is the child, that tiny creature which must be born and grow strong and which alone gives meaning to the whole life-struggle. . . .

32 Official encouragement of marriage

The Weimar Republic had in fact not seen the expected improvements in openings for the employment of women because of the reluctance of the authorities to encourage rapid change, the increased competition for jobs and the restricted labour market following the Depression. In 1933, the Nazis used the need for dealing with the question of unemployment to discriminate, firstly against women in positions of political importance, and then more generally against married women in paid jobs. The idea had been favoured in Weimar days, but the Nazi Government made it official with the law of 30 June 1933, which decreed that only unmarried women over 35 (who were not Jews or married to Jews) could be appointed to permanent posts in the public service. By way of encouragement, women who gave up their jobs on marriage were entitled to apply for a marriage loan according to section 5 of the Law for the Reduction of Unemployment (1 June 1933):

The Reich encourages marriages in accordance with the following regulations.

Marriage Loans, section 1

1. People of German nationality who marry one another after this law has come into force can on application be granted a marriage loan of up to 1000 Reichsmarks. The application for the marriage loan can be made before marriage. The amount is paid only after the conclusion of the marriage. The conditions which must be fulfilled before the grant of a marriage loan are as follows:

(a) That the future wife has spent at least six months in employment in Germany between 11 June 1931 and 31 May 1933.

(b) That a banns has been issued by the Registry Office and that the future wife gives up her job at the latest at the time of the wedding or has already given it up at the time the application is made.

(c) That the future wife pledges herself not to take up employment so long as her future husband receives an income (within the meaning of the Income Tax Law) of more than 125 Reichsmarks a month and so long as the marriage loan has not been fully paid off. . . .

The marriage loan is paid in the form of vouchers. These entitle one to purchase furniture and household equipment in retail shops which are prepared to accept vouchers. The vouchers will be redeemed by the Finance Offices in cash. . . .

33 *Fritz Reinhardt on the economic recovery, 29 January 1935*

The programme expressed an ideological tenet of the Nazis, the principle that women should stay at home. By offering marriage loans on this condition and by making the provision that one quarter of the loan should be cancelled on the birth of each child, it was hoped to withdraw females from employment and replace them by males and also to increase the birth rate. Two years later Reinhardt, State Secretary in the Reich Finance Ministry, claimed substantial success for this aspect of the programme, though as far as female employment was concerned the success was to be merely temporary:

... 5. The granting of 365,591 marriage loans making a total amount of 200 million Reichsmarks up to 31 December 1934 on the basis of the Law for the Promotion of Marriages of 1 June 1934.

The effect of this measure alone:

Reduction in the unemployment figure of at least 500,000 and reduction in the financial requirement of unemployment benefits by approximately 250 million Reichsmarks.

Significant increase in the number of marriages and births. The number of marriages for 1933 was already 27·3 per cent higher than that of 1932. For the first six months of 1934 there is the following picture:

First six months

	1933	1934
Marriages	252,592	334,567
Births	490,340	576,843

Significant increase in the number of households and in the demand for furniture, household equipment and small apartments. . . .

34 *Frick's guidelines on the employment of women civil servants and teachers*

Protests were made from 1933 even by pro-Nazi women's associations concerned at the prospect of discrimination against all employed women, such as the Ring of National Women which wrote to Hitler in April 1933 approving of the removal of women civil servants for political reasons but complaining that 'the position of these women are not filled by other women, but men take over their posts'. In response to further complaints, Frick, Minister of the Interior, wrote in October 1933 to local authorities that there was no general law against women in official positions, although he admitted that, other things being equal, there existed a preference for a male applicant:

As I understand from numerous petitions, a strong sense of disquiet prevails among women civil servants, teachers and employees about the way in which they have been affected by measures of retrenchment carried out by different Reich, state and municipal authorities. It must be pointed out that different authorities evidently take action on the assumption that in the National Socialist State female officials

Key to Illustrations

(Numbers refer to photographs)

PLANTS AS MATERIALS FOR ARTISTIC DESIGN

A. PLANTS FOR STRUCTURE IN DESIGN

   1. Canopy, shelter   2, 3, 4

   2. Area of Space Definition

      a. High, above eye level
         (1) Blocking vision, for privacy   5, 6, 7
         (2) Filtering vision   8, 9, 10

      b. Low, below eye level
         (1) Informal mixed borders, beds   11
         (2) Low border and pattern hedges   12, 13

      c. Ground patterns, groundcovers   14, 15, 16

B. PLANTS FOR ORNAMENTS

   1. Texture in foliage   1, 20, 21, 22, 23

   2. Forms
      (1) Natural   1, 18, 19
      (2) Sheared   19

   3. Color and Fragrance   17

LANDSCAPE DESIGN CREDITS

Doan R. Ogden — 1, 3, 5, 16
Hubert B. Owens, FASLA — 4, 6, 10
Clermont H. Lee, ASLA — 7
Beatrix Farrand, ASLA — 9, 17, 18, 21, 23
T. Miesse Baumgardner & Associates — 11, 12, 13, 19
Ellen Shipman — 14
Lewis Clarke, ASLA — 20
Samuel E. Monk, ASLA — 22

PHOTOGRAPHIC CREDITS

Frazier Smith — 1, 3, 4, 5, 6, 7, 10, 11, 12, 16, 19, 22
Gottscho-Schleisner, Inc. — 13, 14
Author — 2, 8, 9, 15, 17, 18, 20, 21, 23

1. Composition of forms and foliage, rich in interest. Yellowwood, Aucuba, Pyracantha. Asheville, N. C.

2. Structure of a tree foliage canopy.

3. The canopy of trees extends the shelter of roof into the garden. Asheville, N. C.

4. A garden of stone paving and groundcovers dominated by a great Water Oak. Athens, Ga.

5. A screen for the Upper South. White
Pine, Juniper, Rhododendron, Dogwood.
Asheville, N. C.

6. A screen for the Piedmont. Loquat, Carolina Laurel-
cherry, Aucuba, Oaks. Athens, Ga.

7. Coarse foliage patterns supplementing a wall enclosing a small city court garden in the Coastal Plain. Loquat, Banana, Ivy, Holly Fern, Sycamore. Savannah, Ga.

8. Trunks of the Crapemyrtle define space without blocking vision.

AREA DEFINITION

9. The casual disarray of the stems of the Sweetbay Magnolia break the view of the border into interesting shapes. Washington, D. C.

10. Crapemyrtles, repeating the verticals of a picket fence, separate a garden from a busy street without blocking vision. Athens, Ga.

11. Beds of Azaleas and groundcovers under a high canopy of Pines defining ground patterns and areas without blocking vision in a typical Coastal Plain garden. Sea Island, Ga.

12. Hedge and dune-like masses of Yaupon Holly defining a seacoast garden. Sea Island, Ga.

13. Informal shrub borders define this garden from the tidal marsh, the horizontal line of which is formalized in sheared hedge patterns. St. Simon's Island, Ga.

14. The formality of stylized architecture echoed in the architectural disposition of plants following a favorite southern tradition. New Orleans, La.

GROUND PATTERNS

15. Simple disposition of few materials in contemporary design. Birch, Yew, and Vinca. Lexington, Ky.

16. Junipers and Perennials over a steep bank, holding soil, directing traffic, and opening view. Asheville, N. C.

17. Sweetautumn Clematis in fleeting contrast with stone and evergreens. Washington, D. C.

18. Flowing living forms of Wistaria against the trim forms of carpentry and masonry. Washington, D. C.

19. Massive forms in chimney, Palmetto trunks and sheared Pittosporum relieved by the light grace of Oleanders. Sea Island, Ga.

20. Small courtyard garden dominated by building walls given light-
ness and space by the fine textures of Bamboo and Crapemyrtle.
Raleigh, N. C.

21. Japanese Maple and Boxwood. Washington, D. C.

22. Bottlebrush, Yucca, Coontie, and Holly Fern. Savannah, Ga.

23. Some basic principles of designing with plants: the Box harmonizes with the refinement of architectural detail which is accented by the bold trusses of Wistaria. Note similar contrasts in the paving pattern. Washington, D. C.

and employees are on principle to be removed from the public service or to be forced from the posts they have held up to now into posts of lower rank and income or into employee status.

I must emphatically point out that the legal position governing such general action against women civil servants and teachers does not cover the handling of the question in this way. In particular, the stipulations of the Law for the Restoration of the Professional Civil Service, which according to the needs of the service make possible the transfer of officials to a lower rank or the retirement of officials who are not yet incapable of service, cannot be used in a general way against women civil servants as mentioned at the beginning.

I consider it fundamentally right that, in the event of males and females being equally qualified for employment in the public service, the male applicant should be given preference. On the other hand, I must point out that in certain fields, namely in the sphere of youth welfare and the care of youth, also to some extent in that of tuition, the needs of the service require the employment of female labour as civil servants and as employees.

A succession of complaints prompts me to call attention to married female civil servants and teachers, who according to the Law on the Legal Status of Female Civil Servants of 30 May 1932 in the form set out on 30 June 1933 (*Reichsgesetzblatt* Pt. I, p. 435), can be discharged only if their economic maintenance seems permanently secured. The relevant stipulations indicate a regulation with exceptions for women civil servants. These provisions must therefore be taken into consideration.

35 *Hitler forbids the admission of women to the practice of law*

In April 1934, the Prussian Government specifically decreed that high positions in the Civil Service should be reserved to men. One way of restricting the number of qualified females seeking employment in the professions was to put a limit on girl students at universities — this also reflected the Nazi belief that women were not suited to academic work — but in fact the proportion of female students was already relatively low. Few women had been appointed to university posts, but they were very numerous among schoolteachers. Official attempts to reduce their number and the pressure applied through the Nazi professional organizations brought no dramatic changes simply because their services were needed. The law was regarded like politics as an occupation only for men, so that Hitler decided in August 1936 that women should no longer act as lawyers and judges, although those qualified in law could continue in administrative work:

Following the conference in your Ministry on 5.viii.1936 concerning the admission of women as lawyers, I have put the matter to the Führer, since, as the course of the meeting showed, the Party has a special interest in these things. He has decided that women cannot become either judges or lawyers. Women trained in law can therefore be employed only in the public service. I particularly request that trouble should be taken to find places there, where possible, for the existing female probationary lawyers.

36 *Hitler's decision creates practical difficulties*

Hitler's measure created problems of re-employment. In January 1937 Roland Freisler wrote to national and local authorities on behalf of the Ministry of Justice, pointing out that women had made an important contribution to the practice of law and that their skills should be employed in suitable positions:

The Führer and Reich Chancellor has decreed that women in future should not be employed as judges or lawyers or admitted as solicitors.

A fairly large number of female probationary judges, probationary lawyers and junior barristers will be affected by this decision. These women have spent considerable sums on their training and in the overwhelming majority of cases have brought it to a successful conclusion (sometimes at very considerable sacrifice) by hard work and application.

Following upon the decision of the Führer and Reich Chancellor, these women lawyers can find employment in the public service only as administrators. The Deputy Führer has expressly desired that existing female probationary lawyers should be found a place there where possible.

Accordingly, I have already accommodated a number of female probationary judges in positions suitable to their training outside judicial work in the administration of the Reich Chamber of Lawyers and the Reich Chamber of Notaries. I have been in touch over the matter of selection with the Reich Leadership of the *Frauenwerk*,[1] which looks after these women.

The Reich Women's Leader has considered employing a number of female probationary lawyers herself in the administration of her organization.

Considering the limited possibilities of employment available to women in the administration of justice, I would be particularly grateful if a number of suitable women with the ability to become judges or junior barristers can be found employment appropriate to their training in their field of work. Suitable permanent employment would be particularly desirable. For especially severe cases of social hardship, employment for one or two years would be welcome. From experience, the applicants are qualified not only for consideration as employees in administration proper but also in such work as the press, periodicals and library matters. In view of the position of female lawyers immediate help seems desirable as soon as possible. I request therefore that existing requirements should be ascertained quickly in your field of occupation and that the result of these findings be communicated to me.

In fact, although as a result of Government measures, 800,000 women were removed from the labour market in 1933–35, by 1936 owing to the boom there were more women employed than when Hitler came to power.[2]

---

[1] The *Deutsches Frauenwerk*, founded in 1933, was a general Nazi organization for women. It claimed 11 million members by the end of 1936.
[2] See below, p. 458.

Religion[1]

The culmination of the Nazi attempt to mould society in accordance with their ideology would have been a fundamental conflict with religion. National Socialism claimed to be totally comprehensive since it aimed to transform not only the State and its institutions but also its substructure—the social system, manners of living and even attitudes to life. Religion, with its influence over certain sections of the population, presented ultimately a rival to Nazi ideology, which assumed many of the characteristics of a religion with its adulation of the Führer and its intense nationalism. Hitler chose for tactical reasons not to provoke a conflict with the Churches until such time as he could deal with the problem without difficulty. In his speech to the Reichstag on 23 March 1933, he had declared that Christianity was 'the unshakeable foundation of the moral and ethical life of our people' and promised that the rights of the Churches would remain unaffected.

37 *Repudiation of 'German Christians' by the Confessional Church*

A number of Protestant leaders had responded with considerable enthusiasm to Hitler's rise to power in 1933 and were affected by the feeling of 'national revival'. But Hitler's announcement of a new constitution for the Protestant Church (July 1933) uniting the 28 Provincial Protestant Churches (*Landeskirchen*) to form one *Reich* Church under a pro-Nazi Reich Bishop, and his promotion of the pro-Nazi 'German Christians', produced strong reactions leading to the establishment of a so-called Confessional Church, whose opposition to the totalitarian claims of the Nazi regime implied a fundamental challenge. This opposition was primarily theological, as seen in the rejection of the 'German Christians' in the Barmen Declaration of May 1934, which reasserted Jesus Christ as the only source of revelation. In October 1934, however, the Confessional Church formally rejected the Reich Church by creating its own government:

1. We declare that the Constitution of the German Evangelical Church has been destroyed. Its legally constituted organs no longer exist. The men who have seized the Church leadership in the Reich and the states have divorced themselves from the Christian Church.

2. In virtue of the right of Churches, religious communities and holders of ecclesiastical office, bound by scripture and confession, to act in an emergency, the Confessional Synod of the German Evangelical Church establishes new organs of leadership. It appoints as leader and representative of the German Evangelical Church, as an association of confessionally determined Churches, the Fraternal Council of the German Evangelical Church and from among it the Council of the German Evangelical Church to the management leadership. Both organs are composed and organized in accordance with the confessions.

[1] For relations between the Churches and the Nazi State, see Chapters 6 and 11, as well as the section on 'Education' in this chapter.

3. We summon the Christian communities, their pastors and elders, to accept no directions from the present Church Government and its authorities and to decline cooperation with those who wish to remain obedient to this ecclesiastical governance. We summon them to observe the directions of the Confessional Synod of the German Evangelical Church and its recognized organs.

The Confessional Church won the allegiance only of a minority of Protestant pastors, the majority of whom gave active support to neither the Confessional Church nor the German Christians. The Confessional Church also suffered from differences of attitude between its leaders in the different regions of the country, but its protests had some effect. The Government came round to the view that the German Christians had acted too brashly and too hastily.

The Catholic Church also reacted strongly to the encroachments of the Nazis in Church affairs. It was at first content with the negotiations of the Concordat of 1933 (see above, Part II, 'The Seizure of Power') but disillusionment set in when it became clear that the Nazis interpreted the Concordat differently from the Vatican. Particular dismay was voiced over the apparent official approval given to the book *The Myth of the 20th Century* (regarded by Catholics as an attack on Christianity) when its author, Alfred Rosenberg, the Nazi ideologist, was given a position involving supervision of cultural affairs.

38 *Good attendance at churches*

The Catholic Church was in a stronger position than the Protestant Church in Germany because it was more united and also more cosmopolitan. Moreover, church attendance was generally higher and more regular among Catholics. This report from the *Landrat* of Bad Kreuznach (February 1936) admitted some of the difficulties met when dealing with the passive resistance of Catholic priests:

The efforts by the Catholic Church, already mentioned last month, to further the consolidation of its supporters by all means have been continued intensively. Catholic churches are full to overflowing. Even in the early hours of the morning the churches are very well attended. At this point, I would like again to refer to the following: it is often the case that Catholic priests appeal from official orders to a contrary statement on the part of their episcopal authorities, or refer the State authorities to higher church authorities. For example, it has never been possible in the whole district to obtain the membership lists of Catholic associations from the priests, as this ostensibly contradicts an order of the bishop. In order to avoid such fiascos, which can be detrimental to the authority of the State, I should like to suggest that in such cases there should first be direct contact with the episcopal authorities. Furthermore, police statements as to the reading out of pastoral letters have probably, in my opinion, little practical value in so far as this reading takes place on principle in all churches on the order of the bishop.

39 *Catholic Bishops' disillusionment with National Socialism*

The Catholic Church, which had felt little sympathy for the democracy of the Weimar Republic, had initially welcomed the Nazi Government because of its anti-Communism and its promise of establishing order in the country. Some of its leaders, like those of the Protestant Church, reacted sharply when the Nazis tried to intervene in the Church's internal affairs. By 1937, when Pope Pius XI issued his encyclical criticizing the position of the Catholic Church in Germany, the situation had worsened and relations between the Catholic Church and the Nazi Government were very strained. On 13 December 1936 the Bavarian bishops had expressed their disillusionment with the Government in their pastoral letter:

After the deplorable fight carried on by Marxists, Communists, Free Thinkers and Freemasons against Christianity and the Church we welcomed with gratitude the National Socialist profession of positive Christianity. We are convinced that many hundreds of thousands are still loyal to this profession of faith and, indeed, we observe with sorrow how others tend to remove themselves from Christian belief and from the programme of the Führer, and by this means put the Third Reich on a new basis, a *Weltanschauung* standing in open contradiction to the commandments of Christianity. This formation of National Socialism into a *Weltanschauung* which cuts it away from any foundation in religion is developing more and more into a full-scale attack on the Christian faith and the Catholic Church. All this bodes ill for the future of our people and our fatherland. Our Führer and Chancellor in a most impressive demonstration acknowledged the importance of the two Christian confessions to State and society, and promised the two confessions his protection. Unfortunately, men with considerable influence and power are operating in direct opposition to those promises and both confessions are being systematically attacked. Certain of those who lead the attack on the Churches wish to promote a united church in which the confession of faith will become meaningless. Most especially they seek to rid Germany of the Catholic Church and declare it to be a body foreign to our country and its people. These folk lack all real understanding of our holy faith and of the Christian religion in any form.

In 1933 a Concordat was signed between the Holy Father and the German Reich. This was done, as is said in the preamble, out of a 'common desire to consolidate and enhance the friendly relations existing between the Holy See and the German State'. But instead of the much wished-for friendship, there has developed an ever-growing struggle against the Papacy, a struggle carried out in writings and speeches, in books and study courses, in organizations, schools and camps. A hate for 'Rome' has been engendered even in the ears of children. . . . Under the Concordat, Catholic organizations and societies were promised protection for their continued existence. But instead of this continued protection, the exact reverse has taken place until by gradual means the continuation of these organizations has been made impossible. . . . According to the Concordat, insults to the clergy were to be punished. But where is the protection against the kind of insults which come in speeches, writings, broadsheets and pictures? Where is the State protection of the honour of clergy when it comes to cartoons and posters which are set before the eyes of children even in the remotest villages? It has been reported to us that an anticlerical cartoon was exhibited in a class-room. When the parish priest urged the teacher to remove it, he refused. . . .

Nothing could be further from our intentions than to adopt a hostile attitude toward, or a renunciation of, the present form taken by our Government. For us, respect for authority, love of Fatherland, and the fulfilment of our duty to the State are matters not only of conscience but of divine ordinance. This command we will always require our faithful to follow. But we will never regard as an infringement of this duty our defence of God's laws and of His Church, or of ourselves against attacks on the Faith and the Church. The Führer can be certain that we Bishops are prepared to give all moral support to his historic struggle against Bolshevism. We will not criticize things which are purely political. What we do ask is that our holy Church be permitted to enjoy her God-given rights and her freedom.

40 The resistance of the Catholic Church to State interference

Church opposition to the Nazis remained of a largely theological nature until the war brought cooperation between the confessions. Opposition was the result of official interference in religious matters rather than of abhorrence at the political methods of the Nazis or their racial policy (on which question the Churches were on the whole notoriously silent). There were limits to the official direction of ecclesiastical affairs. The Gestapo could ban the distribution of pastoral statements, but could not prevent priests from reading them out in church. In 1940 efforts to control religious festivals aroused strong resistance:

The concluding reports on Corpus Christi Day permit the generalization that the decree of the General Plenipotentiary for the Reich Administration concerning the switching of Corpus Christi as a public holiday, in accordance with Reich regulations, from 9 May 1940 to Sunday 26 May 1940 was simply sabotaged by the Church and the population. Immediately after its publication the decree was the subject of lively discussion and the reaction of the clergy was in general that the celebration of Corpus Christi on a Thursday was the law of the Church and must be upheld by the Catholic population. The Bishop of Fulda even took the view that such a switch could only be undertaken by the Church or the Pope himself, that interference with this canonical and most solemn religious festival was inadmissible and the State decree invalid. . . . The position adopted uniformly by almost all the Church authorities finally led to Corpus Christi being celebrated as a religious festival and work stopped on that day. This was particularly true of the countryside and especially of the mainly Catholic parishes.

Hess had warned in a speech to Party leaders in September 1938 that 'a religion that has influenced, indeed dominated, the life of a people for two thousand years cannot be destroyed or overcome by external measures'. As the Führer's Deputy, he was presumably expressing Hitler's own views at the time. The war changed the situation as it created new possibilities for the application of Nazi ideology (for instance, racial policy) and brought to the fore men who favoured more radical policies. Martin Bormann, who rose high in the Nazi hierarchy during the war and enjoyed increasing influence over Hitler, had made little secret of his long-standing antagonism toward religion. An order sent to the Gauleiters in June 1941 outlined his uncompromising views:

41 Bormann declares Christianity to be irreconcilable with National Socialism, June 1941

The concepts of National Socialism and Christianity are irreconcilable. The Christian Churches build on people's ignorance and attempt to preserve the ignorance of as wide a section of the population as possible. National Socialism, on the other hand, is based on scientific foundations. Christianity has immutable tenets, laid down nearly 2000 years ago, which have increasingly petrified into dogmas incompatible with reality. National Socialism, on the other hand, if it is to continue to fulfil its task, must always be in accordance with the latest findings of scientific research.

The Christian Churches have always recognized the dangers which threaten their existence in the form of exact scientific knowledge. They have therefore endeavoured by means of pseudo-science, which is what theology is, to suppress or falsify scientific research with their dogma. Our National Socialist ideology is far loftier than the concepts of Christianity, which in their essential points have been taken over from Jewry. For this reason also we have no need of Christianity.

No human being would know anything of Christianity if it had not been drilled into him in his childhood by pastors. The so-called 'dear God' does not by any means give young people advance notice of his existence. Astonishingly, for all his omnipotence, he leaves this to the efforts of the pastors. If, therefore, in the future our youth learns nothing of this Christianity, whose doctrines are far inferior to ours, Christianity will disappear of its own accord.

It is also surprising that before the beginning of the present era nothing was known of this Christian God. Further, since that point in time the vast majority of the earth's inhabitants have never learned anything about this Christianity; so, according to the arrogant but Christian doctrine, they were damned from the start.

If we National Socialists speak of belief in God, we do not understand by God, as the naive Christians and their spiritual camp followers do, a human-type being sitting around somewhere in space. Rather must we open people's eyes to the fact that, apart from our small planet which is very unimportant in the universe, there are an inconceivably large number of other bodies, innumerable additional bodies, which like the sun are surrounded by planets and these in turn by smaller bodies, the moons. The natural force by which all these innumerable planets move in the universe we call 'the Almighty' or 'God'. The claim that this world force is concerned about the fate of every single being, of the tiniest earth bacillus, or can be influenced by so-called prayers or other astonishing things, is based on a proper dose of naïveté or else on a calculating shamelessness.

As opposed to that, we National Socialists set ourselves the task of living as naturally as possible, that is to say, biologically. The more accurately we recognize and observe the laws of nature and of life, and the more we adhere to them, so much the more do we conform to the will of the Almighty. The more insight we have into the will of the Almighty, the greater will be our successes.

It follows from the irreconcilability of National Socialist and Christian concepts that we must reject any strengthening of existing denominations or any demand by Christian denominations in the process of emerging. We should not differentiate here between the various Christian denominations. For this reason too the thought of establishing a Reich Evangelical Church by merging the various Evangelical Churches has been definitely given up because the Evangelical Church is just as hostile to us as the Catholic Church. Any strengthening of the Evangelical Church would merely redound to our disadvantage.

It was a historical mistake on the part of the German emperors of the Middle Ages that they repeatedly created order at the Vatican in Rome. It is always an error, into which we Germans unfortunately fall too often, to attempt to create order where we ought to have an interest in disunity and separation. . . .

In former generations the leadership of the people lay exclusively in the hands of the Church. The State limited itself to issuing laws and decrees and primarily to administration. The real leadership of the people lay not with the State but with the Churches. The latter exerted through the priest the strongest influence on the life of the individual human being, on families and on the community as a whole. . . . The State was dependent on the aid of the Church. . . .

The ideological dependence of the State on the Church, the yielding of the leadership of the people to the Church, had become a matter of course, so that nobody dared oppose it seriously. To refuse to accept this as an incontrovertible fact from the beginning was considered absurd stupidity until just before the take-over of power.

For the first time in German history, the Führer has the leadership of the people consciously and completely in his own hands. In the Party, its components and its affiliated organizations the Führer has created for himself, and thereby for the German Reich, an instrument which makes him independent of the Church. All influences which might impair or damage the leadership of the people exercised by the Führer with the help of the NSDAP must be eliminated. More and more the people must be separated from the Churches and their organs, the pastors. Of course, from their own viewpoint, the Churches must and will defend themselves against this loss of power. But never again must influence over the leadership of the people be yielded to the Churches. This influence must be broken finally and completely.

Only the Reich Government and under its direction the Party, its components and affiliated organizations, have the right to the leadership of the people. Just as the deleterious influences of astrologers, seers and other quacks are eliminated and suppressed by the State, so must the possibility of Church influence also be totally removed. Not until this has happened does the leadership of the State have real influence over its individual citizens. Not until then are people and Reich secure in their existence for the future.

It would only repeat the fatal mistakes of past centuries if we were to contribute in any way to the strengthening of one of the various Churches, in view of our knowledge of their ideological hostility towards us. The interest of the Reich lies not in conquering but in preserving and strengthening ecclesiastical particularism.

13   The Economy, 1933–39

When the Nazis took office, they had no coherent economic programme. Hitler's economic priorities were, first, to solve the unemployment and agrarian problems in order to win support for the new regime, and secondly, to establish Germany's military strength. But in January 1933 it was by no means clear how these aims were to be achieved. Before Hitler came to power, Nazi economic thinking had had basically three main themes, and these themes reflected the various phases through which the Party had moved since its foundation in 1919. In the first place, there were the attitudes which lay behind the Twenty-Five-Point Programme of 1920.[1] This programme reflected the economic outlook of the urban lower-middle class. It was hostile to the rentier class, to big business, and above all to high finance and the stock market (Sections 11, 13, 14). It also expressed the hostility of the small shopkeepers and artisans to the big department stores and consumer cooperatives and demanded special consideration for the small man (Section 16). Secondly, there was the agrarian programme which the Party had developed in order to exploit the discontent of the rural population in the years 1928–33. In this programme the main emphasis was on the need to achieve self-sufficiency in agriculture, to restrict imports, and to protect the peasantry from falling into debt. Finally, there was the influence exerted by the increasing contact with industry during the years 1930–33. During this period, with the help of middlemen such as Funk,[2] Keppler[3] and Schacht,[4] industry had succeeded in establishing some links with the Party leadership even though the exigencies of propaganda, particularly during the anti-Papen period (August–November 1932), meant that the Party took a rather hostile line in public.

These three themes – artisan anticapitalism, agrarian autarky, and the need to cater for the interests of industry – were by no means compatible with one another. The anticapitalism of the lower-middle class Party membership, which was particularly prevalent in the SA, was completely contrary to the interests of industry. The policy of self-sufficiency in agrarian products was also incompatible with the interests of industry as it was organized at the time. Industry was dependent on exports; and increasingly

---

[1] See above, pp. 37ff.
[2] Walther Funk, a former editor of a Berlin business paper, had joined the Nazis in 1930.
[3] Wilhelm Keppler was a businessman who joined the Nazis in 1931.
[4] See below, pp. 386ff.

during the 1920s these exports had been arranged through trade agreements with other countries by which Germany undertook to import agrarian produce in exchange. A policy of agrarian self-sufficiency leading to restrictions on agrarian imports would almost certainly result in retaliatory measures being taken against German industrial exports. It would also increase the price of food and therefore put pressure on industry to grant a corresponding increase in wages.

The 'seizure of power', January–June 1933

The main objective before Hitler, as he took office at the end of January, was the winning of the election in March. So far as economic policy was concerned, he contented himself with a general commitment in his Appeal to the Nation to solve what he described as the two major economic problems – unemployment and the agrarian crisis.[1] He gave no details of how he proposed to do this. Indeed, on 8 February he informed his Cabinet that they 'should avoid all detailed statements concerning an economic programme of the Government'. Hitler was anxious to secure the widest possible support before the election and therefore did not wish to risk alienating any social or economic group by putting forward specific proposals at this stage.

1 *Regulation of the Reich Commissioner for the Economy, 13 May 1933*

Very soon, however, in the 'revolution from below' which received great impetus from the March election, the local Party and SA organizations tried to take the initiative in putting into effect the economic principles embodied in the 1920 Programme. The tradesmen, artisans and unemployed who filled the ranks of the SA believed that with Hitler's appointment the opportunity to eliminate their business competitors for which they had been waiting so long had at last arrived. As a result SA and Party 'commissars' moved into businesses and in some cases started to order the sacking of Social Democrat workers and the employment of Nazis in their place. Pressure was particularly strong from the so-called 'Combat League of Middle Class Tradespeople' which embraced the artisans and small shopkeepers in the Party. These small traders had long resented the dominant influence of the big department stores and consumer cooperatives. Indeed, in the period before 1933, the Nazis had exploited this resentment as one of their major propaganda themes. This Combat League now organized boycotts of department stores and cooperatives and interfered in business in various other ways. Soon the disruption of business activity became such a problem that the Government and Party authorities were obliged to intervene:

The organization of the Combat League of Middle Class Tradespeople is an

[1] See above, p. 164.

instrument for carrying out specific economic duties and the setting of these tasks is the sole responsibility of the leadership of the Reich Combat League.

Under no circumstances do the following form part of these duties: the appointment of commissars, the coordination of associations and plants, the dismissal and replacement of undesirable people, the exercise of direct influence on prices or of direct influence on business activity.

These tasks have been delegated to the state and local authorities as well as to the Reich Commissioners for the Economy and their representatives and delegates. All offices of the Combat League, therefore, are strictly forbidden to take unauthorized action of the kind described above. Contravention will from now onwards be punished by the law.

> [signed] DR WAGENER, Reich Commissioner for
> the Economy and Head of the Economic
> Department of the NSDAP

> [signed] DR VON RENTELN, Leader of the Reich
> Combat League

2 Excerpt from a letter from Göring and Hugenberg[1] to von Renteln, 2 June 1933

Even recently the complaints about interference by the Combat League have not ceased, despite the fact that 'coordination' can no longer be used as an excuse for this interference. In particular, public bodies and business institutions are suffering from these interventions by the Combat League. For example, frequently during elections to the Chambers of Industry and Commerce, owing to the intervention of the Combat League, which is naturally more representative of the interests of the small business, medium-sized and large businesses have been excluded from participation in the leadership of the Chambers.... We therefore request that in future all interference in public bodies and business institutions and in their associations should cease.

3 Hess on the attitude of the Party towards department stores, 7 July 1933

The local Party and SA organizations nevertheless continued their harassment of the department stores. They justified their behaviour by the claim that they were after all only acting on Point 16 of the 1920 Programme. But the Nazi leadership was forced to take a wider view. The destruction of the department stores would mean putting thousands of employees out of work; it would also jeopardize their suppliers. Finally, the banks had millions of marks invested in loans to these stores. The elimination of the department stores would therefore cause widespread economic disruption at a time when it was essential for the Government to improve the economic situation. The department stores were now, in fact, in such a critical position that the Government was forced to bail out one of the biggest, the firm of Tietz, with a large loan, despite the fact that it was Jewish. In order to prevent the local Party organizations from destroying the department stores,

---

[1] Now Minister of Economics.

Rudolf Hess was forced to issue the following directive to the Party on
7 July 1933:

The attitude of the NSDAP toward the 'department store question' is in
principle unchanged. Its solution will follow at the appropriate time in accordance
with the National Socialist programme. In view of the general economic situation,
the Party leadership considers action intended to paralyse department stores and
similar institutions to be inadvisable for the time being. At a time when the
National Socialist Government sees its main task as helping as many unemployed
citizens as possible to find work and bread, the National Socialist movement must
not counteract this by taking away their jobs from hundreds of thousands of
workers and employees in department stores and in the firms dependent on them.
The sections of the NSDAP are therefore forbidden to undertake further action
against department stores and similar firms until further notice. On the other hand,
it is forbidden for members of the NSDAP to make propaganda for department
stores.

4 *A local Nazi boycott of department stores, Christmas 1933*
Although this directive averted the collapse of the department stores, it did
not bring the harassment completely to an end. During the following years
the local Party organizations continued to subject the department stores to
various kinds of sanction, such as this boycott organized by the Dortmund
local branch:

We expect all our members and their relations to pay close attention to the following
brief instruction:
Racially conscious Germans make all their purchases for the Christian festival of
Christmas only in Christian German shops, whose owners share our ideology.
They support German retail trade and German craft. They despise those weak
characters who have the nerve to buy presents for the most German of festivals
from people who cannot have any feeling for the values of our blood or the
sacredness of our creed.
Keep away from Jews and the friends of Jews!
Set an example as National Socialists and avoid firms, stores and department store
palaces which, contrary to National Socialist principles, still exist.
Show by your own attitude and by enlightening those around you that you are
National Socialist fighters.
Then you will be able to celebrate a German Christmas with a contented heart.

5 *The Adolf Hitler Fund of German Industry*
The 'revolution from below' had also resulted in the various Party
organizations demanding sums of money from firms and businesses. This
caused increasing annoyance to industry, particularly because it was carried
out on an entirely *ad hoc* and arbitrary basis. Some firms were required to
subscribe to several collections—for the SS, the SA, the local Party etc.—
while others were not asked at all. On 6 April, Krupp von Bohlen had been

appointed head of the Reich Association of German Industry by his fellow industrialists on the strength of his good connexions with the Nazis. At the end of May, Krupp took the initiative in systematizing these *ad hoc* collections in the form of an 'Adolf Hitler Fund of German Industry' by which all industrial firms agreed to pay 0·05 per cent of their annual wage and salary bills to the Party. The following printed circular was issued on 1 June 1933:

In order to replace the numerous individual collections of the most diverse authorities and federations of the NSDAP, a central collection from all branches of German industry has been organized under the name: 'Adolf Hitler Fund of German Industry'. The management of the fund lies in the hands of a management committee composed of representatives of the branches of industry concerned. Dr Krupp von Bohlen und Halbach has taken over the chairmanship of the committee.

The branches of industry have undertaken to raise within one year, more specifically during the period from 1 June 1933 to 31 May 1934, a fixed amount in the manner most convenient for them in each individual case, and to remit the amounts collected to the management committee.

The Reich Federation of German Industry and the Federation of German Employers' Associations request their member associations and firms to support the collection with all means at their disposal. We expect the energetic collaboration of all our organizations and of all plants and the personal active cooperation of their leaders. It is a case of acting quickly and generously, of making the administration simple and economical, and of avoiding all red tape.

For the Reich Federation of German Industry:
[signed] KRUPP VON BOHLEN UND HALBACH
For the Federation of German Employers' Associations:
[signed] KOETTGEN

The 'Adolf Hitler Fund of German Industry' is based upon an agreement between the Reich leadership of the NSDAP and leading representatives of German industry.

It is the purpose of the fund to put at the disposal of the Reich leadership the funds required for the unified execution of the tasks which fall to the lot of the SA, SS, Stahlhelm, HJ, political organizations, etc.

[signed] RUDOLF HESS

In a sense this parallels the preference of the Civil Service and the legal authorities to systematize political and racial discrimination rather than having to continue to tolerate the arbitrary actions characteristic of the seizure of power. In return for this gift, on 31 May, Hitler granted industry a reduction in social insurance contributions and various tax concessions.

The work creation programme

After the election Hitler could afford to turn his attention to the economy. The economic crisis which began in 1929 had been primarily responsible for the electoral success of the Nazi Party and Hitler was well aware that the stability of his regime would depend on whether or not it could solve Germany's economic difficulties. The most immediate problem was the unemployment situation. In their measures for dealing with unemployment the Nazis began by putting into effect plans which had been worked out by their predecessors, the Schleicher Government. On his appointment as Chancellor at the beginning of December 1932, Schleicher had appointed a Reich Commissioner for Employment with the task of working out an emergency programme for the creation of work. The Reich Commissioner, Dr Gereke, produced a scheme which included for the first time a programme of public works which were to be financed by the Reich, state and local governments. The President of the Reichsbank and the Economics and Finance Ministers, however, out of financial conservatism, restricted the amount of money which the Reich would guarantee to 500 million Reichsmarks. This programme had just been authorized when Schleicher was dismissed and replaced by Hitler.

6 *Hitler insists on priority for rearmament*

Hitler now put this public works programme into effect. Furthermore, he made clear his intention of using it to carry out projects which would assist rearmament. Thus, he replied to a proposal by the Ministry of Transport to build a reservoir, as described in an excerpt from the minutes of a Cabinet meeting on 8 February 1933:

The Reich Chancellor stated that in judging the request by the Minister of Transport, another decisive consideration had to be taken into account. Germany was now negotiating with foreign countries about her military equality of rights. The recognition of a theoretical equality of rights was bound to follow in the very near future. But Germany could not content herself with that. This theoretical recognition must be followed by practical equality of rights, that is to say, by German rearmament. The world, especially France, was entirely prepared for German rearmament and regarded it as a matter of course. The next five years in Germany had to be devoted to rendering the German people again capable of bearing arms [*Wiederwehrhaftmachung*]. Every publicly sponsored measure to create employment had to be considered from the point of view of whether it was necessary with respect to rendering the German people again capable of bearing arms for military service. This had to be the dominant thought, always and everywhere.

The Reich Minister of Labour supported these statements of the Reich Chancellor, but added that besides the purely military tasks there was also other economically valuable work which ought not to be neglected.

The Reich Minister of Transport pointed out that the development of German waterways was also a military necessity. In the event of an emergency the entire German traffic system must be in order, and this included the operation of the waterways.

The Reich Commissioner for Air felt he must emphasize on the other hand that the improvement of the German highway system was even more important.

The Reichswehr Minister expressed the point of view that in the first place the immediate needs of the Army had to be considered. The German Army was disarmed to such an extent that the prime necessity was to provide the material foundation for armaments. Only after the emergency armament had been completed would it be possible to tackle larger tasks.

The Reich Chancellor again stressed that for the next 4–5 years the main principle must be: everything for the armed forces. Germany's position in the world depended decisively upon the position of the German armed forces. The position of the German economy in the world was also dependent on that.

The Reich Cabinet decided to have the total budget for 1933 submitted first, then to examine what could be done especially for the armed forces, and finally to see what funds were left for the development of the waterways, especially for the building of a reservoir in Upper Silesia, now under discussion.

Hitler's determination to use the public works programme to promote rearmament also had the advantage of disguise. The projects of the public works programme which were financed by the Reichsbank would not appear in the budget of the Ministry of Defence and would therefore not come to the notice of the Allies. In fact, during 1933, the Ministry of Defence was not in a position to spend more than 50 million Reichsmarks in addition to what had already been budgeted for. But up to 1936, 200 million Reichsmarks of the public works programme had been devoted to military projects.

7 *Law to Reduce Unemployment, 1 June 1933*

Apart from carrying out Schleicher's emergency programme, Hitler introduced a new programme based on plans drawn up by Fritz Reinhardt, the Nazi State Secretary in the Ministry of Finance:

SECTION I: WORK CREATION
Article 1

(1) The Reich Minister of Finance shall be empowered to issue Labour Exchequer Bonds to the amount of one billion Reichsmarks for the promotion of national work and in particular for the following purposes:

1. Repairs and improvements to administrative buildings and apartments, bridges and other building projects of the states, local authorities and other public bodies.

2. Repairs to the apartments and offices of agricultural undertakings, the sub-division of apartments and alterations to other rooms in apartment blocks in order to create small apartments.

3. Suburban housing estates.

4. Agricultural settlement.

5. River works.

6. Installations to provide the population with gas, water and electricity.

7. Building work below ground level on the part of the states and local authorities.

8. Payments in kind for those in need.

(2) The promotion of the projects referred to in Sub-Section (1), Nos. 1, 3, 4, 5, and 6 will take the form of loans. Only projects which are of economic benefit and which the owner would be unable to carry out with his own resources in the foreseeable future qualify for support.

(3) The promotion of the projects referred to in Sub-Section (1), Nos. 2, 7, and 8 will take the form of subsidies. . . .

Article 2

The following regulations apply to the subsidies for the building work below ground level referred to in Article 1, Sub-section (1), No. 7:

1. Subsidies may be granted only for projects which are of economic benefit and which the owner would be unable to carry out with his own resources in the foreseeable future.

2. The projects must begin on 1 August 1933 at the latest.

3. All projects must be carried out with manual labour except when mechanical aids are essential and when the restriction to manual labour results in excessive expense.

4. Only native unemployed workers may be used except where the nature of the particular work requires the employment of skilled workers. . . .

SECTION II

Tax concessions for the purchase of replacements. . . .

SECTION III

Voluntary donations for the promotion of national work. . . .

SECTION IV

The transfer of female labour to domestic employment. . . .

SECTION V

The encouragement of marriage [see p. 365 above].

This programme combined extensive provision for public works with tax incentives to private industry. This technique was favoured by industry and had already been used by Papen's Government in 1932.

Finally, in September 1933, the programme of work creation was completed by a law which initiated the construction of a network of autobahns. This was not an original idea of the Nazis. Already during the 1920s a pressure group had been founded to urge the building of a motorway from the Northern Hansa cities through Frankfort to Basle, the *Verein zur Vorbereitung der Autostrasse, Hansastädte–Frankfurt–Basel* (HAFRABA). A small section of this projected route had been built by 1933 as well as a so-called *Autostrasse* from Cologne to Bonn. The onset of the depression, however, brought these plans to a halt. Nevertheless, the work-creation programmes launched by Brüning, Papen and Schleicher in 1932 had included extensive roadworks.

It appears that the Nazis adopted the idea of the motorway primarily as a means of providing work for large numbers of unemployed and as a prestige project rather than from military motives. Certainly the autobahns played an important part in the work-creation programme and by the end of 1934 210,000 people were working directly on the autobahns, quite apart from all those involved in supplying the materials and equipment.[1]

8 *Level of unemployment at the end of every month in the years 1933–39*

	1933	1934	1935	1936	1937	1938[2]	1939
January	6,013,612	3,772,792	2,973,544	2,520,499	1,853,460	1,051,700	301,900
February	6,000,958	3,372,611	2,764,152	2,514,894	1,610,947	946,300	196,800
March	5,598,855	2,798,324	2,401,889	1,937,120	1,245,338	507,600	134,000
April	5,331,252	2,608,621	2,233,255	1,762,774	960,764	422,500	93,900*
May	5,038,640	2,528,960	2,019,293	1,491,235	776,321	338,400	69,600
June	4,856,942	2,480,826	1,876,579	1,314,731	648,421	292,200	48,800
July	4,463,841	2,426,014	1,754,117	1,169,860	562,892	218,300	38,400
August	4,124,288	2,397,562	*1,706,230†*	1,098,498	509,257	178,800	*34,000†*
September	3,849,222	2,281,800	1,713,912	*1,035,237†*	*469,053†*	156,000	77,500
October	3,744,860	*2,267,6574*	1,828,721	1,076,469	501,847	163,900	79,400
November	*3,714,646†*	2,352,662	1,984,452	1,197,140	572,557	*152,400†*	72,600
December	4,059,055	2,604,700	2,507,955	1,478,862	994,590	455,700	104,400

* 216,000, including Austria and the Sudetenland.
† The italicized figures are the lowest level in each year.

Agricultural policies

The other main economic problem which Hitler had publicly committed himself to solving was the agricultural crisis. Twenty-nine per cent of the population were engaged in agriculture and the rural population had provided the backbone of the Party's electoral support between 1930 and 1933. Moreover, during the last months of 1932 there had been signs of growing disillusionment with the Party owing to its 'left-wing' anti-Papen attitude. Finally, Nazi ideology attributed disproportionate importance to the agricultural sector both on economic and on racial grounds. From an economic point of view agriculture was regarded as of primary importance because of its significance in the event of war and also because of the alleged importance of the rural population as consumers of industrial products. From a racial point of view the Nazis regarded the peasantry as physically and in their mental outlook the most healthy section of the population. All these factors contributed to the importance of the agrarian question in Hitler's mind. On 8 February 1933, he informed his Cabinet of the need 'to satisfy the wishes of at least one section of the nation, namely the German peasantry'.

Initially, agrarian policy was formed by Alfred Hugenberg, the leader of the German Nationalists. Hugenberg combined the posts of Economics Minister and Minister of Agriculture, but concentrated his attention on agriculture which was the main concern of his supporters, the Prussian Junkers, and other landowners. In his first weeks in office Hugenberg introduced a ban on the foreclosure of farms for debt valid until 31 October 1933. He also increased tariffs for the most important agrarian products. In

[1] See R. J. Overy, 'Transportation and Rearmament in the Third Reich', *Historical Journal*, 1973.
[2] From 1938 onwards the figure given is to the nearest hundred.

March he introduced a plan for the compulsory addition of butter to margarine and for reducing the production of margarine to 60 per cent of current production. The result of this measure was to increase the price of fats by between 40 and 50 per cent. Finally, the Government wrote off part of the debts of the farming community at the expense of the banks and other creditors, including the rural artisans.

These one-sided measures in the interests of agriculture and particularly the marked increase in the price of fats were unpopular with the general public and therefore provoked the hostility of the Party. Despite his desire to conciliate the agricultural population, even Hitler began to have second thoughts. At this stage (March 1933), however, Hitler was still dependent on the Nationalists, particularly since in this case they had the support of Hindenburg. He was therefore obliged to accept the Hugenberg policy.

Soon, however, Hugenberg's position was undermined both within the agricultural sector and within the Government. Even before 1933, the Nazis had managed to acquire considerable influence within the various agricultural organizations and so they had no difficulty in 'coordinating' these organizations when it was no longer necessary to conciliate the Nationalists. During April and May 1933, the Nazi agricultural expert, Darré, took over the agricultural organizations and when Hugenberg resigned as Minister of Agriculture at the end of June, Darré replaced him. During September, Darré integrated all organizations involved in agriculture to form a huge new corporate-style organization known as the Reich Food Estate. All those engaged in agriculture, whether in production, processing, or distribution, were obliged to become members of this organization and it set up an elaborate marketing organization which controlled the supply and pricing of agricultural produce.

The Reich Food Estate led a semi-autonomous existence linked with both the Government and the Party and yet basically independent of both. It was the first example of State functions being taken over by a Party organization which then became directly subordinate to the Führer. It was an example which was to be followed by the SS and the German Labour Front. The reason why agriculture was coordinated to a far greater extent than industry was largely that even before 1933 the majority of the agricultural population and the various organizations had already been converted to Nazism. There was not, therefore, the same resistance as there was from industry.

9 *The Reich Entailed-Farm Law, 29 September 1933*

Darré was one of the ideologically most fanatical of the Nazi leaders and, on 29 September 1933, he introduced one of the first pieces of Nazi legislation which was primarily ideological in content, the Reich Entailed-Farm Law:

By upholding the old German custom of entailment, the Reich Government wishes to retain the peasantry as the blood spring of the German nation.

The peasant farms are to be protected from heavy indebtedness and from being split up in the course of inheritance, so that they may remain in the hands of free peasants as the inheritance of their kin.

It is intended to work towards a healthy distribution of agricultural units, since a large number of viable small and medium-sized farms, distributed as evenly as possible over the whole country, forms the best guarantee for the maintenance of the health of the nation and of the State.

The Reich Government therefore promulgates the following law.

The basic principles of the law are:

An agricultural or forestry property consisting of at least 7·5 hectares and at most 125 hectares is an entailed-farm provided it belongs to a person qualified to be a peasant.

The owner of the entailed-farm is called a peasant.

Only German citizens of German blood or of that of a similar race and who are respectable are eligible to be peasants.

The entailed-farm is passed on undivided to the heir.

The rights of the co-heirs are limited to the remaining property of the peasant. Those descendants not qualified to be heirs receive a dowry and occupational training corresponding to the resources of the farm; if through no fault of their own they get into difficulties, they will be permitted to seek refuge at home.

The right of inheritance cannot be excluded or limited by instructions because of death.

The entailed-farm is absolutely barred from encumberment and is inalienable.

. . .

5. The creation of an entailed-farm through special dispensation.

(1) The Reich Ministry of Food and Agriculture may, after consultation with the District [*Kreis*] Peasant Leader and the *Gau* Peasant Leader, permit exceptions to the requirements of section 3.

[These requirements referred to the maximum size of the farm — 125 hectares — and to the need for the farm to be operated without farm steading.]

(2) But a size in excess of 125 hectares should normally only be permitted:

1. When it appears imperative owing to the type of soil or the climate.

2. When it concerns a farm which is economically self-contained and whose estates have been rounded off and when it can be proved to have been in the possession of the family of the peasant for more than 150 years.

3. When a German who has made a particular contribution to the welfare of the German people is to be honoured either personally or through his descendants.

4. When the family which resides on the farm has created works of value there (for example, buildings of artistic interest or of importance in the history of art) for which a size of no more than 125 hectares would provide an inadequate economic foundation.

(3) The precondition that the farm should be capable of being farmed without farm steading can be lifted only if special operating conditions require the farm steading. . . .

38. Foreclosures for debt cannot take place on an entailed-farm.

Under these provisions the peasantry acquired security against foreclosure although at the price of a loss of freedom to sell or mortgage the property. It was a price which, after the previous years of crisis, some were prepared to pay. According to Gestapo reports during 1933–34, the law was welcomed by the heavily indebted peasants, whereas the better-off believed that it would protect the incompetent from the consequences of their inefficiency and benefit them at the expense of the efficient. There was also some resentment at the ban on mortgages which would in effect discriminate against younger children who were not heirs by making it more difficult to provide for them when they got married. In any case, the law only applied to approximately 35 per cent of the units of agricultural production, and subsequent revisions of the law which tightened the provisions on credit and efficiency made it even more difficult to establish an entailed farm.

Apart from the setting up of the Reich Food Estate and the Reich Entailed-Farm Law, Darré's replacement of Hugenberg had led to no fundamental change in agricultural policy. Darré continued Hugenberg's policy of agricultural protection and of increasing the price of foodstuffs. This aroused social discontent particularly because during the first years the regime prevented wages from rising to meet the increased cost of living, thereby protecting industry at the expense of the consumer. This discontent was sometimes articulated by the Party, especially in industrial cities such as Hamburg.

The policies of Schacht

One of the most important decisions which Hitler took during his first weeks in office was to appoint Dr Hjalmar Schacht on 16 March 1933 to the Presidency of the Reichsbank. Schacht's predecessor, Hans Luther, was a very conservative financier who had insisted on restricting the previous government's attempts to provide State finance for the work-creation programme for fear of encouraging inflation. When Luther endeavoured to impose the same restrictions on Hitler he was forced to resign. In Schacht, Hitler found an ideal replacement for the awkward Luther. Schacht had been President of the Reichsbank in the 1920s, had resigned over the Young Plan and had joined the 'nationalist opposition' to the Republic. During 1931, he had established links with Hitler and had continued to support him even when his prospects had not looked bright. Hitler was fortunate in finding in Schacht someone who was both a sympathizer and an acknowledged expert with whom the business community could feel secure. But Schacht was above all a brilliant financier and he now devoted his considerable gifts to the economic consolidation of the Nazi regime and, in particular, to facilitating the rearmament programme.

10 *The financing of rearmament by 'mefo' bills*

Schacht at once began to develop the methods of deficit financing which had been practised only tentatively by his predecessors and to use them to finance rearmament. One of his most important innovations was the so-called 'mefo' bills. After the war Emil Puhl, a director of the Reichsbank, described to the Nuremberg Tribunal how this method worked:

. . .

Dr Schacht, President of the Reichsbank, after considering various techniques of financing, proposed the use of 'mefo' bills to provide a substantial portion of the funds needed for the rearmament programme. This method had as one of its primary advantages the fact that secrecy would be possible during the first years of the rearmament programme and figures indicating the extent of rearmament which would have become public through the use of other methods could be kept secret through the use of 'mefo' bills.

'Mefo' bills, abbreviation for 'mefo-wechsel', were drawn by the armament contractor and accepted by the *Metallurgische Forschungsgesellschaft G.m.b.H.*[1] These bills ran for six months with extensions running for three months each consecutively. The total life of these bills varied and in some instances exceeded four years. The Reichsbank could discount the original bill any time within its last three months. The co-endorser and drawer did not have to accept any liability. (This provision results from a guarantee of the bill by the Reich.)

These 'mefo' bills were used exclusively for financing rearmament, and when in March 1938 a new finance programme discontinuing the use of 'mefo' bills was announced by Dr Schacht, there was a total volume outstanding of twelve billion marks of 'mefo' bills which had been issued to finance rearmament. One of the primary reasons for discontinuing financing rearmament with 'mefo' bills was that by the spring of 1938 it was no longer considered necessary to keep the progress of German rearmament secret. The rearmament boom had by then reached such proportions that it became possible by taxation and by the sale of Government securities to raise sums which could never have been raised when the rearmament programme acceleration began in 1935.[2] . . .

During 1934–35, the mefo bills accounted for 50 per cent of arms expenditure. From then onwards, however, as the economy recovered and it became possible to finance rearmament from Government loans and taxation and as the need for secrecy decreased, they declined in importance. Instead of redeeming them when they became due, however, Hitler pressed for the issuing of more as a means of expanding Government credit, with the result that they contributed to the inflation which gathered pace after 1936.

---

[1] This company was formed in May 1933 by four armament firms but existed on paper only and served as a front for the Reichsbank, which was legally prohibited from discounting Government bills.

[2] In fact the 'mefo' bills were introduced in 1933.

11 *Schacht's policy on foreign debts*

During 1933-34, however, Germany's rearmament programme was threatened by two major problems: the problem of Germany's foreign debts, and the problem of the balance of payments. On the question of foreign debts, Hitler's Government was in a better position than any of its predecessors in one sphere—reparations. Hitler reaped the fruits of Brüning's long negotiations with the Allies which had resulted in the cancellation of reparations at the Lausanne Conference in June 1932. Yet Germany still owed substantial debts on loans which had been raised to pay the reparations under the Dawes and Young Plans. In addition, there were a large number of commercial debts outstanding. Schacht's policy on German foreign debts was described by Emil Puhl:

After Hitler came to power and after Schacht returned to the presidency of the Reichsbank, the problem of Germany's long- and medium-term indebtedness was met by the declaration of a transfer moratorium. By law, starting 1 July 1933, German debtors were compelled to make payments in Reichsmarks (instead of the foreign currency in which the debt might have been incurred) on all interest and amortization payments of foreign debts incurred before the July 1931 crisis to the *Konversionskasse für Auslandsschulden* [Conversion fund for foreign debts] which was under the supervision of the Reichsbank. The law was not applicable to debts for which standstill agreements had been concluded, the Dawes loans, the Young loans, or other foreign loans for which special arrangements were made. It was left to the discretion of the Reichsbank to determine when, if ever, transfer into foreign currency should be made from the funds of the *Konversionskasse*. Immediate threats of retaliatory measures by foreign countries brought a partial payment of interest charges in foreign exchange and in 'scrip' which were sold at a substantial discount. However, after 1 July 1934, a complete transfer moratorium was put into effect and no more foreign exchange transfers for payment of interest and amortization took place, as funding bonds were offered the foreign creditor as payment. This was an arrangement made by the Reichsbank board under the leadership of Schacht.

This policy met with considerable opposition from the creditor countries and if the countries concerned had taken a united stand on the issue, Germany would have been forced to divert foreign exchange from paying for raw material imports for the rearmament programme towards paying off her debts. Yet the decline in international economic cooperation as a result of the depression meant that Germany could exploit the self-interest of the various powers and make bilateral agreements with each one individually.

The second major problem facing the Government during 1933-34 was the balance of payments. During 1933, there was a favourable trade balance of 667 million marks. This was partly because of a decline in food imports as a result of Hugenberg's protectionist measures. But in 1934 the German balance of payments showed a deficit of 284 million marks.

This adverse balance of payments situation was essentially a result of two separate developments. In the first place, the programmes of rearmament and work creation required large amounts of raw materials much of which had to be imported, and they also increased consumer demand with the same result. Secondly, whereas most countries had devalued their currency since 1931, Germany had insisted on retaining the old parity of the mark for fear of public reaction. German exports therefore tended to be too expensive compared with those of other countries. In any case, as a result of the economic crisis many countries had introduced protectionist measures of various kinds.

By the middle of June 1934, the gold and foreign exchange reserves in the Reichsbank had sunk to only 100 million marks and the Government was forced to take emergency action. Foreign exchange controls had in fact been introduced as early as August 1931, but only in the form of the allocation of a fixed quota of foreign exchange to importers, without any attempt by the Government or the Reichsbank to specify what the foreign exchange should be used for. This measure, however, had clearly proved inadequate to deal with the foreign exchange crisis which developed during 1934. From 25 June onwards, therefore, the Reichsbank was forced to allocate foreign exchange on a day-to-day basis, giving out no more foreign exchange than it received. Although a list of priority categories was drawn up, only a few of these could in fact be satisfied. This meant that a number of vital raw materials could no longer be imported, and this in turn meant that the work-creation programme and therefore also the rearmament programme were threatened.

This threat to the rearmament programme prompted the intervention of the armed forces. The Wehrmacht was discontented with the Minister of Economics, Dr Kurt Schmitt. They considered he was not firm enough and they disliked his economic policy. Schmitt wished to solve the unemployment problem by increasing the purchasing power of the masses through reducing the unemployment insurance contributions of the workers. The effect of this policy of increasing consumption would, however, be an increase in the demand for consumer goods and thus an increase in imports which would worsen the foreign exchange situation. Furthermore, an increase in consumption would mean a competition for scarce raw materials between the consumer goods industries and the armament programme. The armed forces received support in their opposition to Schmitt from industry, which resented his dislike of cartels.

12 *Colonel Thomas on the economic crisis of 1934*

The initiative was now taken by Colonel Georg Thomas, the head of the Defence Economy and Weapons (*Wehrwirtschaft und Waffenwesen*) Bureau in the Wehrmacht Office. In a memorandum dated 20 June 1934 which

reached Hitler's desk Thomas pressed the view of the armed forces that
decisive action must be taken to solve the foreign exchange crisis:

The Reich Defence Ministry has for years been pointing out the necessity of
preparing the economy for the event of war. It has demanded stockpiling, revealed
the dangers of the loss of foreign exchange and the collapse of exports for the
defence of the country and has especially requested the regulation of the peacetime
economy in accordance with the needs of war. Only the present Reich Government
has decided to fulfil these demands, but unfortunately economic developments
threaten to nullify these efforts which have hardly begun.

The information from industry and the reports from the supervisory offices for
raw materials show clearly that the raw materials situation is becoming daily more
acute. Not only does this endanger the Government's work programme, but also
the basis for an operational commitment of the Wehrmacht is becoming more and
more remote and everywhere the question is being asked, What is the point of a
larger army if it lacks supplies, its lifeblood? The raw materials situation is taken
far more seriously by the business community than by the Reich Economics
Ministry, and since everybody is clear about the fact that we are in the middle of
an economic war, it is incomprehensible that decisions are not taken to overcome
the danger which threatens. For months we have noticed the drain of foreign
exchange followed by the melting away of stocks of raw materials, but so far there
has been no firm intervention to remove the danger, with a few exceptions which
have proved insufficient. What has happened to all the lessons we have learned from
the Great War in the economic field? Because of struggles between capitalist
interest groups, the wishes of Party offices, and the misguided interventions and
opinions of individuals, no decisions are taken. . . .

The economic crisis, which is imminent because of the raw materials and
foreign exchange situation, is recognized in all informed quarters; the will of the
Führer to overcome it is irreversible. Why is the nation not urged to undergo self-
denial and restrictions in order to overcome this economic crisis? The measures of
individual leaders of the Labour Front run directly counter to these requirements.
In this situation employees should not be lectured about the necessity for a higher
standard of living, which leads everywhere to the desire for wage increases. The
Labour Front imposes financial demands on employers, which small and medium-
sized industry cannot endure in the long run and which are not intelligible so long
as the Labour Front spends large amounts on buying luxurious houses and
similar extravangances. Actions of this kind weaken the financial power of industry
and, what must be particularly avoided, weaken confidence in the leadership.

These impressions of economic life today keep reappearing and can now no
longer be wished away with hopeful optimism. They are supported by the news
about the harvest situation which may well give cause for further disquiet about
the economy. It must be clear that in overcoming the crisis we have to fight for
time, that the economy will not survive the coming struggle if this conflict between
the various authorities and the present indecisiveness of the economic leadership
continues.

The whole situation calls for a resolute and unified economic leadership which
can direct the work of the Ministries of Economics, Agriculture, Labour, and
Finance, the Reichsbank and all offices of the Labour Front by dictatorial methods.

If one returns to question (b)[1] posed at the beginning, one must come to the unequivocal conclusion that, with regard to the situation of the German economy described above, the economic crisis represents a serious threat to the defence of the country and that in these circumstances the economy is not in a position to meet the supply requirements of the Wehrmacht in its enlarged form.

As the Ministry responsible for the security of the Reich, the Reich Defence Ministry must now demand sweeping measures, since otherwise the military measures being undertaken will no longer be matched by the measures for economic defence.

I wish to make the following proposals to deal with this situation:

1. The Führer should assume economic leadership. A permanent official should be appointed as his subordinate with the title of Economics Deputy of the Führer, together with an adviser on industry, agriculture, commerce and banking respectively, and also one liaison officer from the Reich Defence Ministry.

The Economics Deputy must be an exceptionally able man, enjoying the confidence of the widest and most authoritative circle and possessing the utmost resources of energy and authority. He must have the power to issue decrees of decisive importance and have the means to carry them through ruthlessly in the face of all authorities and Party offices.

The Reich Ministries of Economics, Agriculture, Labour and Finance, the Reichsbank, the leaders of industry and the Labour Front shall be subordinate to him.

2. All Party and other offices should be prohibited from carrying out any economic measures which do not come from the Economics Deputy and have not been approved by him.

3. The branches of the economy which are important for war and are still unattached should be integrated in a planned economy.

For this purpose the following are necessary:

The creation of trade monopoly offices for all raw materials which are important for war.

The detailed regulation of the import, export and supplies of all materials pertaining to war.

An immediate start with this process of mobilization [*Erschliessung*] and a clear lead from the Government in building up the country's sources of raw materials.

The establishment of a central office for all foreign trade.

4. The nation should be thoroughly informed about the serious state of the economy, and determined measures should be taken to train the people in thrift and moderation.

5. Measures should be taken to overcome this year's bad harvest.

Thomas therefore advocated that Hitler should take over the direction of the economy himself and should nominate a deputy with dictatorial powers in the economic field. Thomas almost certainly envisaged Schacht

---

[1] This question, which appeared earlier in the memorandum, ran as follows: 'What effect does the current economic situation have on the maintenance of the Army in the event of war and how will this influence the expected increase in German defensive strength through the accelerated reconstruction of the Army?'

for this position of 'economic dictator'. On 28 June, Schmitt fell ill and went on leave and, on 2 August, Schacht was designated acting Minister of Economics. In the meantime, on 3 July, a law was passed giving the Minister of Economics dictatorial powers.

At first sight, it seems surprising that Hitler should have agreed to such a concentration of economic power (Reichsbank and Ministry of Economics) in the hands of a non-Party man. It is probable that the economic crisis, which coincided with the SA crisis,[1] gave him very little choice. The purge of the SA represented a necessary concession to the Army and the business community and the same is almost certainly true of the appointment of Schacht. Schacht was the one man who commanded sufficient respect both at home and abroad and sufficient financial ability to master an economic crisis which threatened the major objectives of the regime.

Certainly the concession was a real one. For the next two years Schacht's position was extremely strong and he was largely successful in resisting attempts by the Party organizations to interfere with the business community. And yet, although from one point of view the appointment of Schacht was a concession by Hitler, Schacht in fact, by solving the economic crisis and by evolving economic techniques to ensure the progress of the rearmament programme, made a considerable contribution to the regime. Unlike Schmitt, Schacht was aware, though he was unable to convince Hitler, that it was impossible to have both guns and butter:

13 *Schacht on the relationship between rearmament and the standard of living, 29 November 1938*

... Reduced to a simple formula, the problem is as follows: The credit money made available for armament purposes produces a demand for consumers' goods through the payment of wages and salaries. The armament manufacturers, however, deliver military goods which are produced but not put on the market. From this follow two consequences: first, care must be taken that aside from armament manufacture sufficient consumer goods are produced to sustain the population including all those working for the armament industry; second, the less there is consumed, the more labour can be used for armaments; but the higher consumption rises, the more manpower must be left for the production of consumer goods. Therefore, the standard of living and the extent of armament production are in an inverse ratio. ...

14 *Schacht's 'New Plan' of September 1934*

In September 1934, in order to deal with the foreign exchange crisis, Schacht introduced a number of new policies. Apart from imposing an absolute moratorium on Germany's foreign debts in order to check the outflow of foreign exchange in the form of interest payments, he also introduced a so-called 'New Plan'. An explanation of the substance of the plan was sent

[1] See above, p. 211.

to all German embassies by Dr Karl Ritter, the extremely influential Director
of the Economics Department in the Foreign Office:

2. . . . In future, all German imports will be regulated and they will be controlled
by Supervisory Offices. Within the framework of a general allotment system the
Supervisory Offices will issue foreign currency permits to importers before transactions are concluded if, judging by the amount of foreign exchange received, it
could be assumed that the foreign currency would be available on the due date.
These foreign currency permits ensure priority for foreign exchange allotments.
Thus, provided that the foreign exchange received comes up to our expectations,
foreign exporters will be given a substantial assurance that their claims will be met
on the date. Where transactions are concluded without a prior foreign currency
permit, however, the importer cannot count on being considered for an allocation
of foreign exchange in the near future.
3. It is assumed under the New Plan that, in view of the decline in German
exports and the consequent decline in foreign exchange receipts, the issue of
foreign currency permits will be to a large degree restricted to vital foodstuffs as
well as to raw materials and semi-manufactured goods. Even here considerable
restrictions will have to be imposed. Outside the foreign exchange plan the system
of barter transactions will be expanded. As regards essential commodities, barter
transactions will be sanctioned provided that they do not require foreign exchange.
In the case of non-essential commodities, an effort must be made to obtain foreign
exchange through barter transactions too, for example by exporting more goods
from Germany than are imported.
4. Treaty arrangements will not be infringed. The import of goods in itself can
continue in the same way as hitherto, but the German importer who concludes
transactions and imports goods without previously receiving a foreign currency
permit will be aware from the outset that he cannot count on an allocation of
foreign exchange. Consequently, in future the foreign exporter will also be able to
satisfy himself as to whether the German buyer and importer will be supplied with
foreign exchange and whether, therefore, he himself can expect payment. Thus
any complaints about allotment of foreign exchange and non-payment will in
future be deprived of justification.
  Where exchange agreements or clearing arrangements are in force, they will not
be affected by the New Plan for the time being, but they must, if necessary, be
adjusted to the new situation by negotiation in the sense that the clearing will
remain limited to certain goods and quantities. Payments agreements containing
the so-called Swedish clause[1] will be applicable only to such goods as are not
subject to special management. As, however, all German importers will be subject
to management, the payments agreements will, although without any formal
infringement of the law, become unworkable in practice. What the effects will be of
this undermining process [Aushöhlung] in respect of the various countries concerned
remains to be examined. . . .

  The principle of this New Plan—the regulation of imports through

---

[1] This referred to Clause 10 of the standstill agreement of 1931 which had been renewed in
February 1933. It dealt with the payment of certain German debts in marks which were paid into
special accounts in Germany and could only be used for authorized purposes such as tourism.

Government supervision of the allocation of foreign exchange—was not new. The New Plan, however, represented a far more comprehensive and detailed application of the principles of exchange control and import regulation than had previously existed. In place of the previous system, by which foreign exchange was allocated *after* the imports had arrived, the New Plan required importers to obtain foreign exchange clearance *before* importing goods. Special supervisory offices were established for each group of commodities which issued permits, and importers were obliged to secure a permit for each individual transaction. This system enabled the Government to plan ahead for imports and to allocate foreign exchange according to its own priorities rather than leaving the decision to the individual importers. It also enabled the Government to determine not only *what* goods and raw materials should be imported, but also *where* the goods should come from. This in turn facilitated a trend which was already apparent in German trade—the trend towards bilateralism.

The introduction of exchange controls in 1931 by several major countries, including Germany, dealt a severe blow to multilateral trade and to the 'most favoured nation' principle. From now onwards, as the various note-issuing banks became unwilling to provide foreign exchange for the payment of imports, there was an inevitable trend towards quotas and barter and clearing agreements by which in effect two countries exchanged goods with one another without recourse to the reserve currencies or even in many cases to their own. This bilateral trade had to be regulated by trade agreements between the two Governments. This gave the Governments power to regulate trade in accordance with political objectives, discriminating between one country and another on diplomatic or strategic grounds.

This tendency had already begun to dominate German trade policy during 1933–34. Germany's main foreign trade problem was that while her imports of raw materials tended to come from overseas, her exports went mainly to Europe. This situation worsened during the economic crisis because the countries exporting raw material tended to be colonies or dominions which now entered preference systems with their mother countries (e.g. the Ottawa Agreement). Germany's exports were still at a disadvantage because of her unwillingness to devalue the mark. In view of this situation, it became the main aim of German foreign trade policy to reorientate German trade to Europe and to those parts of the world which were not subject to colonial preference agreements, in particular South America. Apart from the economic aspect, however, there were political considerations which played a part in this decision. It had always been an important part of the economic policy of the German Right in general and the Nazis in particular, to make Germany as self-sufficient as possible—for strategic reasons. The lesson of the Allied blockade during the First World War had been learnt. By acquiring sources of raw materials in south-east Europe rather than overseas, Germany would be in a far more independent economic position in the event of war, for it was assumed that German economic penetration would have turned south-east Europe from a French into a German sphere of influence.

15 *Circular of the Foreign Ministry on commercial policy*

This trend in German foreign trade policy was described by the German Foreign Office in an explanatory circular to its embassies in June 1934. After discussing the period before 1933, the circular continued:

2. New methods in commercial policy:

Even where the treaties concluded by Germany during the above-mentioned period continue in force, their fundamental principles have been radically altered by the world economic situation. This applies above all to the 'most favoured nation' principle and the question of import restrictions. The 'most favoured nation' principle which, under normal economic conditions and with the possibility of free competition in all markets, had proved in general to be the best method of commercial policy, could not be maintained in its original form under the pressure of the crisis situation. The repercussions arising from the extension of the commercial concessions granted to one country to the imports of all other most favoured nations could not be tolerated at a time of general shrinkage in world trade without grave detriment to home production. Therefore, and *this not only in Germany but in practically all States*, efforts have been made to exclude or at least minimize these undesirable effects as far as possible. The following measures have best served this purpose in German commercial policy during the past year: Monopoly management of a number of the most important products, the introduction of embargoes on imports whilst simultaneously setting quotas, and the increased application of tariff quotas. Import and tariff quotas have sometimes been introduced unilaterally and sometimes by means of treaties. In so far as the 'most favoured nation' treatment, whether under the provisions of a treaty or *de facto*, still exists today, such treatment in effect applies only to tariff rates, which have, however, nowadays lost a great deal of their significance for trade as compared with restrictions on imports and foreign exchange. The 'most favoured nation' treatment, however, no longer applies to the quota system, which has a far stronger influence on the exchange of goods, although efforts are still widely being made to preserve the outward appearance of the 'most favoured nation' treatment.

(a) *Monopoly management*

Since the spring of 1933, German agricultural policy has increasingly gone over to subjecting the most important agricultural products to monopolistic management in order to regulate the home market. At present this system includes the following products: milk products (butter and cheese); eggs; grain, maize, oil cake; livestock and livestock products; animal fats (bacon, lard, tallow); oil seeds.

Monopolistic management is conducted in the following way: The products so managed, irrespective of whether they originate at home or abroad, may be put on the market only after a so-called acceptance certificate (*Übernahmeschein*) has been issued by the competent Reich office. These regulations create neither monopoly of production by the Reich nor a State trading monopoly. Nevertheless they enable the Reich to exert extensive influence on internal German consumption both in respect of home production and in respect of imports. . . .

V. The concept of barter in German commercial policy
German import requirements, particularly in respect of raw materials and consumer goods, are, in spite of the decline in purchasing power, still an important factor in a highly industrialized country with a population of about 65 million. This factor will in future be made use of even more than was possible under the unrestricted application of the 'most favoured nation' treatment, for the purpose of making producers and suppliers of these raw materials and consumer goods aware of the necessity of accepting increased imports of German industrial products in return.

VI. Possibilities of reorientating German imports
Closely bound up with the objectives of the barter system is the question of how far it is possible to transfer German imports of raw materials and consumer goods to the countries which take German manufactures in larger quantities than do those countries which have previously been supplying us.

It is a general aim of German commercial policy to transfer the purchase of raw materials and consumer goods from Africa and from the British overseas territories (Ottawa policy) to countries which offer greater future possibilities to German exports, as for instance South America and the Dutch Indies.

VII. New trade treaties concluded by Germany in the course of the past year
The principles of German commercial policy as expounded above have been set down in various forms in fresh treaties concluded by the Reich Government during the course of the last eighteen months.

Particularly noteworthy in this connection are two further treaties of a special kind which have been concluded in the course of this year and which have political significance above their actual commercial content, namely the treaties with Hungary and Yugoslavia. These treaties are designed to create in Hungary and in Yugoslavia two points of support for German policy in the Danubian region, in order above all to counteract French and Italian policy directed against German policy in the Danubian region. In view of the special purposes which these two treaties serve, a system of secret financial privileges has been embodied therein whereby both countries, without being granted open preferences, are in fact by means of subventions obtaining preferential treatment of their exports to Germany in comparison with their competitors. The Reich Government have in this case consciously made certain financial sacrifices in the interests of German foreign policy in south-east Europe. Nevertheless it was clearly established when these decisions were taken that such procedure was only justified by the special reasons in favour of the conclusions of both treaties and that to apply these methods to commercial policy in general could not be considered, if only on account of the heavy calls on Reich finance which would result therefrom.

In fact, for a time after 1933, Germany carried out a policy of economic exploitation in the Balkans by using her position as a massive buyer of foodstuffs and raw materials. The Balkan countries were handicapped by the fact that owing to the slump they could not find export markets for their produce, particularly since their price level was high by world standards. Only Germany was prepared to buy these expensive commodities. She was able to do so by a technique developed by Schacht whereby Germany built up a large trade deficit with these countries. The imports were paid for in the form of special mark accounts which remained frozen in Germany until they were periodically released by special agreement with the countries. These countries were then obliged to use these mark accounts either to buy German goods or to invest in their countries in plant which would produce goods which Germany required. The German Government fixed the exchange rate at a relatively high level so that these German exports were expensive and thereby balanced out the expensive imports. By this method Germany was able to acquire imports of raw materials on credit, to subsidize her exports, and to acquire economic influence over the Balkan countries. After a time, however, these countries began to resist this type of pressure and to demand payment for their goods in foreign exchange and in cash. It was only after the German take-over of Austria and Czechoslovakia in 1938–39 that Germany acquired a dominant economic position in south-east Europe.

To sum up, then, just as the regime used the economic necessity for a work programme, for the purposes of rearmament, so it exploited the general trend towards Government regulation of the economy, which was accelerated by the world economic crisis, for its political and military objectives. By subjecting her foreign trade to strict Government control through highly specific foreign exchange regulations and bilateral trade agreements, Germany was able to subordinate foreign trade to her political goals of rearmament and of the economic penetration of south-east Europe for strategic and diplomatic purposes. Yet it might be argued that the requirements of Germany's economic situation took first place in the shaping of policy and that their coinciding with those imposed by her political and military aims was an effect rather than a cause. It is certainly true that Germany's rearmament programme and her aim of maximum economic self-sufficiency benefited enormously from the breakdown of the world monetary system and multilateral trade, just as her foreign policy was facilitated by the collapse of international cooperation. On the other hand, Schacht's New Plan was not the only possible response to the economic situation. In July 1934, the Mayor of Hamburg, Karl Krogmann, put forward an alternative scheme which envisaged a liberalizing of foreign trade, emphasized the need to encourage exports, and advocated the replacement of strict import controls by a more flexible system. This plan had the backing of influential figures in the worlds of finance and commerce. Nevertheless it was rejected by the regime because, unlike Schacht's New Plan, it did not ensure priority for those raw materials which were essential for the rearmament programme; that is to say, the New Plan was evolved as much to meet political and military requirements as the obvious economic ones. Similarly, it was not necessary to spend large sums from the work-creation programme on rearmament; they could just as well have been spent on housing.

The Four-Year Plan, 1936–39

Schacht's New Plan solved the balance of payments crisis of 1934 and in the following year there was a trade surplus. But during the second half of 1935 an adverse trend developed, and early in 1936 fears grew of an even worse balance of payments crisis than that of 1934. The New Plan had been unable to alter fundamentally the basic factors governing Germany's balance of payments position. These were, first, the fact that since 1933 the 'terms of trade' had moved against Germany. Between 1933 and 1936 export prices declined by 9 per cent on average while import prices rose by 9 per cent. Thus Germany had to export 18 per cent more in 1936 in order to be able to import the same amount as in 1933. Schacht had in fact introduced measures to try to encourage exports. Thus he forced creditor countries to take payment of German debts in the form of special marks which could be used only for buying German goods or for travel in Germany. He also introduced a levy on firms which was used to subsidize exports. Yet these measures could only mitigate the second basic problem, which was the enormous increase in Germany's demand for imports owing to the work-creation and rearmament programmes. Moreover, the revival of the economy at home meant that firms found it far more attractive to sell on the home market than to try to export in the face of protectionist measures abroad which had contributed to a sharp decline in world trade.

The third basic problem was the conflict between 'guns and butter'. Since 1933, German agricultural production had failed to keep pace with the rising demand which followed increasing employment. This was partly because the Reich Food Estate had discouraged expansion in order to maintain high prices. The most serious shortage was of fats and meat. The regime – and here the Party authorities were particularly adamant – felt that it could not afford to damage its prestige by introducing rationing. During 1935, Darré, the head of the Reich Food Estate, demanded from Schacht large allocations of foreign exchange for the purpose of importing butter, vegetable oil and fodder. Schacht was opposed to this because, with the shortage of foreign exchange, such a grant would compel a reduction in the import of industrial raw materials and therefore would damage the rearmament programme. Hitler, characteristically, was loth to make a decision between the two and appointed Göring to arbitrate in the dispute. For Göring, fear of discontent over high food prices and of the reaction to the introduction of rationing, which seemed the only alternative, proved decisive and he came down in favour of Darré. Clearly, however, the import of agricultural products could not permanently take precedence over industrial raw materials without undermining the rearmament programme. Indeed, in December 1935, Schacht informed the Defence Minister, Blomberg, that he was unable to provide the necessary foreign exchange to pay for a doubling of copper and lead imports, as requested by the armed forces, and that raw material supplies for rearmament could not be guaranteed even at the existing level. The need to find a solution to the problem was therefore pressing.

One way out of the difficulty would have been to increase exports in order to provide the foreign exchange to pay for raw materials. This was urged by Schacht, although he appreciated that, considering the international trade situation, it could only be a medium- to long-term solution. Moreover, the problem was that this solution contradicted the principles of his New Plan. Germany could hardly carry out a policy of ruthless import controls and bilateralism and at the same time expect other countries to welcome her exports. Above all, an expansion of exports would mean a reduction in the rearmament programme, something which the regime was not prepared to tolerate.

If for these various reasons imports could not be paid for by exports, the alternative was to try to cut down on imports and meet the demand for raw materials as far as possible by expanding home production. Such a policy of maximum economic self-sufficiency fitted well with the ideas of autarky which had found expression in the Nazi agricultural programme of 1930 and which were current among influential circles outside as well as inside the Party. It was not only or even primarily economic factors which provided the main force behind this thinking but rather the military and strategic implications of such a policy. The experience of the Allied blockade in the First World War had demonstrated the dangers to Germany of dependence on foreign suppliers of vital raw materials in the event of war.

An attempt to expand agricultural production was, indeed, already in progress in the form of the so-called 'Production Battle' which began in the autumn of 1934. But the problem here was that agriculture was increasingly having to compete with industry for manpower, and industry could afford to pay higher wages.[1] One way out of this dilemma would have been the growing mechanization of agriculture, but this required extensive capital investment by individual farmers, and severe restrictions had been placed on loans and mortgages by the Reich Entailment Law. In any case, it was difficult to expand production of agricultural machinery in view of the priority given to rearmament. As a result, the achievements of the 'Production Battle' were comparatively small. By 1938–39 Germany was still importing 17 per cent of her agricultural needs (1934: 20 per cent) and in particular was dependent on imports for 45 per cent of her fats and 30 per cent of her fodder.

[1] For the labour situation, see below, pp. 454ff.

Just as crucial as the need to expand agricultural production, however, was the need to provide industrial raw materials, above all, oil, rubber, and metals. For by 1936 Germany was having to buy the bulk of her requirements on the world market and in cash. The Romanians, for example, were now insisting on payment in cash for their oil. A solution to this problem was now offered by the giant chemicals firm of I G-Farben. During the 1920s they had developed techniques for the synthetic manufacture of oil and rubber. Because these processes were expensive, the firm had been unsuccessful in its attempts to persuade previous German Governments to underwrite their development. In the winter of 1933, however, a director of I G-Farben, Carl Krauch, persuaded the new regime to sign an agreement, the so-called Feder-Bosch Agreement, which guaranteed, for a period of ten years, a price and a market for oil produced by the hydrogenation process. From then onwards I G-Farben lobbied intensively for further Government support for the programme and, in the context of the chronic crisis in foreign exchange and raw materials, it gained influential converts, of whom the most important was Göring, Chief of the Air Force. Fuel was of vital importance to the new Luftwaffe and Göring was determined to secure supplies at any cost. He evidently convinced Hitler of the need for more action in the sphere of raw material production and on 4 April he was appointed by Hitler Commissioner of Raw Materials with authority to give orders to the departmental ministers on matters of foreign exchange and raw materials.

During the summer, however, the crisis intensified. Munition factories were only producing 70 per cent of their capacity because of the shortage of raw materials stemming from the lack of foreign exchange. Hitler now became convinced that if the momentum of the rearmament programme was to be sustained, a reorientation of the economy in the interests of maximum self-sufficiency in raw materials was necessary. This would subordinate it even more directly to the needs of rearmament than had Schacht's New Plan.

The trend towards autarky, however, did not go unchallenged. Schacht had resented Hitler's appointment in 1934 of Keppler to head a special office for raw materials with the aim of replacing foreign raw materials with German ones as far as possible. And although Hitler had not given Keppler much support, Schacht was aware that the recent appointment of Göring represented a far greater danger to his position. It was, however, not simply a question of power but of policy. Although Schacht had accepted the Feder-Bosch Agreement, he was suspicious of the production of synthetic raw materials. He believed that they were uneconomic and that it was far cheaper to import the raw material itself. In an attempt to win the support of the Defence Minister, he argued: 'If we now proclaim to the world yet again our determination to achieve economic independence, we will be cutting our own throats because we can no longer last out the necessary transition period. In addition, it must be continually emphasized that German raw materials are at the moment much too expensive to be used in goods intended for export, and only exports can make possible further rearmament.' To this appeal Blomberg replied, characteristically: 'Herr Schacht, I realize you are absolutely right but I am convinced that the Führer will find a way out of all these difficulties.' Schacht's doubts were shared by the influential Reich Price Commissioner, Carl Goerdeler, later a leader of the opposition to Hitler. In a memorandum Goerdeler urged a large cut in raw material imports and a return to freer trade. In the context of the 1936 situation, however, this was tantamount to advocating a return to mass unemployment and was therefore ruled completely out of court.

In their opposition to a policy of autarky, Schacht and Goerdeler had the support of commerce and the more export-minded sections of industry, particularly coal, iron and steel. It was in the light of this opposition that, some time during August, Hitler composed the following memorandum, one of the basic documents of the Third Reich:

16 *Hitler on the tasks of the Four-Year Plan, 1936*

This memorandum was given to me personally by A.H. in 1944 with the following statement:

The lack of understanding of the Reich Ministry for Economics and the opposition of German business to all large-scale plans induced him to compose this memorandum at Obersalzberg.

He decided at that time to carry out a Four-Year Plan and to put Göring in charge of it. On the occasion of Göring's appointment as the official in charge of the Four-Year Plan he gave him this memorandum. There are only three copies, one of which he gave to me. . . .

[signed] ALBERT SPEER

The political situation

Politics are the conduct and the course of the historical struggle of nations for life. The aim of these struggles is survival. Even ideological struggles have their ultimate cause and are most deeply motivated by nationally determined purposes and aims of life. But religions and ideologies are always able to impart particular bitterness to such struggles, and therefore also to give them great historical impressiveness. They leave their imprint on centuries of history. Nations and States living within the sphere of such ideological or religious conflicts cannot opt out of or dissociate themselves from these events. Christianity and the barbarian invasions determined the course of history for centuries. Mohammedanism convulsed the Orient as well as the Western world for half a millennium. The consequences of the Reformation have affected the whole of central Europe. Nor were individual countries—either by skill or by deliberate non-participation—able to steer clear of events. Since the outbreak of the French Revolution the world has been moving with ever-increasing speed towards a new conflict, the most extreme solution of which is Bolshevism; and the essence and goal of Bolshevism is the elimination of those strata of mankind which have hitherto provided the leadership and their replacement by world-wide Jewry.

No nation will be able to avoid or abstain from this historical conflict. *Since Marxism, through its victory in Russia, has established one of the greatest empires as a forward base for its future operations, this question has become a menacing one. Against a democratic world which is ideologically split stands a unified aggressive will, based on an authoritarian ideology.*

The military resources of this aggressive will are in the meantime rapidly increasing from year to year. One has only to compare the Red Army as it actually exists today with the assumptions of military men of ten or fifteen years ago to realize the menacing extent of this development. Only consider the results of a further development over ten, fifteen or twenty years and think what conditions will be like then.

Germany

Germany will as always have to be regarded as the focus of the Western world against the attacks of Bolshevism. I do not regard this as an agreeable mission but as a serious handicap and burden for our national life, regrettably resulting from our disadvantageous position in Europe. We cannot, however, escape this destiny. Our political position results from the following:

At the moment there are only two countries in Europe which can be regarded as standing firm against Bolshevism—Germany and Italy. The other nations are either corrupted by their democratic way of life, infected by Marxism and therefore likely to collapse in the foreseeable future, or ruled by authoritarian Governments, whose sole strength lies in their military resources; this means, however, that being obliged to protect their leadership against their own peoples by the armed hand of the Executive, they are unable to use this armed hand for the protection of their countries against external enemies. None of these countries would ever be capable of waging war against Soviet Russia with any prospects of success. In fact, apart from Germany and Italy, only Japan can be considered as a Power standing firm in the face of the world peril.

It is not the aim of this memorandum to prophesy the moment when the untenable situation in Europe will reach the stage of an open crisis. I only want, in these lines, to express my conviction that this crisis cannot and will not fail to occur, and that Germany has the duty of securing her existence by every means in the face of this catastrophe, and to protect herself against it, and that this obligation has a number of implications involving the most important tasks that our people have ever been set. *For a victory of Bolshevism over Germany would lead not to a Versailles Treaty but to the final destruction, indeed to the annihilation, of the German people.*

The extent of such a catastrophe cannot be estimated. How, indeed, would the whole of densely populated Western Europe (including Germany), after a collapse into Bolshevism, live through probably the most gruesome catastrophe which has been visited on mankind since the downfall of the states of antiquity. *In face of the necessity of warding off this danger, all other considerations must recede into the background as completely irrelevant.*

Germany's defensive capacity

Germany's defensive capacity is based upon several factors. I would give pride of place to the intrinsic value of the German people *per se*. The German nation with an impeccable political leadership, a firm ideology, a thorough military organization, certainly constitutes the most valuable factor of resistance in the world today. Political leadership is ensured by the National Socialist Party; ideological solidarity has, since the victory of National Socialism, been introduced to a degree that has never previously been attained. It must be constantly deepened and strengthened on the basis of this concept. This is the aim of the National Socialist education of our people.

The development of our military capacity is to be effected through the new Army. *The extent of the military development of our resources cannot be too large, nor its pace too swift*. It is a major error to believe that there can be any argument on these points or any comparison with other vital necessities. However well-balanced the general pattern of a nation's life ought to be, there must at particular times be certain disturbances of the balance at the expense of other less vital tasks. *If we do not succeed in bringing the German Army as rapidly as possible to the rank of premier army in the world so far as its training, raising of units, armaments, and, above all, its spiritual education also is concerned, then Germany will be lost!* In this the basic principle applies that omissions during the months of peace cannot be made good in centuries.

Hence all other desires without exception must come second to this task. For this task involves life and the preservation of life, and all other desires—however understandable at other junctures—are unimportant or even mortally dangerous and are therefore to be rejected. Posterity will ask us one day, not what were the means, the reasons or the convictions by which we thought fit today to achieve the salvation of the nation, but *whether* in fact we achieved it. And on that day it will be no excuse for our downfall for us to describe the means which were infallible, but, alas, brought about our ruin.

Germany's economic situation

Just as the political movement among our people knows only one goal, the preservation of our existence, that is to say, the securing of all the spiritual and other prerequisites for the self-assertion of our nation, so neither has the economy any other goal than this. The nation does not live for the economy, for economic leaders, or for economic or financial theories; on the contrary, it is finance and the economy, economic leaders and theories, which all owe unqualified service in this struggle for the self-assertion of our nation. Germany's economic situation is, however, in the briefest outline as follows:

1. We are overpopulated and cannot feed ourselves from our own resources.

2. When our nation has six or seven million unemployed, the food situation improves because these people lack purchasing power. It naturally makes a difference whether six million people have 40 marks a month to spend, or 100 marks. It should not be overlooked that a third of all who earn their living is involved, that is to say that, taken as a proportion of the total population, through the National Socialist economic policy about 28 million people have been afforded an increase in their standard of living of, on average, from at least 50 marks a month to at most 100–120 marks. This means an increased and understandable run on the foodstuffs market.

3. But if this rise in employment fails to take place, the effect of undernourishment will be that a higher percentage of the population must gradually be deducted from the body of our nation, so far as its effective contribution is concerned. Thus, despite the difficult food situation, the most important task of our economic policy is to see to it that all Germans are incorporated into the economic process, and so the prerequisites for normal consumption are created.

4. In so far as this consumption concerns articles of general use, it can be satisfied to a *large* extent by an increase in production. In so far as this consumption falls upon the foodstuffs market, it cannot be satisfied from the domestic German economy. For, although the output of numerous products can be increased without difficulty, the yield of our agricultural production can undergo no further substantial increase. It is equally impossible for us at present to manufacture artificially certain raw materials which we lack in Germany or to find other substitutes for them.

5. There is, however, no point in endless repetition of the fact that we lack foodstuffs and raw materials; what matters is the taking of those measures which can bring about a *final* solution for the *future* and a *temporary* easing of conditions during the *transitional* period.

6. The final solution lies in extending our living space, that is to say, extending the sources of raw materials and foodstuffs of our people. It is the task of the political leadership one day to solve this problem.

7. The temporary easing of conditions can be achieved only within the framework of our present economy. In this connexion, the following must be noted:

(a) Since the German people will be increasingly dependent on imports for their food and must similarly, whatever happens, import a proportion at least of certain raw materials from abroad, every effort must be made to facilitate these imports.

(b) An increase in our own exports is possible in theory but in practice hardly likely. Germany does not export to a political or economic vacuum, but to areas where competition is very intense. Compared with the general international economic depression, our exports have fallen, not only *not more*, but in fact *less* than those of other nations and states. But since imports of food on the whole cannot be substantially reduced and are more likely to increase, an adjustment must be found in some other way.

(c) It is, however, impossible to use foreign exchange allocated for the purchase of raw materials to import foodstuffs without inflicting a heavy and perhaps even fatal blow on the rest. *But above all it is absolutely impossible to do this at the expense of national rearmament.* I must at this point sharply reject the view that by restricting national rearmament, that is to say, the manufacture of arms and ammunition, we could bring about an 'enrichment' in raw materials which might then benefit Germany in the event of war. Such a view is based on a complete misconception, to put it mildly, of the tasks and military requirements that lie before us. For even a successful saving of raw materials by reducing, for instance, the production of munitions would merely mean that we should stockpile these raw materials in time of peace so as to manufacture them only in the event of war, that is to say, we should be depriving ourselves during the most critical months of munitions in exchange for raw copper, lead, or possibly iron. But in that case it would none the less be better for the nation to enter the war without a single kilogram of copper in stock but with full munition depots rather than with empty munition depots but so-called 'enriched' stocks of raw material.

War makes possible the mobilization of even the last remaining supplies of metal. For it then becomes not an *economic problem*, but solely a *question of will*. And the National Socialist leadership of the country will have not only the will but also the resolution and the toughness necessary to solve these problems in the event of war. But it is much more important to prepare for war in time of peace. Moreover, in this respect the following must be stated:

There can be no building up of a reserve of *raw materials* for the event of war, just as there can be no building up of foreign exchange reserves. The attempt is sometimes made today so to represent matters as if Germany went to war in 1914 with well-prepared stocks of raw material. That is a lie. No country can assemble in advance the quantities of raw materials necessary for war lasting longer than, say, one year. But if any nation were really in a position to assemble those quantities of raw material needed for a year, then its political, military and economic leaders would deserve to be hanged. For they would in fact be setting aside the available copper and iron in preparation for the conduct of a war instead of manufacturing shells. But Germany went into the world war without any reserves whatsoever. What was available at that time in Germany in the way of apparent peacetime reserves was counterbalanced and rendered valueless by the miserable war stocks of ammunition. *Moreover, the quantities of war materials that are needed for a war are so large that there has* NEVER *in the history of the world been a real stock-piling for a period of any length!* And as regards preparations in the form of piling up foreign exchange it is quite clear that:

1. War is capable of devaluing foreign exchange at any time, unless it is held in gold.

2. There is not the least guarantee that gold itself can be converted in time of war into raw materials. During the world war Germany still possessed very large assets in foreign exchange in a great many countries. It was not, however, possible for our cunning economic policy-makers to bring to Germany, in exchange for them, fuel, rubber, copper or tin in any sufficient quantity. To assert the contrary is ridiculous nonsense. For this reason, and in order to secure the food supplies of our people, the following task presents itself as imperative:

It is not sufficient merely to establish from time to time raw material or foreign exchange balances, or to talk about the preparation of a war economy in time of peace; on the contrary, it is essential to ensure all the food supplies required in peacetime and, above all, those means for the conduct of a war which can be secured by human energy and activity. I therefore draw up the following programme for a final provision of our vital needs:

I. Parallel with the military and political rearmament and mobilization of our nation must go its economic rearmament and mobilization, and this must be effected in the same tempo, with the same determination, and if need be with the same ruthlessness as well. In future the interests of individual gentlemen can no longer play any part in these matters. There is only one interest, the interest of the nation; only one view, the bringing of Germany to the point of political and economic self-sufficiency.

II. For this purpose, foreign exchange must be saved in all those areas where our needs can be satisfied by German production, in order that it may be used for those requirements which can under no circumstances be fulfilled except by imports.

III. Accordingly, German fuel production must now be stepped up with the utmost speed and brought to final completion within eighteen months. This task must be attacked and carried out with the same determination as the waging of a war, since it is on the discharge of this task, not upon the laying in of stocks of petroleum, that the conduct of the future war depends.

IV. The mass production of synthetic rubber must also be organized and achieved with the same urgency. From now on there must be no talk of processes not being fully determined and other such excuses. It is not a matter of discussing whether we are to wait any longer; otherwise time will be lost, and the hour of peril will take us all by surprise. Above all, it is not the job of the economic institutions of Government to rack their brains over methods of production. This has nothing whatever to do with the Ministry of Economics. Either we possess today a private industry, in which case its job is to rack its brains about methods of production; or we believe that it is the Government's job to determine methods of production, and in that case we have no further need of private industry.

V. The question of the cost of producing these raw materials is also quite irrelevant, since it is in any case better for us to produce expensive tyres in Germany which we can use, than to sell theoretically cheap tyres, but tyres for which the Minister of Economics cannot allocate any foreign exchange, and which therefore cannot be produced for lack of raw materials and consequently cannot be used at all. If we really are obliged to build up our domestic economy on autarkic lines, which we are—for lamenting and harping on our foreign exchange plight will certainly not solve the problem—then the price of raw materials individually considered no longer plays a decisive part.

It is further necessary to increase German iron production to the utmost limits. The objection that with German ore, which has a 26 per cent ferrous content, we cannot produce pig iron as cheaply as with the 45 per cent Swedish ores, etc., is irrelevant; we are not faced with the question of what we would *rather* do, but what we *can* do. The objection, moreover, that in that event all the German blast-furnaces would have to be converted is equally irrelevant, and, what is more, this is no concern of the Ministry of Economics. The job of the Ministry of Economics is simply to set the national economic tasks; private industry has to fulfil them. But if private industry thinks itself incapable of doing this, then the National Socialist State will know how to resolve the problem on its own. In any case, for a thousand years Germany had no foreign iron ores. Even before the war, more German iron ores were being processed than during the period of our worst decline. *Nevertheless, if there is still the possibility of our importing cheaper ores, well and good. But the future of the national economy and, above all, of the conduct of war, must not depend on this.*

Moreover, the distillation of potatoes into alcohol must be prohibited forthwith. Fuel must be obtained from the ground, not from potatoes. Instead it is our duty to use any arable land that may become available either for human or animal foodstuffs or for the cultivation of fibrous materials.

It is further necessary for us to make our supplies of *industrial* fats independent of imports as quickly as possible. This can be done by using our coal. This problem has been solved by chemical means and the technique is actually crying out to be put into practice. Either German industry will grasp the new economic tasks or else it will show itself incapable of surviving any longer in this modern age in which a Soviet State is setting up a gigantic plan. *But in that case it will not be Germany that will go under, but at most a few industrialists.* Moreover, the extraction of other ores must be increased, *regardless of cost*, and, in particular, the production of light metals must be increased to the utmost limits, in order to produce a substitute for certain other metals.

Finally, it is also necessary for the rearmament programme to make use even now whenever possible of those materials which must and will replace high-grade metals in time of war. *It is better to consider and resolve these problems in time of peace than to wait for the next war and only then, in the midst of a multitude of tasks, to try to undertake these economic researches and experiments with methods.*

In short, I consider it necessary that now, with iron determination, a 100 per cent self-sufficiency should be attained in every sphere where it is feasible, and that not only should the national requirements in these most essential raw materials be made independent of other countries, but we should also thus save the foreign exchange which in peacetime we need for our imports of foodstuffs. *In this connexion, I want to emphasize that in these tasks I see the only true economic mobilization and not in the throttling of armament industries in peacetime in order to save and stockpile raw materials for war.*

But I further consider it necessary to make an immediate investigation of the outstanding debts in foreign exchange owed to German business abroad. There is no doubt that the outstanding claims of German business abroad are quite enormous. Nor is there any doubt that behind this in some cases there lies concealed the contemptible desire to possess, whatever happens, certain reserves abroad which are thus withheld from the grasp of the domestic economy. I regard this as deliberate sabotage of our national self-assertion, that is to say, of the defence of the Reich, and I therefore consider it necessary for the Reichstag to pass the following two laws:

1. A law providing the death penalty for economic sabotage, and
2. A law making the whole of Jewry liable for all damage inflicted by individual specimens of this community of criminals upon the German economy, and thus upon the German people.

Only the fulfilment of these tasks, in the form of a Several Years Plan for rendering our national economy independent of foreign countries, will make it possible for the first time to demand sacrifices from the German people in the economic sphere and in that of foodstuffs. For then the nation will have a right to demand of their leaders, whom they blindly acknowledge, that they should not only talk about the problems in this field but tackle them with unparalleled and determined energy, not only point them out but solve them.

Nearly four precious years have now gone by. There is no doubt that by now we could have been completely independent of foreign countries in the spheres of fuel supplies, rubber supplies, and partly also iron ore supplies. Just as we are now producing 700,000 or 800,000 tons of petroleum, we could be producing 3 million tons. Just as we are today manufacturing a few thousand tons of rubber, we could already be producing 70,000 or 80,000 tons per annum. Just as we have stepped up the production of iron ore from 2½ million tons to 7 million tons, we could process 20 or 25 million tons of German iron ore and even 30 millions if necessary. There has been time enough in four years to find out what we cannot do. Now we have to carry out what we can do.

I thus set the following tasks:

I. The German armed forces must be operational within four years.

II. The German economy must be fit for war within four years.

17 *Cabinet meeting on the introduction of the Four-Year Plan, 4 September 1936*

On 4 September, Göring read out Hitler's memorandum to the Cabinet and emphasized its implications for the economy:

. . .

SECRET REICH MATTER

Minutes of Cabinet Meeting
of 4 September 1936, 12 noon
Chairman: Minister-President Colonel-General Göring.
Reich Minister of Defence Field-Marshal von Blomberg.
Reich Bank President and Provisional Reich and Prussian Minister of Economics Dr Schacht.
Reich Minister of Finance Graf Schwerin von Krosigk.
Prussian Minister of Finance Prof. Dr Popitz.
State Secretary Koerner.
Economic Adviser of the Führer Keppler.
State Councillor Neumann.
Chief of Staff of the Reich Peasant Leader Dr Reischle.
Keeper of the minutes: Lt.-Col. Löb of the General Staff.

Min.-Pres. Göring: Today's meeting is of greater importance than all previous meetings.

At the last Cabinet meeting of 11 August 1936 it was agreed that supplementary material was needed in order to make it possible to reach a decision.

Meanwhile new trouble has arisen, especially in connexion with non-precious metals and rubber; even the Führer has been drawn into this affair. . . .

. . . Certain persons have been asked for memoranda on the basic conduct of the economy. So far only one has been presented, by Dr Goerdeler, and it is absolutely useless. In addition to many other erroneous ideas it contains the proposal for a considerable limitation of armaments.

In this connexion it should be stated that the mandate of the Colonel-General [as Commissioner for raw materials] refers to the 'ensuring of armaments' which must rather be speeded up than slowed down.

The Führer and Reich Chancellor has given a memorandum to the Colonel-General and the Reich Defence Minister which provides general instructions for putting it into effect.

It starts from the basic premise that the showdown with Russia is inevitable. What Russia has done in the field of reconstruction, we also can do.

Just what sort of risk is it that our industry is afraid of, compared to the risk in the sphere of foreign affairs which the Führer runs so continually?

The Führer is about to have a memorandum issued concerning the financial angle of this problem.

Research on the problem of increasing exports, for instance, has shown that there are hardly any fundamentally new ways to be found. It will not be possible to create a balance of foreign exchange merely by means of exports. The 'New Plan' of the Reich Minister of Economics is acceptable in its basic features, but it can be improved in detail.

The Colonel-General reads the memorandum of the Führer.

The Colonel-General is responsible for the execution of the tasks outlined in the memorandum.

If war should break out tomorrow we would be forced to take measures from which we might possibly still shy away at the present moment. They are, therefore, feasible. Two basic principles:

1. We must strive with the greatest energy for autarky in all those spheres in which it is technically possible; the yearly amount of foreign exchange savings must still surpass that of the first proposal made by the raw materials and foreign exchange staff anticipating savings of 600 million Reichsmarks.

2. We have to tide over with foreign exchange all cases where it seems necessary for armaments and food.

In order to provide for foreign exchange, its flow abroad must be prevented by every means; on the other hand, whatever is abroad must be collected.

The Führer is going to speak very soon to the industrial leaders and disclose to them his basic ideas.

In view of the authority of the State the necessary measures are definitely feasible. Frederick the Great, to whom reference is being made from the most diverse quarters, was in his financial policy a strong inflationist.

Through the genius of the Führer things which were apparently impossible have very quickly become reality; most recent example: introduction of the two-year military service and recognition on the part of France that we need a stronger Wehrmacht than France herself. The tasks now ahead of us are considerably smaller than those we have already accomplished.

All those measures which can be carried through with domestic German money are possible and should be carried out. By their means the requirements of industry and food supply needing foreign exchange must be given a lower priority.

All measures must be taken as if we were actually at the stage of imminent mobilization.

The execution of the order of the Führer is an absolute command.

End of meeting: 1300 hrs.

18 *Decree on the Execution of the Four-Year Plan, 18 October 1936*

The realization of the new Four-Year Plan as proclaimed by me at the Party Congress of Honour [*Parteitag der Ehre*] requires the uniform direction of all the powers of the German nation and the rigid consolidation of all pertinent authorities within Party and State.

I assign the execution of the Four-Year Plan to Minister-President General Göring.

Minister-President General Göring will take the necessary measures for the fulfilment of the task given him, and in this respect he has authority to issue legal decrees and general administrative regulations. He is authorized to hear and to issue instructions to all authorities, including the Supreme Authorities of the Reich, and all agencies of the Party, its formations and affiliated organizations.

ADOLF HITLER

Armed with these far-reaching powers, Göring set about establishing an organization for the putting of the Four-Year Plan into operation. In this he followed two different lines of approach. On the one hand, he established a separate Four-Year Plan organization. This consisted of six departments responsible for (1) the production of German raw materials, (2) the distribution of raw materials, (3) the labour force, (4) agricultural production, (5) price supervision, and (6) foreign exchange matters. The responsibility for the production of raw materials was then distributed between an Office for German Raw Materials and an Office for the Planning and Production of Industrial Fats. The coordination of these six departments was carried out by Ministerialdirektor Neumann of the Prussian State Ministry, who was simultaneously head of the Four-Year Plan department for foreign exchange.

The most important of these departments was the Office for German Raw Materials, which was responsible for the main objective of the Four-Year Plan—the production of raw materials. It was headed by a Colonel Löb, who came from Göring's Air Ministry. The office was staffed by a combination of Air Force officers and representatives of private industry, of whom the most important was Carl Krauch of I G-Farben who was responsible for research and development in the vital chemicals sector. At the beginning of 1938, Krauch replaced Löb, and the Office for German Raw Materials was transformed into the Reich Agency for Economic Consolidation (*Reichsstelle für Wirtschaftsausbau*), a separate Reich authority. Under Krauch there occurred a switch in emphasis within the plan from a general expansion of the raw materials sector to a concentration on specific items which were most urgently needed for rearmament purposes: oil, rubber, light metals and, in particular, gunpowder and explosives for which a special 'express plan' was introduced. This new 'Krauch plan', introduced on 30 June 1938 and intended to cover a period of four years, reflected the new tempo in German foreign policy during 1938 and significantly the 'express plan' was intended to increase Germany's capacity in the areas it covered so that by the end of 1939 it would have reached 'the maximum level of productive capacity achieved in the World War'.

The emergence of Krauch as the most influential figure within the Four-Year Plan organization under Göring set a pattern for the employment of representatives from private industry in semi-official capacities which from now onwards became a characteristic feature of German economic organization. It provided both expertise and administrative flexibility, but at the cost of undermining the structure of the Civil Service, since these men from industry were outside the Civil Service hierarchy and subordinate only to Göring. There has been some controversy among historians, particularly between Western historians and those from East Germany, about the significance of that close relationship between private industry and the Nazi State of which this is by no means the only instance. Historians in East Germany seek to show that the regime was being used by 'monopoly capital' for its own ends and was, indeed, to a large extent its creation. Western historians, on the other hand, tend to argue that it was the state that used industry rather than the other way round, and that politics rather than economics provides the key to understanding the regime.

Although a separate organization was created for the Four-Year Plan, Göring simultaneously followed another line of approach by appointing the State Secretaries in the Ministries of Labour and Agriculture to head the Labour and Agricultural departments in his Four-Year Plan organization. In this way, he effectively coordinated the two Ministries in the interests of the Four-Year Plan. The Ministers of Labour and Agriculture (Seldte and Darré) increasingly found their power being drained off by way of their State Secretaries to the Four-Year Plan organization which had the mighty Göring behind it, and behind him Hitler. Their own lines of communication with the Führer were not nearly so good.

During the following months, Schacht also shared this experience. Increasingly he found his previous power over the economy being undermined by decisions of the Four-Year Plan taken independently of the Economics Ministry in spheres which had hitherto been within its sole competence. Thus, in 1937, a mining ordinance taking over a mining company was issued by the Four-Year Plan, despite the fact that this sphere came under Schacht's responsibility as Minister of Economics. This brought to a head Schacht's growing discontent with what he regarded as the excessive speed of rearmament and the priority given to the uneconomic production of raw materials instead of resources being devoted to exports. After a rather acrimonious correspondence with Göring, he offered his resignation as Minister of Economics, which was eventually accepted on 26 November 1937. He was replaced by the pliable Walther Funk, so that in effect the Ministry of Economics had now also been absorbed within the power orbit of the Four-Year Plan.

The Four-Year Plan, then, represented a reorientation of the economy in the interests of the manufacture of synthetic raw materials and of an increase in the production of Germany's own sources of raw materials, such as coal and iron ore, even where these were uneconomic compared to the price levels of the world market. The following figures show the degree of success achieved in reaching the targets in the most important spheres:

19 *German production increases in the sphere of the Four-Year Plan*

(in thousands of tons)

Commodity	1936 output	1938 output	1942 output	Plan target
Mineral oil*	1,790	2,340	6,260	13,830
Aluminium	98	166	260	273
Buna rubber	0·7	5	96	120
Nitrogen	770	914	930	1,040
Explosives	18	45	300	223
Powder	20	26	150	217
Steel	19,216	22,656	20,480	24,000
Iron ore	2,255	3,360	4,137	5,549
Brown coal	161,382	194,985	245,918	240,500
Hard coal	158,400	186,186	166,059	213,000

* Including synthetic petrol.

20 *The state of German armaments in May 1939*

The most striking failure to match the target was in synthetic petrol, despite the fact that, in the years 1937–42, 40–50 per cent of total investment under the plan went into the production of synthetic fuel. In fact, although the production of synthetic fuel increased by 130 per cent in the years 1936–39, it still only covered 18 per cent of the demand. A major problem was the long time taken by the construction of the factories, which only really began to make themselves felt during the war. In general, by the outbreak of war, Germany was still dependent on foreign sources of supply for one-third of her raw material requirements. Moreover, despite the Four-Year Plan, the German economy had been subjected to no more than partial mobilization for the purposes of rearmament and large areas of it remained relatively unaffected.

In view of this situation, Georg Thomas, the Chief of the Wehrmacht Economic Office, now promoted to General, concluded that Germany's preparations for war were satisfactory in terms of operational units and equipment (armament in breadth), but inadequate in terms of the economic resources necessary for fighting a long war (armament in depth). In fact, however, this situation coincided with Hitler's strategic ideas. Hitler believed that Germany had not the resources with which to fight a long-drawn-out war against several opponents at once. The Four-Year Plan was in his eyes a stop-gap measure to avoid the worst bottlenecks until Germany could conquer the supplies of raw materials she needed. To achieve these conquests Germany must take on her opponents individually and, by concentrating her limited but well-equipped forces, knock them out one by one in lightning wars. This so-called *Blitzkrieg* strategy had also the advantage that it did not require the total mobilization of the nation which he thought might undermine the popularity of the regime.

In the following lecture given at the Foreign Office on 24 May 1939, Thomas gave his assessment of the situation, particularly as regards the question of armament in breadth and armament in depth. In fact, he tended somewhat to exaggerate the degree of readiness of the German armed forces at the level of operational equipment. As he himself was to note later, at the outbreak of war in September 1939 there were shortages of between 45 and 95 per cent in the four months' supplies of the various types of munitions which were regarded by the Army High Command as the minimum required for war:

I

I begin with the state of German rearmament. You have already been given a survey of the present organization of the Wehrmacht by the various sections of the Wehrmacht so that I can be brief and will only cover the development of rearmament.

You know that the *Diktat* of Versailles had limited the number of German divisions to seven, that an air force was prohibited, and that the Treaty completely forbade the Navy to build ships of over 10,000 tons or submarines. The production of arms, ammunition and military equipment was limited to a few authorized plants. All other establishments had been systematically destroyed. Until the end of 1933, despite secret camouflaged attempts, no essential change occurred in the situation, so that we can state that the present rearmament represents the work of four years.

The 100,000-man Army of 7 infantry divisions and 3 cavalry divisions compares today with a peacetime army of 18 corps headquarters [*Generalkommandos*], 39 infantry divisions, among them 4 fully motorized and 3 mountain divisions, 5 Panzer divisions, 4 light divisions and 22 machine-gun battalions. In addition to this, there is on the border a large number of permanent border protection units. Although any larger-scale procurement of new arms for the 100,000-man Army was out of the question, nevertheless the development of new types was busily carried on in secret, and so it was possible to equip our present Army in all fields with the most modern weapons and it is certainly unrivalled throughout the world for its entire infantry armament and the large number of its types of guns. Completely new, and developed only in the last five years, are the five Panzer divisions, the modern battle cavalry, and the light divisions, the light cavalry.

Conditions in the field of war material are the same. The entire equipment of the armoured divisions and the light divisions has been newly built. This achievement can be fully appreciated only by one who knows what it means to produce, after a ban of fifteen years on these armaments, a tank fit for combat which will satisfy the modern requirements of speed, cross-country mobility and armour.

In addition, an enormous number of special motor vehicles, sometimes of the most difficult construction, has been developed and procured, and the artillery has been partly motorized and provided with the most modern sound- and light-measuring equipment. The great increase in technical troops makes special demands on the armament industry.

Besides this manifold rearmament there is the construction of border fortifications first begun in the east and started in the west as soon as the situation permitted. You have all seen the concentration on the development in the west during the last year. In this connexion I want to mention that the construction of modern fortresses makes the highest demands on the armament firms which build turrets for tanks.

The prewar peacetime Army was increased from 43 divisions to 50 divisions in the period from 1898 to 1914, that is, in sixteen years. Our rearmament from 7 infantry divisions to 51 divisions represents, as I have already stated, the work of four years.

The Navy in 1933 had, in addition to a few obsolete prewar ships of the line, 1 armoured ship of 10,000 tons, 6 light cruisers and 12 torpedo boats. Since 1933 we have put into service 2 battleships of 26,000 tons each, 2 armoured ships of 10,000 tons each, 17 destroyers and 47 submarines, a total tonnage of 125,000. Also launched were 2 battleships of 35,000 tons, 4 heavy cruisers of 10,000 tons, 1 aircraft carrier, 5 destroyers and 7 submarines totalling 106,000 tons. The launching of additional ships is impending.

The Luftwaffe has risen again and today has a strength of 260,000 men. Today the Luftwaffe already possesses 21 squadrons consisting of 240 echelons. It is in the process of being increased. The anti-aircraft arm, with its four types, is certainly the most modern in the world and already embraces almost 300 anti-aircraft batteries. Anti-aircraft guns of still larger calibres are being introduced.

The German armament industry has been developed to the same extent. Out of the few factories permitted by the Versailles Treaty has risen the mightiest armament industry now existing in the world. Its performance has partly equalled the German wartime performance, and partly even surpassed it. Germany's crude steel production is today the largest in the world after America's, aluminium production exceeds that of America and the other countries of the world by a considerable margin. The output of our rifle, machine-gun and artillery factories is at present larger than that of any other State. Our powder and explosive production in the next year will again reach the volume of the Hindenburg programme.[1]

And yet, despite this extraordinary feat of reconstruction, to which the Four-Year Plan in particular has greatly contributed, there are still considerable deficiencies in the sphere of our economic armament. . . .

In conclusion we can state that the total German rearmament, in the field of personnel as well as of war material, represents an achievement of the German people probably unique in the world, and a testimony to a resolute leadership and to the energy and creativeness innate in the German people. The great efforts of German industry and of the German people in both finance and hard work have undoubtedly yielded the desired result and we can perceive today that German armament in its breadth and its state of preparedness has a considerable start over the armament of all other countries.

But if one compares the armament situation not in terms of its breadth and preparedness, but in terms of the depth of armament or, to put it in another way, the possibility of endurance in the event of a new world war, the picture looks different. . . .

II

Gentlemen! All the time I have been in charge of my department, I have always pointed out the difference between armament in breadth and armament in depth.

[1] The expanded armament programme of 1916.

By armament in breadth I mean the number and strength of the armed forces in peacetime and the preparations made to increase them in the event of war.

Armament in depth, on the other hand, embraces all those measures, particularly those affecting materials and of an economic nature, which serve to provide supplies during war and therefore strengthen our powers of endurance.

We are all clear about our present superiority in breadth and in the initial striking power of our armament; now we must analyse whether we can retain this superiority in an armaments race and thereby achieve superiority in depth of armament.

Allow me first to say a few words about the dangers which can develop if too much attention is paid to armament in breadth at the expense of armament in depth.

We all know that in every war, soon after the beginning of operations, a request comes for new formations and that then all available resources are recklessly released to provide these new formations. At the same time, there is a request for increased amounts of munitions and all the other necessities, and woe betide the leadership of economic warfare if it is not in a position to fulfil these demands owing to a lack of reserves of finished goods or raw materials and semi-finished products. Here again the old proverb still holds good: 'Save in time of plenty and you will have something in time of need.' You will understand if, particularly at the present time in which the sections of the armed forces are considerably enlarged every year, I emphasize in all seriousness the need of improving our armament in depth. . . .

The information which we have so far received does not indicate that the western Great Powers are as yet pursuing rearmament with the same energy as we are. But should the political situation lead to a long-drawn-out armaments race we must of course realize that the Western Powers, considering the capacity of their economies for producing armaments, will be in a position to catch up with the German lead in $1-1\frac{1}{2}$ years. The combined economic strength of Britain, America, and France is in the long run greater than that of the Axis Powers and in an armaments race the Western Powers will not have the same difficulties which Germany and Italy will always have on account of their lack of raw materials and manpower. If it comes to such an armaments race and then to a war the result of that war will, in my opinion, depend on whether the Axis States succeed in bringing about a decision by a quick decisive blow. If they do not succeed in this, if it comes to a struggle like that of the world war, then the depth of military economic power, that is, the powers of endurance, will decide the issue.

It is not my task to speculate on the possible success or failure of such a lightning war [*Blitzkrieg*]. I myself do not believe that a conflict between the Axis Powers and the Western Powers will be a question of a lightning war, that is, a matter of days and weeks. As far as I am concerned, as Chief of Defence Economic Staff, it is essential for the armaments industry to be prepared for a long war. Our preparations must concentrate on strengthening our armament in depth as much as possible.

There are three particularly important points which must chiefly concern us in this connexion:

    1. The securing of the German food situation;[1]

[1] Thomas emphasizes in particular the shortage of fats.

2. The securing of iron ore supplies;

3. The oil and rubber question. . . .

. . . Another problem is that considerable financial resources are called for and are employed on projects which do not serve German armament and could be postponed for a few years. At the moment our German economy is not 100 per cent employed but 125 per cent. And these superfluous 25 per cent are the contracts which bring disorder into the economy and lay upon us a considerable financial burden.[1] In our present military and economic situation, we must in my opinion follow one path only, that of bringing back the old order into the economy and concentrating all our economic resources on the strengthening of our economic armament.

Concentration of our resources must be our watchword in all spheres, in personnel as in materials, in the regulation of manpower as in the distribution of raw materials and machinery. . . .

21 *Estimated investment in the German economy, 1928–38, classified in relation to military potential*

(in billions RM)

Year	Total investment	Military investment (a)	Basic (incl. Four-Yr. Pl.) (b)	Industry (Four-Year Plan only)	Major transport and roads (c)	Civilian economy (c)
1928	13·8	0·5	2·7	—	1·3	9·3
1933	6·8	1·0	0·5	—	0·8	4·5
1934	10·6	3·4	1·0	—	1·2	5·0
1935	14·4	5·0	1·6	—	1·4	6·4
1936	21·1	9·3	3·0	(0·8)	1·6	7·2
1937	23·2	9·5	4·3	(1·5)	1·8	7·6
1938	29·8	13·6	5·6	(2·0)	2·6	8·0
Totals						
1933–8	105·9	41·8	16·0	(4·3)	9·4	38·7

(a) Military expenditure for buildings, armaments, ships, vehicles, industrial subsidies, etc. Excludes administrative and personnel expenditure.

(b) Includes: Mining and metallurgy; chemical and fuel industries; other producer goods; machinery, automotive and electrical industries; locomotives and cars; ship-building; power and water; iron, steel and metal-working; optical and precision instruments.

(c) Agriculture, light industries, post office and communications, civilian construction (private, state, municipal, and NSDAP).

[1] e.g. the contracts for Party offices and other prestige building projects which Speer describes in his memoirs *Inside the Third Reich* (London 1970), pp. 73ff.

22 Gross national product and military expenditure in Germany, the United States and Britain, 1929–45

Year	Germany			United States			Britain		
	RM billions			$ billions			£ billions		
	GNP	Mil. exp.	Per cent	GNP	Mil. exp.	Per cent	Natl. inc.	Mil. exp.	Per cent
	(a)			(b)			(c)		
1929	89	0·8	1	104	0·7	1	4·2	0·1	2
1932	58	0·8	1	59	0·6	1	—	0·1	—
1933	59	1·9	3	56	0·5	1	3·7	0·1	3
1934	67	4·1	6	65	0·7	1	3·9	0·1	3
1935	74	6·0	8	73	0·9	1	4·1	0·1	2
1936	83	10·8	13	83	0·9	1	4·4	0·2	5
1937	93	11·7	13	91	1·0	1	4·6	0·3	7
1938	105	17·2	17	85	1·0	1	4·8	0·4	8
1939	130	30·0	23	91	1·3	1	5·0	1·1	22
1940	141	53·0	38	101	2·2	2	6·0	3·2	53
1941	152	71·0	47	126	13·8	11	6·8	4·1	60
1942	165	91·0	55	159	49·6	31	7·5	4·8	64
1943	184	112·0	61	193	80·4	42	8·0	5·0	63
1944	—	—	—	211	88·6	42	8·2	5·1	62
1945	—	—	—	214	75·9	36	8·3	4·4	53

(a) For the years 1939–43, includes Austria and Sudetenland. Figures are rounded to the nearest billion.

(b) Figures are rounded to the nearest billion.

(c) Britain's gross national product may be estimated at about one billion above national income, resulting in a slightly downward revision of the percentages calculated here. For example, military expenditures calculated against gross national product would give 7 per cent in 1938, 18 per cent in 1939, and a peak of 57 per cent in 1942.

23 German Visible Foreign Trade: Exports and Imports 1928–1938
(in millions RM)

Year	Imports	Exports[1]	Balance	Imports	Exports[1]	Balance	Imports	Exports	Imports	Exports
	a) At current prices			b) At 1928 prices			Movement of prices 1936 = 100		Movement of volume 1928 = 100	
1928	14,001[2]	12,276[2]	−1,725	14,001	12,276	−1,725	204·1	169·8	100	100
1929	13,447	13,483	+36	13,512	13,669	+157	203·1	167·6	96·5	111·3
1930	10,393	12,036	+1,643	12,039	12,958	+919	176·1	157·7	86·0	105·6
1931	6,727	9,599	+2,872	10,156	11,771	+1,615	135·1	138·4	72·5	95·9
1932	4,667	5,739	+1,072	9,466	8,123	−1,342	100·6	120·0	67·6	66·2
1933	4,204	4,871	+667	7,627	9,312	−1,685	92·2	108·5	66·5	62·1
1934	4,451	4,167	−284	9,809	6,810	−2,999	92·4	103·9	70·0	55·5
1935	4,159	4,270	+111	8,956	7,334	−1,622	94·7	98·8	64·0	69·7
1936	4,218	4,768	+550	8,610	8,092	−518	100·0	100·0	61·5	65·8
1937[3]	5,468	5,911	+443	10,089	9,360	−729	110·6	107·1	72·0	76·2
1938[4]	5,449	5,257	−192	10,792	7,937	−3,455	103·1	112·4	85·5	69·2

[1] From 1928 to 1932 including reparations deliveries. [2] Corrected totals.
[3] From 1937 onwards including silver. [4] Excluding trade with Austria.

Imports 1928–1938: subdivided into agricultural and industrial goods
(a) At current prices

Year	Total [5)6)]	AGRICULTURE					INDUSTRY				
		Total	Live animals	Foodstuffs		Luxuries (e.g. tea and coffee)	Total	Raw materials	Semi-finished goods	Finished goods	Returned goods [6)]
				Animal	Plant						
1913	10,769·7	4,111·4	299·7	906·5	2,452·7	462·5	6,658·3	3,762·0	1,850·4	1,045·9	—
1928	14,001·3	5,721·9	144·8	1,493·9	3,380·3	702·9	8,279·4	3,968·8	2,503·2	1,807·4	—
1929	13,446·8	5,380·6	149·7	1,544·5	2,943·1	743·3	8,066·2	3,927·4	2,374·0	1,764·8	—
1930	10,393·1	4,229·7	118·3	1,310·3	2,166·1	635·0	6,163·4	2,904·4	1,848·1	1,410·9	—
1931	6,727·1	2,783·2	54·9	857·1	1,432·7	438·5	3.943·9	1,832·2	1,145·3	966·4	—
1932	4,666·5	2,132·7	34·3	593·8	1,182·1	322·5	2,533·8	1,271·7	704·3	557·8	—
1933	4,203·6	1,629·7	30·9	432·5	869·9	296·4	2,573·9	1,367·6	701·4	504·9	—
1934	4,451·0	1,543·2	33·3	385·7	827·5	296·7	2,907·8	1,540·7	791·5	575·6	—
1935	4,158·7	1,435·2	45·1	405·5	704·9	279·7	2,723·5	1,567·9	747·5	408·1	—
1936	4,217·9	1,499·4	96·3	443·7	670·2	289·2	2,718·5	1,571·1	750·0	397·4	—
1937	5,468·4	2,045·1	107·5	479·7	1,135·2	322·7	3,373·1	1,996·2	980·3	396·6	50·2
1938	6,051·7	2,393·8	186·8	508·7	1,332·7	365·1	3,607·4	1,991·4	1,139·8	476·2	51·2

Imports 1928–1938: subdivided into agricultural and industrial goods
(b) At 1928 prices

Year	Total [5)6)]	AGRICULTURE					INDUSTRY				
		Total	Live animals	Foodstuffs		Luxuries (e.g. tea and coffee)	Total	Raw materials	Semi-finished goods	Finished goods	Returned goods [5)]
				Animal	Plant						
1913	14,599·9	5,870·1	307·8	1,232·0	3,599·5	730·8	8,729·8	4,967·4	2,206·9	1,555·5	—
1928	14,001·3	5,721·9	144·8	1,493·9	3,380·3	702·9	8,279·4	3,968·8	2,503·2	1,807·4	—
1929	13,511·9	5,522·9	150·2	1,555·7	3,114·2	702·8	7,989·0	3,980·5	2,308·3	1,700·2	—
1930	12,039·0	5,013·8	122·0	1,489·0	2,701·4	701·4	7,025·2	3,617·2	1,995·9	1,412·1	—
1931	10,156·4	4,245·9	71·1	1,233·1	2,339·1	602·6	5,910·5	3,140·7	1,700·4	1,069·4	—
1932	9,464·6	4,212·1	71·2	1,179·9	2,420·1	540·9	5,252·5	3,045·9	1,417·8	788·8	—
1933	9,311·9	3,601·9	69·0	921·6	2,045·8	565·5	5,710·0	3,425·4	1,508·9	775·7	—
1934	9,809·4	3,676·8	71·2	856·1	2,107·2	642·3	6,132·6	3,447·8	1,768·8	916·0	—
1935	8,956·2	3,180·6	85·1	892·0	1,575·4	628·1	5,775·6	3,423·9	1,695·8	655·9	—
1936	8,610·0	3,194·0	166·9	887·5	1,494·2	645·4	5,416·0	3,155·9	1,640·3	619·8	—
1937	10,089·3	4,133·6	168·2	990·9	2,262·1	712·4	5,876·5	3,486·5	1,786·7	603·3	79·2
1938	11,973·3	5,018·5	276·6	1,077·6	2,854·5	809·8	6,878·8	3,812·3	2,303·6	762·9	76·0

[5] Up until 1936 the returned goods are included in the totals of the individual goods.
[6] Until 1936 excluding silver.

Exports 1928–1938: subdivided into agricultural and industrial goods
(a) At current prices

| Year | Total 5)6) | AGRICULTURE | | Foodstuffs | | | INDUSTRY | | | | Returned goods 5) |
		Total	Live animals	Animal	Plant	Luxuries (e.g. chocolate)	Total	Raw materials	Semi-finished goods	Finished goods	
1913	10,097·2	1,213·8	7·4	57·0	1,050·7	98·7	8,883·4	1,346·9	1,082·7	6,453·8	
1928	12,275·6	787·8	18·8	51·1	651·3	66·8	11,487·8	1,498·0	1,491·5	8,498·3	—
1929	13,482·7	869·9	22·0	56·7	721·5	69·7	12,612·8	1,582·0	1,596·3	9,434·5	—
1930	12,035·6	660·7	68·7	77·9	450·0	64·1	11,374·9	1,332·5	1,333·2	8,709·2	—
1931	9,598·6	483·8	46·9	64·1	318·7	54·1	9,114·8	989·6	985·1	7,140·1	—
1932	5,739·2	260·0	14·5	35·8	177·8	31·9	5,479·2	577·6	556·3	4,345·3	—
1933	4,871·4	222·3	9·0	29·3	146·4	37·6	4,649·1	515·9	473·7	3,659·5	—
1934	4,166·9	150·3	3·8	21·3	89·0	36·2	4,016·6	463·5	404·7	3,148·4	—
1935	4,269·7	95·7	2·9	13·4	49·6	29·8	4,174·0	446·7	415·7	3,311·6	—
1936	4,768·2	87·6	2·6	9·7	45·4	29·9	4,680·6	419·2	459·1	3,802·3	—
1937	5,911·0	88·8	2·8	9·6	45·7	30·7	5,820·8	577·6	543·2	4,700·0	1·4
1938	5,619·1	66·7	2·0	9·7	30·0	25·0	5,549·0	534·3	473·0	4,541·7	3·4

Exports 1928–1938: subdivided into agricultural and industrial goods
(b) At 1928 prices

| Year | Total 5)6) | AGRICULTURE | | Foodstuffs | | | INDUSTRY | | | | Returned goods 5) |
		Total	Live animals	Animal	Plant	Luxuries (e.g. chocolate)	Total	Raw materials	Semi-finished goods	Finished goods	
1913	14,885·6	1,612·4	12·8	85·7	1,360·2	153·7	13,273·2	1,947·8	1,324·1	10,001·3	—
1928	12,275·6	787·8	18·8	51·1	651·3	66·6	11,487·8	1,498·0	1,491·5	8,498·3	—
1929	13,669·2	950·2	19·5	56·0	803·7	71·0	12,719·0	1,632·5	1,636·9	9,449·6	—
1930	12,957·5	877·6	78·1	87·1	641·0	71·4	12,079·9	1,549·7	1,460·9	9,069·3	—
1931	11,770·6	778·4	68·7	84·0	555·7	70·0	10,992·2	1,421·5	1,330·9	8,239·8	—
1932	8,122·8	490·4	27·2	56·4	362·6	44·2	7,632·4	1,062·5	981·9	5,588·0	—
1933	7,627·1	520·7	17·1	47·5	409·8	46·3	7,106·4	1,016·8	943·0	5,146·6	—
1934	6,810·3	349·2	5·6	35·0	262·1	46·5	6,461·1	936·4	858·9	4,665·8	—
1935	7,333·6	169·6	3·9	22·4	101·6	41·7	7,164·0	932·1	938·3	5,293·6	—
1936	8,091·6	159·4	3·9	14·3	93·8	47·4	7,932·2	833·5	989·1	6,109·6	—
1937	9,360·0	154·9	2·8	15·3	85·2	51·6	9,202·6	1,014·3	1,059·5	7,128·8	2·5
1938	8,491·9	121·2	2·0	19·4	57·3	42·5	8,364·0	866·7	885·3	6,612·0	6·7

5 Up until 1936 the returned goods are included in the totals of the individual goods.
6 Until 1936 excluding silver.

14   Labour

One of the basic aims of the Nazi Party had been to win the workers. This aim was expressed even in the name of the Party—the National Socialist German Workers' Party. Hitler had seen the *raison d'être* of the Party in the attempt to win the workers away from 'Jewish' Marxism and Internationalism and for nationalism and antisemitism. This he believed to be the prerequisite for German expansion. Yet, in the period before 1933, the workers had on the whole remained loyal to the Social Democratic Party. The more radical of them tended to support the Communists rather than the Nazis. The National Socialist Factory Cell Organization (NSBO), which had attempted to provide a Nazi alternative to the trade unions, had had little success.

The 'seizure of power'

On coming to power, then, the Nazis were determined to eliminate hostile working-class organizations and to win the support of the workers for the new State. There were three different trade-union organizations for manual workers: the so-called Free Trade Unions which were close to the Social Democratic Party and were by far the largest; the Catholic Christian Trade Unions which were quite influential in the Catholic industrial areas such as the Rhineland and were close to the Centre Party; and finally, the small Hirsch-Dunker unions which were liberal and tended to be nationalist in outlook. These divisions within the trade-union movement now weakened it in the face of Nazism.

1 *Law on Factory Representative Councils and Business Organizations,*
   4 April 1933

The Nazis struck first at the Free Trade Unions as part of their campaign against the Left. During March, a number of trade-union offices were ransacked by the SA and many of their officials were arrested and beaten up.[1] Furthermore, during March many leading Socialists and Communists were purged from the works councils in the factories by the SA and the NSBO. Despite their pressure, however, in the works council elections in March, the NSBO candidates still only won 25 per cent of the vote. The regime was therefore obliged to take official action to coordinate the works councils. On 4 April, Nazi control over the works councils was ensured by law:

[1] See above, pp. 180ff.

The Reich Cabinet has passed the following law which is proclaimed herewith:

CHAPTER I: FACTORY REPRESENTATIVE COUNCILS

Article 1

1. The Reich authorities can postpone the elections for the Factory Representative Council for the Reich, parts of the Reich or for individual enterprises until 30 September of this year at the latest, for reasons of public safety and order.

2. If the elections are postponed the existing Factory Representative Council will remain in office. It is only necessary to fill vacancies in Factory Representative Councils caused by the dismissal of members if the number of its members has fallen below half of the legal number of members, or if they number less than three. The new members of the Factory Representative Council required for its minimum strength will be nominated from the eligible workers by the Reich authorities.

Article 2

The Reich authorities can cancel the membership of members who are opposed to the spirit of the State and the economy. It can appoint new members to the Factory Representative Councils from the eligible workers to replace the members who have been dismissed....

2 *Statement of the Executive Committee of the General German Trade Union Federation to the Government, 9 April 1933*

Yet even in April 1933 some trade-union leaders still hoped that the purge would be restricted to political organizations and that they would be able to come to an arrangement with the new regime by adopting a non-political stance. This attitude reflected an influential strand in trade-union thinking which had first manifested itself in the cooperation which the Free Trade Unions had given to the military authorities during the First World War. The Executive Committee of the umbrella organization of the Free Trade Unions offered its cooperation in reorganizing the trade unions:

Loyal to its duty to cooperate in the construction of a social order for the German people, in which the basic rights of the workers are secured in accordance with their national importance in the State and the economy, the General German Trade Union Federation[1] declares itself willing to place at the service of the new state the labour force's own organization which the trade unions have devoted years of activity to creating.

The trade unions recognize now as before that their own freedom of action must be limited by the higher law of the State acting in its role as the representative of the whole national community. The State must have the right to intervene to regulate and establish order within the economy; its duty is to create an economic constitution which binds the economic leadership to the fulfilment of overall economic obligations, because only in this way is it possible to achieve unity between the leadership of the State and of the economy.

The trade unions are therefore prepared to cooperate in the corporative structure of the German economy as planned by the Government in the conviction that,

[1] *Allgemeiner Deutscher Gewerkschaftsbund* (ADGB).

just as the Government decisively maintains the primacy of the Reich over the
states, it will also ensure that the higher law of the needs of the economy as a
whole will prevail over all tendencies towards disunity.

The ADGB welcomes the efforts to unify the trade unions. It will therefore
gladly assist the new State in its attempt to carry out this unification and will put
its experience at its disposal.

This reorganization of trade-union law will inevitably require new regulations
for State supervision of the self-administration of the labour force.

In order to ensure both that the measures planned by the Government are
uniformly carried out and that the trade unions can cooperate effectively, and in
order to restore to the German workers and the German economy a sense of
security which is necessary in the interests of the community as a whole, the
Executive Committee of the ADGB recommends the appointment of a Reich
Commissioner for the Trade Unions.

3 *Nazi plan to take over Free Trade Unions, 21 April 1933*

But the Nazis had no intention of compromising. It was essential that they
should control the organization of labour. On 21 April 1933, plans were
therefore drawn up to take over the trade unions which had already been
weakened by the excesses of the 'revolution from below' in the previous
month.[1] Both planning and execution were to be carried out by the Party
under the supervision of Dr Robert Ley, the head of the so-called Political
Organization of the Party:

On Tuesday, 2 May 1933, the coordination [*Gleichschaltungsaktion*] of the Free
Trade Unions will begin.

The direction of the entire operation lies in the hands of the Action Committee.
The Action Committee is composed as follows:
Dr Robert Ley, Chairman;
Rudolf Schmeer, Deputy;
Schuhmann, Commissioner of the General German Trade Union Federation
(ADGB);
Peppler, Commissioner of the General Independent Employees' Federation
(AFA);
Muchow, Organization;
Bank Director Müller, Acting Director of the Bank for Workers, Employees and
Officials;
Brinckmann, Acting Chief Cashier;
Biallas, Propaganda and Press;
All the acting directors of the unions belong to the enlarged Action Committee.

The essential part of the operation is to be directed against the General German
Trade Union Federation (ADGB) and the General Independent Employees'
Federation (AFA). Anything beyond that which concerns the Free Trade Unions
is left to the discretion of the Gauleiters.

The Gauleiters are responsible for the establishment of coordination in the

[1] See above, pp. 180ff.

individual areas. Those concerned in the operation should be members of the National Socialist Factory Cell Organization.

S A as well as S S are to be employed for the occupation of trade-union properties and for taking into custody the people concerned.

The Gauleiters must proceed on the basis of the closest understanding with the appropriate *Gau* factory cell leaders.

The action in Berlin will be carried out by the Action Committee itself.

In the Reich the following will be occupied: the headquarters of the unions; the trade-union buildings and offices of the Free Trade Unions; the party buildings of the Social Democratic Party of Germany in so far as trade unions are lodged there; the branches and pay offices of the Bank for Workers, Employees and Officials, Ltd; the district and local committees of the General German Trade Union Federation and of the General Independent Employees' Federation.

The following are to be taken into protective custody: all trade-union chairmen; the district secretaries and the branch managers of the Bank for Workers, Employees and Officials, Ltd.

The chairmen of local committees as well as the employees of unions are not to be taken into protective custody but are to be urged to continue their work.

Exceptions are to be made only with the permission of the Gauleiters.

The taking over of the independent trade unions must proceed in such a way that the workers and employees will not be given the impression that this action is aimed at them, but, on the contrary, at a superannuated system which does not conform with the interests of the German nation.

The provisional local leadership of the General German Trade Union and of the General Independent Employees' Federation is to be taken over by a commissioner of the National Socialist Factory Cells Organization.

Negotiations with the authorities and other organizations are to be immediately put into the hands of the newly installed commissioners.

All funds and accounts of the independent trade unions are to be blocked immediately and to remain so until Thursday afternoon 1800 hours. In so far as incumbent cashiers are permitted to remain in office they will be subject to the authority of a commissioner. All receipts for payments must be countersigned by the commissioner.

After lifting the blocking of the funds, the usual payments for the support of individuals must be unconditionally assured, to avoid creating a feeling of uneasiness among members of the trade unions.

Mass meetings are to be arranged as soon as possible, to be freely attended by all trade-union members. In these meetings the significance of the action must be explained and it must be pointed out that the rights of the workers and employees are being unconditionally guaranteed. . . .

It must be understood that this operation is to proceed in a highly disciplined fashion. The Gauleiters are responsible for this: they are to keep the direction of the operation firmly in hand.

4 *Proclamation of the Action Committee for the Protection of German Labour, 2 May 1933*

The Nazis disguised their intentions with a propaganda campaign stressing their sympathy with the workers. On 1 May, this culminated in massive parades and a big speech by Hitler to celebrate May Day, which of course traditionally had been a Socialist festival. On the following day, detachments from the various Nazi organizations occupied the Free Trade Union offices throughout the Reich, confiscated their funds and arrested their leaders. Ley then issued a proclamation in which he frankly recognized that support from the workers for the new regime was inadequate:

German workers and employees! Working people in town and country! The bells have rung in honour of work. The entire German nation has sung the praises of the working man with a strength and an enthusiasm without precedent and thus has done honour to itself and the creative spirit. The wheels stopped. The sound of the anvil was not heard. The miner came out of his mine. Everybody had a holiday.

What trade unions of all shades, red and black, Christian and 'free' have not even come near to achieving, what even at the height of Marxism was only a shadow, a feeble, miserable imitation compared to the gigantic thing of yesterday, National Socialism has achieved at its first attempt.

It puts the worker and the peasant, the artisan and the employee, in short all working people, at the centre of its thought and action and therewith at the centre of the State, and it renders the grabbers and the functionaries harmless. Well, who was that servant of capitalism, that reactionary who was out to oppress you and rob you of your rights? Was it those red criminals who for years have abused you, well-meaning, honest and decent German workers, in order to deprive you and with you the whole German people of your rights? or we, who amidst unspeakable suffering and sacrifices fought against these insane and crazy ideas of devilish Jews and their cronies? Three months of National Socialist Government have already proved to you: Adolf Hitler is your friend! Adolf Hitler struggles for your liberty! Adolf Hitler gives you bread!

Today we are opening the second chapter of the National Socialist revolution. You may say, You have absolute power; what more do you want? True, we have power, but we do not yet have the whole nation, we do not have you workers 100 per cent; and it is you whom we want. We will not let you alone until you give us your entire and genuine support. You too shall be freed from the last Marxist manacles, so that you may find your way to your people.

For we know that without the German worker there is no German nation. And above all we must prevent your enemy, Marxism and its satellites, from stabbing you again in the back.... It is not as if we wanted to disrupt and destroy the unions. On the contrary, we have never disturbed anything which has, in any way, value for our people and we shall never do so in the future; that is a rule of National Socialism. This certainly goes for the unions which serve with hard work and were built up by the pennies taken from the pockets of the workers. No, workers! Your institutions are sacred to us National Socialists. I am myself the son of a poor peasant and I know what poverty is. I myself spent seven years in one of the biggest industries in Germany[1] and I know the exploitation of anonymous capital; above all I know its stingy commercial methods of business, for in 1928 I was sacked for my opinions.

Workers, I swear to you we shall not only preserve everything which exists, we

---

[1] Ley had been an industrial chemist with IG-Farben.

shall build up even further the protection of the worker's rights, so that he can enter the new National Socialist State as a completely worthwhile and respected member of the nation.

Workers and peasants on a broad front, together with the professions and skilled labour—in this way we shall build a new Reich of well-being, honour and freedom. Forward with Hitler for Germany!

5 *Official statement on the coordination of the Free Trade Unions*

For this action there was no legal foundation whatever. But, two days later, the following 'official statement' appeared in the Party paper, the *Völkischer Beobachter*. An action was also brought against the leaders of the trade unions which enabled a warrant to be issued for confiscation of trade-union property. It is one of the first examples of what was to become a common practice in the Third Reich—the retroactive legitimizing of arbitrary actions.

According to official sources, the action taken against the Free Trade Unions corresponds completely with the struggle against Marxism which has been proclaimed by the Führer, Adolf Hitler. The Reich Government believes that Marxism must not be allowed to hide behind the trade unions and to continue the struggle in disguise. The measures were not directed against the workers as such, but were aimed at guaranteeing to the workers their money and their full rights.

A few days later, the Hirsch-Dunker unions 'voluntarily' subordinated themselves to Ley's Action Committee. The Christian Trade Unions were spared for a time because of the intention of making a Concordat with the Papacy. At the end of June, however, when the Concordat had been secured, they too were disbanded. In the meantime, in May, Ley had announced the amalgamation of the other trade unions to form a new organization, the German Labour Front.[1]

The organization of German Labour: the Trustees of Labour and the German Labour Front

6 *Law on Trustees of Labour, 19 May 1933*

The NSBO had always tended to contain the most socially revolutionary elements in the Party and now its leaders attempted to exploit their new power to force wage concessions from the employers, to compel employers to dismiss Social Democrat workers and replace them with unemployed Nazis, and generally to interfere with management. This activity, however, provoked the hostility of business which the regime was anxious to conciliate. On 19 May, therefore, the ultimate authority for the regulation of wage agreements, which had previously been negotiated between the trade unions and employers, was handed over to new *State* officials—the Trustees of Labour. There were thirteen of these, each covering a separate district, and they were subordinate to the Reich Ministry of Labour:

[1] *Deutsche Arbeitsfront* (DAF).

The Reich Government has decided on the following law, which is hereby promulgated.

Section 1
1. The Reich Chancellor appoints Trustees of Labour for the large economic regions upon the proposal of the competent state governments and in agreement with them.
2. The Reich Labour Minister will assign the Trustees either to the participating state governments, if they agree, or to the Reich authorities.

Section 2
The Trustees are to regulate the conditions for the conclusion of labour contracts pending a new revision of the social constitution. This practice is to be legally binding on all persons and replaces the system founded on combinations of workers, on individual employers, or on combinations of employers. . . .
2. Moreover, the Trustees are also to supervise the maintenance of peace between employers and labour.
3. Furthermore, they are to be convoked for their cooperation in the preparation of a new social constitution.

Section 3
The Trustees are empowered to request aid from the competent Reich and state authorities for the enforcement of their regulations. They should contact the state government or one of its designated authorities before carrying out their measures, even though there is a danger of delay.

Section 4
The Trustees of Labour are bound by the directives and decrees of the Reich Government.

Section 5
The Reich Minister of Labour in agreement with the Reich Minister of Economics will issue the necessary regulations for the enforcement of this law.

7 *The activities of a Trustee of Labour, 1933–34*
This law represents another example of the reaction against the Party's 'revolution from below' and typically it took the form of strengthening the State authorities and of regulating their position by legislation. At this period one of the main tasks of the Trustees was to intervene to prevent interference by the NSBO officials in labour disputes:

Düsseldorf-Oberkassel, 23 March 1934
Theodor Hutmacher, Assistant to the Trustee of Labour for the Economic Area Westphalia and Branch Leader of the Western branch in Gau *Düsseldorf*
To the Reich Chancellor Adolf Hitler

My Führer!
On starting work this morning, I received the confidential information that the Trustee of Labour for the Westphalia district, Dr Klein, has been transferred to

Bremen by the Reich Minister of Labour. I consider this extremely dangerous for the future of the state.

Before the take-over of power, I worked in various ironworks and foundries, and was simultaneously a political leader in a Communist stronghold in *Gau* Düsseldorf. From my observations during the prewar, war, and postwar periods and the present, I think I have gained enough experience to be a good judge of affairs. After the take-over of power, I was commissioner of the Chamber of Industry and Trade in Düsseldorf and was in charge of Jewish affairs and foreign-exchange questions. I carried out these tasks under the guidance of Dr Klein and in collaboration with the *Gau* leadership, in accordance with the new regime, and in the spirit of my Führer as well as that of my local National Socialist leaders. With the introduction of the Trustees of Labour, Party comrade Dr Klein summoned me and transferred to me all labour questions in so far as they still needed to be dealt with. For ten months, the Trustees of Labour and I have stood between the devil and the deep blue sea: workers on one side, employers on the other.

The law of 19 May concerning the Trustees of Labour was very vague [*dehnbar*] and, by summoning all his strength and working day and night, Dr Klein mastered the growing disorder which was often reminiscent of class war. Since I alone intervened in disputes throughout the whole economic district of Düsseldorf, I am the best judge of how dangerous it is for the National Socialist State and for peace and order to remove the authority which Dr Klein represents and his knowledge and ability which has served the workers and the economic leadership. This would involve the danger of the non-National Socialist workers and a section of the employers again getting the upper hand. Frequently I came out of negotiations in which strikes and demonstrations were threatened. I rarely met a workers' leader who did not demand the arrest of his employer right at the start of negotiations, the moment after he had greeted me. During night-long negotiations in the Ruhr area I often had to threaten the NSBO agents and works council chairman with the Gestapo in order to achieve peace and order in the labour sphere. My conception of my duty, which was drummed into me by Dr Klein, has made me the worker most hated by the NSBO and the DAF far beyond the boundaries of the Düsseldorf district.

In the NSBO, which usually took part in negotiations between leader and retinue,[1] I found still, to a frightening degree, the spirit of pure class war. But I always managed with Dr Klein's help to keep it in check so that we obtained the best results for the State, the economy, as well as for the retinue. I have often sat in shabby clothes among miners in the Ruhr area, accompanied them on their way to and from the pit (as if I was looking for work) in order to find out the mood of these people. They have faith in our Führer all right but they often do not know how to give it expression. I fear that if Dr Klein is moved, these people, under new leadership, will fall back into the old ideas just as Marxism would have it: living well and sacrificing nothing.

In March 1933, I was elected a city councillor in Düsseldorf and, as the representative of the workers, I signed the letter conferring honorary citizenship on my Führer. Shortly afterwards, I was forced willy-nilly away from the task allotted me by having largely to take the side of the employers because the class war spirit

---

[1] *Gefolgschaft*, i.e. the employees in the factory; see below, p. 428.

on the part of the retinue threatened to ruin the economy and therefore people's jobs. . . .

8 *Law for the Ordering of National Labour, 20 January 1934*

Although probably envisaged as a temporary measure, these Trustees of Labour acquired increasing control over the regulation of wages and conditions of work at the expense of both employers and workers. The powers of the Trustees were defined more specifically in the Law of 20 January 1934 for the Ordering of National Labour which became the basic law governing labour in the Third Reich.

The Reich Government has decided to enact the following law which is hereby promulgated:

SECTION I: THE LEADER OF THE PLANT AND THE COUNCIL OF TRUST

Article 1
The employer works in the factory as leader of the plant, together with the employees and workers who constitute his retinue, to further the aims of the plant and for the common benefit of nation and State.

Article 2
1. The plant leader makes the decisions for the retinue in all matters concerning the plant in so far as they are regulated by this law.
2. He is responsible for the well-being of the retinue. The retinue owe him loyalty according to the principles of the plant community. . . .

Article 5
1. Councillors of Trust recruited from the retinue act in an advisory capacity to the leader of a plant with as a rule at least twenty employees. They constitute, with the leader and under his direction, the Council of Trust of the plant.
2. Those persons who do piecework at home, and who work primarily for the same plant either alone or with their families, also count as retinue in the meaning of the regulations concerning the Council of Trust.

Article 6
1. It is the duty of the Council of Trust to increase the mutual confidence within the plant community.
2. It is the task of the Council of Trust to discuss all measures concerning the improvement of output, the form and enforcement of the general conditions of labour, especially the plant regulations, the enforcement and improvement of safety measures, the strengthening of the ties between the members of the plant themselves and their ties with the plant, as well as the welfare of all members of the community. Furthermore, it is their task to resolve all disputes within the plant community. Their views must also be heard before any decision on punishment for the violation of the plant rules.
3. The Council of Trust can charge certain Councillors of Trust with the carrying out of certain of its tasks. . . .

Article 9

1. Every year in March the leader of the plant, in collaboration with the representative of the National Socialist Factory Cell Organization, shall make a list of the Councillors of Trust and their deputies. Thereupon the retinue shall vote on the list in secret ballot.

2. If there is no agreement between the leader of the plant and the representative of the National Socialist Factory Cell Organization as to who shall be proposed as Councillors of Trust and their deputies or if a Council of Trust is not formed for other reasons, in particular if the retinue does not agree to the list, the Trustee of Labour can appoint the requisite number of Councillors of Trust and deputies. . . .

Article 16

A majority of the Council of Trust of a plant can without delay appeal in writing to the Trustee of Labour against decisions of the plant leader concerning the formulation of the general conditions of employment and in particular regarding the establishment of rules (Article 6), provided the decisions appear to be incompatible with the economic or social situation of the plant. The effectiveness of the decision made by the plant leader will not be impaired by the appeal. . . .

SECTION II: TRUSTEES OF LABOUR

Article 18

1. Trustees of Labour shall be appointed for large economic regions of which the boundaries shall be fixed by the Reich Minister of Labour in cooperation with the Reich Minister of Economics and the Reich Minister of the Interior. They shall be Reich officials and shall be under the supervision of the Reich Minister of Labour. The Reich Minister of Labour in conjunction with the Reich Minister of Economics shall decide on their headquarters.

2. The Trustees of Labour are bound by the directives and instructions of the Reich Government.

Articles 19

The Trustees of Labour shall ensure industrial peace. In order to fulfil this task they shall carry out the following:

1. They shall supervise the setting up and operation of the Councils of Trust and give decisions where disputes occur.

2. They shall appoint Councillors of Trust for plants and remove them from office in accordance with subsection (2) of Article 9, subsection (2) of Article 14, and Article 15. [Article 14 (2): If the Labour Trustee considers the Councillor of Trust unsuitable from a technical or a personal point of view. Article 15: The Labour Trustee appoints new Councillors of Trust when no more substitutes are available.]

3. They shall decide appeals from Councils of Trust in accordance with Article 16.

4. They shall decide proposed dismissals in accordance with Article 20 [requiring the employer to inform the Trustee of redundancies of more than 10 per cent of the labour force].

5. They shall supervise the observance of the provisions regarding the plant rules (Articles 26ff.).

6. They shall lay down principles and collective rules under the conditions specified in Article 32 [giving the Trustees the right to fix minimum conditions of employment].

7. They shall cooperate in the exercise of jurisdiction of the Courts of Social Honour (in accordance with Articles 35ff.).

8. They shall keep the Reich Government informed regarding the development of social policy in accordance with detailed instructions issued by the Reich Minister of Labour and the Reich Minister of Economics. . . .

Article 22

1. Anyone who repeatedly and wilfully contravenes the written instructions of the Trustee of Labour, which have been issued in the course of his duties, will be punished with a fine; in particularly serious cases a prison sentence may be imposed in place of the fine or in combination with it. . . .

SECTION III: PLANT REGULATIONS AND WAGE REGULATIONS

Article 26

In every plant in which there are as a rule at least twenty employees and workers the plant leader shall issue in writing plant regulations for the retinue of the plant (Article 1).

Article 27

(1) The following conditions of employment are to be included in the plant regulations:

1. the beginning and ending of the normal daily hours of work and of the breaks;

2. the times for the payment of remuneration and the nature thereof;

3. the principles for the calculation of piece or contract work, if work is done on a piece or contract basis in the plant;

4. regulations on the nature, amount and collection of fines if provision is made for them;

5. the grounds on which employment can be terminated without notice, in cases where this does not rest on statutory grounds;

6. the utilization of remuneration forfeited by the unlawful termination of employment in cases where the said forfeiture is prescribed in the plant regulations or in the contract of employment or in statutory provisions.

(2) In so far as regulations on the compulsory content of the plant regulations going beyond the instructions of subsection (1) are contained in other legislation or decrees, they retain their validity.

(3) Apart from the rules required by law, rules on the amount of remuneration and on other aspects of employment can be included in the plant regulations, as well as rules on discipline in the plant, the behaviour of the employees in the plant, the improvement of safety etc.

Article 28

(1) The imposition of penalties on employees is permitted only for offences against the discipline or security of the plant. Financial penalties must not exceed half the average daily earnings; but for serious and specified offences fines of up to the full amount of the daily earnings may be imposed. The Reich Minister of Labour determines how the fines are to be utilized.

(2) The penalties are imposed by the plant leader or a person designated by him after consultation with the Council of Trust (Article 6), if there is one.

SECTION IV: THE JURISDICTION OF THE COURTS OF SOCIAL HONOUR

...

Article 36
(1) Serious breaches of the social duties based on the plant community will be dealt with in the Courts of Honour as offences against social honour. Such offences shall be deemed to have been committed in the following cases:

1. when an employer, a plant leader or any other person in a supervisory capacity abuses his authority in a plant by maliciously exploiting the labour of any member of his retinue or by wounding his sense of honour;

2. when a member of the retinue endangers industrial peace in the plant by maliciously provoking other members of the retinue, and in particular when a Councillor of Trust wilfully interferes unduly in the conduct of the plant or continually and maliciously disturbs the community spirit within the plant community;

3. when a member of the plant community repeatedly makes frivolous and unjustifiable complaints or applications to the Trustees of Labour or obstinately disobeys instructions given to him in writing;

4. when a member of the Council of Trust reveals without authority any confidential information or technical or business secrets which have become known to him in the performance of his duties and have been specified as confidential matters.

(2) Civil servants and soldiers are not subject to the jurisdiction of the Courts of Social Honour. . . .

Article 41
(1) Breaches of social honour are to be judged on the application of the Trustee of Labour by a Court of Social Honour which is to be set up for each district in which there is a Trustee of Labour.

(2) The Court of Social Honour is to be composed of a member of the judiciary, appointed by the Reich Minister of Justice in cooperation with the Reich Minister of Labour, as chairman, and a leader of a plant and a Councillor of Trust as assessors. Leaders of plants and Councillors of Trust are to be chosen from short lists drawn up by the German Labour Front in accordance with Article 23; they are to be chosen in the order in which they appear, though it is desirable that persons should be chosen who are in the same line of business as the accused. . . .

This law was drawn up by the Ministry of Labour in consultation with the Ministry of Economics. Apart from strengthening the hand of the Ministry of Labour, it was shaped also by the interests of the employers. The civil servant in the Ministry of Labour responsible for drafting it, Dr Werner Mansfeld, had previously worked for an association representing the interests of mine-owners. The law gave extensive powers to the Trustees of Labour, who were given the final decision on most matters. Secondly, it strengthened the hands of the employers at the expense of the workers. The employer could draw up his own plant regulations. The Councils of Trust were only a pale reflection of the works councils which they replaced. Furthermore, when in 1935 the results of the elections to the Councils of Trust proved unsatisfactory, even this feeble form of workers' representation was rendered completely sterile by the ending of elections to the councils. Finally, the power of the unions to protect their members against unjust actions by the strike weapon was replaced by the new Courts of Social Honour and this also represented a loss of power by the workers. In so far as they were used to protect workers, these Courts acted mainly against small businessmen and artisans, where conditions tended to be bad, and even then only in glaring cases of injustice such as the physical ill-treatment of apprentices. Out of a labour force of over 20 million only 516 cases were brought to the Courts in the years 1934–36 and of these only just over 300 ended with a definite penalty.

In the Law for Ordering National Labour the Labour Front was hardly mentioned and was given only a subordinate role compared with that of the Trustees of Labour. For a long time, it was uncertain exactly what form the Labour Front would take. The following account by Ley of the first months of the Labour Front illustrates the completely *ad hoc* way in which the Nazi regime established itself. There was no coherent planning but merely vague ideas which were taken up or dropped in response to the requirements of the developing situation. Individuals were given jobs to do and had to see what they could make of them.

9 *The Report of Dr Ley to the Fifth Annual Congress of the German Labour Front, 11 September 1937*

When, in April 1933, I received the order from the Führer to take over the trade unions, I did not receive it because I was an expert on the trade unions. I hardly knew how many trade unions there were and I did not know the differences between them. I knew least of all about the way in which they were financed, about their structure and about their economic enterprises. In a word, I went there as a layman and I think I was myself more surprised than anyone to have been given the job. It was not as if we had a complete programme that we could haul out and according to which we could set up the Labour Front. Instead I received the Führer's order to take over the trade unions and then I had to see what I could make of it.

As you know, we were not given a legal status, we were not integrated in the State in any way. On the contrary, after the take-over of the trade unions I went to the Führer a few days later to report that I had taken over all the trade unions. When I said it was now time for us to receive a legal status and be recognized by the State as the Labour Front, the Führer replied in his benevolent, fatherly way: 'Let us wait and see what becomes of this changeling.' He did not want to give legal status to a chaos that was not yet sorted out, he did not want to create a public corporation with a constitution and statutes. The Führer indicated that this had to develop first.

I can say to you frankly, Party comrades, that I felt embittered and defeated then because I saw how everyone else was getting laws and then developing their organizations on the basis of these laws. I almost thought at the time that the Führer mistrusted me since he did not give me the same.

When we took over the trade unions, what did we find, what was there in existence?

Ideologically speaking, the class war was anchored in the trade unions and the trade unions lived off this. On the one side stood the employers' associations, on the other side the employees' associations. The whole thing was seen as ordained by God. Nobody would ever have doubted that the Lord himself wanted it this way and that this could not be changed, that this was a natural law: that there were classes, that one had to recognize these classes, that they fight one another and that they each had to represent their interests as parties confronting one another.

Ideologically speaking, that was the state of affairs which we found.

Apart from that, there was ideological chaos and muddled ideas about a corporate system. This was true of all of us. It only needed two National Socialists to meet and talk about the corporate system and there were bound to be ten different opinions, because each of these two had so many opinions on the corporate system. In practice, I have never met two National Socialists who were of one opinion on the corporate system. It was a real catastrophe in June and July 1933. I can tell you I did not sleep for several nights on account of the corporate system because I could not make head or tail of it and I began to believe I was more stupid than the others. But I did not want to accept this. So I bought all sorts of coloured pencils and made drawings and plans for days and nights on end. There were conferences. The others kept quiet and pretended to be unwilling to reveal their knowledge. They pretended to be very clever.

This corporate system turned out to be an absolute chaos of ideas, a complete muddle. I then tried to study Othmar Spann.[1] But he is unclear and confused like Marx. It is the language of the Jew, the old Moses which no German can understand. It is the language of Bolshevism and the Jew, the language of the Jesuit, the language and learning of Jesuit Rome which he speaks, mixed up with bits of National Socialist thought, of completeness and unity, and then again with Marxist thought, in short, a philosophical muddle which nobody understands. In a word, I was very unhappy during those days of June, July and August 1933.

As a third source of ideas, there was the NSBO, a Party institution, the factory cell organization. I must confess that until then I had dealt with it only on business. It was subordinate to me in my function as inspector under Strasser and I had the task of supervising it, of authorizing or not authorizing circulars and of supervising the finances, etc. I did not do all these things with great enthusiasm. Something prevented me from taking it seriously. Now I know what stopped me then. I can tell you today: the NSBO was, ideologically speaking, just as badly constructed. It did not fit into our National Socialist ideology and it was intentionally constructed like that by Herr Strasser. It was intended to become his power base and serve his treason. So he vetoed employers joining it. If it is intended to be a factory cell the employer must of course be represented as well. That is quite clear.

Thus the NSBO was essentially founded on the lines of the class war just like the trade unions. There was no difference of thought and ideology. People said it should be set up in the factories as a rival undertaking to the trade unions. I do not want to detract from the tremendous value which the NSBO had for our struggle. On the contrary, I would like here to sing the praises of all the men and

[1] An Austrian professor who advocated the corporate system.

women in the factories who took upon themselves a martyrdom of suffering during the time of struggle, who as individual NSBO members sometimes stood up to a horde of Marxists and who fought tenaciously and fanatically. But that does not prevent one from recognizing that the NSBO did *not* represent the ideology we National Socialists represent and must represent.

So at that time I found: the class struggle in its purest form, represented by the trade unions and employers' associations; a corporate structure, that is to say, essentially the class struggle, only in a different disguise; and the attempt by Strasser to introduce this divisive trade union element into the Party via the NSBO. . . .

10 *Proclamation to all working Germans, 27 November 1933*

At first, the Labour Front contained only the various trade unions which had been taken over as well as the NSBO. Hitler, however, who needed the cooperation of industry, was determined to ensure that the Labour Front did not become a giant trade union representing the interests of the workers against the employers. He wished it to contain both employers and workers and to concentrate on propagating social harmony by indoctrination. On 27 November 1933, Ley was obliged to sign a joint declaration with the Minister of Economics, the Minister of Labour and Hitler's economic expert, Keppler:

The German Labour Front is the organization for all working people without reference to their economic and social position. Within it workers will stand side by side with employers, no longer separated into groups and associations which serve to maintain special economic or social distinctions or interests. The value of personality, no matter whether of worker or employer, shall be the determining factor in the German Labour Front.

In accordance with the will of our Führer, Adolf Hitler, the German Labour Front is not the place for deciding the material questions of daily working life, or for harmonizing the natural differences of interest between individual workpeople.

Methods of procedure will soon be formulated to regulate work conditions which will assign both to the leader and to the retinue of a plant the position prescribed to each by the National Socialist ideology.

The high aim of the Labour Front is to educate all Germans who are at work to support the National Socialist State and to indoctrinate them in the National Socialist mentality. In particular, it undertakes the indoctrination of those people who are called upon to play an influential part in the plant in the organs of the social constitution, the labour courts, and social insurance.

On 7 December 1933 the principles contained in this proclamation were enshrined in a reorganization of the Labour Front. The 'coordinated' blue-and white-collar worker unions which had hitherto formed the basis of the Labour Front were abolished and replaced by so-called Reich Plant Communities. These plant communities contained both the employers and employees of the various plants, and the significance of the reform was that the Labour Front was not to become a massive trade union representing the workers and employees against the employers.

Ley had no objection to the role assigned to the Labour Front of promoting social harmony by indoctrination. He was not, however, content for the Labour Front to be subordinate to the Trustees. Ley was an extremely ambitious man and the organization of the Labour Front itself, which expanded into an enormous *apparat* of 30,000 functionaries, acquired its own momentum. Part of the strength of the Labour Front was its close link with the Party. Ley was not only head of the Labour Front but also chief of staff of the political organization of the Party. These two organizations were closely linked and added weight to each other. Ley, therefore, was determined to exploit his strong position to expand his own authority and that of the Labour Front. The local Labour Front officials too regarded themselves as the representatives of the Party in the economic and labour spheres and did not hesitate to apply pressure on employers whom they regarded as uncooperative, even if this meant exceeding their authority under the Law for Ordering National Labour. This law was in fact deeply resented by the Labour Front as a sell-out to industry and the Ministry of Labour, that is, to non-Party elements.

11 *Decree of the Führer on the Nature and Goals of the German Labour Front, 24 October 1934*

On 24 October 1934, however, Ley succeeded in persuading Hitler to sign a decree which went a long way towards reversing the balance of power created by the Law for Ordering National Labour, for it expanded the authority of the Labour Front at the expense of both employers and Trustees who were in effect subordinated to the Labour Front:

Article 1
The German Labour Front is the organization of creative Germans of brain and fist.

In particular, the members of the former trade unions, the former white-collar workers' unions and the former employers' organizations are united in it as members with equal rights.

Membership in professional, social, economic or ideological organizations cannot be a substitute for membership in the German Labour Front.

The Chancellor of the Reich can decree that professional [*ständisch*] organizations which have been recognized by law belong corporatively to the German Labour Front.

Article 2
The goal of the German Labour Front is to create a true national and productive community of all Germans.

Its task is to see that every single individual can take his place in the economic life of the nation in an intellectual or physical condition which enables him to work as effectively as possible, thereby ensuring the maximum benefit for the national community.

Article 3
The German Labour Front is a branch of the NSDAP in the meaning of the Law for Securing the Unity of Party and State, issued on 1 December 1933.

Article 4
The leadership of the German Labour Front is the responsibility of the NSDAP.

The Reich Organization Leader[1] is the leader of the German Labour Front. He is appointed by the Führer and Reich Chancellor.

He appoints and dismisses the other leaders of the German Labour Front.

These posts should be given in the first instance to members of the existing branches of the NSBO and of the NS-Hago[2] which are in the NSDAP, and further to members of the SA and SS.

Article 5
The regional organization of the Labour Front corresponds to that of the NSDAP.

The goal of an organic order as laid down in the programme of the NSDAP determines the professional organization of the German Labour Front.

The Reich Organization Leader of the NSDAP determines the regional and professional structure of the German Labour Front, which will be published in the service book of the German Labour Front. He decides who belongs to and who may become a member of the German Labour Front.

Article 6
The accounts of the German Labour Front are under the control of the treasurer of the NSDAP on the basis of the first executive decree enforcing the Law for Securing the Unity of Party and State, issued 23 March 1934.

Article 7
The German Labour Front has to secure labour peace by evoking sympathy among the plant leaders for the justified claims of their retinue and appreciation among the retinue for the position of their plant and what is practicable for it.

The German Labour Front has the task of finding the balance between the just interests of all participants which is in accordance with the basic principles of National Socialism and which reduces the number of cases which are to be referred to the state agencies which are solely responsible according to the law of 20 January 1934.

The representation of all the participants which is necessary for the process of conciliation is the exclusive task of the German Labour Front. It is prohibited to create other organizations in this field or to permit their activities.

Article 8
The German Labour Front is responsible for the National Socialist Organization, 'Strength through Joy'.[3]

---

[1] Until 12 November 1934 'The Chief of Staff of the Political Organization' — merely a change of title.

[2] *Nationalsozialistische Handwerks- , Handels- und Gewerbe-organisation*: the National Socialist Craft and Trade Organization.

[3] See below, pp. 438ff.

The German Labour Front must provide for technical training.

Furthermore, it must fulfil the tasks which have been assigned to it by the law of 20 January 1934.

Article 9

The property of the former organizations mentioned in Article 1 of this decree, including their welfare and insurance organizations, property administrations and business enterprises, constitutes the property of the German Labour Front. This property is the original capital of the German Labour Front.

The German Labour Front, through its welfare organization, shall guarantee the means of existence to each of its members in case of need, in order to facilitate the progress of the most able Germans or to help them to secure an independent livelihood, if possible on their own land.

Article 10

This decree comes into effect on the day of its publication.

This decree, however, had not been discussed, let alone approved, by the ministries affected (Labour and Economics) or by Hess's office and it immediately provoked strong protests from all of them. At this stage, Hitler was anxious not to antagonize Schacht or industry and therefore he was obliged to retreat. He did not withdraw the order, for this would have been too great a blow to his prestige. It was merely ignored by everybody from then onwards with the tacit approval of Hitler(!).

12 *The Leipzig Agreement of 21 March 1935*

Furthermore, in 1935, Schacht insisted on further definition of the responsibilities of the Labour Front in relation to industry in the so-called Leipzig Agreement which was signed by the Ministers of Economics and Labour on the one hand and by Ley on the other. This agreement, though in theory absorbing the employers into the Labour Front, prevented the Labour Front from claiming any independent economic role by making the office of the Reich Economic Chamber (representing industry) the economic office of the Labour Front and by subordinating it to the Economics Ministry.

I

The Council of the Reich Economic Chamber, in which the directors of the Reich Groups and Main Groups and the directors of the Economic Chambers are represented, after being convoked by the President of the Reich Economic Chamber and the head of the DAF, joins with the Reich Labour Council, which is composed of the heads of the Reich Plant Committees and the district officers (after the Reich reform the *Gau* officers) of the DAF, to form the Reich Labour and Reich Economic Council. The Reich Minister of Labour and the Reich Minister of Economics are to be invited to its sessions. The main task of the Reich Labour and Reich Economic Council is above all to discuss questions of economic and social policy which are of mutual interest, the establishment of cooperation between all sections of the DAF based on mutual trust, and the reception of announcements from the Government and from the leadership of the DAF.

The office of the Reich Economic Chamber is to be also the Economic Office of the Labour Front which is subordinate to the Reich Minister of Economics.

In the regions the council of the Economic Chamber joins with the regional labour council of the DAF to form the Regional Labour and Economic Council corresponding to the pattern at the Reich level of the DAF. The tasks of the regional Labour and Economic Councils correspond to the tasks of the Reich Labour and Economic Council. The executive of the Regional Economic Chamber will be also the Regional Economic Office of the Labour Front. . . .

Although this agreement represented a setback for Ley, he was still determined to ensure for the Labour Front the all-embracing role envisaged by the 1934 decree. Thus in 1936 he issued a commentary to the decree which re-emphasized the Labour Front's claim to total authority in the economic sphere. In 1938 he went even further and tried to claim for the Labour Front a position which would have made it superior even to the Party itself. But in pursuing this course he only succeeded in uniting against him all the other leading figures in Party and State and as a result this last great attempt to expand his authority failed.

'Beauty of Labour' and 'Strength through Joy'

With the proclamation of 27 November 1933 the Labour Front had in effect been allocated the functions of ensuring harmony within the factories, of increasing productivity, and in general of reconciling the working class to the loss of its freedom to organize itself. In order to fulfil these functions, on the same day Ley established two organizations within the Labour Front— 'Beauty of Labour' (*Schönheit der Arbeit*) and 'Strength through Joy' (*Kraft durch Freude*).[1] The function of 'Beauty of Labour' was to persuade employers to improve the working conditions within the factories. To this end, the organization initiated a series of propaganda campaigns with the titles: 'Clean people in a clean plant', 'Greenery in the factories', 'Fight against noise', 'Good lighting—good work', 'Good ventilation in the work place', 'Hot meals in the plant'. According to official estimates of the Labour Front which, it was admitted, were not very adequate, these campaigns produced the following results by 1939:

13   *Results of the campaigns launched by 'Beauty of Labour'*

Total number of factory inspections	67,000
Improvements to work rooms	26,000
Improvements to factory yards and the creation of lawns	17,000
The provision of washing facilities and changing rooms	24,000
The provision of canteens and rest rooms	18,000
The provision of sports facilities	3,000

Total cost: RM 900 million

[1] Called at first 'After Work', following the Italian fascist organization, *Dopolavoro*.

The function of the organization 'Strength through Joy' was to organize the leisure time of the labour force in the interests of the regime. This was carried out with the aim of ensuring maximum relaxation in order that the worker could return to work refreshed and therefore at his most efficient. It was also used to encourage a sense of egalitarianism and community spirit. This was intended not only to compensate for, and divert attention from, the regimentation of life, but also to render more tolerable the inadequacy of the rise in wages which the workers might have hoped for from the increase in national production since 1933 but which was ruled out by the paramount need to restrict consumption if rearmament was to go ahead. Much was made of the fact that thanks to 'Strength through Joy' ordinary people could now participate in luxury pursuits hitherto reserved for the rich such as sea cruises and the prospect of ownership of motor-cars (Hitler laid the foundation stone of the Volkswagen factory on 26 May 1938). Much was also made of the importance of sport as a means of encouraging both the physical health of the people and a 'healthy mental attitude'. In 1936 sports and physical training were introduced into factories and every youth in employment was obliged to spend two hours of his working week doing physical exercises. In the view of the Labour Front it was 'of great political importance that the community spirit associated with physical exercise can make a considerable contribution to the highest principle of National Socialist working life – the unity of the plant in the spirit of the plant community'.

The Labour Front was also successful at exploiting the personal ambitions of the workers for the purposes of the regime. Thus the National Trades Competition, inaugurated in 1933 for apprentices and later expanded to adult workers, offered advancement to the able and ambitious, while simultaneously raising the standard of work all round, and thereby helping to provide the skilled workers so necessary for the rearmament programme.

Running through all the activities were two themes. In the first place, there was the determination to submerge the individual in the mass (in Nazi terminology 'the community'). Secondly, and as a crucial aspect of this, there was an attempt to persuade the workers to regard their work not purely in material terms as a means of earning a wage in order to finance their private activities, but in idealistic terms as a service to the community and therefore their highest duty in life, indeed the main reason for their existence. The continual endeavour of the Labour Front was to substitute psychological motivations for work in place of material motivations. It was an attempt to overcome the alienation of the modern industrial worker by submerging him first in the 'factory community' and then in the 'national community'. He was given a form of status instead of higher wages. This was the essence of their conception of Socialism. Yet these communities were in fact nothing but a mass of individuals manipulated by the organizations of the regime. The effect of this, it was hoped, would be to generate enormous productive energy and at the same time to make the labour force a totally pliable instrument in the hands of the regime. The following documents illustrate these various aspects of the Labour Front's activities. They come from official publications of the Labour Front.

14 *Leisure-time activities organized by 'Strength through Joy' in 1934 and 1938*

	1934		1938	
	number	*participants*	*number*	*participants*
Concerts	1,020	576,594	5,291	2,515,598
Popular entertainments	725	285,037	54,813	13,666,015
Operas, operettas	959	540,841	12,407	6,639,067
Theatre	2,839	1,581,573	19,523	7,478,633
Variety, cabaret	1,315	481,855	7,921	3,518,833
Evening variety shows	3,189	1,228,457	10,989	4,462,140
Films	3,372	316,968	3,586	857,402
Exhibitions	72	237,632	555	1,595,516
Guided tours	1,528	90,242	676	58,472
Others	9,653	3,772,464	15,084	11,118,636
Events for the Autobahn workers	—	—	13,589	2,658,155
Total	24,672	9,111,663	144,434	54,568,467

15 *Sports organized by 'Strength through Joy'*

Type of course	1937	1938	of whom were female
Basic course	4,988,103	4,088,469	2,417,531
Special gymnastics	151,687	136,601	131,229
Light athletics	448,902	304,278	107,995
Swimming	1,809,873	1,582,427	710,416
Boxing, wrestling, etc.	208,762	203,252	8,415
Games	223,426	202,853	82,549
Water sports	19,393	9,641	5,399
Winter sports	53,839	92,631	55,656
Special sports	235,242	211,078	99,474
Youth in employment	1,262,267	3,004,071	140,720
Factory sports	—	12,297,026	2,048,200
Others (sailing, seaside resorts)	—	247,304	128,488
Total	9,401,494	22,379,631	5,936,072

16 *Holidays and trips organized by 'Strength through Joy'*

	participants	
	1934	1938
Vacation journeys	—¹	1,447,972
Short trips	2,120,751	6,811,266
Cruises	61,151	131,623
Hikes	99,408	1,937,850

17 *Motives behind the activities of the German Labour Front*

If any institution of the National Socialist State has convinced the rest of the world that in Germany the national community and Socialism do not simply exist on paper but have become a living reality, it is the National Socialist Community 'Strength through Joy' [KdF]. One can no longer conceive of Germany without KdF as the expression of the affirmation of life of our people. Here I wish only to highlight a few aspects of the work of KdF in order to deduce its basis and intentions from its effects, its aspirations from its achievements. German male and female workers are getting to know their homeland and the world through their holidays. The prerogatives of property over the beautiful things and comforts of life have been removed. It is no exaggeration to say that for millions of Germans KdF has made the world beautiful again and life worth living again. For reasons of self-preservation and in order to gain for itself the place among the nations appropriate to its greatness and befitting its achievements the German nation is compelled to make the fullest use of its labour resources. It is all the more necessary to ensure not only sufficient leisure time but also that this leisure time really enables the individual to relax. For this reason KdF ensures that everybody can travel, and entirely according to his own tastes, no matter whether the mountains or the sea provide him with greater relaxation. There is probably no better proof of the Socialist significance of the NS Community 'Strength through Joy' than the fact that hundreds of thousands have travelled into the wide world in our KdF ships. Not only has the KdF organized a travel and hiking programme but the idea of 'Beauty of Labour' has ensured that the factories are once more worthy of a human being. This too has a deeper significance. People can produce more in clean, airy and bright workplaces. . . .

One of the most important tasks of the German Labour Front is vocational training. Vocational training is not only a priority in view of the Four-Year Plan in order to make every working citizen into as valuable a worker for the nation as possible; it is also important for the individual. It is after all a fact that with few exceptions the man who gets on in life is the man who achieves the most. The few geniuses who starved because nobody recognized their importance are exceptions that merely prove the rule. It is well known that the German worker in particular has always felt a deep need to continue his studies because he has felt that he could only improve his social position by new achievements. In addition there is the current shortage of skilled workers. The German Labour Front has done, and is still doing, almost everything possible to alleviate this shortage. The establishment

¹ In fact, though no overall figure is available, the official record states that 'the first KdF vacation trains started on 17 February 1934. Twelve trains went to twelve different *Gaue*.'

of training centres, the construction of training shops, the additional training of engineers and technicians, a comprehensive specialist press, the encouragement of technical colleges—these are the methods which the German Labour Front has adopted in the sphere of vocational training. The Reich Trades Competition, the Competition for German Factories, the programme for encouraging gifted people, the encouragement of the idea of craft work, also help to increase the productivity of our people. . . .

18 *An improvement in status and working conditions as a substitute for wage increases*

The Deputy Führer [Hess] began[1] by making the point that he was aware that some employees still hold against us the fact that, whereas we are always talking about the increase in production and the growth in the national product, our wages have not been correspondingly increased, so that in reality the employees are not sharing the fruits of this increase in production: 'I can only reply to them that the swimming pool in his plant, the canteens, the improvements in working conditions, all the advances in the social field which were endlessly described earlier [at the meeting], all these things are in the final analysis the result of the increase in production from which the individual benefits as part of the community. And the individual could only properly assess the significance for him of the increase in production, if its main result, namely, the weapons of our armed forces, did not exist.'

It is therefore of great importance that we should assess the social position of the German worker, not on the basis of 'an increase in wages or no increase in wages', but from a consideration of what position the workers, the employees or the small tradesmen now hold within the national community. And in this case one need only go through Germany with one's eyes open to discover that the ordinary citizen can do things which in other countries are open only to a privileged class but never to the workers. . . .

19 *A claim that 'Strength through Joy' was transforming social life*

Out of the experience of the worker must be created the world picture of a new culture which is rooted in the living nationality [*Volkstum*]. Then the working man will become capable of recognizing his worth and he will be assisted in achieving an idealistic appreciation of his existence in the material sphere of life. The significance of his life must lie once more in work as the highest precept and the highest duty. Such an attitude will enable the individual to see his destiny in art as well. The work of 'Strength through Joy' is essentially the struggle for the soul of the worker, for leisure time and holidays presuppose the toil of the working day.

The comradely experience of work and the equally comradely community experience of leisure time belong together; in them lies the idea of social life itself. The 'Strength through Joy' land and sea trips mean far more than social travel in the normal sense: their value lies neither in the type of transport nor in the destination of the journey, but solely in the community experience. It is the great experience of nature which provides the best prerequisite for comradeship, so that one can say that these trips undertaken together and truly experienced represent

[1] At a meeting of the Reich Chamber of Labour, 30 April 1938.

the beginnings of a transformation of social life: a new type of culture is in process of being born. And by making the industrial and rural population aware of one another's style of life and needs one expands their vision and at the same time awakens the seeds of a culturally creative energy. . . .

20 *Hitler's speech on the Labour Service, May Day 1934*

Another institution which combined material and ideological functions was the Labour Service.[1] This had been inaugurated at the end of the Weimar Republic as a means of absorbing unemployed by putting them to work on projects which required a large amount of labour such as the reclamation of land and the digging of canals. The Nazis had regarded it with a certain amount of suspicion before coming to power because it tended to be run by other political organizations. Soon after coming to power, however, they saw its advantages both from a practical and from an ideological point of view. From a practical point of view it absorbed young people from the labour market and therefore opened scarce jobs to family men. Later when unemployment ceased to be a problem and a labour shortage developed, it provided cheap labour for projects of land reclamation for the 'battle of agricultural production'. The ideological advantages were that it provided an opportunity for giving young men political indoctrination and pre-military training. It also stood as a symbol for the 'Socialist' principles of the regime. Thus early on it was made obligatory for students so that they should learn to respect manual labour and from 1935 it was made compulsory for all. Hitler referred to this aspect in a speech on May Day 1934, an occasion which he invariably used to emphasize this aspect of Nazi ideology:

We want to destroy the arrogance with which unfortunately so many intellectuals feel that they must look down upon labour, and on the other hand we wish to strengthen in them self-confidence through their consciousness that they too can perform bodily work. But beyond this we wish to contribute to the mutual understanding of the different classes in order to reinforce the tie which binds together the community of the people. . . . We all know that it is not words or outward professions that lead to the establishment of this community; that needs an inner unlearning, a new education of the people.

The gigantic organizations of our movement, their political bodies as well as the organizations of the SA and the SS, the building up of the Labour Front just as much as the organization of the Army, these are all national and social smelting-furnaces in which gradually a new German man will be formed.

Sickle and hammer were once the symbols of the German peasant and the German workman. The arrogance and unreason of a *bourgeois* age have sacrificed and lost these symbols. Men have praised and admired artists, architects, and engineers; they have spoken of German science, German handicrafts, German business life, but the working man they have for the most part forgotten. . . . The National Socialist State will put an end to this unhappy development. The hammer

[1] The Labour Service was, however, independent of the Labour Front.

will become once more the symbol of the German worker and the sickle the sign
of the German peasant, and with them the intellect [*Geist*] must conclude an
alliance that nothing shall dissolve.... Today, on May Day, we meet to celebrate
the fame of the army of those millions who, as unknown and nameless Soldiers of
Work, in the sweat of their faces, in town and country, in the fields, in the factory
and the workshop, cooperate to produce those goods which rightly raise our people
into the ranks of the civilized nations of the world and enable it to hold that place
of honour.

It is difficult to assess the degree to which the Labour Front succeeded in
achieving its various objectives. It seems probable that some workers were
impressed by the atmosphere of egalitarianism which was created and by the
greater possibilities for social mobility offered by such mechanisms as the
National Trades Competition and the Adolf Hitler Schools. Above all, the
various organizations of the Party, including the Labour Front, offered
positions conferring status to tens of thousands of people who had previously
been condemned to boring, anonymous lives. On the other hand, it is
doubtful whether the working class was as impressed by the activities of the
Labour Front as by the solution of the unemployment problem. It was this
more than any other single factor which won support for the regime among
the mass of the population. The memory of the Weimar Republic for
most people was dominated by the last three years of crisis. It was the contrast between these years of poverty and unemployment and the rearmament
boom of the Third Reich which shaped the attitudes of many people
toward the regime. Nevertheless, it is equally true that, quite apart from the
former Socialists and Communists who were engaged in active opposition, a
significant number of workers remained obstinately unimpressed and
engaged in passive resistance of one kind and another.[1]

Problems created by the rearmament boom — and solutions

Government intervention in the labour market began already in the years
1933–36. In the first place, the Trustees of Labour cooperated with the
employers in ensuring that wage rates did not rise above the level of 1933.
They were helped by the fact that, since there was a large pool of unemployed,
there was little pressure on wages. Secondly, a decree of 26 July 1934
enabled employers to make a considerable number of exceptions to the
Eight Hour Day limit on hours of work. Finally, a number of measures
were passed enabling the Government to exercise more control over the
employment of labour. The Labour Exchanges were subordinated to the
Ministry of Labour and on 10 August 1934 a decree was issued giving

---

[1] For examples see below, p. 455.

the official Labour Exchanges a monopoly in the supply of labour, thereby facilitating State intervention in the labour market. On 26 February 1935, 'work books' were issued for all employees containing details of their qualifications and the details were filed by the Labour Exchanges. This provided the necessary information for any future direction of labour. In addition, two measures were passed which introduced controls in specific areas of the labour market. On 15 May 1934, a law was passed which required agricultural workers to obtain permission from their Labour Exchange before accepting employment in industry. In December similar restrictions were imposed on the movement of metal workers in order to prevent workers from being lured to the more lucrative aircraft industries of central Germany.

21 The labour situation in 1936

During 1936, however, the effects of the rearmament boom began to make themselves felt. Shortages of skilled labour began to appear in important sectors of industry and it became increasingly difficult either to maintain wage rates at the 1933 level or to enforce the decrees restricting the freedom of movement of agricultural and metal workers. This was because employers, anxious to acquire labour, cooperated with their employees in evading the restrictions. These developments, however, had serious economic and social implications, as was pointed out in a memorandum to Hitler from the Ministries of Economics and Labour, dated 6 October 1936:

I. *The shortage of skilled workers and its effects*
1. As a result of the strong revival in the German economy, a severe shortage of skilled workers has developed in the building trade, in the building materials industry and in the metal industry; furthermore, the satisfaction of the labour requirements of agriculture is causing difficulties. The number of workers lacking in these branches of the economy cannot of course be estimated in statistical terms, but according to the available reports it runs into tens of thousands. And the demand will increase still further. For the new aircraft factories alone, 50,000 more metal workers will shortly be needed. The introduction of the two-year military service will make the shortage of workers even worse. Cuts in production which must be expected in view of the present raw material and foreign exchange position will not for the time being bring the economic sectors referred to here, particularly the building industry, any relief.
2. This shortage of workers has produced many undesirable repercussions both economic and social. Under the pressure of delivery schedules which are too short, particularly for public contracts, the contractors feel compelled to use any means to get hold of the workers needed to fulfil the contracts. Since the Labour Exchanges are no longer in a position to provide the necessary workers, many contractors under the pressure of circumstances take the law into their own hands and in so doing follow paths which conflict with business ethics. Thus they frequently make attempts to poach skilled workers from other firms in order to carry out the contracts to which they are committed without any consideration for other factory leaders who have trained these skilled workers. The method of 'poaching workers'

by the offer of excessively high wages is always successful. The wage increases occur so precipitately and so much at random that they can no longer be regarded as desirable from the point of view of social policy. On the contrary, they have serious economic and political repercussions in that they provide, if not a reason, at least an excuse for price increases such as have already occurred with building materials. The size of the wage increases is considerable. Rates of even three times the tariff minimum are being paid; in addition there are the overtime earnings for a working day of up to fourteen hours. These abnormal wages are especially prevalent in industries which have public contracts to fulfil, so that in the end the increase in earnings in the boom jobs is at the expense of the nation as a whole since the contractors undoubtedly pass on their increased costs, if they can, to the Government. The firms with big export business, which depend on a very fine calculation of prices and therefore cannot carry out similar wage increases, are badly hit by the migration of skilled workers. As a result of this, exporting is made more difficult and the desire to export diminishes.

The conditions described above have an extremely adverse effect on the worker's loyalty to his factory and on work morale. The frequent and unregulated switching of jobs produces discontent in the factories. In many instances people leave their factory without giving notice or provoke dismissal by undisciplined behaviour or inadequate work performance. Even strike attempts on the part of the favoured categories of workers (to get further wage increases) are unfortunately no longer exceptional. The flight from the land (the drift from agricultural work to better paid jobs, particularly in the building trade) is encouraged by these developments. Finally, discontent is growing among the workers who are employed in those branches of the economy which have not been so strongly affected by the recovery or are being hit by the shortage of raw materials. Those fellow citizens whose earnings are often down to subsistence level and for the time being cannot be significantly improved are beginning to feel that their situation shows unfair discrimination when they cannot help noticing that the skilled workers in trades which are particularly favoured by State contracts are now earning several times their own wages, though they are already better off than they are.

3. This unsatisfactory situation has developed into a serious threat to the great political tasks of the State and must be remedied without fail in order to safeguard the carrying out of the defence programme and of the new Four-Year Plan, including the Battle for Agricultural Production. For it has already become apparent that numerous building projects and other contracts placed by the armed forces cannot be carried out to schedule because there are not enough workers or they cannot be found in time, and it was only with the greatest difficulty that the labour force for the harvest could be organized. Apart from this a successful solution to our defence and raw material projects requires that the present wage and price levels be kept stable; but the existing situation exposes them to a growing upward pressure. Thus the elimination of these evils is of decisive importance for the carrying out of the special commission which the Minister-President Goring has received.

II. *Inadequate remedies proposed*
Before going on to discuss the content of the draft bill, it is necessary to elucidate why other conceivable remedies of a less drastic nature should not succeed:

1. Measures to increase the supply of suitable labour are no longer possible because all the appropriate methods in this connexion have already been used. All those people in the relevant trades—that is, the building trade, especially bricklayers and carpenters, and in the metal industry, fitters, lathe operators, milling operatives, smiths, sheet metal workers—who are known to be unemployed are not sufficient to meet the shortage even if they could all be employed. But apart from this the available unemployed are in some cases unemployable or only partly employable, and some appear in the statistics only because they were changing their jobs on the day of the survey and therefore were temporarily unemployed. It can therefore be assumed that among the ranks of the unemployed there are no more reserves to cover the shortage. Moreover, the Reich Institute for Labour Exchange and Unemployment Insurance has exhausted the possibilities of adjustment between different areas (the transfer of skilled workers from surplus areas to areas of shortage). In our experience only a small number can be re-trained and this takes too long to solve the present difficulties as does the training of apprentices.

2. Changes in wage policy are just as incapable of eliminating the difficulties outlined above as are the measures hitherto taken. The idea of fixing maximum wage rates, which has been suggested by various people and which is intended to prevent the unscrupulous poaching of skilled workers by the offer of higher wages, would be a breach of one of the basic principles of the Law for the Organization of National Labour. If it was put into practice it would have the effect at once of making the maximum wage the minimum wage and would leave no scope for rewarding people according to individual performance. It is probable that the maximum wage rates would be circumvented by disguised benefits and, as a result, the same situation as we have now would develop at the new level of maximum wage rates; this has been proved by an attempt which was undertaken along these lines in Danzig. It would hardly be possible to prevent such attempts at circumvention since in these cases (unlike the cases in which less than the minimum wage is paid) neither party would complain. In the final analysis, then, the fixing of maximum wage rates could weaken the authority of the State without achieving the desired effect. In addition, changes in wage policy cannot eliminate the shortage of workers.

3. Even a sharper control of prices when awarding public contracts cannot be effective on its own. It is nevertheless urgently necessary, not only for general fiscal reasons, but also in order to counteract dubious methods of 'poaching workers'. These methods can be employed only when the contractor is not obliged to calculate very carefully what price he should charge. Like tougher price controls, a more generous calculation of delivery dates, which are often much too short, could remove many faults. Only recently those responsible for awarding public contracts again had their attention drawn to this point in the circular issued by the Reich Ministries of Labour and Economics. . . .

22 *Report of the Reich Statistical Office: the development of earnings in the first quarter of 1937*

. . . Hourly wages have generally increased. This time, owing to seasonal factors, only the consumer goods industries have had no share in this increase. The production goods industries, above all the trades indirectly or directly involved in armaments, are almost entirely responsible for the increase in wages here mentioned.

Thus, hourly wages in the spring of 1937 are approximately 8 per cent (December 1936: 7·3 per cent), weekly earnings approximately 19 per cent above the level of autumn 1933. In assessing these figures, however, it must be borne in mind that only averages are given here which include the numerous instances of considerably higher wage increases as well as those of lower increases or even wage decreases. Thus 2·5 billion of the increase in the total earnings of German workers from approximately 12 billion in 1933 to 18·6 billion in 1936 consist of increases in hourly wages and increased earnings due to a longer working week, while the rest can be ascribed to the re-integration of unemployed citizens in the production and distribution processes. . . .

Among the various groups of workers the skilled workers were most able to improve their hourly wages during the spring of 1937. But it is noticeable that the increase in earnings is higher among female workers than among male. This phenomenon is the more remarkable since, owing to the lack of labour in many jobs, the percentage of female workers is increasing again and many female workers, who had already left their jobs some time ago because of the replacement of female labour by male labour which has been advocated since 1933, are only now resuming work again, usually with relatively low pay. Although they bring down the average worked out here with their low starting pay, hourly wages of female workers have risen more than those of male workers. . . .

23 *Hitler's Ordinance on the 'National Socialist Model Plant', 29 August 1936*

With the increasing tempo of rearmament after 1936, tension developed between the Ministries and the Army on the one hand and the Party and the Labour Front on the other. The Ministries and the Army wished to concentrate all resources on the rearmament programme and in particular to keep wages down. The Party and the Labour Front, on the other hand, were primarily interested in maintaining public morale and in particular in winning the workers' confidence in the regime. They also wished to assert the authority of the Labour Front as compared to the Government agencies. To this end, they were quite prepared to apply pressure on the employers to bring about wage increases or improvements in working conditions. In 1936, Ley persuaded Hitler to institute a competition between factories to encourage them to improve their working conditions as part of the 'Beauty of Labour' programme:

Plants in which the leader and his retinue have realized most completely the idea of the National Socialist plant community as expressed in the Law for the Organization of National Labour in the spirit of the German Labour Front may be awarded the title of
'National Socialist Model Plant'
This award will be made by me or by an authority commissioned by me, on the advice of the German Labour Front.

The award is made for the duration of one year; it can be re-awarded. The award will be withdrawn if the prerequisites for the award are no longer present.

The award will be made on the national holiday of the German nation and will take place through the handing over of a document to the leader of the plant.

The document shall state the reasons for the award.

A plant which has been awarded the title 'National Socialist Model Plant' is entitled to fly the flag of the German Labour Front with a golden wheel and golden fringes.

This ordinance comes into effect immediately.

24 *Opposition from the Ministry of Economics to the Factory Competition*

This, however, was strongly resented by the Ministry of Economics, particularly since the criteria laid down by the Labour Front for the award included not only matters of social policy but also a more general economic assessment of each firm. This is clear from a letter to Göring, dated 24.ii.37:

I consider that it is impossible to hold the competition instituted by the Führer decree of 29.viii.36 at the present time. The putting into effect of the Four-Year Plan and the rearmament programme already requires the total commitment of the whole economy and therefore of every single plant. It is for this very reason that we must at all costs avoid subjecting the plants to new demands which the factory competition would inevitably involve and which would divert them from their primary tasks, particularly those which are essential to the State. . . .

Furthermore, I cannot support the draft regulations of the Labour Front for the following basic reasons:

In the first place, I must object to the fact that, contrary to the sense and the wording of the Führer's decree, economic aspects also are to be taken into consideration for the judgement. It is absolutely clear from the Führer's decree that the plants are to be judged only on the basis of their social policy. Moreover, the fact that the Labour Front has been given responsibility for selecting the plants which are to be considered for the award shows that the question of social policy was to be the decisive factor in the award.

The draft regulations, however, show on the contrary that in its evaluation of the plants the DAF wishes to go far beyond the bounds set for it, since to a large extent it uses purely economic factors as its criteria and brings under consideration the whole economic attitude of the plants. I need only refer here to some examples mentioned in the draft: rearmament, Four-Year Plan, the acquisition of foreign exchange, increase in exports, etc. Apart from the fact that this is not the function of the DAF, it does not possess the necessary economic experience for it. Such a comprehensive evaluation of the plants would also interfere with the exclusive responsibilities of State agencies, including the Delegate for the Four-Year Plan [Göring]. Finally, there is the danger that a faulty economic assessment could introduce confusion and disruption into the economy, thereby endangering the smooth execution of the tasks to which the State has given prime importance.

If therefore, in view of all this, the criteria for the judging of the factory competition for the award of the title of Model Plant are restricted to social conditions, the Trustees of Labour in particular ought to be officially involved, since they have been given the duty of supervising social conditions in the factories under the Law for the Organization of National Labour. . . .

The following documents illustrate further this tension between, on the one hand, the requirements imposed by the central economic objective of the regime, that is to say, rearmament, and on the other hand, the need to conciliate the workers and consumers. The basic conflicts of interest between employers and employees, between rulers and ruled, had not been removed by Nazi propaganda about a 'national community' or a 'plant community'. Since the various elements in the pluralist system of Weimar had been absorbed into official organizations of one sort and another, the conflicts were transferred from society to the State itself. They became aspects of the struggles between the rival bureaucracies competing for spheres of authority. The Party and the Labour Front based their claim to authority on their alleged popular support and on their function as intermediaries between the people and the State. The Gauleiters and the Labour Front, therefore, became to a limited extent and for tactical reasons defenders of the interests of the workers and consumers against the ministerial bureaucracy, the Army and the employers:

25 *Memorandum of the Reich Ministry of Labour on Interference by the Labour Front (undated, c. Jan. 1938)*

Summary
The cases combined under 'interference by the Labour Front' can be grouped in two categories, apart from a few irrelevant exceptions. They are the cases which:
1. show evidence of efforts to exclude the Reich Trustees of Labour as far as possible;
2. aim at direct control over labour conditions and their improvement, frequently in opposition to the line of social policy laid down by the State. Several methods have been chosen to carry out these aims:

(a) through the labour committees.
   Here the Labour Front tries to achieve results with far-reaching social implications by psychological pressure on the employers in the negotiations of the labour committees; these results are then passed on to the participants with the 'expectation that these decisions will become part of the factory regulations'.

(b) by direct influence on the drawing up of factory regulations.
   The Labour Front tries to obtain direct control of the factory regulations in order to gain influence over the shaping of factory conditions and in order to limit the effects of the external regulations laid down by the Reich Trustees of Labour.

(c) by direct influence on the individual employer for the purpose of improving labour conditions.
   The Labour Front urges the plant leaders in direct negotiations to make substantial social improvements, pointing out that rejection of these requests would be an expression of anti-social attitudes. . . .

26 *Hess directs the Party not to advocate wage increases, 1 October 1937*

The Führer has repeatedly stated that under the present circumstances wage increases must lead to price increases. This in turn will lead to the endless vicious circle familiar to the German people from the time of the inflation. Wage increases, therefore, can only be damaging rather than beneficial to the general public and to the individual, and so must be avoided at all costs.

A gradual general rise in the standard of living can only take place if that part of national production which has been tied up for years in the elimination of previous damage and in the measures which are necessary to secure German living space, and which to some extent must always be tied up, becomes smaller than it is at present. And even then this can occur only if that part of the production which can be exploited directly or indirectly for raising the general standard of living has been correspondingly enlarged.

It follows from this that there is a binding obligation on all Party offices, their subdivisions and affiliated organizations, to desist from trying to win popularity by propagating and publicly advocating wage demands and from any attempt to press such demands by more or less forceful means.

Attempts to bring about wage increases in a firm which is fully employed, and then to make similar demands for all similar firms, must be resisted in view of the Führer's orders and of the extensive economic planning which will presumably still be necessary for a long time and which we must pursue if only in the interests of the Four-Year Plan.

The fact that the economic position of large sections of our people is not what we would wish and are striving for is the fault of the political, economic, and trade-union leadership of the postwar years.

One must not overlook the importance of the fact that the virtual elimination of unemployment at the present time is due solely to the Führer, his movement and his colleagues.

The honest intentions of the Führer should be sufficient guarantee for every German citizen that everybody will get his share as quickly as possible and that unusually high profits which are being made here and there will on the other hand be used to a very considerable extent in meeting general charges. With this kind of tax legislation and economic planning they will be utilized in every instance to increase production which is the decisive factor for raising the general standard of living. If particular cases of hardship should occur anywhere owing to the level of wages, the advice of the authorities responsible for the investigation and removal of such hardship should of course be sought.

Apart from this all Party offices and their organizations must assist the Führer in the solution of his great tasks by faultless behaviour over the whole wage question and must encourage an awareness of those tasks and understanding for his attitude on the wages question among all classes of the population.

27 *Decree for the Implementing of the Four-Year Plan concerning the payment of wages on public holidays, 3 December 1937*

Despite this directive from Hess, however, Gauleiter Bürckel of the Rhine-land Palatinate, a particularly impoverished *Gau*, initiated a campaign for the payment of wages on public holidays. Reluctantly, the ministerial bureaucracy agreed to this measure in a decree signed by Göring:

The carrying out of the Four-Year Plan makes additional demands on all members of the retinue. Wage increases cannot be granted as compensation. But in order that

those collaborating in the Führer's great work should be able to enjoy their public
holidays I decree the following:
1. For the working time lost because of New Year's Day, Easter and Whit Monday,
as well as the two days at Christmas, the members of the retinue are to be paid
regular wages. This does not apply if New Year's Day and the Christmas days
fall on a Sunday. The official regulations or factory (service) regulations can be
used to determine what counts as regular wages. . . .

28 *Decree on the fixing of wages, 25 June 1938*

It was not really necessary, however, for the Party or the Labour Front
to press for wage increases, since the shortage of labour, or at least of skilled
labour, ensured that wage rates rose. Rising wages, combined with the
shortage of consumer goods owing to the emphasis on rearmament, posed
the threat of inflation. To meet this threat the Government introduced a
measure signed by Göring, giving the Trustees of Labour power to fix maximum wages:

The carrying out of measures for the defence of the Reich and of the Four-Year
Plan requires stable prices and wages. In accordance with the Decree for the
Implementing of the Four-Year Plan of 18 October 1936, I therefore decree the
following:

1. The Reich Trustees and Special Trustees of Labour are to supervise wages and
work conditions and to take all measures necessary to prevent any weakening of
the rearmament drive or of the enforcement of the Four-Year Plan through the
trend of wages or of other conditions of work. They are authorized in particular
to fix maximum and minimum wages with binding effect in the economic branches
selected by the Reich Minister of Labour, even to the point of altering factory
(service) regulations and labour contracts.

2. Those who act contrary to or evade the measures taken by the Reich Trustees
or Special Trustees of Labour on the basis of this decree will be punished by a
prison sentence and a fine of unlimited amount, or with one of these penalties.
Prosecution will only be initiated at the request of the Reich Trustee or the Special
Trustee of Labour.

3. The Reich Minister of Labour will make the regulations necessary for the
enforcement and supplementing of this decree.

29 *Report by the Reich Statistical Office on wage developments in the second
   quarter of 1938*

. . .

Summary
The most striking aspect of the development of wages since spring 1938 is the fact
that weekly earnings are not rising more sharply than hourly wages, as in the first
years after the take-over of power, but that on the contrary hourly wages are rising
noticeably compared with a relatively small increase in weekly earnings:

2nd quarter of	Hourly wages (% rise)	Weekly earnings (% rise)
1937	0·1	0·7
1938	0·7	0·4

The main causes of rising wages during this period are neither an increase in productivity through longer working hours, nor, as is shown by other documents, increased production within the same time; it is mainly the increase in hourly wage rates that has led to increased hourly and weekly wages. This is a serious phenomenon which is being firmly dealt with by the Reich Trustees since the Decree on the Fixing of Wages.

30 *Reports by the Reich Trustees of Labour on the enforcing of the Decree on the Fixing of Wages in the fourth quarter of 1938*

... The Reich Trustees have taken action on the basis of the Decree on the Fixing of Wages against a number of unsatisfactory phenomena. Several Reich Trustees followed the example of the Reich Trustee of Saxony in prolonging the period for giving notice to three months. A ban on giving notice had to be imposed on certain firms.[1] On the whole, individual measures have increased compared with general collective measures. That is mainly so with regulations on the fixing of maximum wages. For instance, the Reich Trustee of Lower Saxony has lowered the piece rate per hour in the building trade which was too high. The Reich Trustee of Nordmark [i.e. Hamburg and Schleswig-Holstein] has fixed maximum wages for the building trade generally. The need for this measure has generally been recognized. None the less, building contractors have repeatedly tried to evade the regulations. The Reich Trustee of Middle Elbe has also laid down maximum wage regulations for the building trade, and these have brought about a considerable degree of stability. The plan is to extend the regulations to the ancillary building trade. Individual regulations have had to be used, particularly in the metal trade. The high wages, and especially the piece rates, which were given and earned in the metal industry have frequently caused justifiable discontent. As already mentioned, an investigation into the wages paid in the metal industry has already been initiated. Further orders of the Reich Trustees deal with breaches of contract [i.e. labour contracts]. The Reich Trustees of Thuringia and East Prussia, following the example of other Reich Trustees, have recently taken action against breaches of contract. As a result, breaches of contract have diminished; but not in agriculture or among maid-servants. Further regulations by the Reich Trustees deal with the poaching of workers, and have forbidden the promising of high wages as a bait, and so forth. . . .

Cooperation with the Labour Front still needs to be improved in some instances. Whereas in some economic districts the measures of the Reich Trustee are actively supported by the *Gau* authorities of the Labour Front, the reports of the Reich Trustees show that this is not so in other economic areas. It is obvious that the Reich Trustees can supervise the numerous measures only to a limited degree. The support of the Labour Front is therefore necessary. But the Labour Front rarely reports unjustified or forbidden wage increases. On the contrary, it has been noted that officials of the Labour Front frequently encourage the leaders of firms threatened by the loss of workers to solve their difficulties by wage increases.

[1] The intention was to prevent workers from giving notice in order to get higher wages elsewhere.

Moreover, the proficiency competition between firms [for the award of the title 'Model Plant'] has often in practice taken a direction which cannot be reconciled with the demands of wages policy. This is all the more deplorable as it is easy to form the opinion that the efforts of the State and those of the Labour Front as delegates of the Party are conflicting in the social sector. . . .

In fact, considering the shortage of labour, the Government was on the whole surprisingly successful at limiting the increase in wages. The following figures show that wages as a percentage of Gross National Product sank during this period. This compares with an increase of 36·5 per cent in the undistributed profits of business from 1933 to 1939:

31 *The development of wages, 1929–39*

(1932 = 100)

Year	Nominal hourly earnings Tariff	Nominal hourly earnings Effective	Effective hourly earnings Real	Effective weekly earnings Nominal	Effective weekly earnings Real	Percentage of GNP formed by wages
1929	122	133	—	149	118	56·6
1932	100	100	100	100	100	57·0
1933	97	97	99	102	104	56·0
1934	97	99	99	110	109	55·5
1935	97	101	99	112	110	54·6
1936	97	102	100	117	112	53·5
1937	97	105	101	121	115	52·7
1938	97	108	104	126	119	52·4
1939	98	111	107	131	123	51·8

32 *Signs of overwork in 1938*

By 1938, the effects of the intensive rearmament programme were beginning to have a serious impact. This was felt in terms both of a deterioration in the health and work morale of the labour force and of the effects of the distortion of the labour market on those occupations not involved in the rearmament programme. Those industries, such as agriculture or handicrafts, which could not afford to compete with the high wages offered by firms engaged on armament contracts were stripped of labour. Here can be seen the bankruptcy of those ideological commitments to the peasantry and the small craftsman which had so dominated the Party's propaganda in its early years. The Party's goals were incompatible. If Germany was to fight a war for *Lebensraum* she needed the most efficient economy possible. She needed big firms not small craftsmen, she needed efficient large farms which could afford to mechanize, not peasant family homesteads. The economic logic of rearmament was inexorable and it spelled the doom of the old economic and social groups which the Nazis had sworn to uphold:

Excerpt from the social reports of the Reich Trustees of Labour for the third quarter of 1938

... The discrepancy between the available labour force and the number of orders has in general led to a considerable increase in hours worked which has been made possible by flexibility in the use of the regulations governing working hours. Fifty-eight to sixty-five hours a week are no longer exceptional. And some factories continue overtime, even when there is a reduction in orders owing to seasonal factors, because they are afraid of losing workers. The extraordinary demands made upon the German workers particularly during the period of tension[1] have on the whole been met without any difficulties. Thus the Reich Trustee of Labour for the Saar-Palatinate reports that it is not uncommon for railway workers, for example, to work up to sixteen hours a day. On being questioned by a commission of inquiry, the railway workers declared that normally they worked for eight hours and rested for sixteen hours, but now they worked for sixteen hours and rested for eight hours because the Führer needed it. . . .

Owing to the tense situation in the labour sphere and the increase in hours of work in nearly all branches associated with it, certain reactions were unavoidable. The number of cases of sickness has risen considerably. . . .

A further reaction against continuous overtime, according to several Reich Trustees, is the tendency on the part of the retinues not to work for more than forty-eight hours a week. If this objective cannot be met, the result is a decline in productivity. There is also occasional absenteeism. Thus on several building sites the workers went home straight after the payment of their wages and did not return to work until Monday or Tuesday. . . .

33 *Reports by the Army Economic Inspectorate[2] on the economic situation, July 1938*

Economic Inspectorate X
. . . Furthermore, there are complaints about a decline in the workers' enthusiasm for work, something on which the Führer always lays stress. In particular, young, untrained, and less able people see the favourable employment situation simply as an opportunity to press for higher wages and as a springboard for getting high wages as fast as possible. If they showed willingness to work hard and well, these workers could earn 20 per cent more. . . .

Economic Inspectorate VII
. . . Although in many cases the Labour Exchange prevents workers from changing their place of employment, the fluctuation of the industrial workers remains considerable. If the Labour Exchange opposes a move from one factory to another, the workers who want to change their jobs make all sorts of attempts to leave their present place of employment and start at a new one. If any such attempt succeeds the method used sets an example for others.

There can be no doubt that the suspension of a large number of workers' freedom of movement which has been prompted by the present shortage of labour is bad for

---

[1] The Czech crisis in September 1938.
[2] These were Army agencies which supervised the carrying out of the rearmament programme.

morale; for in this way many workers, and particularly the most able among them, are deprived of the opportunity of improving their economic position and even, in some cases, of creating a new livelihood for themselves. The deal which can be offered to the worker if he stays in his previous factory usually bears no comparison with the improvement he could achieve by changing his employment. As a result, the worker is much worse off than members of other professions who have the opportunity of getting on in their profession through hard work and efficiency.

All the measures taken so far against the shortage of labour have been unable to prevent it from being at the present time worse than ever. In July several firms asked the Munich Labour Exchange for eighty-five workers on the basis of OKW regulations on 'priority demand for labour for contracts for the armed forces'. But the Labour Exchange could only find three workers. Several firms asked the Munich Labour Exchange for several hundred workers for work not concerned with Army contracts, but the Labour Exchange could only provide twelve.

The long-term effects of the labour shortage are particularly bad for agriculture; if this labour shortage persists or gets even worse, there will be nothing left for it but to go over to more extensive forms of cultivation. Agriculture now yields about the lowest return of the whole German economy. It is therefore in no position to pay high wages. The craft trades also, particularly the smaller firms, suffer from the shortage of labour for, like agriculture, craft trades often have only a weak capital basis, and only a few possess substantial cash reserves. Since the profitability of the various branches of industry varies, there is a noticeable migration of workers from those branches which are less successful to those which are doing well; for the better a branch of industry is doing, the higher the wages it tends to be able to pay its workers. This migration from those branches of the economy which are doing badly to those which are doing well has recently occurred mainly at the expense of agriculture and of the craft trades. It will continue as long as the shortage of labour lasts in Germany, unless drastic measures are taken. Only when it has been stopped can agriculture be given effective assistance. Only when the German economy has been more or less restored to normality and workers do not always find employment and high wages in industry will they return to agriculture on their own initiative, as was always so after previous industrial booms. . . .

34 *A crisis in agriculture: the Reich Minister of Labour to the Head of the Reich Chancellery, 4 February 1939*

. . . Following on from these general comments, I now wish to refer to the particularly difficult labour situation in agriculture.

In 1933, 2,230,000 non-family workers were employed in agriculture, horti-culture, and animal-breeding. As is shown in the Work Book census of the middle of last year, this number has now fallen to 2,030,000, i.e. by 200,000 or nearly 10 per cent. But it is probable that the number of independent and family employees in agriculture has also dropped sharply. In 1933 there were engaged in agriculture, apart from the $2\frac{1}{4}$ million non-family workers, another 2·2 million independents and $4\frac{1}{2}$ million family workers. Unfortunately there are no statistics on the last two groups. But even on the most optimistic estimate it must be assumed that, in view of the increased flight from the land, agriculture has perhaps $\frac{1}{2}$ million fewer workers at its disposal in 1938 than in 1933. The reasons for this development are well known: the difference between working conditions and living conditions in the towns compared with the countryside, the excessive opportunities for employment in industry, particularly in the building industry which is closely related to agriculture, and the call-up to labour service and military service.

Considering the increased demands made upon agriculture by the battle for self-sufficiency, this drop of approximately ½ million workers is particularly serious.

Over the last few years, therefore, I have tried within my own sphere to alleviate the shortage of labour in agriculture by taking appropriate action in the labour field, and will endeavour to expand these measures in the coming year. I would like to mention in this connexion the recent extension of the year of compulsory domestic service to all female youth who wish to take up a career and the increased importing of foreign agricultural workers within the limits permitted by the foreign exchange situation. Negotiations for the year 1939 have already been concluded with a few states particularly with Italy. With others, and particularly with Poland, they are at the moment still in progress.

35 A crisis in the social building programme, 1939

Although rearmament was the main reason for the pressure on resources, the situation was made much worse by the prestige building projects initiated by Hitler himself—the so-called Führer buildings—and by the various Party offices. The result was that Germany could not even accommodate the increase in the birthrate which it had encouraged as an ideological goal in order to remove women from employment and to provide cannon fodder for the future:

Report of the City President of Berlin to the Reich Economics Minister, 8 January 1939

VIII. The Berlin construction industry

... And in the framework of the latest projects of the Plenipotentiary-General for the Regulation of the Building Industry [Fritz Todt] the municipal building projects for Berlin—administrative buildings and housing—are only in seventh place in the order of priorities laid down by the decree of 9 December 1938. Although the so-called replacement housing programme has been given the same priority as the Führer buildings, I regard it as urgently necessary for demographic-political reasons that, in view of the catastrophic shortage of accommodation, all apartment building projects, at least in Berlin, should be given the same priority as the Führer buildings.

The same thing should happen with the numerous outdated administrative buildings of the Berlin city administration. In the district of Spandau, for example, the shortage of space in schools is so catastrophic that it has produced numerous complaints from the population. The effects of this lack of school space are gradually becoming a threat to the health of German youth. Whole classes are now having to be taught in corridors. Attempts to alleviate the situation by the use of huts are of no avail because it is just as impossible to get material for them as for large buildings. This intolerable situation as to the accommodation of classes will get worse because from Easter 1939 the bulge years of 1933–34 will reach school age. Such social buildings should not be subordinate to the Führer buildings any more than housing. To put them in seventh place is no more compatible with the principles of a healthy social policy than with recent attempts to increase the population. . . .

36 *Decree on the Re-employment of Women in receipt of Marriage Loans,*[1]
    5 February 1937

The drain on manpower resulting from the introduction of compulsory labour service and of conscription in 1935 compelled the regime to retreat from its ideologically-based commitment to keep women at home. In fact such was the pull exerted by the labour shortage that by 1936 there were already 1,200,000 more women employed than when Hitler came to power in January 1933 and this increase continued as the rearmament boom built up. Nevertheless, ideological objections to the employment of women continued to be prevalent—Hitler himself was sensitive on this issue— and they were to have some influence during the war.[2] The following decree is an expression of the retreat on the part of the regime from its earlier hostility to the employment of women:

According to section 1 of the Family Benefits Law of 30 March 1936, the wife of a National Serviceman who is called up for the armed forces, or of a man liable for Labour Service who is called up to do his Labour Service, receives benefits to ensure her receiving the necessities of life. These benefits are . . . only to be granted if the wife cannot secure the necessities of life through her own efforts, in particular by working.

In these circumstances, the maintenance of the ban on the employment of wives who have received a marriage loan and whose husbands have been called up to the armed forces or to the Labour Service would not be in accord with the regulations of the Family Benefits Law which is intended to reduce the amount of benefits to the absolute minimum in order to relieve the Reich treasury.

On the basis of section 1 of the 6th Decree concerning Marriage Loans,[3] I permit wives who have received a marriage loan to take up employment, provided their husbands have been called up for the Labour Service or for training by the armed forces.

37 *Decree on the guaranteeing of manpower for tasks of special political*
    importance, 22 June 1938

As we have seen, the market mechanism operated fairly successfully in supplying labour to firms engaged in the rearmament programme, but as the diplomatic situation became more and more tense during 1938 Hitler decided to strengthen his position by building a line of fortifications along the frontier with France, the West Wall or so-called Siegfried Line. This required a crash programme, for which, owing to the labour shortage, there were simply not enough people available. The Government had anticipated

---

[1] For the provisions on marriage loans, see above, p. 365.
[2] See below, pp. 647–8.
[3] This decree of 28 July 1936 empowered the Reich Finance Minister to grant exceptions to the ban on the employment of women in receipt of marriage loans.

the need for civil conscription in the event of war in an unpublished statute of May 1935. But this statute was now superseded by a decree which became known as the Decree on the Duty of Service:

In order to be able to make available the labour necessary for particularly important tasks which, for political reasons, cannot be postponed, the possibility must be created of relying temporarily on labour employed elsewhere. In accordance with the Decree of 18 October 1936 for the Implementing of the Four-Year Plan I therefore decree the following:

1. The President of the Reich Institute for Labour Exchange and Unemployment Insurance can require German citizens to do service for a limited period in a workplace assigned them or to undergo a special training course.

2. The general service and social insurance regulations are valid for this new position in service or training. The position in service or training can, however, be dissolved only with the consent of the President of the Reich Institute for Labour Exchange and Unemployment Insurance.

3. Those people signed up for service and training who are employed at the time of their call-up must be given leave for the duration of their service. During their leave of absence the previous position in employment must not be cancelled. The person signed up for service cannot claim compensation and other fees from his previous employment during his leave of absence. The time spent fulfilling the service obligation based on this decree is considered as employment time in his previous job.

4. The regulations necessary for the execution and enforcement of this decree are laid down by the President of the Reich Institute for Labour Exchange and Unemployment Insurance.

5. This decree comes into effect on 1 July 1938.

Workers could now be compulsorily directed to jobs considered of importance to the State, and in February 1939 new regulations extended the decree to foreigners living in Germany and laid down that workers could be conscripted for an indefinite period. Apart from the West Wall, workers were conscripted to build the Four-Year Plan plants and to man the munitions industries. In all, over a million workers were conscripted, but of these less than 300,000 on a regular basis, out of a total work force of some 23 million. Indeed, such was the discontent aroused by the measure and the resultant low productivity that the authorities soon had second thoughts. In November 1939, Hitler insisted that workers should be employed in their home towns — a characteristic surrender to working-class discontent.[1]

[1] cf. T. W. Mason, 'National Socialist Policies towards the German Working Class, 1925–1939' (D.Phil. Dissertation, Oxford 1971), pp. 718ff.

15 Antisemitism, 1933–45

The 'seizure of power', 1933–34

When Hitler came to power in 1933, the antisemitic aims of the NSDAP became official policy. Initially, however, circumstances determined the course of Nazi Jewish policy. The new regime wished to consolidate its power and to avoid provoking strong reactions against too hasty and radical measures. Uncertainty about domestic opinion and concern that foreign disapproval might result in economic reprisals explain this cautious attitude. The Nazi leadership feared that actions against the Jews might get out of control and cause embarrassment. It wished to maintain control over Jewish policy and not to allow the Party to run ahead of its leaders.

1 *Outrages against Jews, spring 1933*

In the context of the 'revolution from below' of March 1933, however, this was difficult to achieve. Thus in the spring of 1933, SA men made numerous if sporadic attacks on Jews and Jewish property. The American Consul in Leipzig, Ralph Busser, reported on 5 April:

> In Dresden several weeks ago uniformed 'Nazis' raided the Jewish Prayer House, interrupted the evening religious service, arrested twenty-five worshippers, and tore the holy insignia or emblems from their head-covering worn while praying.
> Eighteen Jewish shops, including a bakery, mostly in Chemnitz, had their windows broken by rioters led by uniformed 'Nazis'.
> Five of the Polish Jews arrested in Dresden were each compelled to drink one-half litre of castor oil. As most of the victims of assault are threatened with worse violence if they report the attacks, it is not known to what extent fanatical 'Nazis' are still terrorizing Jews, Communists, and Social Democrats, who are considered as favouring the old parliamentary regime in Germany.
> Some of the Jewish men assaulted had to submit to the shearing of their beards, or to the clipping of their hair in the shape of steps. One Polish Jew in Chemnitz had his hair torn out by the roots.
> The involvement of foreign Jews brought protests from diplomatic representatives in Germany.

2 *The Party Boycott Order, 28 March 1933*

At the end of March, perhaps partly in order to gain some sort of control over the antisemitic actions of the local Party and SA units, the Government gave its blessing to an official Party boycott of Jewish shops in retaliation for the campaign abroad against Nazi atrocities. Julius Streicher, the rabidly antisemitic Gauleiter of Franconia, organized action committees to promote the boycott, and SA men were stationed in front of Jewish shops to 'warn' intending customers. But the action failed to arouse public enthusiasm and the planned mass meetings did not take place. The American Consul in Leipzig noted that the boycott was 'unpopular with the working classes and the educated circles of the middle classes'. The Party order of 28 March was published in the *Völkischer Beobachter* the following day:

1. Action committees in every local branch and subdivision of the NSDAP organization are to be formed for putting into effect the planned boycott of Jewish shops, Jewish goods, Jewish doctors and Jewish lawyers. The action committees are responsible for making sure that the boycott affects those who are guilty and not those who are innocent.
2. The action committees are responsible for the maximum protection of all foreigners without regard to confession, background or race. The boycott is purely a defensive measure aimed exclusively against German Jewry.
3. The action committees must at once popularize the boycott by means of propaganda and enlightenment. The principle is: No German must any longer buy from a Jew or let him and his backers promote their goods. The boycott must be general. It must be supported by the whole German people and must hit Jewry in its most sensitive place. . . .
8. The boycott must be coordinated and set in motion everywhere at the same time, so that all preparations must be carried out immediately. Orders are being sent to the SA and SS so that from the moment of the boycott the population will be warned by guards not to enter Jewish shops. The start of the boycott is to be announced by posters, through the press and leaflets, etc. The boycott will commence on Saturday, 1 April on the stroke of 10 o'clock. It will be continued until an order comes from the Party leadership for it to stop.
9. The action committees are to organize tens of thousands of mass meetings, which are to extend to the smallest villages for the purpose of demanding that in all professions the number of Jews shall correspond respectively to their proportion of the whole German population. To increase the impact made by this action, this demand is limited first of all to three fields: (a) attendance at German schools and universities; (b) the medical profession; (c) the legal profession. . . .

During April several measures against the Jews were introduced, among them their exclusion from the Civil Service (see above, pp. 229–30). Hitler's sensitivity to opposition was shown by the exemption, made on President Hindenburg's personal intervention, of those Jewish civil servants who had fought or lost relatives in the First World War. Prohibitions were also placed on Jewish doctors working in hospitals and on the appointment of Jewish assistant judges in Prussia. These were professions in which Jews tended to specialize. In Hamburg, for instance, Jews were only 3 per cent of the population but they accounted for 40 per cent of the doctors, 30 per cent of the lawyers, and 10 per cent of the judges. A further measure designed to isolate the Jews and reduce their contact with the rest of the German population was the Law against the Overcrowding of German Schools, of 25 April 1933, which restricted the number of Jews admitted to schools, colleges, and universities to the same proportion as that of 'non-Aryans to Aryans' in the total German population.

3 *The Reich Minister of the Interior tries to enforce legality in Jewish policy, January 1934*

As far as the Party militants were concerned, however, the pace was not fast enough. As a result, tension between the local Party and S A militants, on the one hand, who wanted to take direct action against the Jews and some of whom were inspired by economic rivalry, and the authorities on the other hand, continued during 1934 and into 1935. As in other spheres, the main burden of resisting the extremists fell on Wilhelm Frick, the Reich Minister of the Interior. This Ministry was the agency primarily responsible for racial questions, changes of name, eugenics, race and naturalization. In January 1934, Frick sent a memorandum to national and regional Government authorities in which he stressed the need to adhere to the letter of the law in the enforcement of legislation affecting the Jews. Clearly this was particularly necessary in the economic sphere where some businesses were apparently anxious to eliminate Jewish rivals by making use of the 'Aryan paragraph'. This practice was not conducive to economic stability which was one of the regime's main objectives.

German Aryan legislation is necessary for racial and State political reasons. On the other hand, the Reich Government has set itself certain limits which must likewise be observed. German Aryan legislation will be correctly judged at home and abroad if these limits are everywhere heeded. It is especially improper and even open to objection for the principles of Para. 3 BBG [Civil Service Law of April 1933[1]], the so-called 'Aryan paragraph' (which has become the model for numerous other laws and orders), to be extended to other fields to which they by no means apply. This is true particularly of the free economy, as the National Socialist Government has always declared.

I therefore repeat my request that infringements of this kind shall be decisively opposed and also that subordinate authorities shall be emphatically instructed that they are to base their measures and decisions only on the valid laws.... Any annulment or extension of Reich laws which are valid can be carried out only by the Reich Government itself according to the Enabling Law, and not by the bodies which administer these laws. They must, on the contrary, apply these laws so long as they are in force and are not to contradict them because they appear not to accord completely with National Socialism.

4 *Hess warns Party militants, April 1935*

In April 1935 Hess felt compelled to issue a confidential order to Party

[1] See above, p. 230.

members warning them not to take the law into their own hands as this would cause friction with the police:

While I can understand that all decent National Socialists oppose these new attempts by Jewry with utter indignation, I must warn them most urgently not to vent their feelings by acts of terror against individual Jews as this can only result in bringing Party members into conflict with the political police, who consist largely of Party members, and this will be welcomed by Jewry. The political police can in such cases only follow the strict instructions of the Führer in carrying out all measures for maintaining peace and order, so making it possible for the Führer to rebuke at any time allegations of atrocities and boycotts made by Jews abroad.

The Nuremberg Laws and Jewish policy, 1935–37

A conference of ministers was held on 20 August 1935 to discuss the economic effects of Party actions against Jews. Adolf Wagner, the Party representative at the conference, argued that such actions would cease, once the Government decided on a firm policy against the Jews. Dr Schacht, the Economics Minister, criticized arbitrary behaviour by Party members as this inhibited his policy of rebuilding Germany's economy. It made no economic sense since Jews had certain entrepreneurial skills which could be usefully employed to further his policies. Schacht made no moral condemnation of Jewish policy and advocated the passing of legislation to clarify the situation. The following month two measures were announced at the annual Party Rally in Nuremberg, becoming known as the Nuremberg Laws. Both measures were hastily improvised (there was even a shortage of drafting paper so that menu cards had to be used) and Jewish experts from the Ministry of the Interior were ordered to Nuremberg by plane. The first law prohibited marriages and extra-marital intercourse between 'Jews' (the name was now officially used in place of 'non-Aryans') and 'Germans' and also the employment of 'German' females under forty-five in Jewish households:

5 *Law for the Protection of German Blood and German Honour,*
  15 September 1935

Entirely convinced that the purity of German blood is essential to the further existence of the German people, and inspired by the uncompromising determination to safeguard the future of the German nation, the Reichstag has unanimously resolved upon the following law, which is promulgated herewith:

Section 1

1. Marriages between Jews and citizens of German or kindred blood are forbidden. Marriages concluded in defiance of this law are void, even if, for the purpose of evading this law, they were concluded abroad.
2. Proceedings for annulment may be initiated only by the Public Prosecutor.

Section 2

Sexual relations outside marriage between Jews and nationals of German or kindred blood are forbidden.

Section 3

Jews will not be permitted to employ female citizens of German or kindred blood as domestic servants.

Section 4

1. Jews are forbidden to display the Reich and national flag or the national colours.
2. On the other hand they are permitted to display the Jewish colours. The exercise of this right is protected by the State.

Section 5

1. A person who acts contrary to the prohibition of Section 1 will be punished with hard labour.
2. A person who acts contrary to the prohibition of Section 2 will be punished with imprisonment or with hard labour.
3. A person who acts contrary to the provisions of Sections 3 or 4 will be punished with imprisonment up to a year and with a fine, or with one of these penalties.

Section 6

The Reich Minister of the Interior in agreement with the Deputy Führer and the Reich Minister of Justice will issue the legal and administrative regulations required for the enforcement and supplementing of this law.

Section 7

The law will become effective on the day after its promulgation; Section 3, however, not until 1 January 1936.

6 *The Reich Citizenship Law, 15 September 1935*

The Nuremberg Laws by their general nature formalized the unofficial and particular measures taken against Jews up to 1935. The Nazi leaders made a point of stressing the consistency of this legislation with the Party programme which demanded that Jews should be deprived of their rights as citizens. The Reich Citizenship Law stripped Jews of their German citizenship and introduced a new distinction between 'Reich citizens' and 'nationals'. Certificates of Reich citizenship were in fact never introduced and all Germans other than Jews were until 1945 provisionally classed as Reich citizens.

Article 1

1. A subject of the State is a person who belongs to the protective union of the German Reich, and who therefore has particular obligations towards the Reich.
2. The status of subject is acquired in accordance with the provisions of the Reich and State Law of Citizenship.

Article 2

1. A citizen of the Reich is that subject only who is of German or kindred blood and

who, through his conduct, shows that he is both desirous and fit to serve the German people and Reich faithfully.

2. The right to citizenship is acquired by the granting of Reich citizenship papers.

3. Only the citizen of the Reich enjoys full political rights in accordance with the provision of the laws.

Article 3

The Reich Minister of the Interior in conjunction with the Deputy of the Führer will issue the necessary legal and administrative decrees for carrying out and supplementing this law.

7 *First Regulation under the Reich Citizenship Law, 14 November 1935*

These laws also paved the way for a more systematic persecution of the Jews, for the Reich Citizenship Law was followed during the Third Reich by a series of supplementary regulations. A major outstanding problem was that of the definition of a 'Jew'. Since the beginning of 1935 the matter had been discussed by Party leaders, who pressed for the application of legislation to all half-Jews. The Nuremberg Laws, drafted by civil servants, failed to provide a clear answer (Hitler had struck out the term 'full Jews' from the draft of the Citizenship Law as it involved a new classification). Dr Bernhard Lösener, a high official in the Reich Ministry of the Interior who had assisted in the drafting of the Nuremberg Laws, produced a memorandum on 1 November which discussed the position of half-Jews. Lösener proposed the inclusion of those half-Jews who were married to a Jewish person and who adhered to the Jewish religion. (The choice of religion for want of a better alternative was inconsistent with Nazi ideology which saw the Jew as a racial rather than a religious being.) Lösener's suggestions were included in the first regulation under the Citizenship Law, issued on 14 November 1935:

Article 1

1. Until further regulations regarding citizenship papers are issued, all subjects of German or kindred blood, who possessed the right to vote in the Reichstag elections at the time the Citizenship Law came into effect, shall for the time being possess the rights of Reich citizens. The same shall be true of those to whom the Reich Minister of the Interior, in conjunction with the Deputy of the Führer, has given preliminary citizenship.

2. The Reich Minister of the Interior, in conjunction with the Deputy of the Führer, can withdraw the preliminary citizenship.

Article 2

1. The regulations in Article 1 are also valid for Reich subjects of mixed Jewish blood.

2. An individual of mixed Jewish blood is one who is descended from one or two grandparents who were racially full Jews, in so far as he or she does not count as a Jew according to Article 5, paragraph 2. One grandparent shall be considered as full-blooded if he or she belonged to the Jewish religious community.

Article 3
Only the Reich citizen, as bearer of full political rights, exercises the right to vote in political affairs or can hold public office. The Reich Minister of the Interior, or any agency empowered by him, can make exceptions during the transition period, with regard to occupation of public office. The affairs of religious organizations will not be affected.

Article 4
1. A Jew cannot be a citizen of the Reich. He has no right to vote in political affairs and he cannot occupy public office.
2. Jewish officials will retire as of 31 December 1935. If these officials served at the front in the world war, either for Germany or her allies, they will receive in full, until they reach the age limit, the pension to which they were entitled according to the salary they last received; they will, however, not advance in seniority. After reaching the age limit, their pensions will be calculated anew, according to the salary last received, on the basis of which their pension was computed.
3. The affairs of religious organizations will not be affected.
4. The conditions of service of teachers in Jewish public schools remain unchanged until new regulations for the Jewish school systems are issued.

Article 5
1. A Jew is anyone who is descended from at least three grandparents who are racially full Jews. Article 2, para. 2, second sentence will apply.
2. A Jew is also one who is descended from two full Jewish parents, if (a) he belonged to the Jewish religious community at the time this law was issued, or joined the community later, (b) he was married to a Jewish person, at the time the law was issued, or married one subsequently, (c) he is the offspring of a marriage with a Jew, in the sense of Section 1, which was contracted after the Law for the Protection of German Blood and German Honour became effective, (d) he is the offspring of an extramarital relationship with a Jew, according to Section 1, and will be born out of wedlock after 31 July 1936.

Article 6
1. Requirements for the pureness of blood as laid down in Reich Law or in orders of the NSDAP and its echelons—not covered in Article 5—will not be affected.
2. Any other requirements for the pureness of blood, not covered in Article 5, can be made only by permission of the Reich Minister of the Interior and the Deputy Führer. If any such demands have been made, they will be void as of 1 January 1936, if they have not been requested by the Reich Minister of the Interior in agreement with the Deputy Führer. These requests must be made by the Reich Minister of the Interior.

Article 7
The Führer and Reich Chancellor can grant exemptions from the regulations laid down in the law.

The administration of this regulation proved complicated because the necessary evidence on family background was not always readily available for distinguishing between the various categories of Jews. Bodies of 'family researchers' were employed to look into the matter but selection was often arbitrary.

8 *Hitler seeks to regulate the pace of Jewish policy*

The Nuremberg Laws introduced a certain degree of stability into the position of Jews in German life if only by systematizing discrimination, thereby reducing the scope for arbitrary actions. There is no doubt, however, that Hitler viewed such legislation as only a stage towards a more thorough solution of the Jewish question, for after the Nuremberg Laws he expressed to Party colleagues his determination to push the Jews out of the professions and into ghettos. But he was in no hurry; in April 1937 he told a meeting of Party district leaders that the final aim of Jewish policy was 'crystal clear to all of us' but that:

All that concerns me is never to take a step that I might later have to retrace and never to take a step which could damage us in any way. You must understand that I always go as far as I dare and never further. It is vital to have a sixth sense which tells you broadly what you can and cannot do. Even in a struggle with an adversary it is not my way to issue a direct challenge to a trial of strength. I do not say, 'Come and fight because I want a fight'; instead I shout at him, and I shout louder and louder, 'I mean to destroy you'. Then I use my intelligence to help me to manoeuvre him into a tight corner so that he cannot strike back, and then I deliver the fatal blow.

9 *The social ostracism of Jews*

Yet despite a reduction in arbitrary terror during these years, at local level the Party and the police continued to apply pressure on the population to ostracize the Jews. The public was often slow to conform to this policy and in February 1936 a local police report from the Rhineland noted:

Unfortunately, many people still regard the Jew as a friend whom they do not want to abandon yet. But enlightenment is progressing in this field also, albeit very slowly with the country population. On 21 February of this year the funeral of a Jewess took place. The population held back and did not take part. A few women who wanted to attend were dissuaded from doing so by the other inhabitants. It was striking that the Jews from all the surrounding areas had come together to show their unity.

10 *Antisemitism and personal relations with Jews*

In Party circles antisemitism was a badge of conformity. Melita Maschmann, who became an official in the BDM, commented after the war to a Jewish friend about the distinction some people made between relations with individual Jews and the acceptance of the official policy of antisemitism:

I had learned from the example of my parents [who were German Nationalist supporters] that one could have antisemitic opinions without this interfering in one's personal relations with individual Jews. There may appear to be a vestige of tolerance in this attitude, but it is really just this confusion which I blame for the fact that I later contrived to dedicate body and soul to an inhuman political system, without this giving me doubts about my own individual decency. In preaching that all the misery of the nations was due to the Jews or that the Jewish spirit was seditious and Jewish blood was corrupting, I was not compelled to think of you or old Herr Lewy or Rosel Cohn: I thought only of the bogy-man, 'The Jew'. And when I heard that the Jews were being driven from their professions and homes and imprisoned in ghettos, the points switched automatically in my mind to steer me round the thought that such a fate could also overtake you or old Lewy. It was only *the* Jew who was being persecuted and 'made harmless'.

11   *The question of emigration*

In this situation those Jews who could afford it were faced with the decision whether or not to emigrate. In 1933, a scheme was initiated called the Haavara agreement, whereby German Jews who left the country for Palestine could transfer their capital by means of trading arrangements designed to promote German exports to Palestine. By 1938 only 170,000 Jews had availed themselves of this opportunity. During the years 1935-38 some Jews who had emigrated returned to Germany under the impression that things had quietened down after the terror of 1933-34. Many Jews with patriotic feelings saw it as their duty to remain in the country and felt bitter towards those who left. In January 1936 a police report referred to meetings of Jewish associations in the Rhineland which discussed this question:

Meetings of Jewish associations have decreased. Apart from the Zionist movement, the Association of Jewish Culture and the Association of Jewish Front Soldiers hold meetings. The meetings gave no cause for complaint, apart from one meeting held by the provincial association of synagogues. At this meeting the lawyer Stern from Berlin spoke to the synagogue congregation in Neuwied. He encouraged people to stay in Germany and warned against hasty emigration.[1] In contrast to the words of the lawyer Stern, Superintendent Dr Kurt Singer from Berlin spoke at a meeting in Koblenz held by the Association of Jewish Culture. In his speech he emphasized that the Nuremberg Laws were beyond discussion; the Jews, especially the young ones, must emigrate.

12   Stürmer *propaganda*

From the Nazi point of view, emigration was not a satisfactory way of dealing with the Jewish question, as only a limited number could leave the country each year. Also the Nazi Government still showed itself very sensitive to foreign opinion. Before and during the Olympic Games in Berlin in 1936 Hitler ordered the temporary removal of anti-Jewish notices throughout the country to impress on the visitors that the situation was not

---

[1] In another account of the speech Stern is reported as saying that the Jews should stay in the country as history had proved this to be right in other countries. All Jews should stand together in times of stress.

as bad as the foreign press had portrayed it to be. A common feature in most towns was the display of placards of *Der Stürmer*, the sensational anti-semitic tabloid of Julius Streicher. These *Stürmerkästen* sometimes included letters from readers, even schoolchildren, to give the impression that the paper's influence was greater than it really was. *Der Stürmer*, which always printed in large letters on its front page Treitschke's saying, 'The Jews are our misfortune', appealed to baser instincts:

The murder of the 10-year-old Gertrud Lenhoff in Quirschied (Saarpfalz). . . . The Jews are our MISFORTUNE!

Moreover, the numerous confessions made by Jews show that to the devout Jew the carrying out of ritual murders is an ordinance. The former Chief Rabbi (and later monk) Teofiti declares that the ritual murders take place especially on the Jewish Purim (in memory of the Persian murders) and Passover (in memory of the murder of Christ).

The instructions are as follows:

The blood of the victims is to be forcibly tapped. On Passover, it is to be used in wine and matzos; thus, a small part of the blood is to be poured into the dough of the matzos and into the wine. The mixing is done by the Jewish head of the family.

The procedure is as follows: The head of the family empties a few drops of the fresh and powdered blood into the glass, wets the fingers of the left hand, then says: 'Dam Izzardia chynim heroff dever Isyn porech harbe hossen maschus pohorus' (Exodus VII, 12) ('Thus we ask God to send the ten plagues to all enemies of the Jewish faith'). Then they eat and at the end the head of the family cries: 'Sfach, chaba, moscho kol hagoym!' ('May all Gentiles perish, as the child whose blood is contained in the bread and wine!')

The fresh (or dried or powdered) blood of the slaughtered child is further used by young married Jewish couples, by pregnant Jewesses, for circumcision and so forth. Ritual murder is recognized by all devout Jews. The Jew believes he thereby absolves himself of his sins.[1]

13 'The Poisonous Mushroom'

It was not typical of the general character of antisemitic propaganda in that it specialized in lurid and suggestive stories, accompanied by large, crudely drawn illustrations. In 1938 *Der Stürmer* published a book for older school-children called *Der Giftpilz* ('The Poisonous Mushroom'). It was written by Ernst Hiemer, editor of Streicher's paper, and contained coloured pictures drawn by the *Stürmer* artist, Philipp Rupprecht. The book began with a mother telling her son Franz during a walk in the forest that there were good and bad people in the world just as there were good and poisonous mushrooms.

[1] This extract, misrepresenting as it does the character of the two festivals of Purim and the Passover, which do not commemorate murders but deliverance from oppression, and embodying alleged quotations from Jewish sacred writings which are not to be found there and are moreover expressed in a tongue that cannot be identified, is a characteristic example of the falsehoods by which Nazi propagandists sought to work upon the ignorance of their readers.

The latter were of course the Jews. Other excerpts were as follows:

'It is almost noon,' says the teacher. 'Now we must summarize what we have learned in this lesson. What did we discuss?'

All the children raise their hands. The teacher calls on Karl Scholz, a little boy on the front bench. 'We talked about how to recognize a Jew'.

'Good! Now tell us about it!'

Little Karl takes the pointer, goes to the blackboard and points to the sketches. 'A Jew is usually recognized by his nose. The Jewish nose is crooked at the end. It looks like the figure 6. So it is called the "Jewish Six". Many non-Jews have crooked noses too. But their noses are bent, not at the end, but further up. Such a nose is called a hook nose or eagle's beak. It has nothing to do with a Jewish nose.'

'Right!' says the teacher. 'But the Jew is recognized not only by his nose ...', the boy continues. 'The Jew is also recognized by his lips. His lips are usually thick. Often the lower lip hangs down. That is called "sloppy". And the Jew is also recognized by his eyes. His eyelids are usually thicker and more fleshy than ours. The look of the Jew is sly and sharp. . . .'

Then the teacher goes to the desk and turns over the blackboard, on its back is a verse. The children recite it in chorus:

> From a Jew's countenance/the evil devil talks to us,
> The devil, who in every land/is known as evil plague.
> If we are to be free from the Jew/and to be happy and glad again,
> Then youth must join our struggle/to overcome the Jew devil. . . .

Inge sits in the Jew doctor's reception room. She has to wait a long time. She looks through the magazines on the table. But she is much too nervous even to read a few sentences. Again and again she remembers her talk with her mother. And again and again her mind dwells on the warnings of her BDM leader: 'A German must not consult a Jew doctor! And particularly not a German *girl*! Many a girl who has gone to a Jew doctor to be cured has found disease and disgrace!'

After entering the waiting-room, Inge had an extraordinary experience. From the doctor's consulting-room she could hear the sound of crying. She heard the voice of a young girl: 'Doctor, doctor, leave me alone!'

Then she heard a man laughing scornfully. And then all of a sudden, absolute silence. Inge held her breath and listened. 'What can this mean?' she asked herself and her heart was pounding. Once again she thought of her BDM leader's warning.

Inge has now been waiting for an hour. She takes up the magazines again and tries to read. The door opens. Inge looks up. There stands the Jew. She screams. She's so frightened, she drops the magazine. She jumps up in terror. Her eyes stare into the Jewish doctor's face. His face is the face of a devil. In the middle of this devil's face is a huge crooked nose. Behind the spectacles two criminal eyes. And the thick lips are grinning. A grin that says: 'Now I've got you at last, little German girl!'

The Jew approaches her. His fleshy fingers stretch out for her. But now Inge has recovered her wits. Before the Jew can grab hold of her, she slaps the Jew doctor's fat face. Then a jump to the door, and Inge runs breathlessly down the stairs. She escapes breathlessly from the Jew house. . . .

The radicalizing of antisemitism, 1938–41

During 1938 the relatively stable position which the Jews had held since 1935 began steadily to disintegrate. This development was part of a general radicalizing of the regime which followed the purge of conservatives in the winter of 1937–38. The process began in the economic field, where the replacement of Schacht as Minister of Economics in December 1937 had removed a conservative influence which had helped to restrain extreme antisemitism in the economy.

Measures taken against Jews before 1938 had affected their way of life in a wide range of activities, professional, cultural, political, personal and also economic. But there was as yet officially no general exclusion of Jews from economic affairs, although discriminative practices had had the effect of restricting their activities. For many years Jewish firms continued to function, some even enjoying Government subsidies. Jewish business skills often proved indispensable. In 1938 the gradually developing practice of the 'Aryanization' of businesses proceeded on a much greater scale. Jews had attempted to evade this practice by transferring their assets in name to 'Germans', but in April 1938 the Ministry of the Interior stepped in to establish some order with a decree demanding the disclosure of Jewish property over the value of 5000 marks and Article 7 of the decree laid down that 'The Deputy for the Year Plan [Göring] is empowered to take such measures as may be necessary to guarantee the use of reported property in accordance with the requirements of the German economy.'

14 *Decree on the changing of first names, 17 August 1938*

Further decrees followed in the summer of 1938, all laying more restrictions and prohibitions on Jewish activities in economic and professional life. On 6 July, changes in the industrial code introduced a total ban on Jews in specified commercial occupations, and the third regulation under the Citizenship Law of 14 July demanded the registration of Jewish businesses. The fourth regulation prohibited all Jewish doctors from treating 'Aryan' patients. Senior Jewish doctors had already been excluded from hospitals since December 1935. On 17 August, in order to facilitate identification, a decree was introduced forcing Jews to adopt Jewish first names:

Section 1
1. Jews must be given only such first names as are specified in the directives issued by the Reich Minister of the Interior concerning the bearing of first names.
2. Section 1 does not apply to Jews of foreign nationality.

Section 2
1. If Jews bear first names other than those authorized for Jews by Section 1, they must, from 1 January 1939, adopt another additional first name, namely 'Israel' for men and 'Sarah' for women.

Restrictions were imposed also on the movement of Jews in Germany. From July 1938 Jews were required to have special identity cards, and on 5 October a new decree on Jews' passports demanded that these should bear the letter J (for 'Jew').

15 *The 'Night of Broken Glass' (Kristallnacht), 9–10 November 1938*

In the meantime, discontent had been building up in the Party over the Government's policy of 'Aryanization', which usually resulted in the transfer of businesses from one large group to another and offered little benefit to the smaller businessman, who was strongly represented in the Party ranks. Appetites had been whetted by the wholesale expropriation of Jewish firms in Austria by Party officials after the Anschluss earlier in the year. In the city of Fürth in Bavaria, which had one of the largest Jewish communities in the country, Gauleiter Streicher attempted to cut across legal procedures by acquiring all Jewish property for the Party in return for derisory compensation. For this action and for the corruption accompanying it he was eventually dismissed, but individual acts of terror increased and went unpunished. Several motives—economic greed, racial hatred, sadism and sheer hooliganism—combined to produce outbreaks of violence which were carried out by SA men, SS groups and aggressive bands of Hitler Youth and were condoned by the police, by this time under the control of the SS. There were now fewer inhibitions about anti-Jewish measures. Not only had Schacht's voice of caution been removed, but Germany's international position was no longer so vulnerable to international pressure. Two weeks after the Munich Agreement, Göring advocated in a speech the vigorous and speedy settlement of the Jewish question and in particular the expulsion of the Jews from the economy. Events were then precipitated by an unforeseen incident, the immediate repercussions of which were somewhat embarrassing to the regime, though, as with the Reichstag Fire, it took full advantage of the situation. On 7 November 1938, Ernst von Rath, a minor official in the German Embassy in Paris, was shot dead by a young Polish Jew named Herschel Grünspan. That evening, Goebbels addressed a gathering of Party leaders in Munich and, as was later revealed in a report of the Party's Supreme Court, he made it clear that antisemitic riots would not be discouraged by the authorities. As a result, the Party leaders present went away and unleashed a pogrom of unparalleled brutality and destruction:

(a) *Secret report of the NSDAP Supreme Court on the antisemitic riots*
On the evening of 9 November 1938, Reich Propaganda Director and Party Member Dr Goebbels told the Party leaders assembled at a social evening in the old town hall in Munich that in the districts of Kurhessen and Magdeburg-Anhalt there had been anti-Jewish demonstrations, during which Jewish shops were demolished and synagogues were set on fire. The Führer at Goebbels's suggestion had decided that such demonstrations were not to be prepared or organized by the Party, but neither were they to be discouraged if they originated spontaneously. . . .

The oral instructions of the Reich Propaganda Director were probably understood by all the Party leaders present to mean that the Party should not appear outwardly as the originator of the demonstrations but that in reality it should organize them and carry them out. Instructions in this sense were telephoned immediately (and therefore a considerable time before transmission of the first teletype) to the bureaux of their districts by a large number of the Party members present. . . . The first known case of the killing of a Jew, i.e. a Polish citizen, was reported to Reich Propaganda Leader and Party Member Dr Goebbels on 10 November 1938 at about 2 o'clock and in this connexion the opinion was expressed that something would have to be done in order to prevent the whole action from taking a dangerous turn. According to the statement by the deputy Gauleiter of Munich–Upper Bavaria, Party Member Dr Goebbels replied that the informant should not get excited about one dead Jew, and that in the next few days thousands of Jews would see the point. At that time, most of the killings could still have been prevented by a supplementary order. Since this did not happen, it must be deduced from that fact as well as from the remark itself that the final result was intended or at least was considered possible and desirable. In which case, the individual agent carried out not simply the assumed, but the correctly understood, wishes of the leaders, however vaguely expressed. For that he could not be punished.

This report estimated the number of Jewish dead at 91. Over 20,000 Jewish men were arrested and taken to concentration camps. Nazi propaganda dressed the affair up as a spontaneous uprising of the German people against the Jews. In fact, the reaction of the public was apparently one of shock. The British *chargé d'affaires* in Berlin claimed that he had not met 'a single German from any walk of life who does not disapprove to some degree of what has occurred'.

(b) Kristallnacht *in Leipzig*
The American Consul in Leipzig, David Buffum, prepared a detailed report (21 November) on the events of the *Kristallnacht* in that city. His account of the violence demolishes any question of strong popular backing for what happened and draws attention to the powerlessness of the public and the refusal of the police to intervene against the outrages:

The shattering of shop windows, looting of stores and dwellings of Jews which began in the early hours of 10 November 1938, was hailed subsequently in the Nazi press as a 'spontaneous wave of righteous indignation throughout Germany, as a result of the cowardly Jewish murder of Third Secretary von Rath in the German Embassy at Paris'. So far as a very high percentage of the German populace is concerned, a state of popular indignation that would spontaneously lead to such excesses, can be considered as nonexistent. On the contrary, in viewing the ruins and attendant measures employed, all of the local crowds observed were obviously benumbed over what had happened and aghast over the unprecedented fury of Nazi acts that had been or were taking place with bewildering rapidity throughout their city. . . .
At 3 a.m. on 10 November 1938 was unleashed a barrage of Nazi ferocity as had had no equal hitherto in Germany, or very likely anywhere else in the world since

savagery began. Jewish buildings were smashed into and contents demolished or looted. In one of the Jewish sections an eighteen-year-old boy was hurled from a three-storey window to land with both legs broken on a street littered with burning beds and other household furniture and effects from his family's and other apartments. This information was supplied by an attending physician. It is reported from another quarter that among domestic effects thrown out of a Jewish building, a small dog descended four flights on to a cluttered street with a broken spine. Although apparently centred in poor districts, the raid was not confined to the humble classes. One apartment of exceptionally refined occupants known to this office was violently ransacked, presumably in a search for valuables which was not in vain, and one of the marauders thrust a cane through a priceless medieval painting portraying a biblical scene. Another apartment of the same category is known to have been turned upside down in the frenzied pursuit of whatever the invaders were after. Reported loss by looting of cash, silver, jewellery, and otherwise easily convertible articles, has been apparent.

Jewish shop windows by the hundreds were systematically and wantonly smashed throughout the entire city at a loss estimated at several millions of marks. There are reports that substantial losses have been sustained on the famous Leipzig 'Brühl', as many of the shop windows at the time of the demolition were filled with costly furs that were seized before the windows could be boarded up. In proportion to the general destruction of real estate, however, losses of goods are felt to have been relatively small. The spectators who viewed the wreckage when daylight had arrived were mostly in such a bewildered mood that there was no danger of impulsive acts, and the perpetrators probably were too busy in carrying out their schedule to take off a whole lot of time for personal profit. At all events, the main streets of the city were a positive litter of shattered plate glass. According to reliable testimony, the debacle was executed by SS men and Stormtroopers not in uniform, each group having been provided with hammers, axes, crowbars and incendiary bombs.

Three synagogues in Leipzig were fired simultaneously by incendiary bombs and all sacred objects and records desecrated or destroyed, in most cases hurled through the windows and burned in the streets. No attempts whatsoever were made to quench the fires, the activity of the fire brigade being confined to playing water on adjoining buildings. All of the synagogues were irreparably gutted by flames, and the walls of the two that are close to the consulate are now being razed. The blackened frames have been centres of attraction during the past week of terror for eloquently silent and bewildered crowds. One of the largest clothing stores in the heart of the city was destroyed by flames from incendiary bombs, only the charred walls and gutted roof having been left standing. As was the case with the synagogues, no attempts on the part of the fire brigade were made to extinguish the fire, although apparently there was a certain amount of apprehension for adjacent property, for the walls of a coffee house next door were covered with asbestos and sprayed by the doughty firemen. It is extremely difficult to believe, but the owners of the clothing store were actually charged with setting the fire and on that basis were dragged from their beds at 6 a.m. and clapped into prison.

Tactics which closely approached the ghoulish took place at the Jewish cemetery where the temple was fired together with a building occupied by caretakers, tombstones uprooted and graves violated. Eyewitnesses considered reliable the report that ten corpses were left unburied at this cemetery for a whole week because all gravediggers and cemetery attendants had been arrested.

Ferocious as was the violation of property, the most hideous phase of the so-called 'spontaneous' action has been the wholesale arrest and transportation to concentration camps of male German Jews between the ages of sixteen and sixty, as well as Jewish men without citizenship. This has been taking place daily since the night of horror. This office has no way of accurately checking the numbers of such arrests, but there is very little question that they have run to several thousands in Leipzig alone. Having demolished dwellings and hurled most of the movable effects onto the streets, the insatiably sadistic perpetrators threw many of the trembling inmates into a small stream that flows through the Zoological Park, commanding horrified spectators to spit at them, defile them with mud and jeer at their plight. The latter incident has been repeatedly corroborated by German witnesses who were nauseated in telling the tale. The slightest manifestation of sympathy evoked a positive fury on the part of the perpetrators, and the crowd was powerless to do anything but turn horror-stricken eyes from the scene of abuse, or leave the vicinity. These tactics were carried out the entire morning of 10 November without police intervention and they were applied to men, women and children.

There is much evidence of physical violence, including several deaths. At least half-a-dozen cases have been personally observed, victims with bloody, badly bruised faces having fled to this office, believing that as refugees their desire to emigrate could be expedited here. As a matter of fact this consulate has been a bedlam of humanity for the past ten days, most of these visitors being desperate women, as their husbands and sons had been taken off to concentration camps.

Similarly violent procedure was applied throughout this consular district, the amount of havoc wrought depending upon the number of Jewish establishments or persons involved. It is understood that in many of the smaller communities even more relentless methods were employed than was the case in the cities. Reports have been received from Weissenfels to the effect that the few Jewish families there are experiencing great difficulty in purchasing food. It is reported that three Aryan professors of the University of Jena have been arrested and taken off to concentration camps because they had voiced disapproval of this insidious drive against mankind.

Sources of information: Personal observation and interviews.

16 *A Nazi's reaction to the* Kristallnacht

Melita Maschmann analysed her own reactions to the events of that night in Berlin and referred to the effect of Party indoctrination in blunting human feelings:

Next morning—I had slept well and heard no disturbance—I went into Berlin very early to go to the Reich Youth Leadership office. I noticed nothing unusual on the way. I alighted at the Alexanderplatz. In order to get to the Lothringerstrasse I had to go down a rather gloomy alley containing many small shops and inns. To my surprise almost all the shop windows here were smashed in. The pavement was covered with pieces of glass and fragments of broken furniture.

I asked a patrolling policeman what on earth had been going on there. He replied:
'In this street they're almost all Jews.'

'Well?'

'You don't read the papers. Last night the National Soul boiled over.'

I can remember only the sense but not the actual wording of this remark, which
had an undertone of hidden anger. I went on my way shaking my head. For the
space of a second I was clearly aware that something terrible had happened there.
Something frighteningly brutal. But almost at once I switched over to accepting
what had happened as over and done with and avoiding critical reflection. I said to
myself: The Jews are the enemies of the New Germany. Last night they had a
taste of what this means. Let us hope that World Jewry, which has resolved to
hinder Germany's 'new steps towards greatness', will take the events of last night
as a warning. If the Jews sow hatred against us all over the world, they must learn
that we have hostages for them in our hands.

With these or similar thoughts I constructed for myself a justification of the
pogrom. But in any case I forced the memory of it out of my consciousness as
quickly as possible. As the years went by I grew better and better at switching off
quickly in this manner on similar occasions. It was the only way, whatever the circumstances, to prevent the onset of doubts about the rightness of what had happened. I probably knew, beneath the level of daily consciousness, that serious
doubts would have torn away the basis of my existence from under me. Not in the
economic but in the existential sense. I had totally identified myself with National
Socialism. The moment of horror became more and more dangerous to me as the
years went by. For this reason it had to become shorter and shorter. But now I am
anticipating. On the 'Night of Broken Glass' our feelings were not yet hardened to
the sight of human suffering as they were later during the war. Perhaps if I had
met one of the persecuted and oppressed, an old man with the fear of death in his
face, perhaps, . . .

17 *Conference on the Jewish question, 12 November 1938*

Goebbels's action in initiating the pogrom had caused extreme irritation to
certain other Nazi leaders, especially Göring, whose responsibilities for the
economy caused him to see the events of the *Kristallnacht* in a different light.
Reactions abroad were highly unfavourable and resulted in a stricter boycott
of German goods. The total damage to property was estimated at around
25 million marks, but much of this was inflicted on property not owned by
Jews (Jewish shopkeepers were often the tenants of German house-owners).
Göring immediately saw Hitler, who had apparently acquiesced in Goebbels's
action, and convinced him of the need for dealing with the Jewish question
more systematically from above. Göring then at once called a conference
on 12 November under his own chairmanship to decide on future policy.
Although he maintained that the problem was 'mainly economic', it was also
much more than that. Certainly, the events of 9–10 November provided
Göring with an opportunity to apply measures which he already had in
mind, but the question was complicated by Party rivalries. Jewish policy
suffered from the fact that responsibility for it was divided between different

authorities. Apart from Göring and Goebbels, those present at the conference included Walther Funk (Economics Minister), Schwerin von Krosigk (Finance Minister), Heydrich (Chief of Security Police), Daluege (Head of the Uniformed Police) and representatives of the Foreign Ministry and insurance companies. Furthermore, the conference did not concern itself solely with economic measures. Goebbels proposed more segregationist restrictions on Jews in social life, and Heydrich hinted at the need to establish ghettos, since the policy of forced emigration with its slow processes did not provide a satisfactory solution to the Jewish question:

Göring: Gentlemen! Today's meeting is of a decisive character. I have received a letter written on the Führer's orders by Bormann, the Stabsleiter of the Führer's deputy, requesting that the Jewish question be now, once and for all, coordinated and solved one way or another. And yesterday once again the Führer requested me on the phone to take coordinated action in the matter.

Since the problem is mainly an economic one, it is from the economic angle that it will have to be tackled. Naturally a number of legal measures will have to be taken which fall within the sphere of the Minister of Justice and within that of the Minister of the Interior; and certain propaganda measures will be taken care of by the Minister of Propaganda. The Minister of Finance and the Minister for Economic Affairs will take care of problems which fall into their respective fields. . . .

Now we have had this affair in Paris, followed by more demonstrations, and this time something decisive must be done! Because, gentlemen, I have had enough of these demonstrations! It is not the Jew they harm but myself, as the final authority for coordinating the German economy. If today a Jewish shop is destroyed and goods are thrown into the street, the insurance company will pay for the damage, which does not even touch the Jew; and furthermore, the goods destroyed come from the consumer goods belonging to the people. . . .

I would not wish there to remain any doubt, gentlemen, as to the purpose of today's meeting. We have not come together simply for more talk, but to make decisions, and I implore the competent agencies to take all measures to eliminate the Jew from the German economy and to submit the measures to me, so far as it is necessary. . . .

Goebbels: . . . Furthermore, my advice is that the Jew should be eliminated from any position in public life in which he may prove to be a provocation. It is still possible today for a Jew to share a compartment in a sleeping car with a German. Therefore, we need a decree by the Reich Ministry of Transport stating that separate compartments shall be available to Jews; in cases where compartments are full up, Jews cannot claim a seat. They will be given a separate compartment only after all Germans have secured seats. They are not to mix with Germans, and if there is no more room, they will have to stand in the corridor.

Göring: In that case, I think it would be more sensible to give them separate compartments.

Goebbels: Not if the train is overcrowded!

Göring: Just a moment. There will be only one Jewish coach. If that is full up, the other Jews will have to stay at home.

Goebbels: Suppose, though, there aren't many Jews going on the express train to Munich, suppose there are two Jews in the train and the other compartments are overcrowded. These two Jews would then have a compartment all to themselves. Therefore, Jews may claim a seat only after all Germans have secured one.

Göring: I'd give the Jews one coach or one compartment. And should such a case as you mention arise and the train be overcrowded, believe me, we won't need a law. We'll kick him out and he'll have to sit all alone in the lavatory all the way!

Goebbels: I don't agree. I don't believe in that. There ought to be a law. Further-more, there ought to be a decree barring Jews from German beaches and resorts. . . . Jews should not be allowed to sit around in German parks. I am thinking of the whispering campaign on the part of Jewish women in the public gardens on the Fehrbelliner Platz. They go and sit with German mothers and their children and begin to gossip and work upon their feelings. I see here a particularly grave danger. I think it is imperative to give the Jews certain public parks, not the best ones, and tell them: 'You may sit on these benches.' These benches shall be marked 'For Jews only'. Besides that they have no business in German parks. Furthermore, Jewish children are still allowed in German schools. That's impossible. It is out of the question that any boy should sit beside a Jewish boy in a German grammar school and take lessons in German history. Jews ought to be eliminated com-pletely from German schools. They ought to take care of their own education in their own communities. . . .

Heydrich: . . . As another means of getting the Jews out, measures for emigration ought to be taken in the rest of the Reich for the next eight to ten years. The highest number of Jews we can possibly get out during one year is 8,000–10,000. A great number of Jews will therefore remain. Because of the Aryanizing and other restrictions, Jewry will become unemployed. The remaining Jews will gradually become proletarians. I shall therefore have to take steps to isolate the Jew so that he won't enter into the normal German routine of life. On the other hand, I shall have to restrict the Jew to a small circle of consumers, but I shall have to permit them certain activities within the professions: lawyers, doctors, barbers, etc. This question will also have to be examined. As for the question of isolation, I'd like to make a few proposals regarding police measures which are important also because of their psychological effect on public opinion. For example, anyone who is Jewish according to the Nuremberg Laws will have to wear a certain badge. That is a possibility which will simplify many other things. I don't see any danger of excuses, and it will make our relationship with the foreign Jews easier.

Göring: A uniform?

Heydrich: A badge. This way we could also put an end to the molesting of foreign Jews who don't look different from ours.

Göring: But, my dear Heydrich, you won't be able to avoid the creation of ghettos on a very large scale in all the cities. They will have to be created.

18 *Decree for the restoration of the appearance of the streets as regards Jewish businesses, 12 November 1938*

Göring acted decisively in enforcing the programme outlined at the conference. Several measures were at once announced on the day of the conference itself. The cost of the damage of the *Kristallnacht* was borne partly by the insurance companies (who compensated for the losses suffered by non-Jewish property owners) and partly by the Jews themselves. Göring decreed that Jewish property owners should meet the costs of repairing the damage done to their property:

1. All damage to Jewish businesses or dwellings on 8, 9 and 10 November 1938 through the indignation of the people over the agitation of the international Jews against National Socialist Germany must be repaired at once by the Jewish occupant or Jewish businessmen.

2. (i) The costs of restoration will be borne by the occupants of the Jewish businesses and dwellings concerned.

(ii) Insurance claims by Jews of German nationality will be confiscated in favour of the Reich.

19 *Collective fine for Jews, 12 November 1938*

A later order permitted Jews to deduct these costs from their contributions towards the collective fine of one billion marks imposed on German Jews by another decree of Göring on the same day:

The hostile attitude of Jewry towards the German people and Reich, which does not even shrink from committing cowardly murder, requires harsh atonement. Therefore, on the basis of the Decree for the Implementing of the Four-Year Plan of 18 October 1936, I make the following Order:

Section 1: The payment of a contribution of 1,000,000,000 Reichsmarks to the German Reich has been imposed on the Jews of German nationality as a whole.

Section 2: Provisions for its enforcement will be issued by the Reich Minister of Finance in agreement with the Reich Ministers concerned.

20 *Decree eliminating Jews from German economic life, 12 November 1938*

The most decisive measure taken on 12 November was Göring's decree excluding Jews from the retail business, thus formalizing the extensive 'Aryanization' of Jewish-owned property which had begun in the autumn of 1937:

On the basis of the Decree of 18 October 1936 for the Implementing of the Four-Year Plan the following is decreed:

Article 1
1. From 1 January 1939 the running of retail shops, mail order houses and the practice of independent trades are forbidden to Jews.

2. Moreover, Jews are forbidden from the same date to offer goods or services in markets of all kinds, fairs or exhibitions or to advertise them or accept orders for them.

3. Jewish shops which operate in violation of this order will be closed by the police.

Article 2

1. No Jew can any longer be manager of an establishment as defined by the Law on the Organization of National Labour, of 20 January 1934.

2. If a Jew is a leading employee in a business concern he may be dismissed at six weeks' notice. After the expiration of this period, all claims of the employees derived from the denounced contract become invalid, especially claims for retirement or dismissal pay.

Article 3

1. No Jew can be a member of a cooperative society.

2. Jewish members of cooperatives lose their membership from 21 December 1938. No special notice is necessary.

Article 4

The Minister of Economics is empowered to issue regulations necessary for the enforcement of this decree with the approval of the Reich ministers concerned. He may allow exceptions in the case of the transfer of Jewish business establishments into non-Jewish hands, or of the liquidation of Jewish business establishments, or in special cases.

21 *The enforcement of the economic legislation against the Jews in 1938*

An administrative order of 23 November provided for the dissolution of all Jewish retail business as a question of principle, while a further decree issued on 3 December legalized the 'Aryanization' of Jewish industrial firms, securities and real estate. Jews were no longer allowed to sell their property. All these measures systematized the process of 'Aryanization' and were intended to assert State control, but the following report of 5 January 1939 to the Reich Minister of Economics by the Office of the City President of Berlin on the final three months of 1938 underlined the discrepancy between the legal requirements and the facts. The execution of the decrees was complicated by other factors: the arbitrary assumption of powers by Party-affiliated organizations and even State authorities; the unfulfilled promise that the independent middle-class businessman would benefit from the abolition of the Jewish-owned chainstores and other large businesses; and generally a whole host of corrupt practices. There was a mad rush to benefit from the 'Aryanization' while it lasted:

• • •

Egoism in economic life

The confused weeks after the new decrees of November 1938 concerning the Jews reflected a coarsening of business methods, perhaps also as a result of the September crisis. Not only in the retail trade, in the competition of applicants for the Jewish retail shops, but in general the impression prevails of an increasingly ruthless exploitation of positions of power. This begins with the fight for the allocation of raw materials, continues with the fight for labour and leads to the ruthless exploitation by people of their own, sometimes merely apparent, financial power, in order to attract workers with wage increases. It sometimes leads to agreements to ignore the wage freeze announced by the Trustee and not even to make an application. The number of interventions on the ground of an alleged acquaintanceship with me of the most superficial kind has increased in influential quarters, despite the fact that such interventions were already criticized by the Party authorities in September 1938 at the beginning of Aryanization. Every group has its favourite for whom it would like to procure, let us say, the plant just ripe for Aryanization. . . .

Such drastic actions as those initiated by the Decree on the Exclusion of Jews from German Economic Life, of 12.xi.38, easily tend to 'get out of hand' at the lower levels of the executive authorities. With the first newspaper announcement or the first announcement by an influential figure on the radio, forces are set in motion which claim the right to carry out such measures themselves, whereas in reality their function is at best advisory. Thus the illegal use of private 'commissioners' has developed, with Jewish owners of plants giving them extensive plenary powers in order to get rid of the factory as quickly as possible (since they hope for the biggest advantage thereby); also, there are attempts at notarial transfers of properties on the basis of such plenary powers, etc. This can be prevented by the issuing, when possible, of executive regulations simultaneously with the basic decree. The main task of my office in the context of Aryanization in retail trade has been to mitigate the uncontrollable actions of such forces.

Arbitrary interpretation of the law

In the same way I have noticed in connexion with the Aryanization programme that legal regulations and decrees are supplemented by a somewhat arbitrary interpretation not only on the part of organizations affiliated to the Party but also on the part of State authorities. Thus, in the process of drawing up the registry of Jewish businesses, a factory was declared Jewish simply because the Aryan proprietress was married to a Jew, although, according to the instructions for the drawing up of this register, there is no such regulation. In fact, according to the edict of the Minister of the Interior of 14.vii.38, the decision is to be made in the light of individual circumstances and according to whether or not the Jewish partner had a dominant influence over the business. The other regulation may even have been avoided on purpose. The further development of legal regulations on the basis of a progressive refinement of the sense of legality within the community is certainly a supplement to legislation which must not be underestimated. It becomes dangerous only if in this sphere, away from the legislator and without knowledge of his motives, the varying strength and power of penetration of the organizations taking part, and of the State and non-State authorities, begin to get out of hand. This happened when the Jews were prohibited from being landlords. Pressure was exerted that Jews should be forced to interpose German administrators over their own house property; basically this was certainly an aim worth striving for, but it was something which had not yet been expressed in legislation (Law for the Alteration of the Industrial Code of 6.vii.38). Thus, letters were written to Jews stating that an administrator had been appointed for their house property and that the owner had to appear at the office so that the 'take-over of administration' might be effected; he was also to bring along any managers who had been appointed by other agencies. He was threatened with 'further measures' if he did not appear. Subsequently, for such measures the explanation was given 'that it was found necessary to keep various Jewish managements under observation during the critical days of November'. Moreover, this procedure was justified since another authority had also given orders for the same property to be supervised. In this way, through the simultaneous actions of two different organizations, several representatives appeared without authority and sometimes even tried to collect the rent. . . .

22 *Restrictions upon Jews in Berlin*

The *Kristallnacht* of November 1938 and the policy decisions following it marked a major stage in the development of Jewish policy since they brought about a greater commitment by the State to settle the Jewish question. With the flood of new legal restrictions on Jews the State machinery became increasingly involved in the administration of this policy. The weaknesses of earlier policies – terror, boycott, legislation and emigration – were becoming clear. The reappraisal after the pogrom revealed glimpses of the more thorough-going policy which led ultimately to extermination. Goebbels's threat to remove Jews from public places was soon carried out, and new regulations for the social segregation of Jews from other Germans pointed towards the creation of ghettos. On 4 December 1938 the Police-President of Berlin issued this order:

In accordance with Reich Police Decree of 28 November 1938 with regard to the appearance of Jews in public, the President for the State Police District of Berlin has issued a first order, which will become effective on 6 December 1938. It decrees that streets, squares, parks, and buildings which come under the restrictions against Jews are not to be entered or driven through in vehicles by Jews of German citizenship or by Jews without citizenship.

If such Jews are still residents of a district which comes under the restrictions against Jews, at the time when this decree becomes effective, they will have to use a permit issued by the police station of that residential district in order to cross the boundary of the restricted area. With effect from July 1939 and thereafter, permits for residents of the restricted area will no longer be issued.

The restrictions against Jews in Berlin include:

1. All theatres, cinemas, cabarets, public concert and lecture halls, museums, amusement places, the exhibition halls at the Messedamm including the exhibition area and radio tower, the Deutschlandhalle and the Sportsplatz, the Reich Sports Field, and all sport places including the ice-skating rinks.
2. All public and private bathing establishments and indoor baths as well as open-air baths.
3. The Wilhelmstrasse from the Leipziger Strasse up to Unter den Linden including the Wilhelmsplatz.
4. The Voss-strasse from the Hermann-Göring-Strasse up to the Wilhelmstrasse.

5. The Reichsehrenmal including the sidewalk on the north side of Unter den Linden from the university to the Zeughaus (Military Historical Museum).

Exempted from articles 1–2 are such institutions and events as are open to Jewish visitors in accordance with properly authorized permission. Intentional or negligent violation will be punished with a fine of up to 150 Reichsmarks or up to 6 weeks' detention.

In addition it is announced, among other things, that even more thorough executive orders will be issued. This restriction against Jews does not apply to foreign Jews. It is probable that the restriction against Jews, which has no time limit, will soon be extended to include a large number of Berlin streets. In this respect the main streets and thoroughfares of Berlin especially come into consideration, because even now, in these streets in particular, Jewry more or less dominates the street scene. The rows of streets in the centre and the north of Berlin, where the Jewish element has predominated for centuries (for example, Münz, the Linien, and Grenadier-Strasse) will probably not be included in the districts banned to Jews. It is therefore advisable for any Jew to start immediately looking for another residence in one of the above-mentioned parts of Berlin, and perhaps to effect an exchange of residence with one of the pure-blood Germans residing there.

Furthermore, the Jews can expect to be restricted to purely Jewish inns in the future.

23 *Further social restrictions upon Jews*

The attempt to enforce a principle always ran up against practical difficulties of administration, in this case the provision of alternative accommodation for those Jews evacuated from certain areas. The anti-mixing regulations were obliged to deal with two fundamental problems, namely, housing and marriage. At the conference on 12 November, Heydrich had raised the question of epidemics breaking out if ghettos were established. He also doubted whether his police could regularly supervise daily life in such ghettos. Göring's answer in his decree of 28 December was to concentrate the Jews in houses instead of areas. Another outstanding matter was the intermarriages which had existed before the Blood Protection Law of 1935. That measure had applied only to marriages contracted after it came into force. In the same decree Göring introduced a new classification in the case of such marriages based on the criterion of the children's religious affiliation. Another determining factor was which spouse was the Jewish partner in the marriage. The Jewish wife was given better treatment than the Jewish husband, presumably because her German husband was assumed to be the owner of the family house:

At my suggestion, the Führer has made the following decisions concerning the Jewish problem:

SECTION A

I. *Housing of Jews*

1(a). The tenant protective law is not, as a rule, to be abrogated for the Jews. On the contrary, it is desired, if possible, to proceed in particular cases in such a way that the Jews are quartered together in separate houses in so far as the housing conditions allow.

1(b). For this reason the Aryanization of house ownership *is to be postponed until the end of the total Aryanization*, that is to say, for the present the Aryanization of houses has to be carried out only in those individual cases where urgent reasons exist. The Aryanizing of industries, businesses, agricultural estates, forests, etc., is to be considered as urgent.

2. Use of sleeping and dining cars is to be forbidden to the Jews. At the same time, no special Jewish compartments are to be established. In addition, the use of trains, streets cars, suburban railways, underground railways, buses, and ships cannot be prohibited to Jews.

3. Only the use of certain public establishments, etc., is to be prohibited to Jews. In this category belong the hotels and restaurants visited especially by Party members (for instance: Hotel Kaiserhof, Berlin; Hotel Vierjahreszeiten, Munich; Hotel Deutscher Hof, Nuremberg; Hotel Drei Mohren, Augsburg; etc.). The use of bathing establishments, certain public places, bathing resorts, etc., can be prohibited to Jews; also health baths particularly prescribed by doctors may be used by Jews, but only in such ways that no offence is caused.

II. Jews who were officials and have been pensioned are not to be denied their pensions. Investigations must be made, however, as to whether these Jews can manage with a reduced allowance.

III. The Jewish welfare organizations are not to be Aryanized or abolished, for so the Jews will only become a public charge; but they may be supported by Jewish welfare organizations.

IV. Jewish patents are property, and as such must be Aryanized. (A similar procedure towards Germany was carried out by the USA and other countries during World War I.)

SECTION B

Mixed Marriages
I,1. *With children* (part-Jews, 1st class)
(a) Where the father is a German and the mother a Jewess, the family may stay in future in its present lodging. The regulations for the exclusion of Jews are not to be applied to such families as far as their housing is concerned.

In these cases, the property of the Jewish mother can be transferred to the German husband or to the mixed children.
(b) Where the father is a Jew and the mother a German, these families are also not to be moved for the present into Jewish quarters, because the children (part-Jew, 1st class) must serve in the labour service and the armed forces in the future and must not be exposed to Jewish propaganda. As far as the property is concerned, one must for the present proceed in such a way that it can be completely or partly transferred to the children.
I,2. *Without children*
(a) If the husband is a German and the wife a Jewess, the provisions of 1(a) are valid accordingly.
(b) If the husband is a Jew, and the wife a German, these childless couples are to be

proceeded against as if they were full-blooded Jews. The husband's property cannot be transferred to the wife. Both husband and wife can be moved into Jewish houses or Jewish quarters.

Especially in case of emigration, such married couples are to be treated as Jews, as soon as increased emigration is begun.

II. If a German wife divorces a Jew, she re-enters the German racial community and all disadvantages for her discontinue.

The Jewish question in terms of numbers was largely an urban matter. According to the 1933 census, one-third of the Jews in Germany lived in Berlin, and 74 per cent of the Jewish population was concentrated in cities with more than 100,000 inhabitants. This tendency increased during the first six years of the Third Reich so that by the 1939 census the proportion of Jews living in large cities had risen to 82 per cent. The Jewish population in Germany (the area confined by the boundaries of 1937) had been reduced during the same period as a result of death and emigration from 515,000 to 350,000, but the acquisition of Austria in 1938, with its relatively large Jewish population of 190,000, reversed the process. Consequently, the policy of emigration received more urgent attention in 1938–39. In August 1938, a Central Office for Jewish Emigration had been established in Vienna to speed up the course of emigration. This solution was soon adopted in Germany itself and involved a scheme to assist poorer Jews to emigrate, whereby richer Jews were obliged to finance the emigration of the poorer. Göring established a central office by decree on 24 January 1939 which was placed under the direction of the Chief of the Security Police, Reinhard Heydrich.

The extermination of the Jews, 1941–45

24 *Hitler threatens destruction of the European Jews in the event of war*

Hitler was increasingly dissatisfied with the progress of antisemitic policy. As Germany moved closer to the possibility of war, his thoughts turned to more radical solutions. In a major speech to the Reichstag on 30 January 1939 he made a chilling prophecy of the destruction of the Jews in Europe should war break out:

One thing I should like to say on this day which may be memorable for others as well as for us Germans. In the course of my life I have very often been a prophet, and have usually been ridiculed for it. During the time of my struggle for power it was in the first instance only the Jewish race that received my prophecies with laughter when I said that I would one day take over the leadership of the State, and with it that of the whole nation, and that I would then among other things settle the Jewish problem. Their laughter was uproarious, but I think that for some time now they have been laughing on the other side of their face. Today I will once more be a prophet: if the international Jewish financiers in and outside Europe should succeed in plunging the nations once more into a world war, then the result will not be the Bolshevizing of the earth, and thus the victory of Jewry, but the annihilation of the Jewish race in Europe!

25 *Göring orders Heydrich to carry out the 'final solution' of the Jewish question, 31 July 1941*

The outbreak of war in 1939 changed the whole aspect of the Jewish question. The possibilities of emigration were automatically narrowed, while the occupation of vast new territories increased the numbers of Jews under Nazi control (Poland had a Jewish community of more than 3 million, constituting 10 per cent of the total population). The war, with the tightened security precautions imposed on the Reich area, allowed the Nazis to pursue a thorough-going policy against the Jews, untrammelled by considerations of foreign opinion. Previously, foreign Jews living in Germany had usually been exempted from antisemitic restrictions, but Nazi wartime successes changed all that. In Poland, Jews were ordered into forced labour, frequent pogroms occurred and ghettos were later established. The SS began to assume more duties dealing with the Jews. In September 1939 Heydrich ordered the first deportations from the Reich area to Poland, and the mass transportation of Jews started in the winter. The German attack on the Soviet Union in June 1941 was a decisive factor leading to the extermination of the Jews, for in Hitler's mind they were the chief propagators of Bolshevism. Hitler had probably decided on the destruction of the Jews in the spring of 1941. Special 'task forces' were formed to carry out this policy, and on 2 July Heydrich ordered them to execute all Communist Party officials and Jews working for the Party and State in the USSR.[1] This order was supplemented by verbal instructions to these groups to include all Jews. On 31 July Göring commissioned Heydrich with the task of carrying out the 'final solution' of the Jewish question:

To complete the task that was assigned to you on 24 January 1939, which dealt with the solution of the Jewish problem by emigration and evacuation in the most suitable way, I hereby charge you with making all necessary preparations with regard to organizational, technical and financial matters for bringing about a complete solution of the Jewish question within the German sphere of influence in Europe.

Wherever other governmental agencies are involved, these are to cooperate with you.

I request you further to send me, as soon as possible, an overall plan covering the organizational, technical and material measures necessary for the accomplishment of the final solution of the Jewish question which we desire.

26 *A request for an explanation of the relationship between the policy of extermination and the needs of war production*

No further distinction was made between Jews, half-Jews and those with

[1] See below, p. 620.

any Jewish background. Himmler forbade any definition of the word 'Jew' and simply ordered that the occupied territories should be cleared of Jews. A major obstacle to the speedy execution of this policy of extermination was the need for Jewish labour, especially in the war production industries. Himmler made exceptions in the case of those Jews whose special skills were highly necessary, but he granted them only as a temporary arrangement. Complaints were made by the occupation authorities about the behaviour of the SS, especially in the eastern territories, where the methods they used were barbaric. In October 1941 the Reich Commissioner for the Baltic States, Hinrich Lohse, prohibited the further shooting of Jews in Lepaya in Latvia, whereupon the SS protested to the Reich Ministry for the Occupied Eastern Territories. The Ministry requested a report from the Commissioner, which was sent on 15 November:

I have forbidden the indiscriminate executions of Jews in Lepaya because they were not carried out in a justifiable manner.

I should like to be informed whether your inquiry of 31 October is to be regarded as a directive to liquidate all Jews in the east. Is this to take place without regard to age and sex and economic requirements (of the Wehrmacht, for instance, for specialists in the armament industry)?

(*note in different handwriting:* Of course the cleansing of the east of Jews is a necessary task; its solution, however, must be harmonized with the necessities of war production.)

So far I have not been able to find such a directive either in the regulations regarding the Jewish question in the 'Brown Portfolio' or in other decrees.

27 *'Economic considerations not a factor in the final solution'*

The Ministry's prompt reply was sent by Otto Bräutigam, head of its political department, and emphasized that economic considerations should not impede the progress of the 'final solution':

The Jewish question has probably been clarified by now through verbal discussions. Economic considerations are to be regarded as fundamentally irrelevant in the settlement of the problem. Moreover, it is requested that questions which arise should be settled directly with the Senior SS and Police Leaders.

Despite further measures to speed up the mass slaughter of Jews, Jewish labour continued to be used almost to the end of the war. In 1944 thousands of Jews were still being employed in war production in Lower Silesia, and some were apparently even taken from Auschwitz to keep the factories going.

28 *Heydrich's Decree on the Identification of Jews, 1 September 1941*

Many restrictions upon Jews which had been introduced in the east were now introduced into Germany itself, including the requirement that Jews should wear the Star of David:

Article 1

1. Jews over six years of age are prohibited from appearing in public without wearing a Jewish star.
2. The Jewish star is a yellow piece of cloth with a black border, in the form of a six-pointed star of the size of the palm of the hand. The inscription reads, 'Jew', in black letters. It shall be worn visibly, sewn on the left chest side of the garment.

Article 2

Jews are forbidden:
a. to leave their area of residence without written permission of the local police, carried on their person;
b. to wear medals, decorations or other insignia.

Article 3

Articles 1 and 2 shall not apply:
a. to a Jewish husband living in a mixed marriage if there are children born of this marriage who are not considered as Jews. This also applies if the marriage is dissolved or if the only son was killed in the present war.
b. to a Jewish wife in a childless mixed marriage for the duration of the marriage.

Article 4

1. Anyone who violates Articles 1 and 2 intentionally or carelessly will be punished with a fine up to 150 Reichsmarks or with imprisonment not exceeding six weeks. . . .

29 *The deportation of the Jews from Germany in 1941*

In 1942 Jews were forbidden in Germany to use public transport without permits allowing them to travel to work, visit restaurants, buy books and even use public telephones. From October 1941 mass deportations from the Reich began. Destinations were usually the ghettos of Lodz, Warsaw, Minsk and Riga. A police official who was responsible for organizing the deportation of one thousand Jews from Düsseldorf in December 1941 described the scene at the station before departure:

The departure of the transport was scheduled for 9.30, so the Jews were got ready at the loading ramp at 4 o'clock. The Reich railways, however, could not assemble the special train so early, apparently because of a lack of staff, so that the loading of the Jews could not be started until 9 o'clock. The loading took place in very great haste since the Reich railways were pressing for the train to depart on time. It was not surprising, therefore, that several wagons were overloaded (60–65 people), whereas others held only 35–40 people. . . . On the way from the abattoir [where the Jews had been collected from all parts of the district] to the loading ramp a male Jew tried to commit suicide by getting himself run over by a tram. But he was caught by the catch bumper of the tram and only slightly hurt. . . . Moreover, an elderly Jewess had left the loading ramp unnoticed and had hidden in a neighbouring house. . . . But a cleaning woman had spotted her, so she was taken back to the transport. The loading of the Jews was finished by 10.15. After shunting several times the train left the goods station Düsseldorf-Dernedorf at about 10.30 for Wuppertal.

30 *The Wannsee Conference, 20 January 1942*

On 20 January 1942, an important conference was held at the headquarters of Interpol at the Wannsee (a lake to the west of Berlin) to coordinate arrangements for the 'final solution'. Those present included Heydrich, Eichmann, other SS leaders and officials from various ministries including Foreign Affairs, Eastern Territories, Four-Year Plan, Interior and Justice. The conference discussed the methods of selection of Jews for deportation, the location of these Jews in Europe and the financing of the whole operation. According to the minutes no specific mention was made of the extermination programme, although that was presumably understood by those attending. In his guidelines for the 'final solution' Heydrich referred to Göring's decree of July 1941 (see above) and underlined the fact that this policy was controlled by Himmler as Reichsführer SS and Chief of Police:

The Chief of the Security Police and the SD, SS Obergruppenführer Heydrich, began by announcing his appointment by the Reich Marshal [Göring] as the agent responsible for the preparation of the final solution of the European Jewish question, and pointed out that this meeting was being held to achieve clarity in basic questions. The Reich Marshal's wish that he should be sent a draft on the organizational, technical, and material matters regarding the final solution of the European Jewish question made it necessary that all central authorities immediately concerned with these questions should deal with them in advance so as to ensure the coordination of the lines to be taken.

The supervision of the final solution of the Jewish question was, regardless of geographical boundaries, centralized in the hands of the Reichsführer SS and Chief of the German Police[1] (Chief of the Security Police and the SD[2])....

III. The evacuation of the Jews to the east has now emerged, with the prior permission of the Führer, as a further possible solution instead of emigration.

These actions, however, must be regarded only as a secondary solution. But already the practical experience is being gathered which is of great importance to the coming final solution of the Jewish question....

In the process of the final solution, the Jews will be conscripted for labour in the eastern territories under appropriate administrative provisions. Large labour gangs of those fit for work will be formed, with the sexes separated, which will be sent to these areas for road construction and undoubtedly a large number of them will drop out through natural elimination. The remainder who survive—and they will certainly be those who have the greatest powers of endurance—will have to be dealt with accordingly. For, if released, they would, as a natural selection of the fittest, form a germ cell from which the Jewish race could build itself up again. (This is the lesson of history.)

In the process of carrying out the final solution, Europe will be combed through from west to east....

[1] i.e. Himmler.
[2] Heydrich, acting for Himmler.

31   *The 'final solution' at Auschwitz*

In December 1941, a permanent extermination camp was opened at Chelmno
in Poland, with staff who had gained experience in gas chamber techniques
through the programme of euthanasia for the handicapped. It was followed
by others throughout 1942 – Belzec in March, Sobibor in May, and Treblinka
in July, and in October gas chambers were installed in the big forced labour
camp of Majdanek. All these camps were in Poland, as was the largest of the
extermination camps which was established at Birkenau alongside the big
labour camp of Auschwitz. From the summer of 1942 onwards Auschwitz-
Birkenau became the main destination of Jews from all over Europe. There
alone, 3–4 million people were put to death. The testimony of the commandant, Rudolf Hoess, to the Nuremberg Tribunal mentioned some of the
methods of extermination used at his camp:

The 'final solution' of the Jewish question meant the complete extermination of
all Jews in Europe. I was ordered to establish extermination facilities at Auschwitz
in June 1942. At that time, there were already in the *Generalgouvernement*[1] three
other extermination camps – Belzec, Treblinka and Wolzek. These camps were
under the command of the task forces of the Security Police and S D. I visited
Treblinka to find out how they carried out their extermination. The Camp Commandant at Treblinka told me that he had liquidated 80,000 in the course of six
months. He was principally concerned with liquidating all the Jews from the
Warsaw ghetto. He used monoxide gas and I did not think that his methods were
very efficient. So when I set up the extermination building at Auschwitz, I used
Cyclon B, which was a crystallized prussic acid which we dropped into the death
chamber from a small opening. It took from three to fifteen minutes to kill the
people in the death chamber, depending upon climatic conditions. We knew when
the people were dead because their screaming stopped. We usually waited about
half an hour before we opened the doors and removed the bodies. After the bodies
were removed our special squads took off the rings and extracted the gold from the
teeth of the corpses.

Another improvement on Treblinka that we made was building our gas chambers
to accommodate 2000 people at a time, whereas at Treblinka their ten gas chambers
only accommodated 200 people each. The way we selected our victims was as
follows: we had two S S doctors on duty at Auschwitz to examine the incoming
transports of prisoners. The prisoners would be marched past one of the doctors
who would make spot decisions as they walked by. Those who were fit for work
were sent into the camp. Others were sent immediately to the extermination plants.
Children of tender years were invariably exterminated since by reason of their
youth they were unable to work. Still another improvement made on Treblinka
was that at Treblinka the victims almost always knew that they were about to be
exterminated whereas at Auschwitz we endeavoured to fool the victims into thinking that they were to go through a delousing process. Of course, they often realized
our true intentions and owing to that we sometimes had riots and difficulties. Very
often women would hide their children under the clothes but of course when we

[1] i.e. that area of Poland which had not been incorporated into either Germany or Russia.

found them we would send the children in to be exterminated. We were required to carry out these exterminations in secrecy but of course the foul and nauseating stench from the continuous burning of bodies permeated the entire area and all the people living in the surrounding communities knew that exterminations were going on at Auschwitz.

We received from time to time special prisoners from the local Gestapo office. The SS doctors killed such prisoners by injections of benzine. Doctors had orders to write ordinary death certificates and could put down any reason they liked for the cause of death.

From time to time we conducted medical experiments on women inmates, including sterilization and experiments relating to cancer. Most of the people who died under these experiments had been already condemned to death by the Gestapo.

32 The destruction of the Warsaw Ghetto, 1943

Himmler pressed for the removal of Jews from the ghettos to Auschwitz and other concentration camps. Ghettos in Poland were to be found in Cracow, Lodz and Lublin, but the largest was in Warsaw, which originally had more than 400,000 Jews. Plans for the clearance of the Warsaw Ghetto were complicated by representations from the armament firms which employed many of the Jews and by the revolt of the Jews themselves when they learnt of the news of their transfer. Immediate action was taken by the SS, and the Ghetto was razed to the ground. Stroop, the SS and police chief in Warsaw, reported:

On 23 April 1943 the Reichsführer SS issued through the higher SS and Police Führer East at Cracow his order to complete the combing out of the Warsaw Ghetto with the greatest severity and relentless tenacity. I therefore decided to destroy the entire Jewish residential area by setting every block on fire, including the blocks of residential buildings near the armament works. One concern after the other was systematically evacuated and later destroyed by fire. In almost every case, the Jews then emerged from their hiding places and dug-outs. Not infrequently, the Jews stayed in the burning buildings until, because of the heat and the fear of being burned alive, they preferred to jump down from the upper storeys after having thrown mattresses and other upholstered articles into the street from the burning buildings. With their bones broken, they still tried to crawl across the streets into blocks of buildings which had not yet been set on fire or were only partly in flames. Often Jews changed their hiding places during the night, by moving into the ruins of burnt-out buildings, taking refuge there until they were found by our patrols. Their stay in the sewers also ceased to be pleasant after the first week. From the street we could frequently hear loud voices coming through the sewer shafts. Then the men of the Waffen SS, the police or the Wehrmacht engineers courageously climbed down the shafts to bring out the Jews and not infrequently they then stumbled over Jews already dead, or were shot at. It was always necessary to use smoke candles to drive out the Jews. Thus, one day we opened 183 sewer entrance holes and at a fixed time lowered smoke candles into them, so that the bandits fled from what they believed to be gas to the centre of the former Ghetto, where they could then be pulled out of the sewer holes there. A great number of Jews, beyond counting, were exterminated by the blowing up of sewers and dug-outs. . . .

Only through the continuous and untiring work of all involved did we succeed in catching a total of 56,065 Jews, whose extermination can be proved. To this should be added the number of Jews who lost their lives in explosions or fires but whose numbers could not be ascertained.

During the large-scale operation the Aryan population was informed by posters that it was strictly forbidden to enter the former Jewish Ghetto and that anybody caught within the former Ghetto without a valid pass would be shot. At the same time these posters informed the Aryan population again that the death penalty would be imposed on anyone who intentionally gave refuge to a Jew, especially on anyone who lodged, supported or concealed a Jew outside the Jewish residential area. . . .

The large-scale action was terminated on 16 May 1943 with the blowing up of the Warsaw synagogue at 20.15 hours.

33 *Himmler on the extermination of the Jews*

Himmler failed to achieve his aim of concentrating the surviving Jews in a few selected areas, but this did not detract from his feeling that the extermination policy was a patriotic mission. In a speech to a group of SS leaders at Posen on 6 October 1943, Himmler said:

I also want to talk to you quite frankly about a very grave matter. Among ourselves it should be mentioned quite frankly, and yet we will never speak of it publicly. Just as we did not hesitate on 30 June 1934[1] to do our duty as we were bidden, and to stand comrades who had lapsed up against the wall and shoot them, so we have never spoken about it and will never speak of it. It was that tact which is a matter of course, and which I am glad to say is inherent in us, that made us never discuss it among ourselves, never speak of it. It appalled everyone, and yet everyone was certain that he would do it the next time if such orders should be issued and if it should be necessary.

I am referring to the clearing out of the Jews, the extermination of the Jewish race. It's one of those things it is easy to talk about. 'The Jewish race is being exterminated', says a Party member. 'That's quite clear, it's in our programme— elimination of the Jews—and we're doing it, exterminating them.' And then they come, 80 million worthy Germans, and each one has his 'decent' Jew. Of course the others are vermin, but this one is a first-rate Jew. Not one of all those who talk this way has witnessed it, and not one of them has been through it. Most of *you* must know what it means when a hundred corpses are lying side by side, or five hundred or a thousand. To have stuck it out and at the same time, apart from exceptions caused by human weakness, to have remained decent fellows, that is what has made us tough. That is a page of glory in our history which has never been written and must never be written, for we know how difficult we should have made it for ourselves if, with the bombing raids, the burdens and the deprivations of war, we still had Jews today in every town as secret saboteurs, agitators and troublemakers.

[1] The night of the Röhm purge.

We would now probably have reached the 1916–17 stage when the Jews were still part of the body of the German nation.

We have taken from them what wealth they had. I have issued a strict order, which SS Obergruppenführer Pohl has carried out, that this wealth should, as a matter of course, be handed over to the Reich without reserve. We have taken none of it for ourselves. Individual men who have lapsed will be punished in accordance with an order I issued at the beginning which gave this warning: Whoever takes so much as a mark of it is a dead man. A number of SS men—there are not very many of them—have fallen short, and they will die, without mercy. We had the moral right, we had the duty to our people, to destroy this people which wanted to destroy us. But we have not the right to enrich ourselves with so much as a fur, a watch, a mark, a cigarette or anything else. We have exterminated a bacterium because we do not want in the end to be infected by the bacterium and die of it. I will not see so much as a small area of sepsis appear here or gain a hold. Wherever it may form, we will cauterize it. All in all, we can say that we have fulfilled this most difficult duty for the love of our people. And our spirit, our soul, our character has not suffered injury from it. . . .

34 The extermination of the Jews

Country	Previous number of Jews	Losses Lowest estimate	Highest estimate
1 Poland	3,300,000	2,350,000	2,900,000 = 88%
2 USSR	2,100,000	700,000	1,000,000 = 48%
3 Romania	850,000	200,000	420,000 = 49%
4 Czechoslovakia	360,000	233,000	300,000 = 83%
5 Germany	240,000	160,000	200,000 = 83%
6 Hungary	403,000	180,000	200,000 = 50%
7 Lithuania	155,000	—	135,000 = 87%
8 France	300,000	60,000	130,000 = 43%
9 Holland	150,000	104,000	120,000 = 80%
10 Latvia	95,000	—	85,000 = 89%
11 Yugoslavia	75,000	55,000	65,000 = 87%
12 Greece	75,000	57,000	60,000 = 80%
13 Austria	60,000	—	40,000 = 67%
14 Belgium	100,000	25,000	40,000 = 40%
15 Italy	75,000	8,500	15,000 = 26%
16 Bulgaria	50,000	—	7,000 = 14%
17 Denmark	—	(less than 100)	— —
18 Luxemburg	—	3,000	3,000 —
19 Norway	—	700	1,000 —
Total		4,194,200	app. 5,721,000 = 68%

PART V Foreign Policy, 1933–39

16 Hitler's Programme

Hitler's diplomatic and strategic programme was shaped by a combination of, on the one hand, ideological tenets most of which were already fixed in his mind before 1919, and, on the other hand, conclusions drawn from European political and diplomatic developments in the early 1920s— conclusions which subsequently had to be modified in the light of developments after 1933.

Hitler began his career as a disciple of the pan-German movement with whose ideas he had been familiar since his schooldays. It was from the pan-Germans that he acquired the basic ideas which determined his outlook on foreign policy. In the first place, he shared the view of nineteenth-century Social Darwinism that human life was a struggle for the survival of the fittest. Secondly, he saw race as the primary factor in history. Finally, he also followed the pan-Germans in their conviction that Germany was becoming overpopulated and required more territory for its survival. Hitler combined these ideas to form a conception of international relations as a struggle between the various nations for the limited amount of land and raw materials available. The function of foreign policy, therefore, was to ensure that Germany could conduct this war for survival from the best possible strategic position.

1 *Hitler's attitude on foreign policy in 1919*

But, in 1919, not only was Hitler's basic outlook on foreign policy derived from the pan-Germans; he also began by sharing their concrete objectives— the revision of the Treaty of Versailles, the unification of all Germans in one Reich, and the acquisition of new land in the form of colonies overseas. This is clear from the first three points in the Nazi Party programme of 1920 which, it seems probable, were inserted by Hitler himself. Moreover, like the pan-Germans, Hitler at this time regarded England and France, not Russia, as Germany's main enemies. Something of Hitler's outlook can be gauged from a speech he made in Munich on 10 December 1919 of which two rather garbled police reports have survived. They show his hostility to England and France and the significance he attached to the loss of the German colonies:

(a) . . . Let us look at our enemies! We can divide them into two groups: one group

497

includes the absolute opponents: England and America;[1] the second group: nations which became our opponents as a result of their unfortunate situation or as a result of their circumstances. Russia was always looking for an outlet to the sea and comes in too. We have been pursuing a Polish policy since Bismarck's time. The so-called Reinsurance Treaty[2] came to an end in 1892 and was not renewed. As a result Bismarck was bitterly attacked [sic]. In 1893 Alexander, the Tsar of Russia, went to Paris. He was applauded and the friendship was forged. And the Germans—well, they are no good at politics: if they don't like something, the State can go to the devil. Italy too originally had nothing against Austria. Men like Holtzendorf [sic], Bismarck, and Ludendorff saw long ago that Italy was not in favour of Germany, it was more likely to take an active part in the war. Serbia and Romania were trying to become Great Powers. Japan had no direct hatred against Germany, it was pursuing world policy.

A count (a shout: 'Bothmer'[3]) said recently: France is pursuing a Continental policy. In fact the French statesmen were pursuing world policy and will continue to do so under our glorious government. In the course of 300 years France has declared war on Germany twenty-seven times. . . .

(b) . . . If whole areas of the world mobilize, one cannot apportion war guilt to a single country. In earlier times English diplomacy has understood how to estrange all the nations from one another in order to secure advantages for itself. The removal of our colonies represents an irreparable loss for us. We are compelled to secure our raw materials from the Allies and at such an expense that we will be excluded from the world market as effective competitors. . . .

Hitler was not, however, committed to the realization of his main goal of German expansion through the revisionist programme. He was prepared to be flexible in the means used to achieve his goal. Above all, he was aware of the need to win allies if Germany were to break out of her isolation and he was prepared to adapt his objectives in order to acquire allies. He therefore soon began to revise his conventional revisionist position in the light of diplomatic developments. The first of these developments was the occupation of Fiume by the Italian nationalist D'Annunzio, on 12 September 1919, contrary to the terms of the Versailles Treaty. This event caused growing tension between Italy and France. By the summer of 1920, Hitler had become convinced that the clash of interests between France and Italy in the Balkans and the Mediterranean would eventually lead to war. Germany should therefore exploit this situation and on 1 August 1920 he asserted: 'The basic demand is "Away with the Peace Treaty!" We must use all possible means to achieve this, primarily the clash of interests between France and Italy so that we can win Italy for ourselves.'[4] The problem was,

[1] Although France is not included here as an 'absolute' opponent, it is clear from the rest of the speech that Hitler regarded it as such.
[2] The treaty concluded by Bismarck with Russia on 18 June 1887, whereby, having already made an alliance with Austria in 1879, he hoped to avoid a one-sided commitment. The treaty was not renewed by his successor, General Caprivi.
[3] A Bavarian federalist.
[4] quoted in Axel Kuhn, *Hitlers aussenpolitisches Programm* (Stuttgart 1970), p. 42. The present section owes much to this work.

however, that under the Versailles Treaty Italy had acquired the German-speaking territory of South Tirol. If Germany were to insist on the unification of all German-speaking people within the Reich as demanded by Point 1 of the Nazi Programme of 1920, a German–Italian alliance would be out of the question. This contradiction was only resolved two years later when at the time of Mussolini's rise to power Hitler offered to sacrifice the South Tiroleans in return for Italian friendship. This was an important decision, for it represented the first occasion on which Hitler sacrificed a vital element of the revisionist programme in the interest of power politics. He justified his decision with the claim that 'in politics there is no room for sentiment, only for cold-bloodedness'.[1]

Hitler, then, was aware of the fact that if Germany was to revise Versailles and to acquire land in the form of colonies, she would need powerful allies to enable her to take on both Britain and France. Italy alone, however, would not be sufficient. Since the Austrian empire had now collapsed, the only other major power left was Russia. Initially, Hitler had not been opposed on principle to an alliance with Russia. Indeed, he made it clear in his early speeches that in his view this should have been the policy of the prewar German Government. After 1919, however, Hitler came increasingly under the influence of a group of Baltic German refugees from the Russian Revolution who had joined the Nazi Party, notably Alfred Rosenberg, a refugee from Reval in Estonia. Rosenberg convinced Hitler that the Bolshevik revolution was the work of Jews, indeed that the Bolsheviks were all Jews. In a speech on 27 July 1920, Hitler asserted that 'an alliance between Russia and Germany can only come about if the Jews are overthrown'.[2] To start with, therefore, he did not entirely rule out the idea of an alliance with Russia because for a long time it was not clear whether or not the Bolshevik regime would survive.

In the meantime, another diplomatic development occurred which brought about a fundamental change in his foreign policy. This was the occupation of the Ruhr by France in 1923.[3] This created a new situation in which Hitler feared that France was bent on the immediate dismemberment of Germany. Furthermore, he became aware of the strength of British opposition to French policy. He became convinced that this represented a basic shift in British policy towards France deriving from fear of French hegemony on the Continent. In the light of this development Hitler came to conceive of the possibility of an alliance between Germany and Britain against France. It is clear that he now regarded France as the greater enemy both because of her immediate threat to Germany's territorial integrity and because, since France was in his view bent on Continental hegemony, she would never allow Germany to regain her lost territory in

---

[1] Speech by Hitler, 14.xi.22, quoted ibid., p. 73.
[2] quoted ibid., p. 53.
[3] See above, p. 53.

Eastern Europe which would be the prerequisite for the attempt to achieve world power status.

An alliance with Britain, however, posed problems similar to those raised by an alliance with Italy. It would be impossible to seek an alliance with Britain while simultaneously trying to win colonies. Yet, if Germany were not to seek colonies, where could she acquire the necessary territory and resources for her surplus population? For even the old boundaries of 1914 had, he believed, been inadequate. It was not until he was in Landsberg prison in 1924 that he produced a solution which would reconcile Germany's need for what he now called 'living space' (*Lebensraum*) with the renunciation of colonies in the interests of an alliance with Britain. His solution was to seek living space in Russia where the Bolshevik regime was now clearly established. In this way, he believed, Germany would avoid the First World War situation of having to fight against both Britain and Russia, a situation which, he argued, had resulted from the prewar German Government's attempt simultaneously to pursue a colonial policy against Britain and a Continental policy against France and Russia. It was a solution which carried overwhelming conviction as far as he was concerned, because it reflected both the elements which shaped his strategy—considerations of power politics and ideology. This programme was elaborated for the first time in his autobiography, *Mein Kampf*, written during 1924–25 from which the following extract is taken:

2 *Hitler's foreign policy aims in* Mein Kampf

The foreign policy of a People's State must first of all bear in mind the duty of securing the existence of the race which is incorporated in this State. And this must be done by establishing a healthy and natural proportion between the number and growth of the population, on the one hand, and the extent and resources of the territory they inhabit, on the other. That balance must be such that it accords with the vital necessities of the people.

What I call a *healthy* proportion is that in which the support of a people is guaranteed by the resources of its own soil and subsoil. Any situation which falls short of this condition is none the less unhealthy even though it may endure for centuries or even a thousand years. Sooner or later, this lack of proportion must of necessity lead to the decline or even annihilation of the people concerned. Only a sufficiently large space on this earth can assure the independent existence of a people.

The extent of the territorial expansion that may be necessary for the settlement of the national population must not be estimated by present exigencies nor even by the magnitude of its agricultural productivity in relation to the number of the population. In the first volume of this book, under the heading 'Germany's Policy of Alliances before the War', I have already explained that the geographical dimensions of a State are of importance not only as the source of the nation's foodstuffs and raw materials, but also from the political and military standpoints. Once a people is assured of being able to maintain itself from the resources of the national territory, it must think of how this national territory can be defended. National security depends on the political strength of a State and this strength, in its turn, depends on the military possibilities inherent in the geographical situation. Thus the German nation could assure its own future only by being a World Power. . . .

Our Movement must seek to abolish the present disastrous proportion between our population and the area of our national territory, considering national territory as the source of our maintenance or as a basis of political power. And it ought to strive to abolish the contrast between past history and the hopelessly powerless situation in which we are today. In striving for this it must bear in mind the fact that we are members of the highest species of humanity on this earth, that we have a correspondingly high duty and that we shall fulfil this duty only if we inspire the German people with the racial idea, so that they will occupy themselves not merely with the breeding of good dogs and horses and cats, but also care for the purity of their own blood. . . .

We National Socialists must never allow ourselves to re-echo the hurrah patriotism of our contemporary bourgeois circles. It would be a fatal danger for us to look on the immediate developments before the War as constituting a precedent which we should be obliged to take into account, even though only to the very smallest degree, in choosing our own way. We can recognize no obligation devolving on us which may have its historical roots in any part of the nineteenth century. In contradistinction to the policy of those who represented that period, we must take our stand on the principles already mentioned in regard to foreign policy: namely, the necessity of bringing our territorial area into just proportion with the number of our population. From the past we can learn only one lesson. And this is that the aim which is to be pursued in our political conduct must be twofold: namely (1) the acquisition of territory as the objective of our foreign policy and (2) the establishment of a new and uniform foundation as the objective of our political activities at home, in accordance with our doctrine of nationhood. . . .

Therefore we National Socialists have purposely drawn a line through the line of conduct followed by prewar Germany in foreign policy. We put an end to the perpetual Germanic march towards the South and West of Europe and turn our eyes towards the lands of the East. We finally put a stop to the colonial and trade policy of prewar times and pass over to the territorial policy of the future.

But when we speak of new territory in Europe today we must principally think of Russia and the border States subject to her. Destiny itself seems to wish to point out the way for us here. In delivering Russia over to Bolshevism, Fate robbed the Russian people of that intellectual class which had once created the Russian State and was the guarantee of its existence. For the Russian State was not organized by the constructive political talent of the Slav element in Russia but was much more a marvellous exemplification of the capacity for State-building possessed by the Germanic element in a race of inferior worth. Thus were many powerful Empires created all over the earth. More often than once, inferior races with Germanic organizers and rulers as their leaders became formidable States and continued to exist as long as the racial nucleus remained which had originally created each respective State. For centuries Russia owed the source of its livelihood as a State to the Germanic nucleus of its governing classes. But this nucleus is now almost wholly broken up and abolished. The Jew has taken its place. Just as it is impossible for the Russian to shake off the Jewish yoke by exerting his own powers, so too it is impossible for the Jew to keep this formidable State in existence for any long period of time. He himself is by no means an organizing element, but rather a ferment of decomposition. This colossal Empire in the East is ripe for dissolution. And the end of the Jewish domination in Russia will also be the end of Russia as a State.

We are chosen by Destiny to be the witnesses of a catastrophe which will afford the strongest confirmation of the nationalist theory of race.

3 Hitler's 'Second Book'

After he had written *Mein Kampf*, Hitler's basic foreign policy objectives did not change. The main purpose of his so-called 'Second Book', written in 1928 but not published, was to justify his assertion of the need to sacrifice German-speaking South Tyrol in the interests of the Italian alliance at a time when the South Tyrol problem was a subject of intense public debate and his own position was under attack. The book was essentially a restatement of the policy set out in *Mein Kampf*, though it did introduce one or two new perspectives.

In the first place, while re-emphasizing that 'in any conflict involving Germany, regardless on what grounds, regardless for what reasons, France will always be our adversary' (p. 128),[1] he now referred for the first time to the strategic threat posed by France's system of alliances in Eastern Europe. Referring specifically to Czechoslovakia and Poland, he pointed out that thanks to these alliances France was 'in a position to be able to threaten almost the whole of Germany with aircraft even an hour after the outbreak of a conflict' (p. 127).

Secondly, he dealt with the argument that Britain would oppose German hegemony on the Continent because of traditional British balance of power policy (pp. 149f.). This he claimed was 'not correct'. For 'England actually concerned herself very little with European conditions as long as no threatening world competitor arose from them, so that she always viewed the threat as lying in a development which must one day cut across her dominion over the seas and colonies'. He cited Britain's attitude to Prussia in the eighteenth century as proof of this. Since Germany did not propose to challenge the British Empire, he argued that Britain would not fear Germany: 'If England remains true to her great world-political aims, her potential opponents will be France and Russia in Europe [since they challenged Britain's imperial position], and in other parts of the world especially the American Union in the future.' This reference to America was not the only one in the book. Indeed, for the first time, Hitler devoted some attention to the United States. He praised Americans as a 'young, racially select people' (p. 100), but hinted at the need 'in the far future to think of a new association of nations consisting of individual States with a high national value, which could then stand up to the threatening overwhelming of the world by the American Union. For it seems to me that the existence of English world rule inflicts

[1] Quotations from *Hitler's Secret Book*, ed. Telford Taylor (New York 1962).

less hardships on present-day nations than the emergence of an American world rule' (p. 209).

Finally, Hitler now spelled out even more explicitly than in *Mein Kampf* the logical conclusion of the Social Darwinist position by pointing out that there was no limit to the expansion of a nation which proved itself racially superior: 'For this earth is not allotted to anyone nor is it presented to any-one as a gift. It is awarded by providence to people who in their hearts have the courage to conquer it, the strength to preserve it, and the industry to put it to the plough. . . . The present distribution of possessions has not been designed by a higher power but by man himself. . . . No. The primary right of this world is the right to life, so far as one possesses the strength for this. Hence on the basis of this right a vigorous nation will always find ways of adapting its territory to its population size' (pp. 15–16).

From the comments and arguments contained in *Mein Kampf* and the 'Second Book', both explicit and implicit, one can construct a foreign policy programme which consisted essentially of five stages. The first stage was the removal of the restrictions on German armaments imposed by the Treaty of Versailles. This was clearly essential if Germany was to operate from a position of military strength. The second stage was the destruction of France's system of alliances in Eastern Europe through which she encircled Germany. This would open the way to the third stage – the confrontation with France. The defeat of France would in turn secure Germany's western frontier so that she could move on to the next stage – the conquest of *Lebensraum* in the east.[1] The conquest of Russia was the crucial stage in Hitler's strategy because it involved the winning of the 'living space' which Hitler regarded as essential to Germany's future. The final stage was, at this time, only a vague concept in Hitler's mind. It envisaged Germany exploiting the newly won resources in Russia to expand outside Europe – possibly through a confrontation with Britain, but preferably in association with Britain against the United States. The logic of Hitler's Social Darwinist position was that Germany, having proved herself the superior racial group, should dominate the world. Hitler had no clear idea of how to achieve these aims beyond his suggestion of German alliances with Britain and Italy. Indeed, the securing of these alliances would give him all the freedom of manoeuvre he needed to fulfil his programme.

Much controversy has arisen over Hitler's conduct of foreign policy. It has been argued, for example, that there was little new about his policies, that Germany was a revisionist power from 1918 onwards, and that Hitler merely carried out what the politicians of the Weimar Republic such as Stresemann would have liked to achieve and were in fact working towards – in short, that Hitler was a conventional German statesman. There is clearly something to be said for this view. The first four stages of Hitler's programme

[1] In fact Hitler was not committed to a policy of defeating France before Russia; he later toyed with the idea of dealing with Russia first.

were certainly by no means original. Thus, the aim of winning living space in the east was part of the *völkisch* programme and had been adopted during the war by, among others, the German war leader, General Ludendorff. Even the fifth stage—world conquest and racial hegemony—may also have been in the minds of some pan-Germans. Secondly, Stresemann and other politicians were undoubtedly working to revise the Versailles Treaties. In particular, they explicitly excluded Germany's eastern borders from the Locarno pact of 1925 which guaranteed the *status quo* on Germany's western frontiers, i.e. they wished to restore to Germany the territory lost to Poland. Moreover, even without Hitler, Germany would clearly have become progressively stronger and would therefore have been more and more tempted to use her strength at least in the form of diplomatic and economic pressure and conceivably by making war in order to revise the Versailles settlement.

Nevertheless, this view is an oversimplification. In the first place, although the Weimar politicians shared the post-Bismarckian commitment to *Realpolitik*, they did not share Hitler's ruthless Social Darwinist vision and racialist theories. Nor had they adopted the pan-German programme. Their revisionism was of a more traditional kind. They thought in terms of the boundaries of 1914, of a restoration of the German colonies, of an Anschluss with Austria, and of a Mitteleuropa in which Germany was economically dominant. Hitler himself was in no doubt about the distinction and would have been horrified to be equated with Stresemann. In his 'Second Book' he summed it up as follows: 'In terms of foreign policy the National Socialist movement is distinguished from previous bourgeois parties by, for example, the following: The foreign policy of the national bourgeois world has in truth always been a border policy; as against that, the policy of the National Socialist movement will always be a territorial one. In its boldest plans, for example, the German bourgeoisie will aspire to the unification of the German nation, but in reality it will finish with a botched-up regulation of the borders' (pp. 44-45). Finally, the Weimar politicians operated according to the conventions of European diplomacy. And while it is true that for a long time the Foreign Office officials acquiesced more or less willingly in Hitler's policies, it is significant that, when Hitler was about to move beyond the traditional methods of German diplomacy in the spring of 1938, he replaced the conventional conservative Foreign Minister, von Neurath, with his lackey Ribbentrop, who had on several occasions already been used to by-pass the Foreign Office. Part of the confusion arises from the fact that up until 1938 or even 1941 Hitler was achieving the goals of conventional German nationalism of which conservatives thoroughly approved, even though they may have had their doubts about his methods. This undoubtedly facilitated the cooperation of the conservative generals and diplomats. It is in the policy pursued in Poland after 1939 and in Russia after 1941 that the distinction between Nazism and conservative German nationalism emerges clearly for the first time. The fact that Nazi policy in the east to some extent derives from ideas expressed in the *völkisch* movement, some of which found their way into official thinking during the First World War, is significant, but it does not justify a blanket equation of Nazism and traditional German nationalism.

Discussion has also raged over the question of whether the war in 1939 was the inevitable outcome of Hitler's aggressive intentions and of the nature of the Nazi regime itself, or whether the circumstances of the inter-war years after Versailles together with the mistakes of other powers were more responsible than has generally been accepted. In particular, it has been denied that Hitler's objectives as outlined in *Mein Kampf* and on subsequent occasions have any real bearing on his foreign policy. One historian has described them as 'day dreams'.[1] It has been pointed out that *Mein Kampf* provides no specific guide to the foreign policy which Hitler carried out between 1933 and 1939, a policy which in fact culminated in a pact with the Soviet Union, the very power which he had claimed to wish to destroy, and in a war with Britain, whom he had originally envisaged as an ally.

Yet it may be suggested that the reason for this disparity between theory and practice is that while Hitler adhered all along to his major objective of acquiring *Lebensraum* in the east, he was not committed to any specific policies for achieving it. In 1924 he had emphasized to a fellow-prisoner in Landsberg the difference between a theoretician and a politician. 'The theoretician must always preach the pure idea and have it always before his eyes; the politician, however, must not only think of the great objective but also of the way that leads to it.'[2] Flexibility was characteristic of his whole approach, at any rate until the war. Thus in the period between 1919 and 1933 he had invariably adapted his tactics to the conditions imposed by a developing situation, first changing from a putsch to a parliamentary tactic and then switching from a demand for a Nazi-dominated Government to the acceptance of a coalition with a strong Conservative contingent. His attitude in foreign policy was similar. For a long time he hoped that he would secure a far-reaching arrangement with Britain, and the Anglo-German Naval Agreement of 1935 seemed to confirm the correctness of his analysis. When an arrangement eventually eluded him and he found himself faced with a threat from the west which represented a permanent obstacle to the achievement of his eastern objective, he postponed his eastern campaign and even allied himself with his intended victim in order to remove the more immediate obstacle, although significantly, even after the outbreak of war, he still hoped that Britain would agree to an alliance. Similarly, although Hitler probably began by merely wishing to detach the smaller powers of Central and Eastern Europe from France and turn them into German satellites, the

[1] A. J. P. Taylor, *The Origins of the Second World War* (London 1963), p. 69.
[2] cf. W. Jochmann(ed), *Nationalsozialismus und Revolution* (Frankfurt 1963), p. 133; see also A. Hitler, *Mein Kampf*, trs. (London 1969), pp. 191-2, where this distinction was reaffirmed.

failure of the Austrian, Czech and Polish Governments to accept the satellite status envisaged for them, their attempt to retain a measure of independence, forced him to go further than perhaps he originally intended at particular stages. He was not, for example, intending an immediate annexation of Austria—he would have been content, for the time being at any rate, with its 'coordination'—but the situation developed in such a way that annexation proved necessary. It would be a mistake, however, to assume from these tactical shifts that he was not guided by any long-term objectives.

Hitler began with several distinct advantages over his predecessors. The reparations issue which had restricted German foreign policy so much in the past had been solved; France had been forced to modify her intransigent line in the light of her experience with the Ruhr invasion and the attitude of her main ally, Britain; above all, the impact of the economic depression had dissolved the ties of international solidarity and had induced everywhere an attitude of *sauve-qui-peut*. It was a situation which provided the necessary freedom of manoeuvre for a power which was bent on exploiting the differences between the other States and on playing them off, one against the other, by means of bilateral rather than the traditional multilateral agreements. Nevertheless, although the diplomatic situation was now distinctly more favourable than that faced by his predecessors, there is no doubt that Hitler exploited his opportunities with exceptional skill. One of his great gifts as a politician was his ability to sense the points of weakness in his opponents' armoury. He sensed the deep unwillingness of the peoples of Western Europe to go to war again. He was aware of the fear of Bolshevism which dominated the European upper and middle classes. He knew that the treatment of Germany under the Treaty of Versailles had left many, particularly in Britain, with a bad conscience. He appreciated that the refusal of the right of self-determination to the Austrian Germans, the creation of German minorities in countries such as Poland and Czechoslovakia, and finally, the imposition on Germany of permanent restrictions while the other powers showed no signs of disarming—that all these aspects of the Treaty appeared to a greater or lesser extent unjust and thus helped to undermine the will of the Allies to defend its principles, particularly if defence of the settlement would involve another major war. Hitler ruthlessly exploited these weaknesses. He combined every move against the Versailles settlement with an assertion of his desire for peace and often with a claim that the particular issue involved represented Germany's final grievance and that in future she would be satisfied; he projected an image of the Third Reich as an anti-Bolshevik bastion against the threat from Soviet Russia; and finally he justified every move against the Versailles settlement in terms of the principles of the settlement itself. Thus, the invasion of the Rhineland and of Austria, and the annexation of the Sudetenland in Czechoslovakia, were all justified on the grounds of national self-determination.

Up until 1939 this tactic proved extremely successful. Yet, from 1938 onwards, he appears to have been governed by a mounting impatience. This impatience may have reflected increasing tensions within the regime itself, it may have reflected a growing fear on Hitler's part that he would not survive long enough to carry out his objectives, or it may simply have reflected his growing self-confidence. Whatever the reason, from 1938 onwards he increased the stakes almost from month to month. His risks were still calculated. It was, for example, a reasonable assumption that the Nazi–Soviet pact of August 1939 would rule out the possibility of Allied intervention in support of Poland in view of their behaviour on previous occasions. Yet Hitler seemed increasingly willing to face the prospect of a general war. It is possible that he believed war to be inevitable; and, since Germany had a head start in rearmament—an advantage which would soon be eroded—it would be better to have war there and then, rather than later. Furthermore, the policy of appeasement had undermined his respect for the capacity of Britain and France to resist him. As a result, when it became clear that, contrary to his expectations, Britain and France would fight on the Polish issue, he did not draw back.

17 Germany Woos Britain and Italy

Conciliation, rearmament and isolation, 1933-35

1 *Hitler's first speech to the generals, 3 February 1933*

Although, once in office, Hitler was obliged to adapt the implementing of his programme to the realities of power, it is significant that on 3 February 1933, a few days after his appointment as Chancellor, he reasserted his general aim of winning living space in the east in a secret speech to a dinner attended by Army and Navy leaders. He was not very specific about his long-term aims in foreign policy, but his main concern at this stage was to win the allegiance of the military leaders, whose attitude had been doubtful at the time of his appointment and whose support he needed for the consolidation of his power. General Liebmann, an infantry commander who was present at the dinner, made notes on Hitler's speech:

The sole aim of general policy: *the regaining of political power*. The whole State administration must be geared to this end (all departments!).
1. *Domestic policy*: Complete reversal of the present domestic political situation in Germany. Refusal to tolerate any attitude contrary to this aim (pacifism!). Those who will not be converted must be broken. Extermination of Marxism root and branch. Adjustment of youth and of the whole people to the idea that only a struggle can save us and that everything else must be subordinated to this idea. (Realized in the millions of the Nazi movement. It will grow.) Training of youth and strengthening of the will to fight with all means. Death penalty for high treason. Tightest authoritarian State leadership. Removal of the cancer of democracy!
2. *Foreign policy*: Battle against Versailles. Equality of rights in Geneva; but useless if people do not have the will to fight. Concern for allies.
3. *Economics*: The farmer must be saved! Settlement policy! Further increase of exports useless. The capacity of the world is limited and production is forced up everywhere. The only possibility of re-employing part of the army of unemployed lies in settlement. But time is needed and radical improvement not to be expected since living space too small for German people.
4. *Building up of the armed forces*: Most important prerequisite for achieving the goal of regaining political power. National Service must be reintroduced. But beforehand the State leadership must ensure that the men subject to military service are not, even before their entry, poisoned by pacifism, Marxism, Bolshevism or do not fall victim to this poison after their service.

How should political power be used when it has been gained? That is impossible to say yet. Perhaps fighting for new export possibilities, perhaps—and probably better—the conquest of new living space in the east and its ruthless Germanization. Certain that only through political power and struggle can the present economic circumstances be changed. The only things that can happen now—settlement—stopgap measures.

Armed forces most important and most Socialist institution of the State. It must stay unpolitical and impartial. The internal struggle not their affair but that of the Nazi organizations. As opposed to Italy no fusion of Army and SA intended—most dangerous time is during the reconstruction of the Army. It will show whether or not France has *statesmen*: if so, she will not leave us time but will attack us (presumably with eastern satellites).

2 *Hitler's 'Peace' speech, 17 May 1933*

During his first years in power, Hitler was obliged to move cautiously. If he was to consolidate the regime, he needed to solve the economic crisis and in order to achieve his foreign policy goals he needed to rearm Germany. All this would take time and during this period he was anxious to avoid unnecessary international tension. The other powers were highly suspicious of the new regime in view of the extreme aggressiveness of previous Nazi propaganda. Thus, in the spring of 1933, Hitler remarked pointedly to Krogmann, the Mayor of Hamburg, that in the circumstances Germany would have to conclude a truce with the European powers for at least six years and that the 'sabre-rattling' of some National Socialist circles was a mistake as Germany had no weapons. His immediate policy therefore was one of apparent conciliation. He protested his desire for peace in a series of speeches in 1933 and followed the same line in several interviews he gave to foreign correspondents. Thus, on the same day as his address to the generals, Hitler spoke with representatives of the Associated Press claiming that 'nobody wishes for peace more than I'. Hitler's first major 'peace speech' was on 17 May in which he disclaimed any wish to subject other nations to German rule. He said that one of the aims of the 'German Revolution' was more

... to re-establish a stable and authoritative Government supported by the will and confidence of the nation which should make our great people an acceptable partner of the other states of the world.

Speaking deliberately as a German National Socialist, I desire to declare in the name of the National Government, and of the whole movement of national regeneration, that we in this new Germany are filled with deep understanding for the same feelings and opinions and for the rightful claims to life of the other nations. The present generation of this new Germany, which so far has only known in its life the poverty, misery and distress of its own people, has suffered too deeply from the madness of our time to be able to contemplate treating others in the same way. Our boundless love for and loyalty to our own national traditions makes us respect the national claims of others and makes us desire from the bottom of our hearts to live with them in peace and friendship. We therefore have no use for the idea of

Germanization. The mentality of the past century which made people believe that they could make Germans out of Poles and Frenchmen is completely foreign to us; the more so as we are passionately opposed to any attempt on the part of others to alienate us from our German tradition. We look at the European nations objectively. The French, the Poles, etc. are our neighbours, and we know that through no possible development of history can this reality be altered.

It would have been better for the world if in Germany's case these realities had been appreciated in the Treaty of Versailles. For the object of a really lasting Treaty should not be to cause new wounds and keep old ones open, but to close wounds and heal them. A thoughtful treatment of European problems at that time could certainly have produced a settlement in the east which would have met both the reasonable claims of Poland and the natural rights of Germany. The Treaty of Versailles did not provide this solution. Nevertheless, no German Government will of its own accord break an agreement unless its removal could lead to its replacement by a better one.

But the legal character of such a Treaty must be acknowledged by *all*. Not only the conqueror but also the conquered party can claim the rights accorded in the Treaty. And the right to demand a revision of the Treaty finds its foundation in the Treaty itself. The German Government, in stating the reasons for the extent of its claims, wishes for nothing more than the results of what previous experience and the incontestable consequences of critical and logical reasoning show to be necessary and just. The experience of the last fourteen years, however, is unambiguous from a political and economic point of view.

Yet, although Hitler adopted a conciliatory line, he combined it with a tough assertion of German interests in those areas where he felt it was most urgent and practical. The most immediate issue in which his Government found itself involved was disarmament discussions with the Western powers. Hitler wished to escape from these irksome negotiations which had begun under his predecessors, and so he claimed equal rights for Germany. He insisted that before Germany disarmed any further it was only right that the other powers should begin disarming as well. This was an argument which was not only popular at home, but also difficult for other countries to dispute. Hitler was well aware of the fact that the other powers and particularly France would never agree to disarm down to Germany's level and when in October 1933, as he expected, the French took a hard line, he could claim with apparent reason that Germany was being discriminated against. He then promptly used this to justify his decision not only to break off the negotiations but also to withdraw Germany from the League of Nations. Then, on 12 November, he held a plebiscite, which produced a 95 per cent vote in favour, showing that his move had wide public approval.

3 Hitler encourages Britain to rearm, 5 December 1933

Hitler now tried to make use of the rearmament issue as a first step towards the agreement with Britain envisaged in *Mein Kampf*. At an interview with the British ambassador, Sir Eric Phipps, Hitler complained that

... Germany's frontier was completely undefended and, as things were at present, the French could walk into the country whenever they liked. Indeed there was a very real danger of some future weak French Government deciding to embark on a policy of foreign adventure in order to divert attention from its weakness at home and to proceed to the occupation of the left bank of the Rhine. This was an intolerable situation for Germany, who was thereby placed in the position of being eternally considered to be a second-class Power. She must also be in a position to throw her weight into the scales at some future time, and, in this connexion, might not Great Britain herself be glad of other alternatives to her present friendships? ...

Hitler then tried to drive a wedge between Britain and France by offering to concede substantial rearmament to Britain, while suggesting that Britain and Italy should combine to force France to come to terms. Phipps continued:

...

6. I enquired what exactly the Chancellor had meant when he had suggested to me in my previous interview that the 'highly armed' Powers should be bound by a species of *Stillstand* agreement to their present armaments. Herr Hitler replied that he had only had in mind France, Poland and Czechoslovakia. So far as Britain was concerned, not only should she not be included in any such standstill agreement, but he would even welcome considerable additions to the British fleet and air force.
7. On the naval side, I remarked that we had often proposed the total abolition of submarines, to which Herr Hitler replied that Germany also would be delighted if submarines could be abolished. He then repeated what General von Blomberg had told me ... that Germany would never dream of competing against England at sea, but would like a few [*ein paar*] big ships after 1935, until which date she would remain within the limits prescribed by the Treaty.
8. The Chancellor declared that he did not believe the present French Government was strong enough to reach any satisfactory comprehensive agreement with Germany. I thereupon asked what procedure he would favour in order to reach an agreement. He replied that if Great Britain and Italy would urge upon France the advisability of concluding an arrangement, at any rate on the basis outlined above, it might induce the French Government to take the necessary decision. ...

Although Britain neglected to take up his proposals, Hitler did not abandon his endeavours to reach an agreement with Britain. In the meantime, however, he moved to isolate France from another direction. On 26 January 1934, he concluded a Non-Aggression Pact with Poland. This was totally unexpected because hitherto German–Polish relations had been poor because of the loss of German territory to Poland under the Versailles settlement. The Weimar Governments had preferred to keep on good terms with Soviet Russia which was equally hostile to Poland. Now Hitler, acting against the counsel of most of his diplomatic and military advisers, reversed this policy. This decision partly reflected his anti-Communist domestic policy. But it was intended, above all, to damage France's system of security alliances in Eastern Europe. For France had concluded an alliance with

Poland in 1921 with the object of containing Germany. Hitler was now exploiting Poland's growing uncertainty of the reliability of France and their common hostility toward the Soviet Union. The pact also had considerable propaganda value for Hitler, who used it as evidence of his peaceful intentions in speeches he made during 1934 and 1935. Sir Eric Phipps, for example, wrote in a report to London that the German agreement with Poland showed Hitler's statesmanlike qualities, since for its sake he was prepared to lose some popularity.

In June 1934, Hitler made his first trip abroad as German Chancellor — significantly to visit Mussolini in Venice. He clearly hoped to pave the way for an understanding with Italy which would lead to the alliance envisaged in his programme. His main task was to try to calm Mussolini's uneasiness about German intentions in Austria. In this he proved unsuccessful. After the war, the German Foreign Minister, von Neurath, who was present at the meeting, recalled that 'their minds didn't meet; they didn't understand each other'.[1] Moreover, after his return to Germany, his attempt to woo Italy and indeed his whole peace policy received a severe setback when Austrian Nazis attempted a *coup d'état* against the Dollfuss Government in Vienna, an attempt which resulted in the assassination of Dollfuss but not in the overthrow of the regime. Whether or not Hitler had approved the *coup* is in dispute; what is clear is that its failure produced serious diplomatic complications, above all with Italy. Indeed Mussolini, who at the time was host to Frau Dollfuss, ordered troops to the Austrian border at the Brenner Pass and relations with Germany became tense.

4 *State Secretary von Bülow on Germany's international position, August 1934*

The Austrian incident came at a time of serious crisis for the Nazi regime. The Röhm 'putsch' had occurred only a few weeks before and had reawakened international suspicion of Nazism. Furthermore, Germany was in the middle of a grave balance of payments crisis which made her extremely vulnerable to international pressure.[2] The State Secretary in the German Foreign Office, von Bülow, stressed the vulnerability of Germany's international position in a memorandum to von Neurath in August 1934:

In judging the situation we should never overlook the fact that no kind of rearmament in the next few years could give us military security. Even apart from our isolation, we shall for a long time yet be hopelessly inferior to France in the military sphere. A particularly dangerous period will be 1934-35 on account of the reorganization of the Reichswehr. Our only security lies in a skilful foreign policy and in avoiding all provocation.

In so doing we must, of course, not only prevent the taking of military measures against Germany such as are being quite openly discussed in military circles

[1] Interrogation of von Neurath at the Nuremberg Trials, *Nazi Conspiracy and Aggression*, Suppl. B (Washington 1948), p. 1492.
[2] See above, p. 389.

abroad. In view of our isolation and our present weakness, economically and as regards foreign currency, our opponents need not even expose themselves to the hazards, the odium and the dangers of military measures. Without mobilizing a single man or firing a single shot, they can place us in the most difficult situation by setting up a financial and economic blockade against us, either covert or overt. In a few of the most important countries 'mobilization measures' for this purpose, within the framework of the economic sanctions in Article 16, have been in readiness for years. Nevertheless, in my view, we need not at the moment fear a preventive war. For France, Britain and others will first wait to see whether, and how, we shall deal with our economic and other difficulties. Their present restraint, however, must not make us think that they would still remain passive if they had nothing more to expect from German domestic difficulties and if we rearmed intensively. France and Britain also would then intervene, the more so as they could not permit an unlimited unilateral German rearmament. It would be wishful thinking to expect them to wait until we are strong enough to be a serious danger to them. They would probably demand guarantees regarding the extent and purpose of our armaments even before we had recovered economically.

The author of this memorandum represented the Foreign Office view, but Hitler himself was not so pessimistic. He had far more insight into the weaknesses of the other powers and in the spring of 1935 he put them to the first major test. By the beginning of that year, the German armed forces were expanding and the Reich Air Ministry was speeding up aircraft production with the result that it was becoming increasingly difficult to disguise the progress of German rearmament. Hitler had been aiming since 1933 to reintroduce general conscription and was waiting for the right moment to announce it. On 4 March 1935, the British defence White Paper gave the increase in German arms as the reason for rearmament plans and six days later the French Government declared that the period of military service would be extended. Hitler responded by cancelling a visit of British ministers to Berlin that week with the excuse of a diplomatic cold and used the opportunity to announce on 11 March the existence of a German air force, and on 16 March a decree introducing general conscription. The decree was coupled with a declaration that Germany had no further intention of observing the defence limitations of the Versailles Treaties.

The other powers attempted to meet the new threat with a concerted response. On 11 April, the prime ministers of Britain, France, and Italy met at Stresa in Italy and afterwards issued a declaration in which they reasserted their determination to protect the integrity of Austria. On 17 April, the League of Nations passed a motion of censure on Germany's action. Finally, on 2 May, France concluded a mutual assistance pact with the Soviet Union.

Germany breaks out of isolation, 1935–37

The formation of the 'Stresa Front' represented the high point of German isolation. It proved a hollow gesture; within three months, Hitler's tactics of trying to win over Britain with concessions on the rearmament issue appeared to have succeeded. In November 1934, Hitler had offered to make a naval agreement with Britain in which Germany would limit herself to building only 35 per cent of the strength of the British surface fleet. Negotiations continued in March 1935 when Sir John Simon, the British Foreign Secretary, and Mr Anthony Eden, the Under-Secretary, visited Berlin to discuss general issues.

5 *The Anglo-German conversations of 25–26 March 1935*

The meetings between Hitler, Simon and Eden, attended also by the German Foreign Minister and Joachim von Ribbentrop, Hitler's expert on English questions, illustrate well the tactics of the two Governments. On the one hand, Britain was trying to tie Germany down by bringing her back into the League of Nations and into the European framework of multilateral agreements. Thus Simon began by stating:

It was the object of British policy to serve peace by securing cooperation amongst all European countries. They hoped Germany would cooperate with all the others. They believed that the future would take on one of two forms: it would either take the form of general cooperation, which Britain greatly desired, or the form of a division into two camps, resulting in isolation on the one side, and the formation of blocs, which might look like encirclement, on the other. He was convinced that the future would develop in one or other of these two ways.

But Hitler wished above all to avoid such multilateral entanglements and preferred the freedom of manoeuvre offered by bilateral agreements. Again he tried to win over Britain to such a bilateral arrangement. This time, however, instead of offering concessions, he applied some degree of pressure, first through colonial demands and later in the sphere of armaments. Thus, in reply to Simon's request that Germany should rejoin the League, he raised in intentionally vague terms the question of colonies:

... The Chancellor then showed his British visitors a diagram indicating the comparative sizes of the European metropolitan countries and their colonies, together with other possessions having economic potentialities. He demonstrated that Germany with her 68 million inhabitants in an area of 460,000 square kilometres, that is to say, with a population density of 137 inhabitants to the square kilometre, had by herself insufficient economic living space [*Wirtschaftsraum*]. It would not do to try to find a solution, only to have it again denounced shortly afterwards, but in the interests of a true peace a solution must be sought which would be permanently acceptable; Britain would thus have pledged herself to Germany and Germany would abide absolutely by her Treaty obligations. He was not asking for the impossible, but for what, in his view, constituted the necessary and reasonable minimum. He recalled that Germany also had made great renunciations. Britain had no interest in making Germany a pariah among the nations, but in bringing her into Britain's own sphere of interest. No one could tell how history might develop. But a time would come when the European nations would have to stand together, and when it would be specially important for Germany and Britain to be standing together. No one in Germany, and least of all the National Socialists, felt any hatred or enmity towards Britain. Nor had they any such feelings towards France, but in view of French complexes it was infinitely more difficult to get on better terms with France. Germany was aware that she could never defend any possible colonial possessions of hers single-handed. But it might also happen that Britain would require outside help to defend her possessions. Should it be possible to find a solution, this might lead not only to cooperation in Europe but to special relations of friendship between England and Germany.

Simon expressed his pleasure at the frank statements made by both sides. He wished to make two observations: The first was that the Chancellor had so expressed his thoughts that they seemed to require closer relations between Britain and Germany than between Britain and France. Britain wanted to be on good terms with Germany, but must not allow this to prejudice her friendship with France. They did not wish to substitute one friend for another. They did not wish to have special engagements with anyone; Britain was an entirely uncommitted member of the Society of Nations. It would not be 'fair' were he to allow the impression to be created that Britain was being disloyal to one friend while seeking another. His second point concerned the colonial question. This would be carefully studied. . . .

During the translation of Simon's remarks, the Chancellor expressed his agreement with the first point (relations with France); as regards the second point, he said that he had no intention of seizing foreign possessions. . . .

On the following day, the discussions concentrated on the armament issue. Hitler repeated his offer of an Anglo-German naval ratio of 100:35 and it was agreed that preliminary naval conversations should be held in London. When the discussions turned to the question of air armaments, Simon asked about the present strength of the German air force. To the astonishment of the British, Hitler replied (untruthfully) that Germany had reached air parity with Britain.

To sum up the significance of the conversations: Hitler had once more suggested Anglo-German cooperation, an offer which had once again been rejected. The British did not want a bilateral agreement with Germany at the expense of relations with France. They hoped rather to bring Germany back into the Concert of Europe, where she could be more easily controlled. The conversations are also significant for the fact that Hitler for the first time introduced new tactics in his relations with Britain. Instead of merely offering concessions, he now also applied pressure — over colonies and over armaments. He was not seriously interested in colonies at this stage; he merely used the issue as a means of convincing Britain of the need to come to terms with Germany and concede her wishes in the Continental field in return for German cooperation outside Europe. Similarly, Germany had by no means reached air parity with Britain, but by lying Hitler was able to apply pressure from another quarter.

Although Britain refused to be drawn into a comprehensive agreement with Germany, Hitler's tactics were partially successful, for, on 18 June 1935, Britain completely undermined the Stresa Front by signing a naval agreement with Germany without having previously discussed the matter with her partners. The agreement allowed Germany to rebuild her navy up to 35 per cent of the strength of the British navy and 100 per cent of the British submarine force. Hitler's directives to the German negotiators had laid down: 'An understanding must be reached between the two great Germanic peoples through the permanent elimination of naval rivalry. One will control the sea, the other will be the strongest power on land. A defensive and offensive alliance between the two will inaugurate a new era.'[1] On hearing the news of the successful completion of the agreement, Hitler described it as 'the happiest day of his life'.[2] He said 'he was convinced that the British regarded the agreement with us in this sphere as only a preliminary to much wider cooperation. An Anglo-German combination would be stronger than all the other powers.'[3]

Soon after the Anglo-German Agreement, the Stresa Front was further undermined by a change in Italian policy towards Germany. Under the influence of a pro-German *Fronde* led by his son-in-law, Ciano, Mussolini was becoming convinced that association with Germany offered the best opportunities for Italian expansion. On 30 May 1935, less than two months after the Stresa conference, the German ambassador in Rome noted that relations between Germany and Italy had improved so much recently 'that one might almost speak of a reversal of Italy's attitude towards Germany'.[4] This trend received added impetus from developments in Abyssinia. Mussolini had assumed that, in return for his cooperation over the German threat to Austria, Britain and France would be prepared to give him *carte blanche* in Abyssinia. His assumption proved erroneous. When the Italians began their invasion in October 1935, the Emperor of Abyssinia appealed to the League of Nations for support. After an attempt to reach a compromise at the expense of Abyssinia had been rejected by British public opinion, the new British Foreign Secretary, Anthony Eden, took the initiative in the League of Nations to impose economic sanctions on Italy.

6 *German policy towards Italy in the Abyssinian crisis*

Germany remained officially neutral on the issue but refused to join the blockade and continued to supply Italy with raw materials. On 17 January 1936, Ulrich von Hassell, the German ambassador to Italy, had an audience with Hitler to report on the political situation in Italy, and three days later made the following report on the meeting:

[1] E. Kordt, *Nicht aus den Akten* (Berlin 1950), p. 100; quoted in A. Kuhn, *Hitlers aussenpolitisches Programm* (Stuttgart 1970), p. 168.
[2] *The Ribbentrop Memoirs* (London 1954), p. 41.
[3] Kordt, *op. cit.*, p. 109.
[4] *Documents on German Foreign Policy,* series C, vol. iv, p. 230.

After a short discussion of the resultant situation, the Führer and Chancellor sent for the Foreign Minister and in the presence of us both drew a picture of the political position as it appeared to him at present. He said he had no illusions at all about the fact that Germany was at present as good as completely isolated. We possessed no really reliable friends. No real trust could be placed in Poland's policy and Italy was herself in a very difficult position. It would be highly undesirable if this isolation should, as the result of a collapse of Fascism in Italy, become a moral isolation as well. We must do everything to prevent the various opponents throughout the world of the authoritarian system of government from concentrating upon us as their sole object. But apart from this it was also in our interests that Italy as a piece upon the European chessboard should not be weakened too much. There was a time, especially after Mussolini's well-known demonstrations at the Brenner Pass, when perhaps we might not have wished to see Italy emerge from the conflict too great or too victorious, but nowadays this danger surely no longer existed to any considerable degree. On the contrary, it was much more to be feared that Fascism, and indeed Italy herself, might be destroyed or at least emerge seriously impaired by the ordeal. We Germans, for our part, could not but wish to make every effort to prevent such a collapse, in so far as we were in a position to do so. He had therefore resolved to continue our benevolent neutrality towards Italy. Indeed, he had even at times considered going further and undertaking some form of action towards peace and thus of mediation in the Italo-Abyssinian conflict. The idea had then again been dropped, but the benevolent neutrality so far observed would continue to be our guiding principle. Similarly he could only welcome it if relations of mutual trust between Italy and Germany were restored. It was a mistake to pursue a policy of emotion in such questions; regardless of what one's own personal feelings might be, it was politically correct to treat the events of 1934 as a closed chapter.

7 The German announcement of the reoccupation of the Rhineland

On 7 March 1936, Hitler exploited the differences between the Western Powers and their preoccupation with the Abyssinian question to spring his next surprise—the reoccupation of the Rhineland which had been demilitarized by the Versailles Treaty. He made this decision in mid-February and took the ratification of the Franco-Soviet Pact by the French Chamber of Deputies on 4 March as a pretext to terminate the Locarno Treaty of 1925 which guaranteed the Franco-German frontier. Relations between Germany and Italy being still somewhat ambiguous, Mussolini had not been informed beforehand. Britain discouraged France from taking action because she did not want to risk war to prevent Germany from walking into her own 'back garden', as one observer put it. Had any action been taken, the German forces would have been vastly outnumbered; but the addition of several police divisions helped to give the impression that the German troops were more numerous than they really were. The occupation of the Rhineland represented not only a great diplomatic *coup*, but also a strategic victory by which Germany had closed a gap in her western flank which had hitherto made her extremely vulnerable to French pressure. Characteristically, Hitler accompanied his aggressive move with a conciliatory gesture. Thus, the announcement justifying the reoccupation contained an offer to sign new agreements:

The German Government have continually emphasized during the negotiations of the last years its readiness to observe and fulfil all the obligations arising from the Rhine Pact so long as the other contracting parties were ready on their side to maintain the pact. This obvious and essential condition can no longer be regarded as being fulfilled by France. France has replied to Germany's repeated friendly offers and assurances of peace by infringing the Rhine Pact through a military alliance with the Soviet Union directed exclusively against Germany. In this manner, however, the Locarno Rhine Pact has lost its inner meaning and ceased in practice to exist. Consequently, Germany regards herself for her part as no longer bound by this dissolved Treaty. The German Government is now constrained to face the new situation created by this alliance, a situation which is rendered more acute by the fact that the Franco–Soviet Treaty has been supplemented by a Treaty of Alliance between Czechoslovakia and the Soviet Union exactly parallel in form. In accordance with the fundamental right of a nation to secure its frontiers and ensure its possibilities of defence, the German Government have today restored the full and unrestricted sovereignty of Germany in the demilitarized zone of the Rhineland.

In order, however, to avoid any misinterpretation of their intentions and to establish beyond doubt the purely defensive character of these measures, as well as to express their unalterable longing for a real pacification of Europe between States equal in rights and equally respected, the German Government declares itself ready to conclude new agreements for the creation of a system of peaceful security for Europe.

Specifically, Germany offered non-aggression pacts with France and Belgium, an air agreement with Britain and even the return of Germany to the League of Nations which it was hoped would prove particularly tempting to Britain.

On 17 July 1936, civil war broke out in Spain; a group of right-wing army officers led by General Franco rebelled against the Government of the Republic, which consisted of a coalition of the Left. Right from the start Germany was involved on the rebel Nationalist side. Her intervention was initiated by the *Auslandsorganisation*, a Nazi organization which controlled relations with Germans living abroad. Its agents in Spain by-passed the Foreign Office and through Party contacts managed to gain direct access to Hitler and win his support for Franco. He agreed to provide the vital transport necessary to bring the elite Moroccan division to the mainland. Italy also soon sent troops and arms to the Nationalists, while Russia supplied the Republicans with arms and Comintern-organized international brigades of foreign Communists and other pro-Republicans.

Intervention in the civil war gave Germany a number of advantages: she had her eye on the valuable raw materials to be found in Spain, iron ore and pyrites, and the war also offered a valuable testing ground for the new German weapons and particularly the air force. But most important were the political factors. In the first place, a pro-German Government in Spain would, it was thought, threaten France and if necessary Britain as well. Secondly, the war would ensure that Italy and France remained in conflict and would therefore bind Italy more firmly to Germany and tie her down in the Mediterranean, leaving Germany a freer hand in the east. Finally, German intervention on the side of the Nationalists could be portrayed by Germany as an anti-Bolshevist move which, it was hoped, would find sympathy with conservative circles in Britain.

8 *Mussolini's speech on the 'Rome/Berlin Axis'*

In the meantime Hitler had taken the opportunity to consolidate friendship with Italy. The Austro-German agreement of 11 July 1936, which acknowledged Austrian independence and attempted to improve relations between the two countries, removed the chief bone of contention between the two Fascist States. In September, Hitler sent the Nazi legal expert, Hans Frank, on an exploratory visit to Rome which resulted in the visit of Ciano, the Italian Foreign Minister, to Germany in the following month. Hitler made special efforts to please the Italians and took a personal interest in the details of Ciano's reception in Munich, which included a gala performance of *Don Giovanni*. After a trip to Berlin, Ciano met Hitler at Berchtesgaden, where the two men signed the secret 'October Protocols' which covered cooperation on a number of points – opposition to Communist propaganda, recognition of Franco as the rightful head of the Spanish Government and an understanding that Germany recognized the Italian empire and had no wish to interfere in the Mediterranean. Hitler referred in grandiose terms to Mussolini as 'the first statesman of the world with whom no one else had the right even remotely to compare himself' and succeeded in overcoming Mussolini's reserve shown during Frank's visit in September. On 1 November, Mussolini made a speech at Milan in which he revealed his satisfaction at Ciano's visit and referred for the first time to a 'Rome/Berlin axis'.

The meeting at Berlin resulted in an agreement between the two countries on certain questions, some of which are particularly interesting in these days. But these agreements, which have been included in special statements and duly signed – this vertical line between Rome and Berlin is not a partition, but rather an axis around which all the European States animated by the will to collaboration and peace can also collaborate. Germany, although surrounded and solicited, did not adhere to sanctions. With the agreement of 11 July there disappeared any element of dissension between Berlin and Rome, and I may remind you that even before the Berlin meeting Germany had practically recognized the Empire of Rome.

Yet, although Hitler had now clearly shifted his main attention to Italy, he did not give up his attempts to win over Britain, the other ally envisaged in his pre-1933 programme, despite a growing sense of disillusionment at the prospects of an agreement. The German ambassador to Britain, Leopold von Hoesch, had died in March 1936, and in August was replaced by Joachim von Ribbentrop. Ribbentrop, a former champagne salesman who had married into a wealthy German champagne firm, had only joined the Nazi Party in 1932. His social contacts, however, had won him a position close to Hitler. In particular, Ribbentrop managed to impress Hitler with his experience of foreign countries, experience which the Führer himself so singularly lacked. After the Nazi take-over Hitler, who wished to lessen his own dependence on the conservative officials in the Foreign Office, relied more and more on Ribbentrop for diplomatic missions to Britain and France. In the spring of 1934, he appointed Ribbentrop his representative for disarmament questions so as to give him official status, and Ribbentrop established his own office, the Ribbentrop Bureau, which became in effect a rival diplomatic service to the Foreign Office. Ribbentrop was particularly associated with Hitler's attempts to achieve an agreement with Britain. Thus, he was given responsibility for the Anglo-German naval negotiations and now Hitler's last words after his appointment to the embassy in London were: 'Ribbentrop, bring me the English alliance.'[1]

At the same time Hitler undertook two further initiatives in the latter half of 1936. In the first place, the balance of payments crisis which broke in the summer of 1936 brought home to him the vulnerability of the German economy and confirmed his conviction of Germany's need for 'living space'. In August, therefore, he inaugurated the Four-Year Plan which was intended to ensure that Germany was economically prepared for war within four years.[2] Secondly, he decided to increase the pressure on England to come to terms. This pressure took the form of an attempt to frighten Britain with the dangers of Bolshevism, as exemplified in Russian intervention in the Spanish Civil War, and to portray Nazi Germany as a bastion of anti-Bolshevism. His aim was to try to persuade Britain that her old 'balance of power' principle was no longer relevant in the light of this new threat and that the opponents of Bolshevism must now stand together. This was the main tenor of Ribbentrop's activities in England and the propaganda was by no means unsuccessful, particularly among the upper classes. Thus, Harold Nicolson, a writer and Member of Parliament associated with the Conservatives, noted in his diary on 16 July 1936 that 'the majority of the National [Conservative and National Labour] Party are at heart anti-League [of Nations] and anti-Russian and what they would really like would be a firm agreement with Germany and possibly Italy, by which we could purchase peace at the expense of the smaller states'.[3]

In the winter of 1936 Hitler added a new dimension to this policy by

[1] *The Ribbentrop Memoirs* (London 1954), p. 62n.
[2] See above, pp. 398ff.
[3] H. Nicolson, *Diaries and Letters*, ed. Nigel Nicolson (London 1966), p. 263.

signing an 'Anti-Comintern Pact' with Japan. This had the advantage of putting added pressure on the British Government, already concerned at the growing Japanese threat to the British position in the Far East. The Pact was not intended as a directly anti-British move. Indeed, Hitler was initially keen that Britain should join it and come to terms with Japan on the basis of their mutual hostility to Russia. But, on the other hand, if Britain was not cooperative then the agreement with Japan would be a useful means of bringing pressure to bear on her to remain neutral in the event of German initiatives directed against other countries. Britain did not join the Pact, but the threat was duly noted. The assessment of the British Chiefs of Staff that Britain had not sufficient forces to take on both Germany and Japan at the same time contributed to the policy of appeasement which was followed over the next three years.

In November 1937, Italy joined the Anti-Comintern Pact. In September, Mussolini had paid a state visit to Germany and, although no formal agreements were signed, Hitler achieved his main object of impressing Mussolini with a display of German power. In addition to the consolidation of the Axis with Italy which removed Austria's main source of support, on 5 November 1937 Germany reaffirmed her determination to maintain good relations with Poland by negotiating a minorities Treaty. In particular, Hitler stated that there would be no change in the position of Danzig, to which Germany had in the past laid claim. With this gesture Hitler secured the neutrality of Poland which was essential, should he wish to move against Czechoslovakia. Although the British were still proving elusive, his position was now sufficiently secure to enable him to move on to the offensive.

9 The Hossbach Memorandum

On 5 November 1937, Hitler called together a group of his most important military and diplomatic subordinates. A report of this meeting, based partly on memory and partly on notes taken at the time, was made five days later by Hitler's adjutant, Colonel Friedrich Hossbach. The surviving version printed here is not the original but a copy of a copy.

This memorandum has been the subject of considerable controversy. It was taken by the Nuremberg Tribunal as evidence of a 'plot' to wage war which had been 'carefully planned', as a blueprint of Hitler's intentions. In fact, it was not a commitment by Hitler to war, for it was not his practice to bind himself in this way. Nor was the memorandum a blueprint; indeed, it omits the most important of Hitler's aims, namely the colonizing of western Russia, probably in order not to frighten his audience with the prospect of a war on two fronts. Moreover, his timetable was wrong and the moves against Austria and Czechoslovakia did not occur in the way he envisaged. A. J. P. Taylor has suggested persuasively that the meeting had little or no significance and must be seen largely as a move in domestic politics. We know that it was called in response to a dispute between Blomberg and Göring over the allocation of raw materials to the armed forces. Blomberg objected to the way in which Göring was exploiting his position in charge of the Four-Year Plan to give preference to his Air Force. Hitler disliked having to arbitrate in such disputes and may have launched out into a general survey of foreign policy in an attempt to avoid committing himself. A more important motive for the speech, however, was probably Hitler's desire to persuade the cautious generals to accept a faster rate of rearmament by impressing upon them the imminent possibility of war. Yet it seems doubtful whether the speech can be attributed solely to limited domestic political motives and disregarded as an expression of serious intentions. It appears rather as an expression by Hitler of a new sense of urgency, of his awareness of the new pressures building up within Germany as a result of the rearmament boom, and of a determination to solve the crisis by pursuing a more aggressive policy abroad before the favourable diplomatic and military situation changed to Germany's disadvantage.

Among the more significant features of the memorandum are, first, the fact that Britain is now coupled with France as a 'hate-inspired antagonist' and both countries are seen as Germany's main adversaries; that is to say, Hitler is now reconciled to the impossibility, at least for the time being, of securing an agreement with Britain. Moreover, his shrewd assessment of the British Government's attitude and its influence on France shows that he was already aware that he could move some way forward without having to fear intervention from Britain and France; Britain's weakness provided an alternative to alliance with her. Secondly, he now sees pressure upon Austria and Czechoslovakia as the next aims of German policy, and clearly as the first stage in the defeat of France and Britain. Furthermore, he sees this as a likely development in the near future. The time factor is, indeed, one of the most significant aspects of the document. The fact that this timetable was wrong is not so important as the fact that he reveals himself to be under the pressure of time, anxious to specify a broad schedule and above all to seize any opportunity which comes up:

Berlin, 10 November 1937

Minutes of the Conference in the Reich Chancellery, Berlin, 5 November 1937, from 4.15 to 8.30 p.m.

Present: The Führer and Chancellor;
  Field-Marshal von Blomberg, War Minister;
  Colonel-General Baron von Fritsch, Commander-in-Chief, Army;
  Admiral Dr R. C. Raeder, Commander-in-Chief, Navy;
  Colonel-General Göring, Commander-in-Chief, Luftwaffe;
  Baron von Neurath, Foreign Minister;
  Colonel Hossbach.

The Führer began by stating that the subject of the present conference was of such importance that its discussion would, in other countries, be a matter for a full Cabinet meeting, but he, the Führer, had rejected the idea of making it a subject of discussion before the wider circle of the Reich Cabinet just because of the importance of the matter. His exposition to follow was the fruit of thorough deliberation and the experiences of his four-and-a-half years of power. He wished to explain to the gentlemen present his basic ideas concerning the opportunities for the development of our position in the field of foreign affairs and its requirements, and he asked, in the interest of a long-term German policy, that his exposition be regarded, in the event of his death, as his last will and testament.

The Führer then continued:

The aim of German policy was to make secure and to preserve the racial community [*Volksmasse*] and to enlarge it. It was therefore a question of space.

The German racial community comprised over 85 million people and, by reason of their number and the narrow limits of habitable space in Europe, it constituted a tightly packed racial core such as was not to be found in any other country and such as implied the right to a greater living space than in the case of other peoples. If there existed no political result, territorially speaking, corresponding to this German racial core, that was a consequence of centuries of historical development, and in the continuance of these political conditions lay the greatest danger to the preservation of the German race at its present peak. To arrest the decline of Germanism [*Deutschtum*] in Austria and Czechoslovakia was as little possible as to maintain the present level in Germany itself. Instead of increase, sterility was setting in, and in its train disorders of a social character must arise in course of time, since political and ideological ideas remain effective only so long as they furnish the basis for the realization of the essential vital demands of a people. Germany's future was therefore wholly conditional upon the solving of the need for space, and such a solution could be sought, of course, only for a foreseeable period of about one to three generations.

Before turning to the question of solving the need for space, it had to be considered whether a solution holding promise for the future was to be reached by means of autarky or by means of an increased participation in world economy.

Autarky
Achievement possible only under strict National Socialist leadership of the State, which is assumed; accepting its achievement as possible, the following could be stated as results:

A. In the field of raw materials only limited, not total, autarky:

1. In regard to coal, so far as it could be considered as a source of raw materials, autarky was possible.

2. But even as regards ores, the position was much more difficult. Iron requirements can be met from home resources and similarly with light metals, but with other raw materials—copper, tin—this was not so.

3. Synthetic textile requirements can be met from home resources to the limit of timber supplies. A permanent solution impossible.

4. Edible fats, possible.

B. In the field of food the question of autarky was to be answered by a flat 'No'.

Hand in hand with the general rise in the standard of living compared with that of thirty to forty years ago, there has gone an increased demand and an increased home consumption even on the part of the producers, the farmers. The fruits of the increased agricultural production had all gone to meet the increased demand, and so did not represent an absolute increase in production. A further increase in production by making greater demands on the soil, which already, in consequence of the use of artificial fertilizers, was showing signs of exhaustion, was hardly possible, and it was therefore certain that, even with the maximum increase in production, participation in world trade was unavoidable. The not inconsiderable expenditure of foreign exchange to ensure food supplies by imports, even when harvests were good, grew to catastrophic proportions with bad harvests. The possibility of disaster grew in proportion to the increase in population, in which, moreover, the excess of births of 560,000 annually produced, as a consequence, an even further increase in bread consumption, since a child consumed more bread than an adult.

It was not possible over the long run, in a continent enjoying a practically common standard of living, to meet the difficulties of food supply by lowering that standard and by rationalization. Since, with the solving of the unemployment problem, the maximum consumption level had been reached, some minor modifications in our home agricultural production might still, no doubt, be possible, but no fundamental alteration was possible in our basic food position. Thus autarky, in regard both to food and to the economy as a whole, could not be maintained.

Participation in world economy

To this there were limitations which we were unable to remove. The establishment of Germany's position on a secure and sound foundation was obstructed by market fluctuations, and commercial treaties afforded no guarantee for their actual observance. In particular it had to be remembered that since the world war those very countries which had formerly been food exporters had become industrialized. We were living in an age of economic empires in which the primitive urge to colonization was again manifesting itself: in the cases of Japan and Italy, economic motives underlay the urge for expansion; with Germany also, economic need would supply the stimulus. For countries outside the great economic empires, opportunities for economic expansion were severely obstructed.

The boom in world economy caused by the economic effects of rearmament could never form the basis of a sound economy over a long period, and the latter was impeded above all by the economic disturbances resulting from Bolshevism. There was a pronounced military weakness in those States which depended for their existence on foreign trade. As our foreign trade was carried on over the sea routes dominated by Britain, it was a question rather of security of transport than of foreign exchange, which revealed in time of war the full weakness of our food situation. The only remedy, and one which might seem to us visionary, lay in the acquisition of greater living space—a quest that has in every age been the origin of the formation of States and of the migration of peoples. That this quest met with no interest at Geneva or among the satiated nations was understandable. If, then, we accept the security of our food situation as the principal point at issue, the space needed to ensure it can be sought only in Europe, not, as in the liberal-capitalist view, in the exploitation of colonies. It is not a matter of acquiring population but of gaining space for agricultural use. Moreover, areas producing raw materials can be more usefully sought in Europe, in immediate proximity to the

Reich, than overseas; the solution thus obtained must suffice for one or two generations. Whatever else might later prove necessary must be left to succeeding generations to deal with. The development of the great galaxies of world politics progressed, after all, only slowly, and the German people with its strong racial core would find the most favourable prerequisites for such achievement in the heart of the continent of Europe. The history of all ages—the Roman Empire and the British Empire—had proved that expansion could be carried out only by breaking down resistance and taking risks; setbacks were inevitable. There had never in former times been spaces without a master, and there were none today; the attacker always comes up against someone in possession.

The question for Germany was: Where could she achieve the greatest gain at the lowest cost?

German policy had to reckon with two hate-inspired antagonists, Britain and France, to whom a German colossus in the centre of Europe was a thorn in the flesh, and both countries were opposed to any further strengthening of Germany's position either in Europe or overseas; in support of this opposition they were able to count on the consensus of all their political parties. Both countries saw in the establishment of German military bases overseas a threat to their own communications, a safeguarding of German commerce, and as a consequence, a strengthening of Germany's position in Europe.

Because of opposition from her Dominions, Britain could not cede any of her colonial possessions to us. After England's loss of prestige through the passing of Abyssinia into Italian possession, the return of East Africa was not to be expected. British concessions could at best be expressed in an offer to satisfy our colonial demands by the appropriation of colonies which were not British possessions, e.g. Angola; French concessions would probably take a similar line.

Serious discussion of the question of the return of colonies to us could not be entered upon except at a moment when Britain was in difficulties and the German Reich armed and strong. The Führer did not share the view that the Empire was unshakeable. Opposition to the Empire was to be found less in the countries conquered than among her competitors. The British Empire and the Roman Empire could not be compared in respect of permanence; the latter was not confronted by any powerful political rival of a serious order after the Punic Wars. It was only the disintegrating effect of Christianity, and the symptoms of age which appear in every country, which caused ancient Rome to succumb to the onslaught of the Germans.

Beside the British Empire there existed today a number of States stronger than she. The British motherland was able to protect her colonial possessions, not by her own power, but only in alliance with other States. How, for instance, could Britain alone defend Canada against attack by America, or her Far Eastern interests against attack by Japan?

The emphasis on the British Crown as the symbol of the unity of the Empire was already an admission that, in the long run, the Empire could not maintain its position by power politics. Significant indications of this were:

(a) the struggle of Ireland for independence;

(b) the constitutional struggles in India, where Britain's half-measures had given the Indians the opportunity of using later on, as a weapon against Britain, the non-fulfilment of her promises of a constitution;

(c) the weakening by Japan of Britain's position in the Far East;

(d) the rivalry in the Mediterranean with Italy who, under the spell of her history, driven by necessity and led by a genius, was expanding her power position, which was inevitably coming more and more into conflict with British interests. The outcome of the Abyssinian War was a loss of prestige for Britain which Italy was striving to exploit by stirring up trouble in the Mohammedan world.

To sum up, it could be stated that, with 45 million Britons, the position of the Empire, despite its theoretical soundness, could not in the long run be maintained by power politics. The ratio of the population of the Empire to that of the motherland of 9:1 was a warning to us, in our territorial expansion, not to allow the foundation constituted by the numerical strength of our own people to become too weak.

France's position was more favourable than that of Britain. The French Empire was territorially better placed; the inhabitants of her colonial possessions represented a supplement to her military strength. But France was going to be confronted with internal political difficulties. In a nation's life, about 10 per cent of its span is taken up by parliamentary forms of government and about 90 per cent by authoritarian forms. Today, none the less, Britain, France, Russia, and the smaller States adjoining them, must be included as factors [*Machtfaktoren*] in our political calculations.

Germany's problem could be solved only by the use of force, and this was never without attendant risk. The Silesian campaigns of Frederick the Great, Bismarck's wars against Austria and France, had involved unheard-of risk, and the swiftness of Prussian action in 1870 had kept Austria from entering the war. If the resort to force with its attendant risks is accepted as the basis of the following exposition, then there remain still to be answered the questions 'When?' and 'How?' In this matter there were three contingencies [*Fälle*] to be dealt with:

Contingency 1: Period 1943-45
After this date only a change for the worse, from our point of view, could be expected.

The equipment of the Army, Navy and Luftwaffe, as well as the formation of the officer corps, was nearly completed. Equipment and armament were modern; in further delay there lay the danger of their obsolescence. In particular, the secrecy of 'special weapons' could not be preserved for ever. The recruiting of reserves was limited to current age groups; further drafts from older untrained age groups were no longer available.

Our relative strength would decrease in relation to the rearmament which would by then have been carried out by the rest of the world. If we did not act by 1943-45, any year could, owing to a lack of reserves, produce the food crisis, to cope with which the necessary foreign exchange was not available, and this must be regarded as a 'waning point of the regime'. Besides, the world was expecting our attack and was increasing its counter-measures from year to year. It was while the rest of the world was still fencing itself off [*sich abriegele*] that we were obliged to take the offensive.

Nobody knew today what the situation would be in the years 1943-45. One thing was certain, that we could wait no longer.

On the one hand there was the great Wehrmacht, and the necessity of maintaining it at its present level, the ageing of the movement and of its leaders; and on the other, the prospect of a lowering of the standard of living and of a limitation of the birth-rate, which left no choice but to act. If the Führer was still living, it was his unalterable determination to solve Germany's problem of space by 1943–45 at the latest. The necessity for action before 1943–45 would arise in contingencies 2 and 3.

Contingency 2:
If internal strife in France should develop into such a domestic crisis as to absorb the French army completely and render it incapable of use for war against Germany, then the time for action against the Czechs would have come.

Contingency 3:
If France should be so embroiled in war with another State that she could not 'proceed' against Germany.

For the improvement of our politico-military position our first objective, in the event of our being embroiled in war, must be to overthrow Czechoslovakia and Austria simultaneously in order to remove the threat to our flank in any possible operation against the West. In a conflict with France it was hardly to be regarded as likely that the Czechs would declare war on us on the very same day as France. The desire to join in the war would, however, increase among the Czechs in proportion to any weakening on our part, and then her participation could clearly take the form of an attack in the direction of Silesia, toward the north or toward the west.

If the Czechs were overthrown and a common German–Hungarian frontier achieved, a neutral attitude on the part of Poland could be all the more surely counted upon, in the event of a Franco-German conflict. Our agreements with Poland only retained their force so long as Germany's strength remained unshaken. In the event of German setbacks, Polish action against East Prussia, and possibly against Pomerania and Silesia as well, had to be reckoned with.

Assuming a development of the situation, leading to action on our part as planned, in the years 1943–45, the attitude of France, Britain, Italy, Poland, and Russia could be conjectured as follows:

Actually, the Führer believed that almost certainly Britain, and probably France as well, had already tacitly written off the Czechs and were reconciled to the fact that this question would be cleared up in due course by Germany. Difficulties connected with the Empire, and the prospect of being once more entangled in a protracted European war, were for Britain decisive reasons against taking part in a war against Germany. France's attitude would certainly not be uninfluenced by that of Britain. An attack by France without British support, and with the prospect of the offensive being brought to a standstill on our western fortifications, was hardly probable. Nor was a French march through Belgium and Holland without British support to be expected; nor would this course be contemplated by us in the event of a conflict with France, because it would certainly entail the hostility of Britain. It would of course be necessary to maintain a strong defence [*eine Abriegelung*] on our western frontier during the prosecution of our attack on the Czechs and Austria. And in this connexion it had to be remembered that the defence measures of the Czechs were growing year by year in strength, and that the actual quality of the Austrian army was also steadily increasing. Even though the populations concerned, especially that of Czechoslovakia, were not sparse, the annexation of Czechoslovakia and Austria would mean an acquisition of foodstuffs for

5-6 million people, on the assumption that the compulsory emigration of 2 million people from Czechoslovakia and a million people from Austria was practicable. The incorporation of these two States with Germany meant a substantial advantage from the politico-military point of view, because it would mean shorter and better frontiers, the freeing of forces for other purposes, and the possibility of creating new units up to a level of about twelve divisions, that is, one new division per million inhabitants.

Italy was not expected to object to the elimination of the Czechs, but it was not possible at the moment to estimate what her attitude on the Austrian question would be; that depended essentially upon whether the Duce were still alive.

The degree of surprise and the swiftness of our action were decisive factors for Poland's attitude. Poland, with Russia at her rear, will have little inclination to engage in war against a victorious Germany.

Military intervention by Russia must be countered by the swiftness of our operations; but whether such intervention was a practical contingency at all was more than doubtful, in view of the attitude of Japan.

Should contingency 2, the crippling of France by civil war, occur, the situation thus created by the elimination of our most dangerous opponent must be seized upon, whenever it occurs, for the blow against the Czechs.

The Führer saw contingency 3 coming definitely nearer; it might emerge from the present tensions in the Mediterranean, and he was resolved to take advantage of it whenever it happened, even as early as 1938.

In the light of past experience, the Führer saw no early end to the hostilities in Spain. If one considered the length of time which Franco's offensives had taken up till now, it was entirely possible that the war would continue another three years. Neither, on the other hand, from the German point of view was a 100 per cent victory for Franco desirable; our interest lay rather in a continuance of the war and in the keeping up of the tension in the Mediterranean. Franco in undisputed possession of the Spanish Peninsula precluded the possibility of any further intervention on the part of the Italians or of their continued occupation of the Balearic Islands. As our interest lay rather in the prolongation of the war in Spain, it must be the immediate aim of our policy to strengthen Italy's rear with a view to her remaining in the Balearics. But the permanent establishment of the Italians on the Balearics would be intolerable both to France and Britain, and might lead to a war of France and England against Italy—a war in which Spain, should she be entirely in the hands of the Whites, might come out on the side of Italy's enemies. The probability of Italy's defeat in such a war was slight, for the road from Germany was open for the supplementing of her raw materials. The Führer pictured the military strategy for Italy thus: on her western frontier with France she would remain on the defensive, and carry on the war with France from Libya against the French North African colonial possessions.

As a landing by Franco-British troops on the coast of Italy could be ruled out, and a French offensive over the Alps against northern Italy would be very difficult and would probably come to a halt before the strong Italian fortifications, the crucial point [Schwerpunkt] of the operations lay in North Africa. The threat to French lines of communication by the Italian Fleet would largely cripple the transportation of forces from North Africa to France, so that France would have only home forces at her disposal on her Italian and German frontiers.

If Germany made use of this war to settle the Czech and Austrian questions, it was to be assumed that Britain, herself at war with Italy, would decide not to act against Germany. Without British support, no warlike action by France against Germany was to be expected.

The time for our attack on the Czechs and Austria must be made dependent on the course of the Anglo-French-Italian war and would not necessarily coincide with the commencement of military operations by these three States. Nor had the Führer in mind military agreements with Italy; he wanted, while retaining his own independence of action, to exploit this favourable situation, which would not occur again, to begin and carry through the campaign against the Czechs. This descent upon the Czechs would have to be carried out with 'lightning speed'.

At the very least, the Hossbach Memorandum gives a valuable insight into Hitler's thoughts at the point when he was about to launch out on a new phase of diplomacy. But there is evidence that it represented much more than this and that in fact it initiated a fundamental shift in German strategic planning.

10 *General Jodl's amendment to 'Operation Green', 7 December 1937*

Hitherto German strategic planning had concentrated on dealing with the threat of a French invasion. Late in 1935 the first major deployment plan, 'Operation Red', was drawn up to meet this eventuality. But the military planners were also obliged to deal with the possibility of intervention by France's ally Czechoslovakia. By 1937 the General Staff had worked out a plan for a pre-emptive strike against Czechoslovakia to forestall precisely such intervention in the case of a war with France—'Operation Green'. On 24 June 1937 a general plan was drawn up which incorporated both 'Operation Red' and 'Operation Green'. In this plan 'Operation Red' took precedence. The extent to which the plan reflected aggressive intentions is in dispute. On the one hand, the preamble to the plan stated that 'the general political situation permits the assumption that Germany need not expect an attack from any quarter', while on the other hand it added that 'a permanent state of readiness of the German Wehrmacht' was necessary 'to take military advantage of any politically favourable opportunities which might arise'. Nevertheless, the emphasis of the plan was in general more defensive than aggressive.

On 7 December 1937, however, following on the Hossbach meeting, the Chief of Operations Staff at OKW, General Jodl, amended the plan in such a way as to give it a definite aggressive slant. From now onwards 'Operation Green' was to take precedence of 'Operation Red' and the invasion of Czechoslovakia was no longer conceived as a pre-emptive strike for essentially defensive purposes but as an 'offensive war' for the purpose of solving 'the German problem of living space':

...

(1) The further development of the diplomatic situation makes 'Operation Red' increasingly less likely than 'Operation Green'. . . .

(3) The political preconditions for the activation of 'Operation Green' have changed, following the directives of the Führer and Reich Chancellor, and the objectives of such a war have been expanded.

The previous Section II of Part 2 of the directive of the High Command of the Armed Forces of 24 June 1937 is therefore to be deleted and replaced by the enclosed new version. . . .

The main emphasis of all mobilization planning is now to be placed on 'Operation Green'. . . .

II. *War on two fronts with main effort in south-east* ('*Operation Green*')

1. *Prerequisites*

When Germany has achieved complete preparedness for war in all spheres, then the military conditions will have been created for carrying out an offensive war against Czechoslovakia, so that the solution of the German problem of living space can be carried to a victorious conclusion even if one or another of the Great Powers intervene against us.

Apart from many other considerations, there is in the first place the defensive capacity of our western fortifications, which will permit the western frontier of the German Reich to be held with weak forces for a long time against greatly superior strength.

But even so the Government [*Staatsführung*] will do what is politically feasible to avoid the risk for Germany of a war on two fronts and will try to avoid any situation with which, as far as can be judged, Germany could not cope militarily or economically.

Should the political situation not develop, or develop only slowly, in our favour, then the execution of 'Operation Green' from our side will have to be postponed for years. If, however, a situation arises which, owing to Britain's aversion to a general European War, through her lack of interest in the Central European problem and because of a conflict breaking out between Italy and France in the Mediterranean, creates the probability that Germany will face no other opponent than Russia on Czechoslovakia's side, then 'Operation Green' will start *before* the completion of Germany's full preparedness for war.

2. The military objective of 'Operation Green' is still the speedy occupation of Bohemia and Moravia with the simultaneous solution of the Austrian question in the sense of incorporating Austria into the German Reich. In order to achieve the latter aim, military force will be required only if other means do not lead or have not led to success.

In accordance with this military objective it is the task of the German Wehrmacht to make preparations so that:

(a) the bulk of all forces can invade Czechoslovakia with speed, surprise and the maximum impetus;

(b) reserves, mainly the armed units of the SS, are kept ready in order, if necessary, to march into Austria;

(c) in the west, security can be maintained with only a minimum of forces for rearguard protection of the eastern operations. . . .

18 The First Phase of Expansion: Austria and Czechoslovakia, 1938–39

The winter of 1937–38 marked the beginning of a new phase not only in foreign policy and strategy but in the development of the regime itself. Hitler now took steps to evict a number of conservatives from influential positions. One factor prompting this move may have been the doubts expressed during the 'Hossbach Conference' of the advisability of Hitler's intentions by Admiral Raeder, Field-Marshal von Blomberg, and von Neurath, the Foreign Minister. Moreover, on 9 November, the Commander-in-Chief of the Army, General von Fritsch, had sent a memorandum to Hitler expressing the concern of the military leaders lest Germany should become involved in a war before her military preparations were complete.

The critical attitude of the Army High Command towards his policy probably decided Hitler to take the first opportunity of replacing the leaders of the armed forces with more pliable men. This was achieved by manufacturing or exploiting personal scandals involving Blomberg and Fritsch and using them as an excuse to ease these men out of their posts. Fritsch was replaced as Commander-in-Chief of the Army by General von Brauchitsch, while Hitler abolished the position of War Minister held by Blomberg and took over from him as Commander-in-Chief of the Armed Forces in addition to the post of Supreme Commander of the Armed Forces which he already held as Head of State. To replace the old Armed Forces Office he established a new High Command of the Armed Forces (OKW) of which he appointed General Keitel, a nonentity, as head. In addition, fourteen senior generals were retired and forty-six others were required to change their commands.

But the purge was not confined to the military. Schacht had resigned as Minister of Economics in November 1937 after differences with Hitler over the pace of rearmament and the undermining of his authority by the growth of Göring's Four-Year Plan Office. His departure and the rise of the Four-Year Plan Office reflected the extent to which the economy had lost its independence and had become subordinate to the political and strategic interests of the regime. The fact that this development benefited certain sections of the economy such as the big chemical trust, IG-Farben, though significant, does not detract from the importance of this development, for IG-Farben were servants of the regime, not vice versa. Lastly, on 4 February 1938, the same day as Hitler made the changes in the military leadership, he appointed Ribbentrop as Foreign Minister in place of Neurath so that the conservative Foreign Office also was now finally coordinated.

This purge of the conservatives marked a new departure for the regime. If June–August 1934 saw the close of the first phase in the 'seizure of power', December 1937–February 1938 marked the beginning of the end of the period of compromise with the conservative elites. This development partly reflected Hitler's growing self-confidence in matters of foreign and military policy. The fact that he had consistently been proved right and his expert advisers wrong over such matters as the introduction of conscription and the occupation of the Rhineland gave him the confidence to take the reins more firmly into his own hands. But the purge also reflected Hitler's decision to increase the pressure in a way which he knew would alienate the conservatives, who were now increasingly concerned at his departure from conventional diplomatic and strategic practices and his embarking on an extreme and hazardous course. Hitler now wanted subordinates who could be relied upon not to question his decisions and who were not inhibited by qualms deriving from morality or tradition or by concern for the preservation of the *status quo*. He was indeed embarking on a course of action which, successful or not, would inevitably shatter that delicate balance between old and new forces which had existed since 1934; in either event it would be the old which would be doomed to suffer.

The Anschluss with Austria, March 1938

Hitler's first initiative after the 'Hossbach Conference' concerned Austria. In the period after the abortive Austrian Nazi putsch of 1934 Hitler had refrained from any overt pressure on Austria in order not to jeopardize the growing *entente* with Italy. On 11 July 1936, an Austro-German agreement was concluded. Germany recognized the sovereignty of Austria, both countries agreed on non-interference in each other's domestic affairs, and Austria promised to follow a foreign policy based on the principle that 'Austria acknowledges herself to be a German State'. The Austrian Government also agreed to give a share of political responsibility to the 'national opposition'. The two Governments, however, had different interpretations of the significance of the agreement. Schuschnigg, the Austrian Chancellor, viewed it as a settlement of differences which relieved him of German pressure. Hitler, on the other hand, saw it as a means of increasing German influence in Austria.

But the process of coordination was not proceeding fast enough for Hitler and the situation was becoming more and more tense owing to the growing conflict between the Austrian Government and the Austrian Nazis. From the end of 1937, therefore, Hitler was looking for an opportunity to speed up the process. Mussolini had informed him on his visit to Germany in September 1937 that he recognized Germany's special interest in Austria. Furthermore, Lord Halifax, who was to become British Foreign Secretary on 25 February 1938, had told Hitler on 19 November 1937 that the British

Cabinet was prepared to accept alterations in the European *status quo*, provided such alterations occurred 'through the course of peaceful evolution' and he specifically mentioned as possible areas 'Danzig, Austria and Czechoslovakia'. The question remained, how was the process of 'co-ordination' to be speeded up? Hitler did not wish to risk an invasion in view of the uncertain attitude of Mussolini and the possibility of Czech or French intervention. Nor did he wish to try another *coup* on the lines of the abortive 1934 *coup* against Dollfuss.

1 *Hitler's demands to the Austrian Government*

The opportunity Hitler was seeking was provided by the Austrian Chancellor. Schuschnigg had been having increasing difficulty with the Austrian Nazis and in January 1938 the police exposed a plot by Tavs, the Nazi leader in Vienna, to stage a *coup*. Schuschnigg took his problem to von Papen, now ambassador in Vienna but in process of being recalled. Papen, who also resented the interference of the Austrian Nazis, persuaded him to seek an interview with Hitler in order to sort the matter out. When Papen informed Hitler of Schuschnigg's desire to meet him, Hitler jumped at the opportunity of putting new pressure on the Austrians. The interview took place in Berchtesgaden on 12 February. Hitler already knew through a security leak of the concessions Schuschnigg was willing to make and proceeded to browbeat him into meeting Germany's demands.

. . . II

(1) The Austrian Government shall from time to time enter into a diplomatic exchange of views on questions of foreign policy of common concern to both countries. Austria shall on request give moral, diplomatic, and press support to the desires and actions of the German Reich, to the extent that circumstances permit. The Reich Government assumes the same obligation toward the Austrian Government.

(2) Federal Chancellor Schuschnigg declares that he is willing to take State Counsellor Dr Seyss-Inquart[1] into his Government and entrust him with Security.

(3) The Federal Chancellor states that the Austrian National Socialists shall in principle have opportunity for legal activity within the framework of the Fatherland Front and all other Austrian organizations. This activity shall take place on an equal footing with all other groups, and in accordance with the constitution. Dr Seyss-Inquart has the right and the duty to see to it that the activity of the National Socialists can develop along the lines indicated above, and to take appropriate measures for this purpose.

(4) The Austrian Government shall immediately proclaim a general amnesty for all persons in Austria punished by the courts or the police because of their National Socialist activities. Such persons whose further stay in Austria appears detrimental to relations between the two countries shall, after an examination of each individual

---

[1] Arthur Seyss-Inquart, who became Minister of the Interior and Security in Schuschnigg's Government, was a Vienna lawyer with pan-German ambitions. Although not formally committed to the Austrian Nazis, he became the chief spokesman for their interests.

case and by agreement between the two Governments, be made to transfer their residence to the Reich.

(5) Disciplinary measures in the fields of pensions, annuities, and public welfare, especially the withholding or reduction of benefits, and in education as well, because of National Socialist activities, shall be revoked and restitution promised.

(6) All economic discrimination against National Socialists shall be eliminated.

(7) The unhindered observance of the press truce agreed upon between the Governments shall be assured by the appointment of Dr Wolf to an important post in the Austrian Press Service.

(8) Military relations between the German and Austrian armed forces shall be assured by the following measures:

    (a) the replacement of General Jansa by General Böhme;

    (b) a systematic exchange of officers (up to the number of 100);

    (c) regular conferences between the General Staffs;

    (d) a systematic cultivation of comradely and professional military relations.

(9) All discrimination against National Socialists, especially that affecting enrolment in and completion of military service, shall be stopped. All past discriminatory actions shall be cancelled.

(10) Preparations shall be made for the intensification of commerce between Austrian and German economies. For this purpose, Dr Fischböck shall be appointed to a leading post.

The Federal Chancellor declares that he is prepared to carry out all measures agreed upon under II (2), (4), (5), (7), by 18 February 1938, subject to the definitive reply agreed upon under II.

2 *Hitler insists on an evolutionary solution to the Austrian problem*

Hitler was satisfied that compliance with these demands would make Austria a satellite of Germany. On 26 February, therefore, when he met five leading Austrian Nazis, he ordered them to remain in Germany for the time being. Wilhelm Keppler, now Hitler's agent in Austria, recorded Hitler's statement of policy at the meeting:

> The Führer stated that in the Austrian problem he had to indicate a different course for the Party, *as the Austrian question could never be solved by a revolution.* There remained only two possibilities: force or evolutionary means. He wanted the evolutionary course to be taken, whether or not the possibility of success could today be foreseen. The Protocol signed by Schuschnigg was so far-reaching that, if completely carried out, the Austrian problem would be automatically solved. He did not now desire a solution by violent means, if it could be at all avoided, since the danger for us in the field of foreign policy became less each year and our military power greater.

Under pressure from German military manoeuvres near the frontier, Austria complied with the German demands and declared an amnesty for political prisoners, mainly Austrian Nazis. Seyss-Inquart, now Minister of the Interior, travelled to Berlin on 17 February to receive instructions from Hitler, and he increasingly dominated the Austrian Government.

Schuschnigg, however, attempted to retrieve the situation by a desperate move. On 9 March, he announced that in three days' time a plebiscite would be held on the question of the independence of Austria.

Hitler was completely taken aback by this bold move on the part of the man who had been so submissive at Berchtesgaden. So far as he was concerned, the whole question had now become a matter of prestige. Furthermore, in view of the voting conditions, he had reason to doubt whether the vote would go in Germany's favour. Voting was restricted to those over 24 (thus excluding many members of the Nazi Party, who tended to be young), there was no up-to-date electoral register, and the wording of the plebiscite question was tendentious. Hitler therefore determined to prevent the plebiscite from taking place and to remove Schuschnigg. Military plans had to be hurriedly drawn up since no preparations had been made for such an eventuality – the only existing plans dealing with Austria were to forestall a restoration of the Habsburg Monarchy, the so-called 'Operation Otto'.

3 Hitler's assurances to Mussolini

A crucial aspect of the situation was the attitude of Mussolini, who had resented not being informed of the Berchtesgaden meeting with Schuschnigg. At noon on 10 March, therefore, Hitler dispatched Prince Philip of Hesse to Rome with a letter justifying Germany's action and giving the following assurances:

I now wish solemnly to assure Your Excellency, as the Duce of Fascist Italy:
1. Consider this step only as one of national self-defence.... You too, Excellency, could not act differently if the fate of Italians were at stake....
2. In a critical hour for Italy I proved to you the steadfastness of my sympathy. Do not doubt that in the future there will be no change in this respect.
3. Whatever the consequences of the coming events may be, I have drawn a definite boundary between Germany and France and now I draw one just as definite between ourselves and Italy. It is the Brenner. This decision will never be questioned or changed.

4 Operation Otto: the invasion of Austria

At two o'clock in the morning of the 11th, Hitler issued Directive No. 1 for 'Operation Otto' which, as the first sentence indicates, still did not commit Germany to an invasion of Austria:

TOP SECRET
1. If other measures prove unsuccessful, I intend to invade Austria with armed forces to establish constitutional conditions and to prevent further outrages against the pro-German population.
2. The whole operation will be directed by myself....
5. The behaviour of the troops must give the impression that we do not want to wage war against our Austrian brothers. It is in our interest that the whole operation

shall be carried out without violence but in the form of a peaceful entry welcomed by the population. Therefore any provocation is to be avoided. If, however, resistance is offered it must be broken ruthlessly by force of arms.

Austrian units who come over to us come immediately under German command. 6. On the remaining German frontiers no security measures are to be taken for the time being.

Hitler now decided to use the threat of an invasion to see how far he could 'coordinate' Austria. He began by demanding the postponement of the plebiscite and the substitution of an alternative question. Then, when this was conceded, he insisted on the resignation of Schuschnigg. When this too was accepted, he demanded the appointment of Seyss-Inquart as Chancellor. Here, however, he came up against an obstacle in the shape of the Austrian President, Wilhelm Miklas, who refused the request and stuck to his refusal despite the threat of invasion. Finally, however, shortly before midnight, Miklas capitulated; but by then it was too late. Hitler had given the order for invasion at 8.45 p.m. and now refused to cancel it despite a request from Seyss-Inquart. In the meantime, he had received news of a broadcast by Schuschnigg ordering the Austrian army not to oppose an invasion. This freed Hitler from the odium of spilling the blood of fellow Germans and from the prospect of foreign intervention.

5 Hitler's reaction to the news of Mussolini's support

Another important factor in his decision not to cancel the invasion was a telephone call which he received from Prince Philip of Hesse at 10.25 p.m. on the 11th. Hitler's replies indicate the degree of his relief at the news of Mussolini's acquiescence in the invasion:

Hesse: I have just come back from the Palazzo Venezia. The Duce accepted the whole thing in a very friendly manner. He sends you his regards.
Hitler: Then please tell Mussolini I will never forget him for this.
Hesse: Yes.
Hitler: Never, never, never, whatever happens. As soon as the Austrian affair is settled, I shall be ready to go with him, through thick and thin, no matter what happens.
Hesse: Yes, my Führer.
Hitler: Listen, I shall make any agreement—I am no longer in fear of the terrible position which would have existed militarily in case we had got into a conflict. You may tell him that I thank him ever so much—never, never shall I forget.
Hesse: Yes, my Führer.
Hitler: I will never forget, whatever may happen. If he should ever need any help or be in any danger, he can be convinced that I shall stick to him, whatever may happen, even if the whole world were against him.
Hesse: Yes, my Führer.

6 *Hitler rejects an offer from Britain, 4 March 1938*

In the middle of the Austrian crisis Hitler received an approach from Britain. The British Government had now decided to try to buy peace in Europe by making concessions outside Europe—in Africa. The offer was prompted by a statement which Hitler had made in the course of his conversation with Halifax the previous November to the effect that 'between Germany and England there was only one difference, namely the colonial question'. The British offer was communicated to Hitler by Sir Nevile Henderson, the British ambassador in Berlin, who was received on 4 March 1938. After stressing the confidential nature of the discussions—'no information would be given the French, much less the Belgians, Portuguese or Italians'— Henderson emphasized that

the offer did not mean a commercial transaction, but an attempt to establish the basis for a genuine and cordial friendship with Germany beginning with an improvement of the atmosphere and ending with the creation of a new spirit of friendly understanding. . . . He stressed the importance of German collaboration in the pacification of Europe, to which he had already referred in previous conversations with Herr von Neurath and Herr von Ribbentrop. This pacification could be furthered by limitation of armaments and by appeasement in Czechoslovakia and Austria. . . .

Concerning the colonies, the British ambassador expressed the sincere willingness of the British Government not only to examine the colonial question, but to make progress towards its solution. Prime Minister Chamberlain had given his full personal attention to this problem. . . .

Henderson then read out a proposal for 'a scheme based on the idea of a new regime of colonial administration in a given area of Africa, roughly corresponding to the conventional zone of the Congo Basin Treaties, acceptable and applicable to all the powers concerned on exactly equal terms'.

Hitler, who according to Henderson was in a bad temper when he arrived, was not impressed. He had raised the colonial issue not for its own sake but in order to persuade Britain to give him *carte blanche* in Europe in return for his dropping it. Now the British were taking him at his word and offering him the precise opposite of what he wanted. He was not prepared to move slowly in Europe for the sake of minor gains overseas. After complaining about the British press, Hitler continued:

. . . that he personally was known as one of the warmest friends of England, but he had been ill-rewarded for this friendship. Perhaps nobody had been oftener and more grievously offended by England than he. It was, therefore, understandable that he had now withdrawn into a certain isolation, which still seemed to him more respectable than to make advances toward someone who did not want him and persistently snubbed him. . . .

Concerning central Europe, it should be noted that Germany would not tolerate any interference by third powers in the settlement of her relations with kindred countries or with countries having large German elements in their population, just as Germany would never think of interfering in the settlement of relations between England and Ireland. It was a question of preventing the continuance or the renewal of an injustice to millions of Germans. In this attempt at a settlement Germany would have to declare most seriously that she was not willing to be influenced in any way by other parties in this settlement. . . .

. . . England need not fear any interference from the Germans. Germany did not meddle in Empire affairs. She was, however, obliged to accept a negative reaction by England when Germany tried to solve her own difficulties. Any attempted settlement toward the east was met by 'No' from Britain and so was the colonial problem, and the British press in particular opposed Germany everywhere and conducted a campaign of slander against this country. . . .

On the issue of the colonies:

The Führer replied that Germany was of course primarily interested in the question of the disposition of her former colonies. Instead of establishing a new and complicated system, why not solve the colonial question in the simplest and most natural way, namely by returning the former German colonies? He, the Führer, must openly admit, however, that he did not consider the colonial problem ripe for settlement as yet, since Paris and London had declared themselves much too firmly opposed to their return. Therefore, neither did he wish to press the issue. One could wait quietly for four, six, eight or ten years. Perhaps by that time a change of mind would have taken place in Paris and London, and they would understand that the best solution was to return to Germany her rightful property acquired by purchase and Treaty. . . .

So far as Hitler was concerned, the British offer was merely a sign that his new policy of intimidating Britain into remaining neutral was proving effective. He now felt all the more prepared to move on to his next objective.

The Czech crisis, 1938–39

While driving into Austria at the time of the Anschluss, Hitler had remarked to his companion, General Halder: 'This will be very inconvenient to the Czechs.' The Anschluss had indeed seriously undermined the position of Austria's neighbour. Yet Czechoslovakia still had a powerful army, well-equipped by the Skoda arms works, and formidable fortifications. Even before 1933, Hitler had regarded the Czechs as a serious threat to Germany both because of their alliance with France and because of their proximity to important German industrial centres, including Berlin, which would be vulnerable to air attack. Moreover, Hitler's own background as a pre-1918 Austrian probably contributed to his attitude a degree of personal animosity, rooted in the Czech–German rivalry of the prewar era. This was accentuated by ideologically based resentment at the fact that Czechoslovakia was a successful democracy. But it was the strategic factor which was decisive. Germany could not dare to launch ambitious plans either in the west or in the east until Czechoslovakia had been dealt with.

The means for dealing with Czechoslovakia lay ready to hand in the country's complicated ethnic structure. The new State, created by the Versailles settlement, contained apart from Czechs and Slovaks a number of minority groups of whom the most important were the three-and-a-quarter million Germans. Most of these lived in the Sudetenland, an area on the northern border with Germany. Hitler now proceeded to use the ethnic diversity of the country as a lever with which to break it up into its ethnic components. The most obvious group with which to start were the Sudeten Germans. For years they had been clamouring for greater recognition of their rights by the Czech Government and there was some justice in their case. But the rise of Nazi Germany had given an added impetus to their demands and in 1935 the German Foreign Office had begun secretly financing the Sudeten German Party, which by 1938 had succeeded in establishing itself as the leading representative of the Sudeten Germans.

7 *Hitler's instructions to the leaders of the Sudeten Germans, 28 March 1938*

After the Anschluss, Hitler summoned the leaders of the Sudeten German Party, Konrad Henlein and Karl Frank, to Berlin and at an interview on 28 March gave them instructions for their future activity:

... The Führer stated that he intended to settle the Sudeten German problem in the not-too-distant future. He could no longer tolerate Germans being oppressed or fired upon. He told Henlein that he knew how popular he, Henlein, was and that he was the rightful leader of the Sudeten German element, and as a result of his popularity and attractiveness he would triumph over circumstances. To Henlein's objection that he, Henlein, could only be a substitute, Hitler replied: I will stand by you; from tomorrow you will be my Viceroy [*Statthalter*]. I will not tolerate difficulties being made for you by any department whatsoever within the Reich.

The purport of the instructions which the Führer has given to Henlein is that demands should be made by the Sudeten German Party which are unacceptable to the Czech Government. Despite the favourable situation created by the events in Austria, Henlein does not intend to drive things to the limit, but merely to put forward the old demands for self-administration and reparation at the Party Rally (23–24 April 1938). He wishes to reserve for later on a suggestion of the Führer's that he should demand German regiments with German officers, and military commands to be given in German. The Reich will not intervene of its own accord. Henlein himself will be responsible for events for the time being. However, there must be close cooperation. Henlein summarized his view to the Führer as follows: We must always demand so much that we can never be satisfied. The Führer approved this view. ...

8 *Henlein's eight demands*

The demands mentioned by Henlein were made at his Party's Congress at Karlsbad on 24 April and consisted of full autonomy for the Sudeten Germans. These demands were intended to be unacceptable to the Czechs but to appear eminently reasonable to foreign opinion who would then gain the impression of Czech obstinacy and injustice:

1. Restoration of complete equality of the German national group with the Czech people;
2. Recognition of the Sudeten German national group as a legal entity for the safeguarding of this position of equality within the State;
3. Confirmation and recognition of the Sudeten German settlement area;
4. Building up of Sudeten German self-government in the Sudeten German settlement area in all branches of public life in so far as questions are involved affecting the interests and affairs of the German national group;
5. Introduction of legal provisions for the protection of those Sudeten German citizens living outside the defined settlement area of their national group;
6. Removal of wrong done to the Sudeten German element since the year 1918, and compensation for damage suffered through this wrong;
7. Recognition and enforcement of the principle: German public servants in the German area;
8. Complete freedom to profess adherence to the German element and German ideology.

At this stage Hitler was in no hurry to solve the Czech question and on 20 May he presented to his generals a draft for an attack on Czechoslovakia ('Operation Green').

9 *Draft for the New Directive 'Green' (Interim)*

1. *Political assumptions*: It is not my intention to smash Czechoslovakia by military action in the immediate future without provocation, unless an unavoidable development of the political conditions *within* Czechoslovakia forces the issue, or political events in Europe create a particularly favourable opportunity which may perhaps never recur.
2. *Political possibilities for commencing the operation*: A sudden attack without convenient outward excuse and without adequate political justification cannot be considered in the present circumstances, in view of the possible results of such action.

   Operations will preferably be launched,

   either: (a) after a period of increasing diplomatic controversies and tension linked with military preparations, which will be exploited so as to shift the war guilt on the enemy.

   But even such a period of tension preceding the war will be terminated by sudden military action on our part with as much of the surprise element as possible, alike in regard to time and extent; .

   or: (b) by lightning action as the result of a serious incident which will subject

Germany to unbearable provocation and which, in the eyes of at least a part of world opinion, affords the moral justification for military measures.

Case (b) is more favourable, both from a military and a political point of view.

3. *Conclusions for the preparation of 'Operation Green'* based on the possible cases mentioned in 2(a) and (b):

(a) For the military operation it is essential to create in the first four days a strategic situation which demonstrates to enemy States which may wish to intervene the hopelessness of the Czech military position, and also provides an incentive to those States which have territorial claims upon Czechoslovakia to join in immediately against her.

In this case the intervention of Hungary and Poland against Czechoslovakia can be expected, particularly if France, as a result of Italy's unequivocal attitude on our side, fears, or at least hesitates, to unleash a European war by intervening against Germany. In all probability attempts by Russia to give Czechoslovakia military support are to be expected.

If concrete successes are not achieved in the first few days by land operations a European crisis will certainly arise. . . .

On the same day, however, rumours spread of German military preparations near the Czech border. In response, the Czech Government ordered a partial mobilization, and Britain and France warned Germany of the consequences if Hitler took any action. Hitler was forced to deny the rumours which were in fact untrue and the foreign press interpreted the affair as a climb-down by Hitler.

10 *General Jodl on Hitler's plans to invade Czechoslovakia*

General Jodl commented in his diary on the effect of this humiliation on Hitler, who returned to Berlin after a week's brooding in Berchtesgaden to tell a conference of military leaders that Czechoslovakia 'must be removed'.

After annexation of Austria, the Führer mentions that there is no hurry to solve the Czech question because Austria has to be digested first. Nevertheless, preparations for Operation Green will have to be carried out energetically; they will have to be newly prepared on the basis of the changed strategic position because of the annexation of Austria. State of preparations reported to the Führer on 21 April.

The intention of the Führer not to touch the Czech problem as yet is changed because of the Czech strategic troop concentrations of 21 May, which occurs without any German threat and without the slightest cause for it.

Because of Germany's self-restraint, its consequences lead to a loss of prestige of the Führer, which he is no longer willing to take. Therefore the new order is issued for 'Green' on 30 May.

11 *Revised version of 'Operation Green'*

II. *War on two fronts, with main effort in South-East*
(*Strategic concentration 'Green'*)

1. *Political assumptions*: It is my unalterable decision to smash Czechoslovakia by

military action in the near future. It is the business of the political leadership to await or bring about the suitable moment from a political and military point of view.

An unavoidable development of events within Czechoslovakia, or other political events in Europe providing a suddenly favourable opportunity which may never recur, may cause me to take warlike action. . . .

A covering letter from Keitel stated that the execution of the plan 'must be assured by 1 October 1938 at the latest'.

Hitler's commitment to an attack on Czechoslovakia by 1 October caused growing concern among the military leaders who doubted whether Germany would be ready for such a war. The Army Chief of Staff, General Beck, in particular, argued that a German conquest of Czechoslovakia would take much longer than envisaged, thus giving the Western Powers plenty of time to take counter-measures. His criticism had the approval of other generals, so that Brauchitsch finally overcame his hesitation and informed Hitler of Beck's views. Hitler responded by calling a conference of the younger military leaders on 10 August to try to win them over.

But Hitler failed to resolve these doubts and some of the generals began to plot his overthrow in the event of war being declared.[1] Their efforts, however, of which the extent is disputed, were nullified by the surrender of the Western Powers over Czechoslovakia. But these efforts showed that the February purge had still not entirely removed the danger from that quarter. Only success would prove decisive.

Unlike his generals, who thought purely in material terms, Hitler's assessment of the situation included the psychological dimension. During the summer he intensified the propaganda campaign against the Czechs and during August and September the German press was full of alleged Czech atrocities against Sudeten Germans. The tactics behind this campaign were to frighten the Western Powers into putting pressure on the Czechs to make concessions. It was hoped that the Czechs would refuse and that the Western Powers would then feel morally justified in washing their hands of Czechoslovakia.

12 *British hopes of a settlement with Germany*

This campaign did not fail to have its effect on the Western Powers. Both Britain and France urged the Czech Government to make concessions to the Sudeten Germans. But when, on 4 September, the Czech Government finally conceded Henlein's demand for autonomy, the Sudeten Germans, following Hitler's instructions to avoid a compromise, evaded the issue by claiming that Czech atrocities precluded further negotiations. The attitude of the British Government at this time may be gauged by an interview on 23 August between the German *chargé d'affaires* in Britain, Kordt, and Sir Horace Wilson, the Prime Minister's closest adviser. Kordt states that he

[1] For further details see above, pp. 301-2.

left Wilson in no doubt 'that we would agree to no solution which left the State intact in its present extent'. He also insisted that Czechoslovakia must end its ties with France and Russia. Yet, he says, Wilson replied that

... a policy of this nature could quite well be discussed with Great Britain. It was only necessary that this policy should not be rendered impossible by the sudden use of force by us. He completely agreed with my remarks on the present unnatural and absurd position of Czechoslovakia. If there was a possibility here of settling the question by peaceful political means, the British Government was prepared to enter into serious negotiations. He asked me if the Führer were prepared to regard such a solution of the Czechoslovak problem as the beginning of further negotiations on a larger scale. The Führer had used the simile to an Englishman (he thought it was Lord Halifax) that European culture rested on two pillars which must be linked by a powerful arch: Great Britain and Germany. Great Britain and Germany were in fact the two countries in which the greatest order reigned and which were the best governed. Both were built up on the national principle, which had been designed by nature itself as the only working principle of human relationship. The reverse of this, Bolshevism, meant anarchy and barbarism. It would be the height of folly if these two leading white races were to exterminate each other in war. Bolshevism would be the gainer thereby.

Wilson then turned to Germany's south-eastern policy. A constructive solution of the Czech question by peaceful means would leave the way clear for Germany to exert large-scale policy in the south-east. He himself was not one of those who held the view that Germany wanted to organize south-eastern Europe and then to use its resources for the annihilation of the British Empire. In these areas he could see possibilities of action for Germany better than any that could be imagined. The Balkan countries were the natural buyers of German manufactured goods, and on the other hand were the natural sources of raw materials essential to Germany. There was no sense in sending a turkey from Budapest to London instead of to Berlin. Neither had Great Britain any intention of opposing development by Germany in a south-easterly direction. Her only wish was that she should not be debarred from trade there. . . .

The implication of this conversation was clear. Britain was quite prepared for Germany to annex the Sudetenland, provided she did it by negotiation. Britain was also willing for Germany to turn the whole of south-east Europe into a German sphere of influence. This, it was hoped, would appease Germany and enable Europe to settle down into a situation where no single power would claim dominance. If, however, Germany insisted on military action, this would have to be resisted, however unwillingly, because such action would imply a German claim to hegemony which would threaten the other major powers. This was to be the basic line followed by Britain throughout the rest of the crisis.

13 *Chamberlain's meeting with Hitler at Berchtesgaden, 15 September 1938*
Hitler's campaign culminated in a violent speech to the Nuremberg Party rally on 12 September in which he demanded self-determination for the

Sudeten Germans and threatened war. This in turn brought to a head the increasing anxiety of the British and French Governments about becoming involved in a war with Germany over Czechoslovakia. Chamberlain decided that a final approach should be made to Hitler to try to reach a peaceful solution. On 15 September, therefore, the British Prime Minister flew to Hitler's residence at Berchtesgaden in Bavaria.

Hitler was delighted. Chamberlain's visit offered him the opportunity of persuading Britain to demand from Czechoslovakia the cession of the Sudetenland. When the Czechs refused, as he assumed they would, Britain would, he believed, wash its hands of Czechoslovakia, and France would be obliged to follow suit. Hitler began the interview by saying that since his youth he had had the idea of Anglo-German cooperation and that although in recent years 'this idealistic belief in Anglo-German racial affinity had suffered very severe blows' he still hoped that 'at the eleventh hour' it would be possible to achieve the agreement he had been seeking. He then came to the crux of the matter. There was, he said, only one problem outstanding, Czechoslovakia, which he would solve by one means or another. He was already forty-nine and if there had to be a world war he would prefer it now rather than later. The question was 'Would Britain agree to the secession of these areas [the Sudetenland] or would she not?' If Britain publicly announced its agreement 'then no doubt it would be possible by this means to bring about a degree of pacification in the regions in question'. Chamberlain replied that he 'recognized the principle of the detachment of the Sudeten areas' and thought that, provided this were done peacefully, it might offer a solution.

14 *Hitler presses the Hungarians to make demands of Czechoslovakia,*
   21 September 1938

Chamberlain then returned to London and under British and French pressure the Czechs agreed to the secession of the Sudetenland. This was of course not at all what Hitler had expected or desired. However, he had taken precautions against just such an eventuality. During the conversation at Berchtesgaden, Chamberlain had asked Hitler whether the Sudeten Germans were all that Germany was interested in or whether 'she was not aiming over and above this at the dismemberment of the Czechoslovak State'. Hitler replied that 'apart from the demands of the Sudeten Germans similar demands would of course be made by the Poles, Hungarians and Ukrainians living in Czechoslovakia which it would be impossible to ignore in the long run, but that he was not of course their spokesman'. Now, however, he proceeded to provoke these demands. Thus, at an interview with the Hungarian Prime Minister and Foreign Minister on 21 September, recorded by an official of the Foreign Office, he

. . . reproached the Hungarian gentlemen for the undecided attitude of Hungary in the present time of crisis. He, the Führer, was determined to settle the Czech question even at the risk of a world war. Germany demanded the entire German area. He was convinced that neither England nor France would intervene. It was Hungary's last opportunity to join in, for, if she did not, he would not be in a position to put in a word for Hungarian interests. In his opinion the best thing would be to destroy Czechoslovakia. In the long run it was quite impossible to tolerate the existence of this aircraft carrier in the heart of Europe. He presented two demands to the Hungarians: (1) that Hungary should make an immediate demand for a plebiscite in the territories which she claimed, and (2) that she should not guarantee any proposed new frontiers for Czechoslovakia. In certain circumstances Hungary might threaten to resign from the League of Nations and to establish a Freikorps. The Czechoslovak problem would be settled by the Führer in three weeks' time at the latest. . . .

The Führer declared further that he would present the German demands to Chamberlain with brutal frankness. In his opinion, action by the Army would provide the only satisfactory solution. There was, however, the danger of the Czechs submitting to every demand. . . .

Prime Minister Imrédy promised to send the Führer today a document, to be treated as confidential, in which Hungarian demands would be set down in detail. The Führer intends to make good use of this document at Godesberg in talks with the British.

Counsellor of Legation Brücklmeier gave me the further information that Ambassador Lipski had been requested to obtain a similar document from the Polish Government. . . .

15 *The meeting between Hitler and Chamberlain at Bad Godesberg,*
    22 September 1938

Chamberlain returned to Germany on 22 September with the Czech agreement to secession in his pocket. At the meeting with Hitler at Bad Godesberg, according to the postwar account of Ivone Kirkpatrick, Head of Chancery at the British Embassy in Berlin, who was present, Chamberlain began by proudly announcing that he had secured the Czech Government's consent:

. . . Mr Chamberlain recalled that at Berchtesgaden Hitler had declared that he would be satisfied with nothing but self-determination, that was to say Anschluss, for the Sudeten Germans. He himself had been unable to give an immediate reply, but he had undertaken to consult his Cabinet and the French Government. He had done so and was happy to say that the British and French Governments agreed in principle. Moreover they had been able just in time to secure the assent of the Czechoslovak Government. The question of principle having been settled, it only remained to discuss the ways and means of transferring the territory in an orderly manner. On this point he had proposals to make which would doubtless be the subject of discussion at the present meeting. The statement was then translated into German. As Schmidt[1] finished speaking, Mr Chamberlain looked inquiringly at Hitler. But Hitler merely gazed down the table and said in a dry rasping voice:

[1] Paul Schmidt, Hitler's official interpreter.

'Es tut mir leid, aber das geht nicht mehr.' And with these words he pushed his chair back from the table, crossed his legs, folded his arms and turned to scowl at Mr Chamberlain. Schmidt translated: 'I am very sorry, but all that is no longer any use.' There was a long pause of pained silence.

That was the atmosphere in which the Godesberg peace negotiations began. Mr Chamberlain, when he had recovered from his amazement, acidly inquired why an arrangement which had been declared satisfactory to Germany a few days before had now become unacceptable. Hitler rather lamely replied that Mr Chamberlain's proposals were no longer sufficient because in the meantime Hungary and Poland had tabled new claims on Czechoslovakia. Hungary and Poland, he added, were good friends and Germany would insist that their claims must be met.

We seemed to have reached a deadlock, but for internal reasons Hitler did not want an early breakdown. So after a considerable period of ill-tempered floundering on both sides he suggested that it might be well to have a look at Mr Chamberlain's proposals in regard to the ways and means of meeting the German demands. Hitler listened to these proposals with increasing impatience and replied that he must decline to accept them on the ground that they involved an intolerable delay. Whilst we were arguing, he said, Germans were being killed by the Czechs, and that was a state of affairs for which he could not be responsible. At intervals little scraps of paper were sent in to Hitler reporting fresh outrages against the Sudeten Germans. No, he shouted, the territory within the so-called language boundary must be ceded at once, without any delay, and occupied by German troops. Mr Chamberlain said that he could not accept an immediate German military irruption. Let Hitler send in police if public order were threatened, but British opinion would be outraged by a military occupation. Hitler must remember that Britain was not ruled by a dictator and that he should take into account the Prime Minister's situation before Parliament and the public. Hitler characteristically retorted that his rule depended on the suffrage of the German people and Mr Chamberlain must take into account the rising anger of the German nation at the Czech maltreatment of Germans. The argument waxed hotly and Schmidt had a trying time.

During his conversation with Chamberlain, Hitler had insisted that the Czechs should evacuate the Sudetenland between 26 and 28 September. On the following day, he postponed the date to 1 October. He claimed this to be a great concession but in fact it made no difference since his military plans for an invasion had all along been fixed for 1 October. Chamberlain agreed to put Hitler's terms to the British and Czech Governments. On 25 September, the British Cabinet decided they could not recommend the terms to Czechoslovakia and, on the following day, Britain promised France support in the event of her becoming involved in a war with Germany in defence of Czechoslovakia. On the same day, Germany was informed of the rejection of Hitler's demands by the Czechs. Yet, far from deflecting Hitler from his proposed course of action, this news made him even more belligerent. In a speech in the Berlin Sports Palace that evening he outdid himself in violent abuse of the Czechs. He warned that he had made the Czech Prime Minister 'an offer which is nothing but the carrying out of what he himself has promised. The decision now lies in his hands: Peace or War.' He ended, however, by publicly thanking Chamberlain 'for all his efforts' and assuring him once more 'that at the moment when Czechoslovakia solves her problems, that is to say, when the Czechs have come to terms with their other minorities, and that peaceably and not through oppression, then I shall have no further interest in the Czech State. And I can guarantee him we want no Czechs.'

16 *The Munich Agreement, 29 September 1938*

In the days following the Sports Palace speech, however, a number of developments caused Hitler to draw back from the brink. In the first place, news came of the beginning of French mobilization and of the mobilization of the British fleet, suggesting that the Western Powers were not bluffing. Moreover, the Army and Navy leaders made clear their doubts of Germany's ability to face a war with Britain and France while simultaneously engaged against Czechoslovakia. Secondly, Göring, whose influence with Hitler was considerable, advised against war, and Mussolini, while assuring Hitler of his support, made clear his concern. Finally, Hitler observed with his own eyes the unenthusiastic response of the German people to the military preparations. Thus, when the British Government appealed to Mussolini to mediate and when Mussolini gave his support to the idea of an international conference to discuss the issue, Hitler grudgingly agreed. It was arranged that a conference between Germany, Italy, Britain and France should be held immediately in Munich. The conference took place on 29 September and the basis for discussion was provided by a memorandum which had been drafted by Neurath, Göring and Weizsäcker in order to circumvent Ribbentrop who was opposed to the idea of a con-ference. The memorandum was then shown to Hitler and, after its approval, was passed to the Italians who then produced it at the conference as if it was their own. Agreement was finally reached on the early morning of the 30th:

Germany, the United Kingdom, France and Italy, taking into consideration the agreement which has already been reached in principle for the cession to Germany of the Sudeten German territory, have agreed on the following terms and conditions governing the said cession and the measures consequent thereon, and by this agreement they each hold themselves responsible for the steps necessary to secure fulfilment:
1. The evacuation shall begin on 1 October.
2. The United Kingdom, France and Italy agree that the evacuation of the terri-tory shall be completed by 10 October, without any existing installations having been destroyed, and that the Czechoslovak Government shall be held responsible for carrying out the evacuation without damage to the said installations.
3. The conditions governing the evacuation shall be laid down in detail by an international commission composed of representatives of Germany, the United Kingdom, France, Italy and Czechoslovakia.
4. The occupation by stages of the predominantly German territory by German troops shall begin on 1 October. The four territories marked on the attached map

will be occupied by German troops in the following order: The territory marked No. I on 1 and 2 October, the territory marked No. II on 2 and 3 October, the territory marked No. III on 3, 4 and 5 October, the territory marked No. IV on 6 and 7 October. The remaining territory of preponderantly German character shall be ascertained by the aforesaid international commission forthwith and shall be occupied by German troops by 10 October.

5. The international commission referred to in Paragraph 3 shall determine the territories in which a plebiscite is to be held. These territories shall be occupied by international bodies until the plebiscite has been completed. The same commission shall fix the conditions on which the plebiscite is to be held, taking as a basis the conditions of the Saar plebiscite. The commission shall also fix a date, not later than the end of November, on which the plebiscite shall be held.

6. The final determination of the frontiers shall be carried out by the international commission. This commission shall also be entitled to recommend to the four Powers, Germany, the United Kingdom, France and Italy, in certain exceptional cases, minor modifications in the strictly ethnographical determination of the zones which are to be transferred without plebiscite.

7. There shall be a right of option into and out of the transferred territories, the option to be exercised within six months from the date of this agreement. A German–Czechoslovak commission shall determine the details of the option, consider ways of facilitating the transfer of population and settle questions of principle arising out of the said transfer.

8. The Czechoslovak Government shall within a period of four weeks from the date of this agreement release from their military and police forces any Sudeten Germans who may wish to be released, and the Czechoslovak Government shall within the same period release Sudeten German prisoners who are serving terms of imprisonment for political offences.

Annex to the Agreement

His Majesty's Government in the United Kingdom and the French Government have entered into the above agreement on the basis that they stand by the offer, contained in Paragraph 6 of the Anglo-French proposals of 19 September, relating to an international guarantee of the new boundaries of the Czechoslovak State against unprovoked aggression.

When the question of the Polish and Hungarian minorities in Czechoslovakia has been settled, Germany and Italy for their part shall give a guarantee to Czechoslovakia.

The Munich Agreement, then, enabled Hitler to march his troops into the Sudetenland on 1 October after all. The fact that this was to be done in stages after international agreement made no difference in practice. The plebiscite envisaged in paragraph 5 was never held and the cession of the Sudetenland, which was followed on 10 October by the cession of Teschen to Poland, meant that Czechoslovakia was now totally exposed to any future attack since the area ceded included the fortifications and the mountains which formed a natural barrier.

17 *Hitler's secret speech to the German press, 10 November 1938*

It has been disputed among historians whether or not Hitler was bluffing all along during the Munich crisis. The majority now believe that he was not bluffing and that he backed out only at the last minute and subsequently regretted the fact. This is the interpretation followed here, and there is evidence from several sources to suggest that, far from feeling elated about the agreement as one would expect had he been bluffing, he in fact resented being, as he thought, cheated of a military victory. Thus, according to Ivone Kirkpatrick, during the conference 'he was obviously in a black mood, furious with the whole business', and on his return to Berlin Schacht overheard him remarking to SS officers: 'That fellow Chamberlain has spoiled my entry into Prague.' On the other hand, it is clear from a speech which he made six weeks later that at any rate by then he had not only become reconciled to being cheated of a war, but was now actually rather proud of his bloodless victory. The following secret speech made to a gathering of 400 representatives of the German press in Munich on 10 November 1938 gives an insight into his thinking at this time. His emphasis on the need to mobilize the nation psychologically is a significant indication of his concern about the lack of enthusiasm shown by the German people for war:

We have set ourselves several tasks this year which we want to achieve through our propaganda—and I consider the press present here among the top instruments of propaganda.

First, the gradual preparation of the German people themselves. For years circumstances have compelled me to talk about almost nothing but peace. Only by continually stressing Germany's desire for peace and her peaceful intentions could I achieve freedom for the German people bit by bit and provide the armaments which were always necessary before the next step could be taken. It is obvious that such peace propaganda also has its doubtful aspects, for it can only too easily give people the idea that the present regime really identifies itself with the determination to preserve peace at all costs. That would not only lead to a wrong assessment of the aims of this system, but above all it might lead to the German nation, instead of being prepared for every eventuality, being filled with a spirit of defeatism which in the long run would inevitably undermine the success of the present regime. It was only out of necessity that for years I talked of peace. But it was now necessary gradually to re-educate the German people psychologically and to make it clear that there are things which *must* be achieved by force if peaceful means fail. To do this, it was necessary not to advocate force as such, but to depict to the German people certain diplomatic events in such a light that the inner voice of the nation itself gradually began to call for the use of force. That meant, to portray certain events in such a way that the conviction automatically grew in the minds of the broad mass of the people: If things cannot be settled amicably, force will have to be used, but in any case things cannot go on like this. This work took months; it was begun according to plan, carried out according to plan, and intensified. Many people did not understand this, gentlemen; many thought all this was rather exaggerated. Those were the over-cultured intellectuals who have no idea, even when the thunder and lightning start, how one gets a nation to stand together.

... Furthermore, it was necessary to use the press and other propaganda methods to influence the enemy which confronted us, namely Czechoslovakia. There may have been some people who did not understand many of the measures taken during the past few years. Gentlemen! After 21 May it was quite clear that this problem had to be solved one way or another [*so oder so*]! Each further postponement could only make it more difficult and make its solution more bloody. Now we know also that it was, I would say, the last moment at which this problem could be solved in the way it was solved. One thing is certain, gentlemen: a delay of only one or two years would have put us into an extraordinarily difficult situation from the military point of view. Our enemies in the rest of the world would have remained. The aircraft carrier in the heart of Germany, i.e. Czechoslovakia, would have strengthened and fortified itself more and more, and gradually all the additional weapons produced by our rearmament programme would have been swallowed up by the task of having to solve this problem first before tackling any other. . . .

I would like to state now that this propaganda has worked superbly this year, quite superbly and that the press has got completely used to this work and that I personally looked through the numerous German papers each day with great pleasure. . . . The greatness of this success became clearest to me at that moment when, for the first time, I stood in the middle of the Czech fortifications. Then it became clear to me what it means to capture nearly 2000 km. of fortifications without having fired a shot. Gentlemen, this time we really have gained 10 million people with over 100,000 square km. through propaganda in the service of an idea. That is tremendous!

Gentlemen, it used to be my greatest pride to have built up a Party that stood behind me steadfastly and fanatically even in bad times—especially in bad times. That was my greatest pride and a tremendous comfort. We must get the whole German people to do this. They must learn to believe in final victory so *fanatically* that even if we were occasionally defeated, the nation would regard it from an overall point of view and say: This is a temporary phase; victory will be ours in the end! It was a Prussian general who best illustrated this character trait—Blücher, the man who was perhaps more defeated than anyone else, but who had a fanatical belief in final victory, and that was what mattered. We must educate our whole nation to that end. They must be educated to the absolute, steadfast, optimistic belief that in the end we will achieve all that is necessary. We can only succeed in this by a continuous appeal to the strength of the nation, by stressing the qualities of the nation and by disregarding the so-called negative sides as much as possible.

To achieve this, it is also necessary for the press in particular to hold blindly to the principle: The leadership is always right! Gentlemen, we must all be allowed to make mistakes. Newspapermen are not exempt from that danger either. But all of us can only survive if we do not let the world see our mistakes but only the positive things. In other words, it is necessary, by removing any possibility of admitting mistakes or of argument, always to stress the correctness of the leadership. That is the decisive point. . . .

18 *Hitler's military directive for the liquidation of the remainder of the Czech State*

Despite his bloodless victory, however, Hitler was by no means satisfied with the Munich Agreement. In particular, he had no intention of giving the guarantee of the boundaries of Czechoslovakia contained in the annex to the agreement. He still found the existence of an independent Czechoslovakia intolerable and it was really only a question of time before he took steps to eliminate it. This intention became clear in the military directive which he signed on 21 October 1938:

The future tasks of the Wehrmacht and the preparations for the conduct of war resulting from these tasks will be laid down by me in a later directive.

Until this directive comes into force, the Wehrmacht must at all times be prepared for the following eventualities:

1. securing the frontiers of the German Reich and protection against surprise air attacks;
2. liquidation of the remainder of the Czech State;
3. the occupation of Memelland. . . .

2. LIQUIDATION OF THE REMAINDER OF THE CZECH STATE
It must be possible to smash at any time the remainder of the Czech State should it pursue an anti-German policy. . . .

In fact, the new Czech Government went out of its way to be accommodating towards Germany. But this was not enough for Hitler. As far as he was concerned, the fact that Czechoslovakia retained some independence and the fact that it still retained a significant army and military resources meant that it represented a troublesome wedge in Germany's south-eastern flank which would still pose a threat to Germany in the event of her being involved in war on her other frontiers. In addition, there was his personal resentment against the Czechs which made him sensitive to the least provocation. In short, after Munich the question was only how and when the remnants of Czechoslovak independence could be destroyed.

19 *Hitler presses the Slovaks to demand independence*

As far as the methods were concerned, the same weapon lay ready to hand that he had used so successfully before—ethnic disaffection. Whereas previously he had used the Sudeten Germans as a lever against the Czech Government, now he proposed to use the Slovaks in a similar role. After Munich, the Czech Government had been forced to give a considerable degree of autonomy to the Slovaks, and Hitler now proceeded to encourage the Slovaks to claim complete independence. Eventually, the Czechs responded to the growing Slovak separatism by dismissing the Slovak Government on 9 March 1939 and by declaring martial law. The new Slovak Government opposed secession and in this it appears to have had the support of the majority of the Slovak people. Hitler, however, had no intention of allowing this opportunity to pass. He now summoned the former Slovak Prime Minister, Tiso, and presented him with an ultimatum: he was either to declare that the Slovaks desired independence, or to stand by and let Hungary, which had designs on Slovakia, take over the country:

... He wanted a final confirmation as to what Slovakia really wanted. He did not want Hungary to reproach him for preserving something which did not want to be preserved.... It was a question not of days but of hours. He had previously said that if Slovakia wished to become independent he would support and even guarantee her efforts in that direction. He would keep his promise so long as Slovakia clearly expressed the desire for independence. If she hesitated or refused to be separated from Prague, he would leave the fate of Slovakia to events for which he was no longer responsible. Then he would look after German interests only, and they did not extend east of the Carpathians. Germany had nothing to do with Slovakia. She had never belonged to Germany.
... The Reich Foreign Minister also emphasized that a decision was a matter of hours, not days. He handed to the Führer a report just received announcing Hungarian troop movements on the Slovak frontier. The Führer read this report, told Tiso of its contents and expressed the hope that Slovakia would reach a decision soon. ...

Tiso then returned to Slovakia and pushed the declaration of independence through Parliament under the threat of German occupation if it were not accepted.

Hitler was genuine in his assurance that Germany had no interest in Slovakia. It was a predominantly agricultural area and its situation posed no strategic threat to Germany. He was therefore content for it to remain a satellite of Germany. It was the Czech areas of Bohemia and Moravia, highly industrialized and strategically important, whose independence Hitler was determined to eliminate. The significance for Hitler of Slovakia's demand for independence was that it enabled the British and French Governments to evade their Munich guarantee of the boundaries of Czechoslovakia on the ground that the State had already disintegrated from within.

20 *Hitler justifies the occupation of the rest of Czechoslovakia*

On 14 March, the Czech Government made a desperate attempt to avert the German invasion. President Hácha and the Foreign Minister, Chvalkovsky, travelled to Berlin to make a direct appeal to Hitler. Hitler, however, had already given orders for the invasion to begin. His justification of his action to Hácha significantly laid stress on the size of the Czech army:

... In the autumn he had not wished to draw the final conclusions because he had thought a coexistence possible, but already at that time, and later during his conversations with Chvalkovsky, he had left no doubt that if the Beneš[1] tendencies did

---
[1] The former Czech President.

not disappear completely he would destroy this State ruthlessly. Chvalkovsky had understood that at the time and had begged the Führer to have patience. The Führer had recognized this, but months had passed without any change taking place. The new regime had not succeeded in making the old one disappear psychologically; he saw this in the press, in propaganda by word of mouth, in the dismissal of Germans, and in many acts which were to him symbolic of the whole situation. He had not understood this at first, but when it had become clear to him he definitely drew his conclusions, for, had things continued to develop along these lines, the relationship with Czechoslovakia would, in a few years, again be exactly where it had been six months ago. Why had Czechoslovakia not at once reduced her Army to reasonable proportions? Such an Army was a tremendous burden for such a State; it made sense only if it supported the State in its role in foreign affairs. As, however, the Czechoslovak State no longer had a role in foreign affairs, such an Army had no justification. He quoted several examples which had proved to him that the spirit in the Army had not changed. This symptom had convinced him that the Army also was a heavy political liability for the future. Add to this the relentless development of a situation of economic stringency, and furthermore the protests from the minorities who could no longer put up with a life of this kind. . . .

21 *The Czech-German communiqué issued on the occupation of the rest of Czechoslovakia, 15 March 1939*

President Hácha was then threatened with the bombing of Prague if he did not order the Czech troops to lay down their arms. After suffering a heart attack, from which he was revived by an injection from Hitler's doctor, he agreed to sign a communiqué which in its unctuous mendacity was remarkable even for the Nazis:

. . . The conviction was unanimously expressed on both sides that the aim of all efforts must be the safeguarding of calm, order and peace in this part of central Europe. The Czechoslovak President declared that, in order to serve this object and to achieve ultimate pacification, he confidently placed the fate of the Czech people and country in the hands of the Führer of the German Reich. The Führer accepted this declaration and expressed his intention of taking the Czech people under the protection of the German Reich and of guaranteeing them an autonomous development of their ethnic life as suited to their character.

PART VI   Germany at War, 1939–45

19 The Successful *Blitzkriege*: Poland and France, 1939–40

The attack on Poland

One of the factors prompting Hitler to destroy the remnants of Czechoslovakia had been the desire to put pressure on Poland. The attitude of Poland would clearly be crucial for future German action either in the east or in the west. Hitler could attack neither France nor Russia without first being sure of Poland. During the winter of 1938–39, he appears to have been moving in the direction of an attack on Russia. Thus he cultivated good relations with France which, on 6 December, culminated in a joint declaration guaranteeing the existing frontier, that is, the abandonment by Germany of Alsace and Lorraine. In return, he clearly hoped that France would cease to interest herself in Eastern Europe despite her alliances with Poland and the U.S.S.R. German relations with Poland had been good since the Non-Aggression Pact of 1934 and, after the Munich Agreement, Poland had acquired Teschen from Czechoslovakia with Germany's connivance. But Hitler now wanted guarantees of Poland's good behaviour; he wanted to turn Poland into a satellite of Germany. Once Poland had accepted this position, he could undertake an attack on Russia with Poland as an ally, or if necessary turn against France.

1 *The German demands on Poland*

As far as Hitler was concerned, the test of Polish willingness to become a satellite was whether or not she would agree to the return of Danzig, a German-speaking city placed by the Treaty of Versailles under the control of the League of Nations, and to a road and rail link through the 'Polish Corridor' which separated East Prussia from the rest of Germany. These demands were first put in a friendly way by Ribbentrop at a meeting with the Polish ambassador, Josef Lipski, on 24 October 1938. Lipski gave an evasive reply. But the Germans were not to be put off and when the Polish Foreign Minister, Beck, visited Berlin in January 1939, Hitler repeated these demands, at the same time hinting at their common hostility to Russia and that Germany would have no objection to Polish acquisitions in the Ukraine:

... On the part of Germany he could state emphatically that there had not been the slightest change in Germany's relations with Poland as based on the non-aggression declaration of 1934. Germany would under all circumstances be interested in maintaining a strong nationalist Poland, quite irrespective of developments in Russia. Regardless of whether Russia was Bolshevist or Tsarist or anything else, Germany's attitude towards that country would always be one of the greatest caution and for that reason she was decidedly interested in seeing Poland's position preserved. Purely from the military point of view the existence of a strong Polish Army meant a considerable easing of Germany's position; the divisions stationed by Poland at the Russian frontier saved Germany just so much additional military expenditure. . . .

From the German point of view the remaining problem in direct German–Polish relations, apart from the question of Memel, which would be settled in the German sense (it appeared that the Lithuanians intended to cooperate towards a sensible solution), was that of the Corridor and Danzig, on which Germany was psychologically very sensitive. . . .

Danzig is German, will always remain German, and will sooner or later become part of Germany. He could give the assurance, however, that no *fait accompli* would be engineered in Danzig.

With regard to the Corridor . . . the necessity for Poland to have access to the sea had definitely to be recognized. In the same way, however, to have a connexion with East Prussia was a necessity for Germany; here too, by using entirely new methods of solution one could perhaps do justice to the interests of both.

If it should be possible on this rational basis to bring about a definitive settlement of the individual problems, which would of course have to do justice to both sides, the time would have come to supplement in a positive sense, in the manner of the agreements with France, the somewhat negative declaration of 1934 by a German guarantee of Poland's frontiers clearly laid down in a Treaty. Poland would then obtain the great advantage of having her frontier with Germany, including the Corridor, secured by Treaty. . . .

Beck's reply, however, was evasive. The Poles were determined to resist their inclusion in Germany's sphere of influence and recognized equally with the Germans that to yield on Danzig would be a tacit acceptance of satellite status. Their attitude has often been interpreted as springing from arrogance; it was certainly based on a gross overestimation of their own strength, most clearly demonstrated by their continuing refusal to contemplate an agreement with Russia. In the light of Hitler's actions during 1938, however, their suspicions of his intentions are more understandable.

2 *Hitler's decision on war with Poland, 23 May 1939*

Three months after Beck's interview with Hitler came the German invasion of Czechoslovakia in which Hitler's motive was probably partly the desire to exert pressure on Poland to come to terms. If so, the impact of the invasion was the reverse of that intended. For Britain, now totally disillusioned by Hitler's annexation for the first time of non-German-speaking territory, decided to try to retrieve the situation by issuing a warning to Germany against further aggression. This warning took the form of a British guarantee of those countries which were regarded as most threatened by Germany—

Poland, Romania and Greece. With a guarantee from Britain (31 March) in their pocket, the Poles were even less willing than before to accede to the German demands.

Hitler was furious at the British guarantee and on 3 April, seeing that now there was much less likelihood of Polish acquiescence, he ordered military preparations for an attack on Poland to begin at any time after 1 September. The directive for 'Operation White' (the attack on Poland), which was issued on 11 April, did not commit Germany to war. Its preamble stated that 'German relations with Poland continue to be based on the principle of avoiding any disturbances. Should Poland, however, change her policy toward Germany, which so far has been based on the same principles as our own, and adopt a threatening attitude toward Germany, a final settlement might become necessary in spite of the Treaty in force with Poland. The aim then will be to destroy Polish military strength, and create in the east a situation which satisfies the requirements of national defence. . . . '

On 23 May, however, when Hitler addressed twelve senior commanders together with Admiral Raeder and Göring it appeared that he regarded war with Poland as inevitable and that the main aim of German diplomacy was to isolate her. Notes were taken by Hitler's adjutant, Rudolf Schmundt:

After six years the present position is as follows:
With minor exceptions German national unification has been achieved. Further successes cannot be achieved without bloodshed.

Poland will always be on the side of our adversaries. Despite the friendship agreement Poland has always intended to exploit every opportunity against us.

Danzig is not the objective. It is a matter of expanding our living space in the east, of making our food supplies secure, and of solving the problem of the Baltic states. To provide sufficient food you must have sparsely settled areas. This is fertile soil, whose surpluses will be very much increased by German, thorough management.

No other such possibility can be seen in Europe. . . .

The Polish regime will not resist pressure from Russia. Poland sees danger in a German victory over the west and will try and deprive us of our victory.

There is therefore no question of sparing Poland, and the decision remains *to attack Poland at the first suitable opportunity.*

We cannot expect a repetition of Czechoslovakia. There will be war. The task is to isolate Poland. Success in isolating her will be decisive. Therefore, the Führer must reserve to himself the final command to attack. There must be no simultaneous conflict with the West (France and England).

If it is not certain that a German–Polish conflict will not lead to war with the West, then the struggle will be directed in the first instance against England and France.

Basic principle: conflict with Poland, beginning with attack on Poland, will be successful only if the West keeps out. If that is impossible, then it is better to attack the West and finish off Poland at the same time.

It will be the task of dexterous diplomacy [*geschickte Politik*] to isolate Poland. . . .

Hitler's first diplomatic success in his preparation for war with Poland was in securing at long last an alliance with Italy. During May, Mussolini had overcome his earlier qualms about tying himself in this way (Berlin had proposed the alliance in October 1938). His annexation of Albania in April, which had been opposed by the Western Powers, had driven him into greater dependence on Germany and so he now agreed to conclude what came to be known as the Pact of Steel on 22 May 1939. Hitler was delighted since he hoped it would increase the pressure on Britain and France to remain neutral.

3 The Non-Aggression Treaty between Germany and the Soviet Union, 23 August 1939

But if Hitler wanted to isolate Poland then clearly an agreement with Russia was essential. For, failing Russian cooperation, the Western Powers would find it impossible to come to Poland's assistance without declaring war on Germany. Britain and Russia were already engaged in negotiations, but neither side took them very seriously. Chamberlain was extremely hostile to the Soviet Union on ideological grounds and also shared the contemptuous view of Soviet military power held by the British General Staff. For Stalin had recently purged several thousand officers from the Red Army and as a result it was widely assumed outside Russia that the Red Army would be ineffective. In any case, the Poles were extremely suspicious of the Soviet Union. Russia too was very wary of committing herself. The abandonment of Czechoslovakia by the Western Powers at Munich and the exclusion of the Soviet Union from the conference had given her good grounds for suspicion. Russia was afraid that Britain and France wished to involve her in a war with Germany while they came to terms with Hitler. In a speech to the Communist Party Congress on 10 March, Stalin had warned that he would 'not let our country be drawn into conflict by warmongers, whose custom it is to let others pull their chestnuts out of the fire'. And in May he replaced Litvinov, who had favoured a pact with the Western Powers, with Molotov as Foreign Minister.

Ribbentrop and Hitler rightly interpreted these moves as signs that the Russians might be prepared to alter their policy towards Germany. German-Russian negotiations proceeded on and off during the summer until, at the end of July, prompted by the initiation of Anglo-Russian military conversations, Germany began to press for an agreement. During August, Hitler, who had now committed himself to an attack on Poland within weeks, became increasingly impatient and, after a personal approach to Stalin, ordered the acceptance of Molotov's draft of a non-aggression pact and agreed to the drawing up of a protocol defining respective spheres of interest in Eastern Europe. On 22 August, Ribbentrop flew to Moscow with Hitler's authority to divide up Poland and Eastern Europe with Russia, and the agreement signed on the 23rd included a secret annex which contained the details of this division of spoils:

The Government of the German Reich
and
The Government of the Union of Soviet Socialist Republics,

directed by the wish to strengthen the cause of peace between Germany and the U.S.S.R. and proceeding upon the basic provisions of the Treaty of Neutrality concluded between Germany and the U.S.S.R. in April 1926, have reached the following agreement:

Article 1. The two contracting parties undertake to refrain from any act of violence, any aggressive action, or any attack against one another, whether individually or jointly with other powers.

Article 2. In case any of the contracting parties should become the object of war-like acts on the part of a third power, the other contracting party will not support that third power in any form.

Article 3. The Governments of the two contracting parties will in future remain in contact with each other through continuous consultation in order to inform each other concerning questions affecting their mutual interests.

Article 4. Neither of the two contracting parties will participate in any grouping of powers which is indirectly or directly aimed against the other party.

Article 5. Should disputes or conflicts arise between the contracting parties regarding questions of any kind whatsoever, the two parties would clear away these disputes or conflicts solely by means of friendly exchanges of views or if necessary by arbitration commissions.

Article 6. The present Treaty is concluded for a period of ten years with the provision that unless one of the contracting parties denounces it one year before the end of this period the duration of the validity of this treaty is to be regarded as automatically prolonged for another five years.

Article 7. The present Treaty is to be ratified within the shortest possible time. The documents of ratification are to be exchanged in Berlin. The Treaty becomes effective immediately upon signature.

SECRET ADDITIONAL PROTOCOL

On the occasion of the signature of the Non-Aggression Treaty between the German Reich and the Union of Soviet Socialist Republics, the undersigned plenipotentiaries of the two parties discussed in strictly confidential conversations the question of the delimitation of their respective spheres of interest in Eastern Europe. These conversations led to the following result:

1. In the event of a territorial and political transformation in the territories belonging to the Baltic States (Finland, Estonia, Latvia, Lithuania), the northern frontier of Lithuania shall represent the frontier of the spheres of interest both of Germany and the U.S.S.R. In this connexion the interest of Lithuania in the Vilna territory is recognized by both parties.

2. In the event of a territorial and political transformation of the territories belonging to the Polish State, the spheres of interest of both Germany and the U.S.S.R. shall be bounded approximately by the line of the rivers Narev, Vistula and San.

The question whether the interests of both parties make the maintenance of an independent Polish State appear desirable and how the frontiers of this State should be drawn can be definitely determined only in the course of further political developments.

In any case both Governments will resolve this question by means of a friendly understanding.

3. With regard to south-eastern Europe, the Soviet side emphasizes its interests in Bessarabia. The German side declares complete political *désintéressement* in these territories.

4. This Protocol will be treated by both parties as strictly secret.

4 Hitler's speech to the Commanders-in-Chief, 22 August 1939[1]

Hitler was convinced that the Non-Aggression Pact with the Soviet Union would ensure that Britain and France would not fulfil their guarantee to Poland. Reports from German visitors to Britain and from the German ambassador had already given evidence of Britain's anxiety to reach an agreement with Germany. On 22 August, the day before the signing of the Nazi-Soviet Pact, Hitler addressed his commanders in his mountain retreat near Berchtesgaden. His speech offers a good insight into his thinking at this time, his assessment of the international situation and the motives which prompted him to act. No official minutes were made at the conference and three separate versions of Hitler's speech have survived which differ from one another to some extent. The version given here is that presented to the Nuremberg Trial and is considered the most reliable. It was compiled from notes made by Admiral Boehm.

The point of the speech was for the Führer to give his assessment of the political situation, to express his views and thereby to strengthen confidence in his decision. For he was determined to act.

In the spring he had intended to postpone the solution of the Polish question, to put it on ice, so to speak, in order first to engage in the conflict in the west which he regarded as *inevitable*. However, as a politician one must not bind oneself to a fixed schedule, one must remain flexible. The preconditions for his original intentions had changed and, moreover, he has never believed that Poland would have kept the Non-Aggression Pact, if Germany had been tied by involvement somewhere else. This was clear from the map and also from the recent attitude of the press which revealed the Poles' most intimate thoughts.

Although this conflict with the Poles was *unwelcome*, it was nevertheless necessary and the political situation was now more favourable to Germany than it might be in a few years' time and for the following reasons:

1. First of all there were the personal factors in our favour:

(a) His own personality as a valuable factor in the life of the German people. He has united the German people, possesses their confidence, and his authority is accepted by them to a degree which no successor would be capable of achieving. At any moment he might be the victim of an enemy or a lunatic, or die of natural

[1] See also the versions in *Documents on German Foreign Policy*, series D, vol. vii, docs. 192 and 193 and *British Documents*, third series, vol. vii, no. 314, enclosure.

causes. His existence therefore was of great importance for the carrying out of the tasks.

(b) The same was true of Mussolini. It was not Treaties with Italy which were decisive but personalities. Mussolini was responsible for her loyalty to the Treaty. The Court was opposed to anything which it regarded as adventurous and would prefer to rest content with what it had already acquired. Mussolini was a man without nerves, as was proved by the Abyssinian conflict.

(c) Franco's personality was also important. The Führer has never expected anything more than benevolent neutrality from Spain. It is still subject to the party interests of several parties. Franco alone guarantees unity and a degree of political continuity.

2. The other side, that of our opponents, presents a negative picture, so far as personalities are concerned. Fortunately for us there were no outstanding personalities.

It is difficult to take decisions which involve spilling blood but for us it is comparatively easy since for us there is only the choice of going through with it or of losing. We can hold out in the present economic situation and with all our resources under strain for perhaps ten or fifteen years, but no longer. We are therefore compelled to take decisions.

Such decisions are much more difficult for our opponents. Their stake would be far greater, inconceivably great, and they would gain virtually nothing.

Our opponents have leaders who are below the average of what one may expect of politicians. They are not men of action.

England has a number of areas of tension: in the Mediterranean, tension with Italy; in Asia, with Japan; in the Near East, England has caused alarm to the Moslems.

If ever the term 'Pyrrhic victory' could be appropriately applied to a nation, then it was to the English victory in 1918. She lost her maritime supremacy and shared it with America, her empire was shaken, Ireland is acquiring independence, the Union of South Africa is also trying to achieve it, the appetite for it in India is on the increase.

Two friends from the 1914–18 war have split off, Russia and Italy.

As far as trade is concerned, England, which thought it would become even richer through a war, has suffered a disappointment. As a result of rearmament, all countries have built their own industries. England's exports have been made more difficult and the old order has been upset.

France is also in a bad situation, chiefly as a result of the lowering of her birthrate.

Other factors in our favour are the occupation of Albania, which in Italy's hands has the effect of keeping Yugoslavia in check. But even Yugoslavia is weaker than Serbia was in 1914, since the Croatians create internal division. Romania is weaker than it used to be, and Hungary and Bulgaria are rearming and mobilizing on its frontiers. Turkey has lost its one great man, Atatürk; the present rulers have petty minds or are under the influence of the pound sterling.

Seen as a whole, therefore, there are a number of favourable circumstances which may not prevail in three years' time.

There is also a psychological aspect to be considered: the last three great events involving Austria, the Sudetenland, and Czechoslovakia are undoubtedly a magnificent political achievement. But it would be extraordinarily dangerous for a country and particularly for its armed forces to regard its military as merely an instrument of political bluff, without having the determination to actually use it. Moreover, from the point of view of a subsequent major conflict in the west which he regards as inevitable, it is militarily advisable *to test the armed forces in a single engagement.*

This now poses the question: *Is there a chance for us to carry out this task without becoming involved in other catastrophes?*

In the first place, it is clear that the state of our present relationship with Poland is intolerable in the long term. For this reason the Führer has made his proposal regarding the cession of Danzig and the establishment of a link through the Corridor. This attempt at *rapprochement* was frustrated by England which got itself into a state of hysteria and prompted Poland to issue insolent notes and to undertake military measures. Unless there is a tolerable relationship between Germany and Poland, intolerable stress is created. As far as England is concerned, however, a continually unstable situation is and was desirable, so that whenever it wishes to attack, it can launch Poland from the other side. But in that case we no longer have the advantage of the initiative. So that from this point of view as well it would be better to act now rather than later.

We must now reject all hollow compromises, the demand for 'gestures of good-will', that language of Versailles which would begin to make itself heard again. We in particular must be very concerned about our prestige which is important for us.

In the Führer's view the danger of the Western Powers intervening in a conflict is not great.

It is true that the carrying out of his plans involves a great risk. It would be a great mistake to believe that politicians receive any instructions from the good Lord. Nobody expects this of a Commander-in-Chief, but they do of a politician. But this is no more the case with a politician than with a Commander-in-Chief. Both must make decisions on their own. We, however, have only the alternative of acting or of being destroyed in the long run.

He, the Führer, might be permitted to make the point that up until now his assessment of the situation during crises had been correct. He recalled the exit from the League of Nations and the introduction of national military service. His advisers had warned him against it for fear of a war and in the latter case had advocated only a restricted number of divisions. But he had stuck stubbornly to thirty-six divisions. He recalled the occupation of the Rhineland. His advisers had advised withdrawing the troops from a number of garrisons as a 'gesture'. Eight days before the occupation Herr Poncet[1] had been to see him and had informed him that as far as France was concerned an occupation of the Rhineland would represent an act of war. But he had stuck to his guns in the face of everybody and had been proved right. There had also been a great risk in the case of Austria, the Sudetenland, and Czechoslovakia, but he had overcome the crisis. It was a simple fact that there were situations which demanded the taking of great risks such as was the case with Hannibal before the battle of Cannae, with Frederick the Great before Leuthen, and with Hindenburg/Ludendorff before Tannenberg. Now, too, there was a great risk which could only be mastered with iron determination.

[1] André François-Poncet, the French ambassador.

The Führer does not believe in intervention by the Western Powers for the following reasons: While both England and France have given Poland a guarantee, in fact France is only in tow behind England. In assessing the situation of the two countries one should note that England has excellent propaganda. In the autumn of 1938 the attitude of many Germans, including those in prominent positions, had given this English propaganda considerable assistance. They maintained both before and during the crisis that England would intervene to support Czechoslovakia, even to the extent of using her armed forces. When this did not happen, they said: 'We give up, the Führer was right after all. He won because he had the stronger nerves and stuck it out.' This was immediately taken note of in England and the Government was bitterly reproached for losing its nerve. If it had not done so, if instead it had accepted the danger of war, the German Chancellor would have given in. This opinion that he, the Führer, was only bluffing and had not really intended to do anything, had made the present situation much more difficult for him.

What is the present military situation in England? The naval construction programme has been only partly carried out and will not show results until 1941–42. There has been no significant increase in land forces. It has been estimated that she could commit three divisions on the Continent; *he would even allow for five or six, but no more.* There had been some success in the air but it was only in its initial stages. The modern anti-aircraft gun had been introduced the previous year; there were about 150–200 guns in the country and the monthly rate of delivery was 15–20. To increase this rate of production would require, even with our superior industry, nine to twelve months in order to increase production from 70 to 90, and even more in England. *So England is vulnerable to air attack.* The English air force itself has only about 130,000 men, whereas we have 390,000.

Political and military complications abroad are therefore unwelcome to England because it has many positions to defend.

One can judge England's assessment of Poland from the loan negotiations. England has rejected Poland's request for an £8 million loan in gold despite the fact that she has recently poured £500 million into China.

When Poland then requested weapons, she was given ridiculous quantities of obsolete material; in other words, her requests for effective assistance were rejected on the grounds that England needed gold and weapons herself. Only credits for other commodities were granted which did not represent effective assistance. Thus England's position is precarious. '*It appears to me, therefore, inconceivable that a responsible English statesman would in this situation incur the risk of a war.*'

France cannot afford a long and bloody war, her birthrate is too low, her war material inadequate. France has been forced into the whole affair against her will and the expression 'a war of nerves' can be appropriately applied to France.

What are the possibilities of intervention on the part of the Western Powers?
1. A blockade, which, however, has not the same importance as before.
2. An attack on land. Here one should consider what it would mean for the French soldiers, who have been trained to think in terms of the *defence* of the Maginot Line, to move out of this defensive line, storm the German West Wall and lose perhaps a quarter of a million men without any guarantee of success. For the German people, who earlier defended shell craters and holes, would certainly hold the West Wall.

Now the Western Powers might perhaps attempt to advance on Germany via neutral territory, and this led the Führer to consider the neutral countries. All these had the earnest desire to remain neutral: the Nordic States unconditionally. Switzerland would open fire on anyone who violated her neutrality; Holland would remain neutral on principle for fear of her Far Eastern colonies being threatened by Japan. Belgium would remain sincerely neutral, less for moral reasons than as a result of her bad experiences during the First World War in which she became the theatre of war and gained nothing. It was inconceivable that England and France would break her neutrality against her will.

It was possible that the declarations of neutrality made by these States had been prompted by England so that, in the event of the outbreak of war between Germany and Poland, they would provide an excuse for England to draw back. She could then say: 'We can't get through the West Wall. A request to Holland and Belgium to be allowed to march through has been rejected. We can't break their neutrality by force—so unfortunately we can't help!'

Now some people say: '*England is getting ready for a long war*; she is expecting or even hoping for one in order to crush Germany as she did after 1914.' *The Führer considers this view to be wrong.* In 1914 nobody reckoned with a long war, let alone wanted one. It was only after the great battles of Tannenberg and of the Marne that everyone realized with horror that there would now be no quick decision, but instead a long war. *Now England also does not want a long war*, since she cannot predict a month ahead what unexpected events might occur in the world. The whole world, however, is aware of our strength in the long run. We entered the world war badly prepared as far as supplies were concerned, with munitions for only a few months, and yet by the end we had enormously increased our production. The present situation, however, is completely different. We are now ready for the economic mobilization of the whole German nation.

Now the Western Powers were hoping that Russia would join in, which, apart from the material support she could offer, would represent an important psychological factor. The decision to risk spilling blood is difficult. One is then inclined to ask: Why me? For this reason England placed her hopes in Russia. But *only a blind optimist could believe that Stalin would be so crazy* as not to see through England's idea of fighting a static war in the west, while *letting Russia bear the main burden of losses* in the east on the lines of the world war. This was the reason why the Western Powers did not want to make any definite commitments, and each time this concrete question arose in the negotiations, they reached an impasse because there was no definite response to it.

But *Stalin must continue to be just as afraid of a victorious army as of a defeated one*.[1] Litvinov's dismissal as Foreign Minister came like a gunshot for the Führer as a sign of a change in Russia's attitude towards the Western Powers. He began a careful change of policy towards Russia, initiated at a reception where he treated the Russian ambassador just as politely as the other diplomats. The same evening the ambassador expressed his thanks for not being treated as a second-class diplomat. Further conversations followed concerning economic matters, which led to a trade agreement. Finally, the Russians put forward proposals for:

[1] In another version this sentence reads: 'Stalin knows that it would mean the end of his regime, no matter whether his soldiers emerged from a war victorious or vanquished.' See *Documents on German Foreign Policy*, series D, vol. vii, p. 204.

1. A Non-Aggression Pact.
2. Mediation between Japan and Russia.
3. A settlement of the question of the Baltic provinces. The Non-Aggression Pact was to be signed on 23 August.

'I have struck this weapon, Russian help, from the hands of the Western Powers. We now have the opportunity of making a thrust into the heart of Poland. The military path is open, so far as is humanly possible.'

The news of the pact has come like a bombshell abroad and is the greatest political event of recent times.

The best description of the situation came from Lloyd George who asked the Government in the House of Commons whether it had secured Russian help before giving its guarantee to Poland. 'If not, then the Government's policy is the most criminal and stupid that one can imagine.'

Naturally, this new course necessitates for him, the Führer, a certain change of course and requires sacrifices. Nevertheless, he believes that the German people will understand him one hundred per cent, and that he has their support. The effect on the Western Powers will be a correspondingly shattering one.

Naturally, the *Western Powers would try to save face*. They may recall their ambassadors; they may institute an embargo on trade.

Only iron determination will be effective against this. We must demonstrate that we have always reckoned with England and France and that Germany will win, provided it remains united. Everything depends on the bearing of every superior; on this depends the conduct of the Wehrmacht, and the attitude of the Wehrmacht will transfer itself to the whole nation. A nation cannot be trained to achieve great feats by a long period of peace but only by becoming used to stress and hardship.

In addition it must be borne in mind that on the other side there are also people with cares and worries. For in the final analysis it is not machines which are wrestling with one another but people. And we have the best people.

It is not true that we collapsed in 1918 as a result of a lack of supplies, because in fact we were better supplied then than in 1915–16. But we lacked the morale [*seelische Voraussetzungen*] for holding out, which is the essential thing. Frederick the Great managed to hold out only because he remained strong in heart until fortune smiled on him again. Firmness and bearing are the secrets of success. He who has chosen to make a hard decision will achieve this firm bearing.

The objective is the elimination and destruction of the military forces of Poland, even if war breaks out in the west. *The quicker we achieve victory in the east, the more chance there will be of limiting the conflict.*

Propaganda will provide an appropriate *casus belli*. It does not matter how credible it is, since whoever wins is in the right.

We must harden our hearts. Anyone who has thought about the world in which we live realizes that its underlying principle is that the best are those who succeed in asserting themselves through struggle. Destiny has made us leaders of this nation and, as a result, we have the task of giving the German people, who are crowded together in a ratio of 140 people to one square kilometre, the necessary living space. When carrying out such a task, the greatest hardness can represent the greatest gentleness.

We can and must believe in the quality of the German soldier. He usually keeps his nerve in a crisis while the leaders lose theirs—for example in the battle of the Marne. The leadership must therefore be as hard as iron.

Once again: speed is essential for the operation, so is adaptability to every new situation which arises and the destruction of the enemy forces down to the last man wherever they show themselves. *That is the military objective which is the precondition for the narrower political objective of a subsequent redrawing of the frontier.*

5 *Hitler's Directive No. 1 for the Conduct of the War, 31 August 1939*

On 23 August, after hearing that the negotiations with Russia were going well, Hitler had provisionally fixed the date for the attack on Poland for the 26th. On the following day, however, Chamberlain responded to the news that the German–Soviet Pact was about to be signed by informing Hitler that Britain was no less determined to support Poland if she were attacked. But he reduced the effect of this step by simultaneously urging negotiations with Poland. Hitler was not impressed and at 3.0 p.m. on the 25th he fixed the date for the attack on Poland for the 26th. An hour later, however, he received news that the Anglo-Polish Treaty, agreed in April, had at last been signed. No sooner had he received this ominous news than he heard from the Italian ambassador that Italy was not yet ready to go to war. In view of these two developments Hitler decided to postpone the attack on Poland scheduled for the following day to 1 September, in order to give himself more time to manoeuvre.

The following days until the outbreak of war were dominated by Hitler's attempt to drive a wedge between Britain and Poland and to try to persuade Britain to force the Poles to come to terms in the same way as the Czechs had been compelled to do. To this end, he dispatched two messages to Britain: one via the German embassy and the other through a Swedish businessman, Birger Dahlerus, who was a friend of Göring. In both these messages he offered to guarantee the British Empire, to give Poland a free harbour in Danzig, and to allow Poland to retain Gdynia and a corridor to it, provided that Britain cooperated in persuading the Poles to give way on Danzig and the Corridor. The British Government was tempted and obviously still hoped that an agreement would be possible, but they insisted on remaining committed to their guarantee to Poland. In this situation the Poles held a trump card which the unfortunate Czechs had lacked. And, although the British urged them to negotiate, they refused to accede to what was interpreted as a German ultimatum which arrived at 7.15 p.m. on the 29th to send the next day a negotiator with full powers, and Britain declined to force them to do so. When the Polish refusal became clear, Hitler went ahead and at 12.30 p.m. on 31 August signed the Directive No. 1 for the Conduct of the War. The war had already been postponed once, a week had been lost and, with the autumn rains not far off, he was under pressure to act even at the risk of Britain and France becoming involved:

1. Now that every political possibility has been exhausted for ending by peaceful means the intolerable situation on Germany's eastern frontier I have determined on a solution by force.

2. The attack on Poland is to be carried out in accordance with the preparations made for 'Operation White [*Fall Weiss*]', with the alterations, in respect of the Army, resulting from the fact that strategic deployment has by now been almost completed.

Assignment of tasks and the operational objective remain unchanged.

Day of attack . . . 1 September 1939
Time of attack . . . 4.45 a.m.

This timing also applies for the Gydnia/Gulf of Danzig, and Dirschau Bridge operations.

3. In the west, it is important that the responsibility for the opening of hostilities should be made to rest squarely on Britain and France. Insignificant frontier violations should, for the time being, be opposed by purely local action.

The neutrality on which we have given assurances to Holland, Belgium, Luxemburg and Switzerland must be scrupulously respected.

On land, the German western frontier is not to be crossed at any point without my express permission.

At sea, the same applies for all warlike actions or actions which could be regarded as such.

The defensive measures of the Luftwaffe are, for the time being, to be restricted to those necessary to counter enemy air attacks at the Reich frontier, whereby the frontiers of neutral States are to be respected as long as possible in countering single aircraft and smaller units. Only if large French and British formations are employed over the neutral States in attacks against German territory and the air defence in the west is no longer assured, are counter-measures to be allowed even over these neutral territories.

The speediest reporting to OKW of any violation of the neutrality of third-party States by our western opponents is particularly important.

4. If Britain and France open hostilities against Germany, it is the task of the Wehrmacht formations operating in the west to contain their forces as much as possible and thus maintain the conditions for a victorious conclusion of the operations against Poland. Within these limits enemy forces and their military economic resources are to be injured as much as possible. Orders to go over to the attack are reserved to me in every case.

The Army will hold the West Wall and make preparations to prevent its being outflanked in the north through violation of Belgian or Netherlands territory by the Western Powers. If French forces enter Luxemburg, the demolition of frontier bridges is authorized.

The Navy will carry on warfare against merchant shipping, directed mainly at Britain. To intensify the effects a declaration of danger zones may be expected. OKM[1] will report in which sea areas, and to what extent, danger zones are considered expedient. The wording of a public announcement is to be prepared in consultation with the Foreign Ministry and submitted to me through OKW for approval.

The Baltic Sea is to be protected from enemy raids. The Commander-in-Chief

[1] *Oberkommando der Marine*: the Naval High Command.

of the Navy will decide whether the approaches to the Baltic Sea should be blocked by mines for this purpose.

The Luftwaffe is, in the first place, to prevent the French and British air forces from attacking the German army and German living space.

In conducting the war against Britain, preparations are to be made for the use of the Luftwaffe in disrupting British supplies by sea, the armaments industry, and the transport of troops to France. A favourable opportunity is to be taken for an effective attack on massed British naval units, especially against battleships and aircraft carriers. Attacks against London are reserved for my decision.

Preparations are to be made for attacks against the British mainland, bearing in mind that partial success with insufficient forces is in all circumstances to be avoided.

6 *The reception of the British ultimatum to Germany, 3 September 1939*

In fact, Hitler still hoped that Britain was bluffing. He hoped that once the war had started and Britain was forced to face the fact that she could not effectively assist Poland, she would accept the inevitable as she had accepted so much already. But this time Britain was not bluffing and although the British Government even now still toyed with the idea of a conference, the mood of the British Parliament and of the British people was such that the Government was forced to issue an ultimatum on 3 September. The German interpreter, Paul Schmidt, recalled after the war the reception of the British ultimatum by the Nazi leaders:

. . . I then took the ultimatum to the Chancellery, where everyone was anxiously awaiting me. Most of the members of the Cabinet and the leading men of the Party were collected in the room next to Hitler's office. There was something of a crush and I had difficulty in getting through to Hitler.

'What's the news?' anxious voices asked. I could only answer: 'Classroom dismissed.'

When I entered the next room Hitler was sitting at his desk and Ribbentrop stood by the window. Both looked up expectantly as I came in. I stopped at some distance from Hitler's desk, and then slowly translated the British Government's ultimatum. When I finished, there was complete silence.

Hitler sat motionless, gazing before him. He was not at a loss, as was afterwards stated, nor did he rage, as others allege. He sat completely silent and unmoving.

After an interval which seemed an age, he turned to Ribbentrop, who had remained standing by the window. 'What now?' asked Hitler with a savage look, as though implying that his Foreign Minister had misled him about England's probable reaction.

Ribbentrop answered quietly: 'I assume that the French will hand in a similar ultimatum within the hour.'

As my duty was now performed, I withdrew. To those in the anteroom pressing round me I said: 'The English have just handed us an ultimatum. In two hours a state of war will exist between England and Germany.' In the anteroom also this news was followed by complete silence.

Göring turned to me and said: 'If we lose this war, then God have mercy on us!'
Goebbels stood in a corner, downcast and self-absorbed. Everywhere in the
room I saw looks of grave concern, even amongst the lesser Party people.

Blitzkrieg in the West

The ease and speed of his conquest of Poland gave Hitler renewed self-
confidence. He was now determined to defeat France in order to leave the
way clear for the main objective, the attack on Russia. In a conversation
with Dahlerus on 26 September he had already 'expressed himself very
sceptically regarding England's real desire for peace'.[1] At the same time, he
probably still retained a slender hope that Britain would now appreciate its
foolishness in having entered a war in support of a guarantee which it could
do nothing effective to fulfil. To encourage this reappraisal, he made a
speech to the Reichstag on 6 October in which, while attacking 'Messrs
Churchill & Co.', he insisted that he was anxious for peace. Significantly,
however, he made no concrete proposals—he had told Dahlerus that 'a
condition for peace discussions would be to allow him a free hand in Poland'.[2]
He clearly hoped to exploit the division within the British Cabinet between
the former appeasers and Churchill, who had just joined the Government as
First Lord of the Admiralty, and also, as he later told the Italian ambassador,
to lay the blame 'for all subsequent developments' on the opposing side.[3]
Three days later, he issued Directive No. 6 for the Conduct of the War in
which he declared: 'If it becomes clear that Britain, and under its leadership
France also, are not prepared to end the war, I am determined to go on to
the offensive without delay.' On 12 October, Chamberlain rejected the idea
of a peace which confirmed Germany's conquests, finally convincing Hitler
that further victories would be necessary in order to force Britain to come to
terms.

7 *Hitler's speech to the Commanders-in-Chief, 23 November 1939*

Hitler now went ahead with his plans for an attack in the west. The offensive
was scheduled to begin on 12 November, but on the 7th it had to be postponed owing to an unfavourable weather forecast. Two weeks later, Hitler
summoned the commanding officers of the three services, who were sceptical
about an attack on France, to the Reich Chancellery to hear his views on
past and future developments. In his account of the past he undoubtedly
argued to some extent *ex post facto*. As far as the future is concerned, his
reference to Russian adherence to the pact 'only so long as Russia considers
it to be to her benefit' and his comment that 'we can oppose Russia only
when we are free in the west' are both significant. His statement that 'for the

[1] DGFP, series D, vol. viii, p. 143.
[2] ibid., p. 141.
[3] DGFP, series D, vol. x, p. 80.

next year or two the present situation will remain' suggests the time-scale according to which he was working at this stage. Finally, the conclusion shows the extent to which his megalomania had progressed. The effect of his speech was to intimidate those in the Army High Command who were opposed to his plans for a western offensive, to which all open opposition ceased thenceforward.

The purpose of this conference is to give you an idea of the thoughts which govern my view of future events, and to tell you my decisions. The building up of our armed forces was only possible in connexion with the ideological [*weltanschaulich*] education of the German people by the Party. When I started my political work in 1919, my strong belief in final success was based on thorough observation of the events of the day and on a study of the reasons for their occurrence. I never, therefore, lost my faith in the midst of setbacks which were not spared me during my period of struggle. Providence has had the last word and has brought me success. In addition, I had a clear understanding of the probable course of historical events, and the firm will to take brutal decisions. The first decision was in 1919 when after long inner struggles I became a politician and took up the struggle against my enemies. That was the hardest of all decisions. I had, however, the firm belief that I would achieve my goal. Above all, I desired a new system of selection. I wanted to educate a minority which would take over the leadership. After fifteen years, I arrived at my goal, after hard struggles and many setbacks. When I came to power in 1933, a period of the most difficult struggle lay behind me. Everything existing before that had collapsed. I had to reorganize everything, beginning with the mass of the people and extending it to the armed forces. First internal reorganization, the removal of symptoms of decay and defeatist ideas, education for heroism. In the course of the internal reorganization, I undertook the second task: to release Germany from its international ties. I would like to mention two points in particular: secession from the League of Nations and denunciation of the disarmament conference. It was a hard decision. The number of prophets who predicted that it would lead to the occupation of the Rhineland was large, the number of believers was very small. I was supported by the nation, which stood firmly behind me when I carried out my intentions. After that came the order for rearmament. Here again there were numerous prophets who predicted misfortunes, and only a few believers. In 1935, the introduction of compulsory military service. After that the militarization of the Rhineland, again a development considered impossible at that time. The number of people who put their trust in me was very small. Then the beginning of the fortification of the whole country especially in the west.

One year later came Austria. This step too was considered doubtful. It brought about a considerable reinforcement of the Reich. The next step was Bohemia, Moravia and Poland. But this could not be accomplished in one campaign. First of all, the western fortification had to be finished. It was not possible to reach the goal in one go. It was clear to me from the first moment that I could not be satisfied with the Sudeten German territory. That was only a partial solution. The decision to march into Bohemia was made. Then followed the establishment of the Protectorate and with that the basis for the action against Poland was laid, but I was not quite clear at that time whether I should start first against the east and then in the west or vice versa. Moltke often made the same calculations in his time. The pressure of events imposed the decision to fight with Poland first. One might accuse me of wanting to fight and fight again. In struggle I see the fate of all beings. Nobody can avoid struggle if he does not want to lose out. The increasing number of people requires a larger living space [*Lebensraum*]. My goal was to create a logical relationship between the number of people and the space for them to live in. The struggle must start here. No people can get away from the solution of this task, or it must yield and gradually die out. That is the lesson of history. . . . If the Polish war was won so quickly, it was owing to the superiority of our armed forces. The most glorious event in our history. Unexpectedly small losses of men and material. Now the eastern front is held by only a few divisions. It is a situation which we regarded previously as unattainable. Now the situation is as follows: Our opponent in the west lies behind his fortifications. There is no possibility of coming to grips with him. The decisive question is: how long can we endure this situation? Russia is at present not dangerous. It is now weakened by many developments. Moreover, we have a Treaty with Russia. Treaties, however, are only kept as long as they serve their purpose. Russia will hold herself to it only so long as Russia herself considers it to be to her benefit. Bismarck thought so too. Think of the Reinsurance Treaty. Now Russia has far-reaching goals, above all the strengthening of her position in the Baltic. We can oppose Russia only when we are free in the west. Further, Russia is seeking to increase her influence in the Balkans and is pressing toward the Persian Gulf. That is also the goal of our foreign policy. Russia will do what she considers is best for her. At the present moment, she has withdrawn from internationalism. If she renounces it, she will go over to pan-Slavism. It is difficult to see into the future. It is a fact that at the present time the Russian army is of little account. For the next year or two the present situation will remain. . . .

Everything is determined by the fact that the moment is favourable now; in six months it may not be so any more.

As the last factor I must in all modesty name my own person: irreplaceable. Neither a military nor a civil person could replace me. Assassination attempts may be repeated. I am convinced of the powers of my intellect and of decision. Wars are always ended only by the destruction of the opponent. Everyone who believes differently is irresponsible. Time is working for our adversaries. Now there is a relationship of forces which can never be more propitious, but can only deteriorate. The enemy will not make peace when the relationship of forces is unfavourable for us. No compromise. Sternness towards ourselves. I shall strike and not capitulate. The fate of the Reich depends on me alone. I shall deal accordingly. Today we have a superiority such as we have never had before. After 1918 our opponents disarmed themselves of their own accord. England neglected the expansion of her fleet. . . .

We have an Achilles' Heel: the Ruhr. The progress of the war depends on the possession of the Ruhr. If England and France push through Belgium and Holland to the Ruhr, we shall be in the greatest danger. That could lead to the paralysing of the German power of resistance. Every hope of compromise is childish: Victory or defeat! The question is not the fate of National Socialist Germany, but who is to dominate Europe in the future. The question is worthy of the greatest efforts. Certainly England and France will assume the offensive against Germany when they have rearmed. England and France have means of pressure to bring Belgium and Holland to request their help. In Belgium and Holland the sympathies are all for France and England. Mention of the incident at Venlo:[1] The man who was shot was not an Englishman, but a Dutch General Staff officer. This was kept quiet in the press. The Dutch Government asked that the body of the Dutch officer be given up. That was one of their greatest stupidities. The Dutch press does not even mention the incident any more. At a given time I shall use that to motivate my action. If the French army marches into Belgium in order to attack us, it will be too late for us. We must anticipate them. One more thing. U-boats, mines, and Luftwaffe (also for mines) can strike England effectively, if we have a better starting-off point. Now a flight to England demands so much fuel that sufficient bomb loads cannot be carried. The invention of a new type of mine is of the greatest importance for the Navy. Aircraft will be the chief minelayers now. We shall sow the English coast with mines which cannot be cleared. This mine warfare with the Luftwaffe demands a different starting-off point. England cannot live without its imports. We can feed ourselves. The permanent sowing of mines on the English coasts will bring England to her knees. However, this can only occur if we have occupied Belgium and Holland. It is a difficult decision for me. No one has ever achieved what I have achieved. My life is of no importance in all this. I have led the German people to a great height, even if the world does hate us now. I am staking my life's work on a gamble. I have to choose between victory or destruction. I choose victory. Greatest historical choice, to be compared with the decision of Frederick the Great before the first Silesian war. Prussia owes its rise to the heroism of one man. Even there the closest advisers were disposed to capitulation. Everything depended on Frederick the Great. Even the decisions of Bismarck in 1866 and 1870 were no less crucial. My decision is unalterable. I shall attack France and England at the most favourable opportunity. Breach of the neutrality of Belgium and Holland is irrelevant. No one will question that when we have won. We shall not bring about the breach of neutrality as idiotically as it was done in 1914. If we do not break the neutrality, then England and France will. Without an attack the war cannot be ended victoriously. I consider it is only possible to end the war by means of an attack. The question whether or not the attack will be successful no one can answer. Everything depends upon the favourable moment. The military conditions are favourable. A prerequisite, however, is that the leadership must give an example of fanatical unity from above. There would be no failures if leaders always had the courage a rifleman must have. . . .

The enemy must be beaten only by attack. Our chances are different today than they were during the offensive of 1918. So far as numbers go, we can deploy more than a hundred divisions. There are reserves of men. The supply situation is good. Moreover that which is not ready today must be ready tomorrow. It is not merely the outcome of a single action that is involved but that of the war itself. What is at stake is not just a single issue but the very existence of the nation.

I ask you to pass on the spirit of determination to the lower echelons.

1. The decision is irrevocable.
2. The only prospect for success lies in the determination of all the armed forces.

The spirit of the great men of our history must hearten us all. Fate demands

[1] A German Secret Service plot by which two British Intelligence officers were lured to the Dutch border and then kidnapped.

from us no more than from the great men of German history. As long as I live I shall think only of the victory of my people. I shall shrink from nothing and shall destroy everyone who is opposed to me. I have decided to live my life so that when I have to die I can stand unashamed. I want to destroy the enemy. Behind me stands the German people, whose morale can only grow worse. Only he who struggles with destiny can have a good intuition. In the last years I have experienced many examples of intuition. Even in the present development I see the work of Providence.

If we come through this struggle victoriously—and we shall—our age will enter into the history of our people. I shall stand or fall in this struggle. I shall never survive the defeat of my people. No capitulation to the enemy, no revolution from within.

The offensive in the west suffered repeated postponements during the winter of 1939–40 and, in the meantime, Hitler's attention was diverted to another area, Scandinavia. There were two spheres in which Scandinavia was of vital importance to the German war effort. In the first place, three-quarters of Germany's iron ore supplies came from Sweden and were transported down the Norwegian coast. Secondly, Germany's main submarine route passed between Norway and the Shetland Islands. With the outbreak of the Russo-Finnish war in December 1939, the Allies were anxious to send help to the Finns, and the Navy now drew Hitler's attention to the very real danger that Britain might occupy Norway and threaten this lifeline. At the end of January, therefore, Hitler decided to use the delay in the west for an occupation of Norway and Denmark. On 1 March, he issued the directive code-named *Weserübung* ('Weser Exercise') and, although the Russo-Finnish war ended on 12 March, thereby reducing the threat from Great Britain, he went ahead and launched the operation on 9 April. Despite opposition from the British navy and a British expeditionary force, by the end of April the success of the operation was assured.

8 *The emergence of the* Sichelschnitt *strategy*

Hitler's attention now reverted once more to the west. Preparations had been continuing all through the winter and, in the meantime, the plans had undergone an important modification. The plans envisaged an attack by three Army Groups—A in the centre, B in the north and C in the south. Under the revised version, Deployment Directive 'Yellow', of 29 October, it was planned that the main thrust should come from Army Group B, which formed the right wing under General von Bock. Its main task would be to occupy Holland and thrust into Belgium north and south of Liège. The main task of Army Group A in the centre under General von Rundstedt would be to cover the southern flank of Army Group B by crossing the Meuse between Fumay and Mouzon and advancing into north-eastern France. Army Group C, under General von Leeb, would cover the Maginot Line further south:

(a) *Deployment Directive 'Yellow'*

1. *General intention.* The attitude of the Western Powers may require the German army in the west to go over to the offensive. All available forces will be committed with the intention of bringing to battle on north French and Belgian soil as many sections of the French army and its allies as possible. This will create favourable conditions for the further conduct of the war against England and France on land and in the air.

2. *Deployment and tasks.* (a) The attack will be made under my command by Army Groups B and A with the aim of destroying the Allied forces in the area north of the Somme and of breaking through to the Channel coast. Army Groups B and A will assemble east of the Reich frontier between Geldern and Mettlach (south of Trier) under camouflage so that they can take up the necessary positions for crossing the frontier within the space of six night marches and attack on the morning of the 7th. The time by which they must be ready will be given separately. Army Group C will have to hold the fortifications in its sector with a minimum of forces. A separate order will deal with the question of simulated attacks. . . .

3. *Tasks of the attacking front.* (a) After breaking through the Belgian frontier fortifications, Army Group B will initially advance in a westerly direction. One attacking force will be sent north of Liège to the area round Brussels, the other south of Liège to the area south and south-west of Namur, so that without loss of time the attack of the Army Group can be continued either in a westerly or in a north-westerly or south-westerly direction depending on the situation. After the breach of the fortified frontier zone, motorized forces must be committed as quickly and in as great a strength as possible. In the area of the northern attacking force they must be pushed forward in the direction of Ghent, in the area of the southern attacking force in the direction of Thuin with the aim, by means of ruthless attack, of preventing the formation of an enemy battle front and so that in mutual cooperation, and following the directives of the Army Group, they may create favourable conditions for the supporting forces to sustain the attack. If necessary, Army Group B will concentrate the motorized units of both attacking forces wherever favourable opportunities exist for a rapid advance. The motorized units of one attacking force must not be allowed to lie idle when they could be effectively employed by the other. With the release of the motorized forces for the advance, their leadership must be separated from that of the infantry divisions which are following. Army Group B will organize the employment of the Army High Commands for the various tasks. The fortresses of Liège and Antwerp are to be surrounded in accordance with the orders of Army Group B. The enemy must be prevented from escaping from the areas of the fortresses. . . .

(b) Army Group A will cover the attack of Army Group B against an enemy advance from the south and south-west. For this purpose it will push its right wing as quickly as possible over the Meuse near and south of Fumay and through the fortified French frontier zone in the general direction of Laon. . . .

This was a rather conventional plan which bore some similarity to that followed in the initial stages of the First World War. It would have come as no surprise to the Allies. Moreover, its objectives were somewhat limited. Hitler was by no means satisfied with the plan, and when it fell into Belgian hands in January he had to abandon it. He now suggested concentrating the attack on the southern Meuse in the direction of Sedan. But the Army High Command regarded this idea as far too daring because the Ardennes hills, through which the attack would have to pass, were considered impassable for tanks. At this stage, Hitler lacked the military self-confidence to press his point. Meanwhile, however, the Chief of Staff of Army Group A, General von Manstein, who was the most brilliant strategic brain on the General Staff, had also expressed his disquiet about the plan for 'Yellow'. He too wished more emphasis to be given to the thrust in the Centre in order to cut off the Allied forces in Belgium on the Somme, and he ascertained from the tank expert, Guderian, that the Ardennes were not impassable provided sufficient tank forces were employed. After securing the backing of his commander, Rundstedt, Manstein pressed his views in several memoranda to OKH.[1] The Army High Command, however, resented this interference which, they may well have assumed, sprang merely from a desire to increase the role of Manstein's own Army Group. They decided therefore to transfer him to a command in eastern Germany, well out of the way. Before he left, however, Manstein succeeded in putting his point of view to Hitler's adjutant and, when Hitler learnt that one of the acknowledged military experts appeared to be thinking along the same lines as himself, he called him for an interview on 17 February 1940. Then, confirmed in his own opinion, Hitler ordered the redrafting of 'Yellow' in accordance with Manstein's plan, thereby transferring the 'centre of gravity' of the attack from Army Group B in the north to Army Group A in the centre. This new draft of 24 February embodied the famous *Sichelschnitt* ('Sickle Cut') strategy which proved so devastatingly successful in May. The key to the plan was that, since the wooded hills of the Ardennes facing Army Group A were considered impassable for tanks, this section of the frontier would be more lightly defended. Then, once through the Ardennes, the tanks would be in the plains of northern France and could make straight for the Channel coast, thereby cutting the Allied forces in half and squeezing the Allies in Belgium between Army Group A in the south and Army Group B advancing from the north. It was perhaps the most brilliant military plan of modern times:

(b) *General von Manstein's suggestions to Hitler made on 17 February 1940 for the alteration of 'Yellow'*

Note

1. *The aim of the western offensive* must be *to bring about the decision on land*. The political and military stakes are too high for partial objectives such as are contained in the existing plan of attack, namely, the destruction of as large a part of the enemy forces as possible in Belgium and the occupation of parts of the Channel coast.

From the outset, therefore, those directing the operations must aim at the destruction of the French powers of resistance.

---

[1] *Oberkommando des Heeres*: the Army High Command.

2. For this it is necessary that, contrary to the deployment directive, right from the start the centre of gravity of the attack should be in the southern wing [the centre], i.e. should be transferred to Army Group A instead of remaining with B or being left undecided. Under the existing plan at best one can only smash the advancing Franco-British forces in Belgium in a frontal attack and throw them back on the Somme, where the operation could come to a standstill.

The southern wing, i.e. Army Group A, must push through southern Belgium over the Meuse and in the direction of the lower Somme. By definitely transferring the centre of gravity in this way, the strong enemy forces which may be expected in north Belgium and which will have been thrown back by Army Group B through frontal attack, will be cut off and destroyed. This will only be possible if Army Group A pushes through quickly to the lower Somme. This must be the first part of the campaign. The second part, the encirclement of the French army by means of a strong right-wing movement, will follow on from it.

3. For such a task it will be necessary to divide Army Group A into three armies. Thus another Army will have to be inserted in its right wing.

The northernmost Army of the Army Group (2nd) has the task of crossing the Meuse and breaking through to the lower Somme in order to cut off the enemy forces withdrawing from Army Group B.

South of that, a second Army (12th) must advance over the Meuse on either side of Sedan and then turn south-westward and, by taking the offensive, defeat all French attempts to mass troops for a counter-attack.

The third Army (16th) has the initially defensive role of covering the southern flank of the operation between the Meuse and the Moselle.

It is essential that the Air Force destroys the French concentration early on, because if the French attempt anything it will be a large-scale counter-attack to the west or on both sides of the Meuse, possibly reaching up to the Moselle.

The idea of committing only the XIX (motorized) Corps to the Meuse near Sedan is a half-measure. If the enemy attack us with strong motorized forces in south Belgium, the Corps will be too weak to destroy these quickly while crossing the Meuse with the remainder of its forces. If the enemy limit themselves to holding the line of the Meuse with forces of some strength, relatively to the present balance of forces, the Corps will not be able to cross the Meuse on its own.

If one is going to commit motorized forces, there must be at least two Corps in the present sector of the Army Group which can cross the Meuse simultaneously near Charleville and Sedan, independently of the commitment of tank forces on the Meuse near Givet by the 4th Army. Thus the XIV Armoured Corps must be placed beside Guderian's Corps from the beginning. It must not be earmarked for the use of Army Group A or B [but definitely for A].

The Führer expressed his agreement with these statements. A short time afterwards, the new and final deployment directive was issued.

(c) *The new draft of Deployment Directive 'Yellow', 24 February 1940*
1. The offensive 'Yellow' is intended to remove the threat of a British occupation of Dutch territory by means of the rapid occupation of Holland, to defeat as many sections as possible of the Anglo-French army by an attack through Belgium and Luxemburg, and thereby to pave the way for the destruction of the military power of the enemy.

The centre of gravity of the attack through Belgium and Luxemburg will lie south of the line Liège–Charleroi.

The forces in action north of this line will break through the Belgian frontier defences. By a further offensive in a westerly direction they will eliminate any direct threat to the Ruhr area from north-east Belgium and draw as large a section as possible of the Anglo–French army toward them.

The forces in action south of the line Liège–Charleroi will force a crossing of the Meuse between Dinant and Sedan (both inclusive) and open up a way through the French frontier defences in the north in the direction of the lower reaches of the Somme.

2. The attack north of the line Liège–Charleroi will be led by the Supreme Command of Army Group B with the 18th and 6th Armies, the attack south of this line by the Supreme Command of Army Group A led by the 4th, 12th and 16th Armies.

Army Group C will tie down the enemy opposite its position and remain prepared to ward off diversionary attacks by the enemy. . . .

5. *Tasks of the Army Groups and initial tasks of the armies.* The task of Army Group B is to occupy Holland by means of motorized forces and to prevent the linking up of the Dutch army with Anglo-Belgian forces. It will destroy the Belgian frontier defences by a rapid and powerful attack and will throw the enemy back over the line Antwerp–Namur.

The fortress of Antwerp will be surrounded from the north and east, the fortress of Liège from the north-east and north of the Meuse. . . . The task of Army Group A will be to force a crossing of the Meuse between Dinant and Sedan (both inclusive) as quickly as possible, while covering the left flank of the whole offensive against enemy attack from the protected region round Metz and Verdun. Then, while continuing to cover the flanks, it will break through in the rear of the French frontier fortifications in the north in the direction of the mouth of the Somme as rapidly and in as great strength as possible. For this purpose Army Supreme Command 2 will be available as an additional Army Supreme Command.

Strong motorized forces in deep formation must be sent ahead of the front of the Army Group towards the Dinant–Sedan sector of the Meuse. Their task is to smash the enemy forces which have advanced into south Belgium and Luxemburg, to gain the west bank of the Meuse in a surprise assault and thereby to secure favourable conditions for the continuation of the offensive toward the west. . . .

9 *The decision to halt before Dunkirk, 24 May 1940*

The German offensive in the west was finally launched on 10 May with twenty-eight divisions under Army Group B in the north and forty-four divisions under Army Group A in the centre. Everything went according to plan. By 24 May the major portion of the British Expeditionary Force and several French divisions were trapped between Army Group B advancing from the north and Army Group A from the south and east. Moreover, the spearheads of the German panzer units of Army Group A were only a few miles from Dunkirk, the only available port of evacuation for the British troops. Yet on that day these tanks received the order to halt, an order which gave the British the necessary breathing space to organize defences so that the evacuation could go ahead:

(a) *War Diary of Army Group A*

24.v.40. . . . At 11.30 the Führer arrives and receives a summary of the situation from the C.-in-C. of the Army Group. He completely agrees with the opinion that the infantry should attack east of Arras while the motorized units should be held on the line Lens–Béthune–Aire–St-Omer–Gravelines in order to 'catch' the enemy who are being pushed back by Army Group B. He gives it added emphasis by stating that it is necessary to conserve the tank units for the coming operations and that a further narrowing of the pocket would result in an extremely undesirable restriction of Luftwaffe operations. . . .

(b) *O K W Jodl Diary*

25.v.40. In the morning the C.-in-C. of the Army arrives and asks permission for the tanks and motorized divisions to come down from the heights of Vimy–St-Omer–Gravelines into the plains towards the east. The Führer is against, leaves the decision to Army Group A. They turn it down for the time being since the tanks must have time to recover in order to be ready for the tasks in the south. . . .

From these documents it is clear that the initial decision to halt was that of von Rundstedt, Commander of Army Group A. When he arrived on the scene Hitler confirmed this decision and made it a Führer command, thereby overriding the Army High Command (OKH). Hitler had been urged by Göring to let the Air Force finish off the retreating British and his own experience of the First World War persuaded him to concentrate on the primary task of defeating France and capturing Paris for fear of the offensive becoming bogged down. Nevertheless, it is clear from the second document that on the following day he left the decision to Army Group A.

The decision to halt caused consternation in the headquarters of OKH, and the Chief of Staff, General Halder, who had become an enthusiastic convert to the 'Sickle Cut', commented bitterly on it in his diary:

(c) *War Diary of General Halder*

25.v.40. The day begins once again with unpleasant arguments between von Br[auchitsch] and the Führer concerning the future course of the battle of encirclement. I had envisaged the battle going as follows: Army Group B would mount a heavy frontal assault on the enemy, which would be making a planned withdrawal, with the aim merely of tying them down. Army Group A, meeting a beaten enemy, would tackle it from the rear and bring about the decision. This was to be achieved by means of the motorized troops. Now the political leadership gets the idea of transferring the final decisive battle from Flanders to northern France. In order to disguise this political aim it is explained that the Flanders terrain with its numerous waterways is unsuitable for tanks. The tanks of the other motorized troops, therefore, had to be halted after reaching the line St-Omer–Béthune.

In other words the position is reversed. I wanted the Army Group A to be the hammer and B to be the anvil. Now B is made the hammer and A the anvil. Since B is faced with an organized front this will cost a lot of blood and take a long time. For the Air Force on which hopes were pinned is dependent on the weather. . . .

At 1.30 p.m. on the 26th Hitler gave the order to continue the advance but the forty-eight hours which had been lost were sufficient to allow the evacuation of the bulk of the B.E.F. during the following week. The evacuation had no effect on the course of the French campaign. Paris was occupied on 14 June and an armistice signed on the 22nd.

Strategic vacillation, June–December 1940[1]

10 *The plan to invade Britain*

Hitler hoped that the defeat of France would make Britain come to terms. On the basis of his reading of history, he believed that Britain intervened on the Continent only when she could use an ally as her 'Continental sword'. Now, with the defeat of France, this sword had been struck from her hands, and, although he began making preparations for an invasion of Britain, this was intended to force her to make peace rather than to destroy her. Thus, after a military conference on 13 July, Halder noted in his diary:

(a) The Führer is most concerned about the question of why Britain will not yet make peace. He sees the answer to this, as we do, in the fact that Britain still has hopes of Russia. He reckons therefore that England will have to be compelled to make peace by force. But he does not like doing this. The reason is that if we crush England's military power the British Empire will collapse. That is of no use to Germany. We would achieve with German blood something which would only be of use to Japan, America, and others.

Three days later, however, the logic of the situation created by Britain's refusal to come to terms compelled him to issue, on 16 July 1940, a directive for the invasion of Britain, Directive No. 16:

(b) *On the preparation of a landing operation against England*
Since England, despite her hopeless situation in the military sense, still shows no sign of willingness to come to terms, I have decided to prepare a landing operation against England, and if necessary to carry it out.

The aim of this operation is to eliminate the English homeland as a base for the carrying on of the war against Germany, and, if it should become necessary, to occupy it completely.

To this end I order the following:
1. The *Landing* must be carried out in the form of a surprise crossing on a broad front approximately from Ramsgate to the area west of the Isle of Wight, in which Luftwaffe units will take the role of the artillery, and units of the Navy the role of the engineers. Whether it is practical before the general landing to undertake *subordinate actions*, such as the occupation of the Isle of Wight or of the County of Cornwall, is to be determined from the standpoint of each branch of the Wehrmacht

[1] This section is especially indebted to Andreas Hillgruber's *Hitlers Strategie: Politik und Kriegführung 1940–1941* (Frankfurt am Main 1965).

and the result is to be reported to me. I reserve the decision for myself. The preparations for the entire operation must be completed by *mid-August*.

2. To these preparations also belong the creation of those conditions which make a landing in England possible:

(a) The English air force must be so beaten down in morale and in fact, that it can no longer display any appreciable aggressive force in opposition to the German crossing.

(b) Mine-free channels must be created.

(c) By means of a closely concentrated mine-barrier the Straits of Dover must be sealed off on both *flanks* as well as the western entrance to the Channel at the approximate line Alderney–Portland.

(d) The area off the coast must be dominated and given artillery protection by strong coastal artillery.

(e) It would be desirable shortly before the crossing to tie down the English naval forces in the North Sea as well as in the Mediterranean (by the Italians), in which connexion the attempt should be made now to damage the English naval forces which are in the homeland by air and torpedo attacks in strength.

3. *Organization of the command and of the preparations.* Under my command and in accordance with my general directives the Commanders-in-Chief will command the forces to be used from their branches of the Wehrmacht. The operations staffs of the Commander-in-Chief of the Army, the Commander-in-Chief of the Navy and the Commander-in-Chief of the Luftwaffe must from 1 August onwards be placed within a radius of at most 50 km. from my headquarters (Ziegenberg). Quartering of the restricted operations staffs of the Commanders-in-Chief of the Army and Navy together at Giessen seems to me advisable.

Hence, for the command of the landing armies the Commander-in-Chief of the Army will have to employ an Army Group headquarters.

The project will bear the code name *Seelöwe* [Sea Lion].

In the preparation and carrying out of the undertaking the following duties will fall to the various branches of the Wehrmacht:

(a) *Army*: Will draw up first of all the operational plan and the transport plan for all formations to be shipped across as the first wave. The anti-aircraft artillery to be transported with the first wave will at the same time be attached to the Army (to the individual crossing groups) until such time as a division of tasks in support and protection of ground troops, in protection of the ports of debarkation and in protection of the air bases to be occupied, can be carried out. The Army further-more will distribute the means of transport to the individual crossing groups and establish the embarkation and landing points in agreement with the Navy.

(b) *Navy*: Will secure the means of transport and will bring them, corresponding to the desires of the Army and according to the requirements of seamanship, into the individual embarkation areas. In so far as possible, ships of the defeated enemy States are to be procured. For every ferrying point it will provide the necessary naval staff for advice on matters of seamanship, with escort vessels and security forces. It will protect, along with the air forces employed to guard the movement, the entire crossing of the channel on both flanks. An order will follow on the regulation of the command relationship during the crossing. It is further the task of the Navy to regulate, in a uniform manner, the building up of the coastal artillery, that is, all batteries of the Army as well as of the Navy, which can be used for firing against sea targets, and to organize the fire control of the whole. As large an amount as possible of *very heavy artillery* is to be employed as quickly as possible to secure the crossing and to protect the flanks from enemy operations from the sea. For this purpose, railway artillery (supplemented by all available captured pieces), less the batteries (K_5 and K_{12}) provided for firing on targets on the English mainland, is to be brought up and emplaced by using railway turn-tables.

Independently of this, the heaviest available platform batteries are to be opposite the Straits of Dover, so emplaced under concrete that they can withstand even the heaviest aerial attacks and can thereby dominate permanently within their effective range the Straits of Dover in any circumstances.

The technical work is the responsibility of the Todt Organization.

(c) *The mission of the Luftwaffe is*: To hinder interference from the enemy air force. To overcome coastal defences which could do damage to the landing places, to break the first resistance of enemy ground troops and to smash reserves which may be coming up. For this mission the closest cooperation of individual units of the Luftwaffe with the crossing units of the Army is necessary. Furthermore, to destroy important transport routes for the bringing up of enemy reserves, and to attack enemy naval forces coming up, while they are still far away from the crossing points, I request proposals on the use of parachute and glider troops. In this regard it is to be determined in conjunction with the Army whether it is worth while to hold parachute and glider troops here in readiness as a *reserve* to be quickly committed in case of emergency.

4. The Wehrmacht Chief of Communications will carry out the necessary pre-parations for communication connexions from France to the English mainland. The installation of the remaining 80-km. East Prussian cable is to be provided for in conjunction with the Navy.

5. I request the Commanders-in-Chief to submit to me as soon as possible:

(a) the intentions of the Navy and Luftwaffe for achieving the necessary conditions for the crossing of the Channel;

(b) the construction of the coastal batteries in detail (Navy);

(c) a survey of the tonnage to be employed and the methods of getting it ready and fitting it out. Participation of civilian agencies? (Navy).

(d) the organization of aerial protection in the assembly areas for troops about to cross and the means of crossing (Luftwaffe);

(e) the crossing and operations plan of the Army, composition and equipment of the first crossing wave;

(f) the organization and measures of the Navy and the Luftwaffe for the carrying out of the crossing itself, security of the crossing, and support of the landing;

(g) proposals for the commitment of parachute and glider troops, as well as for the detailing and command of anti-aircraft artillery, after an extensive occupation of territory on English soil has been made (Luftwaffe);

(h) proposals for the setting up of the operations staffs of the Commanders-in-Chief of the Army and of the Navy;

(i) the attitude of Army, Navy and Luftwaffe on the question whether and what subsidiary actions *before* the general landing are considered practical;

(k) proposals of Army and Navy on the overall command *during* the crossing.

11 *Hitler's peace offer in his Reichstag speech of 19 July 1940*

But three days later, on 19 July, in a speech to the Reichstag Hitler made a final attempt to persuade Britain to negotiate a peace settlement. Again there were no concrete proposals. It was merely assumed that Britain would have to accept the German conquests.

... Mr Churchill has just declared again that he wants the war. About six weeks ago he began to fight in the sphere in which he seems to think he is particularly strong, namely the air war against the civilian population, though under the pretence that the targets are important for the war effort. Since Freiburg[1] these targets have been open cities, market towns and villages, houses, hospitals, schools, nursery schools and whatever else is being hit.

So far I have hardly bothered to respond to this. But that need not mean that this is or will remain my only answer.

I am quite aware of the fact that people will suffer incredible misery and misfortune from our impending response. Naturally this will not affect Mr Churchill, for he will certainly be in Canada where the property and the children of the most important people who have an interest in the war have already been taken. But for millions of other people there will be great misery. And perhaps Mr Churchill should believe me for once when I prophesy the following:

A great empire will be destroyed. A world empire that I never intended to destroy or even damage. But it is clear to me that the continuation of this struggle will end with the complete destruction of one of the two opponents. Mr Churchill may believe that this will be Germany. I know that it will be England.

At this hour I feel compelled by conscience once more to appeal to reason in England. I believe I am in a position to do this because I am not the vanquished begging favours. As victor, I am speaking in the name of reason. I can see no reason why this war should go on.

I regret the sacrifices it will demand. I would like to spare my own people them also. I know that millions of German men and youths are aglow with the thought of at last being able to face the enemy who has declared war on us for the second time and for no reason.

But I also know that there are many wives and mothers at home who, despite their readiness to make the utmost sacrifices, are clinging to this last hope with all their hearts.

Mr Churchill may reject this declaration of mine by shouting that it is only the product of my fear and my doubts of final victory. But at least I have relieved my conscience before the events that threaten. ...

Britain's refusal to come to terms coupled with the political drawbacks and technical difficulties involved in an invasion of Britain placed Hitler in a dilemma. He could not sit tight and adopt a 'hedgehog position' for the simple reason that in the long term Germany's control of central and western Europe was threatened not so much by Britain, but rather by the intervention of the other world powers—Russia and the United States. If

[1] On 10 May 1940 German planes dropped bombs on Freiburg in error and the blame was put on the British.

Germany did nothing, her political and economic dependence on the Soviet Union would increase. Russian supplies of oil, grain and other raw materials under the economic agreement between the two countries had now become essential to the German war machine. And Stalin made it abundantly clear that he would claim a reward for his neutrality. He had been disconcerted by the speed of Germany's victory over France and during June, without consultation, Russia had occupied the Baltic States, which had been assigned to her under the 1939 pact, and began to apply pressure on Romania, Germany's main source of oil imports. This was a defensive move on the part of the Russians who wanted as large a buffer area as possible between themselves and Germany, but it was highly unwelcome to Hitler in view of his long-term objectives in the east. And it was not only Russia that Hitler had to consider. The United States also posed a threat. For, although at this time her Army was far too small to intervene, the lesson of 1917 was not lost on Hitler and he realized that, with America's enormous resources now being devoted to rearmament, she would soon be able to intervene decisively on the side of Britain.

In this situation, there were three possible strategies. In the first place, he could try to defeat Britain directly – by an invasion. Secondly, he could try to approach the same goal indirectly by attacking the British position in the Mediterranean and the Middle East with the help of Italy, Spain and Vichy France, and threaten the British position in the Far East by encouraging the Japanese to take the offensive in the Pacific. Russia might even be persuaded to switch her emphasis from the west to the south toward the Persian Gulf and India. Finally as part of this indirect strategy he could intensify the U-boat campaign against British shipping. These strategies would either destroy Britain as a power or force her to come to terms. In either case this would remove, for the time being at any rate, the basis for American intervention and would secure Germany's rear for an attack on Russia. The third alternative strategy would be to try to defeat Russia in a *Blitzkrieg*. This would then give Germany the security and the basis of raw materials necessary to defeat Britain and, if necessary, the United States. This had essentially been the strategy contained in his original programme which had been upset by the entry of Britain into the war.

During the following months, Hitler oscillated between these three strategies, sometimes pursuing them simultaneously. His decisions were shaped, as always, by a combination of his assessment of the situation and ideological factors. As far as he was concerned, both pointed in the direction of an attack on Russia. But it was too late in the year for a Russian campaign and so in the meantime he toyed with the first two strategies of concentrating on defeating Britain.

12 *The initial decision to attack Russia*

Why, then, did Hitler decide on the need to attack Russia? Apart from the

ideological aspect – the fact that this had formed the core of his programme –
there were also strategic considerations involved and these may even have
been decisive. He had become convinced that Britain's refusal to come to
terms derived from her hopes of Russia as a substitute 'Continental sword'
for France and of future American intervention. In this situation and in the
light of the political and technical problems associated with an invasion of
Britain he decided that the best plan would be a *Blitzkrieg* against Russia.
The defeat of Russia would, he thought, not only remove the threat from that
quarter and destroy British hopes; it would also free Japan to expand in the
Pacific. This in turn would threaten the United States, which, in order to
concentrate on this threat, would have to remain neutral in the war between
Britain and Germany. Hitler first mentioned the idea of an attack on Russia
to General Jodl during the French campaign. But his first reference to it as a
definite objective occurred at a military conference on 21 July. Ten days later,
at another conference of military leaders, Halder noted in his diary Hitler's
assessment of the situation:

Führer:
(a) Stresses his scepticism regarding technical feasibility; however, satisfied with
    results produced by Navy.
(b) Emphasizes weather factor.
(c) Discusses enemy resources for counteraction. Our small Navy is only 15 per
    cent of enemy's, 8 per cent of enemy's destroyers, 10–12 per cent of his motor
    torpedo boats. So we have nothing to bring into action against enemy surface
    attacks. That leaves mines (not 100 per cent reliable), coastal Artillery (good!),
    and Air Force.
    In any decision we must bear in mind that if we take risks, the prize too is high.
(d) In the event that invasion does not take long, our action must be directed to
    eliminate all factors that let England hope for a change in the situation. To all
    intents and purposes the war is won. France has stepped out of the set-up
    protecting British convoys. Italy is pinning down British forces.
    Submarine and air warfare may bring about a final decision, but this may be
    one or two years off.
    Britain's hope lies in Russia and the United States. If Russia drops out of the
    picture, America too is lost for Britain, because elimination of Russia would
    tremendously increase *Japan's power* in the Far East.
    Russia is the Far Eastern sword of Britain and the United States pointed at Japan.
    Here an evil wind is blowing for Britain. Japan, like Russia, has her programme
    which she wants to carry through before the end of the war.

[*marginal note:*]
The Russian victory film on the Russo-Finnish war!
*Russia is the factor on which Britain is relying the most. Something must have
happened in London!*
The British were completely down; now they have perked up again. Intercepted
telephone conversations. Russia is painfully shaken by the swift development of
the Western European situation.

All that Russia has to do is to hint that she does not care to have a strong Germany, and the British will take hope, like one about to go under, that the situation will undergo a radical change within six or eight months.

With Russia smashed, Britain's last hope would be shattered. Germany then will be master of Europe and the Balkans.

Decision: Russia's destruction must therefore be made a part of this struggle. Spring '41. The sooner Russia is crushed, the better. Attack achieves its purpose only if Russian State can be shattered to its roots with one blow. Holding part of the country alone will not do. Standing still for the following winter would be perilous. So it is better to wait a little longer, but with the resolute determination to eliminate Russia. This is necessary also because of contiguity on the Baltic. It would be awkward to have another major power there. If we start in May '41, we would have five months to finish the job in. Tackling it this year would still have been the best, but unified action would be impossible at this time.

13 *The alternative strategy: indirect attack on Britain*

By the middle of September, it had become clear that the Luftwaffe had been defeated in the Battle of Britain. As a result, on 17 September, the invasion was postponed indefinitely and then, on 12 October, put off until the spring. In view of Hitler's Russian plans this was tantamount to a cancellation of the operation. Since it was far too late in the year for an attack on Russia, Hitler was obliged, for the time being at any rate, to fall back on the remaining alternative strategy—that of trying to create a coalition of powers which would be able to attack Britain indirectly, in the Mediterranean and North Africa, and which would put sufficient pressure on the United States to ensure that they remained neutral.

The entry of Italy into the war had given the Axis powers the opportunity to strike telling blows in the Mediterranean through which ran Britain's vital links with her oil reserves in the Middle East and with India and the Far East. The problem was that relations between Germany and Italy were from the beginning plagued by a total lack of coordination which sprang from Mussolini's determination to fight 'not with Germany, not for Germany, but only for Italy alongside Germany',[1] an attitude which was paralleled by Hitler's conception of 'a policy of separate spheres' in which Germany would concentrate on northern Europe, while Italy would be left free to establish a new version of the Roman Empire in the south. The stalemate in northern Europe which set in with the frustration of the invasion of Britain, however, obliged Germany to direct her attention towards the Mediterranean as the only sphere, apart from the bombing offensive, in which the war could be effectively continued against Britain. The question was, Should Germany henceforward concentrate on the Mediterranean as the main area of attack and regard the defeat of Britain as the primary

---

[1] quoted in Lothar Gruchmann, 'Die "verpassten strategischen Chancen" der Achsenmächte im Mittelmeerraum 1940–41', *Vierteljahrshefte für Zeitgeschichte*, Bd. 18 (1970).

objective, or should this be considered a temporary measure, a stop-gap operation undertaken during the period before the attack on Russia could get under way?

The Mediterranean strategy was pressed strongly by the armed forces and in particular by the Naval High Command under Admiral Raeder. Already, during a conference on 6 September, Raeder had pressed Hitler to concentrate on capturing Gibraltar and the Suez Canal as an alternative to the risky venture of an invasion of England. Three weeks later, after the postponement of the invasion and having learnt of the plans for an invasion of Russia, Raeder requested an interview with Hitler *tête à tête*. Afterwards he explained in a minute that 'it was my fear that the war might go off on the wrong track and turn away from the main danger, which was Britain, which prompted me to seek the interview *tête à tête* with the Führer':[1]

Report of the Commander-in-Chief, Navy, to the Führer on 26 September 1940 at 1700 hours. (Without witnesses.)

The Commander-in-Chief, Navy, requests permission to give the Führer his views on the progress of the war, including also matters outside his sphere of operations.

The British have always considered the Mediterranean the pivot of their world empire. Even now eight of the thirteen battleships are there; strong positions are held in the Eastern Mediterranean; troop transports from Australia and New Zealand have been sent to Egypt and East Africa. While the air and submarine war is being fought out between Germany and Britain, Italy, surrounded by British power, is fast becoming the main target of attack. Britain always attempts to strangle the weaker enemy. Germany, however, must wage war against Great Britain with all the means at her disposal and without delay, before the United States is able to intervene effectively. For this reason the Mediterranean question must be cleared up *during the [coming] winter months*.

(a) *Gibraltar* must be seized. The Canary Islands must be secured beforehand by the Air Force.

The *Suez Canal* must be captured. It is doubtful whether the Italians can accomplish this alone; support by German troops will be needed. An advance from Suez through Palestine and Syria as far as Turkey is necessary. If we reach that point, Turkey will be in our power. The Russian problem will then appear in a different light. Basically, Russia is afraid of Germany. It is doubtful whether an advance against Russia from the north will then be necessary. There is also the question of the Dardanelles. It will be easier to supply Italy and Spain if we control the Mediterranean.

Protection of East Africa is assured. The Italians can wage naval warfare in the Indian Ocean.

An operation against India could be feigned.

(b) The question of *North-West Africa* is also of decisive importance.

All the indications are that Britain, with the help of De Gaulle France, and

---

[1] quoted in M. Salewski, *Die deutsche Seekriegsleitung 1935-1941* (Frankfurt am Main 1970), vol. 1, p. 284.

possibly *also of the U.S.A.*, wants to make this region a centre of resistance and to establish air bases for attacks on Italy. Britain will try to prevent us from gaining a foothold in the African colonies.

In this way Italy would be defeated.

Thus action must be taken against *Dakar*. The U.S.A. already has a consul there, the Italians two representatives, and we are not represented *at all*. The economic situation will quickly deteriorate, but the attitude towards the British is *still* hostile. In spite of demobilization there are still about 25,000 troops left in this area; in the neighbouring British territory, on the other hand, there are only about six to eight battalions. The possibility of action on the part of France against the British is therefore very promising. It is very desirable that support be given to the French, possibly by permitting the use of the STRASBOURG.

It would be advisable to station air forces in Casablanca in the near future. In general, it appears important to cooperate with France in order to protect North-West Africa—after certain concessions have been made to Germany and Italy. The occupation of France makes it possible to compel her to maintain and defend the frontiers advantageous to us.

The Führer agrees with the general trend of thought. When the alliance with Japan has been finalized he will immediately confer with the Duce, and possibly also with France. He will have to decide whether cooperation with France or with Spain is more profitable; probably with France, since Spain demands a great deal (French Morocco) but offers little. France must guarantee beforehand to fulfil certain German and Italian demands; an agreement could then be reached regarding the African colonies. Britain and the U.S.A. must be excluded from North-West Africa. If Spain were to cooperate, the Canary Islands, and possibly also the Azores and the Cape Verde Islands would have to be seized beforehand by the Air Force.

An advance through Syria would also depend on the attitude taken by France; it would be quite possible, however. Italy will be *against* the cession of the Dardanelles to Russia. Russia should be encouraged to advance towards the south, or against Persia and India, in order to gain an outlet to the Indian Ocean which would be more important to Russia than the positions in the Baltic Sea.

The Führer is also of the opinion that Russia is afraid of Germany's strength; he believes, for instance, that Russia will not attack Finland this year.

The Führer is obviously hesitant about releasing additional French forces at Toulon; he feels himself bound by previous decisions.

With the invasion of Britain frustrated, and faced with a delay of eight months before the attack on Russia could go ahead, Hitler now went some way towards adopting this strategy of an indirect offensive against Britain. His first move was to conclude a Tripartite Pact with Italy and Japan on 27 September. He hoped thereby to intimidate the United States with the threat of a war on two fronts—a hope which proved futile. Next, Hitler concentrated on trying to broaden this coalition by securing the adherence of Vichy France and Spain, both of which would be valuable as a spring-board for an attack on the British positions in the Mediterranean area. In particular, Hitler was thinking of an attack on Gibraltar.

This strategy, however, had its problems. In the first place, Hitler regarded the Mediterranean as Mussolini's sphere of influence and he was anxious not to offend the Duce by too great an interference in that area. In particular, the problem of reconciling French, Italian and Spanish interests in the area was acute. Secondly, Hitler was unwilling to tie down large German forces in the south, for his main objective remained an attack in the east in the following spring though he was not yet totally committed to it. Finally, his hopes of achieving even a limited success by capturing Gibraltar were destroyed by the attitude adopted by Spain and France. Both countries were unwilling to become involved while the issue of the war was still in doubt. Moreover, Spain was heavily dependent on imports by sea and the sea was controlled by the British navy. Despite a personal visit by Hitler towards the end of October, both General Franco and Marshal Pétain refused to give more than moral support. Even Italian support proved more of a hindrance than a help because of the incompetence of the Italian armed forces, which had to be bolstered by German divisions. How successful the Mediterranean strategy would have been is a moot point: it is unlikely to have led to a different outcome to the war, though it might well have substantially altered its course, had it been fully applied. As it was, Hitler never regarded it as anything more than a diversion. His main concern continued to be Russia.

14 *The Hitler/Ribbentrop/Molotov conversations of 12–14 November 1940*

In the meantime, relations with Russia had entered an awkward phase. Not only was Russia suspicious of the Tripartite Pact, she was also particularly concerned about German actions in two especially sensitive areas, Finland and Romania. Despite the fact that Finland had been assigned to the Russian sphere of influence under the Nazi-Soviet Pact of August 1939, Germany was endeavouring to retain some influence in that country because it was a vital supplier of nickel. Partly in order to assert this influence, Germany sent a number of troop transports through Finland to German bases in northern Norway, a move which was resented by Russia and raised suspicions of future German intentions. Romania was of even greater economic importance to Germany than Finland because of her oilfields, which provided a substantial proportion of German oil supplies. During the autumn of 1940, Hitler took steps to turn Romania into a virtual satellite of Germany. Russia too, however, regarded Romania as an important sphere of interest, and was seriously concerned about the German move. In view of these developments, Russia pressed for an explanation of German policy and, at the beginning of November 1940, Molotov, the Russian Foreign Minister, visited Berlin for consultations. Hitler decided to use this opportunity to try to draw Russia into his grand coalition against Britain, and thereby to redirect her interests away from the Balkans, where they conflicted with those of Germany and Italy, and towards India and the Persian

Gulf which was a British sphere. In his talk with Molotov, Hitler painted a grand vista:

After the conquest of England the British Empire would be apportioned as a gigantic world-wide estate in bankruptcy of 40 million square kilometres. In this bankrupt estate there would be for Russia access to the ice-free and really open ocean. Thus far, a minority of 45 million Englishmen had ruled 600 million inhabitants of the British Empire. He was about to crush this minority.

He wanted to create a world coalition of interested powers which would consist of Spain, France, Italy, Germany, Soviet Russia and Japan, and would to a certain degree represent a coalition, extending from North Africa to Eastern Asia, of all those who wanted to be satisfied out of the British bankrupt estate. To this end all internal controversies between the members of this coalition must be removed or at least neutralized. For this purpose the settlement of a whole series of questions was necessary. In the west, i.e. between Spain, France, Italy and Germany, he believed he had now found a formula which satisfied everybody alike. It had not been easy to reconcile the views of Spain and France, for instance, in regard to North Africa; however, recognizing the greater possibilities for the future, both countries finally had given in. After the west had been thus settled, an agreement in the east must now be reached. In this case it was not a matter only of relations between Soviet Russia and Turkey, but also of the Greater Asian sphere. The latter consisted not only of the Greater East Asian sphere, but also of a purely Asiatic area oriented toward the south, which Germany even now recognized as Russia's sphere of influence. It was a matter of determining in bold outlines the boundaries for the future activity of peoples and of assigning to nations large areas where they could find an ample field of activity for fifty to a hundred years.

15 *The Russian reaction to Hitler's grand design*

How seriously Hitler regarded this attempt to win over Russia, it is difficult to say. In any case, whatever hopes he may have had in this direction, whatever doubts he may have had about the advisability of the attack on Russia, were removed by Molotov's reaction to the German suggestion. The Russians were not interested in grand designs for the future, they were concerned about concrete issues in the present. They were not to be diverted from their concern with the questions of Finland and Romania and they showed that they regarded the whole of eastern Europe and even Sweden as an object in which they had a legitimate interest. As Molotov told Ribbentrop at their last meeting,

... For the Soviet Union, as the most important Black Sea Power, it was a matter of obtaining effective guarantees of her security. In the course of her history, Russia had often been attacked by way of the Straits. Consequently paper agreements would not suffice for the Soviet Union; rather would she have to insist on effective guarantees of her security. Therefore this question had to be examined and discussed more concretely. The questions which interested the Soviet Union in the Near East concerned not only Turkey but Bulgaria, for instance, about which he, Molotov, had spoken in detail in his previous conversation with the Führer.[1] But the fate of Romania and Hungary was also of interest to the Soviet Union and could not be immaterial to her in any circumstances. It would further interest the Soviet Government to learn what the Axis contemplated with regard to Yugoslavia and Greece, and likewise what Germany intended with regard to Poland. He recalled the fact that, regarding the future form of Poland, a protocol existed between the Soviet Union and Germany, for compliance with which an exchange of opinion was necessary. He asked whether from the German viewpoint this protocol was still in force. The Soviet Government was also interested in the question of Swedish neutrality, and he wanted to know whether the German Government still took the stand that the preservation of Swedish neutrality was in the interests of the Soviet Union and Germany. Besides, there existed the question of the passages out of the Baltic Sea (Store Bælt, Lille Bælt, Öresund, Kattegat, Skagerrak). The Soviet Government believed that discussions must be held on this question similar to those now being conducted about the Danube Commissions. As to the Finnish question, it was sufficiently clarified during his previous conversations with the Führer.

The Germans were assuming that the war against England had already actually been won. Therefore if Germany was 'waging a life-and-death struggle against England', as had been said in another connexion, he could only construe this as meaning that Germany was fighting 'for life' and England 'for death'. As to the question of collaboration, he quite approved of it, but he added that they had to come to a thorough understanding. All these great issues of tomorrow could not be separated from the issues of today and the fulfilment of existing agreements. The things that had been begun must first be completed before they proceeded to new tasks.

---

[1] Molotov had asked what the German reaction would be to a Russian guarantee for Bulgaria.

20 From *Blitzkrieg* to World War, 1941–45

1 *Hitler's directive for the invasion of Russia, 18 December 1940*

The failure of the conversations with Molotov, together with the refusal of Spain and France to cooperate in the Mediterranean, confirmed Hitler in his determination to attack Russia in the following spring and on 18 December he issued a military directive for the invasion of Russia which was to be code-named 'Operation Barbarossa'. This confirmed the initial planning which had been going ahead since August:

The German Wehrmacht must be prepared *to crush Soviet Russia in a quick campaign* (Operation Barbarossa) even before the conclusion of the war against England.

For this purpose the *Army* will have to employ all available units, with the reservation that the occupied territories must be secured against surprises.

For the *Luftwaffe* it will be a matter of releasing such strong forces for the Eastern campaign in support of the Army that a quick completion of the ground operations can be counted on and that damage to eastern German territory by enemy air attacks will be as slight as possible. This concentration of the main effort in the east is limited by the requirement that the entire combat and armament area dominated by us must remain adequately protected against enemy air attacks and that the offensive operations against England, particularly against her supply lines, must not be permitted to break down.

The main effort of the *Navy* will remain unequivocally directed against England, even during an Eastern campaign.

I shall order the *concentration* against Soviet Russia possibly eight weeks before the intended beginning of operations.

Preparations requiring more time to get under way are to be started now, if this has not yet been done, and are to be completed by 15 May 1941.

It is of decisive importance, however, that the intention to attack does not become apparent.

The preparations of the High Commands are to be made on the following basis:

I. *General purpose*

The mass of the Russian *Army* in western Russia is to be destroyed in daring operations, by driving forward deep armoured wedges; and the retreat of units capable of combat into the vastness of Russian territory is to be prevented.

In quick pursuit a line is then to be reached from which the Russian air force will no longer be able to attack the territory of the German Reich. The ultimate objective of the operation is to establish a cover against Asiatic Russia from the general line Volga–Archangel. Then, in case of necessity, the last industrial area left to Russia in the Urals can be eliminated by the Luftwaffe.

In the course of these operations the Russian *Baltic Sea Fleet* will quickly lose its bases and thus will no longer be able to fight.

Effective intervention by the Russian *air force* is to be prevented by powerful blows at the very beginning of the operation.

II. *Probable allies and their tasks*

1. On the wings of our operation the active participation of *Romania* and *Finland* in the war against Soviet Russia is to be expected.

The High Command will in due time arrange and determine in what form the armed forces of the two countries will be placed under German command at the time of their intervention.

2. It will be the task of *Romania* to support with selected forces the attack of the German southern wing, at least in its beginnings; to pin the enemy down where German forces are not committed; and otherwise to render auxiliary service in the rear area.

3. *Finland* will cover the concentration of the German *North Group* (parts of the XXI Group) withdrawn from Norway and will operate jointly with it. Besides, Finland will be assigned the task of eliminating Hangö.

4. It may be expected that *Swedish* railroads and highways will be available for the concentration of the German North Group, from the start of operations at the latest. . . .

Before the attack could go ahead, however, an awkward situation which had developed in the Balkans had to be cleared up. It was a result of Italy's abortive attempt to capture Greece with an attack launched from Albania on 28 October 1940. This attempt by Mussolini to realize Italian ambitions in the Mediterranean had not been coordinated with Germany and went directly counter to the German interest in keeping the Balkans quiet preparatory to the attack on Russia.[1] But Mussolini had resented Hitler's failure to give him adequate warning of German actions and now paid him back in his own coin. The whole affair illustrated the dangers of the lack of coordination between the Axis Powers. Not only did the Italian attack fail to make headway, but it opened the way for Britain to establish bases in Greece, as an ally, and thereby exposed the Romanian oilfields and the southern flank of the German offensive in Russia to Allied air attacks. Hitler was obliged, therefore, in order to clear the British out of Greece, to launch on 6 April a campaign in the Balkans which included at the last minute an attack on Yugoslavia, where a pro-British Government had just been installed by means of a *coup*. Although the German offensive was quickly successful, it did mean a postponement of the Russian campaign by four weeks and the southern prong of the German advance was slightly weakened

[1] For a different interpretation of the Balkan question, see Martin L. Van Creveld, *Hitler's Strategy 1940–1941: The Balkan Clue* (Cambridge 1973), which appeared after the present work had gone to press.

by the diversion of troops. In his last days, Hitler blamed Mussolini for the loss of the war owing to this postponement, which meant, he maintained, that the German armies had not time to defeat Russia before the onset of winter. This, however, was undoubtedly an exaggeration. Apart from anything else, the muddy conditions in western Russia in spring would not allow an attack before June.

2 *Rapid change in assessment of the progress of the Russian campaign, July–August 1941*

Operation Barbarossa began on 22 June 1941 and initially the German armies made rapid progress. Stalin had ignored warnings of the attack from the Allies and from his Intelligence, because he could not believe that the Germans would dare to initiate a war on two fronts. He assumed the German preparations were bluff designed to force him to be more conciliatory. And, indeed, in the months preceding the attack he had made serious attempts to be conciliatory. As a result, the Germans were able to take full advantage of the element of surprise and in the first two days half the Russian air force was wiped out on the ground. Whole Russian armies were soon surrounded and it appeared as if the *Blitzkrieg* strategy would once more be successful.

Before the campaign both Hitler and the German military leadership had totally underestimated the strength of the Red Army, arguing partly from the purge of officers in 1937 and partly from its poor performance in the Russo–Finnish war of 1939–40. They estimated that the Russians would be defeated in a matter of two to three months, and this opinion was shared by most military experts in the Allied countries. This helps to explain what in hindsight appears to be the incredible folly of the German attack. During August, however, they began to become aware of the size of the task they had taken on. This changing appreciation of the situation is evident in the entries in General Halder's diary:

3.vii.41
On the whole, then, it may already be said that the aim of shattering the bulk of the Russian army this side of the Dvina and the Dniepr has been accomplished. I do not doubt the statement of the captured Russian Corps CG that, east of Dvina and the Dniepr, we would encounter nothing more than partial forces, not strong enough to hinder the realization of German operational plans. It is thus probably no overstatement to say that the Russian campaign has been won in the space of two weeks. Of course, this does not yet mean that it is closed. The sheer geographical vastness of the country and the stubbornness of the resistance, which is carried on with every means, will claim our efforts for many more weeks to come.

11.viii.41
The whole situation makes it increasingly plain that we have underestimated the Russian colossus, who consistently prepared for war with that utterly ruthless

determination so characteristic of totalitarian States. This applies to organizational and economic resources, as well as to the communications system and, most of all, to the strictly military potential. At the outset of the war we reckoned with about 200 enemy divisions. Now we have already counted 360. These divisions indeed are not armed and equipped according to our standards, and their tactical leadership is often poor. But there they are, and if we smash a dozen of them, the Russians simply put up another dozen. The time factor favours them, as they are near their own resources, whereas we are moving farther and farther away from ours. And so our troops, sprawled over an immense front line, without any depth, are subjected to the enemy's incessant attacks. Sometimes these are successful, because in these enormous spaces too many gaps have to be left open.

3 *The proposal of the Commander-in-Chief of the Army for the conduct of the Eastern Campaign, 18 August 1941*

Towards the end of August, a vital decision had to be taken on the further conduct of the Eastern Campaign. The German invasion force was divided into three Army Groups—North, Centre and South. The question was, on which of these should the main emphasis of the German advance lie? The Army High Command advocated that the main thrust should come from Army Group Centre towards Moscow because the Russians would commit the bulk of their forces for the defence of Moscow. The Germans would thus have the opportunity of destroying the bulk of the Russian forces at one blow and also of capturing the valuable industrial area around Moscow:

1. *The enemy situation*
The distribution of the enemy forces indicates that at the present time, after the annihilation of the enemy forces facing Army Group South and with the impending successes of Army Group North, the bulk of the intact military forces of the enemy is in front of Army Group Centre. The enemy therefore appear to regard an attack by Army Group Centre in the direction of Moscow as the main threat. They are employing every means (troop concentrations, fortifications) in order to block this attack. It is unlikely that the enemy will significantly weaken their forces in front of Army Group Centre in order to reinforce those in front of Army Groups South and North. It is more likely that, in view of their increasingly evident shortage of forces, they will attempt to achieve a tight defensive position by pulling back advanced outposts, thereby shortening the front as much as possible.

2. *The objective of the operation*
The further objectives of Army Groups South and North are, apart from the defeat of the enemy forces confronting them, in the first instance to capture essential industrial areas and to eliminate the Russian fleet. The immediate objective of Army Group Centre, on the other hand, is, above all, the destruction of the strong enemy forces confronting it, thereby breaking down the enemy's defences. If we succeed in smashing these enemy forces, the Russians will no longer be capable of establishing a defensive position. This will create the necessary conditions for the occupation of the industrial area of Moscow. Only the elimination of this industrial area, together with the successes of Army Groups South and

North, will remove the possibility of the enemy's rebuilding their defeated armed forces and re-establishing them on an operationally effective basis.

The decision about the operational objective for Army Group Centre must take into account the following basic points:

(a) The time factor. The offensive by Army Group Centre cannot continue after October on account of weather conditions. The suggested offensive in the direction of Moscow can be carried out as far as can be judged within this time limit. On the other hand, this whole period will be required in view of the distances involved and the resistance of the enemy. As a result, we will not be able to push forward with the motorized units on their own without support from the infantry.

(b) Even after refuelling, the motorized units can only be effective over short distances and with diminishing combat strength. As a result, they must be only used for the essential tasks involved in the decisive operation.

(c) The suggested operation can only be successful if the forces of Army Group Centre are systematically concentrated on this single goal to the exclusion of other tactical actions which are not essential for the success of the operation. Otherwise, time and energy will not suffice to deal a decisive blow against the enemy forces confronting Army Group Centre and their sources of supply during the course of this year. This, however, must remain the objective of the military leadership. Army Group South and Army Group North will be able to fulfil the tasks assigned to them with their own resources. . . .

4 *Hitler's reply to the proposal of the Commander-in-Chief of the Army, 22 August 1941*

Hitler, however, was more concerned with political and economic aspects. He wanted to link up with Finland in the north by capturing Leningrad which would also cut off Russia's access to the Baltic. In the south he was anxious to capture the rich agricultural area of the Ukraine and to secure the oilfields on the Black Sea coast. He also believed that a German advance on the Caucasus would apply pressure on Turkey to enter the war on the German side. He regarded the capture of Moscow as of lesser significance than these objectives in the north and south. Finally, he was tempted by the opportunity of encircling the huge Russian forces concentrated around Kiev. He therefore rejected the OKH memorandum and ordered part of the forces of Army Group Centre to be switched to Army Groups North and South and insisted that the advance on Moscow should be postponed until the objectives in the north and south had been achieved. It was a decision which had momentous consequences:

The proposal drawn up by the Commander-in-Chief of the Army on 18 August 1941 for the future operations of Army Group Centre in conjunction with Army Groups South and North prompts me to go over once again the salient points in this campaign.

1. The objective of this campaign is finally to eliminate Russia as a Continental ally of Great Britain and thereby to remove from Britain all hope of changing the course of events with the help of the last remaining Great Power.

2. This objective can only be achieved:
   (a) through the annihilation of the Russian combat forces;
   (b) through the occupation, or at least destruction, of the economic bases which
are essential for a reorganization of the Russian armed forces.

One must point out in this connexion that the destruction or removal of essential
sources of raw materials is more decisive than the occupation or destruction of
industrial manufacturing plant. . . .

In accordance with the initial decision on the relative importance of the individual combat zones in the east, the following are and remain the most essential
points:

1. The destruction of the Russian position in the Baltic, and
2. The occupation of the Ukrainian areas and those round the Black Sea which are
essential in terms of raw materials for the planned reconstruction of the Russian
armed forces.
3. As already mentioned, in addition, there is the concern for our own oil in
Romania and the necessity of pressing on as fast as possible to a position which
offers Iran at least the prospect of assistance in the foreseeable future.

As a result of the circumstances which have developed, partly because an order
of mine or rather of the OKW was ignored, Army Group North is clearly not in a
position, within a short space of time and with the forces at its disposal, to advance
on Leningrad with a right flanking movement and thereby to be certain of surrounding and destroying this base and the Russian forces defending it. The situation now
demands that Army Group North should be rapidly supplied with the forces which
were intended for it at the beginning of the campaign since it is numerically weaker.
I hope that the three divisions which are being sent will suffice to enable Army
Group North to achieve its objective and to deal with any crises. The cleaning up
and securing of its south-eastern flank can, however, only be carried out by forces
of Army Group Centre.

The faster Army Group North is enabled to clear up its position, i.e. to sur-
round or destroy the Russian opponent through the support of the forces transferred to it by the Army and through the concentration of the Air Force by the
Reich Marshal, the more quickly will the forces of this Army Group, particularly
the motorized units, become available. Then they can use the motorized units put
at their disposal by Army Group Centre to concentrate on their sole remaining
objective, namely to help the advance of Army Group Centre on Moscow.

Just as important, however, in fact even more important, is the clearing up of
the situation between Army Group Centre and Army Group South.

This is a strategic opportunity such as fate only very rarely provides in war.
The enemy is in a salient nearly 300 kilometres long, triangular in shape and surrounded by two Army Groups. It can only be destroyed if at this time Army
Group considerations are not allowed to predominate but are subordinated to the
interests of the overall conduct of the campaign. The objection that time would
then be lost and that the units would no longer be technically equipped for their
advance on Moscow is not decisive in view of this opportunity. The suggestion
that Army Group South should also contribute to this task can be disregarded.
For the decisive point is whether it can contribute. If it can, all the better; if not,
then its task must under no circumstances be therefore neglected and in consequence
remain uncompleted. . . .

The objection that time would be lost and that the attack on Moscow might occur too late or that the tank units would then be unable to fulfil this task for technical reasons is not valid; since after the destruction of the Russian forces, which are still threatening the flank of Army Group Centre, the task of advancing on Moscow will not be more difficult, but considerably easier. For either the Russians will withdraw part of their forces from the central front to cover the gap opening up in the south, or they will immediately bring up the forces which are being created in the rear. In either event, the situation will be better than if the Centre Group tried to advance with the undefeated Russian 5th Army as well as the Russian forces east and west of Kiev acting as a continual threat to its flanks and with the Russians able, in addition, to bring up new formations from the rear as reinforcements. . . .

For these reasons, I am unable to give my general approval to the draft submitted to me by the Army on the further conduct of the operations.

5 *An OKW memorandum on the strategic situation approved by the Führer*

Germany's strategic situation in the late summer of 1941 was summed up by the High Command of the Armed Forces in the following memorandum:

13.ix.41

. . .

For our own prosecution of the war, therefore, the following is necessary:

1. The next and decisive war aim is the collapse of Russia, which must be achieved through the commitment of all the forces which can be spared from the other fronts. If it proves impossible to realize this objective completely during 1941, the continuation of the eastern campaign has top priority for 1942. The acquisition of territory on the southern flank will have great political and economic implications.

Our main aim must be to achieve an alteration in our favour in the political attitude of Turkey. This would significantly improve the military situation in the south-east.

2. Only after the exclusion of Russia as a power factor will it be feasible to concentrate on the battle in the Atlantic and in the Mediterranean against Britain, if possible with the help of French and Spanish bases. Even if Russia was largely crushed by the end of the year, the army and air forces necessary for decisive operations in the Mediterranean, the Atlantic and on the Spanish mainland will not be available until the spring of 1942.

3. It is important that political and military contacts with France and Spain should not be broken off before next spring. On the contrary, they should be strengthened in order to keep France in tow and to continue to persuade her to strengthen West Africa from a military point of view to resist any Anglo-American attack. The difficulty for us, as far as France is concerned, is the need to take into account the rightful interests of our Italian ally. But from a military point of view she is absolutely essential if we are to defeat Britain in the foreseeable future, and therefore she must be approached.

4. On this expanded basis, then, the increasing U-boat offensive can only receive more support from the Air Force from next spring to enable it to continue the blockade of England with greater success.

5. Operations in the eastern Mediterranean are only feasible when the Transcaucasus has been reached.

6. The invasion of Britain can only be seriously considered if, despite the collapse of Russia, all means fail to get Spain or France to take part in the war on the side of the Axis, and if, on account of this, the battle of the Atlantic is not sufficiently successful to ensure the defeat of Britain by this method.

6 *The Commander-in-Chief of Army Group Centre on the reasons for the reverse in front of Moscow, 7 December 1941*

When the advance of Army Group Centre on Moscow began again on 2 October 1941, many of the motorized units were only at 30-40 per cent of their full strength. Moreover, the onset of the autumn rains slowed down the advance, since only tracked vehicles could move effectively through the mud. And then the Russian winter set in early and with full force. The warnings of the Army High Command in their August memorandum on the time factor and the technical problems now proved correct. It was a premiss of the *Blitzkrieg* strategy that Russia would be defeated before the onset of winter. As a result, the German army was not equipped with winter clothing, nor was German military equipment and transport designed for the conditions of the Russian winter. With supply lines already over-extended, the breakdown in transport, made worse by existing shortages of locomotives and rolling stock, was potentially disastrous. Then, on 5 December, with German spearheads in the northern suburbs of Moscow, the Russians launched a massive counter-offensive both north and south of Moscow with fifty-seven fresh infantry, and seventeen armoured, divisions drawn largely from Siberia and well equipped for winter fighting. Writing two days after the counter-attack began, the Commander-in-Chief of Army Group centre, von Bock, reviewed the factors which had led to that situation:

... Three things have led to the present crisis:
   1. The setting in of the autumn mud season.
      Troop movements and supplies were almost completely paralysed by the mud-covered roads. It is no longer possible to exploit the victory of Vyazma.
   2. The failure of the railways.
      Weaknesses in the organization, a shortage of wagons, of locomotives and of trained personnel—the inability of the locomotives and the equipment to withstand the Russian winter.
   3. The underestimation of the enemy's resistance and of his reserves of men and material.
The Russians have understood how to increase our transport difficulties by destroying almost all the bridges on the main lines and roads to such an extent that the front lacks the basic necessities of life and of fighting equipment. Ammunition, fuel, food, and winter clothing do not reach the front line. . . .
   The Russians have managed in a surprisingly short time to reconstitute divisions which had been smashed, to bring new ones from Siberia, Iran, and the Caucasus up to the threatened front, and to replace the artillery which has been lost by

numerous rocket launchers. There are now twenty-four more divisions in the sector of this Army Group than there were on 15 November. By contrast, the strength of the German divisions has sunk to less than half as a result of the unbroken fighting and of the winter, which has arrived with full force; the fighting strength of the tanks is even less. The losses of officers and N.C.O.s are terribly high and at the moment replacements for them are even more difficult to get than new troops. . . .

Hitler's Army commanders advised a withdrawal to less exposed positions. Hitler, however, feared that a retreat might become a rout. On 16 December, therefore, he ordered all the German armies to stand firm and fight. Generals who withdrew were dismissed. On the following day, he accepted the resignation of the Commander-in-Chief of the Army, General Brauchitsch, and took over the High Command of the Army himself. A few days earlier, Halder had noted in his diary, 'The C.-in-C. is little more than a postman', and from then onwards Hitler's interference at all levels of Army operations increased still further. His order did, however, have the effect of stabilizing the situation and on 15 January 1942 he gave permission for a withdrawal to winter positions.

7 *The German declaration of war on the United States, 11 December 1941*

The reverse in front of Moscow was a disastrous setback for Germany because it represented the bankruptcy of their whole *Blitzkrieg* strategy. They were now faced with a long war on two fronts, the very situation which Hitler had planned to avoid. Moreover, in the same month, Germany's strategic situation suffered another devastating blow from a different area, a blow that was partly self-inflicted. On 7 December 1941, Japan attacked the United States fleet at Pearl Harbor. Hitler had envisaged the alliance with Japan as a means of attacking Britain's Far Eastern position and of intimidating the Americans into maintaining their neutrality. He had not envisaged a Japanese attack on the United States. Even so, under the Tripartite Pact of September 1940, Germany was not bound to come to Japan's assistance unless Japan was attacked by another power. Germany, therefore, was not bound to join Japan in the war against America. Now, however, overestimating Japanese strength, Hitler convinced himself not only that the Japanese attack was to Germany's advantage, but that Germany should also declare war on the United States. He had long resented American assistance to Britain and he now believed that, if Germany declared war on the United States, this would simply replace a virtual state of war with an actual one. He failed to appreciate that if the United States was not at war with Germany there was the possibility that she would turn her attention away from helping Britain in Europe to her own problems in the Pacific. Moreover, American help for Russia in the form of supplies of war material helped the Russians to make a more speedy recovery:

...

Mr Chargé d'Affaires: The Government of the United States of America, having violated in the most flagrant manner and in ever increasing measure all rules of neutrality in favour of the adversaries of Germany and having continually been guilty of the most severe provocations toward Germany ever since the outbreak of the European War, provoked by the British declaration of war against Germany on 3 September 1939, has finally resorted to open military acts of aggression.

On 11 September 1941, the President of the United States of America publicly declared that he had ordered the American Navy and Air Force to shoot on sight at any German war vessel. In his speech of 27 October 1941, he once more expressly affirmed that this order was in force.

Acting under this order, vessels of the American Navy, since early September 1941, have systematically attacked German naval forces. Thus, American destroyers, as for instance the *Greer*, the *Kearney* and the *Reuben James*, have opened fire on German submarines according to plan. The Secretary of the American Navy, Mr Knox, himself confirmed that American destroyers attacked German submarines.

Furthermore, the naval forces of the United States of America under order of their Government and contrary to international law have treated and seized German merchant vessels on the high seas as enemy ships.

The German Government therefore establishes the following facts:

Although Germany on her part has strictly adhered to the rules of international law in her relations with the United States of America during every period of the present war, the Government of the United States of America from initial violations of neutrality has finally proceeded to open acts of war against Germany. It has thereby virtually created a state of war.

The Government of the Reich consequently discontinues diplomatic relations with the United States of America and declares that in these circumstances brought about by President Roosevelt Germany also, as from today, considers herself as being in a state of war with the United States of America.

Accept, Mr Chargé d'Affaires, the expression of my high consideration.

RIBBENTROP

8 *The Battle of Stalingrad, July 1942–January 1943*

During the summer of 1942, the German armies managed to make up for their setback in the previous winter, advancing rapidly south-eastwards. Hitler concentrated on trying to destroy the economic basis of the Russian war effort by capturing the oilfields of the Caucasus and the industrial Donets basin. Then, he hoped, he would be able to establish an 'Eastern Wall' from Archangel in the north to Astrakhan in the south, behind which Germany could bring her whole armed strength to bear on the defeat of Britain. In this, however, he overreached himself. Instead of concentrating his forces either on the capture of the key city of Stalingrad or on the Caucasus, he divided them. While the 1st and 4th Panzer Armies were sent to attack Rostov and advance into the Caucasus, the 6th Army was left to advance on Stalingrad alone in what Hitler assumed was just a mopping-up operation. When it became clear that Stalingrad was a tough proposition, the 4th Panzer Army was diverted to the city, thereby critically weakening the Caucasus offensive. The battle for Stalingrad began on 17 August, and on the 23rd the 6th Army received the order to take the city. Although in the course of the autumn the Germans managed to capture nearly the whole of the city, Russian resistance was bitter, and assisted by supplies and heavy artillery support from across the River Volga. By November the northern flank of the German forces between Voronezh and Stalingrad, which was manned mainly by Hungarian, Italian and Romanian troops, had become dangerously exposed to a counter-attack and in the meantime the Russians had been quietly preparing a massive counter-offensive. Hitler's generals advised him to withdraw to a less vulnerable position, but he was determined to capture the city. Apart from its importance as the hub of Russian transport and communications in the south-eastern part of European Russia, the name of the city had symbolic significance. In a speech to his old Party comrades at the annual reunion in commemoration of the Munich putsch, Hitler committed himself to its capture:

(a) *Hitler's speech in the Löwenbräu Cellar in Munich, 8 November 1942*

... I have always been ridiculed as a prophet. Innumerable people who laughed then do not laugh now, and those who laugh now will perhaps after a time stop laughing. Realization of this will spread from Europe throughout the whole world. International Jewry will be recognized in all its devilish power, we National Socialists will see to that. In Europe this danger has been recognized and State after State is imitating our legislation. So in this gigantic struggle there is only one possible outcome: complete success. ... What our soldiers have achieved in terms of speed is tremendous. And what has been achieved this year is enormous and historically unprecedented. The fact that I don't do things the way other people want—well, I consider what the others are likely to think and then I do things differently on principle. So if Mr Stalin expected us to attack in the centre—I had no intention of attacking in the centre. Not only because Mr Stalin may have believed that I wanted to, but because I was not interested. I wanted to get to the Volga at a certain point near a certain town. As it happens, its name is that of Stalin himself. But please do not think that I marched there for that reason—it could be called something quite different—I did so because it is a very important point. Thirty million tons of transport can be cut off there, including nearly nine million tons of oil. All the wheat from the vast Ukraine and the Kuban area converges there in order to be transported north. Manganese ore is mined there; it is a huge reloading point. I wanted to take it and, you know, we are being modest, for we have got it! There are only a few very small places left. Now others are saying: 'Why don't you fight more quickly then?' Because I do not want a second Verdun there but I prefer to do it with quite small detachments of assault troops. Time is no object here. Not a single ship is now getting up the Volga. And that is the decisive thing! ...

The decisive factor in this war is, Who deals the final blow? And you may be sure that it will be us!

The diary of the High Command of the Wehrmacht continues the story:

(b) *Excerpts from the diary of the High Command of the Armed Forces,*
     November 1942–January 1943

7 November 1942. The Chief of the General Staff of the Army reports at the
briefing that, according to agents' reports, a Supreme Council Meeting [*Kronrat*]
took place on 4 November in Moscow at which all the Commanders-in-Chief were
present. At this meeting it was decided to carry out a major offensive either on the
Don front or in the Centre by the end of the year. . . .

19 November 1942. During the day, alarming reports arrive from the Chief of the
General Staff of the Army concerning the Russian offensive which has long been
awaited by the Führer and which began this morning in the sector held by the
3rd Romanian Army.[1]

20 November 1942. The Chief of the General Staff of the Army reports that the
Russians have driven a deep wedge into the 3rd Romanian Army sector. The
situation is not yet clear. In the afternoon, the Führer orders the evacuation of the
Army High Command 11 from Vitebsk to the Army Group B in order that it may
take over the High Command for the Don region with the 3rd and 4th Romanian
Armies, the 4th Panzer Army and the 6th Army subordinate to it.

21 November 1942. The Russian breakthrough in the front of the 3rd Romanian
Army between Kletskaya and Serafimovich has deepened considerably. By midday
on 20 November Russian tank spearheads had reached the Guryev region in the
upper Liska valley and the area to the south. South of Stalingrad too and in the
Kalmyk steppes the Russians have launched an attack with strong forces and large
numbers of tanks against the eastern flank of the 4th Panzer Army and the 4th
Romanian Army.

In the evening, the Führer orders the 6th Army, whose headquarters is apparently
in Kalach, to hold the western and southern corners of their position under all
circumstances.

22 November 1942. The two wedges of the major Russian offensive in the Don–
Volga region have joined together near Kalach. In consequence, the 6th Army is
surrounded between the Volga and the Don. . . .

25 November 1942. The 6th Army which is now surrounded has held its fronts,
though its supply situation is critical and, in view of the unfavourable winter
weather and the enemy superiority in fighters, it is very doubtful whether the 700
tons of food, ammunition, fuel, etc. per day, which the Army has requested, can be
transported to the pocket by air. Air Fleet 4 has only 298 transport planes, whereas
500 are required. The General in command of the VIII Flying Corps in action
near Stalingrad, Colonel-General Freiherr von Richthofen, has therefore suggested to the Führer that the 6th Army should for the time being retire to the
west in order to be able to go over to the offensive later. But the Führer rejected
the idea from the outset. . . .

23 January 1943. . . . The Führer has replied in the negative to the question put by
Zeitzler[2] yesterday evening as to whether the 6th Army could now be permitted to

---

[1] North-west of Stalingrad.
[2] General Kurt Zeitzler was the new Chief of the Army General Staff. Halder had been dismissed
in the autumn because of disagreement over Stalingrad.

capitulate. The Army must fight on to the last man in order to gain time. General Paulus replied to a radio message in this vein from the Führer which was sent to the 6th Army: 'Your commands will be carried out. Long live Germany!'
28 January 1943. The main subject of discussion at the briefing today was the re-establishment of the 6th Army, which the Führer wishes to be carried out as quickly as possible.
31 January 1943. In the morning the last radio message from the Southern Group of the 6th Army arrived from Stalingrad.
2 February 1943. In the morning the last radio message from the Northern Group of the 6th Army arrived. The Foreign Armies East section of the General Staff of the Army [German Intelligence] assesses the number of Russian units which will have become available through the annihilation of the 6th Army at 107 divisions and 13 tank regiments.

In the Stalingrad pocket the Germans had lost twenty-two divisions and a number of Romanian units, comprising in all some 330,000 men.

In the meantime, Germany had suffered two other serious military setbacks. At the end of October 1942, the British and Commonwealth 8th Army had defeated the German Africa Corps at El Alamein in Egypt. And, on the night of 7–8 November 1942, American and British troops landed on the coast of Morocco and Algeria and had soon occupied the whole of French North Africa up to the Tunisian border. By 13 May 1943 all but 650 men of the Axis forces in North Africa had been captured.

Finally, on 24 May 1943 the Commander-in-Chief of the German U-Boats reported that 'in May for every 10,000 tons of enemy shipping sunk one U-Boat was lost, whereas not long ago the figure was one U-Boat lost for every 100,000 tons'. Of these U-Boats 60 per cent were apparently 'almost certainly', and 15 per cent 'possibly', sunk by air attack.

These months, then, from October 1942 to May 1943, mark the turning-point of the war. From now onwards, instead of dictating events to his opponents, Hitler was forced to react to moves made by others. Only occasionally did he launch major initiatives of his own, notably the Kursk offensive in July 1943 and the Ardennes offensive of December 1944. At Kursk he threw his best troops and most modern tanks into a desperate attempt to break through the Russian lines, only to have them ground down by the Russian forces which could then break through the weakened German defences. In the Ardennes his last desperate gamble on breaking through the Allied lines to capture Antwerp was quickly nipped in the bud.

9 *Hitler still believes that Germany will dominate the world, 8 May 1943*

It is an indication of Hitler's megalomania that in May 1943 he was still talking in terms of Germany dominating the world. According to Goebbels, he addressed a meeting of Party leaders along the following lines:

The Führer gave expression to his unshakeable conviction that the Reich will be the master of all Europe. We shall yet have to engage in many fights, but these will undoubtedly lead to magnificent victories. Thereafter the way to world domination is practically certain. To dominate Europe will be to assume the leadership of the world.

In this connexion we naturally cannot accept questions of right and wrong even as a basis of discussion. The loss of this war would constitute the greatest wrong to the German people, victory would give us the greatest right. After all, it will be only the victor who can prove to the world the moral justification for this struggle. . . .

We still have so many chances to hand that we can await further developments with a clear conscience. The Führer rightly recalled that his prophecies in 1919, 1920 and 1921 seemed insolent and impudent. Today they are proved to have been the results of his realistic thinking and of his comprehensive view of the general situation. We must never have the slightest doubt of victory. The Führer is firmly determined in all circumstances to fight this fight through to the end.

By March 1944, the Russian armies had crossed the old Polish frontier and had entered Romania. After a pause for the spring thaw, they renewed their advance on 20 June. It was in the east that the vast bulk of the German forces were concentrated and the inexorable Russian advance implied the inevitable defeat of Germany—it was now only a question of time.

10 *Teleprinter message from Field-Marshal Rommel to Hitler on the situation on the invasion front, 15 July 1944*

In the meantime, the Western Allies had landed in northern France on 6 June 1944. Within six weeks, the German commander in Normandy, Erwin Rommel, was reporting to Hitler that the situation was becoming desperate and was urging him to negotiate:

The situation on the Normandy Front is becoming more difficult every day.

As a result of the fierceness of the fighting, the extremely large amounts of material used by the enemy, particularly in terms of artillery and tanks, and the impact of the enemy air force which is in absolute control of the combat area, our own losses are so high that they seriously reduce the operational effectiveness of our divisions. Replacements from the homeland are few and, owing to the difficult transport situation, only reach the front after several weeks. Compared with the loss of approximately 97,000 men, including 2160 officers and among them 28 generals and 354 commanding officers, i.e. on average 2500–3000 men per day, we have so far received only 6000 men. The losses of material by the troops in action are also extremely high and only a small amount can be replaced, e.g. out of 225 tanks only 17.

The new divisions which have been sent are inexperienced in combat and, in view of the small amount of artillery and anti-tank weapons at their disposal, are in the long run incapable of successfully repulsing major offensives which are preceded by several hours of artillery bombardment and heavy air attacks. As has been demonstrated by the battles so far, even the bravest troops are destroyed piecemeal by the amount of material employed by the enemy.

The supply situation is so difficult, because of the destruction of the railway network and the vulnerability of the roads to air attack up to 150 kilometres behind the front, that only the most necessary supplies can be brought up and we have to economize carefully, especially on artillery and mortar ammunition. We can no longer send significant numbers of new troops to the Normandy front. The enemy front line units, on the other hand, receive new forces and supplies of war material every day. Our Air Force has no effect on the enemy supply lines. The pressure of the enemy is becoming greater and greater.

In these circumstances, we must assume that the enemy will succeed in the foreseeable future—a fortnight to three weeks—in breaking through our own front line, above all, that held by the 7th Army, and will go forward deep into France. The consequences will be incalculable.

The troops are fighting everywhere with heroism, yet the unequal struggle is coming to an end. I must request that you draw the necessary conclusions from this situation. I feel myself duty bound as Commander-in-Chief of the Army Group to make myself clear.

Hitler refused to accept this analysis of the situation and shortly afterwards Rommel was ordered to commit suicide in the aftermath of the 20 July plot. But although the Germans did succeed in staving off an Allied victory, which some had expected by the end of 1944, and even launched a counter-attack, this was only at the expense of weakening their eastern front. The end came at Rheims on 7 May 1945, when General Jodl and Admiral von Friedeburg signed an unconditional surrender of all the German forces which was presented to them jointly by the representatives of Great Britain, the United States, the Soviet Union, and France.

11 *Numbers killed during the war*

Although the invasion of France had accelerated Germany's defeat, it did not basically alter the military situation. It was Russia which in Churchill's phrase had 'torn the guts' out of the German military machine. The significance of the Allied invasion proved to be that it ensured that Western Europe, including Western Germany, did not fall within the Russian sphere of influence. The figures of those killed during the war provide an indication of the relative significance of the various fronts:

Soviet Union:	over 20 million	(13·6 million soldiers)
Germany:	over 7 million	(4·2 million soldiers, more than two-thirds of them in the Russian campaign)
United States:	259,000	(in both the European and Pacific theatres)
Great Britain:	386,000	(including 60,000 civilian air raid victims)

21 The Ideological War

The outbreak of war had important implications for the ideological programme of the Nazis.[1] During the period of diplomatic tension of 1938–1939 the Nazi regime had begun to move away from the period of comparative moderation which had followed the revolutionary years of 1933–34. The years 1938–39 had, for example, seen an increasingly ruthless persecution of the Jews. With the outbreak of war this trend was vastly accelerated. Since 1933 the Nazis had been promoting the psychological as well as the military preparation of the German people for war. Now the crisis situation created by the war provided them at last with the opportunity of carrying out the racialist programme which represented the core of National Socialist ideology. As Goebbels wrote in 1943, the Führer 'is right in saying that the war has made it possible for us to solve a whole series of problems which could never have been cleared up in normal times. The Jews will certainly be the losers in this war whatever happens.' It is important to emphasize this ideological aspect because there is a temptation to become mesmerized by the tactical agility of Hitler's diplomatic and strategic manoeuvres into concluding that he was a pure opportunist whose ideological principles were merely a façade.

It was in the east that the racialist programme found full expression. For the war in the east was something very different from that waged in the west or in North Africa. In the west and in Africa it was a more or less conventional war. There were, it is true, a number of atrocities and the Gestapo actions against the resistance movements in the occupied territories showed their characteristic ruthlessness. Men were conscripted for labour in Germany and the Jews were rounded up. Nevertheless, the basic distinction between the two areas remains. It is significant, for example, that the Jews in the west were transported to the east for liquidation. For the war in the east was an ideological war and this ideological aspect emerged as soon as Poland had been conquered.

1 *Decree of the Führer and Reich Chancellor to strengthen German Nationhood, 7 October 1939*

Responsibility for the enforcement of the racialist programme embodied in Nazi ideology, a programme which involved the deportation and subsequent extermination of the Jews, the deportation of Slavs and the settlement of

[1] See also the last section of Chapter 15, pp. 485ff above.

Germans, was placed in the hands of Himmler and the SS. Himmler formed five *Einsatzgruppen*, or task forces, each 400–600 strong, to follow the German troops into Poland and murder the Polish upper class. These forces were drawn from the Security Police and the SD. Within the first few weeks they had killed many thousands of aristocrats, priests and intellectuals. On 7 October 1939, Hitler appointed Himmler Reich Commissioner for the Strengthening of German Nationhood. His initial function was to deport Poles and Jews from the Polish provinces annexed to the Reich and to replace them with German settlers:

The consequences of the Versailles Treaty have been removed in Europe. Now the Greater German Reich has the opportunity of admitting into its territory and resettling those Germans who had to live abroad, and to arrange the settlement of the racial groups, within its sphere of interest, so as to improve the dividing lines between them. I entrust the Reichsführer SS with the execution of this task according to the following regulations:

I

The Reichsführer SS has the duty in accordance with my directives:
1. of repatriating persons of German race and nationality now resident abroad who are considered suitable for permanent return to the Reich;
2. of eliminating the harmful influence of those alien parts of the population, which constitute a danger to the Reich and German community;
3. of forming new German settlements by the transfer of populations and in particular by settling the German citizens and racial Germans returning from abroad.

The Reichsführer SS is authorized to issue such general instructions and to take such administrative measures as may be necessary to carry out these duties.

In order to carry out the tasks given to him under Article I, No. 2, the Reichsführer SS can assign specific settlement areas to the sections of the population concerned.

II

In the occupied former Polish territories the Head of the Administration in the Ober-Ost area carries out the task assigned to the Reichsführer SS in accordance with the latter's general instructions. The Head of Administration Ober-Ost and the subordinate administrative officers of the military districts are responsible for the executive measures. These measures must then conform to the requirements of the military leadership.

Persons who are given special missions in the execution of this task will not be subject to military jurisdiction in that respect.

III

The tasks assigned to the Reichsführer SS with regard to the reorganization of German agriculture will be carried out by the Reich Minister for Food and Agriculture following the general directives of the Reichsführer SS.

For other matters connected with his duties within the territory of the German Reich, the Reichsführer SS will make use of the existing authorities and institutions of the Reich, the states and the municipalities as well as all other public bodies and the existing resettlement associations.

If agreement required by law and administrative organization cannot be reached about a specific measure between the Reichsführer SS and the competent senior Reich authority in the operational area of the Commander-in-Chief of the Army, my decision must be sought through the Reich Minister and the Head of the Reich Chancellery.

IV

Negotiations with foreign Governments and other authorities as well as with racial Germans, as long as they are still abroad, will be conducted in cooperation with the Reich Minister for Foreign Affairs.

V

If land is required for the settlement within Germany of repatriated German citizens or racial Germans, the law of 29 March 1935, concerning land acquisition for defence purposes, and its executive regulations will be applied to provide the necessary land. The tasks of the Reich Agency for Land Acquisition will be taken over by an agency designated by the Reichsführer SS.

The Reichsminister for Finance will provide the Reichsführer SS with the funds necessary for the execution of these measures.

With the powers delegated to him under this decree Himmler was able to establish his own administrative apparatus within the occupied territories, subordinate only to the Führer, and was authorized to give orders to the civil authorities within the sphere of his own responsibilities.

Poland was now divided into three parts. The western areas which had belonged to Germany before 1918 were incorporated in the Reich, either in the existing *Gaue* of East Prussia and Silesia or to form the new *Gaue* of Wartheland and West Prussia. Central Poland was placed under German administration, forming the so-called '*Generalgouvernement*' under Hans Frank, the head of the Nazi Lawyers' Association, as Governor-General. The eastern parts were occupied by Russia under the terms of the secret annex to the Nazi-Soviet Pact of 24 August 1939.[1]

2 *Hitler's instructions for the occupation of Poland*

Hitler's determination to treat the *Generalgouvernement* as an area for ruthless exploitation emerged in his instructions for the occupation of Poland. Significant is his determination to keep Poland entirely distinct from the Reich, so that it was not subject to the Reich bureaucracy which might otherwise interfere in the enforcing of the racialist programme:

1. The armed forces should welcome the opportunity of avoiding having to deal with administrative questions in Poland. On principle there cannot be two administrations.

[1] See above, p. 561.

2. Poland is to be made autonomous. It will be neither a separate part of the German Reich nor an administrative district of the Reich.

3. It is not the task of the administration to turn Poland into a model province or a model state in accordance with the principles of German order; nor is it its task to put the country on a sound basis economically and financially. The Polish intelligentsia must be prevented from forming itself into a ruling class. The standard of living in the country is to remain low; it is of use to us only as a reservoir of labour. Poles too are to be used for the administration of the country. But the formation of national political groups will not be permitted.

4. The administration must work on its own responsibility and must not be dependent on Berlin. We do not want to do anything there which we do in the Reich. Responsibility does not rest with the Berlin ministries, since no German administrative unit is involved. The accomplishment of this task will involve a hard racial struggle [*Volkstumskampf*] which will not permit any legal restrictions. The methods will be incompatible with the principles which we otherwise adhere to. . . .

5. *Our interests are as follows*: The territory is important to us from a military point of view as an advanced jumping-off point and can be used for the strategic concentration of troops. To that end, the railways, roads and lines of communication are to be kept in order and utilized for our purposes. Any tendencies toward stabilizing the situation in Poland are to be suppressed. 'Polish muddle' must be allowed to flourish. The fact that we are governing the territory should enable us to purify the Reich territory also of Jews and Polacks. Collaboration with the new Reich *Gaue* (Posen and West Prussia) only for resettlement purposes (compare Himmler mission). Purpose: Shrewdness and severity must be the maxims in this racial struggle in order to spare us from having to go into battle again on account of this country.

3 *Some Army attitudes to the SS atrocities in Poland*

The brutal policies initiated by Himmler in his capacity as Reich Commissioner for the Strengthening of German Nationhood horrified the Army units occupying Poland. This disgust was expressed in complaints to the Army High Command. The High Command, however, realized that Himmler was carrying out Hitler's orders and, although Himmler was obliged to give a lecture to the generals explaining his policies, he pointed out that he was only carrying out the Führer's policies. The attitude of sections of the Army is apparent in the following excerpts from a memorandum, dated 6 February 1940, by Colonel-General Blaskowitz, commander of the Ober-Ost military region. It was the second such memorandum by Blaskowitz, a man who was not one of the leading opponents of Hitler among the generals, being a typical professional soldier of limited horizons. His protest cost him a Field-Marshal's baton.

. . .

It is misguided to slaughter tens of thousands of Jews and Poles as is happening at present; because, in view of the huge population neither the concept of a Polish State nor the Jews will be eliminated by doing so. On the contrary, the way in which this slaughter is being carried out is causing great damage; it is complicating the problems and making them much more dangerous than they would have been with a considered and systematic approach. The consequences are:

(a) Enemy propaganda is provided with material which could nowhere have been more effectively devised. It is true that what the foreign radio stations have broadcast so far is only a tiny fraction of what has happened in reality. But we must reckon that the clamour of the outside world will continually increase and cause great political damage, particularly since the atrocities have actually occurred and cannot be disproved.

(b) The acts of violence against the Jews which occur in full view of the public inspire among the religious Poles not only deep disgust but also great pity for the Jewish population, to which up to now the Poles were more or less hostile. In a very short time we shall reach the point at which our arch-enemies in the eastern sphere—the Pole and the Jew, who in addition will receive the particular support of the Catholic Church—will, in their hatred against their tormentors, combine against Germany right along the line.

(c) The role of the armed forces who are compelled impotently to watch this crime and whose reputation, particularly with the Polish population, suffers irreparable harm, need not be referred to again.

(d) But the worst damage which will accrue to the German nation from the present situation is the brutalization and moral debasement which, in a very short time, will spread like a plague among valuable German manpower.

If high officials of the SS and police demand acts of violence and brutality and praise them publicly, then in a very short time we shall be faced with the rule of the thug. Like-minded people and those with warped characters will very soon come together so that, as is now the case in Poland, they can give full expression to their animal and pathological instincts. It is hardly possible to keep them any longer in check, since they can well believe themselves officially authorized and justified in committing any act of cruelty.

The only way of resisting this epidemic is to subordinate those who are guilty and their followers to the military leadership and courts as quickly as possible.

The C.-in-C. of the southern section of the front, General of the Infantry Ulex, expressed himself on 2 February 1940 as follows:

To the C.-in-C. East
Spala

The acts of violence by the police forces which have increased recently demonstrate a quite incredible lack of human and moral feeling, so that it can be called sheer brutalization. And even so I believe that my headquarters only hears of a small number of the acts of violence occurring.

It seems as if the superiors privately approve of this activity and do not wish to intervene.

I see the only way out of this ignoble situation, which besmirches the honour of the whole German nation, in the recall and disbanding at a stroke of all the police units, including all their superior officers and all those leaders in the departments of the 'General Government' who have witnessed these acts of violence for months, and their replacement by sound honourable units.

[signed] ULEX

. . .

The attitude of the troops to the SS and police alternates between abhorrence and hatred. Every soldier feels repelled and revolted by these crimes which are being perpetrated in Poland by nationals of the Reich and representatives of the State authority. He does not understand how such things can happen with impunity, particularly since they occur, so to speak, under his protection.

Every police search and confiscation is accompanied by a tendency for those of the police involved to rob and plunder. It is clearly the normal custom for confiscated articles to be distributed among the police and SS units.

In a conference with the Governor-General on 23 January 1940, Major-General Rührmann reported to the representative of the Four-Year Plan that his skilful director of external departments, a certain Captain Schuh in the cavalry, had succeeded in getting the SS to give up large quantities of watches and gold objects.

Considering such a state of affairs it is naturally not surprising that the individual uses every opportunity to enrich himself. He can do this with no danger to himself, since if everybody steals the individual thief need fear no punishment. There is no doubt that the defenceless Polish population, who have to look on at these crimes and are driven to despair by them, will give fanatical support to any revolt or movement of vengeance. Many people who have never thought of revolt before will use every opportunity of organizing one and will flock to support it, determined to fight. The large peasant population particularly, which, if treated reasonably and objectively by the German administration, would have worked calmly and peacefully for us, is being driven by force, so to speak, into the enemy camp.

The resettlement programme is causing especial and growing discontent throughout the country. It is obvious that the starving population, which is fighting for its existence, can only observe with the greatest concern how the masses of those being resettled are left to find refuge with them completely penniless and, so to speak, naked and hungry.

It is only too understandable that these feelings reach a pitch of uncontrolled hatred at the numbers of children dying of starvation on every transport and the wagons of people frozen to death.

The idea that one can intimidate the Polish population by terrorism and rub their noses in the dirt will certainly prove to be false. This people's capacity for enduring suffering is too great for that. . . .

4 The Euthanasia Order, 1 September 1939

Not only was policy towards the Jews deeply affected by the outbreak of war. Hitler also seized the opportunity created by the new situation to initiate a measure which he had long planned. Already on 14 July 1933, a law had been passed permitting the sterilizing of the mentally and physically handicapped, whose handicaps appeared probably hereditary. In 1935 Hitler had told the Reich Doctors' Leader, Dr Wagner, that 'in the event of a war he would take up the question of euthanasia and enforce it' because 'he was of the opinion that such a problem could be more easily solved in wartime since opposition which could be expected from the Churches would not play so significant a role in the context of war as at other times', and therefore 'in the event of war, he intended to solve the problem of the asylums in a radical way'.[1]

Since euthanasia was illegal according to German law and attempts to legalize it proved abortive for fear of public opinion both at home and abroad, the programme could not be put in the hands of the normal State machinery. In characteristic fashion, therefore, a special agency was set up to handle the matter under Philipp Bouhler, the head of Hitler's private office, the Führer's Chancellery. Hitler told Bouhler that 'he wanted a completely unbureaucratic solution to this problem because he did not want a department such as the Ministry of the Interior, which was stuck in a rut, taking on such a difficult assignment'.[2] Since some formal authority was necessary to show to other departments who might become indirectly involved, Hitler, at the end of October 1939, signed the following order on a sheet of personal notepaper which was backdated to 1 September:

Reichsleiter Bouhler and Dr. med. Brandt are authorized to extend the responsibilities of certain doctors, to be specified by name, so that they may grant euthanasia to those who, so far as can be foreseen after the most careful consideration of their illness, are incurable.

All the organizations involved received euphemistic cover names. Section II of the Führer's Chancellery, which superintended the programme, was given the title of 'Reich Committee for the Scientific Registration of Serious Hereditary Illnesses, Berlin W9, P.O. No. 101' (*Reichsauschuss zur wissenschaftlichen Erfassung von erb- und anlagebedingten schweren Leiden*), the committee of doctors responsible for selecting the victims was the Reich Working Group for Asylums (*Reichsarbeitsgemeinschaft Heil- und Pflege-Anstalten*), and the agency which organized the transport of the victims was the Welfare Transport Company for Invalids Ltd (*Gemeinnützige Kranken Transport GmbH*), known as 'Gekrat' for short. The handicapped people were taken to five or six different asylums where they were either gassed or killed by injections. This part of the programme operated under the auspices of the Welfare Foundation for the Benefit of Asylums (*Gemeinnützige Stiftung für Anstaltspflege*), which employed reliable SS and Party members. It was financed by the Reich Treasury of the Party in order to avoid State regulation. Between January 1940 and August 1941 60,000-80,000 handicapped people were murdered. The 'Action T4', as it came to be known, was finally halted by an order of Hitler to Bouhler dated 24 August 1941, though several thousands subsequently fell victim to '*wild*' or unauthorized euthanasia. The reason for halting the programme was pressure of public

---

[1] quoted in Lothar Gruchmann, 'Euthanasie und Justiz im Dritten Reich', in *Vierteljahrshefte für Zeitgeschichte* (1972), p. 238. I have relied heavily on this article for this document.
[2] ibid., p. 241.

opinion. This received some indirect support from the bureaucracy, particularly in the Ministry of Justice, which resented the way in which the action was being carried on outside the law. This made their position in relation to the population which came to them for redress extremely difficult.

5 *Himmler on the need to propagate children of good blood*

The following documents speak for themselves and illustrate the lengths to which ideological fanaticism was taken:

Berlin, 28 October 1939

Every war is a drain on the best blood. Many a victory of arms has been at the same time a crushing defeat for the life force and blood of a nation. . . .

The old proverb that only he can die in peace who has sons and children must again hold good in this war, particularly for the SS. He can die in peace who knows that his clan and everything that his ancestors and he himself have wanted and striven for will be continued in his children. The greatest gift for the widow of a man killed in battle is always the child of the man she has loved.

Beyond the limits of bourgeois laws and conventions, which are perhaps necessary in other circumstances, it can be a noble task for German women and girls of good blood to become even outside marriage, not lightheartedly but out of deep moral seriousness, mothers of the children of soldiers going to war of whom fate alone knows whether they will return or die for Germany. . . .

During the last war many a soldier decided from a sense of responsibility to have no more children during the war so that his wife would not be left in need and distress after his death. You SS men need not have these anxieties; they are removed by the following regulations:

1. Special delegates chosen by me personally will take over in the name of the Reichsführer SS the guardianship of all legitimate and illegitimate children of good blood whose fathers were killed in the war. We will support these mothers and take over the education and material care of these children until they come of age, so that no mother and widow need suffer want.

2. During the war, the SS will take care of all legitimate and illegitimate children born during the war and of expectant mothers in cases of need. After the war, when the fathers return, the SS will in addition grant generous material help to well-founded applications by individuals.

SS men and mothers of these children which Germany hopes for, show that you are ready, through your faith in the Führer and for the sake of the life of our blood and people, to regenerate life for Germany just as bravely as you know how to fight and die for Germany.

Berlin, 30 January 1940

My order of 28 October 1939, in which I reminded you of your duty if possible to become fathers of children during the war, is known to you.

This publication which, drawn up decently and construed in a decent sense, states and openly discusses actual problems, has led to misconceptions and misunderstanding on the part of some people. I therefore find it necessary that every one of you should know what doubts and misunderstandings have arisen and what there is to say about them.

1. Objection has been taken to the clear statement that illegitimate children exist,

and that some unmarried and single women and girls have always become mothers of such children outside marriage and always will.

There is no point in discussing this; the best reply is the letter from the Führer's Deputy to an unmarried mother which I enclose together with my order of 28 October 1939.[1]

2. The worst misunderstanding concerns the paragraph which reads: 'Beyond the limits of bourgeois laws and conventions, . . .'. According to this, as some people misunderstand it, SS men are encouraged to approach the wives of serving soldiers. However incomprehensible to us such an idea may be, we must discuss it.

What do those who spread or repeat such opinions think of German women? Even if in a nation of 82 million people some man should approach a married woman from dishonourable motives or human weakness, two parties are needed for seduction: the one who wants to seduce and the one who consents to be seduced.

Quite apart from our own view that one does not approach the wife of a comrade, we think that the German woman is probably the best guardian of her honour. Any other opinion should be unanimously rejected by all men as an insult to German women.

Furthermore, the question is raised why the wives of the SS and police are looked after in a special way and are not treated the same as all the others.

The answer is very simple: Because the SS through their willingness to make sacrifices and through comradeship have raised the necessary funds, through voluntary contributions from leaders and men, which have been paid for years to the *Lebensborn* ('Lifespring') association.

After this statement, all misunderstandings should be cleared up.

But it is up to you SS men, as at all times when ideological views have to be put across, to win the understanding of German men and women for this sacred vital issue of our people which rises superior to all cheap jests and mockery.

Field Command Post
Hegewald, 15 August 1942

SS Order to the Last Sons
SS Men!

1. As last sons you have been withdrawn from the front line by the Führer's orders. This step has been taken because nation and State have an interest in your families not dying out.

2. It has never been the way of SS men to accept fate and not contribute anything to change it. It is your duty to ensure as quickly as possible by producing children of good blood that you are no longer last sons.

3. Endeavour to guarantee in one year the survival of your ancestors and your families so that you may be available once again to fight in the front line.

6 *Hitler's directives for the administration of occupied Russia*

With the invasion of Russia, Hitler was determined to extend his racialist

---

[1] In his letter Hess promised that illegitimate children of 'good blood' would have 'war father' entered in the birth register and that the mother would in future be addressed as 'Frau'. He summed up the situation by arguing that 'the family is the basic cell of the State; but, despite this, a nation cannot, especially during wartime, do without the encouragement of racially healthy heirs'.

programme to the area which he had long marked out as Germany's 'living space'. In March 1941, therefore, he laid down the following regulations for the occupation of Russia in which he entrusted Himmler with 'special tasks' which 'result from the necessity of finally resolving the conflict between two opposing political systems' and which he could carry out 'independently':

...

2. As soon as military operations are concluded *the Russian territory* which is to be occupied is to be divided up into individual States with *Governments of their own* in accordance with special instructions:
From this follows:

(a) *The area of operations* created by the advance of the Army beyond the frontiers of the Reich and the neighbouring countries is to be limited in depth as far as possible. The Commander-in-Chief of the Army has the right to exercise executive power in this area and may delegate his authority to the Supreme Commanders of the Army groups and armies.

(b) In the Army's area of operations the Reichsführer SS is entrusted on behalf of the Führer with *special tasks* for the preparation of the *political administration*, tasks which result from the necessity of finally resolving the conflict between two opposing political systems. Within the framework of these tasks the Reichsführer will act independently and on his own responsibility. The executive power vested in the Commander-in-Chief of the Army (OKH) and the agencies to which it may be delegated by him will not however be affected by this. It is the responsibility of the Reichsführer SS to ensure that military operations are not affected by measures taken in the discharge of his task. Details will be settled directly between the OKH and the Reichsführer SS.

(c) As soon as the area of operations has reached sufficient depth, it is to be *limited in the rear*. The newly occupied territory in the rear of the area of operations is to be given its own *political administration*. For the present, it is to be divided, according to its ethnic [*volkstumsmässig*] basis and the positions of the Army groups, into North (Baltic countries), Centre (White Russia) and South (Ukraine). In these territories the *political administration is to be taken over by Commissioners of the Reich* who receive their orders from the Führer. . . .

7 *The principles of the SS*

Himmler summed up the principles which the SS were to apply in Russia in a speech to SS leaders in Posen on 4 October 1943:

...

One basic principle must be the absolute rule for the SS man: we must be honest, decent, loyal, and comradely to members of our own blood and to nobody else. What happens to a Russian or to a Czech does not interest me in the slightest. What the nations can offer in the way of good blood of our type we will take, if necessary by kidnapping their children and raising them here with us. Whether nations live in prosperity or kick the bucket[1] interests me only in so far as we need

---

[1] *Verrecken*, a slang term, used of cattle.

them as slaves for our *Kultur*; otherwise, it is of no interest to me. Whether 10,000 Russian females fall down from exhaustion while digging an anti-tank ditch interests me only in so far as the anti-tank ditch for Germany is finished. We shall never be rough and heartless when it is not necessary, that is clear. We Germans, who are the only people in the world who have a decent attitude towards animals, will also assume a decent attitude towards these human animals. But it is a crime against our own blood to worry about them and give them ideals, thus causing our sons and grandsons to have a more difficult time with them. When somebody comes to me and says, 'I cannot use women and children to dig the anti-tank ditch; it is inhuman, it would kill them', then I have to say, 'You are a murderer of your own blood because if the anti-tank ditch is not dug, German soldiers will die, and they are sons of German mothers. They are our own blood.' That is what I want to instil into the SS and what I believe I have instilled into them as one of the most sacred laws of the future. Our concern, our duty is our people and our blood. It is for them that we must provide and plan, work and fight, nothing else. We can be indifferent to everything else. I wish the SS to adopt this attitude to the problem of all foreign, non-Germanic peoples, especially Russians. All else is vain, false to our own nation, and an obstacle to the early winning of the war. . . .[1]

If the peace is a final one, we shall be able to tackle our great work of the future. We shall colonize. We shall indoctrinate our boys with the laws of the SS. I consider it to be absolutely necessary to the life of our peoples that we should not only impart the meaning of ancestry, grand-children and future, but feel these to be part of our being. Without there being any talk about it, without our needing to make use of rewards and similar material things, it must be a matter of course that we have children. It must be a matter of course that the most copious breeding should be from this racial elite of the German people. In twenty to thirty years we must really be able to provide the whole of Europe with its ruling class. If the SS together with the farmers, and we together with our friend Backe,[2] then run the colony in the east on a grand scale, without any restraint, without any question of tradition, but with nerve and revolutionary impetus, we shall in twenty years push the national boundary [*Volkstumsgrenze*] 500 kilometres eastwards.

Today I have asked the Führer that the SS, if we have fulfilled our task and our duty by the end of the war, should have the privilege of holding Germany's most easterly frontier as a defence frontier. I believe this is the only privilege for which we have no competitors. I believe that not a single person will dispute our claim to this privilege. We shall be in a position there to exercise every young age-group in the use of arms. We shall impose our laws on the east. We shall charge ahead and push our way forward little by little to the Urals. I hope that our generation will successfully bring it about that every age-group has fought in the east, and that every one of our divisions spends a winter in the east every second or third year. Then we shall never grow soft, then we shall never have SS members who come to us only because it is distinguished or because the black coat will naturally be very attractive in peacetime. Everyone will know: 'If I join the SS, there is the possibility that I may be killed.' He has contracted in writing that every other year he will not dance in Berlin or attend the carnival in Munich, but that he will be posted to the eastern frontier in an ice-cold winter. Then we will have a healthy

---

[1] For the part of this speech dealing with the Jews, see above, pp. 492–3.
[2] Herbert Backe had replaced Darré as acting Minister of Agriculture on 23 May 1942.

elite for all time. Thus we will create the necessary conditions for the whole Germanic people and the whole of Europe, controlled, ordered and led by us, the Germanic people, to be able, in generations to come, to stand the test in her battles of destiny against Asia, which will certainly break out again. We do not know when that will be. Then, when the mass of humanity of 1–1½ milliards lines up against us, the Germanic people, numbering, I hope, 250–300 millions, and the other European peoples, making a total of 600–700 millions (and with an outpost area stretching as far as the Urals, or in a hundred years beyond the Urals), must stand the test in its vital struggle against Asia. It would be an evil day if the Germanic people did not survive it. It would be the end of beauty and of *Kultur*, of the creative power of this earth. That is the distant future. It is for that we are fighting, pledged to hand down the heritage of our ancestors.

We see into the distant future, because we know what it will be. That is why we are doing our duty more fanatically than ever, more devoutly than ever, more bravely, more obediently and more thoroughly than ever. We want to be worthy of being permitted to be the first SS-men of the Führer, Adolf Hitler, in the long history of the Germanic people stretching before us.

Now let us remember the Führer, Adolf Hitler, who will create the Germanic Reich and will lead us into the Germanic future.

Our Führer Adolf Hitler
Sieg Heil!
Sieg Heil!
Sieg Heil!

8 *Hitler's speech to the Commanders-in-Chief of the Armed Forces on ideological warfare in Russia, 30 March 1941*

But although Hitler could rely on Himmler's SS, he was not so certain of the attitude of the Army to ideological warfare. Later in March, therefore, Hitler outlined what would be involved in the war with Russia to a conference of military leaders. He drew a distinction between the war in the east and the war in the west and demanded that the Army should not allow any qualms to interfere with the extermination of Bolshevism. This was to be accomplished by killing the Communist intelligentsia and the political commissars attached to the Red Army. Halder recorded Hitler's comments in his diary:

Struggle between two *Weltanschauungen*. Devastating assessment of Bolshevism: it is the equivalent of social delinquency. Communism is a tremendous danger for the future. We must get away from the standpoint of soldierly comradeship. The Communist is from first to last no comrade. It is a war of extermination. If we do not regard it as such, we may defeat the enemy, but in thirty years' time we will again be confronted by the Communist enemy. We are not fighting a war in order to conserve the enemy.

Future State structure: North Russia belongs to Finland. Protectorates for the Baltic States, Ukraine, White Russia.

Fight against Russia: destruction of the Bolshevik commissars and the Communist intelligentsia. A new intelligentsia must be prevented from emerging. A primitive Socialist intelligentsia is sufficient there. The struggle must be fought against the poison of subversion. It is not a question of court martials. The leaders of the troops must know what is involved. They must take the lead in the struggle. The troops must defend themselves with the methods with which they are attacked. Commissars and G.P.U. people are criminals and must be treated as such. That does not mean that the troops need get out of hand. The leader must draw up his orders in accordance with the sentiment of his troops.

The struggle will be very different from that in the west. In the east toughness now means mildness in the future. The leaders must make sacrifices and overcome their scruples.

On 6 June 1941, on the basis of Hitler's statements, the High Command of the Armed Forces (OKW) drew up the so-called Commissar Order which laid down that Red Army political commissars should be segregated from other prisoners on capture and then be handed over to the SS for liquidation. Many generals were shocked at the breach of international law which was involved and were concerned for the discipline of their troops. In practice some carried it out, others circumvented it or ignored it. It was, however, only under the pressure of Russian resistance that, on 6 May 1942, Hitler ordered that 'as an experiment the lives of the Soviet Commissars and Politruks should be spared in order to strengthen the inclination of encircled Russian forces to desert and surrender'.

9 *Heydrich's basic instructions to the Task Forces (*Einsatzgruppen*),*
2 July 1941

The main role in the extermination policy was played by the SS and, in particular, by so-called 'Task Forces' of the Security Police and SD which followed behind the Army. These groups, of which there were four (A, B, C and D), varied in size between 500 and 1000 men and consisted of ordinary police and Waffen SS. Their commanders were senior members of the Security Police and SD. Verbal orders given to the Task Force commanders before the invasion were summarized by Heydrich in a minute issued to the four top SS officials (*Höhere SS und Polizei Führer*) in Russia:

. . .
4. EXECUTIONS. The following will be executed:
All officials of the Comintern (most of these will certainly be career politicians);
Officials of senior and middle rank and 'extremists' in the Party, the Central Committee, and the provincial and district committees;
The People's Commissars;
Jews in the service of the Party or the State;
Other extremist elements (saboteurs, propagandists, snipers, assassins, agitators, etc.); in so far as in individual cases they are not required, or are no longer required, for economic or political intelligence of special importance, for future security police measures, or for the economic rehabilitation of the occupied territories. . . .

No steps will be taken to interfere with any purges that may be initiated by anti-Communist or anti-Jewish elements in the newly occupied territories. On the contrary these are to be *secretly encouraged*. At the same time every precaution must be taken to ensure that those who engage in 'self-defence' actions are not subsequently able to plead that they were acting under orders or had been promised political protection. Special care must be taken in regard to the shooting of doctors and others engaged in medical practice. . . .

10 *A Task Force in operation*

. . .

Task Force A, after preparing their vehicles for action, proceeded to their area of concentration as ordered on 23 June 1941, the second day of the campaign in the east. Army Group North consisting of the 16th and 18th Armies and Panzer Group 4 had left the day before. Our task was to establish personal contact quickly with the commanders of the armies and with the commander of the rear area. It must be stressed from the outset that cooperation with the armed forces was generally good; in some cases, for instance with Panzer Group 4 under Colonel-General Hoeppner, it was very close, almost cordial. Misunderstandings which cropped up with some authorities in the first days were cleared up mainly through personal discussions. . . .

At the start of the eastern campaign it became obvious that the special work of the Security Police had to be done not only in the rear areas, as was provided for in the original agreements with the High Command of the Army, but also in the combat areas, and this for two reasons. On the one hand, the development of the rear area of the armies was delayed because of the rapid advance and, on the other hand, the countering of Communist activities and the fight against partisans was most effective within the area of actual fighting—especially when the Luga sector was reached.

In order to carry out the Security Police duties, it was desirable to move into the larger towns alongside the armed forces. We had our first experiences in this connexion when a small advance detachment under my leadership entered Kaunas together with the advance units of the armed forces on 25 June 1941. When the other larger towns, especially Libau, Mitau, Riga, Dorpat, Reval, and the larger suburbs of Leningrad were captured, a detachment of the Security Police was always with the first Army units. Above all, Communist functionaries and Communist material had to be seized, and the armed forces themselves had to be secured against ambush inside the towns; the troops themselves were usually not able to take care of that owing to their small numbers. For this purpose, immediately after the town had been captured the Security Police formed volunteer detachments from reliable inhabitants in all three Baltic provinces; they carried out their duties successfully under our command. For example, it may be mentioned that the armed forces suffered not inconsiderable losses through guerrillas in Riga, on the left of the Dvina river; on the right bank of the Dvina, however, after these volunteer detachments had been organized in Riga, not a single soldier was injured, although these Latvian detachments suffered some killed and wounded in fighting with Russian stragglers.

Similarly, native antisemitic forces were induced to start pogroms against

Jews during the first hours after capture, though this inducement proved to be very difficult. Carrying out orders, the Security Police were determined to solve the Jewish question with all possible means and most decisively. But it was desirable that the Security Police should not put in an immediate appearance, at least at the beginning, since the extraordinarily harsh measures were apt to cause a stir even in German circles. It had to be shown to the world that the inhabitants themselves took the first action by way of natural reaction against the repression by the Jews over several decades and against the terror exercised by the Communists during the preceding period. . . .

11 *Führer Conference on occupation policy in Russia, 16 July 1941*

On 16 July 1941 Hitler held a conference at which he defined the objectives of Germany's occupation of Russia and appointed those who were to run the German administration in Russia—the Reich Commissioners. Rosenberg had already, on 20 April 1941, been appointed Minister for the Eastern Territories. The minutes of the conference show not only Hitler's determination to exploit Russia but also the beginnings of the clashes of policy and personality which were to bedevil the German occupation of Russia. Rosenberg, himself a Baltic German, wished to distinguish between Great Russia and the other States such as the Ukraine and the Baltic States. In the latter he wished to encourage independence movements and to set up a chain of satellite States between Germany and Great Russia. Göring, who was in charge of the economic exploitation of Russia, Himmler, who was responsible for the enforcement of the racial policies, and Koch, the Reich Commissioner for the Ukraine, had no sympathy with Rosenberg's scheme and no intention of allowing themselves to be restricted by his Ministry for the East. As far as they were concerned, all Russians were the same and should be exploited as ruthlessly as possible:

Unsigned memorandum[1]

A conference attended by Reichsleiter Rosenberg, Reich Minister Lammers, Field-Marshal Keitel, the Reich Marshal [Göring], and myself was held today by order of the Führer at 3.00 p.m. in his quarters. The conference began at 3.00 p.m. and, including a break for coffee, lasted until about 8.00 p.m.

By way of introduction the Führer emphasized that he wished first of all to make some basic statements. Various measures were now necessary; this was confirmed, among other events, by an assertion made in an impudent Vichy newspaper that the war against the Soviet Union was Europe's war and that therefore it had to be conducted for Europe as a whole. Apparently by these hints the Vichy paper meant to say that it ought not to be the Germans alone who benefited from this war, but that all European States ought to benefit from it.

It was essential that we should not proclaim our aims before the whole world; moreover, this was not necessary, but the chief thing was that we ourselves should know what we wanted. In no case should our own way be made more difficult by superfluous declarations. Such declarations were superfluous because we could do

[1] Prepared by Bormann.

everything wherever we had the power, and what was beyond our power we would not be able to do anyway.

What we told the world about the motives for our measures ought therefore to be conditioned by tactical reasons. We ought to proceed here in exactly the same way as we did in the cases of Norway, Denmark, Holland and Belgium. In these cases too we said nothing about our aims, and if we were clever we would continue in the same way.

We shall then emphasize again that we were forced to occupy, administer and secure a certain area; it was in the interest of the inhabitants that we should provide order, food, traffic, etc.; hence our measures. It should not be made obvious that a final settlement is thereby being initiated! We can nevertheless take all necessary measures—shooting, resettling, etc.—and we shall take them.

But we do not want to make enemies of any people prematurely and unnecessarily. Therefore we shall act as though we wanted to exercise a mandate only. It must be clear to *us*, however, that we shall never withdraw from these areas.

Accordingly we should take care:

1. to do nothing which may obstruct the final settlement, but to prepare for it only in secret;

2. to emphasize that we are liberators.

In particular:

The Crimea must be evacuated by all foreigners and be settled by Germans only.

In the same way the former Austrian part of Galicia will become Reich territory.

Our relations with Romania are at present good, but one does not know what our relations will be at any future time. This we have to take account of, and draw our frontiers accordingly. One ought not to be dependent on the good will of other people; we have to arrange our relations with Romania in accordance with this principle.

In principle we have now to face the task of cutting up the giant cake according to our needs, in order to be able, first, to dominate it, second, to administer it, and third, to exploit it.

The Russians have now given an order for partisan warfare behind our front. This partisan war again has some advantage for us; it enables us to exterminate everyone who opposes us.

Principles:

Never again must it be possible to create a military power west of the Urals, even if we have to wage war for a hundred years in order to attain this goal. All successors of the Führer must know: that security for the Reich exists only if there are no foreign military forces west of the Urals; that it is Germany who undertakes the protection of this area against all possible dangers. Our iron principle must be and must remain:

We must never permit anybody but the Germans to carry arms!

This is especially important; even when it seems easier at first to enlist the armed support of foreign, subjugated nations, it is wrong to do so. This will prove some day to be absolutely and unavoidably to our disadvantage. Only the German may carry arms, not the Slav, nor the Czech, nor the Cossack, nor the Ukrainian!

On no account should we apply a wavering policy such as was done in Alsace before 1918. What distinguishes the Englishman is his constant and consistent following of *one* line and *one* aim. In this respect we must learn absolutely from

the Englishman. We ought therefore never to base our actions on individual contemporary personalities; here again the conduct of the British in India towards the
Indian princes, etc., ought to be an example: It is always the soldier who has to
consolidate the regime!

We have to create a Garden of Eden in the newly-won Eastern territories; they
are vitally important to us; as compared with them, colonies play only an entirely
subordinate part.

Even if we divide up certain areas at once, we shall always proceed in the role
of protectors of what is right and of the population. The terms which are necessary
at this time should be selected in accordance with this principle: we shall not speak
of new Reich territory, but of the task which became necessary because of the war.

In particular:

In the Baltic territory the country up to the Dvina will now have to be administered in agreement with Field-Marshal Keitel.

Reichsleiter Rosenberg emphasizes that in his opinion a different treatment of
the population is desirable in every Commissariat. In the Ukraine we should start
with attention to cultural matters; there we ought to awaken the historical consciousness of the Ukrainians, establish a university at Kiev, and so forth.

The Reich Marshal on the other hand states that we have to think first of
securing our food supply; everything else can come later.

(Incidental question: Is there still anything like an educated stratum in the
Ukraine, or do upper-class Ukrainians exist only as emigrants outside present-day
Russia ?)

Rosenberg continues, that in the Ukraine also certain efforts towards
independence should be encouraged....

There ensues a rather long discussion as to the qualifications of Gauleiter
Lohse,[1] who has been considered by Rosenberg for Governor of the Baltic area.
Rosenberg emphasizes again and again that he had approached Lohse already and
it would be very embarrassing if Lohse were not appointed; for the western part
of the Baltic country, Kube[2] was to be appointed, but as subordinate to Lohse;
for the Ukraine, Rosenberg proposed Sauckel.[3]

The Reich Marshal, however, emphasizes the most important criteria which for
the time being must be exclusively decisive for us: securing of food supplies, and as
far as necessary, of the economy; securing of the roads, etc.

The Reich Marshal emphasizes that Koch[4] should either be considered for the
Baltic area because he knows it very well, or that he should receive the Ukraine
because he is the person with the greatest initiative and the best training.

The Führer asks whether Kube could not be appointed as Reich Commissar for
the Moscow area; Rosenberg and the Reich Marshal both thought that Kube was
too old for this position.

Upon further representations Rosenberg replied he was afraid that Koch might
soon refuse to obey his (Rosenberg's) instructions; Koch had, by the way, said
this himself.

[1] Gauleiter of Schleswig-Holstein.

[2] Former Gauleiter of Kurmark. He became General Commissioner of Byelorussia.

[3] Gauleiter of Thuringia. In fact he became head of labour mobilization in 1942; see below,
pp. 647ff.

[4] Gauleiter of East Prussia and well known for his ruthlessness.

As against that, the Reich Marshal pointed out that it was after all not possible for Rosenberg to guide every step of the appointees; rather must these people work quite independently. . . .

The Führer emphasizes that the Ukraine will undoubtedly be the most important district for the next three years. Therefore it would be best to appoint Koch there; if Sauckel were to be employed it would be better to use him in the Baltic area. . . .

The Reich Marshal emphasizes that he intends to assign to Gauleiter Terboven[1] the exploitation of the Kola Peninsula; the Führer agrees.

The Führer emphasizes that Lohse, provided he feels equal to this task, should take over the Baltic area; Kasche, Moscow; Koch, the Ukraine; Frauenfeld, the Crimea; Terboven, Kola; and Schickedanz, the Caucasus.

Reichsleiter Rosenberg then broached the question of providing for the security of the administration.

The Führer tells the Reich Marshal and the Field-Marshal that he had always urged that the police regiments be provided with armoured cars; this has proved to be most necessary for police operations within the newly occupied Eastern territories, because a police regiment equipped with the appropriate number of armoured cars could of course perform much service. Otherwise, though, the Führer pointed out the security protection was very thin. However, the Reich Marshal was going to transfer all his training fields to the new territories, and if necessary even Junker 52s could drop bombs in case of riots. Naturally this giant area would have to be pacified as quickly as possible; the best solution was to shoot anybody who looked askance.

Field-Marshal Keitel emphasizes that the inhabitants themselves ought to be made responsible for their affairs because it was of course impossible to put a sentry in front of every shed or railway station. The inhabitants had to understand that anybody who did not perform his duties properly would be shot, and that they would be held responsible for every offence. . . .

A longer discussion takes place concerning the authority of the Reichsführer SS; obviously all the participants have at the same time in mind the authority of the Reich Marshal.

The Führer, the Reich Marshal, and others reiterate that Himmler was to receive no other authority than he had in Germany proper; but this much was absolutely necessary.

The Führer emphasizes repeatedly that this quarrel would soon subside in practice; he recalls the excellent cooperation between the Army and the Luftwaffe at the front. . . .

Thus Rosenberg, nominally in control of German occupation policy in Russia, was forced in practice to share power with Himmler's SS and with the economic agencies of Göring. Furthermore, the Reich Commissioners, Erich Koch of the Ukraine, and Hinrich Lohse of Eastland (the Baltic States and Byelorussia), although in theory subordinate to Rosenberg, in fact acted almost entirely independently. As senior Gauleiters, they considered themselves Rosenberg's equals and made full use of their right of direct

[1] Gauleiter of Essen. He became Reich Commissioner in Norway.

access to Hitler. In this they received the support in Hitler's headquarters of Martin Bormann, who wished to extend the influence of the Party machine in the east. These personal rivalries were important in view of the different policies adopted by the various organizations. Rosenberg's Ministry of the East was trying to pursue policies designed to win over sections of the Russian population. The SS, the economic agencies and the Party, on the other hand, were bent on ruthlessly exploiting Russia's resources of raw materials and manpower in the short-term interests of the German war machine. Unlike Rosenberg's Ministry they made no distinction between different nationalities and different classes within the Russian population. They regarded all the inhabitants as sub-humans who merely stood in the way of future colonization. This was the attitude of Hitler himself and he threw his weight on the side of the Party and the SS. Thus, according to General von Manstein, on 1 July 1943, Hitler 'declared that promises to Soviet nationalities are not to be contemplated during the war because of the effect on our own soldiers. They must know what they are fighting for, namely living space for their children and grandchildren. The mistake in the First World War was that we did not have any aim.'

12 *Official German criticism of occupation policy in Russia, 25 October 1942*

The policy of forced conscription of labour, usually under the most brutal conditions, and the ruthless exploitation of the peasantry, which was particularly notorious in the Ukraine under Koch, proved counterproductive. It was only in 1943 that any attempt was made to conciliate the Russian population and by then the damage had been done. The following memorandum by Otto Bräutigam, the head of the Main Political Department of the Ministry of the East, although it probably exaggerates the possibilities open to the German occupation in terms of winning over the population, is a damning analysis of German occupation policy in Russia. The combination of ideological blindness and lack of ordinary human sensitivity which marked their policies was to cost the Germans dear:

In the east, Germany is carrying on a threefold war: a war for the destruction of Bolshevism, a war for the destruction of the Greater Russian empire, and finally a war for the acquisition of territory for colonial settlement and for economic exploitation. . . .

. . . It was soon apparent that, because of the vast areas involved and the enemy's inexhaustible reserves of manpower and material, the war could not be decided in a short time by arms alone, but that as in all great wars of recent times a disintegration of morale would also have to take place, and that in the final analysis the war would have to be transformed into a civil war, especially since the German armed forces do not intend to occupy the whole territory of the Soviet Union. . . .

As we all know, the peoples of the Soviet Union have been through very difficult times. Their wishes are therefore incredibly modest, even in the political sphere. A form of administration which was not intent simply on plunder and exploitation and which abolished Bolshevist methods would have kindled the greatest enthusiasm and would have put at our disposal a mass consisting of millions. And the enthusiasm in the occupied territories in the east would have had its impact on the powers of resistance of the Red Army. It would have been easy to persuade the Red Army man to say to himself: 'I am fighting for a system which is far worse than that which I can expect in the event of a defeat. Under the Germans things will be much better than they have been up to now.' If this view had become general among the members of the Red Army, the war would soon have been over.

Appreciating this, the Main Political Department believed it to be its primary duty to devote its energies towards assisting the combat troops with a propaganda campaign aimed at crippling the powers of resistance of the Red Army and in this way at shortening the war. Among the measures proposed for the attainment of this goal there are two of particular importance which differ essentially from Bolshevist policies: the Agrarian Decree and religious freedom.

In view of the exceptional significance of the agrarian question in the Soviet Union, the Main Political Department had demanded even before the beginning of the eastern campaign that the kolkhoz[1] be dissolved and an individual agrarian economy be reintroduced. This proposal was turned down by the Four-Year Plan with the remark that organizational changes were not to be considered during the war. So not before August of last year was it possible to put through an increase in farmland.

But before this plan could be realized, the Four-Year Plan had recognized that the fierce pressure of the whole peasant population for the dissolution of the collective farms would have to be met in some way in the interests of production. The demand of the Main Political Department for the dissolution of the collective farms found expression in the new Agrarian Decree.[2] A few months had been sufficient to make clear, not only to all the Wehrmacht units down to the youngest lieutenant in the most forward position, but also to the military posts at home and to the civil administration in the occupied Eastern territories, the need for reform in the constitution of the kolkhoz. The only exceptions to this general recognition of the situation were the two Reich Commissioners, whose disagreement unfortunately caused a delay of several weeks. The new Agrarian Decree was published shortly before the spring planting and was made the basis of a big propaganda campaign in the territories by the press and propaganda departments of the Main Department.

1. Its immediately successful result was a hitherto inconceivable productivity on the part of the population in the spring planting, which could be undertaken despite unfavourable conditions. In spite of this, there has been no lasting effect on the enemy so far. Naturally enemy propaganda has countered our Agrarian Decree with every means available. Their main argument was that it was only a promise which aimed at temporary tactical successes, and that Germany intended later to make use of the land exclusively for her own purposes. This argument found support in the very slow enforcement of the decree, which is to be partly attributed to practical reasons (lack of surveyors, land registration, survey instruments etc.).

It was intended that, during 1942, 20 per cent of the collective farms would be transformed into agricultural cooperatives. The enlarging of the farmland,

[1] Collective farms.
[2] Published on 26 February 1942.

which forms the main criterion of a communal economy and which should have been carried through everywhere immediately, particularly since it was decreed in August 1941 as mentioned above, has still not been achieved with even 10 per cent of the collective farms. The transformation into agricultural cooperatives was only begun a short time ago and, according to the directives of the Farmers' Leader, Körner,[1] at the end of August, it is not to reach more than 10 per cent this year. Considering this state of affairs, it is understandable that large sections of the Ukrainian peasantry are under the influence of enemy propaganda and have lost faith in the seriousness of our intentions.

Freedom of religion was also intended to produce a propaganda shock effect. But after months of negotiations, it was eventually decided to make no formal announcement of religious freedom, but to let it come into force as quietly as possible. As a result the propaganda effect amounted to nil.

When the Main Political Department noticed the hesitation over the decision in the church question, it looked for a substitute in another means of propaganda, in the question of returning property rights to the individual. In this the whole world could be clearly shown that National Socialism decisively repudiates Bolshevist measures of expropriation and would introduce a new property law. The first precondition for the use of this as a propaganda slogan would have been the immediate suspension of the expropriation measures in the Baltic States, which Bolshevism had ruled for less than a year and where consequently one could have reverted to the previous property arrangements without further ado. But, to the absolute astonishment of the population, the German administration preferred to play the role of receiver of the goods stolen by the Bolshevists. The necessity of the restoration of private ownership for the correct psychological handling of the population was referred to by all the General Commissioners in the Baltic States. It is intended, as is well known, to win this population for German nationality [*Deutschtum*]. Yet even after the Four-Year Plan gave up its original objections in recognition of the fact that further delay in the restoration of private ownership would also damage German economic interests, a basic commitment to the restoration of the pre-Bolshevik property situation did not follow, although the refusal was contrary to all political sense and was based merely on the unfounded objection of the Reich Commissioner.

Again a vital weapon for the disintegration of the enemy front had been wrested from our hands, a weapon whose effects should not be underestimated. For the expropriation of private property by the Bolshevists without compensation had at the time aroused the horror not only of bourgeois circles in Russia, including the better-off peasants, but of the whole civilized world. The world, including the labourers and peasants of the Soviet Union who were disillusioned with Bolshevism, now awaited a clear policy on this question from Germany. This silence on the part of Germany was obviously of use to the enemy propaganda which could argue persuasively to the Soviet masses that Germany did not plan to restore individual ownership.

The Main Political Department has, moreover, always emphasized that the eastern peoples must be told something concrete about their future. It referred to the fact that if we do not counteract the Stalinist propaganda, the peoples would be bound to succumb to this propaganda, i.e. they would believe that Germany

[1] Hellmut Körner, chief of Koch's agricultural section.

intended to enslave them. The Main Department has therefore, in accordance with numerous suggestions from Wehrmacht departments, repeatedly referred to the advisability of assurances from an authoritative German source being given the Slav peoples of the east as regards their future. The best method, it was suggested, would be the establishment of a sort of counter-government to Stalin with a captured Red General or, if one wished to avoid the term 'government', then just a defector General somewhat after the model of de Gaulle, who could become the focal point for all Red soldiers dissatisfied with Stalin. The correctness of this conception has been subsequently confirmed by countless statements of prisoners of war who have all stated independently of one another that the total silence of Germany with regard to the future of Russia leaves it open to people to fear the worst. Many would like to desert, but they do not know to whom they are going. Under the banner of a recognized counter-revolutionary leader they would fight gladly and bravely against the Bolshevist regime.

All the suggestions concerning this were in essence rejected. Permission for front-line duty was secured only for units of the Turkish and Caucasian peoples and finally, after several refusals, for the Estonians as well. Because of the difficulty of recruiting troops, the units in general turned to the enlistment of prisoners of war and civilians, primarily for service in the rear areas. But they were employed even in the front line and fought excellently. Not until the last few weeks, under the pressure of danger from the partisans, was the formation of native units allowed, and then only for action against the bandits. But even this measure will remain ineffective so far as propaganda is concerned, if their commitment at the front is not permitted and if a personality with a big name is not put at the head of the units.

In order to achieve its goal outlined above, the Main Political Department was compelled to rescind or at least to alter substantially measures introduced on the German side which strengthened the enemy's powers of resistance.

Here one should mention the treatment of prisoners as a factor of primary importance. It is no longer a secret from friend or foe that hundreds of thousands of them have literally died of starvation and cold in our camps. It is alleged that there were not enough supplies of food on hand for them. But it is strange that food supplies are lacking only for prisoners of war from the Soviet Union, while complaints about the treatment of other prisoners—Poles, Serbs, French and English —have not been voiced. It is obvious that nothing was more calculated to strengthen the resistance of the Red Army than the knowledge that in German captivity they were faced with a slow and painful death. It is true that the Main Political Department has by unceasing efforts succeeded in achieving a substantial improvement in the lot of the prisoners of war. But this improvement is not to be ascribed to political acumen, but to the sudden realization that our labour market urgently needs replacements. We now experience the grotesque spectacle that after the tremendous starvation of prisoners of war, millions of labourers must hurriedly be recruited from the occupied Eastern territories in order to fill the gaps which have appeared in Germany. Now the question of food was no longer important. With the usual unlimited abuse of Slav people, 'recruiting' methods were used which can only be compared with the blackest periods of the slave trade. A veritable man-hunt was launched. Without regard for health or age people were shipped to Germany, where it soon turned out that well over 100,000 had to be sent back because of serious illness and other disabilities. It needs no elaboration to appreciate that these methods, which of course are being applied in this form not to nationals of enemy countries like Holland or Norway, but only to the Soviet Union, have their repercussions on the resistance of the Red Army. In fact we have made it very easy for Soviet propaganda to increase hatred of Germany and of the National Socialist system. The Soviet soldier fights more and more bravely despite the efforts of our politicians to find another name for this bravery. More and more valuable German blood must flow in order to break the resistance of the Red Army. Of course the Main Political Department has struggled ceaselessly to put the methods of roping in workers and the treatment of the workers in Germany on a rational foundation. Originally it was intended in all seriousness to get maximum performance out of the workers sent to Germany with minimum nourishment. Here also it was not political insight that led to an improvement, but the most elementary knowledge of biology. Now 400,000 female household workers are to go to Germany from the Ukraine and already the German press is announcing publicly that they are to have no right to free time, that they will not visit the theatre, cinemas or restaurants, and that they can only leave the house for three hours a week at the most, apart from exceptions in the line of duty.

In addition there is the question of the treatment of the Ukrainians in the Reich Commissariat itself. With unequalled presumption we ignore all political experience and, to the joyful astonishment of the whole coloured world, treat the peoples of the occupied Eastern territories as second-class whites, to whom providence is alleged to have given the task of slaving for Germany and Europe. They are allowed only the most limited education, and can be given no welfare services. We are interested in feeding them only in so far as they are still capable and they are given to understand that in every respect we regard them as inferior.

In view of this situation, one can state the following:

1. As the population has become aware of our true attitude towards it, so to the same degree has the resistance of the Red Army and the strength of the partisan movement increased. The feats of arms of our magnificent Army have therefore been neutralized, just as in 1918, by an inadequate political policy. Our political policy has forced both Bolshevists and Russian nationals into a common front against us. The Russian is today fighting with exceptional bravery and self-sacrifice for nothing more or less than the recognition of his human dignity.

2. Our political policy of using the Ukraine as a counterweight against mighty Russia, against Poland and the Balkans and as a bridge to the Caucasus, has proved a complete fiasco. The 40 million Ukrainians who greeted us joyfully as liberators are today indifferent to us and are already beginning to swing into the enemy camp. If we do not succeed in checking this situation at the last moment, we risk the overnight emergence in the Ukraine of a partisan movement which would not only eliminate the Ukraine as a source of food supply, but would also tie up the reinforcements of the German army, threaten its existence and thereby involve the danger of a German defeat. . . .

22 War and the Economy

The *Blitzkrieg* economy, 1939–41

Although German rearmament had progressed further than that of the other powers before the war, Germany had by no means a full war economy in 1939, for the civilian sector had not been substantially reduced. The economy was geared to Hitler's *Blitzkrieg* strategy which envisaged a series of short wars and did not require the degree of economic mobilization necessary for a longer war. This situation of partial economic mobilization did not change fundamentally until the crisis in Russia in the winter of 1941–42 demonstrated the failure of the *Blitzkrieg* strategy.

1 *Hitler restates the economic principle of the* Blitzkrieg *strategy*

The *Blitzkrieg* strategy had been largely dictated by Hitler's awareness that the German economy had not the resources for such a long war – a lesson taught by the First World War. The aim of the *Blitzkrieg* was precisely to win for Germany the resources necessary to sustain a World Power role. In the meantime, economic planning for the war had been based on the two basic principles of armament in breadth rather than armament in depth and the principle of autarky embodied in the Four-Year Plan.[1] The outbreak of war increased the pressure for armament in breadth at the expense of reserves of raw materials. The principle was restated by Göring to a sceptical General Thomas in January 1940:

> *Minutes of conference with Field-Marshal Göring*
> *at Karinhall, 30 January 1940*
>
> Field-Marshal Göring began by informing me of the Führer's intentions and of the economic measures resulting therefrom. He stated:
> The Führer is firmly convinced that he will succeed in reaching a decision in the war in 1940 by a big attack in the west. He reckons that we shall gain Belgium, Holland and northern France and he, the Führer, had estimated that the industrial areas of Douai and Lens and those of Luxemburg, Longwy and Briey could replace the supplies of raw materials from Sweden. The Führer had therefore now decided to utilize our reserves of raw materials without regard to the future, at the expense of possible subsequent war years. The Führer is convinced of the correctness of this decision since in his view the best way of building up stocks is the building up of stocks not of raw materials but of finished war material. Furthermore, one must bear in mind that, if the air war were to begin, our factories could

[1] See above, pp. 398ff.

also be destroyed. Furthermore, the Führer is of the opinion that the main thing is to reach maximum effort in the year 1940 and that one should therefore postpone programmes which only produce results later on, in order to accelerate those producing results in 1940.

So far as our work is concerned, therefore, the conclusion is to exploit everything to the utmost in 1940 and thus to exploit reserves of raw materials at the expense of later years. It will be necessary to act in future according to this principle.

I replied to Field-Marshal Göring that I was grateful for this clear programme, but that I advised him to build up reserves of finished war material also, as experience shows that war material which is ready to hand is always put into action at once and used for setting up new formations. We would therefore have to put on the brakes in this respect so that one day we are not faced with big surprises. Field-Marshal Göring agreed.

In fact, however, the expansion of chemical production, particularly synthetics, set in motion by the Four-Year Plan continued. On 5 December 1939 a Reich Office for Economic Expansion (*Reichsamt für Wirtschafts-ausbau*) had been established by Göring under Carl Krauch which was in effect a sort of Chemicals Ministry with the responsibility of overseeing a significant sector of German war production. In 1940 Krauch became chairman of the board of IG-Farben and his new department was described by one observer as 'a nationalized IG'.

2 *Hitler asserts the need for conquests in view of the inadequacy of autarky*

The principle of autarky, as embodied in the Four-Year Plan, had been dictated by an attempt to increase Germany's freedom of manoeuvre by escaping as far as possible from her dependence on imported raw materials. Yet this had been essentially a programme designed to meet the limitations imposed by peacetime. In his Four-Year Plan memorandum, Hitler had insisted that 'the definitive solution lies in an extension of our living space, that is, an extension of the raw materials and food basis of our nation'. In stating this he was merely restating the policy he had laid down in *Mein Kampf*, and he had always envisaged Russia as providing the necessary 'living space'. With his failure to defeat Britain and his decision to attack Russia, Hitler now abandoned his reliance on autarky within the confines of Germany itself. He reverted to his fundamental belief in the necessity for the conquest of living space in Russia. Only the vast resources of Russia would offer Germany the possibility of real autarky:

Berlin, 20 June 1941

MEMORANDUM
The new conception of the Führer, explained to me by Minister Todt,[1] confirmed later by Field-Marshal Keitel, is as follows:

[1] Fritz Todt, Minister of Munitions since 17 March 1940.

Paragraph 1

The course of the war shows that we went too far in our efforts toward autarky. It is impossible to try to manufacture everything we lack by synthetic processes or other measures. For instance, it is impossible to develop our motor fuel manufacturing capacity to a point where we can be entirely dependent on it. All these attempts at autarky require a tremendous amount of manpower, and it is simply impossible to provide it. We must choose another way. What we need but do not have, we must conquer. The manpower required for this will not be as great as that currently needed for the running of the synthetic factories in question. The aim must be to secure all territories that are of special interest to us for the war economy, by conquering them.

At the time the Four-Year Plan was established, I issued the statement in which I made it clear that a completely autarkic economy is impossible for us, because the manpower requirement will be too great. Nevertheless, my solution was always to provide the necessary reserves for missing stocks or to secure the delivery in wartime through economic alliances. . . .

[signed] THOMAS

3 *No conscription for married women*

Blitzkrieg principles also ruled the Government's attitude to labour conscription. There was virtually no attempt to reduce the use of labour in non-essential industries and offices. In particular, there was no attempt to introduce conscription for women. The basic policy regarding the employment of women was laid down at the beginning of the war in the following directive of the Ministry of Labour dated 7 September 1939:

1. State Secretary Dr Syrup has decided that married women who have hitherto not been in employment will continue not to be liable for labour conscription unless they wish to volunteer for the labour mobilization programme entirely of their own free will. The regional labour exchanges are to be informed accordingly.

2. *To the Presidents of the Regional Labour Exchanges* (*personal*)
Subject: Circular of 3.vii.39

In the circular referred to above I have laid down that in peacetime women who have domestic and family responsibilities are not to be called up unless they were previously in employment and unless their family circumstances and health have changed in the meantime.

Even under the present circumstances, I do not consider it advisable to utilize married women who were not previously in employment unless the women volunteer for the labour mobilization programme entirely of their own free will. I request, therefore, that you ensure that the above-mentioned instructions contained in the circular continue to be applied.

The manpower requirements for plants engaged on projects of national importance must be met by exploiting all other possibilities (the employment of labour from plants engaged on non-priority projects, particularly of female workers and employees who become available through the closing down of such plants, by exchanging labour between different areas, volunteers, etc.). If this should prove impossible please inform me of the fact.

4 *The War Economy Decree, 4 September 1939*

The attempt to combine a heavy rearmament programme with a largely unchanged civilian sector had created serious problems. In the period before the war, this policy had subjected the economy to serious strains, notably shortages in raw materials and skilled labour.[1] At the outbreak of war, therefore, the authorities seized the opportunity of using the crisis as an excuse to reverse the process of rising wages and increasing bonuses which had resulted from the labour shortage. On 4 September, a War Economy Decree was issued which attempted to reduce wages and abolish various bonuses:

The safeguarding of the frontiers of our fatherland necessitates big sacrifices from every German citizen. The soldier is protecting our homeland with his weapons at the risk of his life. In view of the extent of this commitment, it is the obvious duty of all citizens at home to put all their strength and resources at the disposal of the nation and Reich, and thereby to guarantee the continuation of an orderly economic life. This means above all that all citizens must impose upon themselves the necessary restrictions on their standard of living. Therefore, the Ministerial Council for the Defence of the Reich decrees with the force of law:

SECTION I: BEHAVIOUR DETRIMENTAL TO THE WAR EFFORT
Para. 1
(1) Anyone who destroys, conceals, or hoards raw materials or products which are essential to the existence of the population and thereby maliciously endangers the supply of these goods will be punished with penal servitude or hard labour. In particularly serious cases the death penalty may be imposed.
(2) Those who hoard bank notes without good reason will be punished with hard labour, in particularly serious cases with penal servitude.

SECTION II: WAR TAXES
Sub-section 1. War surtax on income tax . . .
Para. 2. Those liable to tax
(1) The Reich will levy a war surtax on income tax.
(2) Those liable to income tax at the standard rate whose income does not exceed 2400 RM are exempt from the war surtax.
Para. 3. Amount of war surtax on income tax
(1) The war surtax on income tax is 50 per cent of the income tax for the tax collection period. . . .

SECTION III: WAR WAGES
Para. 18
(1) The Reich Trustees and Special Trustees of Labour on instructions from the Reich Minister of Labour will adjust wages immediately to wartime conditions and will fix a compulsory maximum limit for wages, salaries and conditions of work.
(2) If new plants or administrative offices are established or reorganized, or if

[1] See above, pp. 416, 444 ff.

workmen or employees carry out a different form of employment than hitherto after this decree has come into effect, the same wage or salary levels apply as for similar plants or administrative offices or as those which are standard for the new occupation. If any doubts arise as to which wage and salary scales should be used, the Reich Trustee or Special Trustee of Labour will make the decisions.

(3) Bonuses for overtime work, and for Sunday, national holiday, and night shifts are no longer to be paid.

(4) Paragraphs 1–3 apply equally to remuneration and other work conditions in home labour.

Para. 19
Regulations and agreements on holidays are temporarily suspended. More detailed instructions on their reinstitution will be given by the Reich Minister of Labour.

Para. 20
The Reich Minister of Labour can make decisions on the announcement and content of wage scales and regular hours of work which deviate from existing regulations. For public administrative offices and plants the Reich Minister of Labour makes these decisions in collaboration with the Reich Ministers concerned.

Para. 21
(1) Anyone who promises or grants wages or salaries or accepts a promise or grant contrary to paragraphs 18–20 of this decree will be punished with a disciplinary penalty in the form of an unlimited fine for each violation. The same punishment will apply to those who demand or grant more favourable working conditions than are permitted according to the regulations of this decree. Appeals to the Reich Minister of Labour against disciplinary penalties are permitted.

(2) In serious cases the punishment is hard labour or penal servitude. Prosecutions will be initiated at the request of the Reich Trustee or Special Trustee of Labour. The charge can be withdrawn. . . .

SECTION IV: WAR PRICES
Prices and charges for goods and services of all kinds must be fixed in accordance with the principles of the war economy.

Para. 23
(1) Prices and charges for goods and services of all kinds are to be reduced in so far as savings in wage costs for goods and services occur as a result of Section III of this decree.

(2) Prices and charges for goods and services of all kinds must in future be based on the wages and salaries permitted according to Section III of this decree, these being treated as the maximum.

(3) Social benefits for the retinue, which are not prescribed as compulsory in laws, decrees, or wage scales, must be used to determine prices and changes only in so far as they are customary for that particular business and are not contrary to the principles of economical business methods.

(4) It is forbidden to demand or permit higher prices or charges than those laid down as permissible in paragraphs 1–3. . . .

SECTION V: FINAL REGULATIONS
Para. 29
According to the directives of the Plenipotentiary-General for the Economy and
the Plenipotentiary-General for the Reich Administration, the responsible
ministers and the Reich Price Commissioner can, in collaboration with one
another, proclaim legal ordinances and general administrative regulations for the
implementing and completion of this decree.
(2) They can transfer to other authorities powers which belong to them under
this decree.

Para. 30
The decree comes into effect on the day of its promulgation.

5 *A Gauleiter complains of the effects of the War Economy Decree*
The wage provisions of this decree caused widespread discontent among the
labour force. Significantly, this discontent was voiced by Martin Mutschmann, the Gauleiter of Saxony, one of the largest industrial areas, in a letter,
dated 2 October 1939, to the Ministerial Committee for the Defence of the
Reich:

In the express letter III 16591/39 of 4 September 1939 the Reich Minister of
Labour has instructed the Reich Trustees of Labour to adjust wages in accordance
with the requirements of the war economy.
The Reich Trustees of Labour in the Defence Economy District IV have
consequently introduced a new settlement of wages and work conditions for all
existing wage scales. In the heavily industrialized *Gau* of Saxony, a particularly
large number of wage scales are due for readjustment.
This measure has produced unrest in the economy which is politically undesirable and has not only economic but above all social side effects in that the
workers fear they are now going to be subjected to strong pressure on wages. This
rigid fixing of upper limits for piecework is felt especially acutely since the consumer goods industries which predominate in Defence Economy District IV
are still understaffed and on account of the war have to work increasingly long
hours. The planned rigid restriction of piecework wages is moreover uneconomical
since it has a negative influence on people's enthusiasm and productivity. This
danger exists particularly in the metal industry, which is so important for the war
economy, because, in the context of the new wage scales, a drastic reduction in
average piecework rates is planned even for this industry.
The fact that the readjustment of wage scales is increasing the previous number
of wage group sub-divisions causes scales to become unduly complicated whereas
they should be fixed as simply and clearly as possible, especially in the present
situation, in order to avoid all possibilities for differences and difficulties.
The plan to pay women less in future, instead of the previously approved equal
pay for male and female labour, provides an undesirable inducement for the
excessive employment of women, particularly in the metal industry.
It seems to me particularly unacceptable that, according to the guidelines given
by the Reich Minister of Labour, e.g. the fixing of maximum wages for skilled
workers in the metal industry, *Gau* Saxony, the most important industrial area in

Greater Germany with a relatively high cost of living, is to be worse off than other industrial areas with more favourable living conditions.

For these reasons I request that you decree that an extensive alteration of the wage system should not be carried out at present and that only a wage freeze should be ordered, to reduce the exaggerated top wages and enticement wages. Such measures will be met with understanding by the workers.

6 *Ministerial discussion on the reintroduction of bonus rates, 10 November 1939*

Such was the sensitivity of the regime to discontent among the working class that the suggestion of Gauleiter Mutschmann to replace the reduction of wage rates by a wage freeze was adopted by the Government. At the same time the Government was considering retreat on another provision of the War Economy Decree—the abolition of Night and Holiday Bonuses in Section III, para. 18 (3). This whole question was aired at an interdepartmental conference which throws interesting light on the labour situation at the beginning of the war and on the way in which the political process operated in the Third Reich. The workers had clearly responded to the cancellation of the bonuses by absenteeism and the Government was forced to adjust itself to that fact by restoring the bonuses although 'the authority of the State would undoubtedly suffer a severe blow' (Thomas). The attempt to compensate for this by reducing the level for income tax exemption could not disguise the fact that the Government had been forced to retreat by pressure from below which had been supported by various Gauleiters. The bonuses for Sunday and night work were restored with effect from 27 November 1939:

Minutes of the interdepartmental conference with the GBW[1] *on 10.xi.39, 11 o'clock.* *Subject of discussion:* Bonuses for overtime, night work, and Sunday work. *Participants:* State Secretary Posse (Economics), State Secretary Neumann (Interior), State Secretary Syrup (Labour), with Ministerialdirektor Mansfeld (Labour), General Thomas, Ministerialdirektor Hedding (Finance), Flottman (Reich Price Commissioner), Ministerialrat Josten (Economics), Dr Rigler (Economics).

State Secretary Posse opened the meeting with the declaration that the Reich Minister of Economics felt obliged to consider the reintroduction of bonuses for overtime, night and Sunday work: (1) because the workers' incomes were no longer sufficient to buy the foodstuffs allocated to them by the rationing regulations; (2) because it had been observed that the ban on bonuses had led to a refusal to do overtime, night and Sunday work and to phenomena which constituted actual sabotage. State Secretary Posse pointed out at the same time that a cancellation of the ban on bonuses would constitute the first official deviation from the War Economy Decree. Simultaneously, this raised the question of the advisability of lowering the level at which incomes became liable to the war surtax on income tax.

[1] Walther Funk, Plenipotentiary-General for the Economy (*Generalbevollmächtigter für die Wirtschaft*).

In the ensuing debate the following points were made: In the armament factories the majority of workers had in fact stayed away on Sundays. Similarly, a decrease in night shifts had been noted (Thomas). In addition to this, the usual absenteeism among building workers on Saturdays after they had received their wages on Fridays was now up to 80 per cent (Mansfeld). Only Sunday and night work was regarded as having any importance (Syrup). Moreover, the bonuses were unjust because they were not uniform. They did not correspond to the actual additional expenditure; very often they did not take into account the double amount of food required by workers, e.g. during night shift, which made a tremendous hole in the worker's budget. In the graphics trade, for example, the cancellation of bonuses amounted to 45–50 per cent. This had already required special regulations (against Amann).

The statement that the workers could not even buy everything due to them on their ration cards could not be true for the average worker. (But it could apply to wages actually below average.) It was a fact that sometimes a worker's large family was entitled to more than they had ever bought before. The growth of black-market food ration card agencies was proof of that. The workers doing the heaviest work received more food than they could use. This was proved by the Pohl memorandum, though it was disputed. So far attempts to achieve the necessary increase in productivity had been made through wage increases. At the moment business was once again demanding such wage increases on a large scale. But today this form of incentive was bound to fail. The average worker did not lack the will to work, but could just take no more. For years he had had to stand up to too hot a pace. This was proved by the sickness reports which had shown a rise in places of up to 50 per cent of the retinue (Mansfeld).

On the other hand there had been no wage cuts, so that if the ban on bonus rates, the only sacrifice the workers had had to make so far, was cancelled, the workers would be exceptionally favoured, they would even profit from the war. War could not be waged if one section of the population, the workers, was wrapped in cotton wool. Moreover, the amount of purchasing power was not being matched by the level of production. It must therefore be skimmed off, otherwise the result would be inflation (Josten).

In this context, the reintroduction of all bonus rates was discussed, together with the simultaneous imposition of the war surtax on all incomes down to subsistence level, thereby cancelling the previous level of 2400 RM (234 RM a month) at which incomes became exempt from the tax. Dr Ley would then probably emphasize the unavoidable cases of hardship in which, for example, a previous surtax of 3 RM could be replaced by one of 6 RM. Such a regulation would hit both the small tradesman and the artisan hard.

Accordingly, a reduction of the exemption level from 234 RM to only 150 RM could be approved, although this reduction of the exemption limit would have undesirable repercussions on people's willingness to work, since no worker would want to work so that his earnings came to slightly over this limit. Ministerialdirektor Hedding declared that the reduction in tax revenues with the reintroduction of Sunday and night work bonuses amounted to 100–150 million RM, or, including overtime bonuses, to 250–300 million RM. As a tax specialist, he would welcome the reintroduction of bonuses with a simultaneous reduction in the exemption limit from 2400 RM to 1800 RM.

The authority of the State would undoubtedly suffer a severe blow if the bonuses were introduced (Thomas). To counteract this impression, the most suitable way would have to be found of compensating for such a concession. In the drafting of the War Economy Decree, which incidentally was done without the participation of the relevant Government departments, the question of bonuses for overtime had been treated from a psychological, not from a material point of view. Undoubtedly it would have been better if the bonuses had never been abolished and if instead the war surtax had been imposed on the workers.

As a result of the discussion, State Secretary Posse will suggest to the Reich Minister of Economics that the Ministerial Council should introduce a decree: (1) to reintroduce the bonuses for Sunday and night work; (2) to lower the level of income giving exemption from the war surtax on income tax from 2400 RM to 1800 RM.

7 *Proclamation by Dr Ley on the reintroduction of night and Sunday bonuses, 19 November 1939*

The Government was of course obliged to bluff in order to disguise its retreat, as is clear from the following extract from the *Völkischer Beobachter* of 20 November, which is also interesting for the pseudo-Socialist slant which it gives to Germany's war aims:

. . .

That is the balance sheet in the social sector of our people after ten weeks of war. At the beginning of the war, the severest sacrifices, the tightening of belts; after ten weeks' life back to normal, only a fraction of the powers have had to be used. That was not because the leadership yielded to your demands, workers, but because everything had been so well prepared that these sacrifices were unnecessary. We should almost be ashamed of our small part in the nation's war sacrifices, particularly when we think of the sacrifice in blood made by the soldiers. All the more reason, then, workers, plant leaders and retinue, why we must vow to do everything which the Führer demands of us. . . .

Workers! Plant leaders and retinue!

I have tried to give you a balance sheet of our fighting nation after ten weeks of war in telegram-style descriptions of the situation.

However, the greatest credit factor in this balance sheet is the fact that the Führer lives!

Germany's position has never been better and that of England has never been so bad. This time we're going to do it! England will be beaten and you and Germany will be free!

Work versus Money bags!
Freedom is ours!

Editorial Comment
Socialist war

. . . The path which the National Socialist Reich has followed since 1933 has been a path of work and hardship, the path of a poor nation. But, at the same time, in this poverty lay our wealth: conscious of the difficulties opening up before us, the whole nation became one big community. We have struggled out of the poverty of the fifteen years of Versailles because all Germans were gripped by the spirit of Socialism, because we did not use our minds and our hands for the advantage and profit of individuals or particular classes, but because the rise of the Reich was to the profit of every working German.

It is because of this that Great Britain has declared war on us. The regime of money grabbers, the bastion of capitalism seeks to strangle the Germany that has given the world the example of a Socialist order. They fear the effects of their position in England itself, even more they fear for their huge colonial empire. Their subjects inside and outside are no longer to have the National Socialist State before their eyes which, by its mere existence, might turn them into rebels against their exploiters.

This means that Germany is waging the war not only for its own existence, but at the same time for *all* oppressed nations of the world. . . .

8 *Security Police directive on measures to be taken in the event of strikes,*
   4 November 1939

Since they did not feel confident enough to ask sacrifices of their population, the regime combined compromise with propaganda and intimidation. The element of intimidation was of course provided by the Gestapo, which issued the following directive on the outbreak of war:

1. In the event of strikes, absenteeism, work sabotage, etc., the following basic measures, which are in line with the 'Principles of Internal State Security During the War' issued by the Chief of the Security Police on 3.ix.39,[1] should be observed:

(1) Immediate intervention by police agencies in the event of any strike and the immediate arrest of all suspects etc. will ensure the ruthless suppression of any complications or attempts to exploit it. The investigations necessary in order to clear up each case completely are to be initiated at once, examining first of all the motivations (economic, political or other) for the undisciplined behaviour of the arrested persons; the political and criminal record, and the economic and other personal circumstances of the arrested employees are to be thoroughly investigated.

(2) As a rule it must also be established whether any abuses or other special circumstances in the plants may have contributed to the incidents in order to ensure that the matter is dealt with, if necessary in collaboration with the responsible State and Party authorities.

(3) In the cases dealt with from here special attention will be given to the question of whether there have been any indications of *Communist or Marxist influence* in connexion with the incidents. Recently it has become particularly evident that illegal Communist pamphlet propaganda is increasingly attempting to incite the German workers to oppose the plant leadership and, particularly in plants important for the Army, to neglect their work. Slogans such as 'Work more slowly', 'Put in lazy shifts' or 'Report sick from time to time' are contained in nearly every Communist pamphlet. Since the beginning of the war these slogans have been given

[1] See below, pp. 655–6.

added emphasis by suggestions that, because of the nutritional deficiencies which have developed, the workers have insufficient energy for proper work and under these circumstances cannot be expected to do the same work as previously.

Considering these attempts to undermine morale, therefore, in all cases of strikes etc. not only should the particular case be cleared up, but the attempt should be made to ascertain whether and to what extent forces hostile to the State are at work here, so that those who may be pulling the strings can be brought to light and, if necessary, liquidated without mercy.

(4) Police offices must report immediately to the head of the Security Police after the speedy clearing up of the incidents, so that a decision may be made on the further treatment of the arrested persons and tough measures may be taken, if necessary, on orders from above. . . .

9 *A worker arrested for absenteeism, 17 October 1939*

Rather than attempting to repress the sort of mass absenteeism which developed in response to the abolition of Sunday bonuses, the Gestapo tended to pick out individuals and make examples of them. Absenteeism could lead to a short spell in prison; agitation encouraging others to strike would result in the offender being sent to a concentration camp:

. . . On 17 October 1939 the metal worker Kreuzpaintner, Sebastian, born 2.ii.20 in Munich, Gärtnerstrasse 24/1b, Aryan, Catholic, was taken into police custody because of repeated, obstinate absenteeism from an armament plant. He will be released in three weeks' time. . . .

The switch to the full war economy in 1942

The German reverse in front of Moscow represented the bankruptcy of the *Blitzkrieg* strategy. Germany now faced a long war. The implications for the German economy were far-reaching. The first effects were felt in the armaments field. At the time of the invasion of Russia, Hitler had actually ordered a reduction in the manufacture of armaments allocated to the Army and a switch of resources to the Air Force. This was fully in accord with the *Blitzkrieg* strategy which envisaged a short war with Russia and then, after the defeat of Russia, the concentration of Germany's resources on the defeat of Britain, for which the burden would fall on the Air Force. The setback in Russia now left no alternative to the reorientating of the armaments programme. The following report, written in March 1942 by Col. Hedler, of the Economic Armament Office (*Wehrwirtschafts-Rüstungsamt*) of OKW, explains how this occurred:

10 *'The Reorientation of the Armaments Programme in 1942'*

. . . [in June 1941] as a result of political developments and the military successes in the Balkans, a reduction in the armaments assigned to the Army and an extension of the Air Force programme seemed practicable. This altered the basis of the previous armaments programme, as is clear from the following Führer Order of 20 June 1941:

'If the armaments assigned to the Army are curtailed, manufacturing plant and labour reserves will become available. Those resources which have become available are to be put at the disposal of the expanded Air Force programme under the direction of the Minister for Armaments and Munitions. Arrangements must be made as soon as possible for the Air Force to contact firms regarding the transfer of production.

'The Reich Minister for Armaments and Munitions will regulate the allocation of these available resources between the special Air Force programme and the most urgent requirements of the Army and Navy.'

The basic guidelines on labour and materials for the future armaments programme were laid down in an expanded Führer Order of 14 July 1941.

According to this, the main emphasis of the whole armaments programme was to be on the expansion of the Air Force. But the securing of the basis of supplies of raw materials had equal priority.

At the same time, there were other urgent programmes, namely,

For the Army: The tank programme for the highly mobile troops which were to be increased considerably, the new programme of the heavy 'Pak' [anti-tank guns] together with carriers and munitions, the programme of additional equipment for expeditionary troops, the Army anti-aircraft gun programme which was given the same priority as that of the Air Force and which forms a single unit of production with it.

For the Navy: The continuation of the U-Boat programme.

Cut-backs were to be made in the following fields: the armament and technical equipment of the troops, the general equipment of the armed forces, the expansion in manufacturing facilities, together with all long-term building projects.

The gunpowder and explosives programme had to concentrate in the first instance on the requirements of the Air Force (bombs, anti-aircraft munitions); the expansion of facilities was to be restricted to the absolute minimum and to the simplest form of construction.

The Army had immediately to adapt its replenishment of armament and equipment as well as the production of new weapons, munition and equipment to the reduced size of the Army in the future. The Navy had to restrict itself to the manufacturing facilities and buildings which were directly connected with the U-Boat programme. It had also to postpone all armament plans which went beyond that. The war against Russia created an entirely new situation. The extraordinarily big successes in the first months of the campaign confirmed us in the hope that the war in the east was to all intents and purposes concluded.

Then, in the second half of November, a change occurred in two senses.

In the first place, the winter began surprisingly early and with an intensity such as had not apparently been experienced for 140 years. This had a very serious effect on the military operations. In addition, the Russians succeeded in bringing into battle new, well-equipped and fresh armies from East Asia which went into the attack with tremendous superiority. As a result of these factors, the offensive came to a halt. Nevertheless, we succeeded not only in fighting off an enemy thrust, but also, through bitter fighting, in checking and repulsing the enemy offensive. Yet, despite this, the war situation had changed and new Führer directives were given:

'The Führer Order of 10.i.42 (Armament 1942)

I

'1. The long term objective remains the same—the construction of the Air Force and Navy for the struggle against the Anglo-Saxon powers. This principle must be taken into consideration in all armament plans and in the measures for carrying them out.

'The conduct of the war during 1942, however, for the time being prohibits any reduction in the armament of the Army in the interests of this objective. On the contrary, the Army must be strengthened and its supplies increased to enable it to fulfil the tasks required of it during 1942.

'2. The armament resources must therefore for the time being be devoted to meeting the increased requirements of the Army.

'The basis for this is provided by the commitment of the raw materials at the disposal of the armed forces as a whole.

'Accordingly, I delegate the Commander-in-Chief of the Armed Forces [Keitel] to undertake the allocation of raw materials for the first six months of 1942, cutting down the shares of the Navy and the Air Force where this is unavoidable.

'The necessary regulations for the increase in the extraction of raw materials, particularly of coal and oil, which are the basis of all armament production, will be announced by the Delegate for the Four-Year Plan [Göring]. . . .'

At a meeting of the Four-Year Plan with the leaders of industry on 15 January [1942] General of the Infantry von Hanneken gave a lecture on 'Production Programmes for the Coming Months', in which he stated among other things that the present industrial programmes were defined by the new war situation. The hope that large numbers of troops would be demobilized, which would have led already to an improvement in the labour situation by this winter, has not been realized. Material and men are increasingly required for the defences in the east. The task of the war economy, therefore, is to produce as large an amount of weapons, munitions and other military equipment as possible and to get it to the troops. There is nothing left for civilian production.

These increased requirements are combined with a labour shortage which will become noticeably worse during the next three months owing to the new drafts to the armed forces. The only substitute for the missing labour force lies in the rationalizing of industry and the mobilizing of all existing reserves, e.g. through the exchange of skilled workers for less qualified ones, the rationalizing of the methods of manufacturing equipment and the concentration of orders in the most efficient plants. Today there are still far too many workers per production plant. The reason for this lies in the unplanned allocation of war contracts among the available plants, which are to a large extent faced with methods of production to which they are not accustomed and the shortest possible delivery dates. Industry must above all adapt itself to a long war.

The crisis created by the reverse in Russia not only compelled industry to adapt itself to a long war; it also forced Germany to accept the logic of a war on two fronts, that is to say, the need to produce as much as possible for the Army while continuing to strengthen the Navy and the Air Force. These multiple requirements necessitated a degree of mobilization of the economy which had been unnecessary under the *Blitzkrieg* strategy.

The first moves in the transformation to a full war economy had been initiated by Fritz Todt. Todt was a civil engineer who had been given the job of organizing the construction of the autobahns and the West Wall. On 17 March 1940 he became the first Reich Minister for Armaments and Munitions. The main reform introduced by him was the establishment of a series of committees—a main committee and sub-committees—for the munitions industry. These committees, staffed by able managers from industry, had the job of rationalizing production in the munitions industry and improving efficiency. Todt had also planned to centralize control over the armaments industry in his own hands.

On 8 February 1942, however, Todt was killed in an air crash. Hitler replaced him as Minister of Armaments by his architect, Albert Speer. Speer had established a relationship of unusual intimacy with Hitler, largely based on Hitler's admiration for Speer's architectural gifts. He tended to see in Speer the architect he might have become himself and half-wished he could have become. But Speer had also impressed Hitler with his administrative abilities in the field of construction, for he had helped stage the Nuremberg rallies and at the beginning of the war had been given responsibility for erecting buildings for the Army and Air Force. With Hitler's full support behind him, Speer was able to put into effect and develop further the policies initiated by Todt.

11 *Decree on the establishment of a 'Central Planning Board' within the Four-Year Plan, 22 April 1942*

The most important reform which Speer persuaded Hitler to introduce was the establishment of a central body exercising control over the whole economy in the interests of the armament programme. This body was called the Central Planning Board. Its influence was based on its control of the allocation of raw materials which gave it control over production in every sphere of the economy. Hitler agreed on 4 April 1942 to the formation of the Central Planning Board and ratified it by decree on 15 April. The formation of a body with such far-reaching authority was bound to affect the powers of the other economic agencies. The Reich Ministry of Economics, for example, now declined even further in importance. For the sake of appearances the Central Planning Board was placed within Göring's Four-Year Plan Office and Paul Körner, an official of the Four-Year Plan, was made a member of the triumvirate. But power lay essentially with the other two members, the Air Force General Erhard Milch and, above all, Speer, who not only had direct access to Hitler but for the next eighteen months or so was on exceptionally cordial terms with him.

On the proposal of Reich Minister Speer in his capacity as Plenipotentiary-General for Armaments in the Four-Year Plan, the Reich Marshal has established a 'Central Planning Board' within the Four-Year Plan. The contents of the decree are as follows:

Berlin, 22 April 1942

In order to guarantee the priority for armaments which has been ordered by the Führer, and in order to concentrate in one decision-making body all the demands which must be made on the economy as a whole during the war, as well as to coordinate the requirements of the armament industry with those of the food supply and with the availability of raw materials and manufacturing facilities within the economy, I decree:

1. A Central Planning Board shall be established within the framework of the Four-Year Plan. It is to be directly subordinate to me.

2. The direction of the Central Planning Board shall be undertaken by Reich Minister Speer, Field-Marshal Milch, and State Secretary Körner working in collaboration.

3. The sphere of activity of the Central Planning Board embraces the whole economy and has among others the following responsibilities:

(a) the power of decision over whether or not new plans are required or whether existing plans should be continued;

(b) the power of decision over whether or not to create new raw material manufacturing plants or whether existing plants should be extended;

(c) the apportionment of existing raw materials, in particular of iron and metals, to those requiring them;

(d) the distribution of coal and energy to manufacturing plants;

(e) the coordination of the requirements for transport throughout the whole economy.

4. Except where I have reserved for myself the power of decision in individual cases, the Central Planning Board makes the final decisions on its own authority on the basis of the powers delegated by me.

5. The Central Planning Board decrees the requisite regulations for the enforcement of this decree.

6. The powers which were delegated to the Plenipotentiary-General for Armaments in the Four-Year Plan by my decree of 1.iii.42 are not affected by this decree.

12 *Statistics on armament production*

The following statistics show the significance of the transition from the *Blitzkrieg* economy of 1939–41 to a full war economy. They demonstrate the head start in rearmament which Germany had in the prewar years but also the speed with which the other powers caught up. Finally, they show the hopeless disparity between the armament production of the Axis and that of the Allied Powers—a ratio of 1:3·4 in 1943, which alone is a sufficient explanation of Germany's defeat.

(a) *The index of German armaments production 1940–44*

January–February 1942 = 100

Year	Total production	Weapons	Tanks	Motor vehicles	Aeroplanes	Ships	Munitions
1940	97	79	36	—	—	11	163
1941	98	106	81	—	97	110	102
1942	142	137	130	120	133	142	166
1943	222	234	330	138	216	182	247
1944	277	348	536	110	277	157	306

(b) *Comparison of the rate of armament production of the combatant powers*

(1944 = 100)

	1938	1939	1940	1941	1942	1943	1944
USA	2	2	5	11	47	91	100
Canada	0	2	6	27	73	102	100
Britain	4	10	34	59	83	100	100
USSR	12	20	30	53	71	87	100
Germany	16	20	35	35	51	80	100
Japan	8	10	16	32	49	72	100

(c) *The armament production of the Great Powers in $ billions at 1944 prices*

	1935–39	1939	1940	1941	increase per cent	1943	increase per cent
USA	1·5	0·6	1·5	4·5	200	37·5	733
Britain	2·5	1·0	3·5	6·5	86	11·1	71
USSR	8·0	3·3	5·0	8·5	70	13·9	64
Total	12·0	4·9	10·0	19·5	95	62·5	221
Germany	12·0	3·4	6·0	6·0	0	13·8	130
Japan				2·0	100	4·5	125
Total				8·0		18·3	129
Ratio of Axis to Allies				1:2·4		1:3·4	

The mobilization of labour, 1942-45

The establishment of the Central Planning Board and the extension of the committee system inaugurated the full war economy in Germany. There was, however, one sector of the economy which lay outside the control of Speer and Central Planning but which was crucial to the full mobilization of the economy, namely, the supply of labour. The problem was that attempts to secure additional labour for the armaments industry would involve withdrawing it from other sectors. This was something to which the Gauleiters, who took a considerable interest in the economies of their areas, objected. Speer therefore advocated the establishment of a post with special powers over the mobilization of labour to which, in his view, a Gauleiter should be appointed, since he would have the necessary weight within the Party to enable him to resist the other Gauleiters. Speer nominated Karl Hanke, the Gauleiter of Lower Silesia, who had been his district Party leader in Berlin and had given him his first architectural assignment for the Party. Bormann, however, wishing to reduce Speer's influence, persuaded Hitler that Hanke was too young and suggested one of his own protégés, Fritz Sauckel, Gauleiter of Thuringia. Thus, on 21 March 1942, Sauckel was appointed Plenipotentiary-General for the Mobilization of Labour.

There were basically two possible solutions to the problem of labour supply, though they were not mutually exclusive. The first was the maximum utilization of all available labour resources within Germany. Here one possibility was to comb out German industry and the State and Party administrations, closing down shops, offices, and factories which were not of vital importance to the war effort, or drastically reducing their staff. Those who became available in this way could then be drafted into the armaments industry or to the front to replace skilled workers.

13 *Ideological barriers to the conscription of women*

There was one other obvious possibility in this connexion – the conscription of women. Speer, in particular, pressed for the introduction of female labour conscription. But Hitler was still not prepared to accept a really tough policy of labour mobilization for the war effort; in particular, he was not prepared to accept female conscription. Sauckel expressed the point of view of Hitler and the Party on this in his statement of 20 April 1942:

... The mobilization of German women for labour is extremely important.

After having acquainted myself thoroughly with the views of both the Führer and of the Reich Marshal of the Greater German Reich, and having examined this most difficult problem through my own extremely careful investigations, I must reject absolutely the idea of conscription in the German war and food industries for all German women and girls.

Although, initially, I myself and probably the majority of the leading figures in the Party and in the women's organization had particular reasons for believing in the need for conscription of women, all men and women in responsible positions in the Party, in the State, and in business should now accept the view of our Führer, Adolf Hitler, with the greatest veneration and the deepest gratitude. For his greatest concern is the health of German women and girls, in other words, of the present and future mothers of our nation.

I cannot enumerate all the reasons which have made me come to this decision. I ask only for confidence in myself as an old and fanatical Gauleiter of the National Socialist Party and that you should believe that this was the only decision possible.

We all agree that this decision may appear unjust towards millions of women who are working in the defence and nutrition industries under the most strenuous conditions, but we also realize that an evil cannot be remedied by expanding it to the ultimate extent.

The only possible way of eliminating the existing injustices and hardships lies in winning the war so that we shall be in a position to remove all women and girls from jobs regarded as unsuitable for women—jobs which are a danger to their health, to the birth-rate of our nation, and to family and national life.

We must also bear in mind that it makes an enormous difference whether or not a woman or girl has been used to working in the fields or in a factory from an early age and whether or not she has proved herself capable of standing this kind of work.

Apart from physical harm, it is the wish of the Führer that German women and girls must be protected under all circumstances from moral and mental harm. . . .

It is doubtful whether these conditions could be fulfilled in the event of mass conscription and employment. In this connexion, it is impossible to compare German women with the German soldier because of the basic difference between men and women, a difference which is determined by nature and race.

Considering the countless men fighting bravely at the front and especially those who have been killed, we cannot accept responsibility for the dangers which would threaten the life of the nation as a result of the labour conscription of women. . . .

14 *The treatment of Polish labour*

The other solution to the labour problem was to increase the use of foreign labour. Foreign labour was already being used to some extent. After the conquest of Poland, the Germans began to recruit Poles for work in the Reich. But voluntary methods proved inadequate and in May 1940 they began to introduce coercion and also to convert Polish prisoners of war into civilian workers. As a result, by the spring of 1942, there were approximately 1,080,000 Polish workers in the Reich. The introduction of coercion represented a victory for the more ruthless and extreme racialist elements in the regime. The attitude of this group, among whom the SS were prominent, which regarded the Poles as racially inferior, emerged in the regulations governing the employment of Polish workers in Germany, which were drawn up by the SS. German employers were informed that 'all social contact between these civilian workers and Germans is forbidden. . . . Germans who endanger the success of these measures, e.g. by collecting money and clothing for Poles, who post letters or buy tickets, who visit inns which are open to Poles during their presence etc., will be called to account. Sexual intercourse between Germans and Polish civilian workers of both sexes will be punished most severely.' Pay for Polish agricultural workers was 'on principle lower than that of German workers'. The SS also informed the Polish workers of their duties:

Duties of male and female civilian workers of Polish nationality during their stay in the Reich

The Greater German Reich provides each and every worker of Polish nationality with work, bread, and pay. It demands in return that everyone carries out conscientiously the work allotted to him and that everyone complies carefully with the laws and orders in force. The following special regulations apply to Polish male and female workers:

1. It is strictly forbidden to leave the place of residence.
2. It is also forbidden to leave the billets during the time of curfew ordered by the police.
3. Public conveyances, such as railways, may be used only after special consent has been obtained from the local police authority.
4. Every Polish male and female worker must always wear visibly the badge issued to him or her. They should be worn on the right breast of every piece of clothing. The badge is to be sewn on to the clothing.
5. Anyone who shirks his work, strikes, incites other workers, arbitrarily absents himself from the place of employment, etc., will be transferred to a concentration camp for forced labour. Sabotage and other serious offences against work- discipline will be punished severely, at least by transfer to a labour training camp for several years.
6. All social contact with the German people is forbidden; especially visits to theatres, cinemas, dances, bars and churches, in company with Germans. Dancing and drinking is allowed only in inns especially allocated to Polish workers.
7. Anyone who has sexual intercourse with a German man or woman, or approaches them in any other improper manner, will be punished by death.
8. Any offence against the orders and regulations issued for civilian workers of Polish nationality will be punished in Germany. Nobody will be sent back to Poland.
9. Every Polish male and every Polish female worker must always bear in mind that they came to work in Germany of their own free will. Anyone who works satisfactorily obtains bread and pay. Anyone who shirks his work or disregards the regulations issued will be taken to account severely, especially during wartime.
. . .

Between the end of the campaign in the west and the spring of 1942 the recruitment of foreign labour was mainly among West European prisoners of war and unemployed workers recruited from the western countries and from Germany's allies, particularly Italy. This policy proved extremely successful and by 1 October 1941 there were 3,507,526 foreign workers and prisoners of war employed in Germany.

With the invasion of Russia vast numbers of prisoners of war were captured. But for fear that the Russians would pollute Germany racially and ideologically, Hitler refused to allow Russian prisoners of war into Germany between June and November 1941. Instead, they were allowed to die of starvation and ill-treatment in prisoner-of-war camps. By February 1942, of the original number of 3,900,000 Soviet prisoners of war only 1,100,000 were left. And yet during those very months Germany was trying, now with diminishing success, to recruit foreign workers in other parts of Europe. This is one more example of ideological blindness interfering with the effective prosecution of the war.

15 *Sauckel's labour conscription programme*

Sauckel had been appointed Plenipotentiary for Labour to recruit the large amount of additional labour which was now necessary for the operation of a full war economy and to replace the increasing numbers of workers drafted into the armed forces. On his appointment, he was given orders by Hitler to recruit the necessary workers primarily from the occupied territories and in particular from the east.

Sauckel embodied these instructions in a programme which he issued on 20 April 1942:

. . .

Our armed forces of Greater Germany have surpassed themselves in heroism and endurance on the Eastern Front, in Africa, in the air and on the sea. To ensure their victory under all circumstances, it is now necessary to produce more and better weapons, equipment and ammunition through the increased efforts and endeavours of the entire German people, that is, of all the productive workers, both intellectual and manual, the women and the whole of German youth.

In this way, the German Home Front will make a decisive contribution towards frustrating our enemy's hopes of once again escaping their total and final defeat.

The aim of this gigantic new labour mobilization is to use the rich and tremendous resources, conquered and secured for us by our armed forces under the leadership of Adolf Hitler, for the armament of the armed forces and also to provide food for the homeland. The raw materials as well as the fertility of the conquered territories and their manpower are to be exploited completely and conscientiously for the benefit of Germany and her allies. . . .

All prisoners of war, actually in Germany, from the territories of the west as well as of the east, must be completely incorporated into the German armament and nutrition industries. Their productivity must be raised to the highest possible level.

It must be emphasized, however, that a tremendous additional quantity of foreign labour must be found for the Reich. The occupied territories in the east will provide the greatest pool for this purpose.

Consequently, it is absolutely essential to use the human reserves of the conquered Soviet territory to the fullest extent. If we do not succeed in obtaining the necessary amount of labour on a voluntary basis, we must immediately institute conscription or forced labour.

Therefore, apart from the prisoners of war still in the occupied territories, we must requisition skilled or unskilled male and female labour from the Soviet territories from the age of fifteen upwards for the labour mobilization.

On the other hand, as things stand at present, one quarter of our total needs of foreign labour can be procured from the occupied territories in the west.

The procurement of labour from friendly and also from neutral countries can cover only a small part of our total requirements. In this connexion, virtually only skilled workers and specialists can be considered.

In order to provide significant relief for the German housewife, especially for mothers with many children and farmers' wives who are extremely busy, and in order to avoid any further danger to their health, the Führer has also charged me to procure 400,000–500,000 picked, strong and healthy girls from the eastern territories. . . .

The employment of all prisoners of war as well as the use of a tremendous number of new civilian workers has become a prerequisite for carrying out the labour mobilization programme in this war.

All the men must be fed, housed, and treated in such a way as to exploit them to the greatest possible extent at the absolute minimum of expenditure.

It has always been natural for us Germans to refrain from cruelty or mean chicanery towards a conquered enemy, even had he proved himself the most bestial and implacable adversary, and to treat him correctly and humanely, even when we expect useful work from him.

So long as the German armaments industry did not make it absolutely necessary, we refrained from using either Soviet prisoners of war or civilian workers, men or women from the Soviet territories under any circumstances. It has now become impossible to maintain this attitude, and the manpower of these people must be exploited to the greatest possible extent.

Consequently, my first measures have been to arrange the feeding, housing and treatment of these foreign workers, in conjunction with the competent Reich authorities and with the consent of the Führer and Reich Marshal of the Greater German Reich, in such a way that maximum productivity will be demanded and obtained.

It must be remembered, however, that the output even of a machine is conditioned by the amount of fuel, skill and care given to it. In the case of men, even of a low type and race, how many more factors must be considered than in the case of a machine!

I could not justify it to the German people, if, after such a tremendous number of men had been brought to Germany, these men, instead of doing highly necessary and useful work, were to become a burden on the German people or even a threat to their health because of blunders made regarding their nutrition, housing and general treatment.

The principles of German cleanliness, order and hygiene must therefore be carefully applied to the Russian camps.

Only in this way will it become possible, without any trace of false sentimentality, to exploit their labour so as to achieve the maximum advantage for the production of arms for the front and for our programme of wartime nutrition. . . .

16 *Party resistance to full-scale mobilization*

Part of the problem was that the Party authorities, and notably the individual Gauleiters, often thwarted attempts to mobilize labour resources for essential purposes. Each Gauleiter had come to regard his *Gau* as his own domain and therefore considered any such attempts as interference in his sphere of authority. They were also concerned about the effects of such measures on morale. The Party was acutely sensitive to anything which might affect the prestige of the regime among the population and of themselves as its representatives. After the war, a member of Speer's staff recounted to the Nuremberg Tribunal his difficulties in this connexion.

Excerpt from the Interrogation on 20 May 1946 of Walter Rohland, former head of the Steel Production Department in the Speer Ministry

Q. You attended the meeting of Gauleiters in the summer of 1943 at which Speer and his assistants made some demands.
A. This happened at the meeting of Gauleiters on 6 October 1943. Speer emphasized the seriousness of the situation and remarked that much depended on whether the political leadership showed an appreciation of the situation. He and his assistants made the following requests: 1. Mobilization of the German labour resources including women. 2. Restrictions on the civilian sector and the transfer of the production of civilian goods to the occupied territories. 3. The employment of foreign labour is and remains an emergency measure. So far as the food situation is concerned, it represents a burden because, in addition to accommodation, additional calories must be provided for them, in order that they can work. If the necessary amount of production is to be achieved, these calories must be acquired. Before even more foreigners are brought into the Reich, however, the reserves of male and female German labour not yet involved in the war effort should be withdrawn from trade and from overstaffed administrative offices right down to the last German who is capable of work. But even with all these measures, the employment of foreigners remains absolutely essential. Sufficient food supplies, decent accommodation, etc. must be supplied, since it is only under such conditions that their enthusiasm for work can be maintained. . . .

Speer referred to the remarkable examples of Britain and the United States in this connexion.[1] There were two meetings. I took part in the one on 6 October 1943. . . .

Following on discussions with Hitler, similar requests were made. In particular we strongly criticized the overstaffing of the administration and the Party offices, as well as the excessive production of consumer goods. At the same time practical suggestions were made for the employment of women. (Abolition of half-day work for women.) We also advocated a reduction in the number of offices and the elimination of duplicate and superfluous office staff. Proposals were made for cuts in the sphere of consumer goods.

[1] In June 1944 Speer pointed out to Sauckel that 61 per cent of women in Britain were working, compared to 46 per cent in Germany. One factor was that, unlike the First World War, payments to the wives of German soldiers were surprisingly generous, so there was little economic pressure on them to work.

In this connexion, Speer referred to the fact that the reduction in Party offices had not yet been carried out. He mentioned the expenses, the grandiose outlay, the employment of Germans on special projects of the political offices,[1] and he demanded, particularly from those bearing political responsibilities and especially from the Party leaders, model personal conduct, not only in theory but also in practice, which was by no means the rule at that time. Hitler admitted that Speer's criticism was valid in principle, but he rejected compulsory employment for women on emotional grounds. Moreover, he did not believe that administrative officials would be able to work effectively in factories or that those who had studied would be any use as factory workers. He made no mention of the workers who had been criticized. On the following day, the Gauleiters themselves appealed to Hitler and put forward their point of view, which was dictated by their own ends.

The negative attitude of the Gauleiters can be explained by the following factors. As a result of the brilliantly successful first two years of the war, no one believed in the necessity for total war. This was particularly true as regards the employment of labour and the reduction in consumer goods. All demands from the Speer Ministry and from the industrial organizations met with the greatest suspicion, and the abilities of these experienced men were neglected. This went so far that the demand of the Speer Ministry for additional labour was no longer taken seriously. Some made accusations that the industrialists were keeping back their skilled workers for their own convenience and were thereby sabotaging the requirements of the Wehrmacht. In addition, they claimed that the labour requirement which was stated was exaggerated, in every sense of the word. Most of the Gauleiters acted from personal ambition and desire for power. They and their political associates rejected every new measure for political reasons but did nothing which might further the general welfare in case it might turn to their own disadvantage. They were supported in this by Bormann in particular, and also by Adolf Hitler himself. The standpoint of the Gauleiters was determined by the view that the total war demanded by Speer would weaken the nation's powers of resistance [by causing discontent]. . . .

[1] Such as prestige buildings for the Party.

23 Civilian Morale

Assessing the morale of the civilian population is one of the most difficult tasks facing the historian of Nazi Germany at war. This is especially so when he lacks the kinds of statistical data available today from opinion polls which, though not always accurate, do at least provide a check on the random and subjective impressions of individual observers. The main source for the following analysis is the reports prepared by the Security Service (SD) of the SS. These SD reports represent analyses of public attitudes which were based on the reports sent in every day by the branches of the SD throughout Germany using information provided by their informants in all walks of life. Clearly they must be treated with caution. The reporters were bound to be careful in passing on criticism of leading members of the regime, particularly of Hitler himself, and of the trend of events. They were not anxious to be accused of disloyalty and defeatism by their superiors. By and large, however, they appear to have retained a remarkable degree of objectivity and it is significant that by the summer of 1944 reports were so pessimistic that Martin Bormann, the head of the Party Chancellery, accused the reporters of defeatism and after July 1944 the national reports ceased.

1 *The attitude of the Berliners to the outbreak of war with Britain and France*

On 3 September 1939, two days after the German invasion of Poland, Britain and France declared war on Germany in fulfilment of their obligations under the guarantee to Poland of 31 March 1939. William Shirer, an American correspondent in Berlin, described in his diary the way the news was received in Germany:

... It has been a lovely September day, the sun shining, the air balmy, the sort of day the Berliner loves to spend in the woods or on the lakes near by. I walked in the streets. On the faces of the people astonishment, depression. Until today they have been going about their business pretty much as usual. There were food cards and soap cards and you couldn't get any petrol and at night it was difficult stumbling around in the black-out. But the war in the east has seemed a bit far away to them—two moonlit nights and not a single Polish plane over Berlin to bring destruction—and the papers saying that German troops have been advancing all along the line, that the Polish air force has been destroyed. Last night I heard Germans talking of the 'Polish thing' lasting but a few weeks, or months at the most. Few believed that Britain and France would move. Ribbentrop was sure they wouldn't and had told the Führer, who believed him. The British and French

654

had been accommodating before. Another Munich, why not? Yesterday, when it seemed that London and Paris were hesitating, everyone, including those in the Wilhelmstrasse, was optimistic. Why not?

In 1914, I believe, the excitement in Berlin on the first day of the world war was tremendous. Today, no excitement, no hurrahs, no cheering, no throwing of flowers, no war fever, no war hysteria. There is not even any hate for the French and British—despite Hitler's various proclamations to the people, the Party, the East Army, the West Army, accusing the 'English warmongers and capitalistic Jews' of starting this war. When I passed the French and British embassies this afternoon, the sidewalk in front of each of them was deserted. A lone *Schupo* [policeman] paced up and down before each....

2 *Gestapo instructions on maintaining internal security during the war, 3 September 1939*

But the regime was taking no chances with the attitude of its population. A decree was immediately issued forbidding people to listen to foreign broadcasts and Heydrich issued the following instructions for the Gestapo concerning 'the internal security of the State during the war':

In order to secure the commitment of all the resources of the nation against any disturbance and sedition, which is essential for the realization of the Führer's aims, the following principles are laid down for the security organs of the Reich to ensure the internal security of the State.

1. Any attempt to undermine the unity of the German people and its determination to fight must be ruthlessly suppressed. In particular, any person who doubts the victory of the German nation or questions the justification of the war is to be arrested.

2. Those fellow citizens, however, who are guilty of mistakes of some kind through personal distress or in moments of weakness must be treated with psychological understanding and efforts must be made to strengthen their will by educative means.

3. Particular attention must be paid to all attempts to influence other people in public in a hostile direction towards nation and Reich—in bars, public transport, etc. In the same way, drastic measures must be taken against any attempt to form groups and rings with the aim of spreading such views and information. If instances occur of public activity or the formation of rings, the suspected persons must in every case be arrested.

4. After the arrest of a suspected person all inquiries necessary to clear up the case must be made without delay. In the course of this it must be established as thoroughly as possible through files available at the State Police offices and at sub-sections of the SD and by interviewing suitable witnesses, and through inquiring at local Party offices, what general attitude and what particular motives were behind the actions of the persons concerned. The Chief of the Security Police must then be informed without delay and a decision requested on the further treatment of the arrested persons, since the ruthless liquidation of such elements may be ordered at a high level.

5. Compatriots who are guilty of lapses not wilfully but for excusable reasons must,

after thorough interrogation on the point, be taken to the head of the State Police office in person, who shall lecture them and admonish them thoroughly. This lecture and warning must be carried out in such a way as to produce loyalty and to strengthen their will. While they must be left in no doubt that they are to expect tougher measures in the event of a repetition, the result of this warning should not be pure intimidation; it should rather have the effect of convincing and encouraging the person concerned. The attention of the relevant Party offices must then be drawn to the compatriot concerned and they must be requested to provide political supervision and supervision in material matters.

6. Appropriate steps should be taken at once against informers who for personal reasons make unjustified or exaggerated reports about compatriots, in the form of a serious warning and, in cases of malice, of transfer to a concentration camp.

7. The heads of the State Police offices are personally responsible for the effective suppression of any sign of defeatism in their area.

3 *The population is united behind the Führer as never before*

German morale was transformed by the victories in the west between April and June 1940. The German population which had begun the war with little enthusiasm was delighted at the speedy and painless successes which their Führer had brought them. The SD report of 24 June 1940 stated:

. . .

Victories and activity of the Opposition
With regard to this question, reports from the whole Reich are unanimous in presenting the following picture:

Under the impression of the great political events and under the spell of military success, the whole German nation is displaying an inner unity and a close bond between the front and the homeland which is unprecedented. The soil is no longer fertile for opposition groups. Everyone looks up to the Führer in trust and gratitude and to his armed forces pressing forward from victory to victory. Hostile activities meet everywhere with sharp rejection.

4 *Hitler's warning to Britain in the Berlin Sports Palace, 4 September 1940*

By September 1940, the euphoria had subsided. It was now clear that Britain was not going to sue for peace and people were impatient for the promised invasion. The fact that Britain even dared to launch small-scale air raids increased the sense of frustration. It was in order to deal with this situation that Hitler issued a warning to Britain at the beginning of September. The speech illustrates the mood in which he made the fatal decision at this time to switch the German bomber offensive from British airfields to London and other cities, thereby destroying any chance of a German victory in the Battle of Britain:

. . .

If people in England are at the moment highly inquisitive and ask: 'Well, why doesn't he come?' I say to them: 'Don't worry, he's coming!' One shouldn't go on being so inquisitive.

This world will be set free. Once for all this nonsense must be stopped by which one nation is able to blockade a continent at will. It must be made impossible in future for a pirate State to follow a whim from time to time and expose 450 million people more or less to poverty and misery. We Germans are fed up with always being told by England to do this or not to do that, perhaps even being told whether Germans may or may not drink coffee. If it does not please England the import of coffee will be stopped. It does not concern me personally. I do not drink coffee. But I am annoyed that others should not be allowed to drink it.

In any case, I find it intolerable that a nation of 85 million people should be punished physically and mentally by another nation whenever it pleases some plutocrat in London. I have held out my hand to England so often with the offer of an agreement. You yourselves know that it was my foreign policy programme. Recently I repeated it for the very last time. Now I prefer to fight until at last a clear decision has been reached.

This clear decision can only be that this regime of mean and pathetic warmongers shall be eliminated and that a state of affairs shall be established which will make it impossible in future for one nation to be able to tyrannize the whole of Europe. . . .

It is wonderful to see our people in war, with their discipline. This is particularly true now when Mr Churchill is demonstrating his invention of night air raids. He does not do this because these air raids are particularly effective but because his Air Force cannot fly over German territory during the day. Whereas German pilots and German planes are over British territory day after day, no Englishman comes over during the day; they hardly even get across the North Sea. So they come during the night and, as you know, drop their bombs at random (without any aim or plan) on civilian residential areas, farms and villages. Where they see a light they drop a bomb.

For three months I have not reacted to this in the belief that they would stop this nonsense. Mr Churchill saw in that a sign of weakness. You will understand that we are now increasingly responding night after night.

And if the British air force drops two, three or four thousand kilograms of bombs, we will drop a hundred and fifty thousand, a hundred and eighty, two hundred and thirty, three hundred, four hundred thousand, a million kilograms in one night. If they announce that they will attack our cities on a large scale—we will wipe out their cities!

We will put these night pirates out of business, so help us God. The hour will come when one of us will crack, and it will not be National Socialist Germany.

Once before in my life I have carried out such a fight to the finish; and then my opponent,[1] who now sits in England on a last island in Europe, was also smashed. . . .

5 *Growing discontent with the delay in the 'big blow' against Britain*

German public opinion, however, soon came to doubt the reality of these threats. The people were becoming increasingly frustrated at Germany's

---

[1] i.e. democracy.

failure to defeat Britain and increasingly disillusioned with the forecasts of the German propaganda machine, as the following SD Report of 7 October 1940 indicates:

It is clear from the *Gau* reports of the past week that large sections of the population are adopting a completely unappreciative and thoroughly uncooperative attitude which expresses itself, in particular, in comments about the press and radio.

1. There are many reports that the excitement after the conclusion of the Tripartite Pact[1] has already been dissipated. Only a few people appreciate that the press dealt with the importance of the event in a thorough and exhaustive fashion. Impatience with the fact that the 'big blow' against Britain has not yet occurred predominates (e.g. Allenstein[2]). People are already switching their attention to other topics (e.g. Dresden). Even interest in military developments has declined most regrettably. Grudgingly and reluctantly the population is getting used to the thought of a second winter of war, and daily worries, particularly about fuel, have come to the surface. The thought frequently comes up that the Tripartite Pact shows that the war has been enormously extended. . . .

2. . . . The pictures of the destruction in England are still thought to be making a considerable impact, particularly those published by the *VB*[3] (e.g. Innsbruck, Berlin). The close-ups of bombed streets, individual blocks, etc., were what the masses wanted to see.

An extraordinarily large number of people, however, have complained about the 'sameness' of the daily reports. People have got used to hearing that the recent attacks were heavier than the previous ones and that they had again had a devastating effect (e.g. Dessau, Bielefeld, Koblenz, Augsburg, Königsberg). People have been asking themselves impatiently how long this situation of daily attacks is going to last (e.g. Karlsruhe). After the Führer's remark, 'Don't worry, he's coming',[4] people were expecting the final operation against Britain to begin soon. In fact, the struggle against England was being fought mainly by the press and with a great use of tough talk. But it was obvious that the press was laying it on thick. One only had to think of headlines like: 'Whole of London in Flames', 'London Air Force Bleeding to Death', 'Death and Destruction in London', 'Life in London Unbearable'. People are surprised that the Londoners are none the less withstanding it. Apparently things were not as the German press had heard from foreign reports — that conditions were already worse than those in Warsaw and Rotterdam (e.g. Frankfurt am Main). A few people interpreted the report that the English had already moved their airfields inland as an important success and an indication of the progress of planned destruction. More often people comment that, according to the press reports, there ought not to be much left of the English air force (e.g. Breslau). People are frequently cynical about the daily reports on the ratio of planes shot down on either side. . . .

3. . . . Like the reports on the evacuation of children, the oral and written reports

[1] Tripartite Pact signed between Germany, Italy and Japan on 27 September 1940.
[2] These towns in parentheses refer to the origin of the reports.
[3] The *Völkischer Beobachter*, the official Nazi Party paper.
[4] See above, p. 657.

on the effects of English bomb attacks have generated a psychosis which has an extremely adverse effect on our propaganda. For example, the guests at the Spa in Baden-Baden who were 'convalescing after the effects of night air raids' continually described their 'war experiences' with the result that the reports in the press and on the radio now meet with considerable mistrust. . . .

6 *The reaction of the German population to the invasion of Russia*

The German invasion of Russia had begun on 21 June 1941. The reaction of the population to the news of the invasion was mixed and uncertain, as is shown by an SD Report of 26 June:

The reports on the war with Russia which have been received in the meantime unanimously confirm that the initial nervousness and shock, which was particularly noticeable among women, lasted only a few hours and, as a result of the comprehensive campaign of enlightenment, has given place to a general attitude of calm and confidence. The mood of the population has swung round to such an extent that most people now tend to have a very low opinion of Russia as a military opponent. In some reports there are warnings of an 'obvious underestimation of the opponent. . . .'

While throughout the Reich there are no doubts about the military situation, here and there fears are emerging that it will be extremely difficult to administer and maintain security in the Russian sphere. In this connexion people continually refer to the lack of manpower everywhere. References to the fate of Napoleon, who was defeated by the expanse of Russia, have been comparatively rare so far.

The strong emphasis on a secret agreement between Russia and Britain has in some cases led to the comment that the British were always excellent at diplomacy and should not be underestimated in this capacity. . . .

. . . The events in the east have injected a new degree of bitterness and hate into the general attitude of the population towards England. They are now again longing for the day on which the attack on the island will at last begin. The fact that the air attacks on England have not slackened has been noted with satisfaction. The continual reports on the numerous English planes shot down are received with particular approval. The promise by Churchill of help to Russia has been received with general amusement. In this connexion people ask how England intends to provide this help. It is true that England's aim of confronting Germany with a new opponent has been achieved, but the account with Russia had to be settled sooner or later. The repeated English air attacks in the west of Germany are attributed to the effects of American aid, with which England is gaining time in order to strengthen her bases of operations. It will be so much the more difficult later on to destroy England in the shortest possible time.

7 *German reaction to the declaration of war on the United States*

The German population also appears to have failed to appreciate fully the significance of American entry into the war. An SD Report of 15 December 1941 indicates this:

The Führer's speech[1] has met with a great response and has left everywhere a sense of security and an awareness of the strength of the Reich.

The declaration of war on the U.S.A. came as no surprise and was considered by many to be simply official confirmation of a situation which in reality already existed. Only among the peasantry were there a very few who reacted with surprise and with a certain anxiety about the addition of another opponent. The creation of clear battle lines, as one section of the population described the new situation, has, according to the majority of the reports, had the effect of relaxing tension, particularly after the surprising successes of our Japanese allies. Many people expressed satisfaction that, in contrast to the Great War, Germany has seized the initiative this time and has therefore convincingly proved to the outside world its strength and confidence in victory.

In the discussions about the Führer's speech there was an emphasis on the Führer's objective and self-confident language, which provided the simple man in the street with a clear picture of the present situation, of the absolute necessity for the declaration of war on the U.S.A., and of the present war as a whole.

. . . The detailed statement of the Führer on German–American relations convinced the population of the necessity for declaring war on the U.S.A. as the only possible answer to Roosevelt's attempts at interference in Europe. In the discussions on this it was repeatedly stressed that Germany had never obstructed the U.S.A., in the slightest way and that therefore the war guilt rested on America alone. She had continually infringed international law and in this way had started the war.

The parts of the Führer's speech which dealt with the war and with the danger to Germany represented by America also did not fail to make an impact. In particular, the disclosure by the Führer that completely impregnable U-Boat bases had been established from Kirkenes to the Spanish frontier had a generally calming effect and also led to speculation that the great U-Boat action forecast on previous occasions by the Führer would now begin. For the time being the population has no clear idea of what effect the war with America will have for Germany. They expect a predominantly defensive strategy with a long-drawn-out overseas war. In this context there are rumours that the Führer's headquarters have already been transferred and that the emphasis of the war is being shifted from east to west.

The way the Führer dealt with Roosevelt received particular attention and approval and there was surprise in some quarters that former World Enemy No. 1, Churchill, had been replaced by Roosevelt. The contrasting of the Führer's personal background as a worker and soldier until his take-over of power with that of Roosevelt who from birth had been predestined to high office in the State met with a response of deep satisfaction and pride. . . .

8 Disillusionment and concern among the population, January 1942

The extent of the crisis on the Russian front during December 1941, however, could not be concealed from the German population. During November and December, the Government had organized an urgent collection of woollen clothing for the troops in the east and this had caused

[1] The speech of 11 December in which Hitler announced the German declaration of war on the United States and abused President Roosevelt.

considerable unease. In fact, Goebbels noted in his diary that up to 20 February 1942, 112,627 cases of freezing or frostbite were reported, including 14,357 third degree cases. Although these figures were kept secret, news of the conditions at the front reached the population at home through letters from their relatives. For the first time the confidence of the German people was severely shaken, as is shown by an SD Report of 22 January 1942:

... It is clear from a number of reports that the impact of the public media of guidance is at the moment greatly impaired. Of the various explanations usually given the following are the most frequent:

People had the feeling that when things were going badly the public media of guidance always preserved an 'official face'. As a result, in such situations large sections of the population no longer regard the press as the best source of information but construct 'their own picture' from rumours, stories told by soldiers and people with 'political connexions', letters from the front and suchlike, often accepting the craziest rumours with an astonishing lack of discrimination.

Also, as regards the reasons for and implications of the wool collection, the event which has affected the population in the civilian sector more than any other since the beginning of the war, the public media of guidance had preserved their 'official face' in the sense of not giving any answers to the questions about the alleged organizational deficiencies of winter planning and the late timing of the collection, questions that were being asked by everybody. People had seen in the dismissal of Field-Marshal von Brauchitsch an indirect reply to the many important questions as to who was responsible for the inadequate winter equipment on the Eastern front. ... People argue that even if winter had begun at the normal time, the preparations would not have been sufficient.

Furthermore, word had got round through numerous rumours that Field-Marshal von Rundstedt was being replaced by Field-Marshal von Reichenau and that moreover Field-Marshal von Bock was no longer at his post. The report of von Brauchitsch's operation, therefore, and the cordial wishes of the Führer for his speedy recovery had been extremely surprising. The allusion to the convalescence now needed by Field-Marshal von Brauchitsch seemed to leave open the possibility of his return one day. The same was true of the report that Field-Marshal von Rundstedt represented the Führer at Field-Marshal von Reichenau's State funeral, when von Reichenau, according to numerous rumours, was supposed to have only just taken over command from von Rundstedt. Finally, the surprise was completed by the new picture which showed Field-Marshal von Bock after a short convalescence together with the Führer. Now the population could not 'make head or tail' of the wool- and winter-clothing collection and the reasons for it. Above all, the question again came up of who was to be held responsible for the situation our soldiers were in, and people speculated on why Field-Marshals who, according to the rumours, had just 'been sacked' were suddenly treated kindly again or brought back, as in the case of Bock. People said that they could no longer find their way about in the confusion between what they 'heard' and what was in the papers.

In connexion with the reports before, during and after the winter- and woollen-clothing collection, the letters from the front and reports of soldiers play a great part according to many statements. Many soldiers reported home absolutely hair-raising accounts of hardships endured, cold, bad nourishment, clothing, etc. . . .

9 *Hitler demands exceptional powers, 26 April 1942*

Instead of the mass mobilization of the German people which was required, but which might threaten the prestige of the regime, Hitler began in a paranoid fashion to seek scapegoats among those in positions of authority who were alleged to be failing in their duty. Goebbels encouraged him in the view that the conservative bureaucracy, and particularly the judiciary, were putting obstacles in the way of the war effort because of their determination to stick to the rules. He further persuaded Hitler to demand from the Reichstag exceptional powers to deal with those who were not fulfilling their duty:

. . .

You, my old comrades in the fight, will not doubt that I am determined to do everything necessary to carry out these tasks.

But to enable me to achieve this I have several demands to make:

I expect the nation to give me the right to intervene immediately and to take the requisite action whenever people fail to obey orders absolutely or to act in the service of the great task in which our very existence is at stake. The people at the front and those at home, our transport system, administration, and justice must be governed by one thought alone—victory. At this moment nobody may appeal to established rights; he must realize that today there are only duties.

I ask the German Reichstag, therefore, for explicit confirmation that I have the right to remind everyone of his duties, to cashier him or to remove him from his office and job, whoever he may be and whatever rights he may have, if, in my opinion, he is not conscientiously carrying out his duties.

This is particularly important, because among the millions of decent people there are only a few individual exceptions. And more important than any rights, and that includes the rights of these exceptions, is the fact that today there is one single common duty.

I am not interested, therefore, in the question of whether or not leave can be given to officials or employees at the present time of crisis, and I refuse to allow any leave which cannot be taken now to be credited for a future occasion.

If anyone has the right to ask for leave it is, in the first place, our front-line troops, and secondly, the workers who are working for the front. And since I have not been able to grant leave to the Eastern front for months, I do not want anybody in some office at home to talk about a so-called 'justified claim' for leave.

Similarly, I expect those engaged in the administration of German justice to understand that they are there for the nation, not vice versa. This means that the world, which also includes Germany, must not be allowed to fall to pieces for the preservation of some legal formula. Germany must live, whatever any formal interpretation of the law may have to say about it. I do not understand, just to cite one example, why a criminal, who gets married in 1937 and then ill-treats his wife until she has a nervous breakdown and dies as the result of a final beating-up, should be condemned to five years' hard labour at a moment when tens of thousands of brave German men have to die to save their wives and children. From now on, I shall intervene in such cases and dismiss judges who clearly do not recognize the needs of the moment.

What the German soldier, the German worker, the farmer, the women in town and country, the millions of our middle classes achieve and sacrifice, all with the one thought of victory, demands a like-minded attitude on the part of those who have been appointed by the people themselves to look after their interests; at this time there are no sacrosanct bodies with established rights. We are all simply obedient servants of the interests of our people. . . .

10 *The Reichstag confers exceptional powers on Hitler, 26 April 1942*

There can be no doubt that at the present stage in the war, in which the German people is engaged in a life-and-death struggle, the Führer must possess the right which he claims to do everything that serves to bring about victory. Therefore, without being bound by existing legal regulations, in his capacity as Leader of the Nation, Supreme Commander of the Armed Forces, Head of the Government and Supreme Chief of the Executive, as Chief Justice and Leader of the Party, the Führer must be in a position to compel, with all the means at his disposal, every German, if necessary, whether he be common soldier or officer, high- or low-ranking official or judge, leading or subordinate official of the Party, worker or employee, to fulfil his duties. In the event of violation of these duties, the Fuhrer is entitled, regardless of so-called established rights, to punish and remove the offender from his post, rank and position, without introducing the prescribed procedures.

11 *Public reaction to the news of the defeat at Stalingrad, January 1943*

The German advances in the summer of 1942 brought about some improvement in morale but then, in the autumn and winter, Germany suffered a number of serious defeats. Above all, there was the defeat of Stalingrad which came as a devastating blow to the morale of the German people as the SD report for 28 January 1943 indicated:

At the moment the whole nation is deeply shaken by the impression that the fate of the 6th Army is already sealed and by concern about the further development of the war situation. Among the many questions arising from the changed situation, people ask above all why Stalingrad was not evacuated or relieved, and how it was possible, only a few months ago, to describe the military situation as secure and as not unfavourable. In particular, people discuss, with a marked undertone of criticism, the underestimate of the Russian combat forces through which now for the second time a severe crisis has been triggered off. Apart from this, our compatriots are once more concerned about various developments in the domestic situation which were partly responsible for this blow hitting us so extremely hard. Despite their readiness to subject themselves to the introduction of total war, many compatriots, particularly those who are politically reliable, say that this step was taken very late. Even if every individual was willing to exclude everything from his private and professional life that was not absolutely necessary for achieving victory, it may be questioned whether the great complexity of public life could be reduced to the necessary level with the speed and intensity needed, but also without going too far. Above all, our compatriots doubt whether it will be possible to distribute the burden of war equally between everybody without distinction. Thus, people fear that with the coming use of female labour the upper classes will know how to escape it. It was regrettable that the Führer by now had not found time to deal intensively with the situation at home. According to all the reports the nation is urgently waiting for a speech by the Führer on 30 January and hoping it will provide an answer to all these questions.

Fearing that an unfavourable end to the war is now possible, many compatriots are seriously thinking about the consequences of defeat. While some people say that 'perhaps it would not be so bad', most people are convinced that losing the war will amount to extinction. Although, on the one hand, this alarming thought strengthens the will to keep going, it causes many people, on the other hand, to be thinking already of the possibilities of a way out in the last resort and to be talking of the final bullet that would still be left when everything was over.

Despite the widespread ill-temper and acute symptoms of depression in some circles, the attitude of our compatriots is strengthening, according to reports from all parts of the Reich. There is every chance, these reports state, that the inner resources of the people now mobilized will prove themselves during the crucial tests to come.

12 *Goebbels's speech on total war, 18 February 1943*

In order to avert a collapse in morale, Goebbels who, almost alone among Nazi leaders, had long been pressing for a more far-reaching mobilization of the nation's resources devised a new propaganda stroke. On 18 February 1943 he made a speech in the Berlin Sports Palace before an audience which had been carefully selected to make it representative of every section of the German people. In this speech, broadcast throughout the Reich, he asked for a mandate for total war:

... To find out what the truth is, fellow Germans, let me ask you a number of questions, which you must answer to the best of your knowledge and conviction. When my audience indicated their spontaneous approval of my demands of 30 January, the next day the British press claimed that it had been a propaganda spectacle and did not represent the true mood of the German people. Well, I invited to this meeting today a cross-section, in the truest sense of that word, of the German people. In front of me sit, row upon row, wounded soldiers from the Eastern front, men with scarred bodies, with legs or arms amputated, men blinded in action who have come here with their Red Cross nurses, men in the prime of life whose crutches are standing in front of them. In between them, I count as many as fifty wearers of the Oak Leaf Cluster of the Knight's Cross, a splendid delegation from our fighting front. Behind them is a block of armament workers from the armoured car factory in Berlin. Behind them sit men from the various Party organizations, soldiers from our fighting forces, doctors, scientists, artists, engineers, architects, teachers, officials, civil servants from their offices and studies, proud representatives of our intellectual life at all levels, to whom the country in this time of war owes miracles of inventiveness and human genius. I see thousands of German women distributed throughout the entire auditorium of the Sports Palace. Youth is represented and so is venerable age. No estate, no profession, no age group was overlooked when our invitations went out. So I can say with justification that facing me is a cross-section of the whole German people, at the front and at home. Is that correct?

(At these words from the Minister, the audience rises from their seats and a 'Yes' from thousands of voices fills the Sports Palace.)

Then you, my listeners, are at this moment representative of the nation. And it is to you that I want to put ten questions which you are to answer with the German people before the whole world, particularly before our enemies who also are listening to their radio sets.

(Dr Goebbels can only make himself heard with difficulty after the questions that now follow. The crowd answers each one with a single roar of approval.)

First: The English allege that the German people have lost their belief in victory. I ask you: Do you believe with the Führer and with us in the final total victory of the German people? I ask you: Are you determined to follow the Führer through thick and thin in the struggle for victory and to put up even with the heaviest personal burdens?

Second: The English allege that the German people are tired of fighting. I ask you: Are you ready with the Führer, and as a phalanx of the home front standing behind the fighting armed forces, to continue this struggle with a fierce determination and impervious to all twists of fate, until victory is in our hands?

Third: The English allege that the German people are no longer in a mood to shoulder the ever-increasing war work demanded by the Government. I ask you: Are you and the German people determined, if the Führer orders it, to work ten, twelve and, if necessary, fourteen and sixteen hours a day and to give your utmost for victory?

Fourth: The English allege that the German people are resisting the total war measures of the Government. (Cries of 'Never! Never! Never!') I ask you: Do you want total war? Do you want it, if necessary, more total and more radical than we can even imagine it today?

Fifth: The English allege that the German people have lost their confidence in the Führer. I ask you: Is your confidence in the Führer greater, more faithful and unshakeable, than ever before? Is your readiness to follow him in all his ways and to do everything necessary to bring the war to a victorious end absolute and unlimited?

I ask you my sixth question: Are you prepared from now onwards to devote all your strength to providing the Eastern front with the men and materials it needs to give Bolshevism its mortal blow?

I ask you my seventh question: Do you swear a solemn oath to the fighting front that the country is behind it, with its morale high, and that it will give everything necessary to achieve victory?

I ask you my eighth question: Do you, especially even you, the women, want the Government to ensure that German women also give all their energies to the carrying on of the war, filling jobs wherever possible to free men for action and so to help their men at the front?

I ask you my ninth question: Do you approve, if necessary, the most radical measures against a small group of people who dodge the call-up and work the

black market, who in the midst of war play peace, and who intend to exploit
people's sufferings for their own selfish ends?

As my tenth and last question I ask you: Is it your wish that even in wartime, as
the Party programme requires, equal rights and equal duties shall prevail, that the
home front shall give evidence of its solidarity and take the same heavy burdens of
war upon its shoulders, and that the burdens be distributed equitably, whether a
person be great or small, poor or rich?

I have asked you; you have given me your answers. You are part of the people, so
your voices have demonstrated the attitude of Germany. You have told our enemies
what they must know to prevent them from indulging in spurious fantasies.

Let us approach the great problems of this part of the war with warm hearts and
cool heads. We enter thereby the path of final victory. It is based on faith in the
Führer. So this evening I point out to the nation once more their great duty. The
Führer expects things from us which will put in the shade everything achieved so
far. We do not want to fail in the fulfilment of what he demands. He will be able
to be proud of us, just as we are proud of him. True men and true women too prove
themselves only in the great crises and upheavals of national life. No one now has
any longer the right to talk of the weaker sex; both sexes now show the same determination to fight and the same strength of mind. The nation is ready for anything.
The Führer has given his orders, we will follow him. If we ever truly believed in
victory, it was in this hour of national reflection and inner revival. We see it right
ahead of us: we have only to grasp it. We have only to resolve to subordinate everything else to its service. This is the order of the hour. And therefore the motto is:
Now let the nation rise and the storm break!

13 *The impact of the speech: SD report of 22 February 1943*

According to the reports we have received, a large section of the population listened
to the speech of Dr Goebbels, despite the fact that its announcement came late
and as a surprise. Furthermore, through the repeat of the broadcast, through its
publication in the press and through the lively discussion of its content, it has
penetrated into the furthest corners of the country. Its effect—and the reports
were unanimous on this—was unusually great and on the whole very favourable.
The morale of the population had reached a low point on account of the most
recent developments on the Eastern front, particularly the evacuation of Kharkov,
and they were longing for a clear explanation of the situation. The speech of Dr
Goebbels, despite its frank description of the seriousness of the situation, had the
effect of easing tension and strengthening confidence and trust in the war leadership. Dr Goebbels understood how to develop an enthusiasm and a spirit like that
in the 'time of struggle' [i.e. before.1933] which communicated itself through the
radio.

The theme of 'imminent danger' confirmed the fear of many people that as yet
there was no question of stabilizing the Eastern front, that the series of setbacks
was not yet at an end and that the war could still take a serious turn. To some
extent, people had only now become aware of the terrible seriousness of the situation. But, though they were shaken, they were not despairing. The population was
grateful to the leadership for speaking frankly at last and for telling the plain
unvarnished truth. But many people had expressed the wish to hear more concrete
details about military developments, in so far as it was compatible with military

security. One or two people commented that Dr Goebbels had 'painted the situation blacker than it was' in order to give emphasis to the measures for total war. In his treatment of these measures Dr Goebbels had 'spoken the mind' of the population, although various people pointed out that his comments did not go beyond the measures and points already known and, as before, people said that total war was being introduced 'very late'. The announcement that the measures would be carried out in the most radical fashion was hailed everywhere. The doubts as to whether they will be carried out in a just manner, applying to all classes, have decreased though they have not yet ceased. . . .

14 *Civilian morale during 1943*

During 1943, Germany suffered more and more setbacks both on the Eastern front and also in Italy. Moreover, the Allies continued a massive air offensive on Germany. Germany's cities were pounded, one after the other, by hundreds of bombers at a time, causing enormous damage. These military setbacks and the air offensive could not fail to have their effect on German morale. But it is difficult to generalize about the state of German morale during this period. Certainly, the SD reports on public opinion during 1943, of which the following examples are representative, chart the growing concern of the population at the outcome of the war. On the other hand, the evidence in terms of rising production during this period suggests that the working population, which had been unwilling to make sacrifices during the early stages of the war, now felt that they were fighting for their lives and were therefore prepared to work as hard as they could and were all in favour of total war. The bombing was really effective only where it concentrated on strategically important targets such as ball-bearing factories and synthetic fuel plants. Indeed, the indiscriminate bombing of the civilian population proved, if anything, counter-productive in terms of morale. Productivity in the cities which had been bombed actually increased. Although most people now had few illusions left about the regime, they were afraid of what would happen in the event of defeat. In his propaganda Goebbels made great play with the threat of Bolshevism in the event of Germany's defeat, and this undoubtedly had a considerable impact. But above all, the knowledge that now 'everybody was in the same boat' produced a sense of national solidarity which the regime had never succeeded in achieving before, despite all its slogans about a 'national community':

(a) *People are worried about their future: SD report of 5 April 1943*

. . . Many individual remarks suggest that a large section of the nation cannot imagine how the war will end. Even if the Soviet Union was decisively defeated this year and even if England too was finished, there would still be a long war with America. In the light of the question, 'how will Germany stand when the war is over?' people discuss future prospects with a good deal of concern. Those belonging to the professions, such as lawyers and doctors, fear they will be turned into civil servants; the civil servants, on the other hand, are concerned about the contempt for them which is spreading among the population and from which they do not feel adequately protected from above. In the circles of medium- and small-sized industry there is the belief that the growth of large concerns and the 'State-capitalist concentrations of power' put their whole future in question. Small shop-keepers and craftsmen are worked up about the closure operation[1] and in many cases fear the 'end of the middle class [*Mittelstand*]'. People were also frequently concerned about the possible loss of their property through the expected tax increases, but also through rumours of capital levies. The rise in prices and the general lower valuation given to money were seen by many people as indicating an inflation. . . .

(b) *People want to see and hear more of the Führer: SD report of 19 April 1943*

. . . It has been emphasized in some reports that the whole population has appreciated the fact that recently they have heard more of the Führer. Judicious and positive-minded citizens have remarked that it is not a good idea for the Führer to remain 'out of sight' for too long. The nation wants to have its close personal relationship with the Führer confirmed by receiving frequent news of him. But in the course of the war it has become rare for a picture of the Führer to appear in the newspapers or in the newsreels; the same is true of speeches by the Führer. A picture of the Führer in which one could see that his hair has not gone completely white, as rumour once had it, would have a more positive effect on the population than many fighting slogans. In order to keep alive the contact between leader and nation, it was frequently suggested that the Führer should be shown not only at highly official occasions and at military conferences, but more often in his personal life, as was done before, at the field kitchen or while having a walk, and that there should be reports on his daily routine, and his remarks and comments should be published. . . .

(c) *Signs of weakening in the attitude of the population: SD report of 8 July 1943*

. . . The telling of vulgar jokes detrimental to the State, even about the Führer himself, has increased considerably since Stalingrad. In conversations in cafés, factories and other meeting places people tell each other the 'latest' political jokes and in many cases make no distinction between those with a harmless content and those which are clearly in opposition to the State. Even people who hardly know each other exchange jokes. They clearly assume that any joke can now be told without fear of a sharp rebuff, let alone of being reported to the police. Large sections of the population and even a section of the Party membership have clearly lost the feeling that listening to and passing on political jokes of a certain type is something which a decent German simply does not do. . . .

15 *A Security Service report on the reaction of the population to German propaganda about Soviet atrocities*

By the winter of 1944 disillusionment with the regime was even more widespread; it was increasingly being blamed for Germany's predicament

---

[1] On 30 January 1943 the Reich Ministry of Economics issued a decree for the closure and amalgamation of some small businesses. The intention was to save manpower for drafting to the front and to save energy (coal etc.).

on the grounds that Nazi crimes were now being avenged by the enemy, as is clear from the following report of the Stuttgart SD section dated 6 November 1944:

... The examples [of Soviet atrocities] from Nemmersdorf in East Prussia have in many cases achieved exactly the opposite of what was intended. Compatriots say it is shameless to make so much of them in the German press. ...

'What does the leadership intend by the publication of such pictures as those in the *NS-Kurier* on Saturday? They should realize that the sight of these victims will remind every thinking person of the atrocities we have committed in the enemy territory, even in Germany itself. Have we not murdered thousands of Jews? Don't soldiers again and again report that Jews in Poland have had to dig their own graves? And how did we treat the Jews in the concentration camp in Alsace? Jews also are human beings. By doing all this we have shown the enemy what they can do with us if they win.' (The opinion of numerous people from all classes of the population.)

'Our leaders should be ashamed of publishing such pictures. How did our people deal with their own German compatriots who were put into concentration camps because they had a different political viewpoint? Weren't our SS people frequently even more cruel towards Germans, their own fellow citizens, than the Russians have been towards the East Prussians? We have shown the others how to deal with political enemies. One cannot reproach the Russians for being as cruel towards other nations as our people are towards Germans.' (A secretary, Party member; similar views held by compatriots of all classes and professions.)

'The pictures in the *NS-Kurier* have shocked me, but not for the reason our propaganda imagines, but only because once again I am forced to see that the good German citizen who never did anything wrong has to suffer for all the atrocities the Nazis committed. The political leadership and above all the SS have the whole German people on their conscience.' (An armament worker.)

'So long as people in Germany don't change their own way of treating human beings, we have no right to be upset at our enemies being cruel. I saw myself how in the Ostend Square in Ostheim forty people were just left to a horrible death in the Pflugfelder Café. ...' (A worker, SS leader.)

'They make a fuss about the Russians because they killed a few people in East Prussia. What does human life mean in Germany?' (A worker.)

Finally, a view one can now hear frequently expressed in various forms:

'People maintain again and again that the Führer was sent to us by God. I have no doubt of it. The Führer was sent to us by God; not to save Germany, but to ruin it. Providence has decided to destroy the German people and Hitler is the executor of its will.'

[illegible signature]
SS Obersturmführer

24 The Disintegration of the Third Reich, 1943–45

During the war important shifts took place within the power structure of the Third Reich. Increasingly, power was accumulating in the hands of Himmler and the SS on the one hand, and Bormann and the Party on the other. Since the beginning of the war, the SS had been able to increase its power through the influence which it acquired in the occupied areas, particularly in the east, through the rapid expansion of the concentration camp system and through the SS troops, the Waffen SS. Between 1934 and 1938 the number of concentration camp inmates was relatively stable at about 10,000. In 1939 this rose to 25,000 and in 1940 to 100,000. Moreover, during the war the camps had acquired two new functions. First, they were responsible for the extermination of the Jews. For this purpose, during 1942–43 special extermination camps were built such as Belzec, Treblinka and, the largest of all, Auschwitz-Birkenau.

1 *The concentration camps transformed into SS labour camps, April 1942*

In addition, however, and to some extent in conflict with this policy of extermination, the SS increasingly exploited its prisoners as an enormous labour force. The prisoners were either hired out to armament firms or else were used in special SS industries. These SS industries developed rapidly during the war and were intended by Himmler to provide the SS with an independent economic basis after the war. The independence of these SS industries and the growing SS labour force in the concentration camps posed a growing problem for Speer who was attempting to coordinate German war production in the most effective way. This change in the function of the concentration camps was initiated in April 1942:

. . .

The Chief of the SS-Main-Office Economics and Administration
Berlin, 30 April 1942
Re: The Integration of the Inspectorate of the Concentration Camps into the SS-Main-Office Economics and Administration.
Reichsführer!
Today I am reporting on the present concentration camp situation and on measures I have taken in order to carry out your order of 3 March 1942.

670

by me, because this is made impossible for me. But all the same I have to bear the whole or at least part of the responsibility for them.

A further result is that the Reich Ministers, the other supreme Reich authorities and other bureaux which come directly under the Führer and which, according to the Führer's instructions, are under my care, when they see that through me they get nowhere, choose other, not always desirable and right, ways to the Führer or address him direct. For the Führer this is an extra burden or, at least, looked at from the point of view of time, a multiple burden!

I have to bear, both from the Führer and from the Ministers, etc., the odium of not having got things done! Further, it puts me in the unpleasant and often embarrassing position of having decisions by the Führer passed on to me in which I did not collaborate at all but for which I have to be responsible. Some of these I have to sign jointly and share responsibility for, without ever having been in a position to draw the Führer's attention to some essential aspects which might have brought him to a different decision. . . .

I believe I can take it for granted that the Führer has not withdrawn from me the confidence which he has so far placed in me and assured me of. Indeed, I am of the opinion that the Führer is simply not told what a great many important matters I have been waiting to put before him and what harm and difficulties will arise if I continue to be excluded as I am at present. I therefore request you, my dear Bormann, to arrange a short interview with the Führer for me simply to clarify these questions. I would not bring any reports with me. I simply consider it my duty to place these questions before the Führer in detail and I hope that he will understand that I am bound to do this. If the Führer is, solely for reasons well known to me, not in a position in the near future to take decisions himself as Reich Chancellor on matters the presentation of which he himself demands of me or which I am in duty bound to place before him, it still remains my duty to explain the position in greater detail and leave him to examine the question of whether he will at least depute certain decisions to other authorities, in so far as they do not have to be taken by him, so that the State machinery does not come to a standstill in those matters which must be decided in wartime too. I particularly emphasize that I am not aspiring to be the authority to whom this duty should be deputed. I would also like to place before the Führer a number of other suggestions which would serve to guarantee the faultless working of the State machinery during the further course of the war, without the direct participation of the Führer. I therefore request you once more to arrange a date for me to report to the Führer as soon as possible, just so as to work out these questions. . . .

I only wish you had recently taken account of my interest, i.e. my cooperation and participation, in the affairs which come within my competence or in affairs in which I must participate in the same manner as I normally used to. I am sorry to say that this has frequently not happened. I only want to remind you of the decree for the creation of the Volkssturm (Home Guard), of your difference of opinion with Minister Frank about the construction of emplacements in the Protectorate and of the last Führer decree about the Youth Leaders of the German Reich without going into details here. Trustful cooperation is only possible if it is mutual. I have always observed this in my relations to you. I have never separately and one-sidedly reported to the Führer on any Party matter or any matter in which the Party was concerned, or in which it was merely interested. I even went so far as invariably to discuss with you in confidence numerous matters which did not require your participation and to deal with them in agreement with you, because I considered this, not indeed necessary, but suitable and expedient. I have never yet claimed to intervene officially in purely Party affairs. I think you must admit this. I am totally unaware of and unable to explain any other grounds you could have for being ill-disposed towards me or for your letting anything come between us, as is already giving occasion for comment by others. I would be most grateful to you if you would be kind enough to inform me frankly of any such grounds. After all, frank talk and honest discussion are always best. All insinuations from outsiders, who may have misinformed you or wrongly influenced you, would thus fall to the ground. Otherwise, they will rejoice at bringing about our estrangement. For our mutual cooperation to date has long been a thorn in the flesh of various people who would have preferred to play us off against each other.

In conclusion, I should only like to repeat what I wrote at the beginning of this letter, namely to express my wish that our official and personal relations should remain in the new year the same as they have been in the past. I am not aware of having disturbed them. It is now your turn to say something—either by letter or by word of mouth. I am always at your disposal to talk things over.

3 *Hitler's destruction order of 19 March 1945*

As the German defences crumbled on all fronts, Hitler came to the conclusion that his regime had failed because the German people had been unworthy of its aims. If the Third Reich was to be destroyed, then neither did the German people deserve to survive. In any event, the alternative was Bolshevism. He was determined, therefore, that the Allies should find Germany a desert, though he justified his order on military grounds:

The fight for the existence of our nation compels us to exploit all means, even within the Reich, which can weaken the enemy's fighting capacity and impede his further progress. Every possibility of doing lasting damage to the striking power of the enemy must be taken advantage of. It is an error to believe that after the recapture of lost areas it will be possible to use undamaged or only temporarily paralysed transport, communication, industrial and supply installations again for one's own purposes. During his retreat the enemy will leave only scorched earth behind him and will abandon all concern for the population.

I therefore order:

1. All military, transport, communication, industrial, and supply installations as well as equipment within the Reich which the enemy might use for the continuation of his struggle now or in the future must be destroyed.

2. The destruction of all military objects, including transport and communication installations, is the responsibility of the military command posts; that of all industrial and supply installations as well as other material is the responsibility of the Gauleiters and Reich Defence Commissioners. The troops must give Gauleiters and Reich Defence Commissioners the necessary assistance for the execution of their task.

3. This order must be made known to all commanders as quickly as possible. Orders to the contrary are invalid.

Speer, however, who as Minister of Armaments had considerable influence over the German economy, managed largely to prevent the carrying out of this order, by instructing plant managers not to destroy equipment which was essential to the existence of the German people.

4 Hitler's Last Will and Testament, 29 April 1945

Finally, as the Russian troops fought their way through the streets of Berlin toward the Reich Chancellery, Hitler composed his 'Last Will and Testament', in which he sought to justify himself before history. Significantly, he ends his political career, just as he had begun it in Munich, with an outburst of antisemitism, the dominant principle of his ideology:

. . .

ADOLF HITLER

My private Will and Testament
As I did not consider that during the years of struggle I could take the responsibility of contracting a marriage, I have now decided, before the closing of my earthly career, to take as my wife the girl who, after many years of loyal friendship, of her own free will, in order to share her destiny with mine, entered this town when it was almost completely besieged. At her own desire she goes as my wife with me into death. It will compensate us for what we have both lost through my work in the service of my people.

What I possess belongs, in so far as it has any value, to the Party; should that no longer exist, to the State; should the State also be destroyed, no further decision of mine is necessary.

My pictures, in the collections which I have bought over the years, have never been collected for private purposes, but only for the extension of a gallery in my home town of Linz on the Danube.

It is my most sincere wish that this bequest may be duly executed.

I nominate as my Executor my most faithful Party comrade, Martin Bormann.

He is given full legal authority to make all decisions. He is permitted to take away everything that has sentimental value or is necessary for the maintenance of a modest simple life, for my brothers and sisters, also above all for the mother of my wife and my faithful co-workers who are well known to him, principally my old Secretaries, Frau Winter, etc., who have for many years aided me by their work.

I myself and my wife, in order to escape the disgrace of deposition or capitulation, choose death. It is our wish to be burnt immediately on the spot where I have carried out the greatest part of my daily work in the course of twelve years' service to my people.

Given in Berlin, 29 April 1945, 4 a.m.

[signed] A. HITLER
As Witness: [signed] NICOLAUS VON BELOW
As Witnesses: [signed] MARTIN BORMANN
[signed] DR FUHR

ADOLF HITLER

My political Testament

More than thirty years have now passed since in 1914 I made my modest contribution as a volunteer in the First World War that was forced upon the Reich.

In these three decades I have been actuated solely by love and loyalty to my people in all my thoughts, acts, and life. They gave me the strength to make the most difficult decisions which have ever confronted mortal man. In these three decades I have spent my time, my working strength, and my health.

It is untrue that I or anyone else in Germany wanted the war in 1939. It was desired and instigated exclusively by those international statesmen who were either of Jewish descent or worked for Jewish interests. I have made too many offers for the control and limitation of armaments, which posterity will not for all time be able to disregard, for the responsibility for the outbreak of this war to be laid on me. I have, moreover, never wished that after the first fatal world war a second against England, or even against America, should break out. Centuries will pass away, but out of the ruins of our towns and monuments hatred will grow for those finally responsible whom we have to thank for everything, International Jewry and its accomplices.

Three days before the outbreak of the German-Polish war I proposed once more to the British ambassador in Berlin a solution to the German-Polish problem, similar to that in the case of the Saar district, under international control. Neither can this offer be denied. It was rejected only because the leading circles in English politics wanted war, partly on account of the business they hoped to gain by it and partly under the influence of propaganda organized by International Jewry.

I also made it quite plain that, if the nations of Europe are again to be regarded as mere shares to be bought and sold by these international conspirators in money and finance, then Jewry, the race which is the real criminal in this murderous struggle, will be saddled with the responsibility. I further left no one in doubt that this time millions of children of Europe's Aryan peoples would not die of hunger, millions of grown men would not suffer death, nor would hundreds of thousands of women and children be burnt and bombed to death in the towns, without the real criminal having to atone for this guilt, even if by more humane means.

After six years of war, which despite all setbacks will one day go down in history as the most glorious and valiant demonstration of the purpose of a nation's life, I cannot forsake the city which is the capital of this Reich. As our forces are too small to make any further stand against the enemy attack on this place and our resistance is gradually being weakened by men who are as deluded as they are lacking in initiative, it is my wish, by remaining in this town, to share my fate with those millions of others who have taken upon themselves to do the same. Moreover, I do not wish to fall into the hands of an enemy who is looking for a new spectacle organized by the Jews for the amusement of their hysterical masses.

I have decided therefore to remain in Berlin and there of my own free will to choose death at the moment when I believe the position of Führer and Chancellor can itself no longer be held.

I die with a happy heart, conscious of the immeasurable deeds and achievements of our soldiers at the front, our women at home, the achievements of our farmers and workers, and the work, unique in history, of our Youth who bear my name.

That from the bottom of my heart I express my thanks to you all, is just as self-evident as my wish that you should, because of that, on no account give up the struggle, but rather continue it against the enemies of the Fatherland, no matter where, true to the creed of the great Clausewitz. From the sacrifice of our soldiers and from my own unity with them unto death will in any event spring up in the history of Germany the seed of a radiant renaissance of the National Socialist movement and thus of the realization of a true community of nations.

Many of the most courageous men and women have decided to unite their lives with mine unto the very last. I have begged and finally ordered them not to do this, but to take part in the further battle of the nation. I beg the heads of the Armies, the Navy and the Air Force to strengthen by all possible means the spirit of resistance of our soldiers in the National Socialist sense, specially bearing in mind that I myself also, as founder and creator of this movement, have preferred death to cowardly abdication or even capitulation.

May it become, at some future time, part of the code of honour of the German officer, as it is already in our Navy, that the surrender of a district or of a town is impossible, and that the leaders here, above all, must march ahead as shining examples, faithfully fulfilling their duty unto death.

Second Part of the political Testament
Before my death I expel the former Reich Marshal Hermann Göring from the Party and deprive him of all rights which he may enjoy by virtue of the decree of 29 June 1941, and also by virtue of my statement in the Reichstag on 1 September 1939. I appoint in his place Grand Admiral Doenitz, President of the Reich and Supreme Commander of the Armed Forces.

Before my death I expel the former Reichsführer SS and Minister of the Interior, Henrich Himmler, from the Party and from all offices of State. In his stead I appoint Gauleiter Karl Hanke as Reichsführer SS and Chief of the German Police, and Gauleiter Paul Giesler as Reich Minister of the Interior.

Göring and Himmler, quite apart from their disloyalty to my person, have done immeasurable harm to the country and the whole nation by secret negotiations with the enemy, which they conducted without my knowledge and against my wishes, and by illegally attempting to seize power in the State for themselves.

In order to give the German people a Government composed of honourable men, a Government which will fulfil its pledge to continue the war by every means, I appoint the following members of the new Cabinet as leaders of the nation:

President of the Reich: Doenitz
Chancellor of the Reich: Dr Goebbels
Party Minister: Bormann
Foreign Minister: Seyss-Inquart
Minister of the Interior: Gauleiter Giesler
Minister for War: Doenitz
C.-in-C. of the Army: Schörner
C.-in-C. of the Navy: Doenitz
C.-in-C. of the Air Force: Greim
Reichsführer SS and Chief of the German Police: Gauleiter Hanke

Economics: Funk
Agriculture: Backe
Justice: Thierack
Education and Public Worship: Dr Scheel
Propaganda: Dr Naumann
Finance: Schwerin-Krosigk
Labour: Dr Hupfauer
Munitions: Saur
Leader of the German Labour Front and Member of the Reich Cabinet: Reich Minister Dr Ley

Although a number of these men, such as Martin Bormann, Dr Goebbels, etc., together with their wives, have joined me of their own free will and did not wish to leave the capital of the Reich under any circumstances, but were willing to perish with me here, I must nevertheless ask them to obey my request, and in this case set the interests of the nation above their own feelings. By their work and loyalty as comrades they will be just as close to me after death, as I hope that my spirit will linger among them and always go with them. Let them be hard, but never unjust, above all let them never allow fear to influence their actions, and let them set the honour of the nation above everything in the world. Finally, let them be conscious of the fact that our task, that of continuing the building of a National Socialist State, represents the work of the coming centuries, which places every single person under an obligation always to serve the common interest and to subordinate his own advantage to this end. I demand of all Germans, all National Socialists, men, women and all the men of the armed forces, that they be faithful and obedient unto death to the new Government and its President.

Above all I adjure the leaders of the nation and those under them to scrupulous observance of the laws of race and to merciless opposition to the universal poisoner of all peoples, International Jewry.

Given in Berlin, this 29th day of April 1945. 4 a.m.

ADOLF HITLER

Witnessed by:

DR JOSEF FUHR   WILHELM BURGDORF
MARTIN BORMANN   HANS KREBS

• • •

List of Sources and Bibliography

List of Sources

Part I: The Rise of Nazism, 1919–33

Chapter 1: The Founding of the Party and the Putsch, 1919–23

1. Ernst Deuerlein (ed.), *Der Aufstieg der NSDAP 1919–1933 in Augenzeugenberichten* (Düsseldorf 1968), p. 60.
2. Ernst Deuerlein, 'Hitlers Eintritt in die Politik und die Reichswehr'. In *Vierteljahrshefte für Zeitgeschichte* 7 (1959), pp. 203ff.
3. *Das Programm der NSDAP und seine weltanschaulichen Grundgedanken* von Dipl. Ing. Gottfried Feder (Munich 1932), pp. 4–6.
4. E. Deuerlein, *Aufstieg*, pp. 100–1.
5. Adolf Hitler, *Mein Kampf* (Munich 1925), p. 356.
6. R. G. Phelps, 'Hitler als Parteiredner: Dokument Nr. 17'. In *Vierteljahrshefte für Zeitgeschichte* 11 (1963), p. 325.
7. Kurt Ludecke, *I Knew Hitler* (London 1938), pp. 699–702.
8. Georg Franz-Willing, *Die Hitlerbewegung. Bd. I: Der Ursprung 1919 bis 1922* (Hamburg and Berlin 1962), pp. 110ff.
9. Deuerlein, *Aufstieg*, pp. 137–8.
10. Albrecht Tyrell (ed.), *Führer befiehl ... Selbstzeugnisse aus der 'Kampfzeit' der NSDAP. Dokumentation und Analyse* (Düsseldorf 1969), pp. 33–4.
11. Werner Jochmann (ed.), *Nationalsozialismus und Revolution: Dokumente* (Frankfurt 1963), pp. 88–9.
12. Deuerlein, *Aufstieg*, p. 144.
13. Tyrell, *Führer befiehl*, p. 58.
14. Deuerlein, *Aufstieg*, pp. 145–6.
15. ibid., pp. 164–6.
16. Ludecke, *I Knew Hitler*, p. 94.
17. Deuerlein, *Aufstieg*, pp. 152–3.
18. Ludecke, *I Knew Hitler*, p. 94.
19. Konrad Heiden, *Adolf Hitler, a Biography* (London 1936), pp. 102–3.
20. Ernst Deuerlein, *Der Hitler-Putsch: Bayerische Dokumente zum 8/9 November 1923* (Stuttgart 1962), pp. 194–5.
21. Deuerlein, *Aufstieg*, p. 192.
22. (a) ibid., pp. 192–3.
    (b) Deuerlein, *Der Hitler-Putsch*, p. 496.
    (c) Deuerlein, *Aufstieg*, pp. 193–5.
    (d) Deuerlein, *Der Hitler-Putsch*, p. 497.
    (e) Deuerlein, *Aufstieg*, pp. 195–6.
    (f) Deuerlein, *Der Hitler-Putsch*, pp. 511–12.
23. Tyrell, *Führer befiehl*, pp. 65ff.

Chapter 2: The Creation of a Nationwide Party Organization, 1924–28

1. Werner Jochmann (ed.), *Nationalsozialismus und Revolution: Dokumente* (Frankfurt 1963), p. 154.
2. K. Ludecke, *I Knew Hitler* (London 1938), pp. 217–18.
3. *Völkischer Beobachter*, 26.ii.25.
4. ibid.
5. Albrecht Tyrell, *Führer befiehl . . . Selbstzeugnisse aus der 'Kampfzeit' der NSDAP* (Düsseldorf 1969), pp. 281–3.
6. Jochmann, *Nationalsozialismus und Revolution*, pp. 207ff.
7. ibid., pp. 212–13.
8. *Nationalsozialistische Briefe*, 15.x.25.
9. *The Early Goebbels Diaries: 1925–1926* (London 1962/New York 1963), pp. 66–7.
10. 'Geschichte der Ortsgruppe Affinghausen/Diepholz', Niedersächsisches Hauptstaatsarchiv, Hanover, Hann. Des. 310 I A, Nr. 60.
11. Albert Krebs, *Tendenzen und Gestalten der NSDAP: Erinnerungen an die Frühzeit der Partei* (Stuttgart 1959), pp. 42–3.
12. 'Geschichte der Ortsgruppe Harlingerode/Bad Harzburg, Niedersächsisches Hauptstaatsarchiv, Hanover, Hann. Des. 310 I A, Nr. 69.
13. Ludolf Haase, *Aufstand in Niedersachsen: Der Kampf der NSDAP 1921–1924* (mimeo 1942), pp. 192–3.
14. Hoover Institution Microfilms. NSDAP Hauptarchiv Reel 6, Folder 17.
15. Martin Broszat, 'Die Anfänge der Berliner NSDAP 1926–7'. In *Vierteljahrshefte für Zeitgeschichte* 8 (1960), pp. 102–3.
16. ibid.
17. Jochmann, *Nationalsozialismus und Revolution*, pp. 241–2.
18. Tyrell, *Führer befiehl*, pp. 235–6.
19. ibid., pp. 163–4.
20. ibid., loc. cit.

Chapter 3: The Emergence of Nazism as a Mass Movement, 1928–33

1. Niedersächsisches Hauptstaatsarchiv, Hanover, Hann. Des. 310 I A, Nr. 17.
2. Niedersächsisches Staatsarchiv, Oldenburg 136 2860.
3. *Das Programm der NSDAP und seine weltanschaulichen Grundgedanken von Dipl. Ing. Gottfried Feder* (Munich 1932), pp. 4–6.
4. *Völkischer Beobachter*, 31.v.28.
5. *Niedersächsischer Beobachter*, 18.xii.29.
6. Otto Strasser, *Hitler and I* (London 1940), pp. 114ff.
7. ibid.
8. E. Deuerlein, *Der Aufstieg der NSDAP 1919–1933 in Augenzeugenberichten* (Düsseldorf 1968), pp. 306–7.
9. (a) Niedersächsisches Hauptstaatsarchiv, Hanover, Hann. Des. 310 I B, Nr. 1.
   (b) ibid.
   (c) ibid.
10. Werner Jochmann (ed.), *Nationalsozialismus und Revolution: Ursprung und Geschichte der NSDAP in Hamburg, 1922–1933* (Frankfurt 1963), pp. 404–5.

11. Bayerisches Hauptstaatsarchiv, Munich, MA 101238.
12. Niedersächsisches Hauptstaatsarchiv, Hanover, Hann. Des. 310 I A, Nr. 35.
13. (a) ibid.
    (b) ibid.
14. Hans Christian Brandenburg, *Die Geschichte der HJ* (Cologne 1968), p. 100.
15. Niedersächsisches Staatsarchiv, Oldenburg, 131 1207.
16. (a) Bayerisches Staatsarchiv (Neuburg a. d. Donau), Bezirksamt Nördlingen, 1315.
    (b) Jochmann, *Nationalsozialismus und Revolution*, p. 405.
17. *Partei-Statistik 1 Januar 1935*. Herausgeber: der Reichsorganisationsleiter der NSDAP (Munich 1935), pp. 155, 162.
18. ibid., pp. 53, 70.
19. E. Matthias and R. Morsey (eds), *Das Ende der Parteien 1933* (Düsseldorf 1960), p. 782.

Chapter 4: The Struggle for Power, 1930–33

1. Nuremberg Document (ND) 2512-PS.
2. Hans-Adolf Jacobsen und Werner Jochmann (eds), *Ausgewählte Dokumente zur Geschichte des Nationalsozialismus 1933–1945* (Bielefeld 1961), Bd. I.
3. National Archives, Alexandria/Virginia microfilm collection, T-81, roll 175, frame 317693.
4. *Documents on British Foreign Policy, 1919–1939*, 2nd series, vol. II, pp. 296–8.
5. N. H. Baynes (ed.), *The Speeches of Adolf Hitler 1922–1939* (Oxford 1942), vol. I, pp. 826–9.
6. Ernst Deuerlein (ed.), *Der Aufstieg der NSDAP 1919–1933 in Augenzeugen-berichten* (Düsseldorf 1968), pp. 353–4.
7. Gordon A. Craig, 'Briefe Schleichers an Groener', *Die Welt als Geschichte* 11 (1951), pp. 130ff.
8. R. G. Phelps, 'Aus den Groener Dokumenten', *Deutsche Rundschau* 76 (1950), pp. 1019f.
9. R. G. Phelps, 'Aus den Groener Dokumenten', *Deutsche Rundschau* 77 (1951), pp. 23ff.
10. Joseph Goebbels, *My Part in Germany's Fight* (London 1938), pp. 77ff. (modified translation).
11. Niedersächsisches Hauptstaatsarchiv, Hanover, Hann. Des. 310 I A, Nr. 37.
12. Walther Hubatsch, *Hindenburg und der Staat* (Göttingen 1966), p. 388.
13. Goebbels, *My Part*, p. 122 (modified translation).
14. Niedersächsisches Hauptstaatsarchiv, Hanover, Hann. Des. 310 I B, Nr. 15.
15. National Archives, T-81, roll 1, frames 11427–11432.
16. Niedersächsisches Hauptstaatsarchiv, Hanover, Hann. Des. 310 I A, Nr. 37.
17. Jochmann, *Nationalsozialismus und Revolution*, pp. 407ff.
18. Hinrich Lohse, 'Der Fall Strasser', Forschungsstelle für die Geschichte des Nationalsozialismus in Hamburg.
19. Deuerlein, *Aufstieg*, pp. 411–14.
20. ND 3309-PS.

Part II: The Seizure of Power, 1933–34

Chapter 5: The 'National Uprising'

1. *Documents on German Foreign Policy*, series C, vol. I, pp. 5–8 (modified translation).
2. Werner Jochmann (ed.), *Nationalsozialismus und Revolution: Dokumente* (Frankfurt 1963), p. 421.
3. Hans-Adolf Jacobsen und Werner Jochmann (eds), *Ausgewählte Dokumente zur Geschichte des Nationalsozialismus 1933–1945* (Bielefeld 1961), Bd. II.
4. Jochmann, *Nationalsozialismus und Revolution*, pp. 424ff.
5. ND EC-439.
6. ND D-203.
7. *The Times*, 21.ii.33.
8. Erich Matthias and Rudolf Morsey (eds), *Das Ende der Parteien 1933* (Düsseldorf 1960), p. 234.
9. ibid., p. 239.
10. Rudolf Diels, *Lucifer ante portas* (Stuttgart 1950), pp. 142–4.
11. *Reichsgesetzblatt*, Jg. 1933, Teil I, Nr. 17, p. 83.
12. Jochmann, *Nationalsozialismus und Revolution*, p. 427.

Chapter 6: The Seizure of Power in the States and the S A / Party 'Revolution from Below' of March 1933

1. Henning Timpke, *Dokumente zur Gleichschaltung des Landes Hamburg* (Frankfurt 1964), pp. 56–61.
2. Rudolf Diels, *Lucifer ante portas* (Stuttgart 1950), p. 200.
3. ibid., p. 199.
4. *Braunschweig unter dem Hakenkreuz* (Zurich 1933).
5. Walther Hofer, *Der Nationalsozialismus: Dokumente 1933–1945* (Frankfurt 1957), p. 55.
6. Diels, *Lucifer*, pp. 192–4, 199.
7. ibid., p. 201.
8. Otto Meissner, *Staatssekretär unter Ebert–Hindenburg–Hitler* (Hamburg 1950), pp. 293–4.

Chapter 7: The 'Coordination' of the Reichstag and of the Political Parties, March–June 1933

1. *Documents on German Foreign Policy* (DGFP), series C, vol. I, pp. 113–16.
2. Max Domarus, *Hitler: Reden und Proklamationen, 1932–1945*, Bd. I (Würzburg 1962), pp. 232–3.
3. Erich Matthias and Rudolf Morsey (eds), *Das Ende der Parteien 1933* (Düsseldorf 1960), pp. 431–2.
4. Hans Müller, *Katholische Kirche und Nationalsozialismus* (Munich 1963), pp. 73–4.
5. Wilhelm Hoegner, *Der schwierige Aussenseiter* (Munich 1963), pp. 92–3.

6. *Reichsgesetzblatt* (RGBl.), Jg. 1933, Teil I, Nr. 25, p. 141.
7. Matthias and Morsey, *Das Ende der Parteien*, p. 643.
8. Joseph Goebbels, *My Part in Germany's Fight* (London 1935), p. 248.
9. Müller, *Katholische Kirche*, p. 86.
10. Matthias and Morsey, *Das Ende der Parteien*, pp. 443–4, 451–2.
11. DGFP, series C, vol. I, pp. 652–3.
12. RGBl., Jg. 1933, Teil I, Nr. 81, p. 479.

Chapter 8: The Revolution Stabilized: Conflict with the SA

1. Hans-Adolf Jacobsen und Werner Jochmann (eds), *Ausgewählte Dokumente zur Geschichte des Nationalsozialismus 1933–1945* (Bielefeld 1961), Bd. II.
2. Quoted in Peter Diehl-Thiele, *Partei und Staat im Dritten Reich* (Munich 1969), p. 95.
3. *Ausgewählte Dokumente*, Bd. II.
4. Henning Timpke, *Dokumente zur Gleichschaltung des Landes Hamburg* (Frankfurt 1964), pp. 217–18.
5. ND 951-D.
6. Heinrich Bennecke, *Hitler und die SA* (Munich 1962), p. 82.
7. *Ausgewählte Dokumente*, Bd. II.
8. Bennecke, *Hitler und die SA*, p. 85.
9. *Ursachen und Folgen: Vom deutschen Zusammenbruch 1918 und 1945 bis zur staatlichen Neuordnung Deutschlands in der Gegenwart*, ed. H. Michaelis *et al.* (Berlin, undated), Bd. X, pp. 168–72.
10. E. von Aretin, *Krone und Ketten: Erinnerungen eines bayerischen Edelmannes*, eds. Karl Buchheim and Karl Otmar von Aretin (Munich 1955), pp. 365–6.
11. H. B. Gisevius, *Bis zum bittern Ende* (Zurich 1954), pp. 142ff.
12. *Deutsche Allgemeine Zeitung*, Nr. 302, 2.vii.34.
13. *Völkischer Beobachter*, 3.vii.34.
14. *Völkischer Beobachter*, 5.vii.34.
15. N. H. Baynes (ed.), *The Speeches of Adolf Hitler 1922–1939* (Oxford 1942), vol I, pp. 311–13.
16. Staatsarchiv, Bremen, N7 P 1a, No. 1149.
17. *Völkischer Beobachter*, 26.vii.34.
18. *Reichsgesetzblatt* (RGBl.), 1934, Teil I, Nr. 89, p. 747.
19. RGBl., Jahrgang 1934, Teil I, Nr. 98.
20. *Völkischer Beobachter*, 21.viii.34.
21. Niedersächsisches Hauptstaatsarchiv, Hanover, Hann. Des., Lüneburg III XXV, Nr. 5.

Part III: The Political Structure of the Third Reich

Chapter 9: Party and State, 1933–39

1. *Reichsgesetzblatt* (RGBl.), I (1933), p. 175.
2. H. Mommsen, *Beamtentum im Dritten Reich* (Stuttgart 1966), pp. 16off.

3. RGBl. I (1933), p. 1016.
4. Hans-Adolf Jacobsen und Werner Jochmann (eds), *Ausgewählte Dokumente zur Geschichte des Nationalsozialismus 1933–1945* (Bielefeld 1961), Bd II.
5. Mommsen, *Beamtentum*, pp. 171–3.
6. ND 138-D.
7. RGBl. I (1935), p. 1203.
8. RGBl. I (1933), p. 173.
9. Bundesarchiv, Koblenz, R 43 II/1345.
10. RGBl. I (1934), p. 75.
11. Bundesarchiv, Koblenz, R 43/II 1376.
12. M. Broszat, *Der Staat Hitlers* (Munich 1969), p. 153.
13. Bundesarchiv, Koblenz, R 43 II/494.
14. F. Heyen, *Nationalsozialismus im Alltag: Quellen zur Geschichte des National-sozialismus vornehmlich im Raum Mainz–Koblenz–Trier* (Boppard am Rhein 1967), pp. 263ff.
15. Niedersächsisches Hauptstaatsarchiv, Hanover, Hann. 80 Hann. II, Nr. 799.
16. H. Frank, *Im Angesicht des Galgens* (Neuhaus bei Schliersee 1955), pp. 466–7.
17. P. Diehl-Thiele, *Partei und Staat im Dritten Reich* (Munich 1969), p. 246.
18. *Memoirs of Ernst von Weizsäcker* (London 1951), pp. 164–5.
19. Frank, *Im Angesicht des Galgens*, pp. 122–3.
20. N. H. Baynes (ed.), *The Speeches of Adolf Hitler 1922–1939* (Oxford 1942), vol. I, pp. 449–51.
21. Mommsen, *Beamtentum*, pp. 146ff.
22. Bundesarchiv, Koblenz, NS-Misch., Nr. 1310.
23. *Parteistatistik*. Stand 1 Januar 1935. Herausgeber: der Reichsorganisations-leiter der NSDAP (Munich 1935).

Chapter 10: Law and Order

1. *Documents on German Foreign Policy*, series C, vol. I, pp. 113ff.
2. *Reichsgesetzblatt* (RGBl.), I (1933), p. 135.
3. M. Domarus, *Hitler: Reden und Proklamationen 1932–1945*, Bd. I (Würzburg 1962), pp. 229ff.
4. RGBl. I (1934), p. 345ff.
5. RGBl. I (1935), p. 839.
6. ND 2549-PS.
7. *Dokumente der deutschen Politik*, Bd. IV (Berlin 1942), p. 337.
8. *Justiz im Dritten Reich*, ed. Ilse Staff (Frankfurt 1964), p. 140.
9. ibid., pp. 69ff.
10. ibid., pp. 72ff.
11. ibid., p. 152.
12. ibid., pp. 123–4.
13. M. Broszat, 'Zur Perversion der Strafjustiz im Dritten Reich. Dokumentation'. In *Vierteljahrshefte zur Zeitgeschichte* 6 (1958), pp. 422–3.
14. (a) *Reichsführer! Briefe an und von Himmler*, ed. Helmut Heiber (Stuttgart 1968), p. 317.
    (b) ibid., p. 75.
    (c) ibid., p. 98.

15. ND 2284-PS.
16. J. Conway, *The Nazi Persecution of the Churches 1933–1945* (London 1968), pp. 153–4.
17. Hans-Adolf Jacobsen und Werner Jochmann (eds), *Ausgewählte Dokumente zur Geschichte des Nationalsozialismus 1933–1945* (Bielefeld 1961), Bd. II.
18. R. Diels, *Lucifer ante portas* (Stuttgart 1950), p. 236.
19. ND 778-PS.
20. ND 775-PS.
21. ND 2107-PS.
22. RGBl. I (1936), p. 487.
23. *Ursachen und Folgen: Vom deutschen Zusammenbruch 1918 und 1945 bis zur staatlichen Neuordnung Deutschlands in der Gegenwart*, eds. H. Michaelis *et al.* (Berlin, undated), Bd. XI, p. 57.
24. ibid., p. 6.
25. T. W. Mason, *Arbeiterklasse und Volksgemeinschaft* (Cologne 1974), No. 34.
26. ND 152-R.
27. ND 84-D.
28. ND 1852-PS.
29. *Justiz im Dritten Reich*, pp. 102–3.
30. ND 654-PS.

Chapter 11: Opposition

1. T. W. Mason, *Arbeiterklasse und Volksgemeinschaft* (Cologne 1974), No. 44.
2. Kuno Bludau, *Nationalsozialismus und Genossenschaften* (Hanover 1968), pp. 218–19.
3. Günther Weisenborn, *Der lautlose Aufstand: Bericht über die Widerstandsbewegung des deutschen Volkes, 1933–45* (Hamburg 1954), pp. 153–4.
4. Walther Hofer (ed.), *Der Nationalsozialismus: Dokumente 1933–45* (Frankfurt 1957), pp. 342–3.
5. *The Von Hassell Diaries, 1938–44* (London 1948), pp. 76–7.
6. ibid., pp. 199–200.
7. Hans-Adolf Jacobsen, *1939–1945: Der Zweite Weltkrieg in Chronik und Dokumenten* (Darmstadt 1962), pp. 610–12.
8. ND 3701-PS.
9. ND 615-PS.
10. Jacobsen, op. cit., pp. 305–9.
11. Hans-Adolf Jacobsen, *Der Zweite Weltkrieg: Grundzüge der Politik und Strategie in Dokumenten* (Frankfurt 1965), pp. 290–5.
12. *The Von Hassell Diaries*, pp. 209–11.
13. Inge Scholl, *Die Weisse Rose* (Frankfurt 1952), pp. 108–10.
14. Hofer, op. cit., pp. 333–5.
15. Roger Manvell and Heinrich Fraenkel, *The July Plot* (London 1964), pp. 253–6.
16. *Aus deutschen Urkunden, 1935–1945* (Allied publication, undated), pp. 289–90.
17. Karl Demeter, *The German Officer Corps in Society and State, 1650–1945* (London 1965), pp. 360–2.

Part IV: The New Social Order: Idea and Reality

Chapter 12: Ideology and Society

1. Walther Hofer (ed.), *Der Nationalsozialismus: Dokumente 1933–1945* (Frankfurt 1957), p. 82.
2. *Ursachen und Folgen: Vom deutschen Zusammenbruch 1918 und 1945 bis zur staatlichen Neuordnung Deutschlands in der Gegenwart*, eds. H. Michaelis *et al.* (Berlin, undated), Bd. IX, pp. 430–1.
3. Joseph Wulf, *Presse und Funk im Dritten Reich* (Gütersloh 1964), p. 79.
4. ibid., pp. 87–101.
5. *Reichsgesetzblatt* (RGBl.), I (1933), p. 713.
6. RGBl. I (1933), p. 661.
7. Joseph Wulf, *Presse und Funk*, p. 111.
8. ibid., p. 146.
9. E. K. Bramsted, *Goebbels and National Socialist Propaganda 1925–1945* (East Lansing, Mich. 1965), pp. 217–18.
10. Hildegard Brenner, *Die Kunstpolitik des Nationalsozialismus* (Hamburg 1963), pp. 177–80.
11. Louis P. Lochner (ed.), *The Goebbels Diaries 1942–3* (Washington, D.C. 1948), pp. 17–18.
12. ND 2529-PS.
13. Brenner, *Die Kunstpolitik*, p. 183.
14. N. H. Baynes (ed.), *The Speeches of Adolf Hitler 1922–1939* (Oxford 1942), vol. I, pp. 589–92.
15. Hofer, *Der Nationalsozialismus*, p. 98.
16. *Völkischer Beobachter*, 7.v.33.
17. Paul E. Kahle, *Bonn University in Pre-Nazi and Nazi Times 1923–1939* (London 1945), pp. 16–17.
18. ibid., pp. 34–5.
19. *Ursachen und Folgen*, Bd. IX, p. 453.
20. ibid., pp. 445–6.
21. *Völkischer Beobachter*, 15.ix.35.
22. ND 2435-PS.
23. F. J. Heyen, *Nationalsozialismus im Alltag: Quellen zur Geschichte des National-sozialismus vornehmlich im Raum Mainz–Koblenz–Trier* (Boppard 1967), p. 213.
24. ibid., p. 257.
25. RGBl. I (1936), p. 993.
26. Heyen, *Nationalsozialismus im Alltag*, p. 227.
27. ibid., pp. 228–9.
28. ND 2436-PS.
29. Melita Maschmann, *Account Rendered* (London 1964), pp. 35–6.
30. ibid., pp. 141–3.
31. *Frankfurter Zeitung*, 9.ix.34.
32. RGBl. I (1933), pp. 326–7.
33. *Völkischer Beobachter*, 31.i.35.
34. Bundesarchiv, Koblenz, R 43 II/427.

35. Ursula von Gersdorff, *Frauen im Kriegsdienst 1914–1945* (Stuttgart 1969), p. 292.
36. ibid., pp. 282–3.

Chapter 13: The Economy, 1933–39

1. *Ursachen und Folgen: Vom deutschen Zusammenbruch 1918 und 1945 bis zur staatlichen Neuordnung Deutschlands in der Gegenwart*, ed. H. Michaelis *et al.* (Berlin, undated), Bd. IX, p. 666.
2. H. Uhlig, *Die Warenhäuser im Dritten Reich* (Cologne 1956), p. 105.
3. ibid., p. 111.
4. ibid., p. 128.
5. ND 151-D.
6. *Documents on German Foreign Policy* (DGFP), series C, vol. I, p. 35.
7. *Reichsgesetzblatt* (RGBl.), I (1933), p. 392.
8. *Dokumente der deutschen Politik*, Bd. V (Berlin 1942), p. 355; *Statistisches Handbuch von Deutschland 1928–1944* (Munich 1949), p. 484.
9. RGBl. I (1933), p. 685.
10. ND 436-EC.
11. ibid.
12. Bundesarchiv-Militärarchiv, Freiburg, WilF 5/ 406.
13. ND 611-EC.
14. DGFP, series C, vol. III, pp. 344ff.
15. DGFP, series C, vol. III, pp. 356ff.
16. DGFP, series C, vol. V, No. 490 (modified translation).
17. ND 416-EC.
18. ibid.
19. D. Petzina, *Autarkiepolitik im Dritten Reich: Der nationalsozialistischen Vier-Jahresplan* (Stuttgart 1968), p. 182.
20. ND 028-EC.
21. B. A. Carroll, *Design for Total War: Arms and Economics in the Third Reich* (The Hague/Paris 1968), p. 188.
22. ibid. p. 184.
23. *Statistisches Handbuch von Deutschland 1928–1944* (Munich 1949), pp. 392–4.

Chapter 14: Labour

1. *Reichsgesetzblatt* (RGBl.), I (1933), p. 161.
2. *Ursachen und Folgen: Vom deutschen Zusammenbruch 1918 und 1945 bis zur staatlichen Neuordnung Deutschlands in der Gegenwart*, ed. H. Michaelis *et al.* (Berlin, undated), Bd. IX, pp. 430–1.
3. ND 2283-PS.
4. *Dokumente der deutschen Politik*, Bd. I (Berlin 1934), pp. 151–3.
5. *Völkischer Beobachter*, 5.v.33.
6. RGBl. I (1933), p. 45.
7. Bundesarchiv, Koblenz, R 43 II/532.
8. RGBl. I (1934), p. 45.
9. *Dokumente der deutschen Politik*, Bd. V (Berlin 1942), pp. 366–9.

10. M. Broszat, *Der Staat Hitlers* (Munich 1969), p. 192.
11. ND 1814-PS.
12. R. Ley, *Deutschland ist schöner geworden* (Berlin 1936), pp. 122–3.
13. *Fundamente des Sieges: Die Gesamtarbeit der deutschen Arbeitsfront von 1933 bis 1940*, ed. Otto Marrenbach (Berlin 1941), p. 325.
14. ibid., pp. 334–5.
15. ibid., p. 350.
16. ibid., p. 355.
17. G. Starcke, *Die Deutsche Arbeitsfront* (Berlin 1940).
18. ibid., p. 143.
19. Willy Müller, *Das soziale Leben im neuen Deutschland* (Berlin 1938), pp. 189–190.
20. N. H. Baynes (ed.), *The Speeches of Adolf Hitler 1922–1939* (Oxford 1942) vol. I, pp. 893–4.
21. T. W. Mason, *Arbeiterklasse und Volksgemeinschaft* (Cologne 1974), No. 3.
22. ibid., No. 31.
23. *Fundamente des Sieges*, p. 326.
24. Mason, *Arbeiterklasse*, No. 64.
25. ibid., No. 99.
26. ibid., No. 60.
27. ibid., No. 55.
28. ibid., No. 133.
29. ibid., No. 132.
30. ibid., No. 137.
31. G. Bry, *Wages in Germany 1871–1945* (Princeton N. J. 1960), pp. 233ff.
32. Mason, *Arbeiterklasse*, No. 147.
33. ibid., No. 145.
34. ibid., No. 154.
35. ibid., No. 151.
36. RGBl. I (1937), p. 24.
37. Mason, *Arbeiterklasse*, No. 110.

Chapter 15: Antisemitism, 1933–45

1. ND PS-2709.
2. *Völkischer Beobachter*, 29.iii.33.
3. *Ursachen und Folgen: Vom deutschen Zusammenbruch 1918 und 1945 bis zur staatlichen Neuordnung Deutschlands in der Gegenwart*, ed. H. Michaelis *et al.* (Berlin, undated), Bd. IX, p. 397.
4. ibid., Bd. XI, p. 159.
5. *Reichsgesetzblatt* (RGBl.), I (1935), p. 1146.
6. ibid.
7. RGBl. I (1935), p. 1333.
8. H. Buchheim, Martin Broszat, H. Krausnick, Hans-Adolf Jacobsen, *Anatomy of the SS State* (London 1968), p. 34.
9. F. J. Heyen, *Nationalsozialismus im Alltag: Quellen zur Geschichte des Nationalsozialismus vornehmlich im Raum Mainz-Koblenz-Trier* (Boppard 1967), p. 146.
10. Melita Maschmann, *Account Rendered* (London 1964), p. 41.

11. Heyen, *Nationalsozialismus im Alltag*, p. 139.
12. ND PS-2699.
13. ND PS-1778.
14. RGBl. I (1938), p. 1044.
15. (a) ND PS-3063.
    (b) ND L-202.
16. Melita Maschmann, *Account Rendered*, pp. 56-7.
17. ND PS-1816.
18. Walther Hofer (ed.), *Der Nationalsozialismus: Dokumente 1933-45* (Frankfurt 1957), p. 295.
19. RGBl. I (1938), p. 1579.
20. RGBl. I (1938), p. 1580.
21. T. W. Mason, *Arbeiterklasse und Volksgemeinschaft* (Cologne 1974), No. 151.
22. ND 2682-PS.
23. ND PS-841.
24. N. H. Baynes (ed.), *The Speeches of Adolf Hitler 1922-39* (Oxford 1942), vol. I, pp. 740-1.
25. Buchheim *et al.*, *Anatomy of the SS State*, p. 68.
26. ND PS-3663.
27. ND PS-3666.
28. RGBl. I (1941), p. 547.
29. Hans Peter Görgen, *Düsseldorf und der Nationalsozialismus* (Düsseldorf 1969), pp. 221-2.
30. W. Hofer, *Der Nationalsozialismus*, pp. 304-5.
31. ND PS-3868.
32. ND PS-1061.
33. ND PS-1919.
34. Hans-Adolf Jacobsen, *Der Zweite Weltkrieg: Grundzüge der Politik und Strategie in Dokumenten* (Frankfurt 1965), p. 186.

Part V: Foreign Policy, 1933-39

Chapter 16: Hitler's Programme

1. (a) R. Phelps, 'Hitler als Parteiredner: Dokument Nr. 1'. In *Vierteljahrshefte für Zeitgeschichte* 11 (1963), p. 290.
   (b) E. Deuerlein, 'Hitlers Eintritt in die Politik und die Reichswehr: Dokument Nr. 16'. In *Vierteljahrshefte für Zeitgeschichte* 7 (1959), p. 209.
2. Adolf Hitler, *Mein Kampf* (London 1939), pp. 523-4, 526, 528, 533.
3. *Hitler's Secret Book*, ed. Telford Taylor (New York 1962).

Chapter 17: Germany Woos Britain and Italy

1. T. Vogelsang (ed.), 'Neue Dokumente zur Geschichte der Reichswehr 1930-1933: Nr. 7'. In *Vierteljahreshefte für Zeitgeschichte* 2 (1954), pp. 432-4.
2. N. H. Baynes (ed.), *The Speeches of Adolf Hitler 1922-1939* (Oxford 1942), vol. II, pp. 1046-8.

3. *Documents on British Foreign Policy 1919–1939*, 2nd series, vol. VI, pp. 152–3.
4. *Documents on German Foreign Policy* (DGFP), series C, vol. III, pp. 329–30.
5. DGFP, series C, vol. III, pp. 329–30.
6. DGFP, series C, vol. III, pp. 1043ff.
7. ND 46-TC.
8. Royal Institute of International Affairs, *Documents on International Affairs 1936* (Oxford 1937), pp. 345–6.
9. DGFP, series D, vol. I, pp. 29–38.
10. ND 175-C; DGFP, series D, vol. VII, pp. 635–7.

Chapter 18: The First Phase of Expansion: Austria and Czechoslovakia, 1938–39

1. *Documents on German Foreign Policy* (DGFP), series D, vol. I, pp. 513–14.
2. ibid., p. 548.
3. ibid., p. 576.
4. ND C-102.
5. ND 2949-PS.
6. DGFP, series D, vol. I, pp. 240ff.
7. DGFP, series D, vol. II, p. 198.
8. ibid., p. 242.
9. ibid., pp. 300–302.
10. ND 1780-PS.
11. DGFP, series D, vol. II, p. 358.
12. ibid., p. 608.
13. ibid., pp. 786ff.
14. ibid., pp. 863–4.
15. Ivone Kirkpatrick, *The Inner Circle* (London 1959), pp. 114–18.
16. DGFP, series D, vol. II, pp. 1014–16.
17. *Vierteljahrshefte für Zeitgeschichte* 6 (1958), pp. 175ff.
18. DGFP, series D, vol. IV, p. 99.
19. ibid., pp. 244–5.
20. ibid., p. 266.
21. ibid., p. 270.

Part VI: Germany at War, 1939–45

Chapter 19: The Successful Blitzkriege: Poland and France, 1939–40

1. *Documents on German Foreign Policy* (DGFP), series D, vol. V, pp. 153ff.
2. ND 79-L.
3. DGFP, series D, vol. VII, pp. 245–7.
4. ND Raeder-27.
5. DGFP, series D, vol. VII, pp. 477ff.
6. Paul Schmidt, *Hitler's Interpreter* (New York 1950), pp. 157–8.
7. ND 789-PS.
8. (a) Hans-Adolf Jacobsen, *Dokumente zum Westfeldzug 1940* (Göttingen 1960), pp. 46–9.

(b) ibid., pp. 155–6.
(c) ibid., pp. 64–5.
9. (a) Hans-Adolf Jacobsen, *1939–1945: Der Zweite Weltkrieg in Chronik und Dokumenten* (Darmstadt 1962), pp. 146–7.
   (b) ibid., loc. cit.
   (c) ibid., loc. cit.
10. (a) ibid., p. 151.
    (b) D G F P, series D, vol. X, pp. 226–8.
11. Hans-Adolf Jacobsen, *1939–1945: Der Zweite Weltkrieg*, pp. 154–5.
12. ibid., pp. 161–2.
13. *Lagevorträge des Oberbefehlshabers der Kriegsmarine vor Hitler 1939–1945* (Munich 1972), pp. 143–4.
14. D G F P, series D, vol. XI, pp. 558–9.
15. ibid., pp. 567–8.

Chapter 20: From Blitzkrieg to World War, 1941–45

1. *Documents on German Foreign Policy* (D G F P), series D, vol. XI, pp. 899ff.
2. Hans-Adolf Jacobsen, *1939–1945: Der Zweite Weltkrieg in Chronik und Dokumenten* (Darmstadt 1962), pp. 252, 262–3.
3. *O K W Kriegstagebuch* (Frankfurt 1961–65), Bd. II, pp. 1052ff.
4. ibid., pp. 1063ff.
5. Hans-Adolf Jacobsen, *1939–1945: Der Zweite Weltkrieg*, pp. 266–7.
6. ibid., pp. 281–2.
7. D G F P, series D, vol. XIII, pp. 999–1000.
8. (a) Hans-Adolf Jacobsen, *1939–1945: Der Zweite Weltkrieg*, pp. 354–5.
   (b) Johannes Hohlfeld (ed.), *Dokumente der deutschen Politik von 1848 bis zur Gegenwart* (Berlin and Munich, undated), Bd. V, pp. 387–91.
9. *The Goebbels Diaries*, ed. P. Lochner (Washington, D.C. 1948), p. 357.
10. Hans-Adolf Jacobsen, *1939–1945: Der Zweite Weltkrieg*, p. 474.
11. Andreas Hillgruber, *Hitlers Strategie* (Frankfurt 1965), p. 577.

Chapter 21: The Ideological War

1. ND 686-PS.
2. ND 789-PS.
3. Hans-Adolf Jacobsen, *1939–1945: Der Zweite Weltkrieg in Chronik und Dokumenten* (Darmstadt 1962), pp. 606–9.
4. L. Gruchmann, 'Euthanasie und Justiz im Dritten Reich'. In *Vierteljahrshefte für Zeitgeschichte* 21 (1972), p. 241.
5. *Aus deutschen Urkunden 1935–1945* (Allied Publication, undated), pp. 173–7.
6. ND 447-PS.
7. ND 1919-PS.
8. H.-A. Jacobsen, *1939–1945: Der Zweite Weltkrieg*, pp. 230–1.
9. H. Buchheim, M. Broszat, H. Krausnick, H-A. Jacobsen, *Anatomy of the S S State* (London 1968), pp. 62–3.
10. ND 180-L.

11. *Documents on German Foreign Policy*, series D, vol. XIII, pp. 149–56.
12. ND 294-PS.

Chapter 22: War and the Economy

1. ND 606-EC.
2. ND 1456-PS.
3. U. Gersdorff, *Frauen im Kriegsdienst 1914–1945* (Stuttgart 1969), pp. 296–7.
4. T. W. Mason, *Arbeiterklasse und Volksgemeinschaft* (Cologne 1974), No. 185.
5. ibid., No. 201.
6. ibid., No. 224.
7. ibid., No. 229.
8. ibid., No. 215.
9. ibid., No. 217.
10. Imperial War Museum, London FD 1434/46, No. 170, WiRüAmt, 'Umstellung der Rüstung', pp. 3ff., p. 42.
11. ND Speer-7.
12. (a) Hans-Adolf Jacobsen, *1939–1945: Der Zweite Weltkrieg in Chronik und Dokumenten* (Darmstadt 1962), p. 565.
    (b) ibid., p. 567.
    (c) ibid., p. 565.
13. ND 016-PS.
14. ND 70-EC.
15. ND 016-PS.
16. ND Speer-42.

Chapter 23: Civilian Morale

1. W. Shirer, *Berlin Diary* (New York 1942), pp. 162–3.
2. T. W. Mason, *Arbeiterklasse und Volksgemeinschaft* (Cologne 1974), No. 180.
3. H. Boberach, *Meldungen aus dem Reich* (Neuwied 1965), p. 95.
4. Max Domarus, *Hitler: Reden und Proklamationen 1932–1945*, Bd. II (Munich 1963), pp. 1576ff.
5. Boberach, *Meldungen*, pp. 104ff.
6. ibid., pp. 158ff.
7. ibid., pp. 198ff.
8. ibid., pp. 211ff.
9. Domarus, *Hitler: Reden*, pp. 1874ff.
10. ibid., loc. cit.
11. Boberach, *Meldungen*, pp. 342ff.
12. Hans-Adolf Jacobsen, *1939–1945: Der Zweite Weltkrieg in Chronik und Dokumenten* (Darmstadt 1962), pp. 380–1.
13. Boberach, *Meldungen*, pp. 359ff.
14. (a) ibid., p. 381.
    (b) ibid., pp. 382ff.
    (c) ibid., pp. 416ff.
15. *Aus deutschen Urkunden* (Allied Publication, undated), pp. 275–6.

Chapter 24: The Disintegration of the Third Reich, 1943–45

1. ND 129-R.
2. (a) Bundesarchiv, Koblenz, R 18/1263.
   (b) ND D-753-A.
3. ND Speer-25.
4. ND 3569-PS.

Select Bibliography

Since this book is intended primarily for those with no German, it seemed pointless to list books in German in the bibliography. We wish, however, to reiterate our debt to the numerous works which have appeared in German and notably to Martin Broszat's outstanding *Der Staat Hitlers* (Munich 1969).

Abel, T. *The Nazi Movement: Why Hitler Came to Power*. New York 1966.
Allen, W. S. *The Nazi Seizure of Power: The Experience of a Single German Town, 1930–1935*. Chicago 1965/London 1966.
Angress, W. T. 'The Political Role of the Peasantry in the Weimar Republic', *Review of Politics*, 1959.
——, and Smith, B. F. 'Diaries of Heinrich Himmler's Early Years', *Journal of Modern History*, XXXI (1959).
Arendt, H. *Origins of Totalitarianism*. New York 1951.
Bethge, E. *Dietrich Bonhoeffer: A Man for Others*. New York/London 1970.
Bracher, K. D. *The German Dictatorship*. New York 1970/London 1971.
Brady, R. A. *The Spirit and Structure of German Fascism*. London 1938.
Bramsted, E. K. *Goebbels and National Socialist Propaganda, 1925–1945*. East Lansing, Mich., 1965.
Broszat, M. *German National Socialism: 1919–1945*. Santa Barbara, Calif., 1966.
Buchheim, H., *et al.*, *Anatomy of the SS State*. New York/London 1970.
Bullock, A. *Adolf Hitler: A Study in Tyranny*. Rev. edn. New York/London 1964.
Burden, H. T. *The Nuremberg Party Rallies: 1923–39*. New York/London 1967.
Carr, W. *Arms, Autarky and Aggression: A Study in German Foreign Policy, 1933–1939*. London 1972.
Carroll, B. *Design for Total War: Arms and Economics in the Third Reich*. The Hague/Paris 1968.
Cecil, R. *The Myth of the Master Race: Alfred Rosenberg and Nazi Ideology*. London 1972.
Cohn, N. *Warrant for Genocide: The Myth of the Jewish World Conspiracy*. London 1970.
Compton, J. V. *The Swastika and the Eagle: Hitler, the United States, and the Origins of World War II*. Boston, Mass., 1967.
Conway, J. S. *The Nazi Persecution of the Churches, 1933–45*. New York/London 1968.
Dahrendorf, R. *Society and Democracy in Germany*. Garden City, N.Y./London 1967.
Dallin, A. *German Rule in Russia, 1941–1945: A Study of Occupation Policies*. New York/London 1957.

Deakin, F. W. *The Brutal Friendship: Mussolini, Hitler, and the Fall of Italian Fascism.* London 1961/New York 1963.

Deutsch, H. C. *The Conspiracy against Hitler in the Twilight War.* Minneapolis, Minn. 1968.

Donohoe, J. *Hitler's Conservative Opponents in Bavaria, 1930–1945: A Consideration of Catholic, Monarchist, and Separatist Anti-Nazi Activities.* Leiden 1961.

Eyck, E. *A History of the Weimar Republic.* 2 vols. Cambridge, Mass., 1962–63.

Fest, J. *The Face of the Third Reich: Portraits of the Nazi Leadership.* New York/ London 1970.

Fishman, S. 'The Rise of Hitler as a beer hall orator', *Review of Politics,* 26 (1964).

Fraenkel, E. *The Dual State.* London/New York 1941.

Franz, G. 'Munich: Birthplace and Center of the National Socialist German Workers Party', *Journal of Modern History,* 29 (1957).

Friedländer, S. *Pius XII and the Third Reich.* New York/London 1966.

——. *Prelude to Downfall: Hitler and the United States 1939–1941.* New York 1967.

Frye, A. *Nazi Germany and the Western Hemisphere 1933–1941.* New Haven, Conn., 1967.

Gehl, J. *Austria, Germany and the Anschluss, 1931–1938.* New York/London 1963.

Gerth, H. 'The Nazi Party, its Leadership and Composition', *American Journal of Sociology,* XIV (1940).

Gisevius, H. B. *To the Bitter End.* Boston, Mass., 1947.

Goebbels, J. *The Early Goebbels Diaries: 1925–1926.,* ed. H. Heiber. London 1962/ New York 1963.

——. *My Part in Germany's Fight.* London 1935.

——. *The Goebbels Diaries, 1942–43.* Garden City, N.J., 1964.

Gordon, H. J. *Hitler and the Beer Hall Putsch.* New York 1972.

Graml, H., et al. *The German Resistance to Hitler.* London 1970.

Guillebaud, C. W. *The Social Policy of Nazi Germany.* Cambridge 1942.

Hale, O. J. 'Gottfried Feder Calls Hitler to Order; an Unpublished Letter on Nazi Party Affairs', *Journal of Modern History,* 30 (1958).

——. *The Captive Press in the Third Reich.* Princeton, N.J., 1964.

Hanfstaengl, E. *Hitler, the Missing Years.* London 1957.

Heberle, R. *From Democracy to Nazism: A Regional Case Study on Political Parties in Germany.* Baton Rouge, Louisiana, 1945.

Heiber, H. *Joseph Goebbels.* London 1973.

Heiden, K. *A History of National Socialism.* London 1934/New York 1935.

——. *Der Fuehrer: Hitler's Rise to Power.* Boston/London 1944.

Heinemann, J. L. 'Constantin von Neurath and German Policy at the London Economic Conference of 1933: Backgrounds to the Resignation of Alfred Hugenberg', *Journal of Modern History,* 41 (1969).

Herwig, H. H. 'Prelude to Weltblitzkrieg: Germany's Naval Policy towards the United States of America, 1939–1941', *Journal of Modern History,* 43 (1971).

Hilberg, R. *The Destruction of the European Jews.* Chicago/London 1961.

Hitler, A. *Mein Kampf.* Boston, Mass., 1962/London 1969.

——. *The Secret Book.* New York 1962.

——. *Hitler's Secret Conversations.* New York 1961.

——. *The Speeches of Adolf Hitler.* 2 vols., ed. N. H. Baynes. London 1942.

Hoffmann, H. *Hitler was my Friend.* London 1955.

Holborn, H. 'Origins and Political Character of Nazi Ideology', *Political Science Quarterly* 79 (1964).

Höhne, H. *The Order of the Death's Head.* London 1969.

Homze, E. L. *Foreign Labor in Nazi Germany.* Princeton, N.J., 1968.

Höss, R. *Commandant of Auschwitz.* London 1959/New York 1960.

Jetzinger, F. *Hitler's Youth.* London 1958.

Kahle, P. *Bonn University in Pre-Nazi and Nazi Times.* London 1945.

Kele, M. *Nazis and Workers.* New York/London 1972.

Klein, B. H. *Germany's Economic Preparations for War.* Cambridge, Mass., 1959.

Klemperer, K. von. *Germany's New Conservatism: Its History and Dilemma in the Twentieth Century.* Princeton, N.J., 1957.

Kochan, L. *Pogrom, 10 November 1938.* London 1957.

Koehl, R. L. *RKFDV: German Resettlement and Population Policy 1939–1945.* Cambridge, Mass., 1957.

Laqueur, W. Z. *Russia and Germany.* London 1965.

Lebovics, H. *Social Conservatism and the Middle Classes in Germany: 1914–1933.* Princeton, N.J., 1969.

Lewy, G. *The Catholic Church and Nazi Germany.* New York/London 1964.

Lipset, S. M. *Political Man.* New York/London 1960.

Loewenberg, P. 'The Psychohistorical Origins of the Nazi Youth Cohort', *American Historical Review*, LXXVII (1971).

——. 'The Unsuccessful Adolescence of Heinrich Himmler', *American Historical Review*, LXXVII (1971).

Loomis, C. P., and Beagle, J. A. 'The Spread of German Nazism in Rural Areas', *American Sociological Review*, 11 (1946).

Ludecke, K. *I Knew Hitler: The Story of a Nazi who Escaped the Blood Purge.* New York 1937.

McRandle, J. H. *The Track of the Wolf: Essays on National Socialism and its Leader, Adolf Hitler.* Evanston, Ill. 1965.

Maschmann, M. *Account Rendered.* London 1963.

Mason, T. W. 'Some Origins of the Second World War', *Past and Present*, XXIV (1964).

——. 'Labour in the Third Reich, 1933–1939', *Past and Present*, XXXIII (1966).

——. 'The Primacy of Politics', in S. J. Woolf (ed.), *The Nature of Fascism.* New York 1969.

Meinecke, F. *The German Catastrophe: Reflections and Recollections.* Cambridge, Mass., 1950.

Milward, A. S. *The German Economy at War.* London/New York 1965.

——. *The New Order and the French Economy.* London/New York 1970.

——. *The Fascist Economy in Norway.* London/New York 1972.

Mosse, G. *The Crisis of German Ideology: Intellectual Origins of the Third Reich.* New York 1964.

—— (ed.) *Nazi Culture: Intellectual, Cultural and Social Life in the Third Reich.* New York 1966.

Neumann, F. *Behemoth: The Structure and Practice of National Socialism: 1933–1944.* London 1944.

Nicholls, A. J. *Weimar and the Rise of Hitler.* London 1971.

—— and Matthias, E. (eds) *German Democracy and the Triumph of Hitler*. London 1971.
Noakes, J. *The Nazi Party in Lower Saxony, 1921–1933*. London 1971.
Nolte, E. *Three Faces of Fascism: Action Française, Italian Fascism and National Socialism*. New York 1966.
Nyomarkay, J. *Charisma and Factionalism in the Nazi Party*. Minneapolis, Minn. 1967.
O'Neill, R. J., *The German Army and the Nazi Party, 1933–1938*. London 1967.
Orlow, D. *A History of the Nazi Party, 1919–1945*. 2 vols. Pittsburgh, Pa. 1969, 1973.
——. *The Nazis in the Balkans: A Case Study of Totalitarian Politics*. Pittsburgh, Pa. 1968.
Overy, R. J. 'Transportation and Rearmament in the Third Reich', *Historical Journal*, 1973.
Peterson, E. N. *The Limits of Hitler's Power*. Princeton, N.J., 1969.
Phelps, R. H. 'Before Hitler Came. Thule Society and Germanenorden', *Journal of Modern History*, XXXV (1963).
——. 'Hitler and the DAP', *American Historical Review*, LXVII (1963).
Pridham, G. *Hitler's Rise to Power: The Nazi Movement in Bavaria 1923–1933*. London 1973.
Prittie, T. *Germans against Hitler*. London 1964.
Pulzer, P. *The Rise of Political Anti-Semitism in Germany and Austria: 1867–1918*. New York 1964.
Rauschning, H. *Hitler Speaks: A Series of Political Conversations with Adolf Hitler on his Real Aims*. London 1939.
——. *The Revolution of Nihilism: Warning to the West*. New York 1939.
Reichmann, E. G. *Hostages of Civilization: The Social Sources of National Socialist Anti-Semitism*. London 1950/Boston, Mass., 1951.
Ritter, G. *The German Resistance: Carl Goerdeler's Struggle against Tyranny*. New York/London 1958.
Robbins, K. *Munich*, London 1970.
Robertson, E. M. *Hitler's Pre-War Policy and Military Plans*. New York/London 1963.
—— (ed.) *The Origins of the Second World War*. London/New York 1971.
Roon, G. van. *German Resistance to Hitler: Count von Moltke and the Kreisau Circle*. London 1971.
Rosenberg, A. *A History of the German Republic*. London 1934.
Rothfels, H. *German Opposition to Hitler*. Chicago 1962/London 1963.
Sauer, W. 'National Socialism: Totalitarianism or Fascism?', *American Historical Review*, LXXIII (1967).
Schleunes, K. *The Twisted Road to Auschwitz: Nazi Policy towards German Jews, 1933–1939*. Urbana, Ill., 1970.
Schoenbaum, D. *Hitler's Social Revolution: Class and Status in Nazi Germany 1933–1939*. New York 1966/London 1967.
Schweitzer, A. *Big Business in the Third Reich*. Bloomington, Ind./London 1964.
Seaton, A. *The Russo-German War, 1941–45*. London/New York 1971.
Shirer, W. *Berlin Diary*. London/New York 1942.
——. *The Rise and Fall of the Third Reich*. New York/London 1960.

Speer, A. *Inside the Third Reich: Memoirs.* New York/London 1970.

Stern, F. *The Politics of Cultural Despair: A Study in the Rise of the Germanic Ideology.* New York 1961.

Strasser, O. *Hitler and I.* London 1938.

Sykes, C. *Troubled Loyalty: A Biography of Adam von Trott.* London 1968.

Taylor, A. J. P. *The Origins of the Second World War.* London 1961/New York 1962.

Thorne, C. *The Approach of War.* London 1971.

Tobias, F. *The Reichstag Fire.* London/New York 1964.

Trevor-Roper, H. *The Last Days of Hitler.* 3rd edn. New York/London 1966.

Turner, H. 'Hitler's Secret Pamphlet for Industrialists 1927', *Journal of Modern History*, XL (1968).

——. 'Big Business and the Rise of Hitler', *American Historical Review*, LXXV (1969).

Watt, D. C. 'The Anglo-German Naval Agreement of 1935', in *Journal of Modern History*, XXVIII (1956).

Weinberg, G. L. *Germany and the Soviet Union, 1939–1941.* New York 1954.

——. *The Foreign Policy of Hitler's Germany, 1933–1936.* New York 1971.

Weizsäcker, E. von. *Memoirs.* New York 1951. Published in England as *Memoirs of Ernst von Weizsäcker.* London 1951.

Wheeler-Bennett, J. W. *The Nemesis of Power: The German Army in Politics 1918–1945.* Rev. edn. London/New York 1964.

Whiteside, A. G. 'The Nature and Origins of National Socialism', in *Journal of Central European Affairs*, No. 17 (1957).

Wilson, L. (ed.) *The Road to Dictatorship: Germany, 1918–1933.* London 1963.

Zeman, Z. A. B. *Nazi Propaganda.* London/New York 1964.

Index of Names